IMPERIAL PLOTS

IMPERIAL PLOTS

Women, Land, and the Spadework of British Colonialism on the Canadian Prairies

SARAH CARTER

UMP
University of Manitoba Press

University of Manitoba Press
Winnipeg, Manitoba
Canada R3T 2M5
uofmpress.ca

Printed in Canada

20 19 18 17 16 1 2 3 4 5

Cover design: Frank Reimer
Interior design: Jess Koroscil
Cover image: Sarah Minnie (Waddy) Gardner on her horse "Fly," Mount Sentinel Ranch, Alberta, 1915. Born Wexford, Ireland, 1879, died Calgary, 1959. Museum of the Highwood, MH995.002.008.

Cataloguing data available from Library and Archives Canada.

ISBN 978-0-88755-818-4 (pbk.)
ISBN 978-0-88755-532-9 (pdf)
ISBN 978-0-88755-530-5 (epub)

This book has been published with the help of a grant from the Federation for the Humanities and Social Sciences, through the Awards to Scholarly Publications Program, using funds provided by the Social Sciences and Humanities Research Council of Canada.

The University of Manitoba Press gratefully acknowledges the financial support for its publication program provided by the Government of Canada through the Canada Book Fund, the Canada Council for the Arts, the Manitoba Department of Culture, Heritage, Tourism, the Manitoba Arts Council, and the Manitoba Book Publishing Tax Credit.

TO MY GRANDMOTHER JEAN MUNN (JENNIE MAY MARSHALL), 1899-1967, BORN ON HER PARENTS' HOMESTEAD, WELLWOOD, MANITOBA.

Photo: Family Collection.

During my stay in Canada I heard a good deal about farming for women, and how they ought to take up homesteads, therefore I was interested to come across the young daughters of a neighbouring farmer, who acted as hired men to their father. Mrs. Anderson [her employer] said they rode wonderfully, could handle a team better than most men, drive the "binders," and do the whole work of a farm; but she considered that the life they led was unsuitable for a woman and was unfitting these girls for becoming wives and mothers in the future—in fact, the feeling of the countryside was strongly against their father.

Ella C. Sykes, *A Home-Help in Canada,* 1912

People are beginning to waken up to the vast conception and imperialistic importance of tendering free homesteads as an inducement to women of strong moral force and high intellectual ability to come to our beautiful West and lend their aid in establishing a Canadian colony, a new and clean colony...

"Homesteads for Women," by "Isobel," *Grain Growers' Guide,* 25 October 1911

CONTENTS

LIST OF ILLUSTRATIONS - XI

LIST OF TABLES - XIV

ACKNOWLEDGEMENTS - XV

LIST OF ABBREVIATIONS - XIX

NOTE ON TERMINOLOGY - XX

INTRODUCTION - 3

CHAPTER ONE - 29

NARROWING OPPORTUNITIES FOR WOMEN: FROM THE INDIGENOUS FARMERS OF THE GREAT PLAINS TO THE EXCLUSIONS OF THE HOMESTEAD REGIME

CHAPTER TWO - 85

"LAND OWNERS AND ENTERPRISING SETTLERS IN THE COLONIES": BRITISH WOMEN FARMERS FOR CANADA

CHAPTER THREE - 147

WIDOWS AND OTHER IMMIGRANT WOMEN HOMESTEADERS: STRUGGLES AND STRATEGIES

CHAPTER FOUR - 207

WOMEN WHO BOUGHT LAND: THE "BACHELOR GIRL" SETTLER, "JACK" MAY, AND OTHER CELEBRITY FARMERS AND RANCHERS

CHAPTER FIVE - 245

ANSWERING THE CALL OF EMPIRE: GEORGINA BINNIE-CLARK, FARMER, AUTHOR, LECTURER

CHAPTER SIX - 287

"DAUGHTERS OF BRITISH BLOOD" OR "HORDES OF MEN OF ALIEN RACE"?: THE HOMESTEADS-FOR-BRITISH-WOMEN CAMPAIGN

CHAPTER SEVEN - 327

THE PERSISTENCE OF A "CURIOUSLY STRONG PREJUDICE": FROM THE FIRST WORLD WAR TO THE GREAT DEPRESSION

CONCLUSION - 375

NOTES - 383

BIBLIOGRAPHY - 423

INDEX - 443

LIST OF ILLUSTRATIONS

Figure 1. Survey map of Township 12, Range 15, West of the Principal Meridian. Archives of Manitoba, N6411. *P. 2*

Figure 2. "Sioux Woman," the daughter-in-law of Hidatsa farmer Maxi'diwiac (Buffalo Bird Woman), demonstrates traditional farming methods, 1912. State Historical Society of North Dakota, item no. 0086-0281. Photo by Gilbert L. Wilson. *P. 32*

Figure 3. An 1882 map for "intending settlers," showing the dominion lands surveyed west of the border of Manitoba. Peel's Prairie Provinces, University of Alberta Libraries, Map 597. *P. 51*

Figure 4. Métis women and men at a sitting of the Métis Scrip Commission at Devil's Lake, Saskatchewan, 1900. Saskatchewan Archives Board, S-B9750. *P. 55*

Figure 5. Patent issued in 1883 to Manitoba homesteader Matilda McAskie. Library and Archives Canada, Western Land Grants, http://www.bac-lac.gc.ca/eng/discover/land/land-grants-western-canada-1870-1930/pages/item.aspx?IdNumber=461605&. *P. 67*

Figure 6. "The Primitive Farmer and Burden-Bearer, South Africa," from Otis T. Mason, *Women's Share in Primitive Culture* (1899), 6. *P. 78*

Figures 7 and 8. The Glynde School For Lady Gardeners in Sussex, England, established by Lady Frances Wolseley in 1902. Papers of the Viscountess Frances Wolseley, Hove Central Library, Hove, Sussex, Commonplace Book no. 196. *P. 99*

Figure 9. Colonial Training Farm at Arlesey, England. *The Bystander*, 16 September 1908, 610–11. *P. 113*

Figure 10. "Canada for Women" promotion, Canadian Pacific Railway, 1910. *Daily Mail*, 2 March 1910, 10. *P. 142*

Figure 11. The Canadian Pacific Railway office, London, wants "settlers, not suffragettes," 1913. Getty Images, no. 3424540. *P. 145*

Figure 12. Englishwoman and Alberta rancher Agnes Bedingfeld. Glenbow Archives, NA-2467-12. *P. 151*

Figure 13. Alberta homesteader Margaret de Tro earned extra income as a "magnetic healer" in Edmonton. *Edmonton Bulletin*, 29 December 1905, 4. ***P. 161***

Figure 14. The auction sale of the estate of Madam M. de Tro of Hardisty, Alberta, in March 1916. *Edmonton Bulletin*, 1 March 1916, 9. ***P. 162***

Figure 15. Rush for Free Homesteads at the Dominion Land Office, Moose Jaw, Saskatchewan, 1908. Peel's Prairie Provinces, University of Alberta Libraries, Postcard 18198. ***P. 181***

Figure 16. Homestead rush at Edmonton, Alberta, 1 September 1908. Peel's Prairie Provinces, University of Alberta Libraries, Postcard 6839. ***P. 182***

Figure 17. Women homesteaders near Square Deal, Alberta, c. 1912. Glenbow Archives, NA-206-27. ***P. 192***

Figure 18. Jane Gentles and sons, First World War. Saskatchewan Archives Board, homestead file 2092263. ***P. 201***

Figure 19. Eva Iddings of Indiana in front of her claim shack near Fort Benton, Montana. Barrows Collection, Overholser Historical Research Center, Fort Benton, Montana, 1910, BC11, 244. ***P. 201***

Figure 20. Ontario sisters Caroline (Carrie) Louise MacGregor and Mary Frances MacGregor homesteaded in Sheridan County, Montana, c. 1909. Courtesy Judy Archer (Carrie's granddaughter), Orillia, Ontario. ***P. 202***

Figure 21. Alice (Alix) Westhead, c. 1906. Glenbow Archives, NA-2925-2. ***P. 213***

Figure 22. Isobel "Jack" May, Sedgewick, Alberta. Currie Love, "Farmer-Boy 'Jack,'" *The Lady's Realm* 31, 181 (1911). ***P. 224***

Figure 23. Louisa Wittrick farmed with "Jack" May, but her responsibilities focused on the domestic realm. Currie Love, "Farmer-Boy 'Jack,'" *The Lady's Realm* 31, 181 (1911). ***P. 225***

Figure 24. May and Wittrick at Sedgewick. Currie Love, "Farmer-Boy 'Jack,'" *The Lady's Realm* 31, 181 (1911). ***P. 225***

Figure 25. The "bachelor girl settler." Currie Love, "Farmer-Boy 'Jack,'" *The Lady's Realm* 31, 181 (1911). ***P. 226***

Figure 26. Qu'Appelle Industrial School students with older generation. Georgina Binnie-Clark, *Wheat and Woman,* 70. ***P. 249***

Figure 27. Indigenous people at Victoria Day/Empire Day at Fort Qu'Appelle, 1912. Georgina Binnie-Clark, *Wheat and Woman*, 178. *P. 250*

Figure 28. Portrait of Georgina Binnie-Clark. Courtesy Mr. Dennis Jenks. *P. 253*

Figure 29. Doukhobor women pulling a plough in Saskatchewan, 1902. Glenbow Archives, NA-670-45. *P. 257*

Figure 30. Press coverage from 1910 of Georgina Binnie-Clark's activities in England and Canada. *Gleichen Call* (Alberta): "Are Booming Canada," 9 June 1910, 7; "Making Girl Farmers," 21 April 1910, 7. *P. 265*

Figure 31. A pupil from Roedean School, Brighton, learning to farm at the Binnie-Clark farm, Fort Qu'Appelle, 1913. Georgina Binnie-Clark, *Wheat and Woman*, 402. *P. 273*

Figure 32. "Land and The Woman," article by Georgina Binnie-Clark and photographs. *Canadian Courier* 12, no. 12, 16 November 1912, 16. *P. 274*

Figure 33. Homesteads-for-British-Women petition. Library and Archives Canada, Record Group 15, Department of the Interior, D-II-1, vol. 1105, file 2876596, pt. 2. *P. 314*

Figure 34. Postcards of supporters of the homesteads-for-women campaign. Library and Archives Canada, Record Group 15, Department of the Interior, D-Ii-1, vol. 1105, file 2876596, pt. 2. *P. 315*

Figures 35 and 36. "Farmerettes" of Ontario c. 1917–18. City of Toronto Archives, William James Family Fonds 1244, items 640 and 640A. *P. 332*

Figure 37. Eaton's Department Store advertisement for "Costumes for the Farmerette." *The Globe* (Toronto), 25 May 1918. *P. 334*

Figure 38. "They Serve France." Canadian Victory Bonds poster. Library of Congress, 2003652830. *P. 336*

Figure 39. "Calgary's Land Army," *Grain Growers' Guide*, 10 April 1918, 32. *P. 339*

Figure 40. "Canada West" poster, 1923. Canadian Pacific Archives, Image no. BR. 194 *P. 374*

LIST OF TABLES

Table 1. The gender of Western Canadian homesteaders and their success rates at "proving up," 1872–1882. *P.69*

Table 2. Numbers of male and female agriculturalists in the Censuses of Canada, with percentages of female agriculturalists. *P.158*

ACKNOWLEDGEMENTS

If I were to identify when the initial seed of this project was planted it would be the first class I taught at the University of Calgary, a full-year night class in 1992–93 on Western Canada. We learn a lot from our students, and in that class one wrote an excellent essay on the homesteads-for-women campaign in Western Canada. It was new to me. Thanks to Richelle Brazunas, wherever you are! Having worked up to that time on how First Nations male farmers were stigmatized and excluded from the commercial grain economy I began to see other forms of exclusion through the distribution of land and roles in the settler colony of the West. And while some women worked to bring about a reconfiguration of this distribution, challenging and calling into question the reigning order of "common sense" about who could farm and own land, they (unfortunately) worked in the interests of a privileged few of British ancestry. Yet even if they had chosen another strategy, they would have found that this "distribution of the sensible" remained intransigent and impervious to calls for change.

I have drawn on archives and libraries in Canada, the U.S, the U.K., and eventually as far away as Australia. I would like in particular to acknowledge the help of the archivists at the Saskatchewan Archives Board, the Archives of Manitoba, the Provincial Archives of Alberta, and the Glenbow Archives. Among the many archivists and librarians who have assisted me, I want to give special thanks to Sharon Maier, Regina Public Library; Susan Kooyman and Doug Cass at the Glenbow; Chris Kotecki and Eric Hallett at the Archives of Manitoba; Philip Hatfield and Carole Holden at the British Library; and Nadine Charabin at the Saskatchewan Archives, Saskatoon. Irene Kerr, Museum of the Highwood, searched their collection and provided the cover photograph for this book. Thanks also to Ken Robison and Henry L. Armstrong of the Overholser Historical Research Center in Fort Benton, Montana.

The Social Sciences and Humanities Research Council of Canada assisted me in this study, as did a Killam Research Fellowship. The research funds available to me as a University of Alberta Henry Marshall Tory Chair have been of critical importance to this project. My research in the U.K. was facilitated by several appointments for which I am very grateful: Eccles Visiting Professorship in North American Studies at the British Library; Visiting Fellow, Institute of Commonwealth Studies, University of London; and Visiting Scholar, Centre of Canadian Studies, University of Edinburgh. I visited the Australian National Archives while a Visiting Fellow at Australian National University's Research School of Social Sciences and its Australian Centre for Indigenous History. Thanks to Philip Davies, Eccles Centre at the British Library; Philip Murphy at the Institute for Commonwealth Studies; Annis May Timpson, Canadian Studies, University of Edinburgh; and Maria Nugent, Australian National University.

Countless scholars over many years have inspired and encouraged me, and helped refine and clarify this project, as have conference sessions and invitations to speak or write. Special thanks to Ashleigh Androsoff, Jean Barman, Philip Buckner, Cathy Cavanaugh, Tonia Compton, Nancy Janovicek, Betsy Jameson, Fran Kaye, Nanci Langford, Briony McDonagh, Linda Mahood, Laurie Mercier, James Muhn, Maria Nugent, Adele Perry, Joan Sangster, Nikki Strong-Boag, Georgie Taylor, Nicola Verdun, and Angela Wanhalla. Thanks to my colleagues at the Universities of Alberta and Calgary.

I am very grateful to my research assistants: Gretchen Albers, Alana Borque, Sydney Budgeon, Suzanne Daugela, Karine Duhamel, Corinne George, Patricia Gordon, Leslie Hall, Michel Hogue, Pernille Jakobsen, Amy McKinney, Erin Millions, Cheryl Purdey, Trevor Rockwell, and Claire Thomson. Special thanks to Catherine Ulmer for her help with the South African Scrip women homesteaders of Saskatchewan, and to Sara Tokay, who has been of great assistance with the many tasks of the home stretch.

The Alberta content of this book was enhanced by the University of Alberta's project Last Best West: The Alberta Land Settlement Infrastructure Project, funded by the Canada Foundation for Innovation, with Peter Baskerville as principal investigator and Sean Gouglas (and me) as co-investigators. The project digitized Alberta homestead files and made them available on the Web. Students and other employees hired for this project created an enormous databank from these files. They also alerted me to interesting homestead stories. Special thanks to Katie Pollock, Leigh Johnson, Silvia Russell, Richard Fletcher, and Melanie Niemi-Bohun as well as to Peter Baskerville and Sean Gouglas.

It was remarkable the number of people who stepped forward with research and stories, sometimes of family members. Judy Archer of Orillia, Ontario, kindly shared the story and photographs of her grandmother and great-aunt who left Ontario to homestead in Montana because they were denied that right in Canada. Thanks to Douglas Ramsay for his research on Agnes Balfour, and to Matthew Ostapchuk for information on Sarah Cleverly. Doris McKinnon provided me with Marie Rose Smith's homestead file. Thanks also to Joan Heggie, Teeside University, who, after hearing a talk I gave at the conference Women and Land in Hull in 2015, dug into the mystery of farmer "Jack" May and made some startling discoveries. I am grateful to Juliet Gayton (Exeter University), who unearthed and clarified information on Alberta rancher Alix Westhead, and also to Lionel de Rothschild, Exbury Estate, and Melanie Aspey, Exbury Archives.

For information on Georgina Binnie-Clark, I am grateful to her great-nephews Dennis Jenks and Richard Jenks. During a visit to Fort Qu'Appelle, Saskatchewan, I received a warm welcome and a great deal of information from the late Lynn Anderson, and from Derek Harrison, Doug and Marg Dawson, and Beverly Van der Breggan.

Editor Gretchen Albers skillfully prepared the manuscript for submission. Thanks to everyone at the University of Manitoba Press, and in particular David Carr, Glenn Bergen, and Jill McConkey. Maureen Epp did an excellent job of copy-editing this manuscript.

A few sections of this book have appeared as: (1) "Britishness, 'Foreignness,' Women and Land in Western Canada, 1890s–1920s," *Humanities Research: The Journal of the Humanities Research Centre and the Centre for Cross-Cultural Research at the Australian National University* 13, no. 1 (2006): 43–60, a special issue from the 2004 conference "Britishness and Otherness: Locating Marginal White Identities in the Empire," Australian National University, Canberra; (2) my introduction to the 2007 reprint of Georgina Binnie-Clark, *Wheat and Woman* (Toronto: University of Toronto Press, 2007); (3) "'Hordes of Men of Alien Race' or 'Daughters of British Blood?' The Homesteads-for-Women Campaign in Western Canada," *Great Plains Quarterly* 29, no. 4 (Fall 2009): 267–86; (4) "'My Vocabulary Contains No Such Word as Defeat': Clara Lynch and Her Battle for Her Alberta Homestead, 1900–1909," *Alberta History* 61, no. 3 (Summer 2013).

Finally, thanks as always to Walter Hildebrandt for his encouragement and assistance, including accompanying me on excursions to prairie archives, museums, and small towns. I dedicate the book to my grandmother Jean Munn, whose Manitoba homestead roots are a point of origin for this study. My other grandmother, Nell Carter, born Nellie Weaver in Dartford, Kent (1882–1973), arrived in Moose Jaw, Saskatchewan, as a bride in 1915. I thought of her, too, as I wrote this book, with its focus on British women, and also about her sisters, who stayed in Kent. Clara, Emily, Florence, and Alice Weaver were all employed from a young age, mainly as teachers, and they did not marry. I am certain that they would have detested the label "surplus" women.

LIST OF ABBREVIATIONS

BWEA	British Women's Emigration Association
CIL	Colonial Intelligence League for Educated Women
CPR	Canadian Pacific Railway
FANY	First Aid Nursing Yeomanry Corps
IODE	Imperial Order Daughters of Empire
OSC	Oversea Settlement Committee
RCI	Royal Colonial Institute
SAS	South African Scrip
SOSBW	Society for the Oversea Settlement of British Women
UFA	United Farmers of Alberta
UJFS	Union Jack Farm Settlement
VBA	Volunteer Bounty Act
WLA	Women's Land Army
WNLSC	Women's National Land Service Corps
YWCA	Young Women's Christian Association

NOTE ON TERMINOLOGY

WHAT DID IT MEAN TO HOMESTEAD?

We think of the term today as synonymous with farming, or generally establishing a home in a rural area. But in Western Canada (and the U.S. West) the word "homesteader" had a much more specific meaning. It meant that you were located on a free grant of 160 acres on offer from the federal government. You paid ten dollars to legally locate there, and you then had to cultivate and live on the land before you legally owned the land. While by no means entirely "free," given the costs involved in establishing a farm, it was much cheaper than purchasing land.

THE DOMINION LAND SURVEY

All of the land in the North-West Territories, with the exception of the "postage stamp" province of Manitoba, was under the control of the federal government after 1870. The survey that began in 1871 affirmed Canadian sovereignty over these lands and facilitated non-Indigenous settlement. The land was surveyed into townships of thirty-six square sections. Each section was one mile square and consisted of 640 acres. Sections were further subdivided into four quarter sections of 160 acres each. Township lines run east and west and were numbered north from the international boundary. The lines that run north and south are range lines. The First or Principal Meridian in Manitoba was located just west of Winnipeg, and additional meridians were added as the survey advanced west. For example, the Fourth Meridian forms the Saskatchewan-Alberta border and bisects Lloydminster.

ADMINISTRATION OF LAND

In 1871 the Dominion Lands Branch, a branch within the Department of the Interior, was created to administer the 1872 Dominion Lands Act. There were Dominion Land Offices in towns and cities of the West, employing agents, sub-agents, and homestead inspectors.

SPECIAL SECTIONS

The odd-numbered sections in each township were railway land grants. The Canadian Pacific Railway was granted 25,000,000 acres. The Hudson's Bay Company was awarded one- and three-quarter sections in each township. Two sections in each township were set aside to support educational facilities and were called school sections. Railway, Hudson's Bay Company, and school lands were available for purchase, and the idea was that as the homesteaders improved their quarter sections they would seek to expand through purchase. The value of the land would increase as the homesteaders improved the land, and other buyers would also be enticed. These sections could also be available for leasing.

ENTRY ON A HOMESTEAD

The even-numbered sections in each township were available as homesteads under the Dominion Lands Act. The homesteader paid a ten-dollar filing fee and chose a quarter section (160 acres). A variety of terms were used for this process: the homesteader "filed on," or "claimed," or "made entry" on a homestead, generally in person at the local land office. Homesteaders often found the land unsuitable and then filled out a Declaration of Abandonment that specified why they were unable to farm or reside on that land, after which they were free to file on another quarter section.

WHO COULD CLAIM A HOMESTEAD?

- Under the Indian Act (1876) no one who was "Indian" could homestead.
- Before 1874, any single woman or any male over the age of twenty-one could homestead. This was changed in 1874 to eighteen years of age.
- In 1876, entry could be made by any person who was a sole head of a family or any male over the age of eighteen. Single women were no longer permitted to homestead. A woman could homestead only if she was a sole head of household with a minor child or children. This was generally interpreted to mean a widow.

PROVING UP

After filing on a quarter section, homestead duties had to be performed for a minimum of three years (and in many cases the process took longer). This process was known as "proving up" or "perfecting" your entry. Duties included residence and cultivation on the homestead to prove that he or she was a bona fide settler. In each year for three years the homesteader had to reside for at least six months on the homestead.

APPLICATION FOR PATENT

At the end of three years, if the homesteader fulfilled all of these duties, she or he gave six months' notice in writing of intention to apply for patent. The homesteader filled out an application for patent or clear title (i.e., outright ownership) that contained information on the applicant and family, including nationality and proof of naturalization and details on breaking/cropping, livestock, and buildings. Two witnesses, usually neighbours, were required to attest to the truth of the application. Application was made before the local land agent or homestead inspector. If the application was approved, a patent would be issued to the homesteader, who was then the owner of the land.

PRE-EMPTION

From 1874 on, a homesteader could obtain a second quarter section of land adjacent to the homestead. At the time of filing on a homestead, the settler could also claim a pre-emption (for an additional ten-dollar filing fee). The homesteader had the right to purchase that land after receiving patent to the homestead and was given three years to make that purchase. Pre-emptions were cancelled in 1890 and restored in 1908, when cultivation requirements were added.

PURCHASED HOMESTEADS

Between 1871 and 1918, a settler could purchase 160 acres of land within a nine-mile radius of his or her homestead at three dollars per acre.

IMPERIAL PLOTS

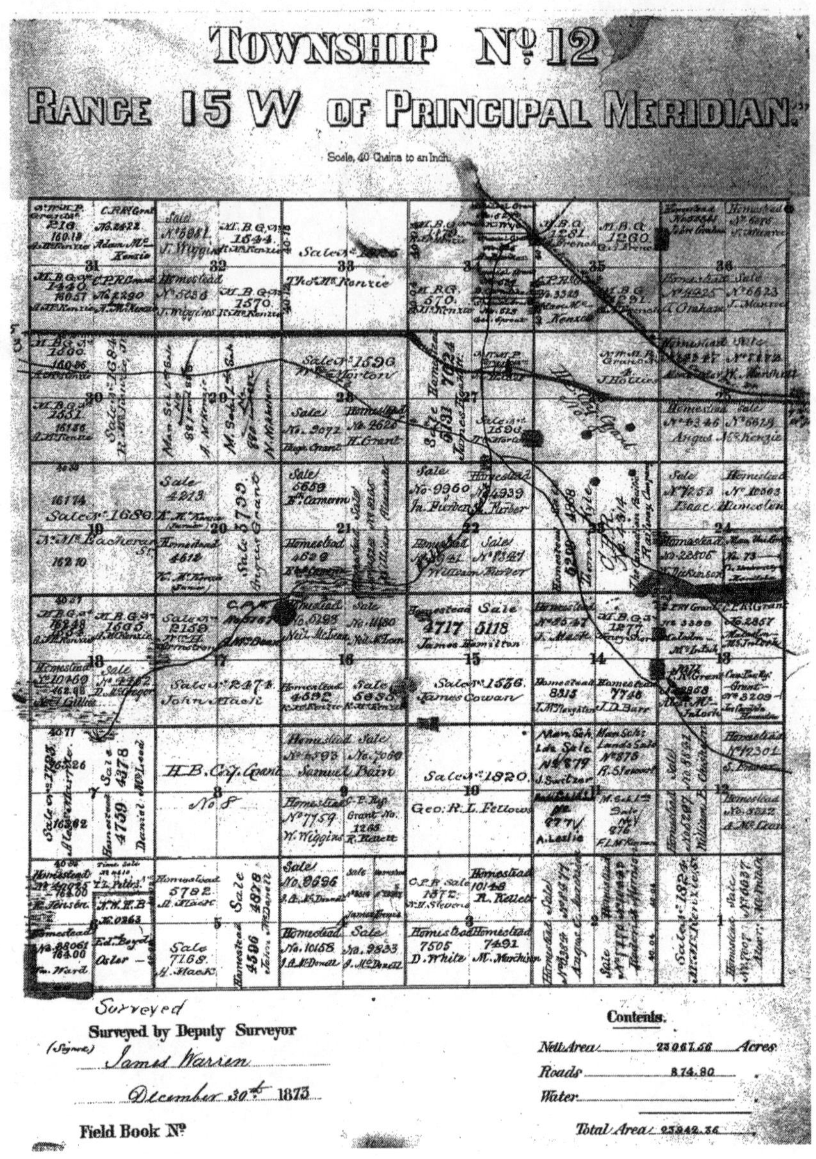

Figure 1. This township map documents the author's family history. Great-great-grandparents John and Mary Graham homesteaded in section 36, and just to the south in section 25, great-grandparents Alexander and Sarah (Graham) Marshall homesteaded. Her grandmother Jennie May Marshall was born here in 1899. Only one woman's name appears on the map, widow Elizabeth Cameron in section 21. Archives of Manitoba, N6411. Dominion Land Survey Township Plan, T12, R15, W, 1873.

INTRODUCTION

The map of perfect geometrical squares from southwestern Manitoba that records the homesteaders of Township 12, Range 15, West of the Principal Meridian is like other maps from across prairie Canada—except that this one documents my own family history. In the late 1870s my great-great-grandparents Mary (Kilgore) and John Graham homesteaded the southwest quarter of section 36. Their daughter Sarah Jane, my great-grandmother, married my great-grandfather Alexander Marshall, who homesteaded the adjoining section to the south, and my grandmother Jean was born there in 1899. Other Grahams married neighbouring homesteaders, and the related families of Grahams, Marshalls, Kilgores, Munroes, and McKinnons helped to form the Wellwood community of Scottish and Irish settlers, some of whom had arrived in Manitoba by way of sojourns in Ontario. Many are buried in the Graham-Munroe cemetery on my great-grandparents' land. In the cemetery you can learn the names of many of the early women settlers, as they are not on the map. Homesteading, the right to a grant of 160 acres, was overwhelmingly a male preserve. Married women were not eligible for the homestead grant and single women were excluded after 1876, leaving only women who qualified as "sole" heads of households, generally widows with children. There is one woman on the map of Township 12, Range 15: Elizabeth Cameron was a widow whose husband, Hugh, died before he "proved up," or fulfilled the residency and cultivation requirements that came with a homestead grant, and so the patent to the land was issued to her.[1] The death of a husband was one of the main ways a woman obtained land in her own name. It is readily apparent from gazing at any township map how land laws and policies were used to shape a society of male heads of household and dependent females, how the land was not neutral, how ideas about proper gender roles were embedded in the landscape. For most women the only way to get land was to get a man, or have a husband die, or be a widow with minor-aged children, which qualified women to enter or file on a homestead of their own.

This book is primarily about the failed effort to redraw maps of prairie Canada to include the names of women. British women spearheaded the charge, and at the height of the campaign in 1908–14 sought to obtain homestead rights for British and British-Canadian women only, excluding "foreign" women and replacing "foreign" men. They aspired to settle on what I am calling "imperial plots" that would have otherwise gone to "ignorant, uncouth, lawless foreigners," or so they argued, so that refined and educated gentlewomen could contribute to the spadework of empire and plant British culture as well as crops.[2] But this book is about more than the campaign to secure homestead rights for "British-born" women; it involves broader questions and debates that took place in both Canada and Britain about the capacity of women to farm, whether it was proper for them to do so, and whether they should participate in activities that threatened to masculinize them and to provide them with independence. It also draws in a much wider ensemble of women agriculturalists than just British women, beginning with the Indigenous farmers of the Great Plains. The book is about how women sought and fought to obtain land and cultivate the prairies, bringing to light many forgotten women farmers and ranchers.

The promoters, planners, and plotters of farming for British women on the Canadian prairies were middle-class or elite and educated women, located mainly in London, who were devoted to the British Empire. They were obsessed with finding solutions to the perceived problem of "redundant," "surplus," or "superfluous" women of the mother country. This book is also about less-privileged women, many British or British-Ontarian and almost all widows, who could spare little thought for the Empire but who came to prairie Canada to claim homesteads to support their families. Many succeeded, others were thwarted, but all faced an obstinate, sceptical, and powerful Canadian federal government bureaucracy. Women with capital who purchased land to farm or ranch on the prairies could escape the surveillance of the bureaucracy that policed the homesteaders, but they were scrutinized in the press and other publications that tended to cast them as abnormal and suspicious. While widespread opposition to the prospect of women farmers began to decline slightly in Britain—where the idea of middle-class women farming small acreages and cultivating the least remunerative and most troublesome crops found a degree of acceptance—powerful opponents in Canada and Canadian officials in England remained fiercely determined to shut almost all windows of opportunity throughout the decades of this study.[3] To find out why this intransigence persisted, the colonial context of prairie Canada is critical.

Prairie Canada was crafted as a colony of the British Empire, and hopes were high for its destiny as the brightest agricultural jewel in the imperial diadem. But the British were to transplant and cultivate not only the crops that would make the prairies the breadbasket of the Empire: here was a "sparsely-peopled or savage-haunted" place where they could plant, grow, and prune a "dominating race." Scotswoman Jessie M. Saxby equated cultivation and farming with civilization, using garden analogies and eugenic allusions in her 1890 book, *West-Nor'-West*, that urged the women and men of Britain to settle on the prairies:

> We should look upon the British Isles as the cradle and nursery of the world—a nursery garden where the best kinds of seedlings and saplings are trained into vigorous young life for the purpose of transplanting into wide gardens, lawns, and woodlands!
>
> What sort of a place would the nursery-garden become, what sort of plants would the promising shoots develop into, if incessant and careful transplanting were not carried out? What sort of credit would attain to the gardener who consigned to his customers only diseased, pining, puny, malformed plants?

> We ought to send to our colonies—to the whole uninhabited, or sparsely-peopled, or savage-haunted places of the earth—"well-assorted specimens" from our home nursery-garden, and our transplanting of those goodly young shoots should be more systematic, more discerning, and more wholesale than it is at present.
>
> ... When shall we fully accept, and show ourselves equal to, our unique destiny—that of a dominating race which must absorb within itself all lower-races, and make itself the ruling power for good of a planet?[4]

During the time frame of this book (the 1870s to the 1930s) most of prairie Canada was gobbled up by white settlers, the squares on the map filled with their names. The Canadian West was a settler colony where First Nations were dispossessed and relegated to small reserves and prevented from obtaining other land on their former territory.[5] As anthropologist Patrick Wolfe writes, settler colonies are driven by a "logic of elimination."[6] Indigenous people were not to play any role in the development of the new economy and society, except to serve as relics of a primitive past that were useful for comparative purposes when demonstrating "strides in the march of progress."[7] "Your noble and idle savage who lives by hunting is dead or doomed," wrote an advocate of settling gentleman English farmers in Canada's West in 1885.[8] "He will not work himself, though he is not ashamed to beg ... Another nobler race, quickened with some of the best blood in the 'old country' ... should be ready to take its place among the masters of the richest parts of a young dominion."[9] Agriculture on reserves was stymied and stifled, a process that was assisted by prevailing views of Indigenous men as inept farmers and shiftless workers.[10] The township of my Manitoba family was on the Treaty One ancestral territory of the Cree and Anishinaabe (Ojibwa or Saulteaux), and there are seven reserves within the boundaries of that treaty occupied by those First Nations. There are also five small reserves of the Dakota, who were not signatory to any treaty.

British settlers were favoured, and they were assigned the task of improving the land, which was considered to be lying "tenantless and silent, only awaiting the Anglo-Saxon race to be transformed into a prosperous and thriving country."[11] As an 1888 promotional publication from Manitoba described the prairie, "Man alone is apparently the missing quantity, and his energy, industry and capital are the required elements in developing the young, but sturdy Dominion into the Greater Britain of the West—the worthy scion of the grand old Motherland across the seas, whose pride is in the colonial gems which adorn the imperial diadem, of which Canada is one of the brightest and most valued jewels."[12]

The use of the term "man" was not in this case intended to extend to and include "woman." The job of empire building was man's work; the white, British, male settler or frontiersman was the heroic figure, taming the "wild frontier into productivity and profitability."[13] A 1910 poem valorizing these men of the far-flung colonies praised their work: "For glory and Empire for home and for beauty; / Away on the fringe of Canadian prairies, / Far up on the heights of African aeries, / Cut off from his kin on Indian stations. / The sentinel frontiersman watches the Nations / In the bush of Australia way over the Seas, / On Islands from Fiji to far Hebrides."[14]

Many (ghastly) poems about the Canadian West, including "The Prairie," by Jack Damusey, celebrated the manliness of empire building and the work of agriculture:

I have place for men
With windy spaces for their square-walled homes;
My lonesomeness awaits the laugh of those who are young.
  Young men I want:
  Young men,
  Stripped,
  Ploughing,
  Building,
  Scheming.
  In sweaty jeans,
Young men with blood and muscles taut and backs of steel
To tame my winds of winter bleak,
To bear my summer's heat.
My breast is rich for them,
But let them be cruel,
Eager like wolves for grain,
I have no valleys for the old;
No sacred woods for ancient gods,
Only the dry, windswept waste
That must be quelled.[15]

Establishing farms was white man's work in the colonies.[16] In *Sowing Empire: Landscape and Colonization,* scholar Jill H. Casid writes that colonial farms and plantations "justified and glorified patriarchally organized and controlled agricultural production and heterosexual reproduction as the necessary bases for family and for national and *imperial* stability, peace and prosperity. At the heart of this mythic construction of empire is the farm—a cultivated, constructed site of agriculture, of nature improved by the intervention of 'man' that functioned as both the material impress and reproducing sign of empire."[17]

In the colony of prairie Canada, the British man would become more manly than his weaker and effete counterpart in the factories and offices of the mother country. Scottish settler Thomas Spence reported from Manitoba in 1879 that "his muscles will be iron, his nerves steel. Vigor will characterize his every action; for climate gives quality to the blood, strength to the muscles, power to the brain."[18] E.B. Osborn, literary editor of the London *Morning Post,* wrote in 1900 that "to live for a year or two in Western Canada is to learn the essential meaning of a man's manhood."[19] As historian Philippa Levine has written, "This vision of masculinity as that which could transform unproductive spaces profitably was simply not on offer to women or to the colonized."[20]

Colonialism, founded on ideas about racial supremacy, reached its apogee at the same time as the consolidation of the liberal political order, supposedly devoted to ideals of freedom and self-government. Patterns of domination, hierarchy, and exclusion were at the core of liberal states, some of which had extensive and powerful empires.[21] Patriarchy was also necessary to the functioning of the liberal order. Historian Adele Perry argues that "imperialism and patriarchy were not complications of or exceptions to the liberal order; they were necessary to its very production." The "liberal order project was predicated on the privatization of women and the relegation of non-Western peoples to various states of reduced humanity, savagery, unfreedom, or containment."[22] The liberal order was premised on the exclusion of women: Liberal subjects were male and European, and they were the genuine political and economic subjects, while "women and racialized people were not so, only potentially so, or at best provisionally and partially so."[23] The liberal male subject was defined through wives' lack of economic autonomy. Wives were virtually excluded from the basic principle of the liberal contract, the right to own property, and while this was challenged and began to erode over the nineteenth century, this study demonstrates how white, mainly British or British-Ontarian settler men continued to secure exclusive rights to property well into the twentieth century through the exclusion of women and Indigenous people. They were assisted in this task by powerful and pervasive ideas of who constituted a capable farmer and landowner, and who was excluded from this category because they allegedly lacked the necessary strength, determination, knowledge, and skills.

If the British man became more masculine by crossing the ocean and settling on the prairies, the British woman was supposed to become even more feminine, her domestic role to be confirmed and preserved. While sailing to the colonies was an act of emancipation for men, firing them with new hopes and aspirations, landing them on their own plots where they could be autonomous and creative, women colonizers were vessels to transport and perpetuate British culture and identity. Women were not to quell the windswept waste. British settler women were to be protected, cared for and cosseted, defined and managed. The colonial tasks assigned to them were to make homes and babies, and it was made virtually impossible for them to do otherwise. This was to be the immutable foundation of the new society, the order of nature. Women were to be models of feminine deportment and conduct and of a cherished gender order that was undergoing turbulent challenge and change in Britain, but was to be transplanted to the colony unspoiled and unsullied. Their central duty and mission was to reproduce and to tame the wild colonial males. As summarized by a promoter: "Colonization without women is futile. Only when women go out at the same time is there a chance of the men settling down soberly and steadily; and besides that, whereas a thousand Englishmen in a colony are a thousand men and no more, every Englishwoman that you take out at the same time carries with her, as it were, four potential English colonists as well."[24]

Feminist scholars have pointed out that "settler colonialism rested on control of female reproduction, not only of indigenous inhabitants, but also of settler women."[25] As historian of Australia Jane Carey has written, if "settler colonialism was driven by the 'logic of elimination' in relation to Indigenous peoples, then the imperative of vigorous white propagation was its necessary corollary."[26] In the Canadian West, the category of "white" was complicated by the presence of the "foreign" migrant, heightening anxieties about the degeneracy of the British fabric of the colony.[27] It was

British women who were to reproduce the most vigorously in the face of these racial anxieties.

British women were not to toil in the fields, to become muscular and masculine, tanned and dark skinned. Impeccable behaviour and demeanour was expected of them, as they were to serve as sharp contrasts to Indigenous women and to peasant settler women from Eastern Europe.[28] In these "primitive" societies, women were understood to be abused and brutalized, made to work outside, while the British allegedly protected and respected proper womanhood by relegating women to the home. The Doukhobors, settlers from Russia, were used to illustrate the stark contrast between the desired and the condemned activities for women. Doukhobor women had hitched themselves to the plough to break land in their settlements and had to "sweat in the fields instead of horses." In Canada they needed to be reclaimed from the "brute level to which they had been degraded, to the home, with its cooking, its spinning and its weaving."[29] Levine writes that "women thus became a fulcrum by which the British measured and judged those they colonized. Women became an index and a measure less of themselves than of men and of societies."[30] In the colonies, British women were to be symbols of cleanliness and purity in contrast to women of other ethnicities, and they were to maintain and display genteel dress and deportment.[31] Kitchen gardens and flower beds were acceptable, as they upheld and perpetuated genteel identities. Farm labour was not acceptable.

British colonial women were, as scholar Anne McClintock writes, "ambiguously placed" within the process of imperial rule: "Barred from the corridors of formal power, they experienced the privileges and social contradictions of imperialism very differently from colonial men … [they] made none of the direct economic or military decisions of empire and very few reaped its vast profits." They were bound in "gendered patterns of disadvantage and frustration," McClintock writes, as it was "white men who made and enforced laws and policies in their own interests." Colonial women held positions of power over colonized women and men and were thus not "hapless onlookers of empire but were ambiguously complicit both as colonizers and colonized, privileged and restricted, acted upon and acting."[32]

In prairie Canada, British women and Canadian-born women of British ancestry did not share in all of the privileges often associated with whiteness, such as the "exercise of power and the expectation of advantages in acquiring property."[33] Whiteness did not equate with power and privilege for other groups in the Canadian West, as certain types of immigrants from Europe were denounced as "foreigners" who were beneath the British. In the Canadian West, a sense of Britishness combined with whiteness to distinguish the elites who would rule from those who would be subject to rule.[34] Frustrated that they were members of this elite yet did not make decisions, did not reap the profits, and did not enjoy all of the privileges and power of that elite, British settler women behind the homesteads-for-women campaign hoped to garner support by articulating an imperialist vision to demonstrate their fitness for the land denied to them yet available to "foreign" men. Situated on their homesteads instead of "foreign" men, British women would transport and transplant British civilization. This campaign also involved the denigration and denouncement of "foreign" women, in order to elevate their own status and bolster arguments for their entitlement. First Nations women were scarcely even in the picture, as they were relegated to reserves and subject to intense surveillance, laws, and policies.

But for British women to establish and operate their own homesteads and farms and work on the land was in direct contrast to their assigned role as models of domestic, feminine demeanour and deportment. Working out of doors was a remnant of an earlier, darker time. Only "primitive" settler women were obliged to labour in the fields and barnyard. There were grave fears that women were "changing to masculinity" as a result of doing work "which men ought to do."[35] According to one expert from 1910, this was a reversion to savagery, as "women in the savage state were so like men in form that it was well-nigh impossible to tell them apart."[36] As this book demonstrates, other British settler colonies shared the same aversion to any public display of women working in the fields. It might be acceptable in England, it was declared in a 1906 letter in an Australian newspaper on "The Female Farmer," because there "surplus" women were "driven into working to support themselves."[37] Where white women were in the minority in a colony, however, they were to revert to their proper vocations as wives and mothers.

If a woman in the prairie West did succeed in obtaining land of her own to farm, she was likely to be seen as suspect, eccentric, and aberrant in her community, belonging in neither the masculine nor the feminine realms. An example was Lizzie Hillis, from Ireland, who homesteaded 320 acres north of Hanna, Alberta, having purchased South African scrip (to be discussed in Chapter 3).[38] Hillis was remembered in her district as being able "to keep up to any man and do any work he did, even hauling bundles on the threshing crew."[39] One year while threshing it took the men "several days before some of them realized she was a woman." She was known as "Old Lizzie," and years of living alone allegedly made her strange, even crazy. She was "famous for taking after people she didn't like with a pitchfork," and that included a priest. Hillis could "hold her own with anybody and cuss like a trooper." While "her batching" was described as "no worse than that of most of the men who were homesteaders," the message was clear that for a woman this was deviant and unacceptable. She made her own clothes out of flour sacks, and one outfit she wore had "a clearly visible 'Alberta's Best' right across her seat." She returned to Ireland in the 1920s and died there. But the story of the Hillis farm did not end there. Her sister Mary came from Ireland to Lizzie's land in the mid-1930s and built a new house with an "absolutely useless" fireplace. According to the local history she was an "old maid and partially paralyzed." Although a nephew lived with her for a time, she was all alone when she "took sick and was found by the neighbors frozen to death under her kitchen table."[40]

Although settler women were to confine themselves to the domestic realm in theory, all women on homesteads—whether widows, daughters, wives, sisters, or mothers; whether British, Doukhobor, or Ukrainian—did a great deal of the physical labour required, particularly in the early years of homesteading and farming. English homesteader Edward West described the work of women in his book *Homesteading: Two Prairie Seasons*:

> One would meet them trudging alone over the prairie, hunting among the bluffs for stray cattle, or see them helping their husbands to dig out stones, or mounted on a plough or disc driving a team of bulls, or hear tales of how they had helped their husbands to dig wells or build the little shack. In some cases they would hold down the homestead with two or three young children while the husband was earning money (getting a "grub stake," as it is called), or even go out themselves to do the same as cooks while their husbands performed the homestead duties.[41]

Local histories often detail the work done by "mother" to secure the homestead. One son of homesteaders near the Montana-Saskatchewan border described how his mother, Mary Kluth, dug rocks and stooked and stacked grain on their land and for neighbours. She gave birth to a son in their homestead shack a day after baking fourteen loaves of bread, and five days later she was cooking for a threshing crew. In 1914 she made fourteen trips across the border to Malta, Montana, "hauling grain one way and bringing back posts, wire, groceries, and the year's needs. Sometimes the weather wasn't too good but most of the time she slept under the wagon. Dad dug rock, tried to get more land broke and looked after us kids while Mother was on the road."[42]

A mother of six small children on a Saskatchewan homestead described the work she performed in 1905 while her husband was away with a threshing crew. This included building their first sod barn:

> The job was hard and we did not have hardly anything to work with. We had gotten a fireguard broken and it was from this that we got the necessary sod. The two oldest children carried the sod between them on a board and I did the building. As this was an exceedingly slow way as the poor children could not carry enough to keep me busy, I made a harness for the cow and made her help us in the hauling the [*sic*] sod. This was a little better but as the harness was not very substantial, it was breaking continually and made things very trying and because of this I had a job every evening of either repairing the old harness or making a new one. The utensils I had to make the sod level with consisted of an old butcher knife and sticks we found lying around. Finally it was completed and a roof was made from poplar poles which we managed to get out of the valley near by.[43]

As women's rights activist Nellie McClung wryly observed in 1916: "Women are doing homestead duties wherever homestead duties are being done ... No person objects to the homesteader's wife having to get out wood, or break up scrub land, or drive oxen, so long as she is not doing these things for herself and has no legal claim on the result of her labour. Working for someone else is very sweet and womanly, and most commendable. What a neat blending there is of kindness and cruelty in the complacent utterances of the armchair philosophers who tell us that women have not the physical strength to do the hard tasks of life."[44]

Yet the conviction that women should not work in the fields and farm their own land, nor be given any official encouragement or sanction to do so, prevailed among lawmakers and other decision makers, and was pressed into service well into the twentieth century. As historian Kathryn Gleadle has argued, the "perpetuation of a dominant discourse concerning the feminized nature of women's public presence obscured cultural knowledge as to the vigorous activities which women often performed on the ground."[45] It was also convenient for authorities to ignore, belittle, or minimize evidence of women's labour on farms.

Englishwoman, journalist, and Saskatchewan farmer Georgina Binnie-Clark challenged the view that British women were incapable of work on the land. In a 1913 presentation on "Land and the Woman in Canada" to the Royal Colonial Institute in London, she made the case that women should farm large acreages and grow grain, the most lucrative crop. Binnie-Clark argued that they were capable of all forms of farm labour, and that British women should be eligible to acquire homestead land so they could play a critical role in the "spade-work of British expansion."[46] She was harshly criticized in the discussion that followed by powerful men in the audience. J. Obed Smith, in charge of the London office of emigration from Europe to Canada and responsible for sending hundreds of thousands of men, women, and children to Canada, was utterly opposed to the idea of women farmers in "this, that, or any other land."[47] He said women were physically incapable of carrying on farming operations, and he "dissociated himself entirely from the idea that a woman alone could pursue general farming in Canada." The next discussant agreed that "it would be most disastrous not only for the woman, but for the reputation of Canada, for any woman to start grain farming in the West."[48]

Influential men like J. Obed Smith and Frank Oliver, minister of the interior from 1905–11, were involved in controversial land speculation themselves, using their positions of influence and knowledge for their own benefit and, in the case of Oliver, to profit his allies and friends.[49] Oliver was particularly adamant and unrepentant that the work of building empire and the profits to be secured were for men only, although this did not include Indigenous men.[50] Oliver was also critical and sceptical of the capacity of "foreign" Europeans to assist in the development and settlement of the West.

All of these groups—women, Indigenous people, Europeans of non-British descent—were marginalized through a variety of political, material, and imaginative systems, or "structures of constraint" that perpetuated subordination and inferiority.[51] The idea that women should not work outdoors was particularly imaginative as it defied what was happening throughout the prairies, where women's work was essential to the establishment of the agricultural economy of the West. But men such as Smith and Oliver had little interest in sanctioning any large-scale change that might undermine the benefits and profits accruing to them and their associates. They had a direct interest in asserting the representational system, however imaginary, that there was a "true" or "normal" gender order that relegated women to hearth and home and banished them from the fields.

A primary reason that women in Canada were denied homesteads was because it would make them "independent of marriage." Frank Oliver believed that "women were already averse to marriage, and he considered that to admit them to the opportunities of the land grant would be to make them more independent of marriage than ever."[52] In my book *The Importance of Being Monogamous*, I detail Canada's determination to impose the monogamous, lifelong, intraracial, and heterosexual model of marriage on the diverse population of Western Canada as central to the nation-building project. The gendered ideals behind the homestead laws, which established the foundation of the economy and society of the prairies, ensured that women had little opportunity to stray from marriage.[53] Nellie McClung summed up this mentality: "The reason given for denying homesteads to women is that it will make them too independent of marriage and it is not independent women we want. It is population … It sounds as if the government was afraid that if women could do anything else, they would not get married."[54]

The useful although imaginary idea that women should not work in the fields was clearly articulated by a Canadian general in 1921, when Canada sought to discourage British women, in particular the land army women of the First World War, from imagining they could come to Canada and work on the land or farm land of their own. Brigadier-General R. Manley Sims said that "it must always be remembered that the Anglo-Saxon never willingly accepts the idea of women for outdoor labor. It is considered, and I think rightly, too heavy for them. It was a war emergency measure and we don't want it continued."[55] This sentiment was echoed by a settler from England who wrote an account of his years in Western Canada and found that "one of the finest of Canadian characteristics [was] the profound reverence with which their women are regarded. Quite rightly they believe that it is not a woman's duty to work the land."[56]

Cora Hind, agricultural editor for the *Manitoba Free Press* and a women's rights activist, was asked by an English journalist in the late 1920s if it was possible for a woman to farm in Canada. Hind replied that while it was possible, she did not advise it, and explained: "You see, a woman can't go on the land as she would in England, for so many of the population of the prairies are low type Central Europeans, who, as a matter of course, make their womenfolk work outside. The result of this is that the Canadian farmer—by that I mean a man of British stock—says, 'I will have no "white" women working on my farm,' for he thinks if he does this he is sinking to the level of the 'bohunk.'"[57] Hind went on to point out that there were only two "real openings for women in Western Canada. The first is domestic work, and the second is more domestic work—marriage to a prairie farmer."[58] There was little hope if even Cora Hind could not advise women to farm in Canada.

That British women colonizers sought land of their own in the colonies has been overlooked in sweeping studies of the "great land rush" or "rise of the Anglo-world."[59] Land seeking has been assumed to be and cast as a uniquely male and particularly British male obsession. Englishman Edward West described his "hunt for homesteads" on the prairies, writing that "it was certainly interesting to see one square half-mile of land after another, with the prospect of owning one of them as a freehold, and one began to wonder if some of the immigration were not due to a sort of hereditary land-hunger, a sort of instinct, inherited from Saxon or other ancestors, to get hold of a bit of Mother Earth, there to have elbow-room and be able to develop ourselves and do our work, without cramping and artificial shackles." British women, too, exemplified this "land hunger" and tried "to get hold of a bit of Mother Earth" to participate in the "great game" and be true partners in empire. As many struggled to make a living to rise above poverty at a time when few vocations were available to them, they may have had even more need and desire for land than did the men, who had far more options.

Frank G. Roe, homesteader, historian, and train engineer, described in his memoir how his mother, Mary Ann Roe, from Sheffield, England, proved up on her homestead in Alberta, earning her patent to her land at the age of sixty in 1902.[60] Her husband and Frank's father died of pneumonia just over a year after arriving in Alberta, after he was "lost on the prairie one night during a terrific rainstorm."[61] Yet Mary Ann Roe persevered and flourished, according to her son, as she was a "born pioneer" who "embraced the new life with joyous eagerness."[62] In her estimation their tiny sod house, "standing on its own acres and ours, was no step down in the world but a decided step up."[63] Frank G. Roe described a "passionate longing" for land that was hardly reserved to men alone:

> It will, one may hope, have been made plain that it was not from any poverty of ideas that such a woman found rest in her soul in the new sphere. Without some historical knowledge of the eviction of the disinherited English peasantry from these ancient "common fields," which once, as their name indicates, were common to themselves conjointly with other classes, it is difficult to realize their passionate longing. The land was to them as the very marrow of their bones. Beyond measure, to such people the possession of acres of their own over which they could stride at will outweighed everything that could be thrown into the scales against it. This was their kingdom and even a sod house could become as a royal palace and she set about to make it one.[64]

Settler women were complicit in the enterprise of dispossessing Indigenous people. They too coveted Indigenous land and resources and were land takers. Migrant women, including those who were British, were homesteaders, speculators, squatters, and purchasers of land, including land fraudulently surrendered on First Nation reserves, and they profited and benefited from the core mission of the colonial project that rested on a foundation of dispossession. But as McClintock reminds us, colonial women were ambiguously complicit; they were both privileged and restricted. They had to struggle for a share in the bounty of Indigenous land, and they faced gendered roadblocks and barriers. As a columnist for the London paper the *Vote* concluded with resignation in 1927, "difficulties, almost insuperable, are put in the paths of women who wish, in our Dominions overseas, to be 'settlers' in the true meaning of the word."[65] British women were largely unsuccessful in their quest for land of their own to farm in prairie Canada, unless they could afford to purchase it.

But through understanding their efforts, their absence from the township maps, as well as the determination of colonial authorities to stymie and prevent them, we can better comprehend how "the vast, fissured architecture of imperialism was gendered throughout."[66]

The ideal of the independent colonial woman farmer was not confined to the British Empire. In German Southwest Africa there was hope that the single woman settler could farm independently, overcoming the prejudices that prevailed at home. Like Georgina Binnie-Clark, and at exactly the same time, travel writer Clara Brockmann promoted the idea of German women as farmers in African colonies.[67] Brockmann was confident German women could do all the farming tasks a man could and also acquire the experience needed in "the handling of their natives." And as we will see in the chapters that follow, women of many nationalities sought to establish themselves as farmers and landowners in British colonies. "I had a farm in Africa, at the foot of the Ngong Hills" is how Isak Dinesen (Karen Blixen), from Denmark, began her memoir *Out of Africa* about her coffee plantation and six thousand acres of land in the British colony Kenya.[68]

While the British colonial context is critical, Canada's proximity to the United States is also essential to understanding the gendered history of the prairies, as the makers of Canada were determined that this British outpost would be forged in the image of the mother country and be distinct from the perceived disarray that prevailed to the south.[69] Canadian laws drawn from the British legal heritage deliberately constituted a world in which white men were the genuine political and economic subjects and women only provisionally so. A British model of gender relations was idealized and emulated, while the perceived gender chaos of the United States was condemned and abhorred. The U.S. West was a much more welcoming environment to migrant women who were single, divorced, separated, or widowed. While still a minority, women homesteaders were significantly more numerous south of the forty-ninth parallel. As historian R. Douglas Hurt has summarized in his recent study *The Big Empty: The Great Plains in the Twentieth Century*, "homesteading offered an irresistible opportunity for thousands of women … who considered a quarter section (160 acres) of land nothing less than the promise of independence, freedom and security."[70] They homesteaded for economic gain and to enhance family landholdings, and male homesteaders did the same. In states such as North Dakota, women constituted approximately 20 percent of homesteaders, and they proved up on their claims as often as—and in some states with a higher degree of success than—their male counterparts. Most were young and single, but there were also older women, many of whom had been widowed or were divorced. (In both the United States and Canada, married women were denied the right to homestead.) Like male homesteaders, they tended to settle among networks of family and friends, and also like male homesteaders, they generally had jobs that provided the capital necessary to establish a farm. Some, like male homesteaders, sold or rented their land after they proved up, while others stayed and kept their land in the family. The proportion of women homesteaders increased on the Great Plains of the United States in the twentieth century. Hurt concludes that "homesteading strengthened the influence of women in their families, and it expanded their work roles in the home and community. Homesteading reinforced the ability of women to act independently as self-determining people who took responsibility for their own lives. By homesteading, single women gained access to property, managed their land, controlled resources, and decided how to spend their money."[71]

Migrant women to Western Canada were deliberately and systematically denied this access to property and the right to manage their own land and resources. The example of the United States as a situation to be avoided was paramount in the justifications Canadian officials provided for denying homestead rights to women. J. Obed Smith told Georgina Binnie-Clark after her 1913 talk at the Royal Colonial Institute in London that Canada had deliberately departed from the U.S. legislation that permitted single women to homestead, as in his view this had led to "disastrous results."[72] Looking back over the twentieth century, and basing his summary on many studies of women homesteaders in the United States, Hurt does not mention any "disastrous results" except that some women consolidated their homesteads with those of their husbands after marriage; that some, like men, failed to prove up; and that some used their land as an investment and moved on. Smith and other Canadian decision makers manufactured an imaginary but useful foil of a foreign land to the south where unscrupulous women were "sham" homesteaders, incompetent farmers, and devious manipulators of the laws.

Over the course of researching and writing this book it became a project of unravelling the profound entanglement of colonial and metropolitan histories, and of discovering how the colonial culture of prairie Canada was constituted through a complex interplay of the local, the region across borders, the national, and the imperial. This book is an effort to write a history that looks beyond the nation in order to "unsettle the naturalness of the nation-state as analytical framework."[73] It is about the circulation of ideas and individuals within the British Empire and across the border shared with the United States. While the book stresses the importance of understanding the projects and the "knowledge," assumptions, or understandings generated from metropoles, it is also about how imperial plots and plans were not monolithic but were contested, debated, and disputed in both the "motherland" and the colony.

I begin with the ancient agriculture of the Great Plains of North America, where women were the farmers, owning their own land and raising produce for sale as well as for their families. The history of Indigenous agriculture is important in understanding that it was not natural or inevitable that women would be virtually excluded from the category "farmer" in the settlement era on the Canadian prairies. That the first farmers were Indigenous women is vital to comprehending why British women colonizers were to symbolize distance, departure, and progression from this earlier and ancient way of life. Chapter 1 then analyzes the gendered and racialized visions that were at the heart of the grid survey and homestead system that blanketed and suffocated Indigenous ways of living on the land. These visions had both American and British imperial antecedents, although there were significant variations in the opportunities for migrant women to own and farm land in British colonies and the U.S. West. There were no obvious and universally shared assumptions about which categories of settler men and women should be given land grants. In prairie Canada, First Nations people were relegated to small reserves where farming was encouraged among males but not females, and on a limited scale that would not require more land. Only a few widows managed to farm on reserves. Land grants to the Métis, called scrip, were issued to men, women, and children, but the scrip system was designed to ensure that they were soon divested of their land. Once this stage was set, the Dominion Lands Act prevailed over the distribution of land on the prairies. Under this legislation, single women could obtain homesteads in prairie Canada, and this chapter traces the history of some of the women who claimed land in Manitoba. This right was abruptly removed in 1876 legislation, however, without discussion or debate, and while no official spelled out exactly why, this chapter speculates on the rationales for this deliberate eradication. From then on it was the white male colonizer only who was to make the wilderness productive and profitable. Single settler women were quickly dispatched and relegated to roles as domestic servants and as potential wives and mothers through this change in legislation. Although their labour on homesteads was expected and required, women were not to be the owners of land unless they were widows with children or could afford to purchase land. Just when the homestead right for most women was removed, one other short-lived opportunity was offered to them: the tree claim, which allowed women and men alike to acquire small plots of land to plant trees. The tree claim concept was soon abandoned, however, as it proved absurd in the prairie environment.

The focus of the second chapter is Britain, and particularly England, where in the nineteenth century the notion of women working in the fields and having land of their own to farm was vigorously debated and discussed. Prominent advocates of agriculture for "gentlewomen" arose by the late nineteenth century and succeeded to some extent in countering earlier views that women working outdoors was not feminine, civilized, or progressive. Farming on a small scale, in groups or settlements of women and concentrating on the "lighter," more feminine branches of agriculture, was one of a number of useful vocations proposed as a solution to a perceived surplus of women. There ought to be an "agricultural brigade of the monstrous regiment of women," as coined by one advocate. By about 1910 there was a "widespread gardening and farming movement among women in England."[74] The arguments and rationales that were advanced in Britain are important to understanding the debates in Canada, particularly during the years of the homesteads-for-women movement.

Opposition to women farmers, gardeners, and horticulturalists remained intense, however, and there were hopes that the colonies could provide a more congenial environment where old prejudices and attitudes might vanish. Chapter 2 also considers the hopes and aspirations for British gentlewomen farmers in the colonies, particularly Canada, a cause that intersected and overlapped with that of sending "surplus women" to the colonies, as advanced by emigration societies and philanthropic individuals. Farming was one of a number of potential vocations for women in the colonies, and it was hoped that farming could attract migrants not drawn to domestic service, even when that was cloaked in more equal and respectable terms as "home help." Many who advocated that British women emigrate to the colonies assumed that ultimately women of superior upbringing would not wish to soil their hands by working on farms, but would instead settle into their proper and expected functions as wives and mothers of a great imperial race on colonial soil. The colonies, including Canada, wanted domestic workers and were interested in few other categories of women. Colonial training schools for young women bloomed across Britain, and while some provided instruction in poultry or horticulture, all concentrated more on the domestic skills required in the colonies.

Increasingly, prairie Canada was seen as the most convivial destination for British women wanting to farm over more problematic colonies such as South Africa, where farm work was performed by "Kaffirs" while the white woman farmer would have to manage and direct their labour. The prairies were seen (incorrectly) as emptier—a virtually Indigenousless land. The trend in favour of farming in prairie Canada is traced in the *Imperial Colonist*, the journal published by the British Women's Emigration Association. Other organizations such as the Colonial Intelligence League, also with headquarters in London, sought to send women to Western Canada to farm. Fiction for girls set in the colonies presented robust and independent heroines who took on arduous outdoor work and often owned or managed land of their own. Advocates of the emigration of British women to prairie Canada included devoted imperialist Flora Shaw, of the *Times* of London, whose proposals were augmented and advanced by Canadian journalist Mary Agnes Fitzgibbon, who advocated a training school for British women in the West that would prepare them to farm land of their own. In the very early years of the twentieth century, promotional publications of the Canadian Pacific Railway also cast women, particularly British women, as efficient owners and managers of farms on the prairies. There were also competing and compelling counter narratives presenting quite an opposite view of the woman settler in the colonies, some fictional and one based on the personal experience of a "Lady Emigrant" to Ontario.

Following the 1876 legislation, there remained one category of women in Canada eligible to file for the homestead grant: those who were the "sole" head of their family. This was interpreted to mean a widow with at least one minor child entirely dependent upon her. A man over the age of eighteen and single was the "sole" head of his family even though he had no children, but the rules were read quite differently in the case of women. Chapter 3 details the experiences of some of these female household heads who homesteaded, many of whom were from Britain. The case of Virden, Manitoba, homesteader Susanna Willis, whose land was expropriated from her, demonstrates how very different rules could be applied to male and female homesteaders. Women who were unable to vote and had no political clout were easily expendable. The Willis case also demonstrates that when women homesteaders ended up with very valuable land, it was coveted by others.

Over the years the categories of eligible women homesteaders were narrowed through rulings and decisions made by bureaucrats as they debated just what constituted a "sole" head of a family. The morality and virtue of the woman homesteader was policed through the legislation and the bureaucracy that interpreted and enforced it. The separated or divorced woman was subject to particularly intense scrutiny, as were those who adopted children because it was often assumed they had done so only to acquire land. Women were tenacious and inventive in their strategies to acquire and keep their homesteads. Through purchasing South African scrip, many women, regardless of marital status, were able to acquire 320 acres of homestead land in Western Canada, but they had to have significant capital to do so, and they were obliged to prove up on their land. A final strategy of women who wanted to acquire land was to cross the border and homestead in the United States, where single women could file on land and where there was greater leniency toward separated or divorced women.

Women were free to purchase land in Western Canada, regardless of their marital status, and if they did they could escape the surveillance of the Department of the Interior, although many were still subject to intense scrutiny and, in some cases, censure. Chapter 4 provides a range of examples of women who bought land as investors, speculators, farmers, or ranchers. Women bought land from the Canadian Pacific Railway, they obtained land through purchasing Métis scrip, and they bought reserve land "surrendered" by First Nations. Jean Laidlaw, for example, originally from England, had a large ranch on Piikani (Peigan) reserve land that was placed on the market despite the protests of members of that First Nation. Some of these women farmers and ranchers attracted considerable attention from the press, becoming minor celebrities. Coverage varied in nature and purpose. Some was purely promotional, in an effort to generate sales of railway land. Feminist journalists were motivated to showcase women successfully establishing farms and ranches to counter prejudice and opposition. Almost all were careful to stress that the women farmers of the Canadian prairies retained their femininity. But some of the press coverage conveyed the message that this was rare, strange, and abnormal work for women. A particular focus in this chapter is the most famous woman farmer of the West, Isobel "Jack" May, who was well-known in

England before she came to Canada. She was featured in articles throughout Canada, the United States, and the British Empire as the "bachelor girl" settler who dressed in "male attire" and had a female companion who took care of the domestic work on their Alberta farm. As a result May was subject to particularly close scrutiny. Some years later English author Patricia Carlisle (known also as Miss Peter Webber) briefly farmed in Alberta, wearing "male attire" and also with a female companion. The prairies, however, proved to be a hostile environment for women who did not conform to feminine ideals.

The other famous Englishwoman farmer of the prairies deserves her own chapter. In 1905 Georgina Binnie-Clark purchased a farm at Fort Qu'Appelle, Saskatchewan. She was a writer and had no experience with farming when she arrived on the prairies that summer to visit her homesteading brother. But from then on she became an ardent promoter of farming as a vocation for British women on the Canadian prairies. Binnie-Clark was also devoted to the British Empire and believed that there were many more women like her who could contribute to the "spade work of British expansion." She not only farmed but published many newspaper articles, lectured in England between 1908 and 1914, and wrote two books about her experiences. For a time Binnie-Clark also trained young Englishwomen in agriculture at her Fort Qu'Appelle farm. Binnie-Clark had even grander schemes that never materialized, including cottage training farms that she hoped could be sponsored by the Canadian Pacific Railway. She was more radical than advocates in Britain, as she was not content with small holdings and "lighter" branches of agriculture, exhorting women instead that growing grain on large acreages was the most profitable return on their investment in land. She disdained housework, far preferred work on the land, and did not speak or write at any time that she or any other woman required a husband. She challenged the idea that women did not have the physical capacity to perform farm work, but unlike "Jack" May, Binnie-Clark was careful to appear in fashionable gowns when she spoke in public (although neighbours recalled her wearing "britches and leggings" on her farm.) She helped inspire the homesteads-for-British-women campaign that originated in 1908, was the first to advocate land grants for British women rather than "foreign" men, and was the central advocate of that cause in England.

Drawn to the suffrage movement and confronting authorities of the Canadian federal government in various departments, however,

Binnie-Clark alienated and aggravated less radical advocates of farming for British women, although she also had influential supporters. She became a lightning rod to those who were utterly opposed to women farmers, such as J. Obed Smith. While Binnie-Clark's 1913 presentation on "Land and the Woman in Canada" to the Royal Colonial Institute was perhaps the greatest achievement of her career and for the cause, it also generated harsh condemnation both in Canada and England. Her 1914 book *Wheat and Woman*, published in England, should have helped to advance the cause of homesteads-for-British-women, but it appeared just before the start of the First World War and interest was diverted to much more pressing issues. Binnie-Clark helped to organize women workers on the land in England during the war, deserting her Saskatchewan farm, and she did not return until the mid-1920s. By that time she had dropped homesteads-for-women, although she continued to promote the settlement of British people in Canada, with an emphasis on families.

While Binnie-Clark focussed on England in her lectures and publications, a homesteads-for-women campaign gained momentum on the prairies, and this is the subject of Chapter 6. The women's columns of the prairie farm journals became the focus of the campaign. Isabelle Beaton Graham of the *Grain Growers' Guide* was the most determined and industrious in generating interest in and support for the cause. In 1910 an initial, Edmonton-based petition calling for homesteads for any unmarried woman in Canada over the age of thirty was organized by an American woman who had hoped to settle in Alberta and was surprised to find she could not homestead in Canada. This initiative did not go far but helped to inspire a much more concerted effort, led by women who took pride in their British ancestry and who eventually settled on the strategy of seeking homestead rights for themselves alone, excluding American and other women viewed as "foreign." Like Binnie-Clark, they advanced an imperialist vision to justify their claims for land over the dubious claims of "foreign" men. As homesteaders they would help to squeeze out undesirable immigrants and cultivate British civilization along with their crops. Many other rationales were advanced: that women were interested in acquiring homesteads, that they had the strength and knowledge to farm, that they would not be lured to the evil cities but rather enjoy healthy lives in the outdoors, and that potential wives would be attracted to the West for the bachelors. Other rationales highlighted fundamental inequalities in Canada's land laws: families of boys could acquire large estates, while those with daughters were penalized. Women had helped establish homesteads all over the West as wives, yet the land was owned solely by the husband who, with the abolishment of dower rights, could sell without even asking his wife's permission. Single women could homestead in the U.S. West, and Canada was losing its "daughters" who headed south. But the rationale that took centre stage was that land should go to cultured and refined women "of British birth," who were "of strong moral force and high intellectual ability," rather than to uncouth "foreigners." This was the core of a petition that was presented to the Canadian Parliament in 1913 with 11,000 signatures. But this tactic created fissures in the campaign, as some regarded it as a "bald piece of discrimination." Opponents in government remained intransigent, even narrowing the eligible categories of women. The idea that women were not capable agriculturalists persisted. Some were convinced that British women were the least likely candidates for the tasks required of homesteaders on the prairies. The strategy of manipulating fears of racial and ethnic "others" in order to assist with the "spade work of British expansion" and to seek an alliance with and win the support of elite males failed. There were fundamental contradictions in the tactics around this petition, as they invoked prejudice and exclusion while calling for equality and justice.

Chapter 7 covers the era from the First World War to the late 1920s, demonstrating that if anything, opportunities for women farmers and homesteaders narrowed over time. The war set back the cause of educated British women farmers in Canada, and although it was revived and invigorated after the war, Canada's "curiously strong prejudice" persisted and became even more entrenched. Despite acute labour shortages, in prairie Canada there was no formal mobilization of women for farm work. This chapter analyzes why this was the case, in comparison to the land armies of the United States and Britain and the "farmerettes" of Ontario. Having told women they were not physically capable of farm work, it would have been difficult for authorities to suddenly reverse this stance maintained over decades and invite them into the fields. During the war and after, pressure to change the homestead legislation to include all—not just British—women continued, and there was hope that women's wartime service would help to bolster the claim. Advocates of emigration for British land army women hoped farm work and land on the prairies could be obtained in recognition of their wartime service. But there was deep and profound opposition at all levels of government in Canada to British land army and ex-service women as settlers unless as domestic workers. The women were viewed as potentially disruptive and troublesome elements whose wartime work experiences conflicted with the "true" and "normal" gendered identities perpetuated on the prairies. In the British settlement schemes of the 1920s there was an emphasis on families, or in the case of single landholders, on male agriculturalists and female domestics. Land and farming in the West remained overwhelmingly masculine, and the First World War helped to further this aim.

The goal of establishing British women homesteaders and farmers on the prairies withered and died in the 1930s. A brief conclusion makes this point by discussing the return of Georgina Binnie-Clark to her Saskatchewan farm and her short-lived and ill-conceived Union Jack Settlement, a plan to plant families rather than single women on imperial plots. There could not have been a worse time to initiate such a venture than the drought and Depression of the 1930s. In 1930, however, women (with the exception of First Nations women) were finally granted the right to homestead in Alberta under new provincial legislation, and hundreds took advantage of this offer. While a study of their experiences awaits their historian, they must have been disadvantaged by the Depression that gripped the prairies. Difficulties they faced would have been compounded by the fact that they had to choose homesteads in areas avoided by previous generations of settlers. The conclusion also discusses the persistent "constraining myths" that reinforce traditional gender relations and continue to marginalize women as farmers.

Imperial plots for British women were thus few by the 1930s, despite decades of effort to establish that they could be capable agriculturalists. They continually confronted the objection that farming would interfere with their ability to perform their most important work as wives and mothers. It was perhaps General Bramwell Booth of the Salvation Army who put this most succinctly in 1921, when he declared that "Canada's two chief needs are a more thorough cultivation of the land and more God-fearing mothers in her homes … there is need all over Canada for more attention to the cultivation of children."[75]

CHAPTER ONE

NARROWING OPPORTUNITIES FOR WOMEN

FROM THE INDIGENOUS FARMERS OF THE GREAT PLAINS TO THE EXCLUSIONS OF THE HOMESTEAD REGIME

"Often in summer I rise at daybreak and steal out to the cornfields; and as I hoe the corn I sing to it, as we did when I was young. No one cares for our corn songs now."[1] These were the words of Hidatsa farmer Buffalo Bird Woman (Maxi'diwiac) around 1912, when she was a resident of the Fort Berthold Indian Reservation in North Dakota. There she farmed a small plot of corn according to ancient methods. By that time there were very few Indigenous people who retained knowledge of their crop production methods, and fewer still who continued to practise them. In Indigenous America, women had been the farmers wherever there was agriculture, including on the Great Plains and in what is now Ontario.[2] They were far more than "gardeners"—the crops of women farmers of the Great Plains were the main economic drivers of their region's economy. These same crops continue to play a major role in the economies of Canada and the United States.[3] The example of the ancient women farmers of the Great Plains demonstrates that it was not natural or inevitable that women were to be virtually excluded from that occupation in Western Canada as intensive settlement and the homestead regime took root. Nor was it inevitable that Indigenous people too were almost completely excluded from the new agricultural economy; both processes took work.

This chapter begins with Plains women agriculturalists and ends with the narrow and confined opportunities for immigrant women to obtain land and practise agriculture that were in place in Western Canada by the mid-1870s. It argues that gendered and racialized visions were at the heart of ideas, policies, and laws about property rights and land apportionment and improvement in Western Canada. Some were borrowed from the United States while others reflected the practices of the British imperial world. Yet women's access to land varied widely in these locations. Ideas, laws, and policies about which categories of women should have land and which could farm land were cultural constructs; they were not shared by all, as the example of homesteading single women in the U.S. West demonstrates. Canada made a very deliberate decision to depart from the U.S. model and ultimately excluded virtually all women but widows from the land grant of the homestead system.

The survey of the land into square homesteads covered and smothered Indigenous ways of living in the West, and it was intended to do so; those defined as "Indian" were denied the homestead land grant and instead relegated to reserves. The rights of immigrant women to homestead in Western Canada changed over the 1870s: single women could file on land until 1876, when the legislation was deliberately changed to exclude them. A significant number of women filed on land in Manitoba in the early 1870s and were more successful than their male counterparts at "proving up" and earning patents to their land. After 1876 there remained only one category of women who could homestead: widows with children. A short-lived opportunity to acquire a small grant of land was extended to all migrant women (regardless of marital status) in the late 1870s under the Forest Tree Culture legislation, but this window too was soon shut, as tree farming proved impractical on the prairies. In a few short years the Great Plains were transformed from a land where women had been the farmers to one where agriculture was overwhelmingly masculine, as was the ownership of land that was the foundation of this economy.

FIRST FARMERS

Agriculture long predated the arrival of Europeans on the northern Great Plains, and women were the farmers, raising corn, beans, squash, melons, pumpkins, and sunflowers. They excelled in the art of plant domestication, developing hardy, early maturing varieties of corn that could flourish even in the short growing season of the northern plains, and that could withstand hail and drought as well as early frost.[4] Dried produce was made into a variety of products for families and communities, as well as for sale to neighbours and to European traders; the women were commercial farmers. For this time and place and available technology, this was large-scale agriculture and should not be dismissed or diminished as "horticulture." It was also more than a trade or vocation; sacred songs and ceremonies were a central component that were critical to the work and success of the farmers and were handed down by women over generations. Indigenous women were deeply attached and strongly committed to caring for the land.

European observers wrestled with the sight of women farmers and traders; their comments generally contained a mixture of praise and disparagement. Describing the Arikara, one of the Upper Missouri village people, Scottish botanist John Bradbury wrote in 1810 that "the women, as is the custom with Indians, do all the drudgery, and are excellent cultivators ... I have not seen even in the United States, any crop of Indian corn in finer order, or better managed than the corn of their villages."[5]

The most northerly of the upper Missouri River village agricultural people have long been assumed to be the Arikara, Mandan, and Hidatsa, but there is archaeological evidence that the village agricultural complex reached farther north into Manitoba. There was an agricultural settlement at Lockport, north of present-day Winnipeg on the banks of the Red River, between 800 and 1700 CE. Archaeology has revealed storage pits, bison scapula hoes, grinding stones for milling seeds, charred corn kernels, and ceramic vessels at this site.[6] There are strong archaeological indications of other early agricultural settlements in Manitoba, although much evidence has been lost because of intensive cultivation of the land. An agricultural earth-lodge settlement of Cree in the Touchwood Hills of present-day Saskatchewan in the early nineteenth century grew "considerable quantities of maize and potatoes."[7]

Hidatsa farmer Maxi'diwiac was born about 1839 in an earth-lodge village along the Knife River in present-day North Dakota and moved to the new Like-a-Fishhook village established in 1845 by the remnants of the Mandan and Hidatsa. In the mid-1880s the people of that village, including Maxi'diwiac, were dispersed onto individual allotments on the Fort Berthold Indian Reservation. Maxi'diwiac passed along her knowledge of agriculture in meticulous detail to anthropologist Gilbert L. Wilson, who

Figure 2. In a field of corn and squash, "Sioux Woman," the daughter-in-law of Hidatsa farmer Maxi'diwiac (Buffalo Bird Woman), demonstrates traditional farming methods of the Great Plains agriculturalists using a bison scapula hoe, 1912. State Historical Society of North Dakota, item no. 0086-0281. Photo by Gilbert L. Wilson.

published *Agriculture of the Hidatsa Indians: An Indian Interpretation* in 1917 (later published as *Buffalo Bird Woman's Garden*). Although Wilson's texts supposedly present the actual words of Maxi'diwiac, this is likely not entirely the case, but her knowledge is there, conveyed in words and sentences that were chosen and written down by Wilson. She did not speak English, so her son Edward Goodbird translated and interpreted her words. The text that resulted from this collaboration provides the most detailed account of Indigenous agriculture ever published, and as Jeffery R. Hanson writes in a new introduction to the text, "One cannot read *Buffalo Bird Woman's Garden* without marvelling at the array of technical skills which Hidatsa women developed and applied to everyday life: agriculture, architecture, construction, storage, crafts, and cooking constitute just a few of the dimensions of knowledge which Buffalo Bird Woman and other Hidatsa women contributed."[8] Men played virtually no role in farming aside from assisting with the harvest and cultivating tobacco.

Maxi'diwiac explained that farmers preferred the bottomlands of the Missouri, where the soil was soft and easy to work, rather than the open prairies, where the soil was hard and dry. Before the introduction of iron implements, they could not have broken the prairie sod, as they used tools fashioned from the shoulder blades of bison. By Maxi'diwiac's time, iron hoes and axes were generally used rather than bison scapula hoes and wooden digging sticks, and her grandmother Turtle was one of the last women to use these traditional implements. Her hoe was precious; she kept it under her bed and "when any of the children of the household tried to get it out to look at it, she would cry, 'Let that hoe alone; you will break it.'"[9]

Farmers had individual plots, although there were also family plots worked with other women family members, particularly daughters. Maxi'diwiac's mother died when Maxi'diwiac was six, but she had three other women she called "mother," sisters of her mother and wives of her father. She was also very close to her grandmother Turtle. These women worked their fields together.[10] To prepare a new plot the land was first cleared, a task the men might assist with. The land was then burned, which "left a good, loose soil."[11] Every spring once the frost was out of the ground, the fields were dug up: "Every foot must be turned up and loosened with the hoe—a slow and toilsome operation."[12]

Most of Maxi'diwiac's narrative is devoted to the intricacies of corn cultivation. She provides a detailed account of the nine varieties of corn raised in her village, including their uses and characteristics. Corn planting started in May and could continue well into June, depending on the variety of seed. Hidatsa women were up before sunrise in planting season, preparing the hills they returned to each year. Of the varieties of corn that were grow, flint was the hardiest, as it could mature in just ten weeks and escape the early frosts of the northern plains.[13]

Platforms or stages were built, where girls and women came to watch the crops, scare off predators, and sing. Maxi'diwiac explained, "We cared for our corn in those days as we would care for a child; for we Indian people loved our gardens, just as a mother loves her children; and we thought that our growing corn liked to hear us sing, just as children like to hear their mother sing."[14] Watching began in earnest in August as the corn ripened. The watchers' songs were usually love songs, as young men of the village would visit the platforms where the girls were stationed.

The corn was threshed in booths, under drying stages. The finest and longest ears of corn were braided, and from these the seed for the next spring was selected, using only the kernels in the centre of the cob for seed. Enough seed for two years was gathered from corn, squash, beans, sunflower, or tobacco, in case of a poor crop the next year. A family's corn supply usually lasted until August of the next year. Supplies were stored in deep cache pits, dug by the women and accessed through ladders. The caches held not only dried corn but dried meat and pemmican and dried wild produce, including berries and "pommes blanches," or prairie turnips. Each family might have up to four cache pits. Fur trader, explorer, and writer Alexander Henry wrote in his journal in 1804 that "so numerous about the village are these pits that it is really dangerous for a stranger to stir out after dark."[15]

Women raised and dried produce for their families and also for sale. Their villages were visited by neighbouring Plains people, who traded their buffalo robes, skin, and meat for corn and other produce. Sometimes the village people travelled out to the plains to trade. Henry described Mandan women preparing for a trade fair: "We observed the women all busy, taking their hidden treasures and making preparations for the approaching fair. I was surprised to see what quantities they had on hand: I am very confident they had enough to serve them at least twelve months without a supply of flesh or anything else."[16] In 1804 Henry accompanied a party of Mandan and Hidatsa to meet the Cheyenne and Arapaho. Henry wrote that the women "had their horses loaded with corn, beans, etc. themselves and children astraddle all over, like farmers going to the mill." They exchanged their produce for "leather, robes, smocks—as if at a country fair."[17]

The agricultural people of the plains also established trade with Euro-American/Canadian traders and explorers. Henry wrote that "we purchased sweet corn, beans, meal and various other trifles. Having bought all we required, which was 3 horse loads, we were plagued by the women and girls who continued to bring bags and dishes full of different kinds of produce."[18] American explorers Meriwether Lewis and William Clark in 1804 bought huge quantities of produce from the Mandan, noting on one occasion that "a number of squaws and men dressed like squaws brought corn to trade for small articles with the men."[19] Describing the trade in corn, geologist Ferdinand V. Hayden wrote that the women of one village sold from 500 to 800 bushels in a season to the American Fur Company and that the trade was "carried on by the women, who bring the corn by panfuls and the squash in strings and receive in exchange knives, hoes, combs, beads, paint etc., also tobacco, ammunition, and other useful articles for their husbands. In this way each family is supplied with all the smaller articles needed for a comfortable existence; and though the women perform all the labor, they are compensated by having their full share of the profits."[20]

Many ceremonies and rituals, both public and private, were involved in achieving successful crops. The cultivated plots were sacred and thought to have souls that had to be cared for like children. The Goose society of the Mandan and Hidatsa, made up of women farmers, was devoted to the rites required to ensure good crops, including fertility and rainmaking rites.[21] The largest and most important ceremony of the society was held when the first water birds arrived; it was believed that corn spirits went south each fall with the water birds, where they were cared for by Old-Woman-Who-Never-Dies.[22] Respected members of the Goose society were believed to have corn spirits in their bodies. Other rituals performed by society members to protect crops included saying a prayer when each seed was planted and rubbing their bodies and clothing with sage each day when returning from the fields. Women farmers left offerings of meat, hide, or cloth. Sacred bundles hung on poles protected the crops. All of the crop was to be cherished and none of it wasted. In the Arikara legend of "The Forgotten Ear," a woman heard a child calling when she was about to leave her field. "She searched and found a small ear of corn she had overlooked, and when she gathered in that ear of corn the crying stopped."[23]

European male observers wrestled with the fact that Plains women worked the land, owned their fields and their crops, and traded their surplus produce. They diminished women's work in various ways. It was often noted that because women were the agriculturalists, men were disdainful of working the land. Artist George Catlin wrote that among the Mandan, "the old women [were] the owners of fields or patches of corn (for such are the proprietors and cultivators of all crops in Indian countries, the men never turning their hands to such degrading occupations)."[24] Another tendency of European observers was to criticize and disparage the skills and technology of women farmers. In his *Ethnography and Philology of the Hidatsa Indians* (1877), Washington Matthews wrote that "their system of tillage was rude. They knew nothing of the value of manuring the soil, changing the seed, or alternating the crops … they had no regular system of fallowing. They often planted a dozen grains of corn or more to the hill, and did not hoe very thoroughly." Matthews saw improvements in farming on the reservations, since ploughs were used, and also because "the men apply themselves willingly to the labors of the field; and the number of working men is constantly increasing."[25] This was not the opinion of Maxi'diwiac, who thought "our old way of raising corn is better than the new way taught us by white men." Maxi'diwiac's people were instructed to plant corn on fields prepared by ploughs on the open prairie, but "these fields on the prairie near the hills I do not think are so good as our old fields down in the timber lands along the Missouri. The prairie fields get dry easily and the soil is harder and more difficult to work."[26]

Rudolph Friederich Kurz (1818–71), a Swiss painter and writer who visited the Upper Missouri village people between 1846 and 1852, carefully weighed the issue and was less condemnatory than others. He believed that "agriculture is the basis upon which is builded [*sic*] every firmly established state. In tilling his land the savage becomes attached to the soil and loyal to his native land. Upon husbandry depends settled habitations, spacious country residences; as the result of husbandry, business thrives, inventions are called into being, arts flourish, sciences are in demand, and laws are enacted for the better morality and better government that is essential to the prosperity of a state." Unlike other observers, Kurz did not dismiss Indigenous agriculture as "gardening" because it was done by women; he wrote that "whether men or women worked the land when they first began to farm is a matter of no consequence. That the Indians did actually cultivate their land throughout the region lying between the Mississippi and the Atlantic Ocean is a fact to which travelers and adventurers who have visited this country since its discovery by Columbus collectively testify—all of them, whether Spaniards, Frenchmen, or Britons." He also defended Indigenous women working the land against claims that this was cruel and brutal treatment: "That Indian women work the land is not due to racial coarseness or brutality but to the fact that the men regard war as their chief aim in life ... According to the contrary argument, European nations, where country women willingly work in the fields, must also be called cruel and brutal. It is far better for women to till the land, which is no disgrace, than to starve or beg alms."[27] Kurz was certain, however, that once the land was densely colonized and settled, Indigenous women "will have to adapt themselves to the same order of things," meaning that they would disappear from fieldwork. To Kurz, women working the land was not the normal or natural gender order.

Even scholars who gained a deep appreciation for the knowledge and skills of Plains women farmers nonetheless labelled their work as "gardening," as somehow less than "agriculture," which was considered the work of modern man. George F. Will and George E. Hyde, who published *Corn among the Indians of the Upper Missouri* in 1917, both praised and diminished the work of women farmers in this passage:

> Most of the early accounts give the impression that the women were drudges who were forced to perform most of the heavy labor, including that of the fields. To those who are acquainted with the Indians it will be easily understood that this conception of the position of Indian women needs to be considerably modified. While there is no question that the women's work was severe, yet there is abundant evidence that the women performed their tasks willingly and took great pride in doing their work well. To those who have seen the Indian woman patiently and solicitously working about her garden it must be evident that she loved her work there and enjoyed it. As a matter of fact in the Upper Missouri region the spring was longingly awaited as the time to commence work on the gardens which furnished much of the pleasure of the

> summer season; and the harvest time, though a season of rejoicing, yet was also a time of regret for the pleasant summer passed.
>
> The Indian woman was a real gardener. Her methods were not those of the bonanza farmer of the present day, but resembled more closely that of the modern market gardener or greenhouse man. She attended to every little detail, working slowly and carefully and taking the utmost pains. She knew the habits of each of her plants and the habits of each separate variety of all the species cultivated, and she worked with careful regard for these differences.[28]

Aside from being skilled in cultivating crops, the Indigenous people of North America, and particularly women, were experts in the science of plants and their environments, and they knew how to sustain and nurture the resources they drew upon for their own purposes and those of future generations.[29] Over millennia they accumulated a vast, specialized, and complex knowledge about plants, their habitats, soil varieties, weather patterns, and seasonal changes. The Blackfoot, for example, drew on approximately 185 species of plants for food, ceremonies, housing, crafts, and medicines.[30]

GENDERED VISIONS: LAND SURVEYS AND GRANTS IN THE UNITED STATES

The land survey that Canada adopted from the United States and that carves up western North America has been described as "one of the most astonishing man-made constructs on earth."[31] The "immaculate grid" of perfect squares is particularly striking from the sky, forming a stunning patchwork quilt.[32] It was not just lines that the surveyors set down on the land, it was a social ideology. As historian Ian McKay has written, "Perhaps the *pièce de résistance* of the Canadian liberal order was to carve upon the map, in lines that majestically remind us of Euclidean geometry and panoptical state power, the perfect geometry of the Province of Saskatchewan: perhaps even more impressive, however, than this quadrilateral demonstration of panopticism was the molecular checkerboard of quarter-sections and individual properties contained within the province's boundaries—a social ideology set down on the land and hence made part of everyday western experience."[33]

The grid, the policies and laws governing who could live on it and who could not, and the enormous bureaucracies needed to apply these rules and regulations moulded and sculpted the societies planted on it. The legacy of those rules remains, just as the grid remains. At the time of his retirement from government service in 1880, Canada's first surveyor general, Colonel John Stoughton Dennis, took pride in his role applying the perfect grid survey and formulating public lands policy in the Canadian West at a time when, in his view, "the country was as a *white* sheet."[34] But the country was far from being a white sheet or blank slate. The West was home to ancient societies, and the grid obscured and ignored land use and tenure systems that were based on generations of accumulated knowledge of and sensitivity to the great variations in the landscape. The grid transformed Indigenous land into the "public domain," meaning it was no longer owned by or available to the First Nations. Surveys created resentment, anger, and resistance. First Nations were excluded from living on the grid and confined to reserves. Immigrant women were discouraged from occupying land on the grid except within family units.

The grid framework was far from a uniquely *Canadian* liberal order that was imposed on the land. The immaculate square survey is also the most obvious example of the long-standing and overwhelming influence of the United States on Canada. The graph paper extends seamlessly across the forty-ninth parallel—a major step toward "continental integration" a century and more before the term was in vogue. As historian Chester Martin writes, the United States was a "veritable quarry" for Canadian policy.[35] The perfect grid system was appealing to both nations because it expedited the mapping, absorption, and individual ownership of the terrain. It permitted the land to be sold, bought, and owned in the most uncomplicated and timely fashion. The grid set the stage for both Canadian and American federal governments to become real estate dealers on a massive scale.

It was American Founding Father Thomas Jefferson who decided after the American Revolution that the simplest, most advantageous method was to survey the land before occupation and divide it into simple squares, replacing the surveying technique known as "metes and bounds," a haphazard system in which parcels of land were described by distinctive characteristics of the landscape and the property lines of previously surveyed lots.[36] The master grid would be formed by "principal meridians" of longitude and "base lines" of latitude.[37] There were to be thirty-six-square-mile "townships" divided into one-square-mile lots called "sections," which were further divisible into half sections and quarter sections.

The grid system had many unique advantages. It facilitated the taking of the land from Indigenous inhabitants, creating instead an army of occupiers on small holdings. It assured clear boundaries and titles, avoiding turmoil and squabbles. Once a parcel of land was surveyed it could be singled out from any other square mile of territory from a land office hundreds of miles away. Every parcel of land had its unique identity.[38] It was an ideal system for buying, trading, and speculating in land. There were disadvantages as well. The survey was laid down without any regard for terrain, climate, or soil. Many of the squares of land throughout North America would prove to be hopeless prospects as farms.

There was much more than commerce, convenience, and mathematics at the heart of the square survey. A desired cultural landscape was to be sculpted through land policies, and ideas of gender and race were at the heart of this ideal society. Jefferson believed that America's virtue rested on an agricultural foundation, and his vision was that these measured boxes would provide the framework around which a democracy would grow. At the centre of this agricultural economy would be the small family farm's independent yeoman—an individual male who was "virtuous, hard-working and faithful to the republic."[39] Jefferson declared in 1787 that "those who labour in the earth are the chosen people of God, if ever he had a chosen people, whose breasts he has made his particular deposit for substantial and genuine virtue."[40] With farmers happily occupying their squares, it would be impossible for wealth and power to become concentrated in the hands of a few. Jefferson's vision was of a white, Anglo-Saxon republic of small-scale farmers, and he had concerns about other types of immigrants.[41] Women were central to this vision as the reproducers of the ideal society of independent yeomen. Women were to be subservient to the yeoman farmer; they were to be on the land but under the control of men. As historian Peter Boag writes, "The land itself then was to play a major role in the preservation of the 'natural' gender order."[42]

Jefferson's system of survey for the land in the western territory was passed by Congress in 1785. The free homestead system came decades later, after acrimonious debate and in stages. The United States Homestead Act of 1862, setting out just who could live on the grid and with what settlement duties or payment, provided that "persons over the age of 21 who were citizens or immigrants who had declared their intention to become citizens" were eligible to file on up to 160 acres of surveyed land on the public domain. A homesteader had to cultivate the land, improve it by constructing a house or barn, and reside on the claim for five years. If these conditions were met (called "proving up"), the homesteader received full title, paying a fee of only ten dollars. Homesteaders could also gain quicker ownership of their land by exercising a "commutation clause" after six months of residence, which allowed them to purchase their homestead at the minimum cash price of $1.25 per acre.

Gender issues were at the heart of the debate over the wording of the U.S. legislation. Determining the eligible and desirable classes of persons for the land grant was not straightforward or obvious. Should only married men be eligible, ensuring that families would be established on the land? Should married men get more land than single men? Should grants of land go to young single men, capable of bearing arms, to build up an army of occupation? What categories of women should be eligible for the land grant? Congressmen changed their minds on the issue over the many years of debate. Proposals included excluding women entirely, permitting only widows with children, and permitting single women with children. There were weighty and lengthy deliberations on the eligibility of abandoned and divorced women. Widows were the most unproblematic category. As historian Tonia Compton argues, widows "had already demonstrated their commitment to the gender order by having married."[43] If they had children, widows were legally considered heads of households, and it was unanimously agreed that the land should go to heads of households. The eligibility of women who had children "out of wedlock" was discussed, and the conclusion was that granting them land was an "utter impossibility," although the stand was later relaxed in practice.[44]

It was assumed from the start (as later in Canada) that a married woman—who was legally, civilly merged with her husband—was under the husband's protection and control, and that for her the homestead privilege was out of the question. The result was that other categories of women, such as those who had never married, as well as widowed or divorced women, were granted this privilege in the U.S. federal legislation of 1862, despite the fact that most other rights of citizenship, such as voting, were denied them at this time.

The place of single women in the homestead scheme was the most perplexing and troubling question. In 1852 one congressman mocked the suggestion that homesteading would benefit "maidens" by asking if it was intended to "propose a clause, providing for all the old maids in the country?"[45] Some argued women would never take advantage of the offer of land because they could not endure the hardships. Compton found that for congressmen it was difficult to accept the idea of single women living by themselves on homesteads. Other objections included that women could be defrauded by devious men who would use them to obtain land. And what would happen when a male and female homesteader married, each having claimed land while single?[46] (This was to become a thorny and vexing issue.) Arguments for the rights of single women to acquire homesteads included "They have as much right there as bachelors," and that "if a female desires to possess a home, and is willing to conform to the requirements of the law, there is no reason why she should be an alien to the justice or the charity of her country. If she is unfettered by marriage ties she has the same natural right to be provided a home from the public domain that the unmarried man of the same age has."[47] Supporters argued that the land grant could serve as a dowry for single women, helping to encourage marriage and ensuring the growth of the population of the West.

The right of single women in the United States to homestead under the 1862 Homestead Act was not the result of, and did not result in, a high estimation of women's ability to farm. Women in the American West had to "negotiate a rocky terrain, littered with the racialized and gendered expectations which accompanied the American efforts to establish an empire in the West."[48] Nor was there any great disruption to the dominant gender order as a result of women's enhanced property rights through the homestead privilege. Women's right to land was still tied to marital status. Women figured largely in debates about homestead bills not because they were ever intended to be the primary beneficiaries of free land measures, nor because Congress intentionally sought to hold out the promise of land ownership to women, but because homesteading was the foundation of the "imperial enterprise" in the West and women were central to this enterprise. White woman loomed large as "wives, mothers, potential wives and former wives through the discussions about free land and western expansion."[49] They were an essential component of the plan to populate the West with the "right kind of Americans."[50] They were to be the foundation of the families of the West and were sent to fulfill traditional gender roles, but at the same time they needed to be adventuresome, plucky, strong, and capable.[51] The role of African American women in homesteading received no attention in debates over the free land grant.[52]

It was not obvious, either, which categories of men should be granted the homestead privilege. Congress debated extensively about whether to include only married men—heads of households—and exclude single men. Race was also an issue. In 1854, for example, a congressman from Alabama proposed that "any single free white male" should be allowed to claim land.[53] The 1862 legislation permitted freed slaves to homestead, and the act also extended land grants to naturalized citizens—those who were not yet but would become citizens. Running through the debates about the various homestead measures was the idea that the process of transforming the land would create and shape American citizens out of foreign immigrants.[54]

There were variations in the land laws of the states and territories, indicating that there was no obvious category of persons for land grants. In Oregon, for example, the Donation Land Claim Act of 1850 granted 320 acres to every unmarried white male citizen over the age of eighteen, and twice that amount (640 acres) to married couples, with the husband and wife each owning half of the grant in their own name. Also eligible for the Oregon land grant were "half-blood" Native Americans.[55] In Texas, the federal Homestead Act did not apply because (as in British Columbia) Texas retained control of its public lands upon admission to the Union. Texas legislators limited the opportunities for single women to homestead, favouring single males and male heads of families. There were, however, approximately 1,500 women who filed homestead claims in Texas between 1845, when Texas was admitted to statehood, and 1898, when homestead land was no longer available.[56]

GENDER AND LAND GRANTS: THE BRITISH IMPERIAL CONTEXT

There was also a British imperial context to the system of survey and land settlement that was adopted in Western Canada. As historian John C. Weaver has explained, in the nineteenth century the globe was "overlaid with rectangles, squares and triangles ... maps defined the empire's nature—transforming the exotic to the knowable, implementing science, dominance and separation."[57] In each colony the appointment of a surveyor general was the first step in establishing a systematic approach to surveying acquisitions.[58] In New Zealand, Australia, and South Africa, the landscape was ordered into individual holdings with reference to longitude and latitude, although rarely was the North American checkerboard adopted completely. New Zealand was the first location of a systematic topographic survey for the purposes of land settlement. As a surveyor in that colony explained: "The main object of a colonial survey is to enable the settlement of the Crown lands to proceed on a system of survey and record, which, for the settler, will give him possession of a definite piece of land which cannot ever after be overridden by a rival claim."[59] A system of registering land rights, linked to the scientific colonial survey, also characterized the white settler colonies of the British Empire. Known as the Torrens system, it was first devised for South Australia in the 1850s.

Throughout the British settler colonies there were significant variations in the opportunities for British immigrant women to obtain land and potentially farm that land; moreover, the rules and regulations did not remain static but continually changed. Historian Kathryn Hunter found that in southeastern Australia the issue of land for single women troubled colonial authorities throughout the nineteenth century.[60] In 1819 Eliza Walsh arrived in New South Wales with her married sister and brother-in-law, and, as she put it, "made up my mind to settle a Farm in this country."[61] She purchased a farm, and then sought more land, asking to have the same grant of land available to male "Settlers according to means," which would permit her to cultivate and raise stock on a larger scale. Governor Lachlan Macquarie refused, stating it was "contrary to late Regulations to give Grants to Ladies." Macquarie explained his reasoning to another official: "I consider it very bad practice (except in some extraordinary and pressing cases of necessity) and very injurious to the Interests of the Colony to give grants of Land to single women. I have declined for some time past making such Grants on the ground that such persons are incapable of cultivating Land, and thereby not adding to the resources of the Colony."[62]

Walsh persisted, pointing out that "it does not appear altogether a just measure to exclude ladies from making use of their money for the benefit of the Colony in consequence of their sex, nor can it be deemed a real objection that a Lady should not be able to conduct a Farm as well as a Gentleman."[63] In the mid-1820s legislators decided that women (and men) possessing capital were eligible to receive grants of land.[64] Walsh eventually received a grant of land but not until 1827.

By the 1860s attitudes about single settler women and land in south-east Australia had shifted, so that married white women were excluded but single women included. Land was then available to any man, widow, or single woman over the age of twenty-one for a price of one pound per acre, and land was surveyed in blocks from 40 to 320 acres.[65] Historian Patricia Grimshaw demonstrated that in the Wimmera district under the terms of the 1869 Land Act, single women over eighteen and widows could select land, while married women could not. Single women were also granted Crown leases. Grimshaw found that single women selected land by or near other family members, helping to increase the size of family holdings.[66] Hunter found land files from the state of Victoria demonstrating that a considerable number of single women selected land and farmed. The probate records also revealed the "constant presence of women in farming in this wheat growing region."[67] In Horsham, female farmers represented 21 percent of probated farmers between 1874 and 1900.[68]

By the late nineteenth century there was concern in Australia that allowing single women to select land was discouraging marriage in the colony.[69] In 1878 the suggestion was made to the Victorian Crown Lands Commission that married rather than single women be permitted to select land, in order to encourage marriage and to allow married couples to increase the viability of their farms.[70] The matter was debated again in 1884, when amendments were made to the Land Bill and one Member of the House of Representatives "pleaded the claim of married women, who are debarred from selecting." In his view married women deserved land more than single women for the following reasons, as described in the newspaper *Border Watch*: "The wives of selectors have been in the colony for years, they have proved themselves excellent colonists, and yet they have fewer rights than the single woman who landed from the old country yesterday… The fairer plan, Mr. Dow thinks, is to permit selection by the mother of families."[71]

One category of married women could obtain land in Australia, although they did not exactly own their land. Through a system of "marriage grants" in South Australia, New South Wales, and Western Australia beginning in 1848, sections of Aboriginal reserve land were granted to Aboriginal women who married non-Aboriginal men.[72] The woman could occupy the land for life and was entitled to enclose, clear, and cultivate the land, and upon her death the licence could be renewed in favour of her "lawful offspring."[73] This was not outright ownership; the state acted as trustee of all reserve land and the woman had permission to occupy the land. As Protector of Aborigines Matthew Moorhouse explained in 1848, the wife would not be disturbed on her land "so long as she lives with her husband and they continue steady and industrious."[74] The policy was intended to encourage legal, Christian monogamous marriage between Aboriginal women and non-Aboriginal men. The land was a form of dowry or enticement, but one that could not become the property of the husband. Such policy was also meant to encourage "steady and industrious" habits. There were changes in the marriage grant system over the years, but versions of it remained until 1911, when attitudes of officials toward these marriages had changed, complications emerged about who could be categorized as Aboriginal, and available land declined. Historians Mandy Paul and Robert Foster found that the records of these grants reveal the persistence of applicants in their struggle for land. Typical was Julia Simpson, who wrote the Protector in 1905: "Will you kindly help me by getting me so many acres of land that I am entitled to ... I think I would be able to get a living here by keeping fowls pigs & also a garden."[75]

New Zealand had similar land enticements as incentives for interracial couples to legalize their marriages.[76] Land grants were awarded to couples from the 1840s, but the system departed from that of the Australian colonies, as the title was in the name of the European husband, although he had no right to sell, mortgage, or lease the land.

THE SURVEY AND LAND GRANTS IN WESTERN CANADA

The grid (with the exception of river lots in some of the settlements that had predated the survey) was quietly and quickly adopted for Western Canada by 1869. This was a departure from the systems of survey used in the older provinces of Canada, where there were several lot and road patterns.[77] That the uniform grid would be imposed on the West was decided with little consultation outside of a small circle, and no debate. The people residing in the West, overwhelmingly Indigenous people—First Nations and Métis—were left completely out of the discussion. Imposing the grid on the West was the task of Surveyor General Colonel John S. Dennis.[78] Dennis consulted with the U.S. Land Office as well as with officials of the

Canadian Crown Land Department in coming up with exactly the same rectangular survey of townships and sections as had been adopted in the United States, with one main deviation: Dennis proposed larger townships consisting of sixty-four squares of 800 acres each. However, this idea was rejected in the interests of perfect, seamless conformity with the U.S. grid.

With the exception of the "postage stamp" province of Manitoba (one-eighteenth of its current size), the land in the Prairie provinces, then called the North-West Territories, and the District of Keewatin became the Dominion of Canada's vast inland empire with a "stroke of the pen" in 1870, and the land remained in federal control until 1930.[79] The Manitoba Act of 1870 provided that "all ungranted or waste lands" were to be administered by the Government of Canada. Canada's secretary of state was responsible for administering this land until 1873, when this responsibility was handed over to the new Department of the Interior. The main discussion about the North-West that took place in May 1869 focused on few details of the survey, as there was a sense that great haste was required to immediately secure the territory for the new Dominion in the face of potential U.S. encroachment.[80] The survey, the maps to document the survey, and a railroad would together declare the land as belonging to Canada, and these needed to be accomplished immediately. There was brief mention of "free grants" of land in the House of Commons in 1869, but no discussion or debate.[81] The survey was needed, and immediately—after that decisions could be made about who would live within the squares.

In the summer of 1869—before the transfer of Rupert's Land (as the Hudson's Bay Company named the territory they claimed) to the Dominion of Canada, before any treaties with First Nations, and before the survey plan was formally approved by order-in-council—Dennis was sent to the Red River settlement to begin the survey of the Principal Meridian. At this time Canada had no legal right to send surveyors west, and they had no authority to begin surveying. Dennis's son later wrote in his history of the surveys made under the Dominion lands system that "in doing this, an approval of the scheme was anticipated which might not have been obtained, but no doubt it was realized that any scheme adopted would, in its main features, resemble the one proposed, and would authorize the survey of the country into rectangular townships."[82] In the fall of 1869, the survey was the catalyst for the "troubles" with the Métis at Red River, under the leadership of Louis Riel. The Métis made up the largest population segment of the Red River settlement and had existing claims to property. Dennis's surveys therefore alarmed them. They resented the fact that they had not been consulted or informed, they feared their land rights would be disregarded, they feared a loss of livelihood, and they objected to the kind of survey that was reshaping the landscape and disregarding their river lots. The complex events that followed are beyond the focus of this book and have been the subject of many studies. The Métis achieved some of their goals through their resistance, including recognition of their French language and Catholic rights, and "provincehood" for Manitoba, although these achievements were ephemeral or soon undermined. They also received a land grant of 1.4 million acres, to be distributed according to an ever-changing set of rules quite distinct from the free homestead system. Thus the land disposal system of Western Canada was immediately more complex than in the United States due to Métis resistance to the survey and the second, complicated tier of land allotment policy devised for them.

When the "troubles" ended the survey continued, with a few deviations for the river lots of the Métis settlements along the Red and Assiniboine Rivers.[83] The new lieutenant governor of Manitoba, Adams Archibald, appointed in 1870, helped to advance the process.[84] He favoured adopting the U.S. survey with no deviations, arguing that this system was known "all over the world to the Emigrant classes" and that "a lot of 160 acres is the acknowledged extent of an Emigrant's requirements for farm purposes."[85] Archibald also looked to the United States in his recommendations regarding regulations governing the distribution of these lands. On 1 March 1871, an order-in-council endorsed the adoption of the American system of survey of townships of thirty-six sections, and the free homestead system, also as administered in the United States.[86] In April 1871 the House of Commons debated some of the details of Canada's homestead legislation.[87] An order-in-council approved on 19 April 1871 amended the policy in the light of some of these criticisms, bringing it even more into line with the U.S. legislation.[88] Canada's 1872 Act Respecting the Public Lands of the Dominion was passed "without opposition and almost without discussion."[89] Ten years earlier the U.S. legislation was a stormy and protracted measure compared to the quiet and quick passage in Canada. A system of road allowances and adjustments for the earth's curvature were the main departures from the U.S. model. The proximity of the American West compelled Canada to adopt a similar approach, and quickly, in order to attract settlers to a setting that was already more daunting because of its colder climate and shorter growing season.[90] It was also difficult to access, until the Canadian Pacific Railway was completed in 1885.

INDIAN RESERVES

As the grid enveloped and altered the homeland of Indigenous people, small "reserves" of land were set aside for those who entered into the treaties that began in southern Manitoba with Treaties One and Two in 1871. According to these agreements, land was granted on the basis of 160 acres per family of five or less (in proportion to family size), although the Dakota received about half that amount of land, as they were regarded as "not British Indians" and were not permitted to enter into treaties.[91] More land was granted in later treaties, but in comparison to the generous grant of 160 acres plus the opportunity to expand through second homesteads and pre-emption available to any male newcomer over the age of eighteen, the reserves were tiny.[92] There were no mechanisms to expand reserve land; sons could not acquire neighbouring land as sons of settlers could under the homestead system. There were, however, detailed provisions under the Indian Act to alienate or "surrender" portions or all of reserves. Nor could any individual identified as an "Indian" obtain land off a reserve.[93] In Treaty Three, the North-West Angle Treaty, reserves were not to "exceed in all one square mile [640 acres] for each family of five, or in that proportion for larger or smaller families."[94]

Within these reserves there was no individual ownership of land, although "location tickets" to small plots were issued to males who could pass these down to heirs. According to the federal Indian Act (1876), these location tickets could be issued to males or females, but in practice they were granted to males only. Women came into possession of location tickets generally only as widows; the widow would receive one-third interest and the rest would go to any children. In 1884 a new clause was added to the Indian Act stipulating that the widow would receive the location ticket "provided she be a woman of good moral character and that she was living with her husband at the date of his death."[95] The result was that widows were virtually the only women who farmed on reserves (just as they were the dominant category of women homesteaders), and they were fairly rare. Implements, oxen, and any other forms of assistance with agriculture promised under treaties were distributed to males, despite the fact that from ancient times women had been the agriculturalists on the Great Plains.

Examples of widowed women reserve farmers include two on a Manitoba reserve in 1895 who had "model homestead[s]."[96] One of them, the "Widow Macleod," had "a very fine new house, costing her some six hundred dollars." She was unusually wealthy. According to the agent, "This was the last of a comfortable competency (eight thousand dollars) left by her father, the late Angus McBeth of the Hudson's Bay Company, a few years ago." Widow Macleod was one of the few reserve farmers who owned oxen, cattle, horses, chickens, wagons, mowers, and horse rakes, and raised grain and potatoes. Acreages under cultivation were tiny compared to the surrounding non-Indigenous farmers. A widow on the Alexander reserve in present-day Alberta was regarded as having a sizeable farm in 1896, with two acres of wheat, an acre each of oats and barley, and three-eighths of an acre of potatoes and vegetables. She also had "a good house, two pretty fair stables, one steer, one heifer, ploughs, harrows, forks and axes."[97] Widows could be moved off their location ticket land, however, at the discretion of officials of the Department of Indian Affairs and be replaced with a man perceived as capable of farming. This was the case with a widow on the Enoch reserve in Alberta who was removed and replaced in 1915 after her son died.[98] She was compensated with $100 from band funds and signed a consent form with her mark.

Virtually excluded from the occupation of agriculture, women on reserves had few means of acquiring income. In southern Manitoba, where the "pass system" meant to keep people on their reserves was generally not enforced, reserve women of the early twentieth century sold their baskets, mats, moccasins, and beadwork off-reserve. They also gathered and sold Seneca root and berries. A few worked as domestics and seamstresses.[99] Some worked in the fields of neighbouring farmers at harvest time. It was a common sight to see them in the harvest fields after the threshing crews were done, "picking up what grain they could gather off the ground around the straw stacks. This grain was put in bags and then loaded on their buggies or wagons to be taken to the local elevators to be sold."[100]

On the Kainai (Blood) reserve in southern Alberta, the largest in Canada, there was only one woman farmer in the 1920s and '30s. Marcia Belly Fat had first worked as a dressmaker in Lethbridge and in the early 1920s returned to the reserve and asked for land that she could

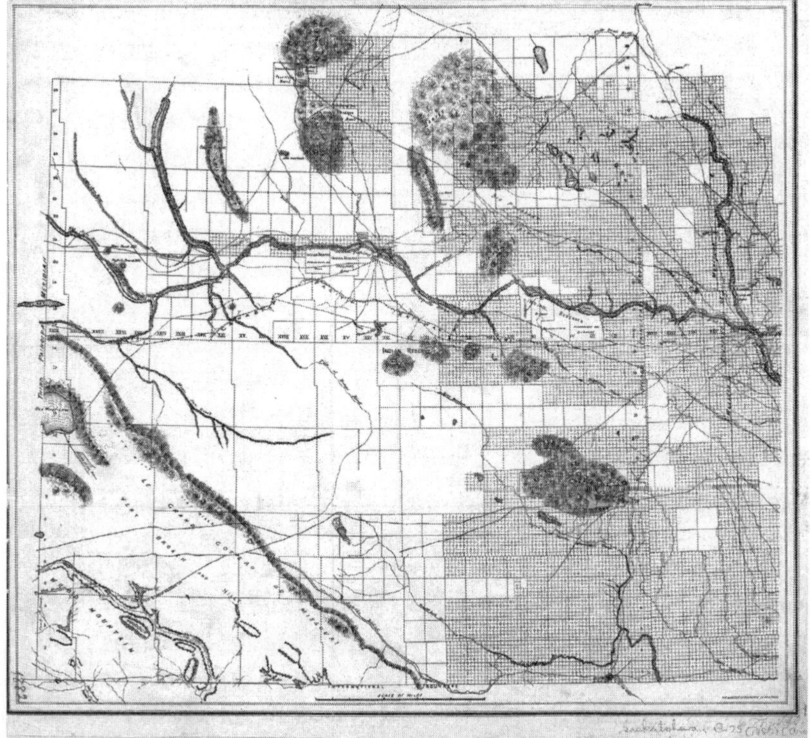

Figure 3. This 1882 map for "intending settlers" shows the dominion lands surveyed to the west of the border of Manitoba. The new and final route of the Canadian Pacific Railway to the south of the Qu'Appelle River and roughly parallel to it is illustrated. Indian reserves of the Treaty Four (1874) people appear on the map, not all in locations well-suited to agriculture. There was soon pressure to "surrender" Indian reserve land that was desirable for farming and close to the CPR. Peel's Prairie Provinces, University of Alberta Libraries, Map 597.

cultivate. She was the only woman to drive a truck, and it was said she "worked like a man."[101]

The possession of land through the homestead system was made possible through the dispossession of the land and resources of First Nations, who were excluded and isolated on reserves. Their economic marginalization and deteriorating health were the results of Canada's nation-building program.[102] Famine followed the disappearance of the buffalo. With poor housing and inadequate substandard rations, reserve people were susceptible to tuberculosis. The completion of the Canadian Pacific Railway in 1885 brought new waves of diseases; as historian James Daschuk writes, the railway was a "fatal disease vector."[103] Prairie reserve populations reached demographic lows by the early 1890s.[104] As their lands were occupied and access to resources restricted, there were, as ethnobotanist Nancy Turner writes, "direct impacts on virtually every aspect of their food systems, technologies, medicines, and Traditional Land and Resource Management Systems, including ceremonial practices and belief systems."[105] Resources, species, and habitats were irrevocably changed.

While officials disregarded and discredited Indigenous peoples' knowledge and systems of caring and managing their land and resources, there was some knowledge exchange, at least in the early settlement era.[106] The daughter of homesteaders in the Cypress Hills of Saskatchewan remembered that the "Indian women were a great help to my mother."[107] They taught her how to keep a fire going, how to clear up diaper rash, how to "wrap the babies Indian style when they were real tiny," and how to preserve berries for winter.

Reserve farmers faced many obstacles, including drought, frost, hail, and prairie fire; they also received little of the assistance promised in treaties in their transition to an agricultural economy. Yet by the late 1880s, agriculture was beginning to succeed on some prairie reserves, prompting their farmers to expand their acreages under cultivation and move in the direction of commercial farming. Yet just at that time reserve farmers were instructed to drastically limit their land under cultivation.[108] The Department of Indian Affairs implemented a "peasant" farming policy on arable reserves in Western Canada that decreed reserve farmers cultivate only an acre or two, grow root crops, use rudimentary homemade implements, and have one cow (rather than cattle herds). The peasant scheme for reserves in Western Canada was devised to ensure that Indigenous farmers did not require any more land and that they not compete with non-Indigenous farmers. It was also intended to assist with the diminution of Indigenous land, which ultimately happened, particularly in the early years of the twentieth century. Agriculture never did become the foundation of an economy that could sustain people on reserves, despite all of the promises made in the treaties.

MÉTIS SCRIP

According to Section 31 of the Manitoba Act of 1870, 1.4 million acres were granted to the Métis of Manitoba. It was decided that those who were categorized as Métis would not be granted reserves, nor would they be given parcels of land that had to be improved over a number of years before patent was granted, as with the homestead system. They were not assisted with agriculture as the treaty people were to a modest extent. Adams Archibald was an architect of the plan, and his goal was to ensure that the land did not long remain in the hands of the recipients. He recommended the land granted to "half-breeds" be surveyed in the same way as other land. He urged that Canada ignore the request of the French Métis to have land laid off in one block, with no right to sell for at least a generation. Archibald was concerned that such land would be "absolutely inalienable" for a long period, which was "feudal."[109] He advocated that the Métis be given outright title to land, an "absolute deed," and he anticipated that they would "as a class, be ready to convert their land into something they can use and will be sure to sell." It is clear Archibald hoped that the granting of outright title would mean that the land would quickly be sold and the Métis dispersed. Archibald described the Métis as "hunters by profession, not farmers. Where the Buffalo go, they go. They could not bear the restraints which cultivation of a farm implies. They would rather forfeit their lots, than settle on them, if by settlement was meant, some degree of cultivation and improvement on the Lots."[110]

Certificates or notes, variously referred to as scrip, warrants, or bounties, were issued in Canada and the United States, and in colonies of the British Empire, as a means of payment for services and claims. In Western Canada there were land bounties for military and police service. Grants of land were awarded to early members of the North-West Mounted Police, to soldiers who participated in the Red River resistance in 1870, in the North-West Resistance of 1885, and in the South African War, although the terms of these varied. Most grants were devised and garnered support as a means of making the West white, military, and masculine, although we will see in a later chapter that purchasing South African scrip became one settler way for women to obtain homestead land in Western Canada.

In settler societies where lands and entitlements were awarded to Indigenous people as individuals rather than as collectives, the result was inevitably more lands transferred to the control of colonial powers or settlers.[111] In Manitoba, adult Métis were granted money scrip that could be exchanged for Dominion lands, while Métis children were granted individual patents to 240 acres. Scrip commissions, inaugurated in 1885, extended the process to the Métis of the North-West. They were offered money scrip (a coupon payable to the bearer and exchangeable at the Dominion Lands Office), or land scrip that required the grantee to be present at a land office to apply the scrip coupon to a legally defined parcel of land (240 acres), for which a patent would be issued. The scrip could be transferred or conveyed prior to the issue of the patent.

"Widespread corruption, if not outright fraud" was the result of the individual and transferable rights awarded to the Métis.[112] William Street, a lawyer from Ontario who was a member of the 1885 scrip commission, described what happened to one Métis woman at Qu'Appelle who reluctantly agreed to receive money scrip, despite the disapproval of her community about participating in the process:

> I prepared, and handed to her, scrip for $160.00, explaining its nature to her, and she went out of the door and was received by a crowd of curious friends, to whom she exhibited her scrip. They were not pleased with her for having allowed herself to be persuaded to come before us, and had almost succeeded in satisfying her and themselves that her scrip was valueless, when Charles Alloway, the agent of a banker in Winnipeg who, with other speculators, had come after us to purchase the scrip from the half-breeds, stepped up and offered her $80 in cash for it. This she gladly accepted, and the money was handed to her in clean, crisp $10 bills. The news quickly spread that we were really giving something which could be turned into cash, and from that hour we were besieged from morning til night by applicants.[113]

Figure 4. Métis women and men at a sitting of the Métis Scrip Commission at Devil's Lake, Saskatchewan, 1900. Scrip was issued to Métis women and girls as well as to Métis men and boys, unlike the gendered restrictions of the homestead system. Saskatchewan Archives Board, S-B9750.

The Qu'Appelle Métis example demonstrates how a community could be quickly "shunted to the fringes of the new society."[114] From at least the 1860s there were many Qu'Appelle Métis engaged in agriculture on an extensive and sophisticated scale, but almost all left their lands in the first few years after the advent of homestead settlement. Historian Lyle Dick has found evidence that they were divested of their lands by fraudulent means.[115] Throughout the prairies there were frauds and abuses that deprived the Métis of most of their land. Speculators used a number of tactics, including forgery and impersonation, to acquire land due to scrip holders. Imposters claimed to be the scrip holders at the land offices. As a columnist wrote in 1911: "There are today in Winnipeg and elsewhere in the West, men who are in the millionaire and near-millionaire classes, who laid the foundation of their fortunes, and made the bulk of them, by their dealings in scrip."[116] These included prominent men such as Donald Smith, Lord Strathcona. Charles Alloway, mentioned in the quotation above, had helped to establish the largest private bank in Canada, Winnipeg's Alloway and Champion Limited.[117] The bank made huge profits by dealing in Métis scrip, reselling lands to other speculators and to settlers. Charles Alloway, who was "at home in the bush and fluent in Indian languages, facilitated most of this business."[118]

Scrip was issued to women and girls as well as to men and boys, so there were many Métis females as well as males who appear in the records of the Dominion lands. The files trace how scrip was acquired and reassigned. In 1905, for example, Isabella Favel made application for a quarter section of land in Saskatchewan, "upon which I desire to locate half-breed land scrip to which I am entitled, and for this purpose I now deliver to Robert McIntosh of Saskatoon, sub-agent for the Regina district, scrip note number A7494."[119] This land was then assigned to Winnipeg lawyer Benjamin Chaffey, who specialized in Métis scrip, and the patent was issued in his name. Chaffey acquired thousands of acres of land in Western Canada.[120] The local history of the Bailey district of Saskatchewan notes that the scrip of three Métis women, Alice McKay, Agnes Archie, and Catherine Maurice, were all transferred to a Duncan McMartin through the work of the Regina law firm Balfour, Martin, Casey and Brown.[121]

Women were among the purchasers of Métis scrip, to be discussed in greater detail in Chapter 4. They included Sarah Green, the English wife of Scotsman John Sanderson, celebrated as Western Canada's homesteader number one, who filed on land near Portage la Prairie in 1871 and received his patent in 1881. Novelist and Manitoba settler Robert J.C. Stead wrote that "although English, she [Sarah Green Sanderson] must have had some of the canny qualities of her husband, for she seized an opportunity to acquire a neighbouring quarter section by means of a half-breed scrip."[122]

HOMESTEAD RIGHTS

The definition of "persons" originally permitted to homestead under Canada's 1872 Dominion Lands Act closely adhered to the U.S. model. Homestead rights were not for First Nations/Native Americans in either nation; they were to be confined to reserves in Canada (reservations in the United States).[123] In Canada the 1876 Indian Act specifically excluded all those defined as "Indian" from the right to homestead.[124] In the Prairie provinces a homestead was available from 1872 to "any person who is the head of a family, or has attained the age of twenty-one years, who is subject to Her Majesty by birth or naturalization shall, after the 1st day of May 1871, be entitled to be entered for one quarter section [160 acres]."[125] The applicant had to pay a ten-dollar filing fee. Patents would not be granted before five years (later reduced to three), when the "settler or his widow" had to satisfy the land office that "he or they have resided upon or cultivated the land for the five years." The homesteader had to prove up by having sufficient acres under cultivation, a habitable dwelling, and living for the required months per year on the land.[126] To receive a patent (title in fee simple or outright ownership) a homesteader who was not a British subject had to be "naturalized." (Naturalization was a process available to every person twenty-one or older who was "not an idiot, lunatic or married woman" who had lived in Canada for not less than three years. The applicant had to then swear an oath of allegiance and an oath that he or she intended to remain in Canada.)[127]

This wording of Canada's original legislation, whether deliberately or not, permitted single women to file for homesteads. In contrast to the U.S. Congress debates about the suitability of women as homesteaders, there were no discussions about the issue in the Canadian House of Commons. If there were private debates, the records do not appear to have survived. An examination of earlier British North American colonial and later provincial legislation reveals that the place of women in free land grants was not obvious and straightforward, or natural. The instructions to Governor James Murray in 1763, for example, gave women—except for Indigenous women (and men)—remarkably equal consideration: "one hundred acres of land [were to] be granted to every person being Master or Mistress of a Family, for himself or herself, and fifty acres for every white or black, Man, Woman, or Child, of which such Person's Family shall consist."[128] Loyalist women acquired free land grants as married women and widows (although these grants were smaller than those received by men), and the daughters as well as the sons of Loyalists were entitled in equal measure to free land. These grants began as 100 acres for a head of household, plus 50 acres for each member of a Loyalist family.[129] Prominent people, including women, got far more. Chief Justice Powell's family received over 12,800 acres; of this his wife and their seven children received 1,200 acres each.[130] An 1848 free grant system for the Crown Lands in the Wellington and Huron districts, however, excluded women, permitting "settlers being subjects of the Queen, males, and not under the age of eighteen years, [to] be assigned each a lot of fifty acres."[131]

The most immediate Canadian precursor to the Dominion Lands Act was the Free Grants and Homestead Act of 1868, a statute of the Legislative Assembly of Ontario that was intended to encourage immigration and settlement. This legislation deliberately included both men and women, without regard to marital status. Following an 1869 amendment, allotments of up to 200 acres were available to any "person … of the age of eighteen years or upwards." The wording of the legislation included both "he" and "she." The person had to swear that he or she was eighteen or older, had not previously located any land under the act, and believed the land was suitable for settlement and cultivation. Patents to the land could not be issued for five years following "settlement duties," which included at least fifteen acres cleared, at least two acres under cultivation each year, and a habitable house built.[132]

The intensive labour that was required in Ontario to first clear the land and the hardships of the immigrant experience were described by English "gentlewoman" Susanna Moodie in *Roughing It in the Bush; Or Life in Canada* (1852).[133] Another memoir, the candid *Letters from Muskoka* (1878), written by an anonymous Englishwoman and published in London, would not have inspired women to take advantage of the free land grants in that region of Ontario.[134] The author was the widow of an army officer; they had been stationed in India, but since her husband's death she had been living in France. Her financial situation was dire, and the move to Ontario was part of a family strategy, as two sons and a married daughter also took up land. A son had gone out to Muskoka a year before. "Emigrant Lady" decided to join him there in 1871, taking with her an unmarried daughter. Her free land grant of 100 acres was beside her son's and son-in-law's grants. While the book contains humour and some happy moments, it is a grim portrait. The author describes life in the "Bush" as dreary, "dull and primitive."[135] There was no church, doctor, or town, nor proper roads to reach any of these. There were "fearfully cold," "dreadful winters of close imprisonment," followed by summers when they were besieged by mosquitoes.[136] The neighbours were all "steerage" class people. It was possible to get a daughter of a settler to work as a servant, but such girls insisted on "a footing of perfect equality with every member of the family, and have no inclination whatever to 'sit below the salt.'"[137] She described local Indigenous people as "degenerate samples of 'Red Men!' The men appeared to me undersized and sinister-looking, the squaws filthy and almost repulsive."[138] All of the settlers had to work desperately hard to clear land before they could cultivate anything. "Emigrant Lady" herself did not do this sort of labour but rather cooked, making do with few ingredients. There was almost no fresh meat, even wild game was scarce. But she wrote that "an Indian officer in our regiment had declared she could make a good curry out of an old shoe," and she persevered.[139] By the end of the second winter, she wrote, "We remain striving, struggling and hoping against hope, that success may yet crown our endeavours."[140]

Part II of *Letters from Muskoka* takes place two years later, but matters have improved little. "Emigrant Lady" feels deceived by the accounts of Muskoka that they had been given before they arrived; the "capabilities of its soil for agricultural purposes have been greatly exaggerated."[141] Years of extensive clearing would be required, and "constant amelioration of the land by means of manure and other applications before it will be capable of bearing heavy grain crops; it is a poor and hungry soil, light and friable." The only reliable crops were oats and potatoes. Her eldest son's health and strength declined, as did her own. They all "looked upon Bush life in the light of exile to a penal settlement without even the convict's chance of a ticket-of-leave."[142] The conclusion to her account of four years on her free grant of land was bleak: "I went into the Bush of Muskoka strong and healthy, full of life and energy, and fully as enthusiastic as the youngest of our party. I left it with hopes completely crushed, and with health so hopelessly shattered from hard work, unceasing anxiety and trouble of all kinds, that I am now a helpless invalid, entirely confined by the doctor's orders to my bed and sofa, with not the remotest chance of ever leaving them for a more active life during the remainder of my days on earth."[143] Perhaps this description of the misery and destitution she endured inspired modifications to homestead legislation in Ontario.

Changes to the Ontario legislation revoked the right of most women to obtain land grants or homesteads in that province, and privileged married men with children. In the 1890s (exact date not clear) the Regulations under the Free Grants and Homesteads Act were altered to narrow the categories of eligible women.[144] Mirroring the changes that were made to the Dominion lands legislation for the prairies in 1876 (to be discussed later in this chapter) free grants of 100 acres were to be available to "a single man over eighteen, or a married man without children under eighteen residing with him, or the female head of a family having children under eighteen residing with her."[145] A free grant of 200 acres was available to "the male head of a family having a child or children under eighteen residing with him … And such male head of a family is permitted to purchase another 100 acres at 50 cents per acre cash." A male head of family, then, was eligible for twice the amount of land as a female head of family, and he had the right to purchase more land at low cost. Some districts of Ontario departed from this model. In the Rainy River district the "male head of a family or the sole female head of a family having a child or children under eighteen residing with him or her may locate for 160 acres, and may also purchase an additional 80 acres at $1 an acre."[146] The term "sole" attached to the female head of family was also used on the prairies to limit the number of eligible women.

British Columbia had separate and divergent land legislation that shifted and changed but eventually provided opportunities for immigrant women that were more generous than those on the prairies. While British Columbia was still a Crown colony, and under 1860 legislation, land could be acquired by "British subjects and aliens who shall take the oath of allegiance to Her Majesty." There was no mention of gender.[147] After 1870, British Columbia designed a land system that was distinct from the Canadian federal government-controlled Crown lands of the three provinces of Manitoba, Saskatchewan, and Alberta (except for a belt of land along the right of way of the Canadian Pacific Railway), which initially offered no opportunity for most immigrant women to acquire land.

Under 1870 legislation for the "pre-emption" of Crown land, "any male person being a British subject, of the age of eighteen years or over" could acquire the right to any tract of unoccupied land.[148] In a 1908 act, however, categories of British women subjects were also permitted to pre-empt Crown lands, including "a widow," "a femme sole who is over eighteen years of age and self-supporting," "a woman deserted by her husband," and "a woman whose husband has not contributed to her support for two years."[149] British Columbia was thus to become a much more welcoming environment for the immigrant woman landowner and farmer than the Prairie provinces were. As in prairie Canada, First Nations in British Columbia were not permitted to pre-empt Crown lands. The 1908 legislation, for example, set out those persons who could obtain land, and continued with "such right shall not extend: a) to any of the aborigines of this continent."[150]

It is likely that in Western Canada, single women and women heads of households were deliberately included in the homestead privilege as it was originally devised, as in the United States. Since there is no evidence of any debate about the issue, however, it is difficult to know for sure. But the precedent of the Ontario legislation and the intense desire to compete with and match the U.S. offer to homesteaders would have compelled this deliberate inclusion. Under Canada's initial legislation, first passed in 1871, it was possible for women heads of families and women who had attained the age of twenty-one to select a homestead. The first published memorandum of 1871 on the Subject of the Public Lands in the Province of Manitoba had provided that "any person who is the head of a family, or has attained the age of twenty-one years" could secure a homestead. This same wording appeared in the 1872 legislation. Chester Martin wrote that the origins of Canada's homestead policy, "direct or indirect, in the United States was conceded on every hand."[151] Yet Canada rather quickly and deliberately took away the privilege of homesteading from single women in 1876, a significant departure from the U.S. legislation.

In both the American and Canadian West the goal of free land and the homesteading scheme was to quickly populate the land with a "preponderance of fit and preferably youthful males." Land policies of both the United States and Canada were "efforts to 'hire' settlers" in order to combat the "Indian's simultaneous claim on public lands and the cost imposed by this dispute over property right."[152] In helping to establish U.S. and Canadian claims in their western territories, homesteading was a "least-cost strategy," a "substitute for direct military force [that] acts to mitigate the costs of violence." A preponderance of fit and preferably youthful males suited this purpose best, and the residence requirement was intended to make them stay put. Settlement had to be scattered to quickly lay claim to vast territories. A homesteader could not reside in a village and head out to the land from there. But restricting the plot size to 160 acres was intended to create relatively dense settlement. Yet in both nations the state had the discretion over where to locate settlers, as homesteading was restricted to surveyed land.

Both Canada and the United States sought to create not just economic development, but a desired social and cultural landscape through land policies. In both nations, administrators were determined to create small-scale holdings reminiscent of an idealized European (particularly British) landscape (despite mounting evidence of environmental limitations). As mentioned, both nations excluded Indigenous people from the homestead privilege, although in the United States, Indian homestead legislation of the 1880s provided some access to land on the public domain. In Western Canada, Métis scrip provided access to individual plots of land. But in both nations the hope was that a white and patriarchal landscape would be created through the homestead system.

In both the United States and Canada, married women were not permitted to homestead. Under the doctrine of marital unity, a married woman had no legal existence. As explained by a commissioner of the U.S. General Land Office in 1864, a married woman's "services and the proceeds of her labor being due and belonging to her husband … that if permitted to enter land because of having arrived at twenty-one years of age, the legal restrictions growing out of her matrimonial relations would at once be violated."[153] A married woman could not apply as "head of the family," because the husband was the "head" during the marriage. This general rule was seriously challenged in the United States in 1882 by Rachel McKee, who applied for a homestead in Colorado where her application was refused because she was married.[154] Her attorney Daniel Witter made some compelling arguments, including that the homestead law allowed anyone over the age of twenty-one to make entry, as the act stated that "every *person* who is the head of a family or who has arrived at the age of twenty-one years … *shall be entitled to enter*" public land. Witter argued Mrs. McKee was a person as defined by John Locke, "a thinking intelligent being that has reason and reflection." He also argued that Congress would have had to have explicitly excluded married women from making entry. Witter further argued that permitting married women to homestead would "give new life to western emigration ... and [would] send tens of thousands of families from poverty and dependence in the over populated east, to prosperity and independence in the new west." The appeal was lost, however, and the McKee decision settled the question of the eligibility of married women to make homestead entries in the United States.[155]

MANITOBA WOMEN HOMESTEADERS WHO FILED BEFORE 1876

Canada's Dominion Lands Act of 1872 originally permitted certain categories of women to homestead—single women and heads of families. And women took advantage of this offer. In the pages of the homestead land registers of the first homesteaders in Manitoba, the names of a few women begin to appear. The early 1870s saw a significant number of women applicants, some single, others widows, although the files do not always provide this information (See Table 1).[156]

The first woman in Western Canada to apply for a homestead in her own name was Mary Walker, who made her entry on land in the House Creek district at the south end of Lake Manitoba in 1872 as homesteader number 214. She died in 1874 before proving up, and her land was patented to her son Peter in 1882, who amassed considerable land in the House Creek district but made his mother's quarter section his home until he sold the land in 1908.[157]

The first woman on the Canadian prairies to receive a patent to her homestead was Isabella McKercher, who entered on a homestead in 1874 at Roseau Crossing, which soon became Dominion City, in south-central Manitoba. She was granted her title to the land in January 1878.[158] She opted to purchase her land after fulfilling some of the homestead requirements, as her land suddenly became very valuable. McKercher came from Ontario with two brothers and her parents, Duncan and Mary, who were the "first white settlers to arrive in Roseau Crossing."[159] She filed on her land in September 1874 and by April 1877, when she swore an affidavit, she had lived on her homestead for fifteen months, and had a house measuring 16 x 12 feet, a stable and wood shed, and four acres under cultivation. In the spring of 1877 it was determined that the Pembina branch of the Canadian Pacific Railway would cross the Roseau River on

McKercher's land, which was thus of "exceptional value," in the words of Donald Codd of the Dominion Lands Branch in Winnipeg. McKercher decided to take the option to purchase her homestead, offered under a section of the Dominion Lands Act, and was likely able to sell the right-of-way at a sizeable profit. When in 1878 the last spike was driven on this branch line, a ceremony was held by the new trestle bridge, barely completed, over the Roseau River. While people took turns driving the spike, Isabella McKercher "was too shy to get up in front of such a gathering, so she held back and watched the others tackle it."[160] That same year she married Alexander Waddell, also a homesteader at Roseau Crossing.

The second woman to prove up was Susannah Jane Kennedy (homesteader number 591), who filed on her land in the Woodlands district in 1873 and received patent to her land five years later.[161] Kennedy appears in the 1881 Manitoba census as born in Ireland, and age eighty.[162] She was illiterate, signing her name on her homestead document with an X. Kennedy sold her original homestead and (incredibly) in 1892, at the age of ninety-four, applied for patent on another homestead, this time in the Souris district, where she was living with an adopted daughter and her husband.

Glimpses of some of the earliest women homesteaders of the Canadian West can be gleaned from the homestead files, and local histories shed light on the identities and experiences of a few, particularly if the names of husbands or fathers or brothers are known. Many were single women to start with who later married. Elizabeth Moffatt, homesteader 615, married John Scott and her patent was thus issued to Elizabeth Scott.

When a woman filed as a single woman, then married before applying for her patent, her husband often (but not always) had to swear an affidavit that his wife was the same person who had filed on land under another name. Malcolm Martin, for example, who married homesteader Kate Smith, had to swear that his wife was the Kate Smith who had entered on land under that name, and that Kate Smith and Kate Martin were one and the same.[163] In 1883 William Ross had to swear that his wife was the same Margaret Campbell who had made homestead entry in 1874, and her brothers Robert and Donald were also asked to add their signatures to the document, verifying that Margaret Campbell and Margaret Ross were one and the same.[164] The records do not always provide the marital status of women homesteaders, as in the case of Mary McLeod, whose land was in the Gladstone district of West Marquette.[165] She filed on her land in 1874, began her residence in 1876, and applied for her patent in

1881, signing her name with an X, as did her witnesses Daniel Reece and John Ross. She was granted her patent to her land in 1882. Women homesteaders varied in age: Jane Leadbeater, who made her entry in 1874, was seventy-two years old when she received her patent in 1887.[166]

These first homesteading women seem to have rarely travelled to Manitoba on their own; some were already residents and others arrived with family. Those whose background is known were not from overseas but from Ontario or Manitoba. Maria Barron filed on land in High Bluff in 1874 and began her residence and cultivation of the land in 1877.[167] Her father was from Scotland and her mother from Ontario. Maria was born in Ontario and came to Manitoba with her parents and siblings in 1874 over the challenging Dawson Trail. Maria married Maxwell Wilton, and her patent was issued to Maria Wilton. The family acquired a lot of land in the High Bluff district.

It can be assumed that some of the women filed along with fathers, brothers, or sons, such as Catherine Doupe, whose entry is beside a Charles Doupe. Sisters filed together as was the case with Mary Matilda Corbett and Sarah Jane Corbett, who claimed homesteads in March 1873. Janet McKercher filed on land close to her parents and brother in 1874. She did not receive her patent until 1906, as her claim was controversial. Although her land had been cropped continuously since 1875, she did not live on her property, keeping house for her parents and then her brother.[168] Two Lipsett women, Phoebe Louisa and Ann Jane, filed with two Lipsett men, Francis W. and James H., in July 1874. All cancelled out, but Caroline Matilda Lipsett, who had filed a few days earlier, eventually proved up in 1891.[169] She was the mother of the other Lipsetts, and perhaps they combined their efforts on her land. Caroline was sixty-four in 1889 when she applied for her patent, declaring that she was a farmer by profession, that her family consisted of herself and eight children, and that when she first occupied her land in August 1875, all of the children were married but one. Her experience, like that of Isabella McKercher, indicates that women could acquire considerable wealth through the right to homestead. Early homesteaders had the right to pre-empt an adjoining quarter section, or to file on a second homestead. Caroline Lipsett became the owner of 320 acres of land in her section, as did other women such as Valletta Jane Nixon, who received her patent to 320 acres under her married last name, Edgar.[170]

It is clear from the register of homesteads in Manitoba that times were difficult, by the number of cancellations as well as the number of years it took to prove up. Persistence was required. Louisa Irvine filed on land in Manitoba in 1874 but did not receive her patent until 1897, when title was issued to her under her married name, Louisa Munro.[171] Weather, poor land, and grasshoppers accounted for delays and abandonments, but homesteaders also encountered bureaucratic problems. Louisa Irvine/Munro first applied for the patent to her land in 1885, claiming that she had lived on her homestead from 1874 to 1877, had built a house, granary, and stable, and had six head of cattle and six sheep as well as one acre under cultivation.[172] She was denied her patent in 1885 because at least fifteen acres under cultivation was required. The case was reconsidered in 1897, when it was noted that "the land is unfit for grain growing" and that regulations had since changed: "more recently it has been customary to accept stock with a smaller amount of cultivation to satisfy the requirements of the Act, where it is clearly shown that the land is unfit for grain growing."[173] It was decided that this was the case and Louisa Munro was finally granted her patent twenty-three years after she first filed on her homestead.

Family strategies included mothers homesteading beside sons. Widow Barbara Scott entered on land next to her son James Scott, who cultivated both his and his mother's land. All of his buildings were on his mother's homestead, however, and this proved a problem as he had not complied strictly with the wording of the legislation. In an 1884 memo, however, officials of the Department of the Interior decided that he had complied with the "spirit" of the law, and he was granted title to his land.[174]

In 1874, the brother of widow Matilda Graham from Ontario filed on a homestead at High Bluff in Marquette West in the name of his sister.[175] She married James McAskie in 1876 in Ontario, and together in 1878 they moved to Manitoba, settled on her claim, and lived there for one year. Her husband then took out a homestead as well, and they moved to his land in 1879, where they were living in 1881 when the land agent at Gladstone told them that "it was not legal for her husband to hold a homestead [and] that one of them must be cancelled." A Matthew Harkness was interested in Graham/McAskie's land and was trying to get her homestead cancelled, or "jump her claim." In 1880 Harkness signed an affidavit (with an X) declaring that Graham/McAskie had not resided on her claim for the last year. In 1881 Matilda McAskie opted to purchase her homestead at one dollar per acre, swearing that the land was "entered by me as a homestead

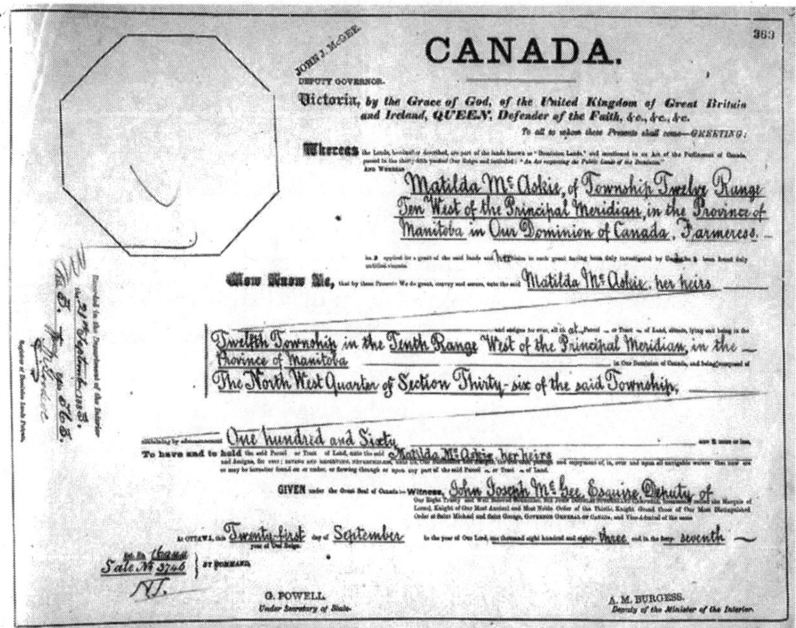

383

JOHN J. McGEE.
DEPUTY GOVERNOR.

CANADA.

Victoria, by the Grace of God, of the United Kingdom of Great Britain and Ireland, QUEEN, Defender of the Faith, &c., &c., &c.

To all to whom these Presents shall come—GREETING:

Whereas [illegible]

Matilda McAskie, of Township Twelve Range Ten West of the Principal Meridian, in the Province of Manitoba in Our Dominion of Canada, Farmeress. [illegible]

Now Know Ye, that by these Presents We do grant, convey and assure, unto the said Matilda McAskie, her heirs [illegible]

Twelfth Township in the Tenth Range West of the Principal Meridian, in the Province of Manitoba [illegible] The North West Quarter of Section Thirty-six of the said Township,

One hundred and Sixty [illegible]

To have and to hold the said Parcel or Tract of Land, unto the said Matilda McAskie, her heirs [illegible]

GIVEN under the Great Seal of Canada:—Witness, John Joseph McGee, Esquire, Deputy of [illegible]

At OTTAWA, this Twenty-first day of September in the year of Our Lord, one thousand eight hundred and eighty-three and in the forty-seventh year of Our Reign.

Sale No 3746 } BY COMMAND,

G. POWELL.
Under Secretary of State.

A. M. BURGESS.
Deputy of the Minister of the Interior.

Figure 5. Patent issued in 1883 to Manitoba homesteader Matilda McAskie, who filed on her homestead in 1874 as Matilda Graham. She was now the owner of the northwest quarter of section 36, township 12, range 10, west of the Principal Meridian. She also acquired an adjoining quarter section, becoming the owner of 320 acres of land. Library and Archives Canada, Western Land Grants, http://www.bac-lac.gc.ca/eng/discover/land/land-grants-western-canada-1870-1930/pages/item.aspx?IdNumber=461605&.

while a widow and a head of a family." She received patent to the northwest quarter section in 1882 and to the northeast in 1883.

Tragedies emerge from the files. Mary Mitchell filed on her homestead in 1873, later becoming Mrs. George Edie. She died in 1877, and her infant child was buried with her. When her husband applied for patent to her land ten years later, there were many hoops to jump through, including finding two people to swear that they had attended Mary Edie's funeral and had seen her buried. The homestead inspector wrote in 1887 that "at the time of her death in 1877 settlers were few and much scattered, and these are the only two in the neighbourhood who were there at the time."[176] Homesteader Hannah J. Whaley also died before she had the chance to prove up on her homestead that she filed on in 1873 in the Pine Creek district, and the patent to her land was issued to her husband Francis Blackmore in 1878.[177]

Conditions were grim for Manitoba's first homesteaders. Plagues of grasshoppers (locusts) were an intermittent problem in Manitoba and the midwestern states to the south, and they returned with a vengeance in 1873–75, devouring all vegetation in their path. There was also a general economic depression to contend with that began in 1873, and in 1874 it was clear that the railway to and eventually through Manitoba would take many more years to build than anticipated.[178] Settlers and Indigenous farmers lacked the equipment and the early maturing varieties of seed suitable to Western Canadian conditions. The number of immigrants plummeted: in 1875 there were 11,970, but in 1876 only between 3,000 and 4,000.[179] Homesteads were deserted. Gerald Friesen writes in his history of the Canadian prairies: "The rate of attrition—the failure of the homesteader to 'prove up' and thus obtain a patent for his quarter-section—was extraordinary. Chester Martin long ago calculated that four in ten prairie homestead applications were never fulfilled. Though admittedly rough, his statistics indicates a rate of failure of 20 per cent in Manitoba (1870–1905), 57 per cent in Saskatchewan (1911–31), and 45 per cent in Alberta (1905–30). This led him to note in his ironic fashion that 'in some respects "free" homesteads have been costly beyond computation.'"[180] The failure rate for the earliest homesteaders in Manitoba was likely much higher than the 20 percent Martin calculated.

Notably, the early women homesteaders of Manitoba were generally more successful than their male counterparts at proving up. For example, of those who filed on land in 1874, 5 percent of the men proved up and

18 percent of the women; in 1875, it was 9 percent of the men and 57 percent of the women; and in 1876, 42 percent of the men and 75 percent of the women proved up. There were women homesteaders who proved up well before John Sanderson, "Western Canada's first Homesteader," who filed on claim one in 1872 but did not receive his patent until 1881.[181]

Year	Total Applicants	Total Male Applicants	Total Men Who Received Their Grant	% of Men Who Were Successful	Total Female Applicants	Total Women Who Received Their Grant	% of Women Who Were Successful
1872	253	245	138	56%	1	0	0%
1873	878	823	377	46%	41	10	24%
1874	1276	416	19	5%	109	20	18%
1875	1931	1920	167	9%	7	4	57%
1876	322	317	132	42%	4	3	75%
1877	964	957	473	49%	7	4	57%
1878	2360	2329	1031	44%	24	14	58%
1879	2746	3574	1906	53%	42	23	55%
1880	2165	2109	1367	65%	30	22	73%
1881	2814	2739	1874	68%	33	23	70%
1882	7644	7494	3861	52%	60	36	60%

Table 1. The gender of Western Canadian homesteaders and their success rates at "proving up," 1872–1882. Note that statistics for applicants of unknown gender are not included in the table. Source: Library Archives Canada, Record Group 15 (Department of the Interior), Homestead Land Registers, vols. 1762–1766, reel T-2.

CHANGES TO HOMESTEAD LEGISLATION: "TO RENDER FEMALES ... INELIGIBLE"

The *Manitoba Free Press* tried to report on the desperate conditions on the prairies while not completely scaring off prospective settlers. But on 7 July 1875 an editorial admitted that the people of Manitoba were in a state of destitution.[182] The crops had failed in some districts for three and in others two successive years: "The question that presents itself for consideration is this: Are the people of the Province, collectively speaking, in possession of the means to purchase their bread, in addition to other necessaries of existence? We answer, they are not." While many of the older settlers had livestock, "the new settlers have but very little, and therefore have scarcely anything to fall back upon, in their day of need." Settlers needed relief, and they needed seed grain for the following spring. While settlers hoped to make a living off of the farm when crops failed, on the railway and city improvements, the market for jobs was saturated.

The "homestead question" dominated the editorials in the *Free Press* in the spring and summer of 1875. Settlement of the province was in a precarious state. There was anger over speculators who, according to the *Free Press*, had filed on homesteads but had no intentions of living on and cultivating their land. Distinctions were drawn between them and the "actual" or bona fide settlers, yet it was admitted that this was difficult to determine under the extraordinary circumstances of the grasshopper infestation.[183] In April 1875 the federal government proposed that lands entered as homesteads and found without occupants in the summer of 1875 would have their entries cancelled, and the *Free Press* had to admit this was not fair under the circumstances, as many "actual" settlers might not be found on their ravaged land that summer. "Scarcely a day elapses that one or more cases of positive hardship, are not brought under our notice."[184] The *Free Press* in 1875 called not for cancellation but for a relaxation of the homestead requirements for a year, as was the case in the Dakota Territory and Minnesota, which were also experiencing the grasshopper devastation. There, settlers were allowed leaves of absence from their land.[185] A problem with the wording of the homestead legislation had also led to some confusion. The original 1872 legislation read that to obtain a patent, proof was required of "having resided upon *or* cultivated the land for three years." According to a letter by a settler in the *Free Press*, many homesteaders believed from this clause that they could cultivate their land without actually having to live there.[186]

On 14 June 1875, an order-in-council was approved in response to a letter from Donald Codd, agent of Dominion lands in Manitoba, reporting on "the depredations of grasshoppers in the Province, and the disastrous effects to the settlements in consequences thereof, unless some special consideration is extended to persons who have taken up homesteads by giving them leave of absence from their farms in order that they may earn subsistence for their families during the prevalence of the plague."[187] Authority was given Codd to relax the rules and regulations so that those whose crops were destroyed and who were actually resident on their homesteads and prevented from putting in a crop because of the plague could, after furnishing unspecified evidence, receive written permission to be absent from their homesteads until 1 July 1876. This period of time could be counted as part of their three years' residence. (This was as recommended by the *Free Press* and adopted from the U.S. model.) Such leave was only to apply, however, to a "bona fide homestead settler."

The Honourable Luc Letellier de Saint-Just, minister of agriculture and immigration in the Alexander Mackenzie government, was sent in August 1875 to Manitoba to determine what measures should be taken to address the situation, including the destitution of the settlers. Letellier de Saint-Just recommended the expenditure of $60,000, authorized by order-in-council in August 1875, to purchase pork, flour, seed wheat, and barley.[188] These were to be distributed as a loan or advance secured on the settlers' lands.

In his October 1875 report to Minister of the Interior David Laird, Surveyor Dennis wrote that he saw signs of hope for the future. The locusts had not left eggs in the soil, as in previous years. Dennis reported that the provision of seed grain and the permission to be absent for twelve months from homesteads had allayed discontent. He found that on the whole the Dominion Lands Act "worked satisfactorily," but that "there are certain important details connected with the operation of the homestead clauses in which it may be improved."[189] From Dennis's wording it appears that Laird agreed with these changes, as he wrote that they had "suggested themselves during your personal experience of the practical working of the law when in Manitoba and the North-West Territories last year." The very first of a list of eight recommended changes was "to render females, not being heads of families, ineligible to enter for homesteads." Dennis provided no explanation for this change. There was no discussion or debate when the changes to the legislation came before the House of Commons. There was no debate about it in the press, and at the time, no protest from individuals or groups.

In May 1876, when the legislation was passed, the *Free Press* explained that the changes had been made with a view to "proper and efficient management" of the land, at the suggestion of the minister or the land agent in the country, "who watches closely the practical operation of existing land laws, and it thus enables him to make valuable recommendations from time to time." The second change mentioned in the same report (the first concerned military bounty warrants) was that "women cannot obtain homestead grants unless they are *bona fide* the independent head of a family."[190] When the amendments based on Dennis's recommendations were passed, homesteads from then on were limited to "any person, male or female, who is the sole head of a family, or any male who has attained the age of eighteen years."[191]

Historians of the settlement era in Western Canada have not mentioned this as a development of any importance or interest, although to prohibit single immigrant women from homesteading was a major departure from the U.S. model that Canada wanted so desperately to match and even exceed. Why did this happen? As mentioned, women homesteaders during that small window of opportunity open until 1876 persisted and proved up on their land at a significantly higher rate than that of their male counterparts, but these statistics would not at that time have been available to policy makers (as it took many years for persistent homesteaders to prove up).

The most significant clue to the perception of the 1870s that Manitoba's single women homesteaders were not bona fide settlers comes from the 1879 observations of David Currie, who visited Manitoba as a special commissioner of the *Montreal Witness.* His letters were published the next year in pamphlet form as *The Letters of Rusticus: Investigations in Manitoba and the North-West for the Benefit of Intending Emigrants.*[192] Currie was sceptical of the capacity and propriety of women farmers, reflecting views that will be further discussed in the next chapter. He believed they were incapable of homestead duties and that it was "unnatural" for women to cultivate land and live on their own. Currie noted the presence of single women homesteaders (and did not seem aware that as of 1876 they were no longer permitted to file on land), and he did not approve, writing that "although the idea of single ladies faithfully performing homestead duties seems unnatural, yet a number of such have secured the land but that they have complied with the terms imposed by the Government is rather doubtful."[193] Currie believed that by contrast, men were complying with the homestead laws: "During my travels over this province I have met with a great many unmarried gentlemen who are fulfilling the letter if not the spirit of the law by 'baching' it on their homesteads; but I have not yet met with a single case where a maiden lady has been honestly endeavouring to comply with the law which gives her a title to her lands."[194]

Currie admitted, however, that he had had little opportunity to observe single women homesteaders at their duties, as he found it difficult and improper for him to either search out or visit them, writing that "indeed any attempt to do so would scarcely seem prudent in a country where the population is so very scattered." Yet he concluded that the "only feasible way by which ladies might faithfully comply with the terms of the law giving them the right to 'homestead' land, is by forming a matrimonial alliance with some gentleman friend, in whose company homestead duties might be faithfully performed."[195]

Currie was also concerned with the potential for fraud, that couples would delay marriage and would acquire more land than they were entitled to. He had heard of engaged couples where the man and woman each secured homestead rights in advance of their wedding, and "by this means acquired double the amount of land that they could legally secure if they had postponed their homesteading until after they became man and wife." He continued that it was "not desirable that persons after becoming 'one flesh' should each reside upon separate homesteads, consequently one of the claims must remain unoccupied." Currie assumed that this was why so many claims were unoccupied and found this "reprehensible," writing that "a large number [of homesteads] remain untenanted with only a few acres brought under cultivation, and perhaps the walls of a home erected, and not a few homesteads remain without any attempts to bring them under cultivation."[196]

In the *Manitoba Free Press* women homesteaders had not been singled out as part of the concern about bona fide settlers, but the serialized account of "How Two Girls Tried Farming," published just at this time, might have encouraged readers to doubt the abilities of women farmers.[197] The account, by Dorothea Alice Shepherd (pseudonym for Ella Farman Pratt), was originally published in the U.S. magazine *Atlantic Monthly* and later as a book. It featured two friends, a "housemaid" and a teacher, who bought a small farm in Michigan after one of them inherited a thousand dollars. "How Two Girls Tried Farming" was a very popular story in the United States, as it was reprinted as a book several times; it was also controversial, raising issues of women's competency to farm on their own. It may have been serialized in the *Free Press* to illustrate the mistakes, trials, and difficulties of women farmers (and they experienced many) and to show that farming was not a "traditional" enterprise for women. The two women of the story succeeded in some respects, although they had to abandon their "small fruits" plan in favour of corn, vegetables, and selling butter and eggs. It concluded with a reminder that for women, ploughing, shovelling snow, cleaning stables, and other chores were "strange abnormal labours … But we do it, therefore others can."[198]

Surveyor Dennis made the recommendation to exclude single women from the homestead grant. Obsessed with the potential of the West, he was very concerned about the depressed conditions and possible collapse of the whole enterprise, and it may have been his personal view that women were not going to make the land productive. It is likely that Dennis shared his opinions with his friend and "most trusted clerk" at the Dominion Lands Branch, Donald Codd, who had been with Dennis on the original survey team sent to Red River.[199] Codd had wide discretionary power in refusing claims, and the dramatic drop in the number of women homestead applicants in 1875 (when there were seven, compared to 109 in 1874), suggests that he may have been refusing or in some way discouraging women from filing on land in advance of the 1876 change in legislation. The decline in applications from women could not have had to do with grasshoppers; there were 1,920 male applicants in 1875, compared to only 416 the year before.

The necessity of wage labour for homesteaders to survive may have been an issue. Male homesteaders worked on railways, in lumber camps, and in the cities, and similar opportunities for women would have been limited. There was some talk of having homesteaders perform statutory labour. In an undated (early 1870s) set of recommendations about how land should be granted, James Cunningham, a member of Manitoba's first legislature of 1870, recommended that every settler be bound to work one day a week for five years on the railway at the rate of one dollar per day. Cunningham estimated this scheme would result in 1,100 men in each township working 250 days a year for five years. While ultimately this measure was not introduced, in any discussion of such a plan, women homesteaders would clearly have been seen as unsuitable candidates.[200]

Speculation about other reasons for limiting women's right to homestead might include the paperwork that was required when single women homesteaders married before they proved up, as discussed above. The case of Matilda Graham/McAskie also illustrates that complications emerged when a woman filed on a homestead as a single woman and then married a man who himself then filed on a homestead: one or the other was obliged to give up the claim, a problem that also emerged in the American West. There the legislation was changed several times to deal with the issue of "entrywomen" who married an "entryman" before proving up, and there were complex and contradictory legal decisions and interpretations on the matter.[201] Bureaucrats at the Canadian Department of the Interior became increasingly obsessed with the opportunities for fraud in acquiring land, and women were seen as particularly suspect.

Citizenship and naturalization may have also been an issue, one that was to complicate the lives of some female heads of households who filed on homesteads after 1876. Upon marriage a woman automatically was given her husband's citizenship; if a woman who had filed on a homestead married a neighbouring homesteader who was not yet a British subject, she lost her ability to apply for a patent until her husband changed his citizenship.

There may have been concerns about the dangers of settlement. The idea of immigrant women alone on isolated homesteads was perhaps unsettling to policy makers and legislators (although they did not waver in the United States, where there was more warfare and thousands more women homesteaders). Supporters of homesteads-for-women understood that the homestead right was rescinded because in the 1870s "Indians were bold and bad" and "lawless" and the railroad was not finished, and "it was considered a big adventure for a hardy man to take up land in the genuinely wild and wooly West."[202] (And they used this as a rationale for having the privilege restored, arguing that this threat from "lawless" Indians no longer existed.)

Many people, women and men, were not prepared for the challenges of life on a prairie homestead. Englishwoman Mary (Mrs. Cecil) Hall described her first thoughts about the prairies in her 1882 book, *A Lady's Life on a Farm in Manitoba*: "O the prairie! I cannot describe to you our first impression. Its vastness, dreariness, and loneliness is appalling."[203] That very year there was a "shocking fatality" in Manitoba that was news across the British Empire.[204] At Meadow Lea, thirty miles west of Winnipeg, a fire broke out during the middle of a roaring blizzard, destroying the home of the Taylor family. The mother and three daughters were all found frozen to death on the prairie.

The idea that women would be poor custodians and cultivators was likely a rationale, as was the idea they would probably be mere investors or speculators in land. In a 1908 article explaining some of the differences between U.S. and Canadian homestead rules, Canada was complimented for its law that "permits a young man to get an early start in life, while it discriminates against those women whose cultivation of the soil is apt to be perfunctory, and the homesteading a mere investment, and favours those cases where there is a real incentive to the making of a living out of the farm for the dependent children."[205] (It was assumed a single male would eventually have children, while a "spinster" would not.)

Robert Rogers, minister of the interior (1911–12) and a politician from Manitoba, stated that while homestead privileges had at one time been available to single women, they "failed to claim them, or having done so, did not fulfil the necessary duties and thus forfeited their rights."[206] This does not appear to have been the case, however; there were significant numbers of women who filed on homesteads during the small window of opportunity available, and they proved up with greater frequency than men. In 1913, a woman journalist with the *Saskatoon Star Phoenix* said that Rogers's explanation sounded "weak and spineless; not in keeping with that pioneer spirit which has made our women remarkable the world over."[207]

A few observers of Manitoba in the mid-1870s took note of the presence of women homesteading on their own. In 1874 the *Toronto Mail* reported that "under the Homestead Law, every individual over twenty-one years of age may take up a free grant of 160 acres of land, and happy are they who have large families of grown children. Our correspondent says he has known single families to have taken up five and even seven homesteads. Father, sons, daughters, maiden aunts and widows being entitled to enter each for 160 acres."[208] This correspondent was not entirely critical of this, it seems, as he said that "it would be of advantage to extend the right to all persons over eighteen years of age, as it would encourage early marriages, and consequent independence, and increase the number of actual farmers." His last comment, however, suggests that he did not include "maiden aunts and widows" in the category of "actual farmers."

Was the homestead privilege taken away from all but widows with minor children because farming and homesteading was not seen as suitably feminine for women colonists? This seems to have been in the mind of David Currie, who wrote that it was "unnatural" for women to perform homestead duties. A woman working in the field was not seen to conform to an idealized British femininity; they were to be delicate and fragile. Predominant representations of Indigenous women played a role by providing a contrast to ideals of a domestic and refined and British femininity. As stressed at the beginning of this chapter, women were the farmers on the Great Plains long before the arrival of Europeans. While Indigenous women working on farms and gardens might not have been very visible to newcomers of the 1870s because this work was being performed on Indian reserves, the representation of "squaws" as exploited and overworked drudges was widely promulgated. The corollary representation was that Indigenous men were reluctant and poor workers who relied on their women for all manual labour, while they relaxed and smoked. Travellers and other writers often commented on this. David Currie's 1879 description was typical: "I observed two native gentlemen reclining on a small straw covered shed, smoking their pipes, seemingly at perfect peace with themselves and all mankind, whilst at the two nearest houses, and within less than one hundred yards of the two smokers, were two native ladies engaged in chopping the night's supply of stovewood from piles of poplar poles. The way that the ladies handled the axe showed plainly that they were no strangers to this occupation."[209]

A Toronto *Globe* correspondent visiting the North-West in 1881 wrote that Indigenous "men are nearly all, in the matter of physical strength, unable to endure manual labour. In the camp the women do all the hard work such as cutting wood etc." The men, by contrast, were "indolent or incapable to do much."[210] Indigenous men were frequently and widely condemned for the fact that women supplied wood for their families, while "they themselves stay in the teepee, smoke, pound the tom tom with a club and see who can tell the biggest lie."[211] The message was that manual labour was unsuitable for colonizing women, who must show superiority to these darker times and ways.

In common with the imperialist rhetoric of other colonial settings, it was white men who stood in contrast to Indigenous males.[212] The white male colonizer would transform the wilderness into productive and profitable terrain. The ideal white male figure was physically capable, courageous, and industrious. The white woman colonizer was not to exemplify these traits.[213] It was vital to demonstrate that the colonizers were superior, that they knew how to treat women in comparison to "savage" societies. Women were the farmers only in "uncivilized" societies, where they were cast as being forced unwillingly into such work by lazy men.[214] In the 1899 book *Woman's Share in Primitive Culture* by Otis T. Mason, a sketch of a sparsely clad woman, hoeing, with her unhappy child strapped to her back, was accompanied by the caption "The Primitive Farmer and Burden-Bearer, South Africa."[215]

Did the arrival of women of varied ethnicities as immigrants play a role in excluding most women from the homestead grant? In this outpost of the British Empire, the colonizers needed to show superiority to the new arrivals of varying non-British origins. Immigrants from other places than the British Isles and Ontario began to arrive in the West in the mid-1870s, when Icelanders settled in the Interlake district of Manitoba and Mennonites from Russia on the plains south of Winnipeg. In these communities, as with the Doukhobors who arrived over two decades later, women worked in the fields and performed other critical manual labour. This was noted by the late 1870s. John Lowe, secretary of the Department

Figure 6. "The Primitive Farmer and Burden-Bearer, South Africa," from Otis T. Mason, *Women's Share in Primitive Culture* (1899), 6. According to British imperialist rhetoric, women were the farmers only in Indigenous societies, where they were cast as unwilling participants forced into the work by Indigenous men.

of Agriculture and a Manitoba farmer (of an enormous farm of sixteen square miles), gave evidence before a federal committee on immigration to Canada that Mennonite women were seen "ploughing in the fields."[216] He also saw "a woman thatching the roof of a building, the materials being handed up to her; and we next saw a girl plastering the outside of a house in apparently a very matter-of-fact way." He saw men, women, and children "going out into the fields to work before the morning was grey. We also noticed these people working until it was dark in the evening." A member of the committee asked Lowe, "Does this kind of work improve the condition of the women, or tend to their refinement?" His reply was that "this must be judged relatively. Their social ideas are certainly, in many respects, very different from ours, and I was told this hard work was considered to be of the highest good to the women. Any finery in dress is rigorously discouraged."[217] It was to become a central rationale of officials, in response to requests for the right of British and Canadian-born women to homestead land, that to have them working in the fields would be "disastrous … for the reputation of Canada."[218] This was not the refined and genteel behaviour expected of them and required to set an example for Indigenous people and other immigrants.

Gardening was acceptable; owning land and farming was not. As historian Dianne Lawrence has written, in the colonies gardens performed added functions. Through their gardens, genteel women colonizers "contributed to the imperial cause by creating order out of chaos of the natural world." Their gardens were small-scale models of the wider imperial project.[219] The flower beds and neat rows of vegetables proclaimed a superior civilization, triumphing over wilderness. Gardening or horticulture for women, rather than commercial farming on land they owned, was less threatening and challenging to the traditional gender order, as discussed in the next chapter. Women homesteaders such as Isabella McKercher could find themselves the owners of land that was very valuable as railroads were built and markets opened. Gender chaos could result if women had the opportunity for independence and incomes of their own. And profits, which were considerable when the economy boomed, would have to be shared. Women were begrudged small acreages while the predominantly male investors and speculators acquired massive landholdings in the West. For all of these reasons, the short-lived and impractical tree culture opportunity was seen as acceptable for women.

A SHORT-LIVED OPPORTUNITY FOR WOMEN: FOREST TREE CULTURE

At the very same time as women, unless they were sole heads of families, were made ineligible to homestead, a new opportunity was offered them for land grants in the West—tree farms, or forest tree culture. Minister of the Interior and Lieutenant Governor David Laird was particularly devoted to this initiative. In his report for 1875, Laird, from Prince Edward Island, wrote that during a trip from Fort Garry to Fort Qu'Appelle in the summer of 1874, "nothing impressed itself upon my mind more than the treelessness of a vast portion of the country over which I passed. Day by day, as I crossed the wide extent of prairies utterly destitute of trees, the question presented itself: How is the settlement of these prairie provinces possible, if the settler is without wood for fencing, building and fuel?"[220] Laird had met with an experienced tree planter in Fargo, North Dakota, and learned how tree culture was to be encouraged there, and he was determined to provide the same opportunities north of the border.[221]

In 1873 the U.S. Congress passed an act encouraging the cultivation of trees on the western prairies. This was available to anyone regardless of gender and marital status; the act stated that "any person who shall plant, protect, and keep in a healthy growing condition for ten years forty acres of timber ... shall be entitled to a patent for the whole of the said quarter-section."[222] In the United States pressure had mounted from the 1860s to address the question of the cultivation of trees for the treeless prairies. As an editorial in an 1866 St. Cloud, Minnesota, newspaper showed, tree culture was considered work for women, who would be better off devoting themselves to the care of groves of trees than the "patchwork quilts and other jim crackery upon which women waste their time and ruin their eyesight."[223]

In his 1875 letter to Laird recommending that females who were not sole heads of families be ineligible to homestead, Surveyor Dennis urged similar legislation to promote forest tree culture in Manitoba and the North-West, which could transform small plots of "apparently worthless" prairie lands into valuable farms.[224] These farms, according to Dennis, would improve the climate and provide fuel, building, and fencing material. Dennis reviewed the U.S. legislation and its early results at length, claiming that in Minnesota alone, "the enormous area of 170,307 acres had been entered under the Acts encouraging tree planting." Dennis's glowing recommendations about tree planting indicate that he saw this as a more suitable task for women. Dennis wrote that "this new industry, if prudently and patiently followed up, is even a surer source of wealth than wheat growing, and without the additional expense and anxiety connected with the latter." He quoted a U.S. expert who asserted that land properly cultivated and planted with trees could be sold for $100 per acre within twenty years.

As historian David M. Emmons has written, the Timber Culture Act of 1873 in the United States was prompted by a theory "which gave expression to both the optimism and the desperation which accompanied the Americans in the settlement of their last frontier."[225] Land previously seen as arid, sterile, and inhospitable had to be transformed into a green, bountiful, appealing prospect for agriculture and settlement. There were many theories about how rainfall could be increased, and the early 1870s saw influential champions of the idea that trees brought rain. The main authority was George Perkins Marsh, author of *Man and Nature* (1864), who predicted that splendid forests could be grown on the plains, checking evaporation and ameliorating the harsh climate.[226] Ferdinand Hayden, director of the U.S. Geological and Geographical Survey of the Territories, found rainfall increasing wherever there were settlers who planted trees, and he was confident that "the Great American Desert had been converted; indeed as a continuous area it has already ceased to exist, even in imagination."[227]

Canada quickly followed with its own measures to bring rain and provide timber to the settlers, and new Forest Tree Culture provisions of Canada's Dominion Lands Act were added in the 1876. Enthusiasm for the measure was expressed in the *Manitoba Free Press*, and an American expert was quoted who asserted that "a grove of trees can be grown as surely as a crop of corn," that within five years ten acres of timber could supply fuel and fencing for a family, that "apparently worthless prairie land" could be sold within twenty years for $100 per acre if planted with timber, and that within ten years lands "properly planted and cultivated with trees will ... realize at the rate of ten to one as compared with the profits attending the raising of wheat."[228]

The 1876 legislation provided women, regardless of marital status, as well as men, the opportunity to acquire land to plant trees: "Any person, male or female, being a subject of Her Majesty by birth or naturalization, and having attained the age of eighteen years, shall be entered for one quarter section or less quantity of unappropriated Dominion lands as a claim forest tree planting."[229] The use of both "he and she" throughout the complicated legislation setting forth the rules and regulations made it clear that this was quite deliberately inclusive. Was this to be a replacement for the right to homestead, offering all women an opportunity for a parcel of land in their own names?

A tree claim was exceedingly complicated and demanding compared to homesteading. The applicant was to select up to 160 acres of land that was "open prairie and without timber." One year after the date of entry on the land the claimant had to have cleared eight acres for tree planting, eight more the second year, and sixteen more within the third year. This acreage had to be planted with trees. After six years, and not before, the claimant could receive a patent if she or he had trees kept in good condition.

Some of the significant differences from homesteading land may have convinced architects of the plan that tree culture was more suitable than homesteading for women. Claimants were not required to build a dwelling and reside on their land; tree farmers, unlike homesteaders, did not have to be isolated and alone living on the prairie. Presumably a tree claimant could live on a family homestead or in a town or city. It took twice as long, however, to be able to apply for patent to the land; homesteaders could apply after three years, while tree claimants had to wait for six years (and later eight). At any time during those six years, the tree grower was liable to forfeiture if he or she was not breaking land, planting, and tending the trees. For homesteaders the precise amount of land to be broken and cultivated each year was not specified until an amendment in 1884 that demanded ten acres a year, which was reduced to five in an 1886 amendment.

Tree claims did not catch hold of the imagination of prospective settlers, either women or men. Few seized the opportunity: in the first six months of 1877 in Manitoba, for example, there were 348 homestead entries and five forest tree culture entries.[230] Problems with the initial legislation were addressed in the 1879 amendments to the Forest Tree Culture legislation.[231] The number of acres that had to be broken each year was lowered from eight to five. Claimants were given two more years to plant and tend their trees; they could not apply for a patent until eight years, rather than six. After eight years the claimant had to prove that "he or she has planted not less than two thousand seven hundred trees on each acre of the portion broken or ploughed and cultivated to crop."

Writing in 1879 for the *Montreal Witness*, David Currie stated that tree claims were being abused, that the scheme "seems also to be only used as a means for securing unlawful possession of Government lands."[232] He had "not yet heard of one acre of these claims being planted with trees" and knew of some who were cultivating grain on their tree claims.

Timber culture was abandoned in the United States in 1891, when the act was repealed by Congress as part of a general reconsideration of land policy. It had been discovered that trees planted on the plains did not bring more rain. According to Emmons, "nature did not prove quite as docile and malleable as the advocates of increased rainfall believed. Drought struck the plains in the mid-70s and again in the mid-80s. Trees planted in response to the Timber Culture Act withered and died."[233] North of the border the same situation prevailed and the program was abandoned even earlier, in 1886.[234] Tree claims proved utterly impractical. There was nowhere to acquire the thousands of seedlings and/or cuttings the tree farmers were to plant. Winds could be severe, dry, and hot. Hail was also a frequent visitor. There was no income for the claimant for six to eight years. Donald Codd reported in 1878 that there were only thirty-five claims under the Forest Tree Culture provisions. Altogether there were only fifty-one tree claims entered in Manitoba.[235] Most were south of Winnipeg along the banks of the Red River, where flooding was also an issue many years. Of these claims, only five patents were ever issued.

Interviewed in 1913 about the homesteads-for-women petition, Isabelle Beaton Graham of the *Grain Growers' Guide* spoke of the short-lived tree claim opportunity: "They [women] were not allowed [homesteads] on the same terms as men, but could have tree claims and must have planted and have growing 500 trees before they could get a patent. Very few made good of course. The proposition was absurd because the trees were almost impossible to obtain, and even when induced to grow could yield no financial returns."[236] Tree planting, another woman journalist wrote in 1913, was "a healthful and interesting occupation ... but when planted heaven sent no manna as fruit thereof. Even if the claimant succeeded in securing and getting into the ground the five hundred birch, elm soft maple etc. for which the Government clamoured she could not make a living out of them. She failed, and though it was from no fault of her own, the privilege was withdrawn."[237]

The right of unmarried women to homestead was abolished in 1876, and the right, however impractical, to tree claim land was removed in 1886. But there did remain one category of eligibility for women—the sole head of family. From 1876 the legislation read: "Any person, male or female, who is the sole head of a family, or any male who has attained the age of eighteen years shall be entitled to be entered for one quarter-section."[238] As understood by Canadian authorities, this meant that only widows with minor children dependent upon them were permitted to homestead.

As the homesteads-for-women campaign grew prior to the First World War, many commented that this was simply not fair. In a 1913 *Saskatoon Star Phoenix* column entitled "No Way for a Single Woman to Get a Farm, Unless She Captures a Man," Valance Patriarche wrote that "a woman who wants a homestead must prove she has been clever and energetic enough to have previously captured a husband and either kept him or let him die. If she has him on hand he obtains the homestead; if she has let him slip away to a better land she is solaced by having the grant made out in her own name."[239] That same year journalist Lillian Beynon Thomas also used humour to criticize the law that seemed far from fair to her, noting that "there are no homesteads for women in Western Canada unless such women care to qualify by killing off any inconvenient husbands they happen to own."[240]

British women interested in farming and owning land in the colonies were urged to emigrate to a not entirely hospitable environment in prairie Canada, and the individuals and associations advocating this, the subject of the next chapter, appeared to know little of the challenges and obstacles that awaited. Canadian authorities wanted British women immigrants, preferably young, single, and robust, who could be wives and mothers. They were not at all interested in encouraging women to settle and farm on their own. They wanted to plant and nurture a traditional gender order, not cultivate new strains of independent women. Neither the unwelcoming conditions nor the discouragement of authorities, however, prevented the creation of a modest momentum for the cause of British "gentle" or educated women farmers for the prairies, which reached its zenith in the years just before the First World War.

CHAPTER TWO

"LAND OWNERS AND ENTERPRISING SETTLERS IN THE COLONIES"

BRITISH WOMEN FARMERS FOR CANADA

At a meeting of the Colonial Section of the Royal Society of Arts in London in March 1913, English travel writer Ella C. Sykes spoke on "Openings for Educated Women in Canada." She stressed the several occupations they might find in that colony, all of which were suitably feminine, and she included farming on a modest scale and "taking up land on their own account." She noted, however, that "so far the Canadian seems to object to women working on the land, the reason of this, perhaps, being that he finds them so valuable in the house." Yet Sykes called on educated women to take up the challenge of this "imperial" work: "Canada has shown unmistakably that she wishes to have the British stamp, and that can never be if the women of our race refuse to do their part … The girl of the right type who cares for the Flag and what it stands for, can be in very deed a missionary of Empire in the Dominion."[1]

One month later, and also in London, English author and Saskatchewan farmer Georgina Binnie-Clark spoke on "Land and the Woman in Canada" to the Royal Colonial Institute. Binnie-Clark was much more radical then Sykes, urging British women to grow grain on large acreages in prairie Canada. "The commercial farmer," she stated, "is not to farm for mere livelihood, she is to farm for independence." Like Sykes,

Binnie-Clark saw this as an imperial enterprise. British women could play a critical role in the "spade-work of British expansion in this, the supreme place of prosperity among British lands." "It is time," Binnie-Clark stated, "to shoulder one's spade and get off into the unknown country where a further stretch of the Empire is calling for the pioneer."[2]

These two talks before prestigious patriarchal colonial institutes represent the apogee, the summit of enthusiasm and optimism for the prospect of British women farmers for Canada. Modest and slow momentum for this cause had been gathering for several decades in Britain, particularly England, and to a lesser extent in Canada. But opposition remained formidable and powerful, and any momentum gained was lost in the First World War. There was a moderate revival of the cause after the war, but the opposition was even more entrenched. This chapter traces the growth of support for the idea of sending British women to Canada to farm, an idea that generated mild support from some and zealous, energetic, and fervent support from a few. Starting in the late nineteenth century, British proponents of agriculture for women, emigration associations, colonial training schools, and imperially minded journalists and travel writers advocated farming and land-owning for "gentlewomen" in the colonies, particularly Canada. A number of factors and causes intersected and overlapped to create modest momentum for this initiative, including alarm about the "surplus women" of Britain, concern about the "surplus men" of the colonies, devotion to the Empire, the push to expand educational, professional, and vocational options for women, the opposition to women farmers or horticulturalists in the "mother country," and the fact that there had to be more options than housework to tempt British women to cross the Atlantic. Fiction for girls and young women set in the colonies presented robust and independent heroines who owned or managed land of their own.

Proponents of sending British women to farm in Canada faced many opponents and obstacles. The colonies wanted women for domestic service, marriage, motherhood, and little else. Gentlewomen were reluctant, however, to cross the seas to scrub floors. There was an effort to camouflage domestic service in the colonies as something acceptable for refined women; they were to be "home helps" and treated as family members, not exploited servants. This subterfuge did not succeed in attracting the "surplus women" in significant numbers, and farming emerged as one option they might pursue in Canada. This would not only be a vocation, it would permit British women to truly be Empire builders. In *A Woman in Canada* (1911), English garden author Marion Cran wrote that the "wild beautiful West" provided opportunities for lives of independence for women willing to give "their best of mind and body for the race and for the Empire."[3]

SHIFTING ATTITUDES IN THE MOTHER COUNTRY

Opinions about the respectability of women working in the fields in Britain shifted dramatically and rapidly throughout the nineteenth century, and varied according to factors such as class, age, marital status, and region.[4] There was heated debate about the suitability of farm work for the educated "gentlewoman," and by about 1900 there had emerged a degree of acceptance, although sceptics and opponents remained.[5] Aspects of these debates and the more tolerant attitude that developed, particularly within England, are an important foundation and context for this study. Advocates of farming for women in the colonies drew on the arguments that were mustered for the same cause in Britain. Among these were that this would solve the "surplus woman" problem, and that farming would provide a healthy and useful vocation. Other rationales were that women's work on the land would remain feminine, because it would be limited to a few acres and to the "lighter" forms of agriculture. They would farm in settlements or clusters of women so that they would not have to hire and oversee labourers, or need expensive machinery. Yet while attitudes changed and a degree of acceptance developed in Britain, the same was not the case in Canada, where opponents resorted to age-old arguments that women working in the fields was an antiquated and despised abomination, a remnant of primitive times. Canada was not to be promoted or crafted as a colony where women did fieldwork. If they did in fact work in the fields (as did happen), this would be ignored and concealed and never officially endorsed or rewarded. Drawing on attitudes that prevailed by the mid-nineteenth century in the mother country, Canadian authorities saw women's confinement to the home and hearth as a key indicator of superiority over earlier, "darker" times, over other nations and colonies, and over the Indigenous peoples of the colonies. Fieldwork was believed to demoralize and uncivilize women; indoors became the only setting for proper femininity.

Promoters of agriculture as a vocation for women were seldom interested in working-class women, as it was presumed they had a natural function or calling—domestic service. They were concerned with educated women of some means, or "gentlewomen." For some advocates, agriculture for women was part of a larger movement to secure women's political, civil, and educational rights, and farming was one profession that could provide economic independence and an alternative to marriage. Others had more conservative objectives. Viewing women as unsuitable for intellectual careers or for professions such as medicine and law, they saw farming as a viable occupation that demanded less mental aptitude and education. Women's fields and gardens would be safe and secure places where they would be kept isolated from the world; there they would be kept busy and not tempted to join in political agitation. Marriage remained the ultimate goal to these thinkers, and a knowledge of farming or gardening had the advantage of remaining useful even after marriage, whereas other professions would have to be abandoned. Yet it is difficult to neatly categorize proponents of agriculture for women into radical and conservative camps, as it was shrewd to pose as non-threatening to the male domain of agriculture and land ownership in the face of fierce and powerful opposition.

WOMEN IN THE FIELDS: A REMNANT OF DARKER TIMES

In 1898 an article on "Ladies as Farmers" proclaimed that in Britain farming was "quite the most fashionable occupation for women nowadays," and that "a craze for agricultural pursuits [had] taken possession of ladies of fashion."[6] English journalist Virginia M. Crawford was more measured but largely in agreement in her article of the same year, entitled "Englishwomen and Agriculture," writing that "the whole question of agricultural employment for women is, so to speak, in the air. It has emerged somewhat suddenly from the sea of future possibilities, and is fast developing into one of the social questions of the day."[7] While "in the air," the question of agriculture as a vocation for women faced formidable opposition from those who insisted it was unbecoming and inappropriate. Crawford argued that an "active and ceaseless" propaganda and public education campaign had to be waged to combat the idea that farm work was unladylike and to supplant it with that of the "dignity and beauty of farm life."[8]

Until the end of the eighteenth century, there was little disapproval of women carrying out farm tasks.[9] But with complex factors such as urbanization, industrialization, and the expansion of the British Empire in the nineteenth century, the practice of women working in the fields came to be seen as backward, alien, a remnant of darker times. As an imperial power, Great Britain had to demonstrate that the women of its nation lived better lives than the Indigenous women of the colonies did. Historian Karen Sayer writes that "as the urban became culturally superior to the rural, English culture was increasingly seen to be superior to that of native populations in the colonies."[10] That the lives of British women were superior to the "downtrodden" dark and alien Indigenous women of the colonies and of "foreign" lands, who were allegedly treated little better than beasts of burden, was a common theme in Victorian imperial travel, missionary, and explorer narratives.[11] As one English traveller to Bukhara (present-day Uzbekistan) observed in in 1835: "The Kaffir women do all the out-door work, and follow the plough; and it is said that they are sometimes yoked in it along with an ox."[12]

Women of the fields who were strong, robust, and energetic questioned and threatened Victorian ideals of passive, weak femininity. They were "unnatural women, unable to fulfill the natural, feminine role of motherhood because of their labour and economic activity."[13] Because they were vigorous, strong, and tanned from their work, women who did farm work crossed "the boundaries of race. They therefore moved into the realm of alien, dark, sensual, sexual womanhood."[14] According to a clergyman: "Not only does it unsex a woman in dress, gait, manners, character, making her rough, coarse, clumsy, masculine, but it generates a further very pregnant social mischief, by unfitting her or indisposing her for a woman's proper duties at home."[15]

Agriculture changed dramatically in nineteenth-century Britain as the consolidation of larger-scale capitalist agriculture and mechanization brought an end to the small-scale farming of cottagers. The vast majority of agricultural workers, whether male or female, became landless labourers. Capitalist agriculture hastened the trend toward women's restriction to a limited range of tasks. Women were pushed into "monotonous, low-status jobs, and [they were] deprived of the range of skills possessed by the farmer's or cottager's wife in the pre-industrial period."[16] The wives of wealthier farmers "began to lead a life more resembling that of the leisured wives of the bourgeoisie."[17] Male married farmers took pride in having wives who did not have to do fieldwork, "apparently adopting the middle-class ideology of domesticity."[18] Farmers' organizations supported women's invisibility from outdoor farm work, arguing for a male breadwinning wage so that women would not have to go to the fields.[19] Since many male farm labourers found themselves out of work due to the mechanization of agriculture, it was useful to insist women did not belong in the fields. Women were unwanted competition because they were paid about half the wage of their male counterparts on the farm. They could get much better wages in factories.

By the late nineteenth century, women who did continue to do farm work had become invisible. It was not respectable to be seen working in the fields; farming was by then "ideologically viewed as 'man's work.'"[20] Outdoor activity was associated with men, while indoors was the respectable setting for women. Women might continue to engage in farm work, "as long as these activities were kept out of sight."[21] The woman who worked in the fields was "a figure of the past, a ghost."[22] These were the attitudes that advocates of farming for women in Britain had to contend with, and these were the attitudes that had a much longer shelf life in Canada, lasting well into the twentieth century.

SMALL HOLDINGS, "LIGHTER BRANCHES" OF AGRICULTURE, AND "FRIENDLY BANDS" OF WOMEN

Advocates of farming for women in the nineteenth century had a variety of arguments that they drew on to challenge these attitudes. One was that women would remain distinctly feminine and would not compete with male farmers, as their work would be relegated to small holdings of a few acres, to the "lighter" forms of agriculture (dairying, poultry keeping, and horticulture), and that they would band together in farm settlements or colonies. Proponents "had to tread a careful line between promoting an unusual career for middle-class women and maintaining a sense of social refinement and feminine respectability. After all, for decades, women had been told that work connected to the land was improper and unwomanly."[23] The result was a division of agriculture into feminine and masculine spheres, with "lighter" agriculture enabling women to "maintain their reputation and dignity," while not posing a direct challenge to male ownership of land and to the more profitable sphere of grain farming and large herds of livestock.

A small-holdings movement of the nineteenth century in Britain, supported by politicians, social reformers, philanthropists, and agriculturalists, constitutes another point of origin for the growing pressure to admit women to the profession of farming.[24] The ideal small holding was a "market garden or family farm large enough to support the cultivator and his family, and small enough to be cultivated by the labor of the occupier and his family without substantial amounts of permanently hired labor."[25] Discussions of the virtues of small holdings intersected with and involved the promotion of even smaller "allotments" of half an acre or less, for the production of vegetables and flowers, as particularly suited to women.[26] The widely held assumption was that women did not have the physical capabilities and strength for larger acreages.[27] Fruit, vegetables, flowers, and ornamental plants were the best crops for the woman small holder, and poultry, dairy cows, and bees were more suitable than livestock such as cattle.[28] The 1903 book *The Lighter Branches of Agriculture*, by Edith Bradley and Bertha La Mothe, is perhaps the fullest articulation of the realms of farm work seen as the province of women.[29] "Petite culture" or the "lighter branches" meant "all the work on the land which required skill rather than mere physical strength. It embraces work in the dairy, work in the garden and greenhouse; supervision of market gardens, culture of fruits, management of poultry and bees."[30]

Supporters of farming as a vocation for women rarely saw this as an individual endeavour. In her introduction to *The Lighter Branches of Agriculture*, Lady Frances Evelyn (Daisy) Warwick, an influential advocate of agriculture for women, wrote that she looked forward to a time when "a number of these settlements working on co-operative lines [would be] dotted all over England."[31] Lady Frances Wolseley, who wrote extensively on horticulture for women and established a school for "lady gardeners" in Sussex, recommended that women garden in colonies, grouping themselves in "friendly bands."[32] Settlements or colonies of women would address the issue of isolation in the country; the gentlewoman needed companions of her own social standing or she might "sink" to the level of her neighbours.

There was heated debate, however, about the future of small allotment farming, which included more radical voices. Among the critics was Louisa Cresswell, the "lady farmer" of Sandringham Estate, a tenant of "Bertie," the Prince of Wales. Cresswell was opposed to small holdings for anyone. After the death of her husband, she farmed 900 acres on the prince's estate for many years (until, she alleged, the prince's hunting parties destroyed her crops.)[33] In her 1881 pamphlet, *How the Farming in Great Britain Can Be Made to Pay*, Cresswell wrote that "the proposal to establish an extensive system of small holdings or petite culture, as it is called, and which is argued by some to be a panacea for all ills, is likely to be a very hopeless undertaking."[34] She championed larger farms: "Upon arable lands, whether they be light, medium or clay, I do not think that 10,000 or 20,000 acres will be too much."[35] "I would also," she wrote, "buy mighty machines and use them whenever practical ... use self binders at harvest and every description of labour-saving machinery that the ingenuity of man can devise." Cresswell predicted (correctly) that there would be a revolution in agriculture with machinery. She was proud to say that her farm, where steam machinery was used extensively, had been "pronounced by one of the keenest judges in England to 'have been left in the highest state of cultivation' and 'as clean as a garden.'"[36]

In her 1883 book, *My Home Farm*, Katherine Burton, who was an experienced tenant farmer, advocated small but not tiny farms for women.[37] She engaged in mixed farming, having dairy cows for milk, butter, and cheese, and raising pigs and sheep, poultry, and vegetables. She farmed for profit and not for family subsistence.[38] Burton was critical of much of the advice given to women farmers: "My own private belief is that the reason for the persistent recommendation of 'poultry farming' to 'ladies' is that gentlemen are aware that it is the most troublesome and least remunerative branch of the business—at least if pursued separately."[39] Prominent English farmer Katherine Courtauld also did not agree that women should pursue only the "lighter branches" of agriculture, instead advocating commercial large-scale farming. She farmed 2,000 acres, and in 1900 employed fifteen men and boys.[40]

"THE AGRICULTURAL BRIGADE OF THE MONSTROUS REGIMENT OF WOMEN"

Rationales for advancing the cause of women as farmers were varied and contradictory. Almost all, however, started with the assumption that there were "surplus women" in Britain who needed occupations or should be shipped off to the colonies (or both). The corollary was the "surplus" of men of the colonies (although this term was not used to describe them) who were in danger of degenerating. The problem of "surplus," "redundant," or "excess" women was first identified in the 1851 British census, which indicated there were 500,000 more women than men in the British Isles.[41] The problematic "surplus woman" was middle class and educated; working-class women were not viewed as "surplus," as they were believed to have occupations suitable to their station in domestic service or factories. Conventional occupations for the genteel single woman were as governess, companion, or seamstress, and these professions were underpaid and overcrowded.[42] Who or what would shoulder the burden of supporting these women? And they were seen as burdens, as encumbrances, as pariahs. Women who did not conform to social expectations of marriage and motherhood had no obvious place in society. As will be discussed in greater detail later in this chapter, shipping "excess" women off to the colonies and dominions was widely seen as the best solution, proposed as early as 1862 by journalist W.R. Greg.[43]

Lady Warwick was concerned with the educated "daughters of professional men" with large families but small incomes. Her object was to provide these daughters with a new field of work and means of livelihood through involvement in light agriculture.[44] Women were advised to "'go back to the land'; they can listen once more to the 'charm of birds,' and 'Nature, that sweet old nurse,' can teach them the wisdom and hope and love." Sending "trained and cultured" women into the country would "have a salutary and energizing effect upon rural England. They can stimulate the local interest in village clubs, in cottage gardens, in the general principles of citizenship of a vast Empire, and in a hundred other ways can help to 'make the path a little brighter where they tread' by their sympathy and comradeship."[45] If "ladies" could show they were healthy and happy working on the land, the more "rustic damsels" would be inspired to follow their lead.

Journalist Virginia Crawford also saw agriculture as a solution to the problem of thousands of women from the country "above the domestic servant class" crowding into the cities, struggling to find work as teachers, governesses, bookkeepers, and secretaries. A few succeeded, but many failed, according to Crawford, losing their health and living a "cramped and anxious existence in lonely lodgings or comfortless boarding houses and ... are thankful in old age to find a refuge in some governesses' institute or home for decayed gentlewomen."[46]

Farming as an occupation would be a blessing to the large number of "idle women" who would never become wives—the "surplus women."[47] An 1879 article in the *Examiner*, "Gardening for Women," began: "What is to be done with our surplus women?"[48] In her reply to an 1897 article entitled "The Monstrous Regiment of Women," Edith Bradley, a social reformer who worked in partnership with Lady Warwick, wrote "The Agricultural Brigade of the Monstrous Regiment of Women," proposing that women farmers could help to solve a myriad of problems facing England and the British Isles, including the "surplus million."[49]

Women of refinement and education were best equipped for the sort of outdoor work advocated by Frances Wolseley. She wrote that "maidservants" were "totally unsuited" to the profession of gardening, which required intelligent and educated ladies, "daughters of professional men."[50] The woman gardener who was untidy, had unkempt hair, disorderly clothing, and bad manners was not to be tolerated. "Maidservants" could work on farms if overseen by a farmer's wife who would "look out for their moral welfare." The men employed in a private garden, according to Wolseley, would not tolerate a young woman of "their own sphere," but would "gladly allow a lady to direct their work."[51] In her 1916 book, *Women and the Land*, Wolseley gave further reasons why only refined and educated women were suited to the work, including that they were "from their earliest days accustomed to riding and hunting; they play golf and out-of-door games, so that exercise in the open air comes to them quite naturally, and in fact many can barely exist without it."[52] Women were required who could direct subordinate workers, and these "should belong to the upper classes or upper middle classes." They had to be able to "command and to exact respect."[53]

Aside from addressing the "surplus women" issue, there were other rationales for involving women in agriculture. All sorts of anxieties that faced the nations and the Empire justified the cause.[54] In "The Agricultural Brigade of the Monstrous Regiment of Women," Edith Bradley wrote that women farmers could mitigate another of the most pressing national and social problems of the day, the "wholesale desertion of the villages for the towns, or the emigration to foreign countries." The "Agricultural Brigade of Women" would "stay the depopulation of our villages" and "keep some of the money in this country which is annually spent on foreign dairy, poultry and horticultural produce."[55] Women of the agricultural brigade would be "bringing back country life to England, and so assist in strengthening, not only the national, but the Imperial life of our Empire."[56]

RADICAL AND CONSERVATIVE ADVOCATES

Supporters of agriculture and gardening for "surplus women" did not all share the same political views. Activists in the women's movement attempted to redefine the problem of "surplus women," arguing that the issue was not the numerical excess but the lack of educational and occupational opportunities that could permit women independence outside of marriage.[57] Useful work would be their salvation; the "unproductive" woman would become productive. Among the earliest of the nineteenth-century advocates of farming and land ownership for women were members of the middle-class feminist Langham Place Group, founded in the 1850s. They organized the Society for Promoting the Employment of Women and campaigned for married women's right to retain their property after marriage, for the right of women to take paid employment, and for wealthy women to own land and take up farming.[58] Jessie Boucherett, the daughter of Lancashire landowners, was particularly devoted to this cause, but it was a small part of a broader campaign to expand women's involvement in skilled trades. She was determined to assist "distressed gentlewomen."[59] In her 1863 *Hints on Self-Help: Advice for Young Women*, Boucherett proposed many professions, including home decoration, photography, nursing, bookkeeping, and shopkeeping. Farming was another idea proposed to enable women to support themselves. Social commentators such as Harriet Martineau wrote extensively about how attitudes needed to change toward women and work, that women as well as men should be educated for work, and that vast numbers of women were already working in industries.[60] Martineau was the author of *My Farm of Two Acres*, first published in 1865, which described her poultry, swine, and dairy enterprises and advocated women's economic independence through small-scale farming.

The significant number of women who operated farms on their own in Britain was cited by champions of women's rights, who raised questions about gender, land ownership, and the vote. Women farmers, who paid taxes and employed men who could vote while they could not, bolstered arguments for an extension of the franchise. Why, it was asked, should a woman farmer "who in every way performs the duties of an employer ... have no vote, whilst the keeper of a low beerhouse close by, who demoralizes laboring men, and is hardly able to write his name, exercises the right from which she is denied."[61] An 1883 petition from 170 women farmers asked Prime Minister William Gladstone why "the oft-time totally ignorant agricultural labourer" should have the vote that was denied to them.[62] Because they did not have the vote, "widows and daughters of farmers are frequently rejected as tenants by large landowners for the sole reason that their sex disqualifies them from giving their landlord that Parliamentary vote which it has been his custom to expect from his tenants, and yet these same women have proved their undoubted business capacity by years of successful management during the illness or incapacity of their husband or father."

In 1884, Conservative Sir Robert Peel spoke of the injustice of women farmers being unable to vote while their male labourers could. He quoted an agricultural expert who stated: "Fancy a woman farming 500 acres of land, and paying the usual contributions to the taxes of the country, having no voice in the representation of the country while her labourers have."[63]

Supporters of women's suffrage saw women gardeners and farmers as natural allies in the cause of the parliamentary franchise. Speaking in favour of women's suffrage at Birmingham in 1891, Millicent Fawcett declared there to be 38,000 female landowners in England and Wales, and of these 20,000 were actively engaged in farming.[64] The census of 1891 "showed that there were 21,692 female farmers and graziers in England and Wales, 564 female occupiers of market gardens or nurseries."[65] Matilda Betham-Edwards, farmer and women's activist, and member of the Langham Place Group, was in favour of votes for women farmers. She wrote that in Suffolk in the early 1860s there were many "lady farmers" who were "widows, sisters and daughters of deceased tenants to whom their lease had been renewed," with one widow leasing the largest farm in the parish.[66]

The more radical advocates of gardening and farming for women advanced the rationale that this occupation could assist a woman in the event of marriage breakdown or the death of a husband or his failure to provide.[67] As the author of a 1905 article observed, marriage "did not necessarily mean for a woman provision for life."[68] "How many women," this author asked, "one has known whose husbands have failed or been disappointed in life, to be thereafter chimney-corner encumbrances, leaving it to the wives to bring up, educate and launch the family?"

There were also those with more conservative views, who did not wish to challenge or upset the gender order, who believed women's destiny was marriage and domesticity, but who nonetheless favoured some expansion of women's occupational opportunities to include certain forms of agriculture. Some advocated gardening or farming because they believed there were an "immense number of women unfit for intellectual work."[69] Farming and gardening was a "reasonable" vocation compared to "unsuitable employments" such as "doctors, lawyers, members of Parliament, and heaven knows what else beside."[70] The life of the gardener, small holder, or farmer was for "our girls whose cleverness mainly lies in their hands ... girls not brilliant at books."[71] There would ever only be a "small minority" of women who "would be able to embrace the learned professions, should those professions be universally thrown open to them."[72]

Conservative advocates of farming for women were careful to stress that the "lady gardener" could retain her femininity. She could perform delicate work that did not require physical strength, such as "budding dwarf fruit-trees ... making cuttings, sowing and collecting seed, gathering and packing fruit, weeding, hoeing and the lighter parts of the tillage."[73] Women gardeners were expected to have limited marketing ambitions and a low public profile; they would not supplant or compete with men gardeners, according to Frances Wolseley. Rather, they would "supplement and increase the good work which men are doing for our land."[74] They would assist by lending intelligence, refinement, and other womanly qualities. Another conservative impulse at work in counselling women to take up farming over other potential occupations, careers, or professions was that it would teach them skills that would remain useful after marriage. Women could garden both before and during marriage, which was still viewed by many commentators as the ultimate objective of a woman's life. As a writer for the *Leeds Mercury* wrote in 1900:

> There is one thing to be said of a training for women in gardening, especially which cannot be stated in reference to many another career for women, namely that, even if the student marries, the value of her training will not be lost, as is so often the case in other branches of industry. It is often said, with truth, that when a father goes to great expense in training his daughter for a profession or business, the outlay may be almost or entirely thrown away in the event of her marrying. But, unless a woman is to pass her life in the heart of a crowded town, training in horticulture will be valuable, and a source of delight to her, however much married she may be.[75]

PREPARING THE SOIL: EDUCATION

An obstacle identified by advocates of gardening, horticulture, and agriculture for women was the lack of available training and education. When Jane Chesney proposed a horticultural college for women in her 1879 article "A New Vocation for Women," it was a "bold suggestion."[76] The lady gardener of her day, Chesney wrote, could learn only by reading, asking questions, and by "sad and bitter experience," and as a remedy she advocated a course of training in horticultural principles and garden economies.

Gradual advances were made in admitting women to horticultural and agricultural education. The Horticultural College at Swanley, Kent, established in 1887, was originally intended for men only, but women were admitted beginning in 1891.[77] By 1899 there were thirty-two women students taking the two-year course, and by 1903 it became a women-only institution, closing its doors to male students.[78] Swanley reflected a shift in horticultural training from an apprentice-based system (that had excluded women) to one based on science and study.[79]

At Swanley the students' time was divided between practical work and lectures. The students produced a regular supply of flowers, fruit, and vegetables for the London market. Professors from Oxford, Cambridge, and London lectured on natural sciences such as botany; geology, and entomology. Some women graduates from Swanley found positions as "gardener's boys" at the Botanic Gardens at Kew, and others at the Royal Botanical Gardens in Edinburgh and Dublin. Soon women trained at Swanley were teaching horticulture at places such as Lady Henry Somerset's Industrial Farm Colony (for "female inebriates") at Duxhurst.

In 1898 the Lady Warwick Hostel in Reading was established, offering courses to women on horticulture, dairy work, market gardening, fruit culture, and beekeeping. The demand was high; there was a full complement of twenty-four students in the first year of operation and soon two more hostels were added.[80] In 1903, Warwick moved her students to Studley Castle in Warwickshire, near her own stately home, Warwick Castle, and established the independent Lady Warwick College. This later become the Studley Horticultural and Agricultural College for Women and remained an all-women institution until it closed in 1969. By 1904, it was reported, there had been 250 graduates of Warwick's college since 1898, and of these twenty-four possessed small holdings of their own that they operated as dairy or poultry farms or market gardens.[81] Other graduates were working at country houses, superintending

Figures 7 and 8. The Glynde School For Lady Gardeners in Sussex, England, established by Lady Frances Wolseley in 1902. The caption written by Wolseley for the top photo (Figure 7) is "Students before they wore the kit invented by Miss [Elsa] More which was after adopted by other women who worked the land," c. 1902–8. In the bottom photo (Figure 8), from 1913–14 the students are wearing the "kit" designed for work on the land. Wolseley and her students encountered criticism such as only a "complete failure as a woman could adopt such a career." Papers of the Viscountess Frances Wolseley, Hove Central Library, Hove, Sussex, Commonplace Book no. 196.

dairies, gardens, and conservatories. In 1905 one journalist proclaimed that Warwick had "convinced her bitterest opponents that in the lighter branches of agriculture—such as dairy work, market gardening, poultry and beekeeping, and in the growing of fruit and flowers—there is a means of livelihood for the gentlewoman in which she can live far more happily than in our grimy cities."[82] Warwick also established in 1899 the Lady Warwick Agricultural Association, and in the same year launched the *Woman's Agricultural Times* as its official organ.

Other educational options included private gardening schools that began to spring up. By 1940 there were some nineteen such schools in England.[83] Among them was Lady Frances Wolseley's school of gardening at Glynde, established in 1901. These schools were the preserve of women with income and the time needed to devote to two or three years of training.[84] Private initiatives included the scheme of Victoria Woodhull on her estate at Bredon's Norton, Worcestershire, where by 1908 there were between twenty-five and thirty women studying agriculture through lectures, reading, and demonstrations.[85] The school's purpose, according to Woodhull (the first woman to run for president of the United States) was not only to address the "surplus women" problem but to "regenerate England," because the "future of the race" was in the land. All of these initiatives stand in sharp contrast to the situation in Canada, where well into the twentieth century there were very few opportunities for women to study agriculture or even horticulture.

"A DELUSION AND A SNARE": OPPOSITION AND DEBATE

The idea that farming was a suitable profession for women and that agricultural education should be available to them was opposed by many. Advocates contended with ridicule and bemusement. The major objection was that farming was a "man's domain": women working in the fields defied a gender order, cast as timeless and traditional, in which they were relegated to hearth and home, and farm work defeminized women, making them unattractive to men. As one anonymous journalist objected in 1910, after noting that women were ploughing fields, this "invaded what I regard as the last ditch of man's domain."[86] He wrote that it was not "good for women to lead laborious days behind the plough. Heavy manual labour produces a rough, unpleasant type of woman, and the only thing it qualifies her for is to plough that lonely furrow in life, which, however suitable to some politicians, is not the true destiny of women."

Critics argued that industries such as cheese making, although once the domain of farm women, were not suitable for gentlewomen because they could be neither "mistress nor maid," and there was nothing in between these two social positions. To be mistress required considerable means, since land, cows, and their own training in the skills required had all to be purchased. Nor could she be a maid; it was not possible for a "young lady ... go into a dairy-farm, in some cheese country, and give her services in return for her training and board." The dairymaid worked for years, "lifting great weights, wielding heavy implements, straining every muscle in her body with reaching over the wide tubs, screwing up the ponderous presses, and turning and weighing the mighty cheeses which the ordinary run of ladies could no more carry to the scale than they could carry the farmhouse to the next parish ... They would find hoeing turnips, or digging potatoes, light work in comparison."[87]

An idea of the nature and intensity of opposition to women in the field is revealed in scrapbooks of clippings and correspondence kept by Frances Wolseley. For example, she received an anonymous postcard that read, "I think if you taught those young ladies how to cook, they would be far more use in the world than [——] up an old garden. P.S. Why don't you teach them housework to make them useful."[88] There was heated debate in the letters to the editor section of *Country Life*, also preserved in one of Wolseley's scrapbooks. As "Cherry Tree" wrote in response to an article about Wolseley's school: "It makes one rather sad to think that an educated woman should be reduced to do the work suitable to a rough uneducated man, losing as she must all feminine grace and charm, and also the vantage ground her education ought to have given her over him. I can scarcely think that any except a girl without any intellectual faculties, and consequently one who could not rise to any position requiring mental gifts, would choose such a career. In other words, I cannot think that anyone not a complete failure as a woman could adopt such a career."[89]

Opponents insisted that training in agriculture was wasted on girls who were destined for marriage. In *The Revival of English Agriculture*, P. Anderson Graham wrote: "Educate women for what purpose you please, and map out the future for them as carefully as if it were to go in a Government survey, Love steps in at the end and upsets all the plans."[90] He was willing to admit, however, that there was a "residue" of "well born women ... who in many cases pass unwedded lives," and he supposed that they might be able to pursue *la petite culture*, although "they certainly cannot do the hard work—no woman can without sinking into the position of a drudge."[91]

Supporters countered with an array of arguments. One wrote in 1891 that "there is something in the female mind that is peculiarly conformable to field culture and the care of stock. I need scarcely point out that ladies have always been the best gardeners, and the more field culture is made to correspond to garden culture the better will it be for all who have to do with the soil in this country."[92] Phillip Astor wrote favourably of "Lady Farmers" in 1900 after a visit to the school at Swanley. The article began with a photograph of students ploughing.[93] He argued that Swanley "proves that women find the work of ploughing quite within their capacity, and do not suffer physically from the hard work. Of course, it is not intended that women should oust men from the work of the fields, but it is considered desirable that they should have a practical knowledge of it."[94]

An 1898 article on "Lady Gardeners" by "Darley Dale" weighed the cons and pros. The profession was not for delicate women, and it would involve sacrifice from any woman.[95] The lady gardener would have to rise early, work hard, stand a great deal, and be exposed to all weathers. She would not have "very white, delicate hands; potting, planting, sowing, weeding, taking cuttings, all spoil hands." Nor would she be able to take care of her complexion, as "she must be exposed to the east winds of spring, the hot sunshine of summer, the gales of autumn, and all the freaks of an English climate." But the lady gardener who made these "sacrifices" to "feminine vanity" would be "a very bright, happy cheerful woman; the freedom of her life, and the exhilarating effect of being so much in the open air, probably contribute to this." The result, according to this author, would be "a thoroughly womanly woman who has gained some masculine advantages without losing any of the tenderer qualities of womanhood."

Yet as the strong opposition illustrates, women seeking an occupation and an income, whether through agriculture or most other professions, were viewed with suspicion.[96] They were "icons of unsettling change."[97] Their independent earnings and autonomy from families were altogether a departure from the white, Anglo-Celtic norm of feminine respectability, a dangerous challenge to the traditional gender order. Low-paid, exploited, wage-earning women were regarded as a moral problem, and reformers devised various techniques of regulating and controlling their activities. Equally unsettling and controversial were the "New Women" of the educated and middling classes.[98] These "New Women" contested Victorian definitions of gender, some fighting for women's rights and seeking professional careers, and some even opting for a single lifestyle. They further fuelled fears that the gender order, the foundation of society, was cracking.

Through expectations of appropriate feminine dress and deportment, women's bodies were moulded to be more docile than men's, and their mobility was much more limited. There were (and remain) norms of feminine motility, a disciplinary regime of femininity that restricts women's posture and movements.[99] Women were (and still are) trained to move with "grace" and not to reach and stretch and extend the body in sports and certain physical tasks. As Sandra Lee Bartky has argued, "the imposition of normative femininity upon the female body required training," and "the modes of training are cultural phenomena properly described as 'disciplinary practices.'"[100] In Victorian times, the clothing worn by middle-class and elite women restricted their movement and ability to do any manual labour. Long skirts, tightly laced corsets, bustles, hoops, weighty petticoats, and high-heeled shoes made it virtually impossible to bend, stoop, or adopt the many other postures agriculture and gardening required. In wearing this gear, women "were suggesting that they had others employed to perform these functions."[101] Thorstein Veblen wrote in his 1894 "Economic Theory of Women's Dress" that the corseted Victorian woman's inability to move was evidence of her role as a decorative ornament who did not have to perform any manual labour, signifying her husband's wealth and power.[102]

Those women who exercised and altered their bodies, becoming strong and athletic, were censured. In a 1900 article on "The Redundancy of Spinster Gentlewomen," the author "T.P.W." criticized women who were "almost wholly given up to outdoor pastimes of a more or less robust and muscular character":

> The very exercise of muscular achievements suitable only for men has the effect of hardening and the roughening the feminine exterior; while it is too often associated with a strident voice, a self-assertive manner, a brusque and abrupt address to malekind, and a general lapse of attractiveness. All of which attributes tend to damp a man's matrimonial intents.[103]

Women with the physical attributes to farm risked being seen as not-women, as desexualized and unattractive and "unnatural."[104] They were "not seen as real farmers by men but as inferior others who try to be like men and cannot therefore be taken seriously."[105] Single women farmers did the work on their own, it was assumed, only because they did not have husbands to do the work. Fathers, brothers, and labourers were seen as indispensable to the woman farmer, confirming that women could not farm without men. Single women farmers might perform the work themselves, but were still not able to farm like men. "Physical strength, sturdiness, aggressiveness, competitiveness, speaking one's mind and dominance" were masculine qualities, while women were to be "slim, fragile, submissive, nurturing, quiet and withdrawn."[106] A single woman farmer was not a potential wife, as she did not embody and perform feminine attributes. She was excluded from both the feminine and the masculine realms.

This was the fate of two sisters, Sarah Spencer and Mary Spencer, who farmed in Sussex. In an 1842 article on "Female Farmers," the author adopted a kindly tone when describing the Spencers, explaining that they farmed because their marriage prospects were slim, that "their persons, though not uncomely, were not so attractive as to flatter them that without fortunes, they could marry advantageously."[107] While the author felt they were farming "without ceasing to be *gentlewomen*" and that their farm was "much to their credit and advantage," he also observed that they were not "popular characters." He wrote: "This was the hard fate of the Spencers, who, instead of gratitude, long experienced little else than discourtesies and opposition in the neighbourhood. The more active of them was called *Captain Sally*; and her sister, her *Man Mary*." Things had not changed dramatically by 1907 when Estelle Long, a "girl farmer," was described as a reclusive character to be shunned.[108] On her eighteen-acre farm in Surrey, she lived in a hut (a "dreary" and "desolate" spot) and did everything herself: "reaps, hoes, sows, kills and dresses her poultry, takes her produce to market, grooms her pony, and cleans the harness and trap, and mows her hay." Long was a graduate of Lady Warwick's school of agriculture, and her father, J. Long, was a professor and authority on agriculture, but none of these credentials made her any less suspect. In her neighbourhood, it was said, "the more superstitious of the villagers look upon her … as having 'turned witch' or something of that sort."[109]

The few single women farmers of Western Canada were to be similarly stigmatized, and well into the twentieth century. Farmers such as Lizzie

Hillis (mentioned in the introduction) and "Jack" May (to be discussed in Chapter 4) were criticized and marginalized. But in the 1890s there was optimism for the cause of the "lady farmer." One advocate declared in 1891 that Queen Victoria herself could be claimed as "the first lady farmer in this country," as she took great interest in her farms and was an "illustrious example" of the fact that "in respect to stock-keeping, women have softer natures than men, and delight to pet and cherish dumb creatures of all kinds."[110] Her "chief source of pleasure" allegedly, was her prize-winning cows.[111] While at Balmoral she personally inspected her home farm every day, particularly the dairy, and she advised on butter and cheese making. The products of her farms were sold in London, and "her thrifty Majesty earns many an honest penny in this way."

Proponents of farming for women had made important advances in challenging the conviction that women who worked outdoors were rough, coarse, indecent, and masculine, insisting instead that respectability and refinement would not be lost. Things had changed from the early 1800s, when a woman with "pretensions to gentility … had to distance herself from farm production."[112] By the early twentieth century, the topic of women in agriculture and horticulture was very popular and highly visible. In 1910, for example, a series of articles appeared in the London *Daily Mail* with headlines such as "The Successful Woman Farmer: How Two Women Run an Agricultural Farm in England," and "The Woman Poultry Farmer: Experiences of a Two-Acre Farm."[113] At that time Georgina Binnie-Clark wrote inspiring columns describing her experiences as a farmer in Saskatchewan (to be discussed in Chapter 5). Yet opposition remained intense, and grew in new directions as the competence of college-trained women farmers was questioned and denigrated. Some advocates for the "gentlewoman" farmer hoped that the colonies might provide a more welcoming and congenial environment, as Binnie-Clark appeared to illustrate.

"SURPLUS WOMEN" FOR THE COLONIES AS "HOME HELPS" … AND FARMERS

A host of keen imperialists devoted to "civilizing" the colonies through the importation of women of the British "race" were active by the late nineteenth century, and they were anxious that women of "superior breeding" and education be pressed into service.[114] "If the Mother Country sends us enough people we shall grow strong as British powers," wrote one staunch Australian imperialist, and "if she does not we shall either evolve quietly into races determined by our alien immigration, or we shall be swamped and effaced by invaders."[115] Women imperialists worked to dispel attitudes of indifference, suspicion, and fear toward the colonies among "refined" women and awaken their sense of patriotism toward the Empire. These transplanted women were to transport British culture and identity to the colonies, and nurture it there. Anxieties about being "swamped and effaced by invaders" were heightened in colonies such as Western Canada, where Americans and ethnically diverse Europeans began to arrive in significant numbers starting in the later nineteenth century.[116]

Promoters of emigration tried to persuade colonial employers of the virtues of educated "home helps," a description that was intended to create a category well above the rank of domestic servants. Women who were home helps would fit comfortably into the family circle, eliminating the need for costly servants' quarters. They would "tackle labour with their hands *and* their brains."[117] Explorer and writer Arthur Montefiore Brice explained in his 1901 article, "Emigration for Gentlewomen," that in the colonies "you have to pay atrociously high wages for a miserable servant, who has vulgar notions of what are her rights and her duties, who cares nothing for your comfort or your welfare, who will not do any work which is distasteful to her, and who leaves you at a moment's notice."[118] A "home help," however, a "healthy amiable woman, educated somewhat, able to cook and clean, sew and mend," would be regarded as "an equal, as a friend, as a member of the family"; she would be treated as "a near relative, even a sister of the mistress."[119]

A problem, however, was that domestic work did not appeal to the educated gentlewomen, despite assurances that being "companion helps" or "home helps" would entail no loss of social status. They were told that they would find adventure, happiness, and quite likely husbands, and would be doing a great service to the Empire. They were "encouraged to see emigration to the colonies and employment in someone else's home as a logical path to financial stability, self-fulfillment, and sanctified heterosexual love."[120] Here the problem of the "surplus" educated woman of the "motherland" intersected with and was seen as a solution to the "servant problem," and to the bachelor (or surplus male) problem in the colonies.[121] White women were needed to work on the farms and ranches of the colonies, rather than the "half-caste or full-blooded native" or whites of the serving class, who were also undesirable.[122]

In the 1880s, a network of female imperialists began "an aggressive long-lasting promotional campaign to entice single women above the working class to emigrate."[123] Various associations were formed, becoming in 1901 the British Women's Emigration Association, established to encourage and assist women of "good character" to emigrate. Domestic service for educated women, thinly disguised as home help, historian Lisa Chilton writes, "was primarily a means to an end—the end being the proper feminization of the empire."[124]

Not all of those concerned with the "surplus women" problem saw emigration to the colonies, where they would perform domestic work and then marry, as the solution. Some feminists criticized emigration as a strategy to discourage activism for women's rights at home, and as a means of maintaining and transplanting to the colonies women's traditional roles as wives, mothers, and moral guardians. Feminists "began to realize that the unclear distinction between emigrating to find work and emigrating to find husbands was embarrassing."[125] The problem, as they saw it, was not "surplus women," but restricted education and employment opportunities.[126] To Jessie Boucherett the solution was not emigration but extending opportunities for occupations and education and reforming the institutions that treated women as unequal to men. Women needed to be trained for occupations and pursuits other than matrimony.[127]

As early as in her 1863 book, *Hints on Self-Help,* Boucherett identified a central conundrum: the colonies were not interested in genteel educated women. It was impossible to persuade potential employers in the colonies that the educated woman made a good domestic servant. Boucherett quoted a Canadian emigration agent as saying that "there exists but a very limited demand in this province for the class of women in question." He warned that "the introduction of such a class into Canada would be attended with consequences far from advantageous," and he requested the Government Emigration Board to "discountenance the emigration to this country of any grade of women higher than the domestic servant." Boucherett wrote that the same answers came from Australia, and continued:

> Now, if this little history of the proposed emigration of educated women were not tragical, it would be comical. England so anxious to send them away, the colonies

> so afraid of having to receive them; England says, "Why don't you go to the colonies? You are not wanted here, you are burdensome to us, and we will gladly pay your passage to get rid of you." The colonies hearing this indignantly exclaim, "For mercy's sake, don't send us your useless creatures! We want men to fell our Woods, cultivate our land, tend our sheep and cattle, and women to cook our dinners, and wash our clothes, but as to educated women, we don't want them, and we won't have them; if they come they will be worse off than at home, for we have no work-houses to put them in.[128]

Boucherett proposed the radical idea (in part tongue-in-cheek) that every young man in England be compelled to emigrate when he reached twenty-one. The scarcity of male labour would mean that women would be employed in many occupations identified as male, enabling the superfluous women to be provided for and thus no longer superflous.[129]

Historian Jane Hammerton argues that female emigration was initially a feminist project in the 1860s but then became an un-feminist project, as supporters of emigration were committed to a separate-spheres ideology. Others have since questioned this interpretation, arguing that female imperialist organizations had powerful links to a broader British women's movement.[130] Lisa Chilton found that the dominant image these organizations created for public consumption celebrated feminine power, nurturing visions of a "new class of women for the colonies." Promoters of emigration saw in the colonies possibilities unavailable in Britain, and had "unbounded faith in the abilities of suitably educated women to be successful in whatever venture they might undertake."[131] In the colonies, they "would carve out meaningful roles and identities for themselves, and … reshape the mutable male environment of the colonial frontier." But as one devoted supporter of emigration of women to the colonies, Lady Knightley of Fawsley, wrote, the goal of marriage and motherhood in the colonies was paramount in the minds of the philanthropists who assisted women to emigrate: "Helping women of every grade to stand for all woman is worth, in Empire building, in evangelizing work, in going where women are prayed for to make homes for good living men, where women can be mothers of quivers full, without fear of there ever being one too many, for there will be plenty of work for every hard-working boy of every class, and a Jack for every Jill."[132]

Aware that domestic service, even when relabelled as the more exalted home help, held little appeal to educated women, some advocates of female emigration to the colonies cast about for other potential occupations, and farming was one that emerged from a "range of possibilities."[133] The promise of land and the vocation of agriculture, it was thought, could be held out as an inducement to emigrate for genteel educated women who would not stoop to domestic service. Proposals included "Tea and Silk Farming in New Zealand" as ideal enterprises for "educated yet reduced gentlewomen."[134] This sort of work would not "rob them of one iota of dignity, or lower them a single inch in the social scale."

Writer Jessie Weston, who was originally from New Zealand but who settled in London, wrote in 1891 in "Hints for the Single Women of the United Kingdom" that there had to be some inducement other than marriage and domestic service for women to leave England for the colonies. "Marriage may not be the desire of many of the female sex in the mother country," Weston wrote, "and still they might be induced to emigrate if sufficient inducement were found."[135] They should become "land owners and enterprising settlers in the Colonies." Weston was sceptical of farming opportunities for women "in a severe climate like that of the Confederation [Canada]," instead advocating agricultural pursuits for women in South Africa, New Zealand, Tasmania, and Australia. She wrote: "All the means of earning a livelihood we have mentioned are of and from the soil, the possession of which in all times and countries is, and has been, the source of dignity and power to its owners. To be the proprietor of an orchard, a honey-farm, a chicken farm, a vegetable farm, would fill the lives of women, now wasting away for want of an object upon which to devote their energies, with an absorbing interest, would make them useful citizens, and add to their happiness. Independence and plenty to do are powerful factors in the total sum of human happiness."[136]

Weston recommended small-scale farming, "which we presume would be the aim of sensible women, who are not likely to ruin themselves with great undertakings, like the male sex have so often done. As in farming, a piece of land from ten to forty acres is a source of greater profit and pleasure than a block of five hundred acres." Farming on a large scale, Weston observed, required "capital, labour, and, more than common sense, knowledge, while the profits are relatively less." Women who farmed on a larger scale, she believed, were successful only if they carried on as widows "what was left in good working order by their husbands." While capital was required for a small farm, Weston saw no reason why women without capital could not emigrate and soon save enough to purchase land.

For Weston, the goal of sending women agriculturalists to the colonies was to preserve rather than challenge the status quo. The "surplus" single women of the United Kingdom were, or sought to be, wage earners, and they thus "help[ed] to block the labour market, thrusting out the heads of families, whether male or female." (In Weston's view, heads of families ought to be the wage earners.) She also believed that sending women to the colonies as a means of addressing "the utter helplessness, the apathy of despair of the poor" "would be more to the credit of the female sex than all their exertions on the Suffrage question," and more useful as well: "A practical exposition of the ability of the female sex to become land-owners and enterprising settlers in the Colonies will be of more material advantage to woman than all oratory and literary efforts to prove the equality of the sexes."[137]

There were many others who chimed in, arguing that occupations other than marriage had to be offered to women sent to the colonies. The author of a 1902 article, "The Need of Women Colonists in South Africa," wrote, "It scarcely sounds decent to cart women out to the colonies for the simple purpose of matrimony, however laudable in itself and approved by ancient precedent. Some women, I am told are not 'nice' to marry, whilst, strange as it may appear to mere men, other women do not care about marriage."[138] This author advocated training for potential women colonists in gardening, poultry raising, and beekeeping.

COLONIAL TRAINING SCHOOLS

Advocates of colonial farming for genteel women from the United Kingdom, concerned that the women would be unaccustomed to manual labour and to farm work, issued calls for training schools.[139] There was a model to emulate: the Colonial College for sons of gentlemen, established in 1887 in Suffolk, where practical as well as scientific instruction was offered on a host of topics, including agriculture, surveying, and forestry. This institution addressed the problem of the "greenhorn" who arrived in a colony, only "to undergo—likely among rough and ignorant strangers—things which his previous bringing-up has rendered distasteful to him … to work in the open fields from dark to dark, to eat the coarsest of prepared food, and to lodge in a wretched shanty."[140]

Around the turn of the century a large number of colonial training schools for females quickly materialized. In most the emphasis was decidedly upon domestic rather than farm work. The earliest to be established was the Leaton Colonial Training Home in Shropshire founded in 1890. The objective was "to give practical training in domestic work to ladies wishing to proceed to the Colonies to join their relatives, or as Companion helps."[141] Pupils were "those of the middle and upper middle class, who have been well educated at school, but who have had little to no training in domestic duties, and who being obliged to work for their living, prefer to try their fortunes abroad rather than to seek employment in England where almost every branch of women's work is overcrowded."[142] Miss A.L. Vernon, the "lady superintendent" of the school, wrote in a 1905 pamphlet on the Leaton Colonial Training Home published by the British Women's Emigration Association that the school was intended to be a

> means of fitting women who have no particular talents or gifts, for a useful, purposeful life, more easily to be found abroad than at home … Anyone who has come much in contact with that most hopeless individual, the middle-aged, unmarried woman with no profession and an income only sufficiently large (and often not even that) to keep herself alive, must desire to save girls of the coming generation from a similar fate. Women of first-class ability will probably always be able to find remunerative employment in England … but to the large class with no special qualifications and not great ability, life in the Colonies offers much brighter prospects.[143]

The "mother country," Vernon wrote, derived the advantage of the "removal of superfluous women," while there was an "even greater gain to the Colonies of receiving capable useful women, who are needed as servants, teachers, or nurses, and ultimately as wives."[144] Vernon admitted that this last consideration was of the utmost importance to all who "see in our Colonies only a Greater Britain which they wish to keep in the hands of English men and women, and to see peopled by the descendants of English parents." Aside from learning how to wash clothes, cook, and scrub floors, pupils learned poultry keeping. The school was located in an "old-fashioned" manor house that did not have "modern conveniences," helping to make the pupils "adaptable and resourceful, and able to do their work with the simplest appliances."[145] The Leaton Colonial Training Home moved to Stoke Prior in 1907, by that time boasting that over 350 women had been trained, and "nearly all have gone to and are living in the Colonies."[146]

In 1902 Lady Warwick established a one-year course of colonial training at her school in Reading and then at Studley.[147] This program placed more emphasis on domestic skills than on farming and/or horticulture, with three months each devoted to "cookery, housewifery, laundry and dressmaking, dairy and poultry-farming, flower, fruit and vegetable gardening."[148] The students were also taught substitutes for ingredients or how to manufacture their own, such as making yeast from potatoes. "Their training in fact, will consist very largely in doing without things," was one description of the colonial course.[149]

The Swanley Horticultural College also established a Colonial Branch in 1902, anticipating an increase in the number of women emigrants to South Africa, offering a one-year course of "practical training in Gardening, Dairying, Poultry, Cooking, Fruit Bottling and Jam Making, Laundry, Hygiene, Sanitation, South African Languages etc."[150] Among the many competing institutions and programs, Swanley was distinct because of its curriculum that aimed at educating women to fill skilled occupations in teaching, gardening, and agriculture in the colonies, although domestic work was also included.[151] The Swanley program also aspired to the goal of settlements or colonies of women engaged in the "lighter branches" of agriculture.[152] By 1909, however, a change in the program's name to the Colonial and Home Domestic Training Branch acknowledged that there were few placements in the colonies of graduates in horticulture.[153]

It seems that very little accreditation or inspection was required to open a training school for women headed to the colonies, and programs proliferated. In 1904 a school in Domestic Training for Gentlewomen: For Colonial and Home Life opened in "a small private Ladies Club in Chelsea at very moderate fees."[154] The pupils were taught plain cooking, house and parlour work, and domestic economy. The school advertised itself as the only residential training school in London devoted to the purpose of colonial training, meant specifically for the benefit of girls who could not afford a long and expensive education. That same year a new Training Home for Ladies opened in Devonshire, where the emphasis

The Bystander, September 16, 1908 611

Getting Ready to be Rough and Ready

A Little Lesson in Chopping Wood

the employers who await them across the water. As a rule, the unfortunate employer has to begin by training the girl, and by the time she is competent she marries and departs to a home of her own, there to go through a similar domestic difficulty.

Practical and Theoretical Training

Miss Turner's pupils certainly show themselves afraid of nothing. In one of our pictures they will even be seen at work digging up a piece of rough ground—"breaking ground" as it is called. Carpentering lessons are also taken, which are necessary for other things besides the making of the *maraicher* frames. There is an excellent horticultural and agricultural library in the farm, and a couple of lectures a week are given in the evenings by the Principal. The students may choose their own subjects, which may be "Catering for a Family for a Week," or "Book-keeping," or "Horticulture." Miss Turner was for several years her father's assistant on a farm of 1,500 acres, and after that she was Vice-Principal at the Glynde School of Gardening; so her experience is wide and varied. One unusual subject she makes a great point of is the carving of joints, as she holds that many shillings a week can be saved by an expert carver.

the women who are wanted in the Colonies. The others are only "superfluous" over there. And if the work is hard, as a well-known professional woman said recently, for one woman of this class who dies of over-work, a hundred die for want of work, or drag out an existence that is not worth living.

A Hint

If all who took the step of going to the Colonies had had previous training in the domestic arts, such as that given at Miss Turner's farm, it would be a happy thing for

Milking Time

Manual Exercise with Spade, Fork, and Barrow: Breaking Ground

Besides ordinary farmwork and housework the pupils are given instruction in the methods of close-cultivation, about which so much has been heard lately, by which out-of-season vegetables may be profitably grown, and the girls are taught how to construct simple "*maraicher* frames," and do simple carpentry jobs which such work necessitates

Figure 9. Article on the Colonial Training Farm at Arlesey, England, "to prepare girls who wish to emigrate for the exigencies of Colonial life." For two years students took lessons in plain cooking, breadmaking, laundry, pickling and preserving, gardening, dairying, poultry and pig farming, carpentry, chopping wood, and digging up rough ground. Arlesey focused on Canada as the destination for its graduates. *The Bystander*, 16 September 1908, 610–11.

was on domestic economy, including cooking, jam making, dressmaking, laundry, plain gardening, simple carpentry, upholstery, butter making, and poultry raising.[155]

The Arlesey House Colonial Training school at Hitchin opened in 1907. Here, as at Studley, the training focused on "making do" when "far from civilization." The practical instruction included "plain cooking, bread making, riding, driving, stable-management, [and] simple carpentry." There was, however, instruction in farming small holdings, and after taking the full two-year course the graduate was pronounced equipped to farm her own land if she so wished. A critic of the school commented on the "vagueness" of the training, as it was not clear for what colony or region of a colony the women were being trained: "You might keep house for fifty years in most parts of New Zealand and never want to do most of the things taught at this school."[156]

Training for Canada was increasingly the focus at Arlesey. Journalist Sarah A. Tooley visited Arlesey in 1910 and wrote an article in the *Globe* (Toronto) on "Training Girls for Life in the Colonies."[157] A conference with the theme of Canada was hosted there that same year. The principal of the school, Miss J.S. Turner, explained that the theme was chosen because "such a very large proportion of the girls who wrote to her about colonial training wanted to go to Canada." In the conclusion to her article Tooley wrote, "The aim of the school is to fit women for colonial life, whether as cultivators of land on their own account, as gardeners, poultry-keepers, or as the wives and mothers of homesteaders." She also noted that Miss Turner had plans to establish branch schools in the various colonies, but this did not materialize in Canada.

Several other colonial training schools were established by 1912. There were so many by this time that staffing them may have constituted one solution to the "surplus women" problem. Battersea Polytechnic offered a three-month program through its Training Department of Domestic Science: Preparation for Colonial Life, which included household management, cookery, laundry work, and needlework. At Lane House, Brandesburton, Hull, a Mrs. Harrison established "a small private colonial Training School Highly recommended and conducted by Ladies. The house stands on its own grounds a few yards away from the farm, and the work is conducted as much as possible as it would be on a Colonial ranch." The training here covered housework, cooking, dairy and laundry, curing bacon and hams, fruit bottling, preserving, poultry raising, beekeeping, and gardening.[158]

In 1914 an Overseas Training School for Women was established at Hoebridge Farm, Woking Surrey, by Rupert Guinness, of the wealthy brewing family. Guinness was a keen agriculturalist, as was his wife, Gwendolen Guinness, who was also involved in emigration societies such as the Colonial Intelligence League. Encouraged by the success of the Emigration Training Farm for young men from the public schools, the Guinnesses extended this work to women and girls. The school was for Englishwomen of the educated class desirous of making homes in the dominions, and its emphasis was on "domestic science." A farmhouse was equipped under the direction of a Canadian woman, a graduate of the Macdonald Institute in Guelph. Housework would be undertaken "according to Canadian practice," and students would learn to cook "all dishes common in Canada." A short course of eight weeks for "Home Makers Overseas" was recommended to all women "going to join husband, brother, or father, as well as for home helps or those to be engaged in the lighter forms of agricultural work such as dairying, poultry raising."[159]

Girls and women who attended the colonial training programs must have come to Western Canada, but there are few traces of their presence. Emma (Roberts) Ducie was born in Yorkshire in 1883 and came with her family to Saskatchewan in 1907.[160] She had attended the Home and Colonial Training College supported by the Anglican Church before coming to Canada, and credited the training college "and its far flung students with making her realize there was a world beyond Great Britain." This may have been an institution that trained teachers rather than providing the sort of domestic colonial training detailed above, which was designed for girls with little interest in intellectual pursuits. Ducie "used her training to advantage" while teaching school in Saskatchewan. She married a homesteader, and they farmed together for forty-two years and raised three children. Ducie organized the local Homemakers Club (later Women's Institutes) and planned reading courses for rural women on topics such as "farming, gardening, international affairs and education."[161]

THE *IMPERIAL COLONIST* AND WOMEN FARMERS FOR THE COLONIES

A growing enthusiasm for sending British women as farmers to the colonies can be traced in the journal the *Imperial Colonist.*[162] In the late nineteenth century the Women's Emigration Society, the United Englishwomen's Emigration Society (renamed in 1901 the British Women's Emigration Association, or BWEA), and the Society for the Overseas Settlement of British Women all worked to ensure that women of "good character" were sent to the colonies, arrived safely, and received adequate reception upon arrival.[163] The BWEA published a monthly journal, the *Imperial Colonist,* inaugurated in 1902 and edited by Lady Knightley of Fawsley, who was devoted to the cause of women's emigration to the colonies and who had a particular interest in agriculture. This organization advocated farming for single women in the colonies, among many other occupations, all rather uneasily alongside an even greater emphasis on domestic service or home help as a training ground for marriage. In the wake of the South African War, that colony was a major focus of the journal when it first appeared, and Fawsley was particularly devoted to South Africa. The *Imperial Colonist* was filled with references to the need for women to transform "the blood-stained veldt" into "a loyal and prosperous community living in peace and harmony beneath the British flag."[164]

But from the first issue of the *Imperial Colonist,* much attention was paid to Western Canada as a destination for girls and women who wanted a life out of doors, as home helps, as mothers' helps, or as sisters helping brothers. Slowly there also crept into the pages suggestions that women might farm land of their own in Western Canada. In any case, they would bring culture, music, and refined ways that would improve the lives of men in the outposts of empire. Founder and first president of the BWEA Ellen Joyce announced in the first issue: "The women wanted in Western Canada are those healthy, countrybred women who love and understand animal life, and who prefer the freedom of the country to the conventionalities of the town. They must be women of some culture, but who have training in domestic arts by practicing them, and who will keep up the tone of the men with whom they mix by music and book lore when the day's work is done."[165]

Despite no expressions of interest in women farmers from any of the colonies, the idea of agriculture as a potential occupation for British women settlers gained momentum in the *Imperial Colonist.* Opportunities for women to study or attend conferences on agriculture before setting out for the colonies were advertised in the journal. In the third issue it announced that Lady Warwick intended to hold a conference of women engaged in the "lighter branches" of agriculture. Small holdings and horticulture were advocated in the journal: raising poultry, dairy, fruit, vegetables, or some combination of these (despite the fact that these sorts of enterprises were not characteristic of successful farms on the prairies). Colonies of small holders close to railways and towns or cities, rather than on the isolated prairies, were proposed. By the twelfth issue (1902), an article on "Woman's Position in Canada" noted that "there is room in the country for single women with a little capital, who may invest in the establishment of poultry farms, either near one or other of the cities within reach of the railway."[166] It was anticipated that the women would first work as home helps, however. In 1903 the journal annouced "offers on the spot" in Calgary "for yeoman class women to go on ranches to join family life; work is hard but life is healthy."[167] Marriage remained the true goal and gauge of success, however; the same issue noted that because so many of the home helps sent to farms had married, there would be many openings in the spring in the "Far West" of Canada.

Details about difficulties, challenges, and disadvantages that awaited women who wanted to farm land in Western Canada were not dealt with in the *Imperial Colonist.* The specifics of the "free" grant of homestead land (160 acres for a filing fee of ten dollars), a privilege available only to widows with children, were not described in any detail. Advertisements that ran in many issues for several years in the *Imperial Colonist* proclaimed "160 Acres in Western Canada Free. Healthy Climate. Good Crops. Free Schools. Light Taxes. Abundant Water," but made no mention that most women were not eligible for this land.[168]

Nor was it ever mentioned that single women could have a free grant of homestead land if they moved to the American West. British women were directed only to the British colonies and encouraged to see themselves as vital to the great British imperial enterprise. The *Imperial Colonist* discouraged emigration of single women to the United States with warnings that there would be no one to meet and house them, which would "leave the Englishwoman stranded," and that she could then be lured by Mormons into a life of polygamy.[169] Women were urged to go to Canada "under our own flag," where they were needed to stem the tide of immigration from the United States into Canada.[170]

Hopes that British women could farm in the colonies were not solely trained on Western Canada, and initially South Africa received a lot of attention. The *Imperial Colonist* reported in January 1904 that the Agricultural Sub-Committee of the South African Colonization Society had devised a scheme for a dairy and poultry farm near Potchefstroom in South Africa.[171] It was to be operated by two graduates from Swanley and ten others who would rent a farm, and there were hopes that this might form the nucleus for a prosperous settlement of women farmers. The scheme did not materialize. This was followed in March 1904 by the announcement of plans for a Women's Settlement in the Orange River Colony, where plots of irrigated land were to be offered to "lady settlers."[172] It was also hoped that women could play a part in the agricultural and horticultural development of the Transvaal, and there were calls in the *Imperial Colonist* for women who had a little capital, some knowledge of climatic and other conditions, and "the tact and power necessary for the management of native labour."[173]

There were many reports in early issues of the *Imperial Colonist* of Swanley graduates being sought in South Africa for positions as gardeners, and of the successes of a few who took up these positions. These reports generally stressed the success of women gardeners in managing "Kaffirs."[174] In February 1906, Mary Hewetson, a former Swanley student and head gardener at Pietermaritzburg, was managing about thirty acres of fruit, flowers, and vegetables, as well as a poultry yard, with the aid of "six Kaffirs."[175] A year later Hewetson had taken up a forty-acre plot of irrigated land of her own in Natal with a woman friend.[176] This announcement, however, was soon followed by "sad news of the death of Miss Hewetson," with no explanation of the cause. Hewetson was heralded in the September 1907 *Imperial Colonist* as "a Pioneer and a most able one in the work of establishing women in agricultural and horticultural pursuits in South Africa."[177] A few months earlier, Mrs. Macdonald, the secretary of the Pietermaritzburg branch of the South African Colonization Committee, had been "murdered by her Indian servant."[178] Following these events there was less promotion in the *Imperial Colonist* on opportunities for women farmers in South Africa. Poultry farms in Natal, it was reported, were precarious because of "thieves and strange new diseases."[179] Vegetable gardening there was "chiefly in the hands of coolies who rent and cultivate most patches by rivers." This was seen to be difficult for the British woman gardener, as "the hard-working, frugal Indian coolie has made market gardening his specialty and it needs skill, perseverance and some little capital in order to compete with him."[180]

Articles on South Africa in the *Imperial Colonist* often focused on topics related to managing local servants. Stories about successful Swanley graduates stressed the proficiency of women gardeners in managing "Kaffirs,"[181] while other articles discussed matters such as "The Wrong Way to Manage Black Servants" and "The Peril of the Black."[182] Even the somewhat successful Mary Heweston had found it a challenge to "manage" her servants; she reported in 1906 that "I have a dozen or thirteen 'boys' of all kinds, some utterly raw, ignorant, unintelligible and stupid—others, with fixed ideas of what they should or should not do—a difficult team to drive, and often at night I wondered how I should get through the next day."[183] A 1919 article on "Empire Migration" warned potential home helps headed to South Africa that the work "may probably be to superintend the native servants, and she must be able to keep them in their right place and prevent any liberties, as familiarity might have terrible results." Yet the author did not want to frighten or discourage, adding: "Not that there need be any fear for the safety of a sensible girl who follows advice, especially where there is a white man to act as protector."[184]

Beyond the *Imperial Colonist*, concerns were being expressed about South Africa as a destination for British women who wanted to farm. In a 1909 presentation to the National Union of Women Workers of Great Britain and Ireland, Frances Taylor spoke on "Conditions of Life for Women in South Africa," emphasizing that it was impossible for white female (or male) colonists to perform manual labour on farms or elsewhere.[185] She explained that "most of the hard work is done by natives, and therefore, unfortunately, manual labour on the part of the superior, or White Race, is looked down upon as derogatory and undignified … How quickly does the girl just arrived to undertake the ordinary duties of a domestic servant learn to say, 'Oh, that is Kaffir's work, I could not possibly do that.'" South Africa did "not want women doing manual labour out of doors, contending that it would bring them down to the level of 'Kaffirs.'"[186] Edith O'Connor, who farmed with her husband in the Transvaal, was more explicit in her explanation of the obstacles to British women farming independently in South Africa, stating that "the attitude of the native toward women is the big and predominant difficulty. Even a small picaninny will be deeply hurt if hit by a woman, it being not the slap, but the sex of the slapper that insults him. Carry this attitude to the grown man, who, in addition to despising women, is uncontrolled in his sexual appetite, and the difficulty for a white woman can be imagined."[187] O'Connor warned that a woman alone on a farm would have to sleep with a revolver handy and to have a guard dog. For many reasons, then, farming for women in South Africa was dismissed as an "absurd expedient."[188]

Agricultural opportunities also existed for British women in New Zealand and Australia, according to the *Imperial Colonist.* Particularly favourable conditions were seen to prevail in New Zealand for small holdings.[189] But increasingly, Western Canada was cast as the most congenial destination for women who wanted to farm. There were none of the problems with "native servants" that prevailed in South Africa; there was plenty of cleared prairie land available; and the climate was healthy and exhilarating. In a 1908 *Imperial Colonist*, for example, a woman reported from "Sunny Alberta," north of Edmonton, that she had bought land adjoining that of her daughter and son-in-law, where she had a poultry farm that made a profitable business through marketing chickens, geese, and turkeys.[190] She wrote that "it is really a very happy life, a quiet one certainly, but have plenty of books and papers, and we are all interested in our poultry, and animals, and gardening, and though it is a very quiet spot the country is most beautiful and life ideal. The climate is cold in winter, but air so clear and dry, one does not feel it as in England."

In 1910 agricultural opportunities for women in the Canadian West began to garner much more attention in the *Imperial Colonist.* It was announced that a colony of women poultry farmers was to be established by the Canadian Pacific Railway at Strathmore, Alberta; the colony would provide eggs and poultry to the transcontinental railway. (The initiative does not appear to have ever materialized.) And as will be discussed in Chapter 5, articles and lectures by Saskatchewan farmer Georgina Binnie-Clark helped to generate interest in farming for English women in the Canadian West.

But calls for British women to farm the prairies also generated criticism and warnings. In 1910 Eileen L. Burns wrote to the *Imperial Colonist* to say that she could "not possibly recommend farming for women in Western Canada." It was unsuitable and impossible. Few women, she wrote, had the physical strength and endurance required, and she continued: "When farming is advocated as a career for women in this country, I most positively and definitely state that it is an absolutely visionary scheme, foredoomed to failure." Burns knew of only a few cases where women had succeeded, apart from widows who carried on with farms that were already "going concerns."[191] (She was the wife of cattle baron and meat packer Patrick Burns, one of the wealthiest men in Western Canada.)

Overall, however, it must be admitted that there were many more articles in the *Imperial Colonist* devoted to opportunities for home helps (as well as for nurses, stenographers, teachers, dressmakers, and tea-shop owners) in Western Canada than to the potential vocation of agriculture for single women. And a great deal of emphasis was placed on the immediate matrimonial destiny of the home helps. A 1902 article declared that so many of the home helps sent out to the "Far West" had married that there would be as many fresh openings in the spring.[192] A primary concern of the journal was to draw attention to the "White Women's Burden."[193] The editorial note in a 1911 issue was typical: "The Empires' call to the women of our race is clear, urgent and inspiring: never before so insistent as it is today. Our young men want mates of their blood in the great sunny uplands of the Empire ... The Dominion needs wives, sisters, mothers, teachers, nurses, domestic helpers and home makers."[194] Women farmers were not on the list.

JOURNALISTS FLORA SHAW AND MARY AGNES FITZGIBBON, AND THE SCHOOL FOR "LADY COLONISTS" IN WESTERN CANADA

Flora Shaw, the colonial editor of the *Times* of London, saw it as the duty of British women to settle the Canadian prairies and wrote a series of columns on the subject in 1898. At that time she did not advocate that women farm land of their own, but she came later to endorse the idea. Others, particularly Canadian journalist Mary Agnes Fitzgibbon, built on Shaw's observations of the needs of the region to point out the potential for women farmers, and together they became linked with the scheme for a school for "lady colonists" on the prairies who would learn the skills required to farm land on their own.

A devoted imperialist, Shaw aspired to advance the cause of the British Empire through her journalism.[195] She was an intense student of what was happening in the colonies, she advocated imperial expansion and colonial economic development, and she sought to influence imperial politics and policy makers. Her work had attracted worldwide press attention and praise by 1898, when she was sent to investigate conditions in the

Klondike, and she welcomed the opportunity because it also allowed her to visit and write about other parts of Canada. As part of a series called "Letters From Canada," Shaw wrote several long articles on the prairies and the ranching, grain, and mixed-farming economies being established there. Her main concern was the preponderance of solitary men on their solitary homesteads, living in tiny, poorly built shacks.[196] The new verb "to batch," she noted, "upon the prairies represents perhaps the *minimum* of pleasure in existence with which man, civilized or uncivilized, has been known to content himself with." Shaw proposed that sisters be encouraged to join their brothers in the enterprise of farming the prairies. This was not a new idea for this journalist; in 1894 she had given a paper to the Royal Colonial Institute in London on the "Australian Outlook," and had called on younger sisters to accompany brothers settling in the colonies.[197]

Shaw did not in her published letters touch on the subject of women farming on their own on the prairies, and did not deal with the thorny issues of ownership of the farm and land that the sister and brother had jointly established, or what would happen to her if the brother married. Shaw's idea of the sister companion to the male homesteader in Western Canada gained supporters, however, who did address these issues. Arthur Montefiore Brice adopted many of Shaw's ideas and phrases but went much further, advocating an equal partnership.[198] Brice wrote that on the Canadian prairies, "brother and sister ... should take up a farm together and work it on terms of equal partnership for ... not less than four or five years." When one or both wanted to marry, "it is only right and practical that then there should be a basis for the equitable division of, or allowance for, the results of their joint labours."

Building on Shaw's proposals, and also publishing in the *Times* of London some months after Shaw's articles about Canada appeared, Canadian journalist Mary Agnes Fitzgibbon (writing under her pen name, Lally Bernard) proposed a scheme for the establishment of a school in Western Canada for lady colonists who would then obtain land there on their own. This would not be for "female emigration in the lower rank of life," but be "in the interests of the numerous gentlewomen who are capitalists in a small way ... Often such is the daughter of a small squire or a land-owner."[199] A few months of practical work at such an institute, Fitzgibbon wrote, would fit a woman to take up land and "invest her capital at a much higher rate of interest in Canada than she could ever hope to get at home." These colonists would be released from the "worrying grind of genteel poverty." Fitzgibbon was eloquent in her call for women to take up this challenge rather than join the "spinster army of Great Britain":

> Granted the lady colonists will have much to learn and much to endure, still how many women have to go about the Continent with some browbeating dowager or spinster aunt, whose petty tyranny leaves her unhappy companion, a nervous wreck of womanhood, to take her place among the spinster army of Great Britain. They cling to their tradition of caste. Let them prove their claim to intrepid blood and face life in this newer Britain, fighting, it may be against the elements and certainly against difficulties and prejudices in their new surroundings. This was surely better than the striving to make a tiny income cover expenses which very probably increase as their already small interest diminishes.[200]

Yet even Fitzgibbon saw these women primarily and ultimately as reproducers of the "race" rather than as farmers. She called on women to help give to the "Anglo-Saxon world a new 'Viking' race" to rule over "the boundless waves of the prairie province, that vast rolling sea of earth ready for the seed man shall scatter and plough." The mothers of this Viking race, in Fitzgibbon's view, should be the "daughters of British gentry ... practical, intelligent and cultured" and trained to "face the vicissitudes of existence in the sparsely populated districts of the North-West." Daughters of British gentry could not simply go upon Canadian farms the way the sons could, they needed training and to be shown that "interesting absorbing work can be found in activities connected with agriculture."

Fitzgibbon was herself struggling with "genteel poverty" at this time. Born Mary Agnes Bernard in Canada, in 1881 at age nineteen she travelled to England with her aunt, Lady Susan Agnes Macdonald, the second wife of Prime Minister John A. Macdonald, and made her debut in London that season.[201] A year later she married an Irish lawyer of titled parentage, Clare Valentine Fitzgibbon. He was a grandson of the Earl of Clare, and the couple socialized among an elite London circle. Their daughter was born in 1885. But when her husband was confined to an asylum in 1896, Fitzgibbon had to find a way to support herself, her daughter, and her mother.[202] She was a gentlewoman thrown on her own resources. She returned to Canada and lived in Toronto with her mother and stepfather, D'Alton McCarthy. McCarthy was killed in a carriage accident two years later. Fitzgibbon became a journalist, publishing mainly in the Toronto *Globe*. (After about 1900 she was known by the name "Mrs. Clare Fitzgibbon," and she also published under the names "Margo Meredith," "Citoyenne," and "Fitz-Clare" as well as "Lally Bernard.") Her fourteen years in England had helped to make her a devoted "Imperial Daughter" who continued to return for visits, attending two coronations and "helping to forge a strong link between Canada and the Mother Country."[203]

Fitzgibbon's 1899 letter to the *Times* on a school for lady colonists was soon followed by a *Times* editorial endorsing the scheme, particularly the idea of a training school, but placing less emphasis on the women farming on their own. The editorial was clearly written by Flora Shaw, and she and Fitzgibbon were together associated with the scheme from then on. Shaw's "Women and Colonial Settlement" began by detailing the number of "surplus" of women that had risen alarmingly in the United Kingdom. Industrious, cheerful, and healthy women were needed in the colonies.[204] The Canadian West was an "admirable field" for the initiation of an experiment of the kind proposed by Fitzgibbon, as the land was cheap, the soil good, markets were at hand, and "nowhere more than the Canadian prairies are women needed for the purpose of investing the bare log houses known as 'shacks' with the comfort and dignity of homes." It was emphasized that there were no physical dangers to be faced on the prairies.

The *Times* editorial endorsed the idea of a training home for women situated in Western Canada, operated at government expense in connection with a system of experimental farms. Women would be instructed in practical agriculture (dairying, gardening, poultry rearing, beekeeping) as well as in household arts, including cooking and laundry. The graduates "might in some instances purchase and work land for themselves," but "in the majority of cases it is supposed that they will in the first instance work in co-operation with their farmer brothers on a system of mutual profit." To keep the cost of this education within reason, Shaw called on the government to at least subsidize such an institution with the assistance of private subscriptions and endowments. She predicted that if such a scheme were successfully inaugurated, other colonies would soon copy the example, and Canada would "render a service to the cause of Imperial consolidation."

Shaw explained why educated and refined women were needed for the colonies rather than working-class women: they were "hardier, more active in out-of-doors habits, better bred and better fed than their contemporaries of the less-favoured labouring classes. They have the intelligence to initiate ... and are driven by the wholesome spur of poverty either present or to come."[205] She concluded with the hope that in one generation it would be commonly accepted that "the young women no less than the young men of the United Kingdom should confidently seek a living wherever the British flag flies in a temperate climate."

The idea of a training school for lady colonists received widespread coverage in English and Canadian newspapers. Some were in favour. An editorial in the *Leeds Mercury* of 12 April 1899 endorsed the scheme of training women in agriculture suitable to the region of prairie Canada. A school was essential for "poor ladies, refined and well brought up, who may desire to exchange the pinched life and narrow means ... for the greater independence, freedom and brighter outlook of which the colonial farm gives the assurance." The editors believed that the Canadian prairies would be the best colonial location for the scheme, as "no better climate could be found, the soil is fruitful, and land so cheap that, we are told, one year's moderately successful crop will cover not only the cost of purchase, but the outlay on production."[206]

Others, however, raised questions about the feasibility of the plan.[207] Fitzgibbon elaborated and developed her scheme and addressed the concerns of critics.[208] She stressed the efficiency of the North-West Mounted Police in ensuring a peaceful and law-abiding country. There was no influx of raucous gold seekers in the region. She faced the question of the cold winters with the reply about the "dry cold" that has since become standard when describing the Western Canadian climate. Fitzgibbon wrote that settlers on the prairies would rather face a temperature of fifty degrees below zero there than "the cold which chilled them to the very marrow while dining in one of England's swagger country houses in November."

In October 1899, Fitzgibbon went to Western Canada for a six-week trip for the purpose of "verifying exactly what life is like at the present there among the educated class of people."[209] She also wanted to explore the feasibility of settling a number of women near Calgary, where they would raise poultry and market garden. Fitzgibbon continued to emphasize that the scheme was meant to promote women farmers, but she argued that they ought to devote their capital and energies to "co-operative small farming, poultry-raising, fruit culture, dairying etc." It was nonetheless a radical plan, as she insisted there was scope for women "as operators on their own account along co-operative lines." If they were "girls," then they should go to the West as "lady helpers" rather than farmers. On this visit she declared Brandon, Manitoba, as a likely site for such a school, in conjunction with the experimental farm there. She also stated that she had submitted a plan to Minister of the Interior Clifford Sifton, "from whom I received a decidedly ambiguous acknowledgement."

Fitzgibbon developed further rationales for choosing Canada over other colonies.[210] In Canada, British women "could go forth and fight their way in any line they may choose, just as their brothers are doing." No "special machinery" was required "for the protection and placing of lonely women." Ignoring the Indigenous population, the writer explained that Canada was a "white man's land from end to end" and added, "There are other Colonies where the 'native' question renders such a line or argument impossible."[211]

"Influential women in the motherland," Fitzgibbon hoped, would lend their assistance to the scheme of a school for lady colonists, but this did not materialize. As one letter to the *Times* replied in response to the initiative, there *was* a training school for lady colonists, the Leaton Colonial Training Home, which not only trained suitable women but weeded out "those who were unfit" before they ever arrived in a colony.[212] Nor did Fitzgibbon succeed in persuading the Canadian government to support the plan. Her own newspaper, the *Globe*, thought private enterprise rather than government should take up the scheme.[213] Despite the fact that no such training school was ever founded in Western Canada, Fitzgibbon's campaign helped to focus aspirations for British colonists and farmers in that region. Fitzgibbon had successfully argued that "of all the colonies Canada has the greatest advantages to offer as a field for the enterprise of the future lady colonist."[214] As Mrs. Archibald Colquhoun stated in her 1904 presentation to London's Royal Colonial Institute on "Women and the Colonies," for middle-class women emigrants "it was to Canada that they must look for their chief field of colonization," if they could be persuaded to have more courage and patriotism.[215]

In her regular columns for the *Globe* as Lally Bernard, Fitzgibbon stressed her "deep interest in the question of agriculture and horticulture as a vocation for women." She wrote, "I am often amused at the scorn with which the majority of people regard the idea of agriculture for women as being practicable and desirable. As a matter of fact, both in the U.S. and Canada farms of all kinds are most successfully run by women, and all branches of horticultural work are being run by women in every part of the world."[216] She compared the opportunities for women to study agriculture in Canada unfavourably to those in Britain and other nations. In a 1901 column she had asked why the government did not open the horticultural department at the Agricultural College at Guelph to women students, given that the head of the department was "most anxious" for this to happen. She noted that "already in Great Britain women are doing most successful work in horticulture ... Lady orchardists and florists are to be found both in the United States and Great Britain and Belgium."[217]

Fitzgibbon was disappointed, however, at the colonial training schools in England, where she found little emphasis on sending student colonists to Canada. The colonial training branch at Swanley, she observed in 1903, was directed toward opportunities in South Africa. She hoped that a patron could supply the school with a kitchen and entire "Canadian outfit" such as would be found in the West. By this point, Fitzgibbon had backed away from promoting colonial training in Canada, writing that it was beyond the means of most women who had to pay for their passage and find a job right away. She now highlighted the domestic skills women needed for Canada and downplayed their potential as farmers and landowners on their own. She often returned to the theme that lady colonists were what the West needed, but placed greater emphasis on their roles as wives, mothers, and home helps rather than as farmers.[218]

THE COLONIAL INTELLIGENCE LEAGUE

Founded in 1910, the Colonial Intelligence League for Educated Women (CIL) was the creation of Caroline (Mrs. Norman) Grosvenor, a novelist and artist, and member of an influential network of elite women interested in the settlement of British women in the colonies.[219] Grosvenor had been an activist with the South African Colonization Society. For her it was an imperial mission and duty for women to emigrate. She believed, however, that girls and women could not be simply sent out as potential wives, and that farming could be the vocation that awaited some of them. Yet the CIL was somewhat cautious and muted in its support for women farmers in Canada, not wanting to appear radical and alienate potential donors and supporters, but instead reflecting the consensus that women were best suited to lighter agriculture on small holdings, clustered in settlements or colonies.

Grosvenor was above all an ardent imperialist, and this was combined with an obsession about the fate of the "surplus women" of the genteel or educated classes. The plan was to send these "superior" women to the colonies, and the focus of the CIL was soon Canada. Here would be employed "a vast amount of splendid material which is now being either wrongly used or entirely wasted"; this would "bring hope and a future to many thousands for whom life at present looks infinitely dark and difficult, and last and most important of all, it will help to keep the British Empire for the British race."[220] Grosvenor was concerned that Englishwomen, "charming, pretty, amiable as they might be[,] are hopelessly unfitted for the life of hard work" that awaited them.[221] In a 1909 column in the *Times* of London, Grosvenor addressed the issue of training Englishwomen for conditions in the colonies. She argued first of all that unmarried daughters *must* go to the colonies where "the very best of our British race are sent to plough their lonely furrow."[222] The women had to be trained, however; they could not simply be sent "on the chance of their meeting suitable husbands," and Grosvenor recommended the Colonial Training College at Stoke Prior. She urged any woman under thirty who had "the ancient inheritance of her race—the spirit of adventure and the longing of a home of her own" to set forth, but to first attend a training home. Small groups of women could establish market gardens, or poultry, dairy, or bee farms.

The three goals and objectives of the CIL, as set out in the first annual report of 1910, were to (1) maintain an "Intelligence Office" in England that estimated the demands for women's work in the colonies; (2) establish in each of the colonies expert agents who would investigate local opportunities and conditions; and (3) establish in each a "Colony of Settlements for Women," where they could be trained for local conditions.[223]

The focus of the CIL was the educated "surplus woman."[224] While other organizations were devoted to sending women to the colonies primarily for domestic service, the CIL would be solely aimed at the "educated gentlewoman, accustomed to country life, with a knowledge of practical affairs, and [who], with a little capital might find an opportunity in some one of the many departments of intensive agriculture." Grosvenor's organization was also determined to gather "intelligence" about conditions in each of the colonies. The existing organizations, Grosvenor thought, provided the machinery for emigration, but there was a "crying need for a proper intelligence department which shall estimate the demand of the Colonies and bring it into relation with the supply which we believe to exist." She wanted to be sure that women left for the colonies only when they were assured of suitable work. The plan was for the CIL to establish in each colony an agency to investigate local needs. And Grosvenor did investigate local needs herself (to some degree), travelling to Western Canada in 1911, 1912, and 1914, quickly focusing on British Columbia as the site for an "agricultural training home" for Englishwomen.[225]

Like many other and earlier advocates of agriculture for "surplus women" in the colonies, Grosvenor sought women who were not interested in intellectual pursuits but instead loved the outdoors. As a novelist, she provided descriptions more eloquent than those of many of her contemporaries and predecessors. Grosvenor "spoke of the girls who have been brought up in the country, who amidst the moorlands of Scotland or Ireland, the dales of the North of England, the broad pastures of the Midlands, or the wind-swept downs of the South, have got into their blood the love of outdoor life, of outdoor things and animals."[226] More than previous advocates of emigration, however, Grosvenor was focused on Canada, and she was more willing to articulate the difficulties to be faced. She outlined these in her most sustained statement on the issue in the *Times* in 1913, under the title "Women Farmers in Canada: A British Farm Settlement."[227] The major problem was that there were no salaried positions for women in Canada on poultry or dairy farms because it was difficult to house them ("hired" men could sleep in rough conditions, but hired gentlewomen could not); because few farmers produced eggs, poultry, and dairy products for market; and because "there exists in Canada a curiously strong prejudice against employing women in outside work."

The structure of the CIL departed to some extent from previous emigration societies, "breaking away from past practices of amateurism and female voluntary work," but the upper-class background of its founders kept it a "patrician organization."[228] Its honorary president was Princess Christian of Schleswig-Holstein, and many elite women and men figured among the benefactors. Historian Andrew Yarmie has argued that the CIL was not as stridently imperialistic as its predecessors, placing less importance on imposing English ideas on the colonies and instead cautioning that the English woman must learn the "ways and ideas" of the colonies.[229] While there was an emphasis on recruiting Englishwomen, the organization also had branch offices in Edinburgh and Glasgow. Some of the members were acquainted with Canada, such as Lady Sybil Grey, daughter of the Governor General of Canada Earl Grey. Lady Grey was an adventurous person (later a decorated nurse wounded in the First World War) who in 1909 visited the Yukon and staked a gold claim in the Klondike.[230]

Echoing the cause of Mary Fitzgibbon, Caroline Grosvenor believed that British women already trained in poultry farming or dairying in the "Old Country" required practical experience in Canada, in farm settlements, where they could learn about local conditions. She decided this following her 1911 visit to Western Canada.[231] The belief that "home help" work was ill-suited to the educated woman was reinforced by the visit that same year of Ella Sykes, mentioned at the outset of this chapter. Sykes volunteered to visit Canada in 1911 on behalf of the CIL to investigate conditions for women in the West. Her book *A Home-Help in Canada* was a result of this visit. She took five temporary "home help" positions in four provinces and was a guest on other farms. Her description of the life of a "home help" was negative, or at best ambivalent, and she did not recommend the work for the educated woman. Skykes was, however, like Grosvenor, convinced that British women needed to seek their fortunes in the colonies, that it was "Imperial work to help girls of a high stamp to seek their fortunes beyond the seas—women who will care for our glorious Flag and what it signifies."[232]

It was after the 1911 visits to Canada of Sykes and Grosvenor that the CIL began planning a farm settlement in British Columbia, which began in 1913 with the purchase of fifteen acres. The Princess Patricia Ranch would train eight to ten women at a time, who would give their labour in return for board and lodging. The settlement would also demonstrate the capacity of British women as poultry keepers and vegetable growers and induce Canadian farmers to employ them. "The Canadian needs 'ocular demonstration' to be convinced," Grosvenor wrote, "but once convinced he will take up a new idea with lightning rapidity." The ranch was to be the first of others, as it was hoped that government aid would fund future such settlements. Grosvenor believed the scheme should appeal to both Canadian and British as "sound Imperial statesmanship." As the first of many in Canada and other colonies, the Princess Patricia Ranch would be a "stepping stone in a big movement, which will be of the greatest possible use in opening up enormous possibilities to women themselves, and to the country of their adoption."[233] Ultimately these settlements would "help to keep British possessions loyal to the flag."[234]

Despite its emphasis on "colonial intelligence," the CIL appears to have gathered very little information on the conditions of farming, ranching, or gardening in Western Canada. In the organization's archival collection there is a substantial bound volume with the title "Colonial Intelligence League Reference Book: Canada" printed boldly on the front, along with "N.B. The contents of this book are strictly private and confidential."[235] Inside, however, there is surprisingly little "intelligence." Most of the pages are blank. On farming there are a few entries, most of which are discouraging. From Calgary in 1912 it was reported that it was not possible for women to find positions there on poultry farms; they would need to work as hired helps, which meant "grinding work." There was also no work in Calgary for women "Jobbing Gardeners" because of the "long idle season. We are so high up that our gardens are always spoilt very early by a crushing frost. Last year it was in August, and after that there is nothing to do but gather up and burn the debris, cover all up with manure and wait until April." The real problem was, "What would they do from October to April?" From British Columbia it was reported that year that land was very expensive to purchase, that it took years to clear land and that it was arduous work: three to five years of "waiting and struggling." Fruit trees did not produce for four or five years. Gardening in British Columbia was "in the hands of the Chinese," and they undersold all others.

The CIL appears to have forged no links with the women who had been attempting to promote and facilitate farming for (British) women in prairie Canada through the homesteads-for-women campaign, to be discussed in Chapter 6. There is no record of any association with Binnie-Clark, for example, whose book *Wheat and Woman* appeared in 1914. Binnie-Clark and others involved in Canada in the homesteads-for-women cause may have been viewed as too radical by membership of the CIL, anxious as the organizers were to raise funds for their "experimental station" in Canada. They likely could not afford to challenge the Canadian federal government in the way that Binnie-Clark and others had. Binnie-Clark spoke to suffrage organizations in England, and many of those involved in Western Canada were also committed to suffrage, dower, and other campaigns that posed fundamental challenges to property and land laws. Binnie-Clark's address to the Royal Colonial Institute in 1913, mentioned at the outset of this chapter and further discussed in Chapter 5, discredited her in the eyes of the Victoria *Daily Colonist* as misleading to emigrants, particularly young women. For this reason it would not have been in the interest of Grosvenor and the CIL to make common cause with Binnie-Clark.

The CIL did, however, attract the notice and participation of Mary Agnes Fitzgibbon. The sole product of her campaign for colonial training for gentlewomen in Canada was the Queen Mary Coronation Hostel for Gentlewomen in Vancouver, British Columbia, founded in 1912 under the patronage of Queen Mary and with funding from Lord Strathcona. Fitzgibbon had moved to British Columbia in 1907, concentrating her energies there with the help of Lady Mary Minto (wife of the former Governor General).[236] This initiative, along with the Princess Patricia Ranch, marked the growing tendency to see British Columbia rather than the prairies as the most suitable destination for the educated British woman emigrant. The hostel was operated in conjunction with the CIL. Unlike other hostels that received Canadian government funding and were intended for immigrant domestics, admission to the privately funded Queen Mary Hostel was restricted to "gentlewoman." For a small fee, English gentlewomen were taught to become competent housewives.[237] Gone was the emphasis on women owning and farming land of their own. They learned to split their own wood and to cook on a wood stove in a "real Western shack" situated on the grounds of the hostel, but that was the extent of their outdoor work. The majority of the women who stayed at the hostel found work in homes or clerical positions.[238]

Yet the CIL's goal of training women to farm persisted (although it was not to last for long). In 1913 there were two women workers at the Princess Patricia Ranch at Vernon, British Columbia, along with a superintendent. Optimism was in the air, as British Columbia's Minister of Agriculture W. Scott was impressed with the potential for dairying, fruit growing, and poultry production. He recommended that the ranch become a government demonstration farm. Critics of the work of the CIL were also emerging. An editorial in a July 1913 *Daily Colonist* of Victoria noted that an organization known as the Colonial Intelligence League had sent young English girls out to British Columbia to "pick berries."[239] The editorial continued: "The *Colonist* points out the absurdity of such girls working in the fields side by side with Indians, Chinese and Japanese. The League that is engaged in this particular form of pumping [*sic*] the white man in to keep the yellow man out knows so little of British

Columbia that it should be renamed the Lack of Intelligence League." According to the editorial, "there is not an educated young woman in British Columbia who would think for a single moment of going out to the berry fields to work side by side with Indians, Chinamen and Japanese."

Mary Agnes Fitzgibbon was opposed to British women picking fruit, considering it a job for Chinese and Indian workers.[240] Caroline Grosvenor did not believe it was suitable, either, but was willing to concede that it depended on the employer. Lady Sybil Grey was entirely opposed to British women fruit picking in British Columbia, "where the work was usually done by Chinese or Indians, and by the less reputable workers of the district."[241]

The *Daily Colonist* was sceptical of the entire idea of women farmers in Canada. Also in 1913, they severely criticized Georgina Binnie-Clark's talk "Land and the Woman in Canada," and her claims that British women could aspire to farm in Canada. The *Colonist* claimed the CIL plans for a farm settlement of women would cause suffering and disappointment. That the organizers were "unintentionally deceiving many of your girls is beyond all question." The Colonial "Lack of Intelligence League" was guilty of "Mischievous Benevolence."[242]

"GIVEN HEALTH AND INDUSTRY THERE IS A FORTUNE WAITING FOR THEM": MARION CRAN AND *A WOMAN IN CANADA*

English writer Marion Cran's voice joined those calling for the "educated gentlewoman" to take up farming in Canada, although she was careful to point out the challenges and obstacles. Cran was a prolific author of gardening books, including *The Garden of Ignorance* (1913), *The Garden of Experience* (1921), and *The Joy of the Ground* (1928), in which she wove the story of her garden on rented property in Surrey with stories of her three husbands, her children and parents, and her problems with finances.[243] Cran used her gardening books to draw attention to inequalities in marriage and other restrictions women of her era encountered. Born in South Africa, she was a devoted imperialist, believing in the superiority of the British "race." Cran was asked by the Canadian government to investigate conditions for British women immigrants in Canada, and her visit took place in 1908, with her findings published as *A Woman in Canada*.[244]

Cran was enthusiastic about the potential of Canada, where she spent six and a half months, finding that "the Englishwoman in Canada is everywhere welcomed and valued. In the North-West, where wives are scarce, a work of Empire awaits the woman of breed and endurance who will settle on the prairie homesteads and rear their children in the best traditions of Britain."[245] Yet she went beyond the demand for women as wives and mothers, arguing that Canada needed "educated, middle-class gentlewomen, and these are not the women to come out on the off-chance of getting married. They may be induced to come to the country if they can farm or work in some way to secure their absolute independence. They want, every nice woman wants, to be free to undertake marriage as a matter of choice, not of necessity."[246] Once settled, these women might "throw in their lot with the bachelor farmers of the prairie and British Columbia," but there had to be more than marriage in order to entice them to immigrate.

A Woman in Canada called on British women to consider farming in Canada. Cran's second chapter, "A Woman Farmer and an Experimental Farm," is about meeting a woman who farmed 600 acres in Ontario, and this example was used by Cran to promote the opportunities on the land. Cran claimed she had never met a woman farmer before and was deeply impressed. The farmer, never named, was dignified and beautifully dressed. She was cultured, "transplanted from the hectic life of Paris and London to this healthy, busy land."[247] Cran quoted the farmer as declaring, "almost passionately," that "it is an indescribable joy, this turning of the wild into fertile plains,—I can never have enough of it,—I do not grudge one second of the work, hard and exacting as it is,—I am repaid a thousandfold when my days and weeks of anxious care are borne into blossom like this."[248]

Leaving Ontario full of enthusiasm for farming, Cran headed west, where she was disappointed to find little evidence of women farmers. She had hoped to find "bachelor women," women "working the land 'on their own,' singly or in clusters," but did not find any and concluded that "there are no women on the prairies except the wives and daughters of farmers, and they are scarce enough."[249] She wondered why women "should not come out and work it as well as men," and did not seem aware that homesteads were not available to most women, writing that as "the labour of 'homesteading' would be very great for women, I can understand their shirking it."[250] "To 'make good' on a free farm," Cran wrote, "a woman would need either much courage and capital, or considerable male labour, besides agricultural skill." She concluded that instead of taking up 160 acres, a woman should buy a small acreage within a few miles of the railway, and that "given health and industry, there is a fortune waiting for them in that marvelous prairie loam, just as surely as for the men who go out to grow wheat and run stock-farms. Above all there is a splendid opening for our women gardeners."[251]

Like most of her counterparts in England, Cran advocated taking up small holdings, writing that men might prefer the "big gamble of wheat growing," but the surer, steadier road to fortune was through vegetable, fruit, and flower growing, and she urged English women to consider farming cooperatively or in colonies: "Here then, is the opportunity for Englishwomen. Let them come out in twos and threes, unless any single woman has sufficient capital, and (just as important) courage for a lonely life; let them settle within marketable driving distance of such cities as Saskatoon, Regina, Edmonton, Calgary, etc., and they will find awaiting them every facility for a life of independence and certain ultimate success in the grandest climate in the world. The brilliant bracing air, the bustle of industry and of hope which pervade the prairies are beyond my powers to describe."[252]

Cran strongly discouraged women from homestead farming.[253] She said it was not women's work, that the land would be so far from a railway that transportation problems would be endless and the loneliness "unendurable." Wheat farming, according to Cran, was for men only. Wheat required large acreages; it was a venture that did not begin to pay until 160 acres were tilled, "a feat which takes some doing in the bush-covered parts of the prairie with only a scrub-plough to help. The ploughing of a few acres, on the other hand, is not a very formidable undertaking, and returns in flowers and vegetables would be steady."[254] Women could improve their smaller acreages at a slower, saner pace. Cran was particularly struck by the potential for women market gardeners at the Winnipeg Horticultural Exhibition, where she saw tomatoes, pumpkins, Swiss chard, cabbage, parsnip wine, cherry wine, raspberry vinegar, and sweet herbs such as thyme, sage, and marjoram. Poultry farming was another option for women in Cran's view, but she believed that British Columbia was a better environment for this industry and for fruit growing.

Cran concluded, however, that the majority of English "bachelor women" were not capable of facing the challenges and toils of life on the prairies.[255] They were "unfitted by our complete civilization." But she felt there were exceptional women, numbering "in the thousands," who were "fearless, enthusiastic, clean-bred." She wrote, "There must be some who have the courage and health to leave the ready-made comforts of the old country, and come into this wild beautiful West, giving their best of mind and body for the race and for the Empire."[256]

FICTION SET IN THE COLONIES AND THE RECONFIGURING OF BRITISH NORMS OF FEMININITY

Adventure fiction for girls set in the colonies bolstered the idea that it was possible to farm or pursue other occupations that might be seen as unfeminine, and thus unacceptable at home, while sharing in the task of building the Empire. In the late nineteenth century, British authors of adventure fiction for girls created independent, resourceful, and courageous heroines who rose to the challenges of the rugged environments they helped to colonize. These began to emerge decades after the appearance of equivalent books for boys by writers such as G.A. Henty and H. Rider Haggard. Author Bessie Marchant set her novels all over the British colonial world, creating robust heroines who took on arduous outdoor work (although most eventually married).[257] Indigenous people are almost absent in her novels except as occasional "expendable obstacles in the path of British rule" and as extra players in the background.[258] Marchant's books inspired her readers to question the idea that "men must work and women must weep." Her readers were "no longer content to be simply backers-up of male empire builders … [they] were seeking new worlds of their own to conquer."[259]

Women's ownership or management of land and their responsibility for crops and livestock are prominent in several of Marchant's novels, as titles such as *Erica's Ranch* suggest. In two of her novels written before the First Wold War, the protagonist is "the sole possessor, in her own right and name" of her "own piece of the Empire."[260] Often the father of the heroine is elderly and incapacitated, and she must run the farm or ranch. The heroines manage land, however, not to "usurp the part of men, but [to] work toward self-sufficiency or the maintenance of family property in their absence."[261] Many of Marchant's stories were set in Canada, including *Sisters of Silver Creek: A Story of Western Canada*. In this novel one of the sisters cultivates the land and attains self-sufficiency, becoming a manager of a jam business as well as a landholder. When she eventually marries, her command of her property and her work is curtailed, but Marchant had other heroines who remained autonomous and unmarried. In novels such as *The Loyalty of Hester Hope: A Story of British Columbia*, the protagonist continues to enjoy hard work on her own land, irrespective of her marriage. Marchant's portrayal of strong and capable heroines presented hard work outdoors, independence, and self-sufficiency as all desirable qualities. Even the artwork on the covers conveyed the message that women could successfully farm and raise livestock.

Other fiction writers of Empire helped women to imagine that they could have an imperial fresh start, take on new occupations, and lead invigorating lives in the colonies. In 1910 Mary Ward (who published under the name Mrs. Humphrey Ward) published her novel *Canadian Born*. The English heroine arrives in Canada as a widow and meets and marries a Canadian, after much consternation about whether she could bear to be transplanted to such an unfamiliar environment.[262] But she and her husband buy a farm (with her money), and she hopes to not only set up a cottage hospital but also establish a "training college for farm-students—girls and boys."[263]

Yet other writers conveyed more conservative messages about the potential for, or the wisdom of, British women farming and owning land in Canada. Scottish journalist and romantic fiction writer Annie S. Swan visited Western Canada several times and wrote a serialized novel, "Prairie Fires," set in Alberta. One of the main characters is a British woman horse rancher, Lady Florence Belfield (Lady Flo), an accomplished rider who excells at "men's talk,—all about wheat, and stock and the breeding of horses."[264] Hilary, the young, naïve, and inexperienced English wife of Robin Merrick, an English homesteader, feels threatened by Lady Flo as her husband admires the horsewoman's knowledge and abilities. Hilary thinks Lady Flo is "half a man," while her husband lectures her: "It's a pity you can't take a leaf from her book, Hilary. Her's [*sic*] is the only attitude possible for a woman in Canada if she's going to make a success of it."[265] Hilary runs away to the United States but the couple reunites before long on the homestead. Hilary should never have been jealous of Lady Flo, it turns out, as her husband far prefers his wife, weak and fragile as she is. Lady Flo is far too masculine for any British settler to consider as a wife. Hilary becomes "the mother of gallant sons and fair daughters ... helping her husband to lift high the standard of life in the new country."[266]

CANADIAN INTEREST IN (BRITISH/CANADIAN) WOMEN AS AGRICULTURALISTS

The topic of middle-class British women as potential farmers did not generate the same degree of interest in late nineteenth-century Canada as it did in Britain. There was no concern about a "surplus women" problem in Canada from which schemes to place women on the land in the colonies arose in Britain. Yet the work of journalist Mary Agnes Fitzgibbon indicates that there was interest in promoting the cause of British women farmers for the prairies.

Benjamin F. Austin, principal of Alma Ladies' College in St. Thomas, Ontario, was one of the few vocal supporters of farming for women. In a chapter entitled "Open Doors for the Women of To-Day" in the 1890 book *Woman: Her Character, Culture and Calling*, he argued that the cultivation of plants, fruits, and flowers was "really adapted to woman's strength and tastes, opening a pleasant, profitable and health-giving occupation to her in the country."[267] He believed that most of the labour required was not as hard as housework. Austin found the example of the United States most compelling, writing that there were "sixty thousand female farmers, or agricultural laborers, in the United States," and that "it is not thought improper for girls who work in the field to wear male attire. By doing so, they escape the cumbersome dress which would drag in the dirt and catch on weeds and briers."[268] Austin asked, "What would some of our small-waisted city belles, so tightly corseted, so unnaturally attired, so enfeebled by irrational modes of dress that a few minutes brisk walk, or the climbing of a flight of stairs throws them into palpitations, think of their sturdy sisters in the far West who plough, sow, pitch, cart and enjoy blessed exemptions from nervousness, heart disease and sick-headache?"[269] In Austin's view, light farm work was vastly preferable, better suited and "far more wholesome in effect on health and happiness than the miserable slave life many women lead in factories, shops and stores where long hours, promiscuous associations and poor pay are the general rule."

Canada's National Council of Women advocated agriculture as a suitable female vocation. Their 1900 publication *Women of Canada: Their Life and Work* included a chapter by Adelaide Hoodless (founder of the Women's Institutes), in which she placed agriculture second on a list of "women's industrial possibilities," after "household arts."[270] Through agriculture, Hoodless wrote, women could play a role in "national development," as it is "pre-eminently the great Canadian industry." The "unlimited possibilities" included dairying, raising poultry, bees, and fruit, and hot-house culture. She saw these as "distinctly feminine agricultural pursuits," in contrast to grain farming and stock raising.[271] Hoodless was an advocate of small holdings and colonies or settlements of women farmers: "The tendency in Canada has been towards the cultivation of large tracts of land which has necessitated a greater expenditure in money and labor than would be possible for the average woman. These conditions, together with their attendant social isolation, have not proved sufficiently attractive to induce women to consider agriculture as a special vocation … Co-operative principles, with regard to farm labor, marketing etc., must prevail where women adopt agriculture as a means of livelihood."[272]

Hoodless believed that agriculture for women would be a "factor in promoting the health and morals of a nation." She was opposed to factory and office work for women, as she believed that women's primary role was as wives and mothers. Hoodless believed women should be educated in practical skills and roles that would strengthen the family. She was a strong advocate of agricultural education for women and of training in domestic or household science, then an emerging discipline that would be known eventually as "home economics." Like some of the advocates of agriculture for women in Britain, she opposed female enfranchisement, arguing that women exercised their influence through their husbands and sons.[273]

In *Women of Canada*, the statistics compiled about women farmers were encouraging. According to the 1891 census there were "11,590 women farmers in Canada. This is an increase of 4,794 in ten years, according to the census of 1881. These women own and work their own farms; 252 of them are in Manitoba, where in 1881 there were only 71."[274]

At a 1909 Toronto meeting of the International Congress of Women, held under the auspices of the National Council of Women of Canada, a great deal of attention was paid to the topic of "Women in Agriculture." Women with capital were called upon to purchase and farm land. They were exhorted not to sell inherited land but to "keep your land; improve it; make it do your work and earn your money for you." They were urged to "study, think, act intelligently; use judgement, study soil conditions and quality … Then set to work to master every detail of the business undertaken."[275] The cooperative or colony farming option was gaining strength. Miss Yates of the Ontario Agricultural College at Guelph urged the "bright-faced women across the ocean" who were "longing to put their powers to the test" to consider farming on the cooperative plan in Canada. Yates stated that "the very energies that are so valued upon the hockey and the gold fields at home are exactly what are wanted here in the game of life that is being played on these farm lands."[276] She suggested that colonies of women could rent or purchase land and grow fruit and raise poultry.

Well into the twentieth century, there were few opportunities for women in Canada to study agriculture or horticulture.[277] The situation was dismal and in stark contrast to the various options in Britain. In Canada, instruction in dairying (at the Kingston Dairy School, the Agricultural College in Guelph, and the Government Dairy School in Winnipeg) was about all that was available to women except at the School of Horticulture at Wolfville, Nova Scotia, where in 1898 eighteen out of forty-nine students were women, and at the School of Agriculture at Truro, Nova Scotia, operated in connection with the Normal School, where all students took the same subjects, including biology, soils, dairying, gardening, and agricultural chemistry. In the agricultural colleges of Ontario, Manitoba, and Saskatchewan, "farmers' daughters" were steered toward courses in "domestic sciences."[278]

Support within Canada for sending educated gentlewomen from Britain to acquire land of their own on the prairies was occasionally expressed. In 1910 Marion Crerar of Hamilton, a regent of the Imperial Order of the Daughters of the Empire, wrote to the *Times* of London to endorse the scheme of settling educated women on imperial plots, although she clearly thought these should be very small.[279] Crerar was motivated by the desire to "draw our beloved countries together" and objected to the "wretched specimens," the "scourings from London streets" who were being sent to Canada. She asked, "Cannot England spare some of her well-bred and refined people to raise the tone of the whole country? Have you not an army of women of education who could be spared to build up this part of our Empire?" Crerar pointed to the great need of such women on the prairies. Here was the chance for "our 'Frontierswomen.'" She endorsed the cooperative plan, suggesting four ladies select a town with a clergyman and buy a little piece of land and a house. One could teach music and lead the choir, another could teach sewing, and one might keep poultry. Together they would be the leaven for the district, they would "be the props of the new and struggling parish, and the one gentle and refining influence on all the farming life around it." The added joy would be that all was done for "King and country." They would not be carrying swords into distant lands like their male counterparts, but would be bringing their refining influence.

THE CANADIAN PACIFIC RAILWAY'S PROMOTION OF THE WEST FOR WOMEN

It was in the interests of the Canadian Pacific Railway (CPR) to appeal to potential purchasers of their land in the West, including women. A series of pamphlets from the early twentieth century, aimed specifically at women, featured stories of women who were capable workers and efficient owners and managers of farms. They were cast as having made substantial fortunes and as supporting large families. The CPR wanted to entice homesteaders who might then be motivated to expand their holdings by purchasing railway lands. In order to compete with the U.S. West, where single women could homestead, the CPR needed to show that there were opportunities for women as well as men in Western Canada. Through its office in London, the CPR bombarded Britain and northern Europe with pamphlets, posters, and maps of Western Canada.[280] Their immigration offices were "seductive parlours designed to trap passing pedestrians" with posters of lush fields of grain and prosperous, happy settlers.[281] Travellers carried the "gospel of emigration" into the British countryside so that according to one historian, "no corner of Britain was left untouched; no station wall or hotel lobby was safe from one of the CPR's poster maps."[282] Travelling promoters gave lectures with lantern slides, and exhibits of posters, photographs, and soil samples were displayed in town halls, at agricultural fairs, and at mechanics' institutes. The CPR also had a horse-drawn exhibition van decked out with prairie products that travelled to small towns. In 1893 the van attracted an incredible 1.75 million visitors in 593 places.[283]

In 1903 the CPR published *Words from the Women of Western Canada*, which featured many women farming on their own.[284] In particular, the opportunities for widows to homestead were highlighted, and the pamphlet also advertised CPR railway lands that were for sale. The successes of women settlers from Britain were emphasized, although women of other ethnicities were mentioned.[285] Women from the "Old Country" included "A Wiltshire Woman," "A Scotchwoman's Success," and "A North of Ireland Woman's Words." There were no women from the United States in the 1903

Figure 10. Through its "Canada for Women" promotion, the Canadian Pacific Railway appealed to Englishwomen living "wasted lives" to emigrate. Allegedly quoting one such woman, the caption read, "Ten thousand Englishwomen could be ranged in a line and shot. No one would be sorry. Everyone would be glad. *There isn't any place for them.*" *Daily Mail*, 2 March 1910, 10.

pamphlet, but Mennonite, Doukhobor, and Romanian women were included, although briefly, and are clustered toward the end of the pamphlet.

Words from the Women of Western Canada cast women as capable owners and managers of farms who still retained their femininity and attended to domestic work as well. They reaped and ploughed, although generally only when the farm was short of male labour. Varied occupations were featured, including a bee farm and a dairy farm. Despite all of this, domestic skills were praised above all, and the pamphlet depicted any unattached women emigrants as destined for marriage. The concluding words were those of an "old timer" who had come to Manitoba in the 1870s.[286] Her message was that "as soon as these women immigrate they are snatched up by the hordes of well-to-do bachelors."

Widows were not the only women featured in the 1903 pamphlet, but they predominated. While the reasons for the deaths of the husbands were not made explicit, readers may have wondered why so many husbands died, often soon after arriving in Canada, leaving their widows to struggle on their own. Despite the rags-to-riches stories of successful, prosperous widows, the ubiquitous death of the husbands may have limited the appeal of emigrating to Canada. In a 1906 pamphlet called *Women's Work in Western Canada: A Sequel to "Words from the Women of Western Canada,"* there was much less attention given to the untimely death of husbands.[287] Perhaps this was because overall the pamphlet featured fewer examples of women homesteaders and placed more emphasis on the wisdom of purchasing CPR land. There was also less attention to women farming and/or owning their land, while the family unit working together was stressed.[288]

There were widows featured in the 1906 pamphlet, however, reflecting the fact that this was still the only way women could obtain homestead land. Maria Bird of Pipestone, Manitoba, formerly of Gloucestershire, ran a prosperous farm and also published stories of prairie life in journals such as *The Family Circle.*[289] Her husband had died shortly after she arrived in the West, and she buried him "on the lone plains which took the last dollar." But "she bravely took up the work of the farm, seven children depending upon her; how she stuck to the plow; stood by the grain stack and put 'Stow-on-the-Wold' vim and vigor into the work." She had found fortune, and so had her children. "How a Widow Won" told the story of Agnes Balfour of Lumsden, Saskatchewan. She had arrived from Ontario as a widow with eight children.[290] Her homestead was "one of the prize places of the west," and her children had all prospered; three daughters settled in the Lumsden area, two sons farmed the old homestead, two other sons were in the mercantile business in that town, and one son was a "leading lawyer" in Regina.

The pamphlet also featured women settlers of means. Under the heading "An Irish Lady's Winnings," Mrs. Westhead of Alix, Alberta, was presented as an example of an independent purchaser/investor in land despite being married.[291] She had bought land on a visit with her husband to Canada, and they then decided to emigrate.[292] Mrs. Westhead was shown as the more active partner in superintending their prairie estate.

The final pamphlet in the CPR series, *Home Life of Women in Western Canada* (1907), also focused on the work of farm wives in partnership with their husbands and on the prosperity of settler families from the "Old Country." It featured very few widows farming on their own. A major message was the dire need of domestic workers. Perhaps as the issue of women and homestead rights began to heat up, with the Canadian government steadfastly opposed, the CPR did not wish to appear to be as welcoming to women as farmers as it had been in earlier pamphlets.

The CPR advertised the West as a destination for "surplus" women of Britain through newspapers such as the *Daily Mail* where a 1910 advertisement, "Canada for Women," showed three women in a wheat field.[293] Right beneath were the words, allegedly from a woman in England who felt her own life to have been wasted: "Ten thousand Englishwomen could be ranged in line and shot. No one would be sorry. Everyone would be glad. *There isn't any place for them.*"

In 1913 the windows of the office of the CPR on Cockspur Street in Charing Cross, London were smashed by suffragettes as part of a campaign to punish businesses for not lobbying in support of votes for women.[294] The CPR boarded up their windows and posted a notice: "We are looking for settlers, not for suffragettes." The suffragette journal *Votes for Women* pointed out that "the Suffragettes *are* settlers."[295] But surprisingly, the CPR advertised extensively in the suffrage journals, including the *Suffragette* and *Woman's Leader and the Common Cause.* A 1913 CPR advertisement "Canada for Women" in those journals showed a young woman with a pail confronting a cow with the caption "Dairy Farming."[296] That same year the CPR placed an advertisement in the *Suffragette*: "A Welcome to Women in British Columbia."[297] The notice began, "In these days of women's independence, when girls set out to earn their own living, it

Figure 11. In 1913, the windows of the Charing Cross office of the Canadian Pacific Railway were smashed by suffragettes as part of a campaign to punish businesses that did not lobby in support of votes for women. The windows were boarded up and the CPR posted the notice, "We are looking for settlers, not suffragettes." Yet the company advertised in suffrage journals, clearly seeing potential settlers and even farmers in suffragettes. Getty Images, no. 3424540.

is perhaps not out of place to point out the opportunities for making a comfortable living out of Dairy Farming, Chicken Raising and Flower Gardening—branches of agriculture in which women are particularly successful." Young women "fond of outdoor life" were urged to club together and run small farms in the Windermere district of British Columbia.

By 1913, as indicated by the talks by Skykes and Binnie-Clark described at the outset of this chapter, there was a great deal of optimism in the air both in Canada and the mother country about the potential for British women to farm land of their own on the prairies. But in all of the ink devoted to this cause—the lectures, organizations, and intelligence-gathering trips—there appears to have been precious little knowledge of or contact with the women who were attempting to homestead or otherwise farm the prairies. Legal obstacles and disadvantages were seldom referred to by the proponents of farms for British women. Ideas about small holdings and the "lighter branches" of agriculture and colonies of women farmers clubbing together could not simply be transplanted to prairie Canada because of environmental and climatic factors, because of the nature of the land survey system, and because markets were small and scattered. Authorities wanted women immigrants, other than those who arrived as members of families, to work as domestic servants and certainly not in the fields (at least not visibly). And while attitudes about educated gentlewomen as potential farmers might have been changing somewhat in Britain at this time, opposition persisted. When women worked on the land there during the First World War (to be discussed in Chapter 7), detractors were many.

Similar objections to women farmers prevailed in Western Canada, well into the twentieth century. On the prairies Indigenous women and some recent immigrant women were condemned as the "beasts of burden" or drudges of their communities. British women were not to stoop to this level; they were to be models of domesticity and gentility and not sweat in the fields. In spite of these admonitions, women—British and of many other ethnicities—laboured in the fields, and some established homesteads and farms of their own, as the next chapter describes.

CHAPTER THREE

WIDOWS AND OTHER IMMIGRANT WOMEN HOMESTEADERS

STRUGGLES AND STRATEGIES

> Mrs. Bachelor [*sic*], a lady farmer … has the finest and earliest fields of spring wheat that I have seen this year. This lady is a widow, but conducts one of the best managed farms I have seen in the West. The grain fields are clean. The plowing is well done, and all the buildings are comfortable and remarkably well kept.[1]
>
> F.W. Hodson, editor of the *Farmers' Advocate*, 1909

F.W. Hodson was describing the fine grain fields of Eliza Ann Batchelor near North Battleford, Saskatchewan. Originally from England, Eliza Ann and her husband, Thomas, first emigrated to Japan, where he was a tobacconist.[2] Their three children were born in Japan. In 1905 they left Japan to homestead in Saskatchewan, and Thomas (aged sixty-four) died a few months later after being thrown from his horse. The children were aged nine, six, and four. Eliza Ann, then forty-nine, completed the homestead duties, earned her patent to the land, and clearly became an accomplished farmer.[3] From 1876 virtually the only way for a woman to obtain a homestead of her own on the prairies was to be or become a widow. As journalist Lillian Beynon Thomas (quoted in Chapter 1) wrote, "There are no homesteads for women in Western Canada unless such women care to qualify by killing off any inconvenient husbands they happen to own."[4]

This chapter is about women who homesteaded land in prairie Canada. While the chapter concentrates on British women, homesteaders of other ethnicities are included, as it is important to recognize that women from many nations were interested in "free" land in Canada.[5] To understand the full range of obstacles they faced and the strategies they adopted, it is necessary to cast a wide net that includes migrant widowed women homesteaders of diverse ancestries along with women from Ontario, Quebec, and other provinces of Canada.

The "imperial plots" thread of this book is not always obvious in this chapter. Most of these women left few records beyond what is available in homestead files and local histories. The existing sources do not indicate whether they were influenced by or associated with the organizations in the mother country advocating farming for British women on the prairies, which focused on single, never-married "surplus women," not widows with children. Organizations such as the Colonial Intelligence League were concerned with educated single "gentlewomen," and the widowed homesteaders of prairie Canada were not necessarily from that class. There are no indications that any of these widows attended the colonial training schools intended to equip the woman settler with the skills she would need; they would not have had the time or income for such training. It is likely that the homesteading widows were motivated more by their personal and family economic situations and needs than by the desire to contribute to the "spade-work of empire."

Chapter 1 ended with the homestead right being removed for most categories of women. As of 1876, a woman (other than an "Indian" under the Indian Act) was eligible to homestead only if she could establish that she was a "sole" head of a family. This was interpreted to mean widows with minor children. A considerable number of women, mainly widows, managed to homestead and prove up on their land in Western Canada, but they faced many roadblocks and obstacles. A complicated welter of Department of the Interior and Department of Justice "rulings" and "opinions"—never debated in Parliament but decided by bureaucrats—governed which women could homestead, and individual cases were carefully scrutinized by officials in Ottawa with the overall goal of severely restricting the numbers of eligible women. Widowed women homesteaders enjoyed privileges that were denied to First Nations people, yet they did not have the same virtually unfettered access to land extended to male migrants. They were under intense scrutiny by the formidable bureaucracy of the Department of the Interior, whose employees were concerned about the most personal details of their lives and were convinced that they would readily resort to devious methods to obtain land. Women fought this bureaucracy and made remarkable efforts to acquire and retain homestead land. Women who were not widows (married, single, divorced, or separated) could obtain 320 acres of homestead land if they could afford to purchase South African scrip, and many did, but they still had to perform all of the homestead duties and were subject to the surveillance of the bureaucracy. Women could also cross the border and settle in the American West, where single women could homestead and where the bureaucracy was much more lenient in permitting divorced, separated, or unmarried mothers to file on land.

A WIDOWED LAND

A ruling that was never clearly spelled out in the Dominion lands legislation, but was made policy, was that to be a sole head of a family a woman had to have a child or children under the age of eighteen. Nor did the Dominion lands legislation ever specify that an eligible woman must be a widow, but in publications of the Lands Branch it was made clear that this was the only category of woman eligible. For example, the 1903 Dominion Lands Branch pamphlet *Homestead Regulations of North-Western Canada* stated that "a woman who is a widow, having minor children dependent upon her, is entitled to a homestead entry."[6] In a 1912 publication of the Grand Trunk Pacific Railway, readers were informed that these children had to be the widow's own: "A widow having minor children of her own dependent upon her for support is permitted to make homestead entry as a sole head of a family."[7]

Widows with their children soon started to arrive in the West to claim homesteads. Like the early male homesteaders in the West, the majority were from the British Isles or Ontario, and were British-Ontarian.[8] In the spring of 1878, Elizabeth McGavin (1838–1904) arrived with her ten children and filed on a homestead at Prairie Grove, Manitoba.[9] She and her husband, James McGavin, were from Scotland and had first immigrated to Paisley, Bruce County, Ontario. It was there that James died in 1877 of food poisoning following a church picnic, leaving Elizabeth with three daughters and seven sons. Elizabeth had family members homesteading in Manitoba, and they headed there, mainly by lakes and rivers, until they landed at the old Lombard wharf in Winnipeg. The family was very poor and lived initially on deer, rabbits, prairie chickens, ducks, and fish. But the children received good educations, and three became physicians, including daughter Jessie Margaret McGavin, who in 1895 graduated in medicine from a Chicago university.

Widow Ann McGregor, from Edinburgh, arrived in Manitoba in the mid-1870s with five sons while three daughters remained in Scotland.[10] She filed on a homestead near Keyes, and three of her sons also homesteaded. From this cluster grew what was known as the McGregor settlement, later renamed Mekiwin, Cree for "gift." Ann McGregor was a midwife in that district and ran the post office out of her home.

Hannah Stott came to Manitoba from England in 1883 with her children. Her husband had been lost at sea in 1877. Through homesteading and purchasing she acquired extensive tracts of land near Brandon, first 320 acres that she sold in 1890, and then another farm that she personally cultivated and improved until her death in 1907.[11]

One of the early homesteaders in the Moose Jaw district of Saskatchewan was Grace Keay, a widow from Edinburgh who settled in the spring of 1885 with her two daughters (aged eleven and eight) and her son (fourteen).[12] It was reported in 1896 that she "works quite a farm," and by 1899 she and her son had together acquired 960 acres.

Homesteading widows were often referred to as "grandma" in their districts. "Grandma" Eleanor Bell Cairns was forty-one when she and her five children from Morpeth, Northumberland, arrived in Manitoba in 1882, together with her father, John Bell, aged seventy-seven.[13] Eleanor entered on a homestead, as did her father. To prove up they were supposed to have separate dwellings, but Eleanor wrote for and received permission to live in one home. The family had some very lean years but persisted, and Eleanor's home became an important community centre, where church services began in 1884. She had the first organ in the district, and dances and musical evenings were held at her home as well. She died at the age of eighty-seven in 1928.

Isabella Beveridge, born on a ship on the Atlantic Ocean as her parents sailed from Scotland to Canada, married Thomas Burns in Ontario in 1865.

Figure 12. Englishwoman Agnes Bedingfeld was the widow of a lieutenant in the Madras Infantry. She homesteaded at Pekisko, Alberta, as did her son Frank, and together they established a prosperous ranch, which they sold in 1919 to Edward, Prince of Wales. Mrs. Bedingfeld was regarded as "one of the most competent agriculturalists and livestock breeders in Alberta." Glenbow Archives, NA-2467-12.

They and their seven children moved to Washington State in 1889, where Thomas died.[14] In 1893 Isabella Burns filed on a homestead in the ranch land of the Pincher Creek district of Alberta and successfully proved up.

Englishwoman Agnes Katherine Bedingfeld (born 1845) was the widow of a lieutenant in the Madras Infantry. The daughter of Robert Cobb, a Norfolk rector, she married Francis William Bedingfeld in 1862 when she was seventeen.[15] He was from the landed gentry, his family occupying Ditchingham Hall, also in Norfolk. Their son Francis, known as Frank, was born in 1866 in Suffolk. After Lt. Bedingfeld died in 1869, leaving Agnes a widow at a young age, she and Frank came to Pekisko, Alberta, in 1883. The next year she filed on a homestead.[16] In her application for patent (acquired in 1899), Agnes stated that she had lived in a tent on her land for a portion of 1883 and built her house in 1884. It was necessary for her to file as soon as she could, as Frank was seventeen when they came to Canada, and if she waited until he was eighteen she would not have been eligible. Mrs. Bedingfeld also worked as a housekeeper for Fred Stimson, of the Bar U Ranch. Frank also homesteaded, and his and his mother's log cabins were built together but on each side of the line dividing their quarter sections.[17] Agnes took out a second homestead adjoining her first and received her patent to this land in 1906.[18] The Bedingfelds eventually owned 1,400 acres and controlled another 4,000 acres through leases.[19] They concentrated on raising Clydesdale horses but also had cattle. Agnes Bedingfeld was regarded as "one of the most competent agriculturalists and livestock breeders in Alberta."[20] She retired to Hertfordshire and she and Frank sold their ranch in 1919, when it was purchased by Edward, Prince of Wales, becoming the EP Ranch.

Christina Anne (Bethune) Ritchie homesteaded in the Blackie region of Alberta, filing on her land in 1904.[21] She was born in Nairn, Scotland, and in 1880 emigrated with her family to the Falkland Islands, where she married Scotsman John T.M. Ritchie. She and her husband, along with their three children, settled in Calgary in 1898. John Ritchie died in 1901, leaving Christina at age thirty-three with thirteen-year-old daughter Jennie, ten-year-old son John, and daughter Dora, sixteen months. Christina Ritchie first had to ask for an extension of six months after filing on her land, as she did not have the resources to settle on her homestead. In a statutory declaration of November 1901, she stated that she had "been waiting for the means to be able to go to said land with my cattle, & as I am a widow with children dependent on me find far more difficulty in getting same than a man would do."[22] According to the entry in the local history, Ritchie arrived at her new home in 1905 with "15 cents in cash, a sack of flour, a pound of tea and 20 pounds of sugar; pretty meagre rations for a new beginning." She eventually had cattle and milk cows, but also worked off the farm. Cattle baron Patrick Burns had a beef camp close to her homestead, and Ritchie took in the laundry, baked, and mended for the cowboys. In 1907 newly arrived neighbours from England set up a training farm for students who were "mostly the rich mens [*sic*] sons and remittance men from England."[23] There were over thirty students, and Ritchie cooked and kept house for them. The oldest daughter, Jennie, also worked off the farm doing general housework. Daughter Dora wrote in the local history book that her mother "kept her homestead free of mortgage—the only piece of land that I know of that didn't become mortgaged at one time or another. Many men lost their land owing to having to mortgage it." In 1908 Ritchie received her patent to her land; in her application she described herself as a "rancher."

Sarah Jane Hill (née Castle), from Sheffield, England, was a widow and mother of eight who homesteaded at Melfort, Saskatchewan (Pleasantdale district), arriving in 1906 with five of her children.[24] She was a nurse and midwife in her district working, with African-Canadian physician Dr. Alfred Schmitz Shadd. With the help of her sons, she cleared and broke bush land and hauled her grain by team and wagon. In the spring of 1920, Hill moved to a son's homestead, where "they worked and cleared the land and farmed together." She was remembered as "one of Pleasantdale's first and great pioneers. She loved the land, people and her family."[25]

Widow Mary Elizabeth Birss arrived in Canada in 1905 from Aberdeen, Scotland, filing on land in the Stonehenge district of southwest Saskatchewan in 1908.[26] Her husband James had died of a stroke in 1894, leaving her to raise their eight children. Three of her sons settled on the prairies, and she later followed them. When she filed on her land she was fifty-two years old, and her youngest child was twelve. She proved up on both her homestead and a pre-emption and with four sons filing on land nearby, they established a considerable Birss empire. Mary Elizabeth died on her homestead in 1937, in the small two-storey home that was built in 1908 and occupied by the Birss family until 1967.

In 1906 widow Frances Powell and her family of four daughters and one son arrived in Lethbridge from Wales. She filed on a homestead in the Coyote Flats district of Alberta.[27] Her brother homesteaded nearby but left for Australia soon after proving up. Frances persisted, however, and became "well known throughout the district as 'Aunt Fanny.' She was a nurse and midwife and "regardless of the weather or of how busy, she was always on hand to take charge if needed."

Eliza (Landymore) Garwood, born in Walsham-le-Willows, England, proved up on a homestead in the Inverlea district near Crossfield, Alberta, in 1907.[28] A widow, she and her two children first settled in Calgary in 1902, then she filed on land near her homesteading brother. Garwood was a nurse in the Crossfield, Carstairs, and Madden districts. She remained on her homestead until her death in 1938.

Catherine Corbet Sommerville, from Glasgow, Scotland, her daughter Margaret and sons John, Hugh, Robert, George, and James settled in the Ghost Pine district of Alberta in 1908.[29] Catherine proved up on a homestead and a pre-emption, becoming the owner of 320 acres, and her sons filed on adjoining land, so the family acquired an extensive tract. According to the local history, the whole family "took a prominent part in the social life of the Ghost Pine community for years."[30] (In the summer of 2014, about 160 family members, all descendants of the Catherine Corbet Sommerville family, gathered at the Sommerville farm, which had been recognized with the Alberta Century Farm and Ranch Award.[31])

In 1912, following the death of her husband and a two-year-old daughter that same year, "Grandma" Barbara Bradshaw, a widow and mother of (originally) eight from Ayrshire, Scotland, travelled to Parkbeg, Saskatchewan, where a son was homesteading.[32] A year earlier another son who had also homesteaded at Parkbeg had been killed in a railway accident. Bradshaw filed on the land of her deceased son and applied for her patent in 1917, swearing that she was "the head of a family having at the time of my son's death 3 minor children to take care of, and at the present time I have one, namely Grace, who will be 15 years in October this year." In her district she was remembered for her love of Robbie Burns and for her "famous Scotch scones."

Entries in the local histories on homesteading widows are often brief. We learn little about "Grandma Holman" except that she was an early Manitoba homesteader and was married several times, as she was described as "nee Harrison—nee Hornsby, nee Ingleby." Ingleby was likely her maiden name, since she was allegedly "a granddaughter of Lord and Lady Ingleby of England. She delivered the babies that were born to other homesteaders' wives."[33] Cathy Jamieson was a Scottish widow who filed on 160 acres in 1896 and later bought another quarter section near Lacombe, Alberta. A lake on her land is named after her.[34] (Given that the lake was also described as a slough, her land was not likely the best.) Jessie Kinnaird, from Alloa, Scotland, "in an effort to keep her family together," followed her three sons to Saskatchewan. In 1912 she filed on a homestead northeast of Gull Lake, bringing her daughter Margaret with her.[35] In the same district was widow Mary Attridge from Tyronne, Ireland, who had settled in Ontario where her husband died in 1905.[36] She was a mother of ten, and her two youngest children were living with her when she filed on a homestead in 1910. Three older sons had homesteads nearby. A "tiny lady, only five feet tall with red hair, [Attridge] was a hard worker. She milked cows, canned fruit … and acted as midwife for many miles around … She occupied her 'leisure time' braiding rugs, making quilts and reading tea cups."

Flora S. Law, known as "Granny Law" (whose full name is not even provided in the local history biography), was a widow from Scotland with seven children. She homesteaded in 1906 in the Swift Current region of Saskatchewan near two of her sons who were already established there.[37] Her home was a stopping place for the North-West Mounted Police and other travellers because it was on the road to Swift Current. Church services were also held at her house. She died in 1917, and her body was taken back to Scotland for burial. Isabel H. Brookes, from England, homesteaded near Moose Jaw starting in 1911, along with her son Harry, and received her patent in 1914.[38] "Grandma" Catherine Gordon, from Scotland, first emigrated with her husband to New Brunswick, where he and six of their children died of tuberculosis.[39] In 1906, at age sixty, she and two of her sons arrived in Saskatchewan, and she entered the next year on a homestead north of Shaunavon, proving up in 1914. Two of her grandchildren were dependent on her, as their parents had died of tuberculosis. Marguerite Douglas, a widow with one child, came from England to Saskatchewan in 1908.[40] She worked as a housekeeper in Moose Jaw while she homesteaded, and by the time she received her patent in 1911 she was married to a neighbour. Martha Lucas, mother of three from Birmingham, filed on land near Lloydminster, Saskatchewan, in 1904 and proved up by 1907. Her husband, a draper, had died of pneumonia.[41]

Sarah Cleveley of Bangor, Wales, was a widow with eight children when she sailed to Canada in 1912, with Edmonton as their destination.[42] In 1914 she filed on land at Roselea, next to a quarter section homesteaded by a son. Sarah married neighbour George McCoy in 1918, but the next year she died in the flu epidemic.

Homestead files leave traces of the widowed women who were not recalled in local histories. Olivia Thompson, from Dublin, Ireland, was seventy when in 1909 she filed on a homestead at Elm Springs, Saskatchewan.[43] She did not strictly qualify, as the youngest of her four children was twenty-two. She had, however, squatted on the land for about seventeen years at the time of her homestead entry, made as soon as the land was surveyed. When she applied for her patent in 1912, she argued that she deserved title to her land as she had broken fifty acres, even though she lived on the adjoining quarter section with her son. She wrote on her statutory declaration of 1912 that "I have lived with my son as I could not live alone & think after being the first white woman in the south country I should be entitled to me deed after living here over 21 years & having done all the improvements."[44] There may have been debate in the land office about Thompson's entitlement, as she did not receive her patent until 1917, when she was seventy-nine years old.

NUMBERS AND DIVERSITY OF WOMEN HOMESTEADERS

While the widows depicted above were British women, the origins of women homesteaders were more diverse. This diversity is important to understanding the narrowness and elitism of the campaign that was launched for homesteads for women of "British birth," to be discussed in Chapter 6. In southwestern Manitoba, however, most of the women homesteaders were British or British-Ontarian. Historian Kathryn McPherson found that between 1872 and 1900 at least 283 women possessed title to 418 quarter sections.[45] Most of this land was purchased, but McPherson found ninety-two women homesteaders, and these were British citizens "by birth" (which would have included those born in Canada). Preliminary results of a database of Alberta homesteaders indicate that up until 1911 there were 1,587 women who had filed in their own names in what became that province.[46] Information on place of birth is available for only 25 percent of these Alberta women homesteaders. Of this 25 percent, there were 126 from the U.S., 128 from Canada, and 75 from the British Isles. (The rest were from Scandinavia, Austria/Hungary, Germany, and Russia). It is notable that women proved up with a greater success than did men. While patent success for male homesteaders was 69 percent, for women it was 85.4 percent.

Census data demonstrate increasing number of women farmers, but their numbers were tiny compared to their male counterparts. In Manitoba in 1881 there were 71 female farmers, and in the Territories, 9. The 71 in Manitoba represented 0.65 percent of the total number of farmers. By 1891 there were 252 women farmers in Manitoba, who were 1.2 percent of all farmers, and in the Territories 102, comprising 1.3 percent. By 1911 there were 3,575 female farmers, 1.4 percent of all farmers, while male farmers totalled 254,561. Also in 1911 there were 83 female ranchers or stock raisers (3,838 male), or 2.16 percent of the total. The 1911 census recorded 52 women gardeners (7.54 percent). In the census of 1921 there were 3,930 female farmers, comprising 1.57 percent. That year there were 65 women ranchers (6.28 percent). By 1931 there was a considerable increase in the numbers of female farmers, with 6,786 female farmers (2.57 percent) and 263,642 male farmers (see Table 2).

My study of the women homesteaders of the Wood Mountain district of Saskatchewan found 114 women who filed in their own names as solo homesteaders. Of these, 57 were widows and 45 of them successfully proved up, receiving patent to their land. There were 34 other solo women who filed on land in their own name, whose marital status is uncertain, and of these 21 proved up. There were 23 women—married, single, widowed, and of unknown marital status—who homesteaded and received patent to their land through South African scrip (to be discussed later in this chapter). There were other ways that women of Wood Mountain acquired land. For instance, if a wife on a homestead was deserted by her husband for a period of five years, and if this desertion was verified by the homestead inspector, his entry could be cancelled and she could make entry.

Most of the widows and other women homesteaders of Wood Mountain filed in the years 1908–11, and most received their patents in 1914. There were three who long predated this land rush, who had been squatters before the land was surveyed. Of the widows who proved up, ten also successfully proved up on an adjoining quarter section acquired as a preemption. Of those whose place of birth is known, only eleven were from the British Isles. Twenty-six were from Canada, the majority from Ontario, and about half that number from Quebec. At a close second were twenty-three women from the United States, followed by England with nine, Romania and Austria six each, Hungary five, and France four. There were two from each of Norway, Sweden, and Germany, and one from each of Ireland and Scotland. Thirteen of these women homesteaders of

		Farmers			Ranchers/Stock Raisers			Gardeners		
		M	F	%	M	F	%	M	F	%
1881	Manitoba	10 818	71	0.65%	N/A	N/A	N/A	36 (No Sex Listed)		
	Territories	822	9	1.08%	N/A	N/A	N/A	2 (No Sex Listed)		
1885 (Territories Only)	Saskatchewan	735	14	1.9%	0 (No sex listed)			1 (No Sex Listed)		
	Alberta	1214	1	0.08%	158 (No Sex Listed)			3 (No Sex Listed)		
1891	Manitoba	20 323	252	1.2%	103	0	0%	59	1	1.6%
	Territories	7 696	102	1.3%	682	21	2.9%	21	0	0%
1911	Saskatchewan	119 934	1587	1.3%	1077	12	1.1%	135	2	1.4%
	Manitoba	61 292	826	1.4%	498	29	5.5%	29	32	52%
	Alberta	69 760	1162	1.6%	2180	42	1.8%	473	18	3.6%
1921	Saskatchewan	114 265	1197	1.04%	713	17	2.3%	130	9	6.4%
	Manitoba	51 003	1151	2.2%	256	14	5.2%	473	8	1.7%
	Alberta	79 115	1582	1.9%	1215	34	2.7%	267	8	2.9%
1931*	Saskatchewan	119 799	2952	2.4%				6 (No Sex Listed)		
	Manitoba	44 371	1493	3.1%				17 (No Sex Listed)		
	Alberta	89 686	2341	2.5%				405	7	1.6%

- N/A indicates nothing listed under that occupation that year
- 1931* Lists Farmers and Ranchers under the same category
- Percentage (%) is representative of female percent, not male, and is calculated by combining total numbers and dividing female number to total number.

Table 2. Numbers of male and female agriculturalists in the Censuses of Canada, with percentages of female agriculturalists.
Source: Canada, Dominion Bureau of Statistics. For 1881, Table 14, 319–20; for 1885, Table 11, 48–50; for 1891, Table 12, 145–146 and 181; for 1911, Table 5, 52–3, 96–7, 228–9; for 1921, Table 4, 242–3, 270–1, 292–3; for 1931, Table 11, 346–7, 358.

Wood Mountain signed with X. Those who signed with an X were mainly from Hungary, Romania, and Austria, although one women of Canadian birth in the Wood Mountain district also signed with an X.

Some homesteading widows in Western Canada had no knowledge of English. Marie Goueffic, from Brittany, France, immigrated to Saskatchewan in 1906 with her four sons, all under the age of twelve.[47] Her husband had died of yellow fever in French Indo-China. They spoke no English. A sister, however, had come to Canada two years earlier and was living at Carlton, Saskatchewan. The Goueffics lived in a crude and cold shack with furniture consisting of a wagon box filled with straw, where they all slept. Marie Goueffic delivered their grain to the closest elevator at Duck Lake, a trip that took three days. The family eventually could afford a "ready-made" house from the Eaton's catalogue, and by the First World War they had the necessary machinery, and an automobile. One of the sons served overseas. A daughter-in-law wrote that Marie, who died in 1926, "did not die of old age. She died from being worn out from all the hard work and hardship she had gone through."[48]

In his study of the Peace River Country of Alberta prior to 1915, historian David Leonard found fifty-eight women who applied for homesteads, and fifty-four others who filed on land "as a free grant or with some form of scrip." Widowed homesteader Katherine Sampson was originally from South Carolina, and she proved up on land in the Grande Prairie district in 1919, becoming the first African-American owner in the Peace River country.[49]

There were also Métis women homesteaders. Marie Rose Smith, originally from Manitoba, ranched at Pincher Creek, Alberta, until the death of her husband. Smith filed on a homestead in the Lethbridge district in 1915, earning her patent in 1923.[50] Julie Rowand (née McGillis) received a patent to her Deville, Alberta, homestead in 1915 when she was sixty-six years old and a widow with no children living with her. She signed her name with an X. Rowland was one of the early settlers in the district and had been a squatter on her land before it was surveyed.[51]

Studies of homesteading on the prairies have demonstrated that the process required income, particularly in the start-up years.[52] As the short profiles of the homesteading widows at the start of this chapter suggest, widowed homesteaders often earned outside income, sometimes significant, sometimes small. Several of those already mentioned were midwives and nurses. Agnes Balfour, who entered on her homestead near Lumsden, Saskatchewan, in 1883 "quickly developed a reputation as a practical nurse and midwife. There was no doctor in the area until 1898, so Agnes tended the sick and delivered the babies for miles around. She was called out at any time of the day or night and never turned down a request for her assistance."[53] Some women homesteaders laundered and baked for neighbouring bachelors, or worked as cooks and housekeepers. Alberta homesteader Florence Lavelle worked as a farm labourer for a neighbour.[54]

Margaret de Tro, homesteader near Hardisty, Alberta, and widow with three sons likely had the most unusual job.[55] When she first began to advertise in Edmonton in 1905 she was "Dr. de Tro: The Lady Healer" but by 1907 had become "Madame de Tro."[56] She was a "magnetic healer," and she established a "Turkish Bath with Magnetic Massage" business that she also called a "sanatorium." According to her advertisement, she could treat "any and all kind of diseases," and she defied "any one to bring anything to my office that I cannot relieve and cure if my advice is strictly complied with." She also offered bathing facilities to the public, including Turkish and vapour baths. All Edmontonians could "afford to be clean and fragrant" if they bathed at her sanatorium, and she asked them to "come and try one: makes old young and cures what ails you."[57] As bathing days were Tuesdays, Thursdays, and Saturdays, it is difficult to determine how much time she spent on her land. She received her patent to her land in 1909 but died in 1913, aged fifty-eight, on her "ranch." She had gone out shooting and did not return. Her friends found her unconscious, lying over her gun, and it was assumed she had been stricken with apoplexy. She was taken to hospital but never recovered.[58] Sadly, the Lady Healer homesteader was unable to heal herself.

HURDLES AND TRIBULATIONS

The experiences of Marion Ferguson Frazer (Pearce) demonstrate some of the obstructions and handicaps the woman homesteader faced.[59] Frazer was from Largs in Ayreshire, Scotland, and she was a widow, nurse, and mother of two young sons in 1905 when she left for North America with her sons and brother, settling first in Virginia on a plantation. A year later the family moved north to Ontario, where Frazer worked as a nurse, and in 1909 she left her sons in the care of her brother to take a job nursing in Regina and explore the opportunities the West had to offer. A year later they joined her there, and in the spring of 1911 they loaded up a wagon and all set out for her homestead about 240 kilometres away at Wood

Dr. M. de Tro

THE LADY HEALER

has now opened a Bath Parlor at her Health Sanitarium on Jasper avenue, second door beyond Kinistino street going east, where all kinds of baths will be given from a plain tub bath to the finest perfumed vapor bath. She kindly solicits the patronage of the public and her prices will be so reasonable that all can afford to be clean and fragrant; the first bath awarded to each patron at half price

Bathing days Tuesdays, Thursdays and Saturdays; at other times, appointment, until further notice.

Yours for Health,

HEALER.

Figure 13. Most homesteaders, whether male or female, had to earn money to help establish their farms and for basic survival in the start-up years. Alberta homesteader Margaret de Tro was a "magnetic healer" in Edmonton from 1906 to 1913 when she was not on her land near Hardisty. She earned her patent to her land in 1909 and died there in 1913. *Edmonton Bulletin*, 29 December 1905, 4.

AUCTION SALE

Of Farm Property Near Hardisty, Alta.

Madame M. De Tro Estate

THURSDAY, MARCH 16th,

A.D. 1916 AT 1:30 O'CLOCK AFTERNOON
Within the Office of
KING EDWARD HOTEL, HARDISTY

The folowing lands will be offered for Sale by Public Auction subject to the reservations and conditions in the grant from the Crown and in the existing Certificate of Title, viz:—

1 N.E. Quarter of Section twenty-two (22) in township Forty-three (43) in range 9 W. 4th Meridian, containing 160 acres more or less.
2 S. ½ of N.W. Quarter of Section twenty-two (22), in township forty-three (43) in range 9 W. 4th Meridian, containing 80 acres more or less.
3 N.W. Quarter of Section sixteen (16), in township forty-three (43) in range 9 W. 4th Meridian, containing 161 acres more or less.
4 N.E. Quarter of Section seventeen (17) in township forty-three (43) in range 9 W. 4th Meridian, containing 161 acres more or less.

The above described lands will be sold each subject to a Reserve Bid. The terms of payment will be one-third (1-3) cash and the balance will be payable in three equal instalments in one, two and three years respectively after the day of the sale, with interest at eight (8%) per annum, the Purchaser to pay any taxes which may be payable under the Unearned Increment Tax Act.

The Purchaser will be required to make a payment of ten (10%) per cent. of the cash payment on the day of the Sale and the balance of the cash payment will be payable to NATIONAL TRUST COMPANY, LTD., at EDMONTON, within 14 days thereafter.

The N.E. ¼ of 22 and the S. ½ of N.W. ¼ of 22-43-9 W 4th Mer., are slightly rolling with good soil and about 100 tons of hay can be cut each year.

The N.W. ¼ of 16 and the N.E. ¼ of 17-43-9 W. 4th Meridian are all fenced, with excellent soil and about 127 acres under cultivation in the year 1915. Buildings not valuable.

For further particulars apply to

National Trust Company, Limited.

Edmonton, Alta., Administrators of Estate of M. de Tro

V. B. ROBBINS, Hardisty, Auctioneer.

ANDREW MYLES, Estates Manager.

Figure 14. The auction sale of the estate of Madam M. de Tro of Hardisty, Alberta, in March 1916 indicates that she had acquired about 562 acres of land. *Edmonton Bulletin*, 1 March 1916, 9.

Mountain. Frazer was forty-seven, her sons were eight and eleven, and her brother was sixty.[60] They were joined by Willie, a cousin from Scotland. None of them had any farming experience, and they were heading toward one of the more desolate and dry regions of the West. Frazer's brother had been a "drayman on a big steam ship," while Willie had been a cook on a sailing vessel.[61]

Within a few months of her arrival, Frazer became Mrs. Pearce, marrying the man from whom she bought her team of oxen. He had filed on a homestead on the same section and the new Mrs. Pearce wrote to the Dominion Lands Office in December 1911 to ask if they could build one house and live together on her land. She added that "we intend making this our home it is not a case of speculation."[62] But these were the cases that land agents were wary of. Had they colluded to obtain two homesteads? Permission was denied. The newly married couple had to each have a residence on their separate homesteads to prove up.[63]

Marriage did not bring an easier life. Marion (Frazer) Pearce continued to nurse and attempted to farm on her very poor land. Her crops often failed. Her husband left her in 1917, abandoning his homestead without proving up, and she asked permission for her son to file on his land. The homestead inspector was sent to report on whether Mrs. Pearce was truly deserted, and he learned through "careful enquiries" that Mr. Pearce was "afraid they [her sons] would shoot him" and had left that part of the country.[64] Eventually her son James was permitted to enter on the land deserted by his stepfather. As Marion Ferguson Pearce, she proved up on her land in 1919. But her homestead file documents the difficult circumstances of farming on what was at best range land, long after she got patent to her land. She was in debt for taxes and seed grain well into the 1920s. The whole region suffered from severe drought from 1918 to 1922; many provincial and federal officials argued that southern Saskatchewan should never have been homesteaded.[65]

Discrimination against women homesteaders such as Marion Frazer (she reverted to that last name in 1924) continued. Once their children grew up, as children tend to do, women homesteaders were not eligible for land offers made to other settlers. In 1928 the outlook brightened for settlers of the Wood Mountain district, as an amendment was passed granting all those who had obtained their patent before 1925 the right to make a second homestead entry on the usual homesteading terms. This was in part a recognition of the very poor land and difficult circumstances everyone in that district experienced. But this opportunity was denied to Marion Frazer. Since her sons were no longer minors, she did not qualify for a second homestead. She was informed by the Acting Commissioner of Dominion Lands: "You obtained homestead entry [in 1911] on the ground that you were a widow with two minor children, aged eight and eleven years, dependent upon you for support. Under the regulations the privilege of a first or second homestead is only extended to a woman who is a widow with minor children dependent upon her. It would appear that you have no minor children now dependent upon you for support and I regret to inform you that you are not entitled to another homestead."[66]

Mary Ann McNab, from Scotland, who settled in 1882 in the Moose Mountain district of Saskatchewan, also struggled to obtain the right to a pre-emption of an additional 160 acres. Her husband Alexander had died a year after they arrived in Saskatchewan, leaving her with two of their children; seven of her other children had also died.[67] McNab continued to live on and prove up on the homestead and was granted patent to that land in 1887, but she wanted to pre-empt another quarter section. In an October 1890 statutory declaration, Mary Ann McNab, then forty-six, wrote that she "intended to take possession of this land last year, but I had both my arms broken and was not able to, I have paid a neighbour to draw the material for a house on the land, and I will take possession shortly. I am most desirous of keeping the land. I have had a very hard time providing for myself and two children."[68]

John Geddes, the Presbyterian minister at Carlyle, Saskatchewan, wrote to the secretary of the Department of the Interior in October 1890, explaining the circumstances of Mary Ann McNab and asking that she be granted the pre-emption.[69] Geddes reminded the government that McNab had lost her husband and seven of her children; accordingly, he asked that the government "consider the number of times she has stood on the brink of the grave." She was a "woman of indomitable courage … obliged to do many things that fall, no doubt, within the province of a man." Geddes further described her as "a talented woman, considering that she got only a common school education in Scotland." In particular, he admired her ability (which would have been rare among settlers) to speak the language of the neighbouring First Nation: "She has learned the Assiniboine language, which I believe she can speak as fluently as English … I have heard her keep up a conversation with the Indians without a stutter." Geddes said that she had many skills, that she was "quite a mechanic," and "likewise a good needlewoman, a laundress, and a weaver; and when occasion is necessary, she can solder tin-plate." She knew "the kinds of prairie weeds and flowers [that] are applied by the Indians in the healing art." (He recommended that she be hired to work among the people of the neighbouring reserve.) Yet according to Geddes, Mrs. McNab's ambition was "to be tilling the ground." She was an excellent gardener, raising many varieties of vegetables; her work "might compare favourably with the crops of any man that has made gardening a profession." The major goal of the letter was that Mrs. McNab be allowed to "perform her duties on her second homestead." Geddes quoted from the Bible—"Plead for the widow" (Isaiah 1:17)—and asked that the government "plead for her against those that would deprive her of one of the chances of making a living." Geddes asked, however, that his name be left out of any investigation that might be made as the "parties against Mrs. McNab are in my congregation." Department of the Interior officials were sympathetic to the claim of Mrs. McNab, and in November 1890 she was given a further opportunity to comply with the conditions of the Dominion Lands Act. Mary Ann McNab received her patent to the pre-emption in 1897.[70]

There were many ways in which the intricacies of the Dominion lands legislation made life difficult for the woman homesteader. She had to build a habitable dwelling and live on her homestead for six months of each year for three years. As was the case with Marion Frazer, if she married after she filed on her land but before she proved up, and if her husband was also a homesteader, they had to have separate residences, each on his or her own land during the six months of the year they were required to perform residency duties. If the woman homesteader had a son who filed on adjoining land, she could not live on his homestead (except during the six months she could be absent). Yet a son could live with her, never build his own shack, and still "perfect" his own entry. The legislation permitted a son who had parents in the vicinity to reside with his parents. The clause specified that the son homesteader could live with "the father (or the mother, if the father is deceased)."[71] But a woman homesteader could not live on her son's homestead and still "perfect" her entry.

This rule was tested in 1898, when Saskatchewan homesteader Louisa Hill asked for permission to reside with her son on his adjoining quarter section and still prove up on her own homestead. Hill was informed that there was "no provision in the law by which you can do residence duties while living with your son … there is no way of meeting your wishes."[72]

Correspondence on the matter continued for several years, with Hill claiming she had to live with her son because of ill health and because she lacked the means to live on her own. In September 1905 she was thrown from her rig and her arm was injured. That December she wrote to land officials that she was "under the impression a mother could live with a son just as a son could live with a mother." But she was wrong. She had to live on her own homestead to perfect her entry. In 1906 it was decided that because she had been under an erroneous impression of the residence requirement, Louisa Hill would be permitted to purchase her land at one dollar per acre, and this payment must have been made because a patent was granted to her in 1907.

The issue of citizenship also complicated the life of the woman homesteader. To receive patent, a homesteader had to be a British subject or be naturalized, which meant an immigrant had to have resided in Canada not less than three years. At that point, "He must take the oath of allegiance, and also an oath that he intends to remain in Canada."[73] This process was available to "every person who is of the full age of twenty-one years, and not an idiot, lunatic or married woman." Upon marriage a woman assumed the citizenship of her husband; if he became naturalized she was automatically naturalized. A woman homesteader, therefore, had to take great care if she married before she proved up. If, for example, she was a British subject either by marriage or birth but married a homesteader from the United States who was not yet naturalized, she would lose her right to her homestead because when she married she would become a U.S. citizen.

This became an issue in the American West among single women homesteaders, particularly those near the border of the United States and Canada. If a single woman homesteader born in the United States married a Canadian (or any other "alien") before she proved up on her land, she would lose her U.S. citizenship and her right to her homestead. The cause of these women was championed in 1917 by Jeanette Rankin, congresswoman from Montana. Campaigning for re-election, she learned that "many of the girls along the border with Canada love Canadian boys and cannot marry them without losing their American citizenship and therefore also their Montana homesteads."[74] Rankin found the situation "ridiculous," saying that "men are allowed to choose their own nations. Women should be accorded the same right." (The U.S. citizenship legislation was changed in 1925 to address this, and the process began in Canada with legislation of 1932.)

DEBATING AND NARROWING THE CATEGORIES OF ELIGIBLE WOMEN: THE CASE OF SUSANNA WILLIS, VIRDEN HOMESTEADER

As the experiences of homesteaders such as Marion Frazer indicate, women contended with vicissitudes and difficulties over and above those that challenged their male counterparts. They held no political clout; they were without votes and without wealth. They could be shoved off their land if it was desired by a neighbour or a speculator. This was the case with homesteader Susanna Willis, whose entry was cancelled because she had valuable land. The stated rationale was that her children were too old; she was likely the first woman to have her homestead cancelled because of this reason. Willis was a widow, originally from Ireland, who had emigrated to Ontario in 1830, and at the time of her 1882 filing on a homestead in Manitoba was about sixty-three.[75] Her land turned out to be very valuable, as it was just where the CPR decided to locate the town of Virden. Land for a townsite was highly sought after, and many speculators tried to anticipate where these sites might be located. Willis was suddenly rendered ineligible to homestead and was told that this was because she did not qualify as a head of family. She had built a house and had part of her land ploughed when she was informed of this, and also told that her land was required for the townsite. However, the main argument used to disqualify her was that while she was a widow and had two sons, she did not have a minor child or children, so she was no longer a head of family.

Willis's case raised many questions at the time and for years later. The *Manitoba Free Press* was sympathetic to her cause, reporting that "a very dirty trick" had been perpetrated on her and suggesting that the CPR wanted her off the land to be able to profit from the townsite:

> The Government appears determined not to do justice to the widow, Mrs. Willis, whose homestead was taken from her last spring on a technicality because it was wanted for the town site of Virden. An Ottawa correspondent states that, failing to obtain any satisfaction from the Local Land Agency, Mrs. Willis appealed to the Government, and a few days ago when her solicitor laid her case before the department, he was told by a government official that the provision in the Land Act enabling widows to acquire homesteads, only applied to widows with very young

> children. A number of other equally brilliant excuses were given for depriving the woman of her homestead at the request of the [CPR] Syndicate.[76]

There was fierce debate, however, about the right of the "Widow Willis" to her land. The *Winnipeg Daily Times* supported the government's stand and insisted that "although a widow, [she] is not a sole head of family in the sense of having a family dependent on her for support ... on the contrary her sons are grown up and have second homesteads and preemptions for themselves."[77] The *Times* stressed that the *Free Press* was trying to present this as the story of an "Irish eviction" and that other issues were involved, including that Mrs. Willis had not improved the land and was two months late in becoming a bona fide resident of her homestead (while the *Free Press* claimed she was delayed by flooding).[78] According to the *Times* there was subterfuge involved, and Willis had filed on land as "simply an attempt to obtain a second homestead for the son in the name of the mother."

The debate continued well into the next century, when it was proven that Thomas Mayne Daly, a Brandon lawyer (and elected mayor of Brandon in 1882) and later minister of the interior, had made huge profits from land sales in Western Canada, including from his "ownership" of land that became the town of Virden.[79] A 1901 Northwest Town Sites Commission found that Daly had entered on the south half of the township in question, while Willis had the northeast quarter as her homestead.[80] She made improvements and was living on her homestead, while Daly had made no improvements and had been in residence there only ten days. Willis's entry was cancelled for the official reason that her son was not a minor, and she received no compensation. Daly, however, made an enormous profit selling his "rights" to the south half for $6,400.

Inquiries revealed the documentary evidence. In May 1882 the CPR land agent at Winnipeg, J.H. McTavish, wrote to C. Drinkwater, secretary of the CPR in Montreal, to the effect that the Willis/Daly section had been chosen for the station and town, and that "Mrs. Willis has failed to comply with the homestead regulations, and I am taking steps to have her entry cancelled. Daly is prepared to abandon if we pay him $20 per acre or $6400.00 cash." Drinkwater replied yes, that they should "deal with Daly and take the necessary steps against the widow Willis." Daly's claim was to be settled from the first sale of town lots in Virden.[81]

The matter was still being discussed in 1908, when the *Brandon Daily Sun* asked, "Would the CPR have made fish of Mr. Daly and fowl of the widow if Mr. Daly had not been backed by the Government at Ottawa? Was Mr. Daly as Minister of the Interior under any obligations thereafter to promote the interests of the CPR?" No one, it seems, thought of asking Susanna Willis herself about the issue.[82] She was still in Virden as late as 1901, when at age ninety-two she was living with her son Thomas (fifty-three), a farmer.[83] At the time she was forced off her land in 1882, Thomas would have been nineteen, just out of "minor" status. Daly, by contrast, has been honoured for his "distinguished legal and political career" by the Historic Sites Advisory Board of Manitoba. There is a plaque outside his home, which is a museum in Brandon, and a pamphlet that recognizes his contribution to public affairs in Manitoba and Western Canada.[84]

WHO IS A "SOLE" HEAD OF A FAMILY?

The wording of the 1876 amendment to the Dominion Lands legislation left room for many questions, including whether in certain cases a "spinster" was a head of household and could homestead. In 1886 there was concern that an amendment to the law was necessary to make it clear that a spinster was not a head of household. The minister of justice concurred with the opinion of William Wilson, law clerk of the House of Commons, that "under no circumstances can a spinster be considered eligible to make homestead entry."[85] Wilson wrote, "I fail to see how a spinster could be the head of a family in terms of the Dominion Lands Act. If she had servants or dependents they would, subject to the terms of their agreements, be free to go when they like and therefore could hardly be deemed to be a family ... I therefore think that the practice which appears ... to have obtained, of refusing them homestead entry is in accordance with the law, and that no amendment of the law in the direction indicated is necessary."[86]

Yet there were rare instances when single women did manage to homestead. Isadore Harkness, a dressmaker at Prince Albert, Saskatchewan, filed on land as a single woman in 1882 and built a home there in February 1883.[87] A document explaining her case over ten years later stated that the Agent of Dominion Lands at Prince Albert "through inadvertence, and apparently under the impression that she was the sole head of a family, granted a homestead entry ... to a spinster."[88] Harkness lived on her land for several months each year (May to November) and in 1885 applied for her patent, having ten acres under cultivation. Her case was delayed, however, for over ten years after her initial application for patent, as the issue of her eligibility was debated at the highest levels of government and of the bureaucracy. In 1895, Minister of the Interior T.M. Daly (who had helped to divest Mrs. Willis of her land) was sympathetic. He thought there was evidence that Harkness was the sole support of her widowed mother and sisters. But Deputy Minister A.M. Burgess looked into the case and found that in fact the mother and a blind brother both had their own homesteads, and the mother was residing with her son. Although Burgess too was sympathetic, he concluded that "we cannot say that she is the sole support or even chief support of the family." Minister Daly referred the matter to the Privy Council, recommending that letters patent be granted, that "it would be a hardship now to deprive Miss Harkness of her homestead on the ground of her ineligibility to obtain a homestead entry, inasmuch as she secured her entry and complied with all the requirements of the law in good faith." Harkness finally was granted ownership of her land in May 1895.

But the majority of single women who inquired about their right to homestead were informed that they were not eligible. Ellen Margaret Cameron wrote to the Department of the Interior from Pittsburgh, Pennsylvania, in 1886, asking whether a head of family in the legislation could be interpreted to mean "a young unmarried lady over 21 years of age who wished to have a homestead of her own independent of other members of the family (as is now quite customary in the United States)."[89] Her deceased mother, she noted, was a Canadian. Cameron was curtly informed in 1887 that "a young unmarried woman does not come under the term 'sole head of a family' existing in the Dominion Lands Act."[90]

The eligibility of women in other categories was debated by officials, including the case in 1893 of Margaret Spence, a Métis woman and mother of "illegitimate children." The evidence before the Departments of the Interior and Justice was that she was not legally married to Thomas Young, but had children with him, and had lived with him on land that "Young squatted upon … and lived thereon until the year 1891, when he left the country."[91] "He had during all that time residing with him a Half-breed woman," was how an official of the Department of the Interior put it. In 1893 Margaret Spence wanted to be allowed to make homestead entry; she and her children were still living on the land, keeping up improvements, and paying taxes. The secretary of the Department of the Interior sought the opinion of the Department of Justice, noting that "the practice of the Department of the Interior has been to interpret the expression 'sole head of family' ... to be restricted to a widow with children some of whom at least are minor, and the Department has refused to recognise the mother of illegitimate children as entitled to make homestead entry." The two departments rummaged about for "the proper definition of the term 'sole head of a family' but did not succeed in finding any record of such an opinion." The Minister of Justice decided that "under the peculiar circumstances of this case ... your Department may properly recognize Margaret Spence as a sole head of family, and permit her to make entry for the land in question."[92] The minister would not, however, "lay down any general rule on the subject." (There is no register of a land patent for Margaret Spence.) Documents pertaining to the scrip application of Margaret and Thomas's daughter Sarah suggest that her parents were in fact married, that her mother was Margaret Young and the widow of Thomas Young, who had died in Alaska in 1889.[93]

The Margaret Spence case led to an intensive effort to create a "general and final ruling" on which women could homestead, and how terms such as "sole" and "head" were to be interpreted. In an 1894 memorandum, a Department of Justice clerk collected definitions of the meaning of the term "head," including "a person to whom others are subordinate" and "the most prominent or important member of any organized body."[94] *Bovier's Law Dictionary* defined "Head of a Family" as follows: "Householder; one who provides for a family ... There must be the relation of parent and child, or husband and wife." Because the term "head of family" could not be said to be a "word of art" (meaning a term that has a precise or specific meaning within a discipline or field), the clerk urged that "the only safe general rules we can lay down must be founded upon a strict construction of the Statute, leaving doubtful cases to be decided according to their special circumstances." It was further noted that "sole was not used in the U.S. legislation." In Canada the designation "sole" head of family was used to exclude a great variety of women, for example someone whose husband might still be alive, although ill or incapacitated. A woman who had adopted or was an older sister of siblings, or was caring for a sibling's children had to have the *sole* legal right to custody or control of children in order to qualify.

An 1895 Department of Justice ruling set out the rights of women to make homestead entries.[95] The most uncomplicated eligible category was that of widow, but the widow had to have a minor child or children—if they were grown the applicant was not eligible. A person was considered a minor in the eyes of the law until age twenty-one. However, if the widow's only child (or only minor child) was a son who had reached the age of eighteen, the widow was no longer eligible, as the son could apply for his own homestead.[96] If her child was a daughter the widow was eligible until the daughter was twenty-one.

The widowed applicant generally had to sign a statutory declaration that she indeed was a widow (although it is not clear just when this became a requirement), and provide the names and ages of her children.[97] If it was later discovered that she was not a widow then she might be disqualified altogether, or she might be permitted to purchase her homestead, generally at a price between three dollars to one dollar per acre, or she could be sent to jail, as discussed in one case below.

According to the 1895 ruling, a married woman deserted or separated with a minor child or children could "sometimes" be the sole head of a family, if the husband was presumed dead, for example, or "where by a *binding agreement* or by the Courts she has been given the custody or control of the children." In this and many other categories, when doubts arose, the cases were to be submitted to the Department of Justice. A married woman separated or deserted and having no children depending on her "cannot be held to be the sole head of a family." Even with children, it was unlikely that a deserted woman would be permitted to homestead. A Mrs. Doig of Regina applied for permission to homestead nine years after her husband deserted her, went to the United States, acquired a divorce, and remarried. The reply to her request was that if she had minor children and had already performed settlement duties on a homestead acquired by her husband she was eligible to apply for title to that land, but if she was applying "with a view to taking out land I should think that it ought not to be granted."[98] Since Mrs. Doig had no children she was therefore not regarded as a sole head of a family, and her application was not granted. Even though her husband had deserted her and remarried, the decision still applied that "a married woman who does not live with her husband, though not divorced under Canadian law, is not so entitled."

Documents had to be produced for the land office, and the files of some women homesteaders or would-be homesteaders include deeds of separation. In August 1913 Amanda Giller, widow and milliner of Grouard, Alberta, wrote directly to the secretary of the Department of the Interior, explaining that she was legally separated from her husband, Dr. Jean Louis Giller, that she was left with three children, and was "absolutely obliged to see to their education, not knowing even where there [*sic*] father is living."[99] She wrote that she was twenty-nine years old and her husband seventy, and the children were two, three, and four. The local land agent had urged her to write directly to Ottawa for permission. She had a legal separation and produced the document, dated 9 June 1913. The document stated that they were from then on to live "separate and apart," that "Amanda Giller shall be as if she were feme sole, and shall henceforth be free from the control and authority of the said J.L. Giller." She was granted custody, but if she failed to provide for "the necessaries of life, or to give them a proper education," she had to deliver the children to her husband. A further provision was that "the said Amanda Giller shall conduct herself as a chaste and good woman and does not endanger at any time the moral welfare of the said children." It is not clear from the file whether she was permitted to enter on a homestead. No patent for land was ever issued to her. An Ottawa memo of 1914 in her file noted that her Agreement of Separation was not "legally sealed," although in the margins an official wrote, "She appears to be entitled under present practice." Perhaps during the many months when she heard nothing back from the Department of the Interior, she decided to pursue other survival strategies.

A major concern about separated women was, as future prime minister R.L. Borden explained in the House of Commons in 1907, that to permit them to file for homesteads would encourage separation, because then both husband and wife could obtain homesteads.[100] (This same reasoning was not applied to separated men.) Rulings with regard to deserted and separated wives were eventually relaxed, but in all cases women had to have minor children. Initially, women who could prove desertion for five years were permitted homestead entry, and in 1920 this was changed to two years, although the Department of the Interior would "order an investigation by a Homestead Inspector regarding the BONA FIDES of the application," and when the report was received, there was no guarantee—the case would be decided on its own merits.[101] In 1914 separated women who could produce a proper agreement of separation could also be considered, and an investigation would be held. The homestead inspector's report had to "clearly show that there is no danger of collusion"—of the husband and wife plotting to both acquire land. Throughout the correspondence of the government officials there was an evident lurking suspicion that deceptive and evasive tactics were being employed to acquire land.

The 1895 ruling on which women were eligible to make homestead entries also stated that a married woman "validly divorced" in Canada and having control or custody of minor children was entitled to be treated as a sole head of a family. A valid decree of divorce had to be submitted with an application. (There were very few such validly divorced women, as divorces were very rare at that time in Western Canada. There were no divorce courts in the Prairie provinces, and divorce was obtained by a special Act of Parliament, an expensive and public procedure. Alberta, for example, had one divorce case in 1906 and one in 1909, these being the only divorces to 1909 since Alberta became a province in 1905.)[102] A foreign decree of divorce would have to be carefully scrutinized for its validity—including American divorces, which were generally not recognized in Canada.

The 1895 ruling declared that "spinsters without any one related or otherwise dependent upon them" were not eligible to file for a homestead, nor were spinsters with servants or employees dependent upon them. Nor was a spinster with dependent brothers or sisters eligible, unless she had been given custody or control through a will or legal instrument or a competent court. There were exceptions, but these were carefully scrutinized. In 1904 Miss Matilda Bucknam requested permission to file on a homestead.[103] Lawyer James MacLean of Yorkton wrote to J.G. Turriff, Commissioner of Dominion Lands in Ottawa, on her behalf and explained that "Miss Bucknam is, and has been the support of her Mother, a widow and an invalid, and her brothers and sisters for many years. One boy, a minor of about 15 years now with her sick helpless mother is entirely dependent on Miss Bucknam for support… Miss Bucknam is desirous of having the privilege of taking up a Homestead in her own name. Her mother could not, owing to ill health, fulfil the homestead duties."[104] The commissioner consented to this, and Bucknam filed on a quarter section near Edmonton, although she later had to abandon the claim, declaring in 1905 that "I am unable to go to live upon it at the present time as the salary I am now earning is necessary to the support of myself and my mother who is a widow."

An unmarried woman with "illegitimate" children depending upon her "may sometimes be eligible as it has been held that a mother has a natural right to the custody of her young children," but every such case was to be decided on its own merits. Generally the Department of Justice refused to recognize the mothers of illegitimate children as entitled to homestead entry, although a few cases were permitted. Initially grandmothers having custody of minor grandchildren were not considered eligible, but this ruling was reversed in 1896. However, in 1916 a widow named Mary Blackstock filed on a homestead, claiming she had a minor child dependent upon her for support, but when it was later shown that this was not her own but her daughter's child, cancellation proceedings were instituted on the ground of fraud.[105]

An unmarried woman with adopted children was not eligible, unless, once again, this was "by virtue of a will or other instrument, or the judgement or order or decree of a competent court." In 1888 Miss Bertha Livingston, who had some of her sister's children depending on her for support, was informed that she was not eligible. In the 1895 case of Eliza McFadden, who adopted the two children of Thomas Hare, it was not sufficient to produce a letter from Hare in which he agreed to relinquish and resign all his legal claims to these children as their parent. McFadden was found not eligible because she could not be considered the *sole* head of a family, as "a father cannot divest himself of his authority over or responsibility for his children by such an agreement."[106]

Replies to enquiries were terse. In 1904 Susan Walper of Yarrow, Alberta, wrote to the secretary of the Department of the Interior asking if she could enter on a homestead.[107] She was thirty-two and single, and had a nephew in her care whose parents had died. She wrote that her "sister's last wish was for me to provide for and bring up the child." She found it hard to make a living, and was ready to move onto the land and "make it a future home for myself and my boy." The answer from P.G. Keyes was simply that "you are not entitled to a homestead entry, as this privilege is restricted to women only who are widows with minor children dependent upon them." This was not what the legislation stated, but this was how it was consistently interpreted.

Proof of legal adoption was required. In 1911, when Miss Marion T. Thompson applied for entry on an Alberta homestead, she had to submit her "Agreement as to Custody of a Child," dated 1908, at Newcastle upon Tyne. Through this agreement, widow Elizabeth Hopwood Thompson of Durham gave "possession and custody of her son James" to her sister Marion Thompson, who agreed to maintain, clothe, and educate him. At the time of the adoption agreement, Marion Thompson was a "spinster" living at the Pioneer Club, Grafton Street, London, which was a women's club devoted to the suffrage campaign and other feminist issues of the day.[108] The club hosted lectures and discussions of a great variety of topics, and the potential for women to farm in the colonies may have been raised by speakers. James was seventeen years old when his adoptive mother filed on a homestead—if she had waited one more year she would not have been eligible. Marion Thompson established a ranch at Swallowhurst, and she was often mentioned in the social columns of the Edmonton and area newspapers (although an adopted son was not mentioned). In a May 1912 issue of the *Edmonton Bulletin*, it was noted that "Miss Marion Thompson leaves next Monday with her maid for her ranch in Swallowhurst."[109] She received her patent to the land in 1915.

While older children could be of assistance to women homesteaders, the presence of young children must have impeded the progress of the farm. Imagine for a moment just how efficiently and quickly the prairies would have been settled if male homesteaders had been restricted to the category of widowers with young children they were solely responsible for. While children were not strictly required to reside on the land with the woman homesteader, the children might have to be produced for the homestead inspector, especially in the case of a widow coming from another country, as "there would be some opening for misrepresentation if a widow … were granted entry merely upon her statement that she has a minor child or her own dependent on her for support, such child not being a resident of Canada."[110]

Wives whose husbands were incapacitated by disease or injury could sometimes be granted the right to homestead, but these appear to have been exceedingly rare. Each case was individually examined, and in each case the applicants had to have minor children. In 1895 Mrs. Catherine Godkin wrote to the Department of the Interior for permission to homestead. She was the mother of four young children, and her husband had been confined in an insane asylum for seven years, with little hope for recovery. The decision was that Mrs. Godkin was not a sole head of her family within the meaning of the statute (presumably because her husband was still alive and thus she was not the *sole* head).[111] In the 1920s this was relaxed to some extent but not automatically; each case was still individually examined. The insane or incapacitated husband could not have previously filed on a homestead, and there had to be no chance of recovery.

Decisions were not always as draconian as with the Godkin case. In 1887 a homestead entry near Yorkton was granted to Mrs. Jane Ferguson when evidence was filed that her husband John was "hopelessly insane."[112]

THE DEVIOUS WOMAN HOMESTEADER

Despite having tried to clearly identify which women could qualify as a "sole" head of household, Dominion lands officials remained concerned about the potential for women to resort to devious means to obtain land. A new clause was added to the "Eligibility for Homestead Entry" section of the Dominion Lands Act in 1897: "If in the case of any woman who, claiming to be the sole head of a family, makes application for a homestead entry, any doubt arises as to the right of such woman to be recognized as the sole head of a family, the Minister may decide from the special circumstances of the case whether such application shall be granted or refused."[113]

Stories of these devious means were many, some true and others embellished. There were women who acquired or tried to acquire homestead land through falsely representing themselves as widows. Some were caught and prevented, while others managed to slip through the cracks of the bureaucracy, possibly because a local land agent and inspector relaxed the rigid rules. Hannah Surrey (née Osborne), from Essex, England, homesteaded in the Maple Creek district of the Cypress Hills. She settled in 1887 with three children.[114] In the entry on Surrey in the local history, the author comments, "Just what prompted a widow with 3 children to choose a four year old prairie town (so far from her native home) to rear her family is question not answered." But the same entry hints at an answer: "She was accompanied by her brother-in-law John Harvey, who also had a young family." A Harvey family genealogist in recent years has (re)discovered that Hannah and John ran away together to Maple Creek.[115] Hannah was the sister of John's wife (Charity Osborne Harvey). The scandal this must have generated would have motivated the couple to seek this distant location so remote from their home. In the 1906 census Hannah Surrey is listed as a "widow" and "sister" of the head of household, John Harvey, who is listed as "married."[116] They had become prosperous ranchers with 200 horses and 700 head of cattle. Hannah remained on the Maple Creek ranch until 1912, when she moved with daughter Jane to Victoria.[117]

Elise Vane was a Manitoba homesteader, filing on her land in 1886. She arrived in Canada in 1882 from England (although she was originally from Germany) with her five children, along with Percy and Alice Criddle and their four children.[118] Both Alice and Elise were Percy's wives and the mothers of his children. Elise Harrer, who changed her last name to Vane when they immigrated to Canada, was the first wife of Percy Criddle (although the term "common law" may be most apt for this marriage, as no marriage certificate has been found). She was German, and they had met in Heidelberg where they were both students. Later she moved to London, where Percy had a wine shop. Criddle then married Alice Nicol in 1874. They all shipped off together and settled north of Treesbank, where the family eventually acquired 6,000 acres.

In Elise Vane's quest for a homestead, both she and Percy Criddle declared that she was a widow. When she applied for her patent to her land in 1889 and was asked to clarify her status as a head of family, she wrote, "I beg to tell you that I have been a widow since Sept. 1874 and that I am a head of a family having five living sons and one daughter. I thought I had already given this information."[119] Further complications arose in obtaining her patent because she had been living with the Criddles and not on her homestead, except for three months of one year, and the land office initially insisted that she had to fully comply with the residency requirements. Vane objected, stating that she was a "widow with scanty means" and would lose her employment as housekeeper. She added that she considered her homestead her "clear and undoubted right."[120] But officials maintained that it seemed she had abandoned her homestead and changed her vocation. Then another complication arose. In January 1890, an anonymous letter arrived at the land office in Winnipeg, stating, "If you take the trouble to look into the record of Mrs. (Miss) Vane … you will find that she is an unmarried woman living as a servant in the house of P. Criddle."[121]

The homestead inspector was sent to investigate. From his interview with Vane, he reported that she was born in Germany of German parents and had married an Englishman in 1864; they lived in England and had five children.[122] Vane stated that her husband had died in England in 1874, but that his death certificate and their marriage certificate were lost in Winnipeg in 1882. The inspector also spoke to Percy Criddle, whom he found to be a "thoroughly reliable man." Criddle stated that Mrs. Vane had been their housekeeper since 1874 or 1875, that "he has known her family for the past thirty years, and that he believes her to have been married and that she has always had a good character." Criddle was one of Vane's witnesses to her application for her patent, swearing that all her information was true. (In a letter to the Dominion Lands Commissioner in Winnipeg, Criddle wrote that he knew the real name of the author of the "scurrilous" letter, suggesting that the writer had reason to profit if Vane's application was rejected and that he wanted the letter so that he could have the handwriting analyzed.)[123] The homestead inspector further reported that other male settlers in the neighbourhood stated that Vane was "a respectable woman and that she is a bona fide settler."

Vane and Criddle persuaded officials that she was a sole head of a family, as letters patent were issued to her in March 1890. In the census for 1891, Elise Vane is identified as a widow, aged fifty; it appears she was living on her own land beside the Criddles, with sons Edwy, nineteen; Harry, eighteen; and Cecil, seventeen.[124] In 1901 she is listed as a "lodger" in the Criddle home and a widow, but she identifies herself as a "farmer."[125]

The experiences of Elise Vane illustrate how women homesteaders were policed and monitored in a way that men were not. Inspectors were sent to see if male claimants were attending to their homestead duties of cultivation and residency but did not inquire into their marital status, their status as a sole head of family, or their morality. A man could have two wives and families and not have his affairs investigated and be declared "thoroughly reliable." Widowed women homesteaders were often assumed to be the opposite—trying to obtain land for devious purposes and through devious means.

"Collusion" was the term often used to describe how a devious woman might conspire with a male partner or fiancé to obtain two homesteads. At an Edmonton land rush on 31 August 1908, there was one woman among the several hundred men waiting to file on homesteads outside the land titles office. She was Margaret Conklin, who told the *Edmonton Bulletin* she was a widow from Michigan.[126] The paper reported that she did not have to stand in line all night, as a "young man saw her intention and offered to hold her place. She had a good night's rest and resumed her stand this morning." She successfully filed on a quarter section. Journalist Gertrude Balmer Watt later wrote of her interview with Conklin as she stood in line.[127] The widow said she was looking for a homestead for herself and her son, who was fifteen: "She knew all about farming; could plough with the best of them; had studied gardening and chicken raising, and loved both occupations. She and her boy would work the farm themselves; she had her eye on a likely spot, which friends had looked over for her."

Just days after the land rush it was reported that Conklin had married Fred Reed, also from Michigan, at Grace Methodist church in Edmonton.[128] Reed had located a homestead on the adjoining quarter section and had been just ahead of her in the line. The *Bulletin* commended this "unique inauguration of a 320 acre farm and wished Mr. and Mrs. Reed their full share of health and happiness," but added that "the subject of a very interesting inquiry would be whether the pair had the matter all arranged before coming to the city, or whether the gallant Reed sort of 'sprung it on her' as they stood in line." No such evidence was ever forthcoming. The couple, however, did not retain both homesteads. Fred proved up upon his and got a patent to his land, but Margaret abandoned her homestead in 1910, for reasons that the file does not reveal.[129] Their story lived on and was retold as the "romance at the land office ... of the bachelor and young widow who filed on neighbouring quarter sections at the same time, compared notes on leaving the office, and in due course were married."[130]

MINISTER OF THE INTERIOR FRANK OLIVER AND FURTHER NARROWING OF OPPORTUNITIES

Under the administration of Frank Oliver, minister of the interior for the Wilfrid Laurier Liberals from 1905 to 1911, the applications of women for homesteads were subject to increasingly intense scrutiny, and many were rejected. Oliver was the member of Parliament for Edmonton and a newspaper publisher, politician, and land speculator who was implicated in many improper land transactions that enriched his friends and supporters, and lined his own pockets.[131] In 1910 Oliver became particularly intransigent, perhaps in response to the growing campaign for homesteads-for-women. In January of that year Oliver "dug his heels in" and declared to employees of the department that the rules were to be rigidly interpreted and applied. In a memorandum to employees, Oliver warned them to guard against fraudulent applications by women. He told them that the homestead privilege was "not to be granted to a widow who is the legal guardian of a minor child, nor to a widow who has an adopted minor child dependent on her for support except in cases where the adoption was made a sufficiently long time prior to the application for entry to satisfy the Department that such adoption was not made for the mere purpose of making her eligible for homestead entry."[132] A few months later he told employees of the Department of the Interior: "No woman should

Figure 15. A land rush was the prairie equivalent of a gold rush. As surveys were completed and new townships opened for entry, hundreds rushed to claim homesteads. Hopeful homesteaders might camp out for days outside the land office. While some land rushes were orderly, others were not, requiring police assistance. There were sometimes stampedes as people rushed to be at the front of the line once the office opened. Rush for Free Homesteads at the Dominion Land Office, Moose Jaw, Saskatchewan, 1908. Peel's Prairie Provinces, University of Alberta Libraries, Postcard 18198.

Figure 16. At the Edmonton land rush on 1 September 1908, Margaret Conklin, a widow from Michigan, was the only woman among several hundred men lined up. She successfully filed on a homestead, and a day later, married Fred Reed, also from Michigan, who had been just ahead of her in the line. Had they "colluded" to obtain two homesteads, it was wondered? While she did not "prove up," her husband did. Homestead rush at Edmonton, Alberta, 1 September 1908. Peel's Prairie Provinces, University of Alberta Libraries, Postcard 6839.

be granted permission to enter for a homestead unless she is clearly eligible to do so under the regulations, that is to say, a widow with minor children dependent upon her for support. This means that a woman who has been abandoned by her husband, or has in some other way become separated from him, is not to be granted homestead entry until her case has been passed upon by the Minister."[133]

Oliver instructed his staff that cases of women applicants "in which there is no merit are to be turned down promptly," and that any case with "some merit" was to be brought to his attention.[134] It was in 1910 that a woman (Elizabeth Edmundson, further discussed below) claiming falsely to be a widow in order to file on a homestead was sent to jail when her husband was brought all the way from Buffalo, New York, to appear at her trial in Medicine Hat, Alberta. This courtroom drama was likely staged with the knowledge and approval of Minister Oliver. And in July 1910 Oliver personally ruled on the homestead application of Mrs. Louisa Pearkes, of Droitwich, England, who was reported to be on her way to join her two sons at Stauffer, Alberta. She had submitted an "uncertified copy of a Deed of separation between herself and George Pearkes" from 1907.[135] Louisa Pearkes had one minor child, a daughter who was nineteen. Oliver denied permission: "The separation is uncertified and too recent. In cases of separation any of less than five years will not be considered." If Oliver was concerned that the mother and sons were of dubious character because of her separation from her husband, he was to be proven wrong. Louisa Pearkes joined her sons with her daughter in Alberta in 1910 and found them living in impoverished circumstances. The sons had not wanted to "add to their mother's problems," as she was separated from their father, and they were clearly receiving no assistance from him.[136] Louisa Pearkes remained separated from her husband, later moving to British Columbia. Her homesteader son George was awarded the Victoria Cross for gallantry in the First World War, and he later became a major general in the Canadian Army, General Officer Commanding-in-Chief Pacific Command, a member of Parliament, the minister of National Defence, and Lieutenant Governor of British Columbia.[137]

In June 1910 Oliver once again proved rigid and intransigent when he decided that Mrs. Oxilla Grant was not eligible for a homestead. Although her daughter was over the age of twenty-one, Grant had provided a statutory declaration and a medical certificate to the effect that her daughter

"Anna Grant, is an invalid and incapable of earning her living by her work." Oliver wrote tersely, "Not eligible daughter is not a minor."[138]

THE PROBLEM OF THE LIVING BUT ABSENT HUSBAND

There were cases when authorities decided that a woman homesteader was not entitled to have entered on a homestead after all because a husband was found to be alive, in the vicinity, or providing support. In some of these instances the woman homesteader was permitted to purchase her land. This was generally a humiliatingly public process, as the matter was referred to the Privy Council, an order-in-council had to be passed, and the result published in the *Canada Gazette* four times.[139] In January 1895, Maria Bell Heath from Ontario was permitted to enter on a homestead near Leduc, having claimed the right to make an entry as she had a deed of separation between herself and her husband. The deed of separation was dated 1880. The matter was referred, however, to the Department of Justice, and there it was decided that "the said deed of separation does not make Mrs. Heath the sole head of a family within the meaning of the Dominion Lands Act to qualify her to obtain a homestead."[140] Presumably because her husband was still alive, Mrs. Heath, whether separated or not, was not considered the sole head of her family. The matter was discussed at the level of the Privy Council, where evidence was presented that Mrs. Heath was "to all intents and purposes a widow and has the care of a family, is desirous of obtaining the said land for the purpose of residing on and cultivating the same." While the council decided that she could not be allowed to homestead, even under the "exceptional circumstances" of the case, it was decided that she be allowed to purchase the land at one dollar per acre.[141] This decision was approved in July 1895, but it still took years for the matter to be settled; she was not granted her patent until 1901.[142]

Women homesteaders who were found to be separated from their husbands rather than widows, as they had claimed, were permitted to purchase their land. In 1907 Margaret Heffernan secured entry to an Alberta homestead, claiming to be a widow with minor children.[143] However, a homestead inspector reported that Heffernan's husband was alive, that they had been separated for about twelve years, and that he still paid her twenty-five dollars per month. The clerk of the Privy Council reported in 1912 that "as Mrs. Heffernan has been receiving support from her husband she is not properly entitled to a homestead entry in her own name." Yet she was permitted "some consideration," as she had completed all of the homestead duties. It was decided that she would be allowed to purchase her land at one dollar per acre.

A woman homesteader who falsely claimed to be a widow, however, could be sent to jail. This was the case with Elizabeth Edmundson, who filed on a homestead near Medicine Hat in 1910. She claimed not only that she was a widow, but that she had the care of a number of small children (also false).[144] In the article on her trial for perjury in the *Medicine Hat Times*, the reporter wrote that she claimed her husband had "been under the sod since May 1, 1906 … What must have been her joy then to see her deceased husband in the courtroom on Saturday afternoon. In fact she seemed so overwhelmed by emotion that she thought it better to make no defence at all to the charge of perjury."[145] Husband William H. Edmundson was brought all the way from Buffalo, New York, to testify that Elizabeth had left him three years earlier with another man who had been boarding with them, taking their son with her. Mr. Edmundson followed his wife to Medicine Hat some time later, "hearing that the son was being badly treated," and placed the son with his sister in Buffalo. Because the husband had been in Medicine Hat in 1907 to collect his son, the police knew that Mrs. Edmundson was not a widow as she claimed. While Elizabeth did not testify, there were hints in the questions of her lawyer that her husband had threatened her with a knife and was a drinker. In giving his decision the magistrate said that he was sorry that the accused had not been examined, as he believed that she had "acted on the instigation of some man … who ought certainly to be brought to justice." While the punishment for perjury was two years in the penitentiary, magistrate O.W. Kealy stated that there were several circumstances that made this case "peculiar." The first was that "he was well aware of the fact that laxity as to the truth in obtaining homesteads was too prevalent altogether. Mrs. Edmundson happened to be the one caught." He was also "sorry that she was a woman, because otherwise he would have imposed the full sentence. He said her offence had been deliberate and was without excuse. He hoped that it would be a warning to others who might be tempted to try similar methods." Elizabeth Edmundson was sentenced to nine months of imprisonment in the Calgary jail.

Delia Bell presented herself as a widow when she first filed on a homestead at Grandview, Manitoba, in 1903.[146] She wrote in June of that year to the land agent that "I am a widow and have never had a homestead. I have 7 children." In the 1881 census, Delia was a Mrs. Wheeler, aged twenty-six, living with her farmer husband George Wheeler and four children in the Lisgar district of Manitoba.[147] In the 1891 census, she was Mrs. Bell, living with her husband W.G. Bell (ten years younger than her), born in Scotland, who was a "stable man"; she had five children with the last names Wheeler and two younger children with the last name Bell.[148] In the 1901 census, she was a "widow" operating a boarding house, with three of her children still with her; their last names were first recorded as "Bell" but then were crossed out and the last name "Whaler" recorded.[149] In 1906 she was back with William Bell and no longer a widow; they were living on a farm in Grandview.[150] In 1911 she was still living with William Bell and two children. These changing identifiers were to cause her problems as a homesteader.

Bell wanted to file on land abandoned by her son who had left for the United States. She was granted entry in 1903, but very soon there were reports from nearby settlers that she was not living on her land and making no improvements. The land agent at Dauphin supported Bell, writing in 1904 that he knew her well as she had "lived in this town for some time where she kept boarders, she is a hard working and industrious woman, who advanced considerable money to her son T.H. Wheeler, who was the former holder of this land and is reported to have disposed of the cattle and equipment, purchased with her money, and left the country. I would ask the Commissioner to grant any protection possible in this case." Cancellation proceedings were abandoned, but there was persistent interest in the land from others who continued to insist that she did not live on or improve her homestead.

In May 1909, however, Delia Bell still did not have patent to her land when the Dauphin land agent reported that although she had made entry as a widow, "I am given to understand that she is not a widow." Months later, in February 1910, the homestead inspector reported that "Mrs. Bell claims that she and her husband were parted for seven years; she worked and was supporting her family and not getting any money from her husband so she considered herself a widow. Her husband came back in 1907." That fall her homestead entry was cancelled. This required an order-in-council (signed by Prime Minister Laurier) stating that Delia Bell had represented herself as a widow when she entered on her land and that "it has since been shown that her husband is alive, and it has been decided to cancel her entry, as she was not eligible to take up a homestead in her own name." It was also found that she had made improvements on the land to the value of six hundred dollars. The order-in-council recommended that she be permitted to purchase her quarter section at the rate of three dollars per acre.[151] Bell never did come up with the funds to complete this purchase, although she (illegally) sold it in 1920 to a cattle dealer, despite being warned in 1916 that the land was not hers to sell.

While a woman separated from her husband might be granted the right to a homestead, the entry could be cancelled if he materialized. This was the case for Margaret Little, of Roblin, Manitoba (originally from Fergus, Ontario), who had been permitted, after "careful consideration" by the Commissioner of Dominion Lands, to enter on a homestead in 1909 after she signed a statutory declaration that she had been deserted and that she had been the sole support of minor children for ten years.[152] A few months after she filed on her homestead, however, questions were raised about her eligibility. In February 1910 her husband, Lemuel Little, filed on a homestead not far from hers and stated to the clerk at the land office that he would live with his wife while he proved up.[153] Immediately the couple was suspected of collusion to obtain two homesteads. The homestead inspector was dispatched to report "very carefully" upon whether Mr. Little had in fact abandoned his wife. The inspector reported that he was a "constant visitor," that there was a bed for him in the house, that he was a horse dentist who was away frequently because of his occupation, and that the neighbours knew nothing of family trouble.[154]

Margaret Little fought back in many letters, arguing that there was no collusion to obtain two homesteads, as she had known nothing of her husband's plans until the homestead inspector told her.[155] She signed another statutory declaration, dated 7 June 1910, that she was the sole support of herself and family, that she had not lived "as wife" with her husband for over eight years, and he had not supported them for over twelve. She admitted he occasionally called at her house to see their sons but that they never had "any business with each other."[156] She further swore that "the neighbours are well aware we are not living together and never will." A few weeks later a neighbour who coveted her land wrote the land office in Dauphin that she was not entitled, as Mr. Little was at home and able to work.[157]

In early December 1910, Margaret Little was informed that her entry was to be cancelled because "the return of your husband removes the reason by which you were granted a homestead. You have no claim whatever to this land which is being re-opened for entry."[158] She continued her letters, writing on 7 December 1910 that "I am only a woman but please give me a hearing."[159] She asked why the land office did not cancel her husband's homestead entry instead, arguing that he would sell his land as soon as he got the patent while she would pass her land to her family after her death. She also announced that she would stay on her land until these false accounts that her husband supported her could be proven. She asked how the government could take from "me what they allowed me to have to help support my family when my husband would not." Then she came up with a brilliant strategy: when her land was thrown open for entry at the land office in Dauphin on 13 December 1910, Margaret Little and her son were at the head of the line, and she entered on the same land in the name of her son Roscoe. Although her son was still only seventeen, the rules permitted her to enter her son on a homestead and reserve the land for him until he would be old enough the following year.[160] Roscoe did eventually receive patent to this land, although it took until 1919 due to various bureaucratic hurdles.[161] Margaret continued to argue with Department of the Interior authorities that she deserved to enter on a homestead, but was told that she did not qualify and that only a widow with a minor child or children dependent upon her for support was eligible. Her husband, Lemuel, proved up on his homestead, and her son Roscoe proved up on the land that she had homesteaded. Of the three Littles, Margaret was the only one never permitted a homestead in her own name.

Margaret Little's quest for a homestead was admired in the *Minnedosa Tribune*. Under the headline "An Enterprising Lady," the article described how she successfully retained "the homestead and also the improvements which she has put upon the place, and to which all will admit she is justly entitled."[162] The tenor and sincerity of her letters suggest that she was indeed the sole support of her family and that her husband, though an occasional visitor to his children, had deserted them. One document in the land file corroborates Margaret Little's claims: her cousin William Hughes, a Manitoba homesteader, wrote to the Department of the Interior in 1903 asking if Little could make a homestead entry, writing that "she has had to support herself and five of a family for the last three years. Her husband has left her and the family to support themselves."[163] Hughes, who died in 1905, left his land to Margaret Little.[164] It is curious, however, that one of the witnesses to his will was Margaret's husband, Lemuel Little.

Clara Lynch (from Iowa) waged an epic battle to secure her Alberta homestead and to prove that she was "worse than widowed" after her husband deserted her.[165] She faced difficulties because of her status as a deserted wife, and because although she claimed to have a son dependent upon her, he was nowhere to be seen. Yet Lynch remained determined, resolute, and tenacious. She wrote to the highest Ottawa officials, consulted a lawyer, and trudged through deep snow to get the signatures of neighbours on a petition supporting her right to homestead. She confronted overwhelming legal and other obstacles, including a neighbour who coveted her land. Her perseverance eventually paid off, but not until 1909, four years after her death.[166] Officials had insisted that she could not be considered a head of household, since "her husband is alive, and is liable to come back any day."[167] In one of many eloquent letters pleading her case, Lynch asked how an official of the Department of the Interior could dare "to assert under the sacred Motto on Canada's shield 'God and my Right,' that I am not the head of a family; if he only knew the man that was my husband, but is such no longer, he would know, that I was *forced* to be the head of the family whether I would or no. I can point you to at least a dozen creatures of the species, male bipeds, in my own immediate neighborhood, who have homestead entry, who are not, and in all human probability, never will be heads of families; I think his lexicon must be an obsolete one."[168]

Still fighting her battle, Lynch died on 5 May 1905 in Edmonton, at age thirty-nine, of "abcess and tuberculosis." Yet the battle for her land was not over; it continued for four years after her death. After a mountain of correspondence, in which officials disagreed about and debated the case, Lynch's estate was finally granted patent to her land in April 1909, but her estate had to pay for it! She never was granted the right to homestead. A sad irony is that if Lynch had remained in the United States or returned there, she would have had no trouble securing a homestead. As a deserted woman, she would have been considered a head of household regardless of whether she had children or not.

SOUTH AFRICAN SCRIP WOMEN HOMESTEADERS

Whether single, married, divorced, or widowed, women could obtain homestead land in Western Canada if they could afford to purchase South African scrip (SAS). These women belong in the chapter on homesteaders because they did not purchase land, they purchased scrip that permitted them to homestead 320 acres. They did not own the land after purchasing scrip; they had to comply with all the rules and regulations involved in proving up and were under the watchful eye of the land agents and inspectors.

In July 1900, Harold Lothrop Borden, a lieutenant in the Royal Canadian Dragoons serving in the South African War (1899–1902), was killed at Witpoort, South Africa. He was just twenty-four, and a promising medical student in his third year at McGill. He was also the only son of Canada's minister of the militia Sir Frederick William Borden. Under the Volunteer Bounty Act (VBA) of 1908, volunteers domiciled in Canada who had served in the South African war, deceased or living (7,300 Canadians), were offered money scrip (sixty dollars) or land scrip that permitted the recipient to enter on 320 acres (two adjoining quarter sections) of homestead land in Western Canada. Recipients of land scrip had to fulfill all of the regular homestead duties of cultivation and residence over three years and could then receive patent to the land. The recipient or purchaser of scrip had to commence residence within twelve months of entry being made. Borden's father was his legal representative, and like many recipients of SAS he opted to sell the scrip, likely through an agent, rather than spending three years fulfilling homestead duties. The purchaser of Harold Borden's scrip, in 1911, was Anna Utech, a married woman with three children, and she successfully proved up on her homestead in Saskatchewan in 1914, earning her patent or outright ownership.[169] Without the option of SAS, Anna Utech would never have qualified for homestead land in Western Canada because she was a married woman. Utech was among about 540 women of all marital and non-marital statuses who took advantage of the rare opportunity offered by SAS to homestead land in Saskatchewan, and some purchased more than one SAS, becoming the owners of not just 320 but 640 acres.[170] These women, and the press attention some of them received, played a vital role in demonstrating that women were interested in obtaining homestead land and that they could successfully prove up on that land. They had to have some capital, as SAS sold for about $800, or more.

The VBA was passed after much discussion and debate in the House of Commons about the value of land grants to the military, but a majority of parliamentarians were eventually persuaded that the scheme could help to build a white, British, masculine West. The grant of land in return for military service was an ancient practice that was incorporated into Canada's Dominion Lands Act in several instances, including after the 1869–70 Red River Resistance and the 1885 North-West Rebellion. The idea was to encourage enlistment, reward service, and foster settlement of loyal, disciplined, men of British ancestry. SAS was intended to reward those who had served but also to attract the right kind of settler. As one member of Parliament stated, "a young man who is sufficiently loyal to risk his life in South Africa is a pretty good kind of man to mix with certain elements that will go into that country."[171] To ensure actual settlement and cultivation the homestead provisions of the Dominion Lands Act had to be complied with. Grantees had to live on the land for six months every year for three years, build a house and not a temporary shack, and cultivate the land. The idea of being able to appoint a substitute, if the grantee decided he did not want to homestead, was a point of considerable debate. The main concern was land speculation—that SAS would be "sold for a song to the scrip shark who has been the curse of the west."[172] But substitutes were ultimately permitted and SAS could be sold to anyone, including women, regardless of marital status, in a twist that parliamentarians never anticipated.

The VBA included one category of women. The definition of volunteers was for the first time extended to female nurses who had served in South Africa, becoming the first exception to the general rule in Canada that women (except sole heads of households with dependent children) were ineligible for homestead entry. There were only twelve nurses from Canada in South Africa, however—not enough to concern Canadian parliamentarians or to constitute a threat to the masculine West. One nurse who sold her scrip was Deborah Jane Hurcomb, who was with the Second Canadian contingent and who died in 1907. Her scrip was purchased by Mary Matalski of Verndale, Saskatchewan, a married mother of sixteen who successfully proved up in 1914.[173]

There was also a high degree of interest in obtaining SAS among Canadian women teachers who volunteered in South Africa, but they were denied this reward. At least forty women teachers from Canada taught in the Boer concentration camps. An appeal was made in the House of

Figure 17. Homesteaders near Square Deal, Alberta, c. 1912. Both women acquired their homesteads through purchasing South African scrip. Johanna Solberg (right) was a stenographer in Bassano, Alberta, and Sebina Jacobsen a dressmaker, also in Bassano, when they filed on their homesteads of 320 acres each. Both were single. Purchasing South African scrip was virtually the only way a single woman could acquire homestead land in Western Canada. Glenbow Archives, NA-206-27.

Commons to have them included in the land grant. Teacher volunteer Winifred Johnston Plowden, whose letter of appeal was read in the House, argued, among other things, that for their loyalty to the British Empire and for all of the hardships they endured, teachers should have land rights over male volunteers who saw no action, or over foreign widows who could claim homesteads the teachers were denied. "From my point of view many of the girls that went out suffered much more hardship than the last military contingent, who only landed at Cape Town and never went up country at all, and got a good grant for that."[174] The teachers were as deserving of government recognition as "some United States or Galician widows who may settle on western lands." "I hope," Plowden wrote, "that the government which has treated outsiders with the greatest generosity will see its way clear to a recognition of the first forty Canadian women who went half way round the world to impress upon a country shortly after its second birth into the British Empire, something of the acknowledged excellence of the Canadian public school system." The reward of SAS was not however extended to the teachers.

Yet teachers were among the women who purchased SAS and homesteaded land in Western Canada. The most celebrated of these was Mildred Williams, who made headlines across North America in May 1910 for her stamina and determination.[175] She was from Lintonville, Minnesota, and had arrived in Canada eight months earlier. Williams was the sole supporter of her widowed mother, and perhaps she had hoped to qualify for a free homestead, but the rules did not permit her because she had no minor child or children dependent upon her for support.[176] Single, in her early twenties, and working as a teacher in Saskatoon, Williams waited for twelve days and nights at the top of the stairs outside of the land office in Saskatoon in order to be able to file on a half section (320 acres) of land near Kindersley valued at eighteen to twenty dollars per acre. Williams purchased the SAS of Frederick Charles Snell, a storekeeper at Pilgrim's Rest, Transvaal, but previously of the Lord Strathcona Horse.[177] He was a North-West Mounted Policeman who had risen in the ranks and served in the Yukon, where he got a grant of land for his service. He was just the sort the legislators hoped to entice to the West, but he decided to stay in South Africa, living out his days there. Instead, Mildred Williams got his 320 acres.

Williams carefully planned her vigil. She employed a woman to bring her meals and soft drinks, and another as a "kind of scout and messenger."[178] She sat in a reclining chair and made a kind of tent over this in the nights. She put up with a great deal of inconvenience during the twelve-day vigil. On her second day, she was challenged by a man who wanted the same property. He allegedly tried to push her off her chair at one point, but Williams's numerous supporters came to her aid, shoving him down the stairs, and he gave up. She successfully filed on the property, and when she emerged from the land office a large number of friends greeted her, cheering and applauding. Williams successfully proved up on this land and became the owner of 320 acres of valuable land. She may have later sold this land, for in 1917 the *Star Phoenix* reported that she had resigned her position as teacher and gone to the Pacific coast.[179]

In May 1910, columnists praised Williams's "energy, determination and patience."[180] Writing in the *Edmonton Bulletin* (ironically, the paper owned by Minister of the Interior Frank Oliver, who opposed homestead rights for most women), Gertrude Seton Thompson predicted that "in three years she will have property worth at the least $10,000.00, and this sum, properly invested, should give her an income of $1,000.00 per year—Bravo!"[181]

Mildred Williams was far from alone. Of the 4,730 SAS entries in the Saskatchewan Archives Board (SAB) database, approximately 11 percent are women. Many of the files contain detailed and rich correspondence, documenting the challenges and difficulties the SAS women faced regardless of their marital status. Among the single women, some had the assistance of brothers or fathers, and the purchase of SAS involved family strategies to expand farms, while others appear to have been totally on their own. Marie Westphal, from Milwaukee, purchased SAS at Kindersley in 1910.[182] She was single and had arrived in the Eatonia area of Saskatchewan to keep house for her homesteading brother Herman. She filed on land previously abandoned by another brother who was unable to take up residence. Marie was single when she proved up, but later married and settled in the district. Together the Westphals amassed considerable acreage in the Kindersley area, as their father also homesteaded nearby at age seventy-one.[183]

Married women could add to family land holdings through purchasing SAS. In the Buffalo Lakes district of Peace River, Alberta, Emma Bradford of Manitoba was the largest single landholder, having proved up on a full section of land after purchasing two SASs. She was married, and along with her husband Andrew "had the largest family holding with seven quarters compiled from three scrips and a homestead, all of which were proven up."[184]

Lottie Kennedy of Winnipeg clearly had little idea of what she was signing up for when her fiancé Edward Baird (a railway mail clerk also of Winnipeg) entered on a homestead in the Maple Creek district of Saskatchewan, and she entered on adjoining land in 1913 through SAS that had been purchased for her by her father as a wedding present.[185] While Kennedy and Baird may have been planning to increase their land base through SAS, neither seemed to be aware that Kennedy would be required to perform actual residence on the land. The couple married and continued to live in Winnipeg. In 1915, Baird's uncle and a member of Parliament for Ontario, E. Guss Porter, wrote Minister of the Interior W.J. Roche to ask if breaking land on Mrs. Baird's homestead could "count as a year's duty without actually going out there to live. They are living in Winnipeg now where he holds a position in the mail service and he does not like to give up his position and go out there to live on the land if it can be avoided." Porter was informed that nothing could be done, that Mrs. Baird had to perform her residence duties, and that "it is only in the case of deceased, insane or physically incapacitated homesteaders that residence is dispensed with." The Bairds began residence duties in 1915, and Lottie Baird was granted her patent in 1918.

Other single women SAS homesteaders were without a family network or strategy. Originally from Norway, Carrie Sveum was a cook for threshers at Olson, North Dakota, and then a cook at a hotel in Swift Current in 1910, when at age thirty-eight she purchased SAS, filing on land at Waldville, Saskatchewan, and successfully proving up in 1914.[186] In 1914 she "travelled to Norway and brought back a husband a Mr. Sagen.[187] Together she and her new husband ran a successful restaurant and "stopping place." When her husband died, she sold her land and moved back to Norway.

The single women who were SAS homesteaders ranged in age, but most were in their thirties or forties, and some were older. Sarah Birtles of Alexander, Manitoba, was sixty-two when in 1913 she applied for patent on her SAS at Colonsay, Saskatchewan.[188] From Yorkshire, Birtles was a nurse who had immigrated with her family to Manitoba in the 1880s.[189] She had some difficulty fulfilling her residency requirement but not because of her age—rather, it was because when she was absent she was proving up on another SAS near Provost, Alberta, securing 640 acres for herself in two provinces. She was short in the residency requirement on her Saskatchewan claim by five days, so that the case was examined by a homestead inspector, who wrote, "The applicant is a spinster 62 years of age having nearly completed her residence duties for this Scrip and at the same time having performed residence duties on another Scrip near Provost Alta. The difficulty appears to be loss of time consumed in moving from one place to the other." The shortages were overlooked, although officials were annoyed, because "it is hardly the intention to allow the same person to locate more than once, although there is no legal objection of course to one person locating as many Volunteer Bounty Warrants as he can provided the ordinary duties can be completed." The same official wrote, "I suppose we should be very careful about establishing a precedent in a case of this sort."

There were other older women who acquired land through SAS. Eliza Birmingham, from Meaford, Ontario, was sixty years old in 1910 (although she may have been trimming a few years) when she received patent to her homestead in the Battleford district of Saskatchewan.[190] Her family then consisted of herself and two grandchildren. A year later she purchased the SAS of Alfred Arthur Lyndon of Toronto, and in 1914 (when she stated she was sixty-seven) successfully proved up on land in the vicinity of her first homestead.[191]

There is no doubt that unlike Sarah Birtles, some single women found it challenging to prove up on one SAS. Like Lottie (Kennedy) Baird, Sophia Brauer, age thirty-four, seemed unaware when she purchased her scrip that she would be required to live on the land and perform homestead duties. Brauer was from the United States and was working as a dressmaker in Swift Current when she purchased SAS and filed on land at Lemsford in 1911.[192] By early October of that year she was wondering if she could take a leave of absence until May, writing to the land office that "I want to stay longer if the weather allows it. But I do not see how I could stay all winter as it is so far from town and such a new country with few conveniences, cold winters and blizzards. I am afraid of perishing out here." She offered to live in Swift Current for the winters. She was told that she had to meet the residency requirements and live for six months of each year on her land except in the case of "serious accident, illness or calamity to the entrant, or to the wife or child of an entrant." Brauer did successfully meet her residency obligations and had sixty acres under cultivation in 1914 when she proved up.

Despite the fact that some of the married women SAS homesteaders had husbands and older children to assist them in proving up, their lives were often more complicated than those of single women SAS homesteaders. Many married women could not (officially) live in their homes with their husbands for six months of each year for three years, because they had to live on their own land to perform their residence duties. Matters become even more complicated when young children were involved. Nellie Jane Sorsdahl filed on land at Macoun, Saskatchewan, in 1910 but did not prove up until 1917.[193] By that time she was the mother of eleven children. She was threatened with cancellation proceedings on several occasions. In her correspondence with the Department of the Interior, Sorsdahl never mentioned the continual arrival of her children as the reason why she had difficulty meeting her residency requirements. In 1911, for example, she asked land officials if she could live with her husband on his SAS and perform her residence duties there, as her "health has been failing." The reply was that "it is regretted you cannot be permitted to live with your husband and thus satisfy the requirements of the Act as to residence ... the regulations require that you shall live upon your own half section for at least six months in each of three years."[194]

Jennie Cochrane, formerly Doyle, of San Francisco (but born in Canada), was the legal representative of her deceased son, George Doyle, a volunteer in the South African War who was granted SAS.[195] Cochrane is the only woman so far located who took up land as a mother of a deceased volunteer. She was fifty years old in 1913 when granted patent to her land at Biggar, Saskatchewan, although the process was not without complications. Early in 1913 she wrote to the Department of the Interior from San Francisco (spelling mistakes in the original):

> I don more than was required of me in Building and also in Breaking paid for every thing out of the way taxes included I wish I never saw the old land at all, for I suffered hardship and privitations enough to kill a dog a yellow dog. of course you are aware that I came by that Government Grant through the Death of my only Son. who was out in South Africa. 23 Rigement Mounted Cavlery. Now I do hope thair will be no more draw backs with regard to getting my patent. I am pretty sick of this and some times I woner if the dear Honourable Government is not trying to grind our lives out. as you know I don everything to the best of my knolledge in getting things fixed properly before I left Biggar in a Leagel way and con do no more.

Jane Gentles was a teacher from England who was married with three sons in 1908 when she purchased SAS. She did not file on land until 1911, when she entered on 320 acres near Saskatoon that had been abandoned by one of her sons.[196] In 1915 the government wanted to cancel her homestead entry, as she had not satisfied the inspector that the necessary homestead duties had been completed; she was ten weeks short of the time required. A neighbour had his eye on her land and had brought out the homestead inspector. But Gentles was teaching in Islington in London, England, at this time. All three of her sons served overseas in the First World War. Her husband stayed behind in Saskatchewan, taking care of her 320-acre homestead as well as one of their sons. Gentles was told by land officials, however, that she needed to be back in Saskatchewan completing her residency requirement. She wrote very vigorously in her own defence, asking that her war work count as residence duties on her land.[197] Gentles was teaching at Drayton Park Boys School, taking the place of a male teacher who had enlisted, and she was in charge of fifty-one boys. "And in that way," she declared, "I am serving my country to the best of my ability." She added as a postscript: "By Royal Proclamation in England any woman who undertakes work and by so doing liberates a man for the service of war is considered to be serving her country as truly as those serving in the trenches. I have given two sons out of three and the 3rd son is anxious to join the colours too but as he is all I have to help me he must stay behind unless it is absolutely necessary then he will join too." Gentles was sent a form to fill out, and in it she stated that "my time [residency on land] is not quite completed but I have given myself and my sons to my country's cause and we are all serving her here at very great sacrifice and ask the department to allow war work time to count as residence duties."[198]

Jane Gentles's land was protected from cancellation until 1 May 1916, but at that time she had still not returned to complete her residence duties. She wrote once again to officials of the Department of the Interior to say that she was she was planning to return in time for seeding, but that "the danger from torpedoes was very great at that time and my boys advised me to stay." Two of her sons were at Ypres; her oldest son should never have been accepted for duty as his sight was only 25 percent normal; and "these are all the children I have and I have given them up to fight the Germans." She concluded, "I think I was entitled to ask you to give me those few weeks time in face of the great sacrifices I had made." Gentles was fifty years old in 1919 when her patent to her land was finally approved.

Of the hundreds of women in Western Canada who acquired homesteads through purchasing South African scrip, few made the headlines, but those who did, such as Saskatoon teacher Mildred Williams, became important to the homesteads-for-women campaign that was gathering momentum just at that time. The SAS women homesteaders demonstrated that women, whether single, married, divorced, or widowed, and regardless of whether they had children, were interested in obtaining homestead land and could successfully prove up on that land. The fact that women had to *purchase* expensive scrip in order to homestead land also highlighted the discrimination at the foundation of the Dominion lands legislation. As columnist Gertrude Seton Thompson wrote in the *Edmonton Bulletin* after describing the vigil of Mildred Williams: "I hope the Dominion government will make a note of this, and give consideration to the question of women being allowed to homestead. That only by buying scrip can they homestead seems unfair. If allowed to take up land at all it should be on the same terms as men—not under almost prohibitive conditions."[199]

HOMESTEADS FOR WOMEN IN THE U.S. WEST

Migrant women could obtain homesteads by heading to the U.S. West, and many thousands of solo women did so.[200] It is important to understand this context and opportunity in order to appreciate the dimensions of the homesteads-for-women debates, to be covered in Chapter 6. Both supporters and critics of the homesteads-for-women movement drew on the example of the "entrywomen" of the American West. It is also vital to understand the dramatic differences between the United States and Canada when it came to the gender of homesteading.

The U.S. rules permitted a much wider diversity of women to acquire homestead land, and overall there was a greater flexibility in how officials of land offices interpreted the regulations, and more acceptance of and assistance to women who would be stigmatized in Canada, such as unwed mothers and divorced women. Widows applying for homesteads did not need to have minor children dependent on them for support as they did in Canada. Single women with adopted children were eligible. Single, unwed mothers were permitted to make entry, even if they were not yet twenty-one years of age.[201] Mormon women who were plural wives were permitted to enter on homesteads because their marriages were not recognized as legal.[202] Deserted and divorced women could homestead without having to have minor children dependent on them. In the United States an abandoned wife or "one whose husband is a confirmed drunkard" was considered the head of a family.[203] A married woman could make homestead entry if she had been "actually deserted" by her husband, or if her husband was in the penitentiary or "incapacitated by disease or otherwise from earning a support for his family and the wife is really the head and main support of the family."[204] Most of this was clearly itemized in U.S. legislation and available in the published guides to prospective homesteaders.

Before 1900 women homesteaders constituted less than 10 percent of all entries in the U.S. West, but their numbers grew dramatically thereafter.[205] Numbers vary; one study of forty-three townships in North Dakota reveals that proportion of women homesteaders varied from 1 percent to 22 percent, with an average of 10 percent.[206] In two counties in Colorado, women entrants were at 11 percent before 1900 while after that date, nearly 18 percent. In the peak years of the homestead rush in Cochise County, Arizona, from 1900 to 1918, 14 to 21 percent of the homesteaders were women.[207] The majority of women homesteaders were single: in North Dakota, for example, 83 percent were single, 15 percent were widows, and 1 percent were divorced.[208] Women homesteaders were as successful at proving up as their male counterparts.[209] Felice Cohn, whose work as a federal assistant superintendent of public sales of Indian lands took her to the land offices of Montana, wrote in 1919 that "the woman homesteader always lives up to the land regulations of the government. The homestead inspectors seldom have occasion to make an adverse report on a woman who is proving up on her land. Every regulation is always faithfully complied with."[210]

Recent studies that focus on counties in the U.S. West demonstrate that women homesteaders were everywhere. In the Yellowstone River Valley between 1909 and 1934, the federal government issued 4,066 land patents in Yellowstone County, and of these 18 percent, or 746, were issued to women who together claimed over 150,000 acres.[211] In Valley County, Montana, which borders on Saskatchewan, there was a similar percentage of women homesteaders. There were over 900 women homesteaders who proved up on homesteads in Valley County. There were likely many more, as the names were taken from 104 plats of townships and ranges, and nearly half of these are missing. Women homesteaders

Figure 18. Englishwoman, teacher, and mother Jane Gentles purchased South African scrip and filed on 320 acres of land near Saskatoon, Saskatchewan, in 1911. In 1915, when Gentles was in London teaching so that a male teacher could enlist, Canadian land officials wanted to cancel her entry. Gentles fought back, arguing that she was "serving her country as truly as those serving in the trenches." She included this photograph of herself and two sons who were at the front. Officials relented and Gentles was granted a patent to her land in 1919. Saskatchewan Archives Board, homestead file 2092263.

Figure 19. Eva Iddings of Indiana in front of her claim shack near Fort Benton, Montana. Eva filed on her homestead in 1910 and proved up in 1912. Three brothers and two aunts also filed on homesteads. Solo women homesteaders, rare in Western Canada, were abundant in the American West. Barrows Collection, Overholser Historical Research Center, Fort Benton, Montana, 1910, BC11, 244.

Figure 20. Canadian women, ineligible to file on homesteads on the Canadian prairies, homesteaded in the American West. Sisters from Ontario Caroline (Carrie) Louise MacGregor and Mary Frances MacGregor homesteaded in Sheridan County, Montana. Carrie earned her patent to just over 156 acres in 1912, and Mary became the owner of 312 acres in 1914. According to an October 1909 description in the local paper, "The Macgregor sisters have a large ranch about five miles down the valley from Redstone.... These girls have a fine dwelling and a good barn and granary, a great deal of the carpenter work being done by themselves. They have a fine bunch of horses, cows, pigs and chickens. They are both college graduates and musicians. It was a great pleasure to visit such well informed people so far out on the frontier." These photographs show the nature and range of their work on their land. Courtesy Judy Archer (Carrie's granddaughter), Orillia, Ontario.

comprised approximately 17 percent, or one-sixth, of the homesteaders in that county.

Like male homesteaders, women often homesteaded in clusters—sisters, cousins, and friends filed together and near each other. Three Chmelik sisters—Anna, Mary, and Emily—from Minnesota, took up adjoining homesteads in Chouteau County, Montana, in 1910. Anna was a teacher and Mary a seamstress. Their brother helped them build their cabins and break sod for their first crops. In 1912 Lena J. Michels and her two cousins, Mary Lambert and Frances Lambert, left South Dakota and filed on adjoining homesteads near Stanford, Montana, by the Genou post office.[212] One settlement in the Hawarden district was called "Ladyville" because of its preponderance of women homesteaders.[213] Daughters arrived with mothers, and all took out homesteads. Homesteaders sometimes built cabins close together but on their own claims, divided by the survey line. For example, Sophia Jefferson and Mildred Hunt filed on adjoining homesteads on the North Bench near Fort Benton in 1910, and their cabins were known in the area as "twin shacks." Often filing on land was part of a family strategy. Daughters could help expand the family land base by taking out homesteads, filing alongside brothers, sisters, fathers, uncles, aunts, or other relatives. Ann Yoctorowic Obie filed on land near the homesteads of her father, sister, and three brothers near Joplin in Liberty County.[214]

The opportunity to cross the border and homestead in the United States was well known to women living in Canada, as discussion of the homesteads-for-women campaign will show. Caroline (Carrie) Louise MacGregor and her sister Mary Frances MacGregor, from Ontario, homesteaded in Sheridan County in Montana. Carrie earned her patent to 156 acres in 1912, and Mary earned her patent to 312 acres in 1914.[215] They pooled resources and established a ranch together, which was described in the 1 October 1909 newspaper *The Searchlight* (Culbertson, Montana): "The Macgregor sisters have a large ranch about five miles down the valley from Redstone … These girls have a fine dwelling and a good barn and granary, a great deal of the carpenter work being done by themselves. They have a fine bunch of horses, cows, pigs and chickens. They are both college graduates and musicians. It was a great pleasure to visit such well informed people so far out on the frontier." Carrie was a graduate of the University of Toronto. She married Rev. William Archer in 1912 and moved to Quebec. Mary married a fellow homesteader Hans Madsen and was the mother of two young daughters when she died in the flu epidemic of 1919.[216] According to her granddaughter Judy Archer, Carrie settled in Montana because the Canadian government would not grant homesteads to single women. Judy Archer writes that "Carrie rode a horse bare back, with a long skirt on. She kept a pistol because the local Indians would ride past the knoll where the house was." As the photographs indicate, the sisters did the work required themselves, in long dresses.

In 1910 Alberta teacher Etta Smalley crossed the border to take up a homestead. Her movements back and forth across the forty-ninth parallel indicate how fluid the border then was. Smalley was originally from Ohio and settled in Alberta in 1904 with her family when her father filed on a homestead at Soda Lake.[217] She completed her Alberta departmental exams in 1906 and attended the Provincial Normal School at Calgary.[218] In 1910 she was teaching at the Bolan Marea School in the Soda Lake district of Alberta, where her students were Ukrainian and Romanian.[219] Smalley boarded with the Woods family, where there were two daughters, and when Mr. Woods and one of the daughters filed on homesteads in Hill County, Montana, Etta decided she would join them. She claimed 320 acres, as she was able to take advantage of the Enlarged Homestead Act of 1909, and proved up while continuing to teach, at first in Alberta and then at Inverness, Montana. She earned her patent to her land in 1914 and that same year married a neighbouring homesteader, Will Bangs. They had four children. They lived at first on Will's homestead and persisted through drought, grasshoppers, and war, even as Inverness and nearby Joplin were "all but abandoned."[220] Will Bangs lost his homestead to the banks in 1926, but Etta retained hers. The family moved into her original homestead shack, and as described in her memoir, they bought a larger house in 1943 and had it moved to her land. The Bangs were still living on her homestead in 1954 when they retired and moved to Havre. Etta Bangs died in 1973 at the age of eighty-seven. In 1980 her homestead was turned over to her grandson Tom.

British women also went to the U.S. West to obtain homesteads, ignoring calls to do their duty to the Empire and settle under the British flag. An example is Jessie de Prado MacMillan from Scotland who acquired 540 acres in New Mexico, and she was not alone; other Scottish women homesteaded nearby, one of whom served as her inspiration in leading her to homestead on Agua Chiquita Creek.[221]

While British women such as MacMillan opted to go to the American West, where homestead land could be obtained by a single female, a great number and variety of women overcame the considerable challenges and obstacles to obtaining homestead land in the Canadian West. Their numbers are difficult to ascertain because of the scattered and fragmentary records they left, but the evidence indicates that women were determined to acquire land and were willing to go to extraordinary lengths to do so. For its part, the Canadian government went to extraordinary lengths to ensure that women had very limited access to land, circumscribing the eligible categories of women and scrutinizing and rejecting their applications.

This scrutiny was intense. A weary and jaded Department of the Interior law clerk, T.G. Rothwell, expressed exasperation in 1914 correspondence that his job allowed no common sense leniency or discretion in interpreting the exact wording of the Dominion Lands Act.[222] Rothwell was dealing with the case of Mary Briggs, a widow of Wood Mountain, and her right to a pre-emption or purchased homestead. She had obtained a homestead through the death of a son, and she was his legal representative. Hers was a complex and unique case in which officials were reluctant to depart one inch from the legislation because that might set a precedent, and Briggs was not strictly entitled to a homestead, although clearly a bona fide settler. Reviewing the case, Rothwell expressed his dismay with the intransigent bureaucrats who were so reluctant to call on the discretionary powers of the minister.[223] He wrote that he himself had "followed a practice that has been incorrectly followed ever since I have been an officer of this Department, over thirty years, a practice to which so many other members of its staff, some of them most capable and hard working officials, are glued—soldered—so closely, that it is not possible to detach them from it. That practice is to construe the provisions of the Dominion Lands Act literally—to give the settler his pound of flesh only, and oftentimes not quite that." Bureaucrats did not care, Rothwell thought, about the central purpose of the act, which was to place agricultural settlers on the land and to afford the subject benefits and privileges. They feared "leaving the well beaten track and establishing a precedent that may bring responsibility, as much as travellers in South Africa fear an approaching South African lion." In an earlier memo he had himself recommended that Mrs. Briggs be turned down in her request, but his assistant, a "Miss Barber," had saved him from "doing a great injustice to Mrs. Briggs."

Rothwell felt it was ridiculous to be concerned about setting a precedent. He believed that another case such as hers would arise "not in a hundred years, and so the granting of a purchased homestead or of a pre-emption to Mrs. Briggs will not form the dangerous precedent I have been warned it is certain to establish if this privilege is given to her."

Migrant women faced vicissitudes, intense scrutiny, and hardships, but they did succeed in acquiring homestead land on the prairies. They enjoyed homestead privileges denied to Indigenous women and men, and participated in land acquisition that dispossessed Indigenous people. But none of these women homesteaders shared in the full range of privileges offered to male homesteaders. Reflecting the larger settlement patterns of the West, women homesteaders were diverse; from the earliest arrivals to the late nineteenth century they were British and British-Ontarian, and after 1900 they came from a variety of European nations and the United States. This diversity would be seized upon and criticized by advocates of homesteads for British-born women, who concluded that the strongest rationale for including British women in the homestead privilege was that it would help to exclude "foreigners" and assist in crafting a British West.

CHAPTER FOUR

WOMEN WHO BOUGHT LAND

THE "BACHELOR GIRL" SETTLER, "JACK" MAY, AND OTHER CELEBRITY FARMERS AND RANCHERS

While migrant women who wished to homestead faced many restrictions, they were free to purchase land in Western Canada if they had the money. They could be single, married, separated, or divorced, young or old, with children or on their own, or in partnership with a female companion. Questions were not asked about their marital or parental status if they had the funds to buy land. As they were not homesteaders, they did not come under the intense oversight of the land office and the homestead inspectors who insisted they be widows with children. Yet women who bought land were still scrutinized, particularly in the press, because they were rare, and they were often cast as aberrant, abnormal, or eccentric, although some of the coverage was celebratory, hoping to widen and sanction such vocational opportunities. This chapter features Isobel "Jack" May, an English farmer who settled (briefly) in Alberta in 1911. She garnered particular attention throughout the British Empire and in the United States because she wore men's clothing and because she most clearly challenged the accepted norms of femininity and the spotlight on the white male pioneer figure. While May was English, this chapter does not focus exclusively on British women, since they were not alone in purchasing land. Purchasers of land, however, were less diverse than women homesteaders because they had to have capital.

INDIAN RESERVE LAND AND MÉTIS SCRIP

Land that was for sale on the prairies included large areas that First Nations were induced to "surrender," severely reducing the size of their reserves.[1] In 1909, for example, a controversial sale of land on the Piikani (Peigan) reserve took place in southern Alberta. Although the majority of male band members (the eligible voters) had opposed the surrender of thirty-six sections, or 23,500 of their 116,000 acres of reserve land, the Department of Indian Affairs declared (fraudulently) that a fair vote was taken.[2] This was part of a pattern of dispossession and diminishment of reserve land throughout prairie Canada. The Piikani applied for an injunction against the advertised sale of their land by public auction at Pincher Creek in November 1909, but this request was denied and the sale took place.

Two quarter sections were purchased by Jean Laidlaw of Ontario and her female partner.[3] Laidlaw was originally from England and was working in Ontario as a kindergarten supervisor when she purchased this land.[4] A 1920 article on Laidlaw is typical of the sort of scrutiny the reasonably rare woman rancher or farmer was placed under. In the Toronto *Globe and Mail* under the headline "Woman Rancher Tells of Life: Miss Jean Laidlaw Runs 320 Acres near Pincher Creek, Alberta: Shows Great Pluck," readers learned that together with a nephew, Laidlaw raised cattle, horses, pigs, and poultry on her land.[5] She was described as "nothing if not feminine. Petite, gentle-voiced, and with dimples that look as if the wearer must have been play-acting when the camera snapped her, arrayed in a pair of overalls, struggling with one or other of the 'chores' that punctuate farm life." Her crop had failed in 1919, but she still had "hope and grit in her heart, ready to take her chances with next summer's weather." The article also noted that Laidlaw's land was on the Piikani reserve, and she had "many amusing stories to tell of farm hands drawn from this tribe," including one "who wound a pink ribbon around his Stetson, "this gay garniture forming the frame of a picture of his girl, which adorned as a buckle might, the upturned brim of his headgear." The message was that both Laidlaw and her hired Indigenous helpers were odd and eccentric presences on an Alberta ranch.

Women purchased Indigenous reserve land after it was "surrendered" for sale for the purpose of speculation. In 1891 the Passpasschase reserve near Edmonton was sold at auction, and purchasers included Nancy Miquelon of Calgary and Belle Thomson of Quebec.[6] In 1902, when the Enoch/Stony Plain reserve was sold, Ellen Carruthers, the wife of the Indian agency clerk, acquired one quarter section.[7] Some of the women purchasers may have been "fronts" for insiders who wanted to try to cover their tracks. For example, in 1903 Maria Allison of Ottawa bought land surrendered on the Michel reserve in Alberta, paying much less than its value. According to historian Peggy Martin-McGuire, Allison was "guided in these purchases by Herbert N. Awrey, a clerk in the Department of Indian Affairs for whom she worked as a janitor. Her bids had been forwarded in a departmental envelope, and included clippings from typed copies of the surveyor's reports."[8] At an auction of reserve land in the Battleford agency in 1905, M.J. Day, the wife of the Indian agent, bought two quarter sections.[9] The auctioneer's wife also bought land. In 1907 Alice Tye, secretary to the Indian agent, bought land surrendered on the Cowessess reserve in Saskatchewan.[10]

Migrant women also acquired land on the prairies through purchasing Métis scrip. As described in Chapter 2, the original Métis recipient of land scrip was required to sign a form that identified the section of land on which he or she desired to locate their scrip. The land was then assigned to the purchaser of the scrip, and the patent issued in his or her name. Susan Jones Willoughby, the wife of prominent Moose Jaw barrister and senator W.B. Willoughby, K.C., acquired a lot of land in this way. She died in 1907, and when her husband died in 1932 it was noted that he "was a heavy landholder in southern Saskatchewan."[11] In 1900, for example, Mrs. Willoughby received patent to 320 acres through "four assignments from Peter Dumont, Francois Gosselin, Emmanuel Gosselin and Norbert McGillis."[12] There are many other examples, including Matilda Bucknam (mentioned in Chapter 3). She was permitted to "scrip" eighty acres of her quarter section and to purchase the rest. Her Edmonton lawyers wrote to Minister of the Interior Oliver, asking that if permission was granted for her to do this, "we will be notified in order that we may hunt up the half-breed for whose scrip Miss Buckman has paid, in order to complete the transaction."[13] Sarah J. Milligan acquired land in the Fort Qu'Appelle region by purchasing the scrip for 240 acres of Samuel George McNab of the Touchwood Hills.[14]

Alberta teacher Victoria Lepage used a variety of tactics including the purchase of Métis scrip to acquire land near Lamoureux.[15] In 1895 she bought a military bounty scrip and located a nephew on a half section of land, assigning him the homestead duties, although he soon abandoned the tasks. She planned to pay cash for eighty acres and "apply a Half-breed land scrip upon 240 acres of the land in question." Lepage purchased the Métis scrip, but for a variety of reasons she was not successful in this complicated venture, and her claim was cancelled. Among the causes was a neighbour (and likely a relative) Charles Lepage, who wanted her land for his son and who complained that no improvements had been made and believed that a single woman teacher was not a suitable owner of land.[16] He wrote the land office that "there are lots of hands who would be too glad to improve [this land] and put them in a shape [*sic*] so that they would be a benefit to the country. The lady I refer to is a school teacher earning $600 a year, and a sure thing she does not need any land to speculate on." The Lepages were originally from Rimouski, Quebec. They came in a large family group to Lamoureux and amassed many sections of land in the district.[17] Victoria Lepage, the youngest of thirteen children, was a celebrated pioneer teacher of Lamoureux but never able to acquire land of her own.[18]

BRITISH WOMEN PURCHASERS OF LAND

Women who could afford to purchase land could be single, married, separated, divorced, or widowed in contrast to homesteading women who had to be widows and mothers. There were no homestead inspectors reporting on whether they conformed to these categories. Local histories provide brief glimpses of some of the women who purchased land. In 1880, Fanny McClure became one of the earliest settlers in the Rapid City district of Manitoba. According to the local history, "she was a wealthy English lady and bought the NW1/4 34-13-19 sight unseen."[19] Her brother, Colonel Thomas Martin, bought an adjoining quarter section. The brother and sister built two houses, and she lived in one with her son and his wife, but she disappeared from the district in the early 1890s. In 1898 Margaret Hunter and three sons, from Callander, Scotland, came to the Tremaine district of Manitoba, where she bought a farm.[20]

"Madame" Simpson (first name not recorded) settled in Grosse-Isle, Manitoba, in 1889 with four sons and one daughter. Originally from Ireland, this Quaker family had allegedly "made farming experiments in many lands ... the south of Ireland, Belgium and France were all tried and found wanting. On this continent they looked through California before winding up their grand tour in this district where they became large land owners." The Simpsons accumulated "some 1600 acres of land."[21]

In 1903 Isabella Wilson, from Wigan in Lancashire, England, arrived in Saskatchewan with two brothers.[22] The two men filed on their free homesteads. As Isabella was not eligible to homestead, she bought a quarter section from a departing farmer and named her farm Broadlands. Neighbours helped her to build her log cabin, and it was to this home in 1905 that she welcomed the remainder of her family members from England, including her mother.

Married women purchased land, and in some cases they were the farmers rather than their husbands, who might still be present but not active on the land. It is a mistake to always assume that the husband was the farmer. The married woman farmer and purchaser of land could, however, encounter legal puzzles and impediments. This was case with Maggie Lindsay, who farmed with her husband near Yorkton.[23] He had bought land from funds that Maggie received from her family in Scotland. When he was unable to meet his payments she offered to make them if he would assign the land to her, and he did. Maggie made all subsequent payments with money from her relatives. The husband owned the adjoining quarter section. Under executions against her husband, the sheriff seized a quantity of wheat grown on her land. The question before the court in 1907 in *Lindsay v. Morrow* was, who owned the grain grown on her land? The creditors claimed that the crops were Mr. Lindsay's, as he did the work and that if otherwise, the onus was on her to establish that the husband was her servant and the farming business really hers. Maggie Lindsay as claimant called her husband as the only witness, and they both testified that "the farming operations were carried on by Mrs. Lindsay with the help of two hired men; that she hired the men and that they took their orders from her ... The husband worked on her land part of the time, but in return received help on his quarter from her hired men." Evidence also showed that she had her own implements, and that she purchased her own seed grain from the government. When the seed arrived she personally took delivery of it. It was found that the proceeds from her farm could not be held liable for her husband's debts.

There are several prominent examples of married British women who were the farmers in the family. Annie E. Williams, from Beaufort, Wales, was an enterprising and accomplished farmer north of Gleichen, Alberta.[24] She and her husband, Frederick C. Williams, first came to Alberta in 1908. She purchased over 500 acres from the Canadian Pacific Railway, establishing Primrose Farm.[25] She became well-known as a "lady farmer." Annie Williams experimented with different kinds of wheat and flax seed. In 1912 she stopped by the office of the local newspaper, the *Gleichen Call*, to report on the excellent results of the Alberta Government Laboratory test of the "Stanley" wheat grown on her farm.[26] In 1913 she had a bumper crop of flax that yielded nearly thirty bushels to the acre, and she had other crops that yielded well, including her oats and spring wheat. Across Alberta she was featured in headlines such as "Mrs. A.E. Williams Receives Big Price for Her Seed Flax," "Mrs. Williams Grows Excellent Flax," and "Lady Farmer Raises Record Crop."[27] (The contribution, if any, of her husband to the farm work was never mentioned.) In 1916 Mrs. Williams purchased, for $12,500 in cash, two other farms that were "some of the very best farm property in the Gleichen district."[28] The Williamses stayed on the farm until 1923, but according to their son, crops were poor in the later years because of hail, frost, drought, grasshoppers, and caterpillars or cutworms.[29]

Alice (Alix) Westhead was another married Englishwoman who was the farmer and rancher in the family. The town of Alix, Alberta, is named for her, and she was featured in the 1906 Canadian Pacific Railway (CPR) pamphlet as a successful farmer, as mentioned in Chapter 2.[30] Westhead was born Alice Charlotte Hall in 1863 in India and in 1881 at Rawalpindi, Pakistan she married her first husband, who died in 1887. As a widow in London in 1891 she married Charles George Westhead.[31] They moved to Alberta in the mid-1890s and established their ranch together, but they drifted apart and she managed the enterprise. She purchased 1,440 acres from the Canadian Pacific Railway, and her husband purchased 480 acres (although it seems that he defaulted on his payments while she paid in full for her land).[32]

She was well-known as a stock-raiser and agriculturalist in her district. Alix Westhead was honorary president of the Alix Agricultural Society in 1910, and the annual ploughing competition took place at her ranch.[33] She was a friend of another famous Alix resident and fellow Englishwoman with family ties to India, Irene Parlby, who became well-known as an Alberta politician and cabinet minister in the United Farmers of Alberta government.[34]

Figure 21. Alice (Alix) Westhead, c. 1906. She was born in Lahore, India, in 1863 and was living in Ireland with her second husband, C.G. Westhead, when they immigrated to Alberta in the mid-1890s. While they established the Quarter-Circle-One Ranch together near the town of Alix (named after Westhead), she was the owner and operator of the enterprise of over 2,000 acres. She returned to England around 1912 and the ranch was sold. Glenbow Archives, NA-2925-2.

In 1911 an article titled "A Woman Rancher in Alberta: A Visit to the Quarter-Circle-One Ranch," by Gertrude E. Seton Thompson, appeared in the *Canadian Home Journal*.[35] Thompson wrote that Mrs. Westhead had arrived in 1895 "from the Old Land with the idea of becoming a rancher, and had acquired over 2,000 acres." According to Thompson, Mrs. Westhead had "expert knowledge on all matters relating to farming, and t[ook] a keen interest in the agricultural interests of the country." Her expertise in matters agricultural, readers learned, had begun on her husband's estate in Ireland, where she had started a creamery. The article made no mention of the presence of her husband.

The point of Thompson's article was that it was Mrs. Westhead who was the rancher. It was Mrs. Westhead who "gives orders to her men and otherwise superintends the running of the ranch." She had sixty beautiful horses. The journalist traced a typical day on the ranch for Mrs. Westhead, which began with breakfast served and cleaned up by her domestic helper "Scotch Jane." Then off to the garden to gather lettuce, peas, beans, and strawberries, followed by butter churning. After lunch and a siesta, Mrs. Westhead drove for tea to a neighbouring ranch. The article concluded, "Mrs. Westhead's success as a rancher should prove encouraging to other women who, having some capital to invest and loving the outdoor life, feel a desire to launch into the wide sphere of farming or ranching." The same year as the article appeared, however, the ranch was sold, and Mrs. Westhead moved first to Edmonton and then to England.[36] The last mention of her in Alberta was in a 1912 publication that stated she "still owns and manages a ranch of some 3,500 acres."[37] There was a hint in this publication that her land had become valuable as it was announced that the town of Alix was to have three transcontinental railways passing through it. After returning to England, Westhead lived in a farmhouse near Exbury and acted as a companion to Mrs. Marie-Louise de Rothschild, when she and her husband Lionel, who created his famous garden there, were in residence.[38]

Journalist Celesta Hamer Jackson (also known as Celesta Grivot de Grandcourt), who first arrived in Alberta on assignment with the London *Daily Mail* in 1911, decided she would take up farming and ranching. She relocated her husband, George, and six children to the prairies, where she acquired 640 acres near Red Deer.[39] The Hamer Jacksons had been experiencing some difficulties and challenges in England. In 1903 George, a London bookmaker, lost all of his money through his speculation on the stock exchange. He had started the business "with a capital of 800 pound, lent to him by his wife."[40] By 1910 George and Celesta were in business together as journalists under the name Hamer-Jackson and Co., when they were accused of copyright infringement for publishing some illustrations without permission.[41] They proposed to make a payment to the plaintiff, who offered to stay the proceedings.

None of this was mentioned in Celesta Hamer Jackson's 1913 account of "How I Made a New Home in Canada," published in the *Daily Mail*.[42] There, she described how she had been attracted by "the wonderful boundless prairies … its freedom from the trammels of civilization." Her husband was "ready to give up everything" (and perhaps he already had). She did not specify how they acquired their ranch of 640 acres, but in 1911 Celesta was one of three purchasers of 160 acres of CPR land that was assigned to her alone in June 1913.[43] Hamer Jackson describes her family arriving with a party of others who were accustomed to "all the comforts that European homes can possibly realise." They lived in tents for three months but then had barns and houses ready. They bought implements and horses, and thoroughbred cattle, pigs, and fowls. The men of the party soon constructed "model" piggeries and poultry houses. In her 1913 article she describes this as a "profit-sharing farm" where no one got a salary, but it seems they all worked for her as the owner-manager. She intended to build a model dairy and a cheese-making factory. Hamer Jackson confessed that "not one of us had real working farm experience … But we all had pluck and perseverance. We all went with a resolve to succeed at all costs."

In newspapers as far away as Australia, Hamer Jackson was described as "the most remarkable woman farmer in the Dominion of Canada."[44] According to one account she had brought thirty people from England to help her, but she was "her own managing director." She was described as a "Canadian rancher" who raised "nothing but thoroughbred stock on her farm." This was achieved despite the fact that "she had no previous knowledge of farming methods," had "capital too trivial to mention," and was a "slip of a woman." None of the press coverage mentioned her husband, other than to note that her family consisted of him and their children; all of the success was attributed to her. In 1914 the press declared that this "Canadian rancher" had "struck the keynote of successful settlement in Western Canada."[45] Hamer Jackson lectured in England on farming in

Canada under the auspices of the CPR, and also published articles with the promotion of Canada to potential British settlers as her main theme.[46]

It is not always possible to determine from the fragmentary evidence whether Englishwomen who farmed the prairies felt they were contributing to the "spade work of Empire," but it seems likely in the case of Hamer Jackson. Her articles indicate she was an imperial enthusiast. She was concerned about the education of the "foreigners" in Western Canada, and about their proclivity to bring with them "racial vices."[47] Imperial views of the savage and civilized and the virtues of the British Empire were expressed in her 1931 book written for children, *Discoverers and Explorers of North America.* It is not clear how long Hamer Jackson farmed. She had moved by 1919 to Edmonton, where she was active in social circles, continued to publish articles, and was secretary of the Edmonton Women's Institute.

As the examples of Annie Williams, Alix Westhead, and Celesta Hamer Jackson demonstrate, women purchased CPR land intending to farm that land themselves. They also purchased CPR land as investors and as speculators. The CPR records for most of them include their marital status, describing them, for example, with terms like "spinster," "wife of …," or "widow." There are seventy-nine records of land purchased by spinsters.[48] Some were resident in the Canadian West. Maggie Dunn, spinster, was a resident of Ellisboro, Assiniboia, when she purchased her land in 1900, and when she paid in full in 1908, she was a Mrs. Merrifield, still of Ellisboro.[49] Others were from distant U.S. locations, including Iowa, Illinois, the Dakotas, New York, and California. Frances Mabel Green, spinster, living in Los Angeles, California, paid for her 160 acres in full at the time of purchase.[50] There were also buyers from England, including Alice Caton, spinster, who was among three purchasers from Blackpool.[51] There are 1,849 records of married women purchasing CPR land, such as "Margaret Ducklow, wife of James Ducklow, Osprey, Ont." who purchased CPR land in Manitoba in 1882.[52] There are 320 records of widows purchasing CPR land.[53]

CELEBRATED WOMEN FARMERS AND RANCHERS

Mary Gilroy, "Bachelor Girl" Farmer of Regina – While farmers and ranchers Annie Williams, Alix Westhead, and Celesta Hamer Jackson received considerable attention from journalists, there were others who were even more celebrated. Regina's Mary Gilroy was one. In her 1907 article "Openings for Women in Canada," author Agnes C. Laut advocated "fruit farming, chicken farming, ranching, even wheat growing" for women and wrote that "the number of women who have done this successfully is legion. I recall a girl who went to the Territories to teach painting. Now the West is not old enough for art. The paints were laid aside, and, as the head of her family of brothers and sisters, she bought land near Regina. On that land the banks advanced money for building and implements. Today the girl drives her own span, and is educating the other members of her family—which she could never have accomplished from art."[54] While the "legion" of women who successfully farmed is a challenge to locate, Laut's Regina farmer was Mary (Marie) Gilroy, "one of the most famous woman settlers of the west."[55] Yet when she died in Regina in 1949, there was little recollection of her achievements. It was noted in the *Leader-Post* (Regina) that "Miss Mary Victoria Gilroy," who died at age eighty-two, had arrived from Barrie, Ontario, in 1882, and that "she was believed to have been one of the first women farmers in Saskatchewan."[56] Little is known about Gilroy aside from the press coverage she received. She was born Mary Gilroy in 1867 in the Niagara district of Ontario. Her parents were from Ireland and her father was a farm labourer.[57]

Gilroy was celebrated by the CPR in their 1903 publication *Words from the Women of Western Canada* under the subtitle "A Bachelor Girl Speaks."[58] She was an important example in the pamphlet because as a single woman she could not acquire a homestead, but she could purchase land, preferably CPR land. According to the pamphlet, Gilroy was not a "'toil-worn farm woman' [but] on the contrary, she appeared a well-to-do business woman, clad in a handsome seal jacket, a neat toque, completely up-to-date driving attire." She described herself as a "genuine farmer … my art is merely a winter's amusement, for I was obliged to give it up as a means of livelihood some years ago." Her health was not good in her home province of Ontario, and she had consulted a physician who "ordered me at once to the North-West, told me to burn my paint brushes and give myself a chance for life by imbibing the pure prairie air." He advised her to work on a farm, but instead Gilroy bought a half section of land. She told the author of the pamphlet that she ran the farm all alone, with one hired man and up to three others during seeding and harvest. Her brother, a student, lived with her, but she managed the work of the farm herself. Gilroy began as a grain farmer only but was considering mixed farming. She had at that time (1903) farmed for seven years, and she operated the plough and the binder and cleaned the stables. The pamphlet stressed her scientific knowledge of agriculture, including the chemical composition of the soil, but this was all acquired through experience. She described herself as

> an enthusiast on prairie farming: why not? From a semi-invalid, existing on a bare living brought in by my paintings, I've grown to be the healthiest of women! Well, no not exactly the "wealthiest" as well, but I've no reason to complain of my financial standing. I don't owe a dollar, I've a clear title to my 320 acres; 240 acres are broken and 210 acres ready for crop another season.... Life on a prairie farm is an ideal existence; that is if you don't get into a "rut." I believe no life is so elevating as farm life; there's no "drudgery" about it unless you let it become drudgery. Yes it means close application: I am up at four every summer morning, but when my day's work is done, I have my books, music and my brush. I've made money from the start: any one can do the same, and if you run over the list of farmers in this district you won't find one failure![59]

In 1906 Gilroy was visited by the Canadian Women's Press Club when representatives toured Manitoba, Saskatchewan, and Alberta.[60] They were looking for "evidence of the success of women in the West" and found it "beyond our ken" that "women entirely ignorant of farming or ranching could make a success in that line of life." Gilroy was cast as fiercely independent and as having great authority over the men she employed. Described once again as "the bachelor girl farmer of Regina," Gilroy "turned the first furrow of our disbelief and planted facts where fancies had grown rampant." She had known nothing of farming when she bought her land eleven years earlier for $2,000. She told the touring press women that "if any men didn't do what I thought was right I discharged them and got others ... Ask anybody for miles around if I can be imposed upon ... I've a 'firing' reputation." The press women also reported, however, that Gilroy had sold her farm and stock for $13,750, a small fortune.

Gilroy was also featured in an article about women farmers in Western Canada in the *Minneapolis Journal* of July 1906, called "How Four Plucky Women Won Out in the Canadian Northwest."[61] It began with "'The bachelor girl farmer' is a personage of whom one hears fifteen minutes after arriving in Regina. 'She's a corkerjack, as you Americans say,' was how one enthusiastic man expressed it."

Selling her farm in 1906 did not mean that Gilroy was excised from further promotion of women farmers. In the 1907 CPR pamphlet *Home Life of Women in Western Canada* she appeared again, although it was noted that she had sold her "country holding for the round sum of $15,000.00."[62] The pamphlet described Gilroy as "one of the big grain growers of the district" and as "one of the most written about business women in the West; her plucky venture, putting her last shilling in a prairie farm, her indomitable energy, spent in a hand-to-hand tussle with fortune." It was reported that she was touring Europe, "taking pleasure from the result of her $2,000.00 investment on the prairie plains!" Gilroy then faded into obscurity and has been forgotten. According to her obituary, she became an insurance "saleswoman" for Mutual Life Assurance Company of Canada.[63] In 1911 she was a "lodger" in a rooming house on Retallack Street in Regina.[64]

Lady Ernestine Hunt: Alberta Horse Rancher – By 1906 "the most adventurous Englishwoman of the day," Lady Ernestine Hunt, a daughter of the Marquis and Marchioness of Ailesbury, had a horse ranch near Calgary of (allegedly) between 30,000 and 40,000 acres.[65] Her ranching activities were widely reported in Canada, the United States, and Britain in part because she was well-known for her exploits long before establishing her Canadian ranch. She was described as "a modern feminine Don Quixote" and as having "crowded into her life more adventures than one usually comes across in the pages of a sensational novel."[66] As Lady Ernestine Brudenell-Bruce, she established a reputation for "handling a yacht … almost equal to the most experienced 'old salt.'"[67] As she told a reporter in 1906, "As long as I can remember I have had a roving disposition, and have been fond of two things—horses and the sea. By the time I was 24 I had been around the Horn, and I was a night staff nurse at Krugersdorp [South Africa] at the time of Jameson raid. A few months later I went to Australia in a sailing boat, returning in another sailer [*sic*]."[68] In order to take command of her own yacht she required a yacht master's certificate, and she attended nautical school in Liverpool but was refused permission to write the final exam because she was a woman. While there she met Harry Brady Hunt from Ireland, and they eloped. He was a mate in the merchant service, and she sailed with him to Japan and many other locations. She also trained steeplechasers in Ireland.

Under headlines such as "Titled Lady Has Ranch in the West" and "Canadian Woman Rancher: The Daughter of a Marquess Ships Horses to England," it was widely reported in 1906 that Lady Hunt was the "only woman that has ever brought livestock across the ocean by herself," from her ranch near Calgary through the port of Montreal.[69] She arrived at the port "dressed in real cowboy fashion. She is a dark complexioned young woman about 28 years of age: wore a sombrero hat, black waist, khaki colored skirt reaching to the knees, leather leggings and shoes. Her hair was cut short."[70] She shipped seventeen horses and personally supervised their conveyance, although they were yet to be broken and were still in a "half wild state." She intended to ship them to her Irish estates at Ballylean, County Clare, and Kilcurly Adare, County Limerick.[71] Several nights on board she had to give up her sleep to calm them. Hunt could "handle them just about as she pleased, although the deck hands found it necessary to keep at a safe and respectful distance."[72] Despite sleepless nights she was "a picture of beauty and health."[73]

Hunt was apparently dividing her time between Ireland and her ranch in Alberta in 1910 when she founded a colonial training school for girls at Cosham Park near Portsmouth. Situated on seven acres of meadow and orchard, the school was intended to train women to be independent once they arrived in the colonies. Hunt had found that "girls who have left boarding school have a great deal to learn before they are fitted to seek a career of independence in the colonies of the empire."[74] She appointed herself the principal of the school, and her aim was to give girls of eighteen or older training in subjects that would be useful to them in "fending for themselves and their homes, whether in the colonies or in England." Graduates who did not wish to go to the colonies were qualified to become matrons, or housekeepers in large households. Horsemanship was the foremost subject. The students were taught to ride sidesaddle and astride, and single and pair driving. Other subjects included cooking, home nursing, first aid, darning, stable work, and gardening. There were to be no servants at the school, as the students were to do all the required work themselves. In summer the students were to sleep in tents.

Whether the school was a success and just how long Hunt ranched in Western Canada are difficult questions to answer, since both ranch and school disappear from view. By 1908 she was busy in England with the First Aid Nursing Yeomanry Corps (FANY).[75] A small organization made up of elite women who owned horses, FANY combined nursing skills with the sense of valour and patriotism of military service.[76] In 1909 it was announced that Hunt was the first woman to receive a commission as lieutenant in the territorial division of the British Army.[77] Reports at the time claimed that she still operated her horse ranch, that it was lucrative, and that "she has a wonderful influence over the wildest horses, so much so that she astonished the cattlemen on her ranch, who declare that she is able to accomplish by mere gentle suasion what ranchmen can only attain by the hardest rough riding."[78]

Grain on a "Stupendous Scale": Ruth Hillman and Fairview Heights Farm, Keeler, Saskatchewan – Ruth N. Hillman, a farmer at Keeler, Saskatchewan, was featured in newspapers as far away as New Zealand and Australia.[79] She purchased her land about 1906, and by 1911 she was operating a "profitable farm of nearly 2,000 acres," despite having no previous farming experience. Hillman was born in St. Paul, Minnesota, and had been a "stenographic reporter" before she "took what capital she had … and staked her savings in Canadian land."[80] There were two years, however, between her purchase and her move, and during that time she allegedly studied and read all she could and made herself aware of the conditions of farming on the northern plains. She learned she needed to avoid "any attempt to transplant the small farming methods of Minnesota to the broad acres of Saskatchewan." Hers was another version of "rags to riches": she declared that "what she has done can be done by any girl working on a small salary. From small beginnings her land grew." The 1911 census shows that Hillman had a large workforce on her farm with a foreman and six labourers, plus her brother, aged fifteen. Her mother, too, was resident on the farm and listed as the head of household.[81]

Also in 1911 it was reported that Ruth Hillman was in St. Paul to secure the cooperation of the Twin Cities "jobbers and manufacturers … in the fight for free trade or reciprocal trade relations."[82] She was quoted as saying, "It would make your heart sick to see how some women and children almost starve themselves in their homestead shacks so that their husbands can raise the money to pay the exorbitant prices charged for American farm machinery." In this account Hillman was a "writer of romances," as well as a manager of a farm "aggregating 20,000 acres."

During the First World War, Hillman was described as breeding Percheron horses and having a wheat crop of 40,000 bushels.[83] In this report her femininity was stressed: she was a "slim little person" with "dainty hands." Hillman allegedly declared that she did not do any of the "actual manual labor": "You see I believe farming is just like any other big business and business systems should be introduced into it. I study for all I am worth, reading up what others have done, noting my mistakes and finding out why they are mistakes ... then when my foreman comes for consultation I know what I want done." She had thoughts about farming as a profession for women: "Women can be successful at it if they make up their minds to work, work, and then work. I can see where they would do splendidly near a big market, but as to away out on the prairie, they must be sure of their physical, moral and mental strength before they attempt it. It is a big test."

Hillman's enormous new house and barn were described in "Who Said Women Can't Farm?," a lengthy feature article by Mary P. McCallum that appeared in a 1918 *Grain Growers' Guide.*[84] At that time she had "one of the finest herds of Percherons in Saskatchewan." Hillman was continuing to study agriculture and to experiment on her own with wheat varieties.

The author of this article concluded that Hillman was "one of a long line of women who are forging for women new links in the chain of world industrialism and professionalism," and that the prairies could now boast many women farmers. Some were small-scale producers with little or no capital who faced "unspeakable adversities," while others, like Hillman, were farming grain on a "stupendous scale." Like Lady Hunt, Hillman also faded from the public eye. The local history reports only that she married Bob Lowe and left her farm, which she called Fairview Heights, during the Depression.[85] At that time she likely got little or nothing for her farm, as it was in the centre of Saskatchewan's Dust Bowl.

Isobel "Jack" May and Her "Ready-Made" Farm at Sedgewick, Alberta – The woman farmer of Western Canada to receive the most acclaim and notoriety was Isobel "Jack" May. Before she left for Alberta in 1911 she was known in England as "Lady Jack," or the "Lady Farmer."[86] She had attracted attention from as far away as New Zealand for her work as a farm labourer and for her attire.[87] Despite all of the press coverage she received, it is difficult to know for certain very much about her background or her own thoughts. There are no sources left by her, just vast press coverage, far from reliable. Most articles about her written after her arrival in Canada claimed that she was a daughter of Admiral Sir William Henry May, Commander of the Atlantic Fleet, and accustomed to mingling with elite society, including royalty, at dinners, balls, and receptions. It is unlikely, however, that she was his daughter, unless she was "illegitimate."[88] Press coverage contrasted her (alleged) former life as the daughter of an admiral with the solitude and demands of life on her Alberta farm. According to one description in a 1912 article entitled "World's Happiest Girl Who Declares She Would Rather Plow Than Go to the Opera," she had been a "frilly, frothy society belle, to whom the theatre, balls and card parties represented all that was worth living for."[89]

According to the press, Jack May, like Lady Hunt, served as a nurse in the South African War.[90] Upon her return to England she enrolled at the Horticultural College at Swanley. After graduation she worked at two farms in Kent. There she attracted attention because of her work on the land and with animals, but also because of her clothing, which was described as "male attire." One of the earliest descriptions of May is from her 1906 appearance as a witness in police court in Bromley, Kent, where her garb attracted much more attention than the details of the case at hand. It was reported that the witness was "a young woman dressed in boys' clothing … Her name is Isabel May. Her hair is cut short and she wears leggings and a cap. The only exception to the male costume is a sort of smock reaching almost to the knees. Miss May, or, as she prefers to be called "Jack" is a most interesting young woman. Her ambition is to be a farmer and with this end in view has taken service with Mrs. Smith at St. Mary Cray. She is handsome and stalwart, and in the farming garb presents quite a picture of strength."[91] The report further noted that May was "certain that women can succeed on a farm if they try," and that no one "doubts her ability as a mower, reaper, or plougher."[92]

According to other reports, May insisted that her garb was feminine and that she was "hurt by the imputation that she wears male attire." She also contended that she "does not work on the land but is engaged upon

Figure 22. Isobel "Jack" May, often referred to as the "bachelor girl settler," was briefly a farmer at Sedgewick, Alberta in 1911–12. Her occupation and her "male attire" attracted press attention from around the globe. This photograph was used widely in the press to illustrate her farm work in Alberta, but it pre-dates her arrival in Canada. She was already a celebrity "lady farmer" before she left England with press attention from at least 1905. Currie Love, "Farmer-Boy 'Jack,'" *The Lady's Realm* 31, 181 (1911).

Figure 23. Louisa Wittrick farmed with "Jack" May, but her responsibilities focused on the domestic realm. Both women purchased "ready-made" Canadian Pacific Railway farms, and together they had 320 acres. Currie Love, "Farmer-Boy 'Jack,'" *The Lady's Realm* 31, 181 (1911).

Figure 24. May (seated) and Wittrick in front of their "ready-made" farm home at Sedgewick. Currie Love, "Farmer-Boy 'Jack,'" *The Lady's Realm* 31, 181 (1911).

Figure 25. A widely published photograph of the "bachelor girl settler." Currie Love, "Farmer-Boy 'Jack,'" *The Lady's Realm* 31, 181 (1911).

ordinary women's tasks, such as milking and butter making. In a later statement however, she said that at the farms in Kent she did every kind of farm work, including mowing, reaping and ploughing."[93] In 1907 she left Kent and operated a flower and vegetable farm of several acres in Norfolk, and it was here that she began to wear trousers.[94] Her goal, once she had enough experience, was to go to Canada and "turn some capital that she has to account in farming on a large scale."[95]

May's arrival in Saint John, New Brunswick, in April 1911 caused a sensation. When the CPR liner arrived with a group of fifty farmers from England headed for the CPR "ready-made" farms in the Canadian West, it was found that one was a female dressed as a male. This became big news, broadcast with headlines such as "Miss Jack May in Male Attire: An Eccentric Young Woman Passenger on the Empress of Britain."[96] According to one description, "A female second cabin passenger who gave her name as 'Miss Jack May,' was detained by the Canadian immigration officials, she being attired in male costume. According to one report she 'shocked the … immigration agents, who had heard of no such thing in this part of the world, where there are no suffragettes or anything of that kind.'"[97] In the record of her arrival she is entered as a male, age 35, then this is crossed out and she is entered into the female column.[98] May readily admitted that "she was one of the opposite sex and said that she and her male companion had worked on a farm in England. She had her hair cropped short, wore leggings and tan boots and a short skirt that was not visible below a man's overcoat. Her age was about 30 and she was rather good looking."[99]

May's "male attire" was regarded not only as odd or perverse but as suspicious, shady, even treacherous. She was "masquerading" as a man. In Canada and the United States, this was a crime. In 1914 at Fort William, Ontario, a woman was sentenced to six months in the penitentiary for "masquerading as a man" and working as a hotel porter.[100] Her defence was she needed to "keep from starving" and that "being in the guise of a girl she was under too great a handicap to make her way in the world." Four years later a woman was sentenced to two years in the Kingston women's prison because she had "posed as a man, had her hair cut in military style, and went so far as donning a man's attire in order to do her bit in a log-driving bee."[101] (This prison sentence, however, raised a "storm of indignation.") In the United States in 1911 a woman musician who dressed in trousers and waistcoats was given sixty days in jail in Portland, Oregon.[102] In passing the sentence, the judge said that "I hope that by the time your sentence has expired your friends will have provided you with clothing suitable to your sex." In 1913 a New York woman was arrested and jailed for "masquerading" as a man; she worked at a bookbindery and dressed as a man to earn better wages.[103]

There was considerable debate about, and mixed reactions to, May's arrival in Canada in "male attire." One rural Alberta newspaper, the *Gleichen Call*, welcomed her: "A woman with energy to study the science of farming and to work it as Miss May has done, would be a decided acquisition to any country, and the fact that she adapted her attire to her work shows her good sense. The sight of a woman in men's attire and doing man's work may be novel, but it does not make her any the less a lady."[104] The *Daily Colonist* of Victoria, British Columbia, was much more critical:

> Most women would rather not have read that this handsome and enterprising young lady considered it expedient to travel in men's costume. If at her work Miss May found it necessary to dress as a man she was certainly under no such compulsion while travelling. Few people find it necessary to wear the uniform of the workshop on the street. "Jack" May... may be a picturesque figure on a railway platform and make a good story for a reporter, but most women would prefer to see their daughters dressed less conspicuously. Conventions are not without meaning and no woman would lightly disregard them.[105]

May stood out and was seen as odd, or worse, not only because of her attire but because of her occupation. She was reported to be "the first woman to undertake farming on an extensive scale in the west."[106] She had successfully applied for one of the CPR's ready-made farms at Sedgewick, Alberta, stating in her application that she had "done every kind of farm work, from that of an ordinary farm hand to bailiff or manager."[107] The ready-made farms were a scheme to help attract the "sons of Britain," instead of peasants from Europe, to settle in Western Canada.[108] Prospective farmers signed up for a plan that was intended to avoid many of the pitfalls of the free homestead system while making money for the CPR, as the farmers had to purchase their land. The settler had to pay a 10 percent down payment plus the cost of the improvements. In the contract the CPR agreed to provide each farmer with a four-room cottage, a barn with hayloft, and to have fifty acres on each farm broken, planted with crops, and fenced before the settlers left the old country. The farms were to be close to a railway, to market, churches, and schools—unlike homesteads, which were often very isolated.

May was fortunate to be accepted into the scheme, as the conditions were that the applicants were to be married men actually engaged in agriculture.[109] May qualified only for the latter. She purchased Farm No. 2 at the Sedgewick colony, consisting of 160 acres, at the price of sixteen dollars per acre. Her land was valued at $2,560 and the improvements at $2,227, for a total of $4,787.[110]

While May was reported to be with a "male companion" when she was detained by immigration officials at Saint John, when she arrived in Alberta her companion was identified as Miss Wittrick of Norfolk. From Wetaskiwin, Alberta, it was reported on 29 April that the two were on their way to Sedgewick: "Miss May is a large property owner in the Old Country, and some six years ago adopted the male attire as a convenience in her duties of managing her large holdings. When they reach their new home Miss Wittrick will do the house-keeping and Miss May will do the farming. It is said that she is thoroughly proficient and can ride a horse or handle a plow like an expert. She also knows livestock and she has plenty of grit and ambition."[111]

In the CPR records of the colony, Louisa May Wittrick had Farm No. 3 on the northwest quarter of the same section (NW 7-43-12-W4) as May's plot. Together they had 320 acres. May purchased her farm on 16 May 1911 and Wittrick, on 24 April 1911. Aside from Wittrick and May there was only one other woman among the Sedgewick ready-made farmers, Caroline Ann Potts (who received no press attention, and there is no record of the results of her farming adventure). In the extensive press coverage of Wittrick and May, Wittrick was always presented as looking after the domestic realm; she did not dress in male clothing. According to one description, the "two young ladies are working in partnership. They find no difficulty in the arrangement, though the average farmer out there assures you that partnerships are unworkable in such a business. Each member is responsible for her own department but is always ready to help the other. Miss Wittrick looks after the dairy and the house … and she is a beautiful butter maker and an excellent cook, but she takes a hand in the field work whenever there's need of extra help."[112] May did the ploughing, discing, harrowing, reaping, and binding, and she also marketed the grain.

Louisa Wittrick wrote a letter to the *Canadian Gazette* in January 1912, describing how the two were coping with their first winter on their farm and, despite noting that it had been as cold as 56 below (Fahrenheit), she was very positive: "Somehow Jack and I have never found one day long enough. We are up at 6:30 and we are at it till past eight at night."[113] It was very dry; the snow covered the ground but was not deep. Their cows and pigs were doing well; Jack had made a shed of saplings and straw. The CPR had dug a second well for them because their first was no good. They had spent a quiet but happy Christmas, enjoying the rest as they had to normally work every day of the week.

The Sedgewick colony farmers had faced some surprises upon their arrival They were angry to learn that the CPR was charging them three dollars an acre more than the price quoted them in England by the company agent.[114] This resulted in a delay in the colonists' taking possession of their land. Edwin and Felicia Snowsell and their two children, from Gloucestershire, who arrived in 1911, were dismayed to find Sedgewick to be a tiny village with one street and "all around bare prairie. Our spirits fell to zero."[115] They also found that the well was not ready on the farm they had purchased. The CPR had done a poor job of ploughing the land. According to Frank Snowsell, the CPR contractors "tried to squeeze the 50 acres out of areas without trees to avoid the added cost of clearing. Since many quarters had over 100 acres of poplar and willow brush with many sloughs, this required some tricky dodging around the wooded areas. Also, cultivating was practically non-existent." No one in the Snowsell family had any farming experience. Son Frank wrote years later, "Dad had never done any farming, nor handled horses or any other animals until he came to Canada. Mother had never cooked a meal, washed clothes, nor done any of the usual prairie housewife's tasks until she arrived in Alberta."[116] They had a poor first harvest due to rain that delayed the harvest, and then frost.

Compared to the Snowsells, Jack May and Louisa Wittrick were well prepared and seemed to thrive, at least according to press reports. An April 1912 report observed that May and Wittrick were "not among the old country people [of the CPR ready-made farms] who because their wheat was frozen left their valuable crop of potatoes to rot in the ground."[117] Their successes were emphasized, and their contentment. They were in Sedgewick for only a few weeks when an article appeared in the *Canadian Courier* called "The Woman Who Never Looks Back."[118] The author of the article, Norman S. Rankin, took his title from a poem by Mary I.S. Schaeffer, a choice that was not apt as the poem was about the farm wife who was "comrade" to her husband:

> We speak of the man who has opened the door
> Of the great teeming West, that has brought to the fore
> The wealth of the prairies—so vast and so wide
> But how many think of the one at his side
> The one who has made him a home in the shack
> His comrade—the woman who never looks back.

Rankin's article exemplifies the intense scrutiny May received. He provided a detailed description of Jack May's appearance, noting that this was the first "out-and-out professional woman-farmer" he had ever heard of: "Her face was pleasant, deeply bronzed, inclined to be square with a broad mouth and forehead over which a thick mass of auburn hair struggled from beneath her tweed cap. Brown eyes twinkled at you. Probably five foot three or four inches in height, she gave the impression of strength and endurance. Her costume—about which so much publicity has ensued—was certainly unique. A cloth jumper over a shirt waist, a cloth skirt, knee length, brown leather leggings and a three-quarter overcoat completed it. And as she strode across the platform with a grip in each hand and her cap set jauntily on the back of her head, one certainly would have thought 'A jolly good-looking fellow.' I did."

Rankin's article included two photographs: one with May on horseback with the caption "Smart and well proportioned, she might have been taken for a college youth"; and the other of her behind a horse and rake with two men with the caption "She finds farming congenial and male costume much more fitted to the work she does than woman's." Rankin clearly struggled with May's attire, writing, "She wears masculine garb because she wants to. One might wonder why she wants to, but it wouldn't do him any good, or bring him any nearer a solution. There's no argument open. She finds farming congenial, and male costume much more fitted to the work she does than woman's. And that's enough."

May was also featured as early as 1911 to help promote the ready-made farms and the CPR. In an article by Currie Love in a pamphlet about the "phenomenal progress" of Calgary and region, the Sedgewick women colonists were highlighted.[119] Love was a Canadian journalist who spent some years as a special writer for the CPR, and she was quite likely working in that capacity when she wrote the article, as it promoted the ready-made farm scheme for British settlers.[120] Love wrote that "women will be interested to know that one of the most successful 'ready-made' farmers is Miss Jack May, daughter of Admiral May, of England, who with her friend Miss Louise Wittrick, has taken 320 acres." Although Love included much of the same detail as others had, she did not mention anything about May's male attire. Love was also interested in promoting the scheme for other women, writing that "a woman needs to be pretty strong to do farm work in a new country but given sufficient capital and common sense any woman can succeed."[121] She urged women to purchase the forty-acre ready-made farms. (The large acreages, grain crops, and equipment such as steam engines were for male farmers, according to Love.) On their smaller holdings, women could grow food for their cows, pigs, and hens. They could also grow various berries and vegetables. Money was required. Advocating poultry farming in particular, Love wrote that "any young woman starting a poultry farm in Alberta should possess capital of from $2,500 to $3,000, ambition, a practical turn of mind, and a goodly amount of determination." She continued: "In these twentieth century days when women are emulating men in almost every department of life, it is not surprising that they should follow masculine example and emigrate to a new country where opportunities are more plentiful than in the Old Land, and where the women who work for a living are neither regarded with suspicion nor ostracised from society."[122]

Currie Love published much of the same material in a 1911 article entitled "Farmer-Boy 'Jack'" in the *Lady's Realm* (London). A story of how "two Englishwomen have solved the problem of work for women," the article began thus: "Though not a suffragette, Miss Jack May, an Englishwoman who has come to Canada to farm her own lands, is an example of what the twentieth century woman can accomplish alone and unassisted."[123] Love emphasized in this article how "all their neighbours thoroughly respect them, and do all in their power to be of service to them." The farm hosted a steady stream of visitors, "anxious to see the two women who have come thousands of miles from home to make a success of farming in Canada."

"The World's Happiest Girl" was how May was described in an article featured in many newspapers in Canada, the United States, and New Zealand in late 1912 and early 1913. May stated (allegedly): "I wouldn't go back to society again for worlds. I would rather plow than go to the opera. I would rather plant corn than attend a pink tea. I much prefer currying my horse to arraying myself in an evening gown. What's a butterfly life in damp and foggy England compared to real life in bright sunshine and bracing cold?"[124] She claimed to "love the freedom of the life here and the highness of things here on the western prairies ... In England one is bound by conventions, as one's fields are girt with hedges. Here I can do as I choose, I would not go back under any circumstances."[125] When May "dressed up" she still refused to be corseted and constricted; rather, she wore "a soft collar and tie, and a peasant smock of navy blue denim, which comes to her knees and is loosely belted around her waist."[126]

The most detailed account of May and her farm is a 1914 article, "Haymaking with Jack May: A Woman's Life on a Canadian Farm" by Currie Love, published in *Quiver*, a London illustrated magazine. Love reported that May did not even own a skirt: "Can't be bothered with the things. Besides, women's fashions change every minute, and I can't afford to keep pace with them. My first reason for adopting men's clothes is that they are comfortable and sensible, and the only safe costume for farm work. Imagine me on a plough in a hobble skirt! Wouldn't I be a fine sight? You're liable to be thrown off a plough every twenty minutes or so, and a skirt would be absolutely dangerous under those circumstances. From wearing men's clothes to work, I gradually adopted them for everyday wear, and now I should be most uncomfortable in conventional feminine garb."[127] According to Love, May was assisted not only by Louise Wittrick but by Miss Grace Hanson, also from England, aged eighteen. Hanson too opted for the comfort and safety of masculine dress: "The very idea of corsets makes her shudder with disgust. 'Nasty stiff things,' she says: 'I wouldn't wear them for anything.'" They had six cows, six horses, seventeen pigs, two dogs, and some hens. There were 150 acres sown of barley, wheat, and oats, and it was reported that May did all her own work with the grain—ploughing, seeding, reaping, and binding. She also did her own carpentry work, building a barn and pigsty as well as shelves for the living room. The women had found their first Canadian winter "delightful." The "long days of bright sunshine and clear, bracing cold [were] so different from the damp fog of England." "We had expected," [May] laughed, "to find an Alberta winter a terrible experience, but we liked it even better than the summer." May declared she would not go back to England except to visit:

> To see my people at home, but not to stay. I like the freedom of life here—the bigness of things. No, I wouldn't go back to stay. I don't believe that Canada is a wonderland. I know you can't pick up gold off the streets, as some of the old-country people believe. I don't think the climate is the best in the world, or that anyone who comes here is bound to become wealthy in a year ... But I do believe that Canada offers the greatest opportunity I know of to a man or woman with a little capital who is not afraid to work ... If you want to work hard, have beautiful soil, own your farm and house, be your own landlord, and have a free, independent life, Canada is the place.

Sadly, Canada was not the place for Jack May. She lasted only a little over a year. Just why she left for good is not clear. When Currie Love's article in *Quiver* was published in September 1914, May had already been gone for nearly two years. In December 1912 the *Sedgewick Sentinel* reported that "Miss Jack May left last week to spend the winter in England."[128] She did not return. The 1 May 1913 issue of the *Sentinel* noted that "Miss Jack May, who went on a visit to the old country last fall, is not returning, she having taken a farm in the county of Shropshire, England."[129] It was further noted in the same issue that "Miss Hanson [the young assistant mentioned in the 1914 Love article] is entering into partnership with Miss Wittrick, in place of Miss Jack May." Finally, this same issue of the *Sentinel* boasted that Sedgewick, particularly Jack May, was featured in a lengthy article in the *Calcutta Statesman* of 2 February 1913.

But Jack May was gone for good. The local history of Sedgewick, published in 1982, provides clues. In her entry on "Miss May Jack and Miss Louise Whittrick [*sic*]," Mary Weber wrote that "Miss May left the farm for Australia in 1913 and Miss Whittrick took over the farm. At this time Mr. David Moore, the recently appointed supervisor of the CPR ready-made farms, bought the west half of section 17 in 1913–15. Mr. Moore and Miss Whittrick were married in Sedgewick in 1914, a most posh ceremony. Two sons were born to them on the farm but the eldest died as an infant. In 1922 Mr. and Mrs. Moore sold the farm, had a sale of their effects and, with their son Jack, about four years old, returned to Ireland."[130]

Jack May disappears from view. Whether she in fact went to Australia or to a farm in Shropshire is unknown. Articles about her as a farmer in

Canada, however, continued to be published, such as Love's 1914 piece in *Quiver*. A popular 1913 article about May was entitled "Society Lady Who Prefers the Plow to the Pink Tea," although it was a re-hash of earlier articles.[131] When speaking before the Royal Colonial Institute in London in 1913, Saskatchewan farmer Georgina Binnie-Clark referred to the injustices of Canada's land laws and the contribution women could make in the "spade work of British expansion in this, the supreme place of prosperity among British lands." She used Jack May as her best example of this potential: "And of the Sedgwick colony in 1911, the verdict from officials, dealers, tradesmen and neighbours concerning the work of Mrs. Jack May and her partner, Miss Louisa Wittrick, on their ready-made farm was, 'The women are the best men of the lot.'"[132] In 1914 an article published in the *Irish Homestead*, and reprinted as "Lady Farmers" as far away as New Zealand, focused on May and Wittrick, and the author had allegedly recently visited them.[133] As late as 1924, May was still being celebrated as one of the "pioneer women of the West" who, along with Miss Wittrick, was "happy and flourishing" on her farm at Sedgewick, that she had in fact long since left.[134] She may have left for personal or economic/agricultural reasons, or a combination of both.

One visitor to the May-Wittrick farm perhaps provides a clue. In his book *Canadian Trails: Hither and Thither in the Great Dominion*, English writer Eldred G.F. Walker described his visit to Sedgewick in the summer of 1912, writing that he had resolved to "go and see the lady settler, Miss Jack May."[135] Walker was welcomed by May and her "lady friend," and he found their home "natty." He described May as liking her farm very much, as having the best dairy cows he had seen in that part of the country, and as having cut plenty of hay. But "a tragedy had nearly occurred the day before, as during the storm the electric fluid had struck the windmill, and running down had found a metallic clothes-line, from which it had flashed into the hen-coop, killing twenty-two chickens and blinding the old hen." Altogether Walker seemed impressed with what they had done, writing that "I had heard of the life of the Wild West, but it did not look as though life was so very wild when these two girls could have a home of their own all alone out on the open prairie."

Walker also reported some discontent among the Sedgewick colony farmers. One complained that he could not get the CPR steam plough to do the promised breaking of the land.[136] Many of the Sedgewick and other CPR colony farmers and homesteaders in Western Canada were soon or eventually discouraged, and sold up or abandoned their land. Their crop of 1911 was very poor, and they had to be provided with seed wheat for their crop of 1912. This seed was full of weeds. They found winters difficult with not enough fuel; their water would be frozen in the morning and their vegetables in the root cellar also froze. The houses that were built for the settlers had no insulation for the winter weather and were built of inferior materials.[137] Elizabeth Snowsell taught school from 1913 to bring necessary income to the farm, as the grain crops could not be relied on. The Snowsells found it essential to hire casual labour, particularly at harvest time. After fourteen years, including several years of crop failures, the Snowsells abandoned their farm, leaving it in the hands of the CPR. Like that of May and Wittrick, the CPR record of Snowsell's contract reads "Status of Purchase: Uncertain." Many other records read "contract cancelled," or "contract surrendered and cancelled." According to an account in the local history of Sedgewick, a great many of the colonists were from cities and had no experience in farming: "Some of them didn't last out the year, and by the time ten years had rolled around, there were very few of those with no farming experience left here."[138]

CPR Sedgewick settler Jim Hallum, who arrived as a boy with his parents, wrote that the colonists were disappointed for many reasons, including the tiny houses, and the fifty acres on each farm that was supposed to be seeded to wheat upon their arrival, but was not.[139] The wells were particularly disappointing, as they were so deep and equipped with steel rods that "in order to pump water from a well like that, it really took some muscle and strength." But there were colonists who persisted under adverse circumstances. Bessie and David Black and their young son came from Essex to Sedgewick in 1912. David died that August,and another son was born two weeks after his death. Yet Bessie Black persisted, with the help of her parents who came out from England in 1913.[140]

There was at least one other woman farmer in the district who appears to have persisted longer than Jack May, although she received very little press coverage by contrast; she must not have donned male attire. Miss Helena Hill of Seattle purchased CPR land near Sedgewick and in the spring of 1911 it was reported that she was sowing 100 acres to flax.[141] Under the headline "Another Woman Farmer," it was reported that Jack May "is to have a rival in her fascinating occupation in Alberta." A Miss Hilliard, also of Seattle, would supervise the house, while Hill developed the farm, and it was further reported that she intended to go into farming on a large scale and bring 640 acres under cultivation. It seems Hill was much more successful than May at farming the prairies. The 7 November 1912 issue of the *Sedgewick Sentinel* noted that "Miss Hill shipped the first car of grain through the Farmers Elevator on Monday."[142] (It was one month later that the same newspaper reported that "Miss Jack May left last week to spend the winter in England"—and never returned.)[143]

DISRUPTING AND TRANSGRESSING: CROSS-DRESSING FARMERS

Just how Jack May understood her own gender and sexual identity cannot be gleaned from the evidence available. Nor can it be known whether she and Wittrick were partners in more than just their farm. The name Jack, however, may have been adopted as a masculine nickname when she was developing a visible lesbian identity, as in the example of her contemporary Vera "Jack" Holme, actress, suffragette, and chauffeur (to the Pankhursts).[144] According to historian Anna Kisby in an article on Holme, "A recurrent theme among Jack's friends is their use of male pseudonyms. Making her identity as a lesbian apparent according to the conventions of the time, Jack's nickname and her masculine dress act as key signals of her sexual identity."[145] As historian Peter Boag has shown in his book *Re-Dressing America's Frontier Past*, "cross-dressers" included a wide spectrum of people. At one end were those for whom "such an act was not crossing at all but was something that came naturally to them, as they really felt themselves to be other than the sex their bodies suggested them to be."[146] At the other end were those "who took on the garb of the opposite sex for purposes unrelated to either sexuality or gender identity." Boag also contends that when cross-dressers are remembered in Western history, a "progress narrative" is invoked that "normalizes the cross-dresser by maintaining that 'she' changed her clothing for some purpose related to securing personal advancement in a world with a deck that was otherwise stacked against her. For example, she might have dressed in male attire to pass herself off as a man so that she could obtain better-paying employment."[147] While Boag admits that there were "logical and practical" reasons why a woman might dress as a man in the nineteenth-century West—for safety, for opportunities, or adventure—digging deeper can reveal a "bonanza" of evidence that "female-to-male cross dressers undertook a change of wardrobe to help them better express feelings of sexual and gender difference."[148] In the case of Jack May, however, it is impossible to "dig deeper"; the sources are not there. Similarly, it cannot be determined from the press reports whether May had aspirations of political equality or economic independence for herself, her partner, and other women.

Did May's male attire make her an oddity, an outcast in the Sedgewick colony and in Western Canada more broadly? Cross-dressers are disruptive figures "invested with potent and subversive powers," as they throw into question the binary categories of "male" and "female."[149] As historian Ann McClintock writes, clothing became "central to the policing of social boundaries."[150] May's transgression of gender, the spectacle of boundaries crossed, clearly fascinated a reading public, but how did her neighbours feel? It is possible that Jack May did not receive a warm welcome from her neighbours in Sedgewick. In all the accounts of women performing farm work in the West, it is extremely rare to learn that they did so in men's clothing. One other example is Patricia Carlisle, an English writer (pen name David Lyle) who purchased the Sunnyslope Ranch of 800 acres near Priddis in 1924.[151] There she was known as "Miss Peter Webber," and the land was jointly worked with "her companion Miss Goppel." They were known in the district as the "farmerettes," as they were "the first women locally to run a farm and operate machinery along with the men." It was explained in the local history that Carlisle did not use her real name in the district because "she was the daughter of a well to do London, England, member of Parliament." These and other stories about her may or may not have been true. It was stressed that she had other abilities normally associated with men, that she was "an expert driver" and a "good shot." She was "extremely venturesome," had "worked for the British Government in Turkey and India," and "during the War she is supposed to have driven an ambulance in Serbia."

Carlisle wore trousers and a cowboy hat.[152] She did all the farm work, including driving a tractor, ploughing, and harvesting. She had a crop of 7,000 bushels in 1925. Yet the local history stressed the somewhat eccentric ways of the "farmerettes." Carlisle and Goppel bought a tractor and grain separator in downtown Calgary and drove them all the way back to their ranch (thirty-seven kilometres), despite the fact that it was forbidden to drive the machines on the pavement in that city.

Like Lady Hunt and the farmer to be discussed in Chapter 5, Georgina Binnie-Clark, Carlisle announced her intention to train English women to farm in Western Canada. (This was one way to solve the need for farm labourers—by using unpaid help who were supposedly in training. As mentioned above, Jack May also had "apprentices.") Carlisle reported that after an interview with her was published in London, she received 500 letters from English women who wanted to emigrate to ranches in Canada immediately.[153] Carlisle was quoted saying that "farming is a profession as suitable for a woman as for a man for mechanical labour saving devices are every year entering more intimately into its operation. Actually it returns more for brains than for the muscle applied to it."[154] In 1925 in London she (allegedly) interviewed 100 women as possible students, and it was announced that Carlisle would return from England to Alberta with a well-known London woman surgeon, three school teachers, and three business women.[155] They were all to receive a "thorough agricultural education and to engage in practical farm work." They would then set up farms of their own near Carlisle's. The plan was that each year several more women would join them.

In 1925 modest press attention was devoted to Carlisle under captions such as "She Writes and Ranches," detailing her first successful crop and the plans for the future—and then no more.[156] The local history entry on the "farmerettes" indicates that this was a brief experiment. The entry on the couple ends with the marriage of Miss Goppel in the fall of 1924 to B.F. Rhodes of Cochrane, Alberta, and "Miss Webber took off for England in November. Returning in 1925 she was on the Walker Ranch, Pine Creek, for awhile."[157]

There are few other examples of women who farmed in "male attire." Mrs. Chamberlain, a widow who established the Chamberlain Ranch at Wood Mountain, Saskatchewan, was one. Many stories were told about her, living without a husband in what was described as a wild and desolate region, where shots could be heard as "rival bands fought on the ranges." This young widow with a daughter reportedly decided it was "no place for an unprotected woman."[158] The only thing she could think of was to "give the appearance of there being a 'man in charge.' One morning she donned her husband's clothes—and for ten years never wore her women's garments again." To the cowboys with whom she had little contact, she was known as the "Yankee chap," and not one "dreamed that the quiet, almost taciturn, slender little fellow who curtly repulsed all offers of help, was other than a man rancher who preferred to be left alone." As her herd grew the "Yankee chap" dealt with the traders and buyers, making shrewd bargains. It was not until the region was settled by families that she revealed the "masquerade."

A "woman who made it alone" in the Millicent district of Alberta, near Brooks, also "put on men's clothing and did all the farm work" after her husband left the farm.[159] She was described in the local history as an odd, eccentric, cantankerous, and amusing diversion from the overwhelming norms of behaviour. Allegedly Jeanette Fleming had decided that her husband had to go back to the United States, as "there can only be one boss on a place." She "led an independent life," and "her main ambition seemed to be to show the world that anything a man could do she could do better." She was recalled as a shrewd bargainer, and her sows raised more piglets per sow than those of her neighbours. She spent hours tutoring the children of the district in mathematics. But overall she was viewed as incompetent: "Being a woman rancher and farmer, she had her own ways of doing things. At one time she kept 500 sheep and they were being killed by coyotes in the night. To combat this, she got 200 lanterns and hung them on the fence posts to keep the coyotes away."[160] She flooded her and a neighbour's land when she attempted to irrigate her own fields. Insisting on never asking for help from her neighbours backfired on one occasion. Fleming was hammering shingles on her roof when her ladder blew down and she was stranded: "She waved to cars that passed by and people waved back thinking that Jeanette was uncommonly friendly that day. Evening came and she was still up on the roof. Finally someone stopped to investigate and helped her down."

Peter Boag concludes in his study of cross-dressing in the U.S. West that it was "clearly a place and process where gender and sexuality were unstable, contentious and transgressive. It was a place where a wide variety of people who did not conform to gender and sexual expectations lived, loved and died."[161] But was this the same north of the forty-ninth parallel? In 1917 at a Liberal convention in Winnipeg, a male farmer delegate objected to a resolution proposing homestead rights for women because "if a woman settled alone in the midst of men who were homesteading rightly or wrongly her name would be tarnished."[162] A single woman farmer would be morally suspect. One who dressed as a man would be even more suspect.

The 1923 novel *Cattle* by Winnifred Eaton (Onoto Watanna) provides a hint of the way in which May and Carlisle might have been received by their neighbours. The central character, Angela Loring, is a cross-dressing farmer who broke her own land, put in her own crop, hayed, and fenced.

An author and screenwriter born in Montreal of Chinese-British ancestry, Eaton lived on a ranch in the Alberta foothills for some years. Her novel *Cattle* is a sharp critique of the treatment of and attitudes toward women in an Alberta ranching community Eaton called "Yankee Valley." The woman farmer in *Cattle* was known as "Mr." Loring in her district: "Her name, it appeared, was Angela Loring, but some wag had named her 'Mr.' Loring, because of her clipped hair and her working-man's attire, and this name stuck."[163] Loring is regarded as a "strange woman" because of her occupation and dress and cropped hair, but also because she wants no contact with her neighbours:

> The woman was a "bug" pronounced the farm people of Yankee Valley. At all events she was the kind of 'bug' they found it prudent to keep at a safe distance. She had met all overtures of friendship with hostility and contempt. She was on her own land. She desired no commerce with her neighbours. She needed no help. It was nobody's business but her own why she chose to dress and live in this way ... Thus she became a sort of bugaboo in the popular imagination, but as time passed the country became used to the woman-hermit and gave her the desired wide berth.[164]

In the novel the local doctor, a beloved figure in the community, takes a great interest in Loring, seeing feminine potential. He lectures her repeatedly about how her dress and occupation were unacceptable: "Her cut hair he denounced unsparingly. No lass, he declared angrily, had a right to cut the hair from her head. Her man's clothes were unqualifiedly disgraceful. Her working the field was against Nature."[165] Loring takes on a young woman assistant, Nettie Day, a single mother who was raped by Bull Langdon, the owner of the biggest ranch in the district. She too cuts her hair, adopts masculine garb, and works the land. Although there is more than a hint that Loring and Day are devoted to each other, by the end of the novel they have reverted to suitably feminine roles: Loring marries the doctor, and Day marries a neighbouring homesteader.

That it was not acceptable for women to dress in male attire, even while performing farm labour, was made clear to the British women who were part of the Princess Patricia Ranch experiment in British Columbia. When in 1913 they wore men's clothing while at work on the farm, they were instructed by their sponsors, the Colonial Intelligence League, to desist for fear that they were creating a poor impression in the community. A new rule was passed that residents "must always wear skirts when working. The wearing of men's clothing is not permitted."[166]

It will remain a mystery why Jack May left her Alberta farm so soon. She had more agricultural experience than the Snowsells, but faced the same challenges. She and Wittrick, like the Snowsells, had to be provided with seed wheat for the crop of 1912. Perhaps she found the press attention and constant visitors overwhelming, although in her own district—at least if the *Sedgewick Sentinel* is any indication—little attention was paid to May. Did the community welcome or ostracize Jack May? Was she excluded from both the masculine and feminine realms of life in the community of Sedgewick? She may have thought she was travelling to a new setting where gender was more flexible, but she was surrounded in Sedgewick by other British settlers. As mentioned in Chapter 2, in England attitudes were being challenged and were slowly changing, but single women farmers were still viewed with suspicion, as "unnatural" women.[167] They were "not seen as real farmers by men but as inferior others who try to be like men and cannot therefore be taken seriously."[168] Jack May was suspect if she demonstrated masculine qualities of "physical strength, sturdiness, aggressiveness, competitiveness, speaking one's mind and dominance."[169] She refused to appear "slim, fragile, submissive, nurturing, quiet and withdrawn." A single woman farmer was not a potential wife, as she did not embody and perform feminine attributes. Louisa Wittrick was a potential wife and could find a place in Sedgewick society, while May could not as long as she farmed and worked in men's attire. Recall the "girl farmer" of Surrey, Estelle Long (introduced in Chapter 2), described as living all alone in a two-room hut with a ferocious mottled mongrel dog in a "dreary and desolate" spot with a "double-barrelled gun by her bed and strong bolts and bars to the windows and strong locks to the door." In her neighbourhood she was regarded as "having 'turned witch' or something of that sort."[170]

WHY THE ATTENTION?

Women farmers and ranchers of the Canadian West received a great deal of attention in the first decade or so of the twentieth century, through CPR promotional pamphlets and in the press. Often the coverage drew heavily on the information provided in the CPR publications, suggesting that the articles were engineered by that corporation. A 1907 article entitled "Women as Farmers: Success of Some Who Have Taken Claims in the Northwest" appears to have been based on a CPR pamphlet. The article featured Mary Gilroy and others, and was placed in newspapers as distant as New York, Michigan, and South Carolina, as well as in the Western Canadian press.[171] "How Four Plucky Women Won Out in the Canadian Northwest," which appeared in the *Minneapolis Journal* in 1906, also drew a great deal on the CPR promotional publications.[172]

A 1910 article by Cynthia Westover Alden in the U.S. *Farmer's Review* drew on some new examples under the headline "Prosperous Women Farmers."[173] Alden reported that she met half a dozen women farmers on her recent trip through Western Canada who were "typical of what a woman can do." There was the "clever widow" of Saskatoon who was originally from Iowa, had invested in land, and made $50,000 in the last year. A woman known only as "Mother" in her district had a blind husband, and she had "carved her fortune from the soil," creating a farm worth $20,000. A farmer still in her twenties "intended to retire in the fall after her wheat was threshed and sold, having made a sufficient fortune to live on the rest of her days." Alden wrote that everywhere she went she "talked with sunbrowned and sturdy women who had as keen an eye for good soil and good crops as any man." She concluded that "if a woman has enough capital to tide her through the first year, and wishes to be independent, she should go back to the land and use her brains and muscle as these Canadian women I met and as hundreds of them are doing every day."

Despite the happy impression left by authors such as Alden that there were numerous "prosperous" women farmers in Western Canada, agriculture and farm ownership on the prairies was overwhelmingly a masculine domain and enterprise. These women illustrated what women could do, and created an impression of a welcoming, even liberating, environment, but they were fairly exceptional cases, and most of the women had been obliged to purchase their land rather than obtain it through homesteading. Why the concerted efforts to present this positive impression and to make relatively rare cases appear typical or representative? This was not unusual or unique to Western Canada; Australia too had celebrated women agriculturalists. Articles such as "Lady Settlers in Australia" featured Geelong sheep farmer Anne Drysdale, "an elderly maiden lady from Scotland," who had rented a farm in Scotland before settling in Australia in 1840 for her health.[174] The sheep farm was run in partnership with Englishwoman

Caroline Newcomb, and together they lived in comfort and prosperity in a fine stone mansion overlooking Port Phillip Bay.[175] Other examples of successful women agriculturalists in Australia included Eliza Forlonge ("Mother of the Australian Wool Industry"), Janet Templeton, Elizabeth Macarthur, and Mary Penfold, and unlike in Canada, many are still remembered and even celebrated today.[176] (The Penfolds are still in the wine, port, and sherry business.[177]) Some of these women were married, but with husbands absent from the colony. Women who owned or leased land and farmed independently however, were the smallest group of rural women, according to an economic history of women in Australia from 1788 to 1850, and very few were recorded as farmers or landholders in documents such as censuses of the period.[178]

The CPR had an obvious interest in promoting the idea that Western Canada was a welcoming environment for women who wanted to farm, in order to compete with the United States, where single women could obtain homestead land, and to promote the sale of railway land. Some of the attention paid to women farmers came from journalists interested in encouraging women to pursue occupations that could provide them with independence outside of marriage.[179] Most of the women farmers, however, were carefully depicted as maintaining femininity even while they undertook labour seen as masculine. The attention paid to Isobel "Jack" May, however, is of a different nature and scale. She traversed boundaries of proper femininity in her male attire, challenging and conflicting with norms of white British femininity. Her exploration of an alternative femininity, her behaviour, and her appearance served to confirm these norms, helping to define and articulate what was going to be considered acceptable and unacceptable in this society in the making.[180] And there was to be little space and scope for the woman farmer.

Even without male attire, the "bachelor girl" was suspect and unwanted. In 1912 the Alberta newspaper the *Redcliffe Review* warned that the "gay, careless life of the bachelor girl is apt to make her self centred and self absorbed. She grows selfish ... and before she knows it life will not be full of bloom and fragrance. There will be barren spots. It will begin to take on the hue of the desert. And unless she heeds these signs of the times she will come to a rather desolate old age."[181] While women who could afford to purchase land avoided the scrutiny of the homestead inspector concerned about their marital and parental status, they were still subject to intense pressure to conform to the norms of acceptable feminine behaviour and attire.

CHAPTER FIVE

ANSWERING THE CALL OF EMPIRE

GEORGINA BINNIE-CLARK, FARMER, AUTHOR, LECTURER

In August 1905, Georgina Binnie-Clark was a thirty-three-year-old writer with no farming experience when she impetuously bought an "improved" farm of 320 acres in Saskatchewan, despite having been in Canada for only a few weeks and despite the advice of family members who told her it was the "maddest thing which you have ever done."[1] Just a few years later she had become the most vocal advocate of "Canadian Farms for English Spinsters" and was well-known for this cause in Canada, Britain, and beyond.[2] Through her writing and lectures, her farming and training of young Englishwomen agriculturalists, Binnie-Clark expressed her allegiance to the British Empire and asserted the superiority of the British, who she assumed should have a privileged status in the colonies. She was part of and a product of the female imperialist network who contributed to the journal the *Imperial Colonist* and who believed that the British Empire was a force for great good in the world. Binnie-Clark also exemplified the new type of woman farmer that began to emerge in England at the turn of the century: not the daughter or widow of a farmer carrying on the family business, but "the unmarried, middle-class educated townswoman, drawn to farming as a profession in which she could potentially secure health, happiness and an independent income."[3] For Binnie-Clark this was to be accomplished in prairie Canada, and she made it her business to encourage others to follow her lead. While the celebrated farmers of the last chapter, many of them British, may have shared Binnie-Clark's enthusiasm for the cause of the British Empire, no records of them remain aside from the press coverage, and their degree of devotion is not clear. But for Binnie-Clark the cause of the Empire was paramount.

Binnie-Clark was more radical than other "genteel" women pursuing a life on the land in that she was not content with the "lighter," feminine branches of dairying, poultry raising, and horticulture; she was a wheat farmer who required a large acreage, and she advised others that this was the wisest and most profitable approach. She was determined not only to farm herself, but to publicize and promote opportunities for interesting and rewarding work for educated women in the colonies, particularly agriculture. Binnie-Clark detested housework and appeared to have no interest in marriage. She contended that women were capable of all categories of farm work. She pursued a demanding sphere of farming that was identified as male. Yet unlike farmer "Jack" May, Binnie-Clark performed her femininity in her lectures by wearing fashionable gowns, and in her writing she adopted a modest and self-deprecating tone. As she wrote in one of the final passages of her book *Wheat and Woman* (1914),

> The faithful chronicle of one's own difficulties may at first thought appear but a poor foundation for one's hope and firm belief that agriculture will prove to be the high-road and foundation of wealth and independence for Woman, but the strength of a chain is its weakest link ... I had no training, inadequate capital, and my commercial instinct, though strong in theory, is weak in practice—I fail to hold my own in buying or selling ... but in spite of this I am still behind my conviction that three hundred and twenty acres of good land in Canada can be working to produce a net profit of £500 per annum to its owner, [and] my weak link is very much stronger.[4]

IMPERIAL DREAMS

A devoted imperialist, Binnie-Clark counted herself among those who were "fighting out the battle of our Empire with the pick and spade on unbroken soil."[5] She was charmed by Quebec City, as it was "stamped with associations which bear the glorious seal of dauntless, deathless, effectual moments in our imperial history, when we English knew how to fight for causes."[6] She was devoted to the "Mother Country" and saw herself as helping to rear the "daughter nation" of Canada, "our most important colony."[7] Western Canada was "unbroken soil," a mutable environment, a tabula rasa. In eloquent passages Binnie-Clark described the beauty of the prairie in all seasons—its vastness and emptiness. This was a blank slate, a white sheet, where educated women from England "would use their inherent personal advantages to carve out strong roles and identities for themselves in the mutable environment of the colonial frontier, to civilise and extend the boundaries of the British world."[8]

Binnie-Clark shared the view that the British Empire would uplift the "darker" races, but this was not her main concern or issue.[9] She devoted only passing attention to Indigenous people in her writing and appeared to know little about them, even though her farm was located on Treaty Four land of the Cree, Assiniboine, and Saulteaux, who were relegated to reserves not far from her property. The non-treaty Dakota (Sioux) were also close neighbours. Her message was similar to that of Lally Bernard/Mary Agnes Fitzgibbon: that Canada was a "white man's land from end to end," and the solitary woman farmer had nothing to fear. Her first book, *A Summer on the Canadian Prairie* (1910), conveyed a typical settler mentality that much was being done to "graft civilization on the aborigines of our colonies with generosity and excellent intention," but that they refused to live in the good houses or till the good farms they were given.[10] A photo in that book of "An Indian's Home on the Prairie" illustrated this point; they were content to live the way they always had, refusing to take advice and farm. An unstated message of the photo was that the land was now in much better hands, for settlers such as Binnie-Clark and other British and Ontarian colonists would cultivate, transform, and altogether improve the acres that until then were dormant. The Treaty Four First Nations had in fact been attempting to farm their reserves since 1874, but faced overwhelming obstacles, including government policies that limited their enterprise to farming tiny holdings using only rudimentary implements, drastically reducing their acres under cultivation and discouraging interest in agriculture.[11] Just at the time Binnie-Clark arrived, Indigenous people were coping with a federal government determined to divest them of most of the best land on their reserves through dubious, and often illegal, land "surrenders."

In *Wheat and Woman* (1914), Binnie-Clark praised the work of missionaries, both Catholic and Anglican, for their "brave, unselfish, dauntless" work.[12] She was particularly keen on the Roman Catholic industrial school for Indigenous children at Lebret in the Qu'Appelle Valley. She approved of the boys being taught useful trades, working in the farm and gardens of the school, so that they would be able to "take possession of the opportunities civilization brought to the wonderful treasure-land of their fathers."[13] All were acquiring "good manners," and the priests and nuns had "most truly bestowed on the children of the darker race the consolation of religion." Yet she admitted a tinge of regret that they had been robbed of their liberty. During a visit to the school "one glorious summer afternoon," she was present when the children were let out to swim and saw how they clearly loved the freedom and release from the confinement of the school: "Suddenly there was the impression of the opening of a great big door and a sense of wide liberty, followed by the crescendoing chorus of joy—then the patter of many bare feet treading the path of pleasure." She wrote that when she left after a visit to the school and was back on the trail by the lake, enjoying the scents and scenes of an evening on the prairie, breathing the "air of liberty," the "fascination of life in the open tugs at the heart-strings [and] you know that the children of Hiawatha pay the price for those opportunities of civilization."[14]

Yet a photograph included in *Wheat and Woman* of four industrial school children with two elders was one of the propaganda images that the Department of Indian Affairs used to demonstrate the contrasts between the old and new generations, conveying the message that being robbed of their freedom was in the children's best interests. They too were the children of Mother Britannia, but they were in need of a stern but kindly guardian. The Indigenous people of Binnie-Clark's district, in her account, were tame, contained, and unable to travel freely as they had, but they were the beneficiaries of colonization. Although this photo emphasized several generations of women, there was almost no mention of Indigenous women in Binnie-Clark's books or articles, and her concerns for women's rights to homestead and farm did not extend to them. In *Wheat and Women* she mentioned an Indigenous woman once.[15] She was "Soo" (Sioux) and had walked from her "village" (presumably the Standing Buffalo reserve) to the Catholic mission at Lebret on Easter morning.

THE PRESENT PHASE OF DEVELOPMENT IN FATHER HUGENARD'S WORK FOR THE MOTHER COUNTRY

Figure 26. From Georgina Binnie-Clark's *Wheat and Woman*, this is a carefully staged photograph of students at the Qu'Appelle Industrial School, allegedly with their parents. It was intended to illustrate the dramatic contrast between the old and young generations. The caption is the original from her book and refers to Rev. Joseph Hugonnard, the principal of the school. Her farm was located not far from the school, on the Treaty Four land of the Cree, Saulteaux, and Assiniboine. A reserve of non-treaty Dakota was also located near Fort Qu'Appelle. Georgina Binnie-Clark, *Wheat and Woman,* 70.

VICTORIA DAY (NOW EMPIRE DAY) AT FORT QU'APPELLE, 1912

Figure 27. The caption "Victoria Day (Now Empire Day) at Fort Qu'Appelle, 1912," conveys the message that the Indigenous people of the West are loyal and grateful to the British Empire. A devoted imperialist, Binnie-Clark believed that the Empire would uplift what she called the "darker" races. Photographs of wheat fields, threshing, and other scenes of the prosperous future of the region constituted sharp contrasts to those of Indigenous people, representing the past. Georgina Binnie-Clark, *Wheat and Woman*, 178.

Her name was "Tosh," and she was deeply religious. Easter day was, according to Binnie-Clark, "a beautiful oasis in her life."

Some Métis men of the Fort Qu'Appelle district were her only Indigenous acquaintances, according to her books, and she hired them to fence her land. (She praised their work, as they did the job thoroughly, and she could pay them by the mile, whereas she had to "feed white men and pay them by day or week for the same job.")[16] Overall, however, Binnie-Clark's writing was not characterized by the same degree of pejorative, negative descriptions of Indigenous people that were to be found in the publications of many of her contemporaries, and she may have been trying to challenge misconceptions and assumptions. When her suspicion that two "half breeds" had stolen her bag of oats proved untrue, and they actually helped her find the oats and hoist them onto her buggy, she "vowed to scorn suspicion and colour prejudice for evermore."[17]

QUESTION MARKS: FAMILY HISTORY AND FICTION

Binnie-Clark seemed an unlikely candidate for the calling and cause of agriculture for Englishwomen in Western Canada. She was born in 1872 in Sherborne, Dorset, the third child of Arthur Walter Binnie Clark, the son of a labourer. Clark was a valet to George Winfield Digby at Sherborne Castle when in 1866 he married Georgina's mother, Maria Setheby, the daughter of a gamekeeper.[18] The Binnie-Clarks were proprietors of the Digby Arms Hotel in Sherborne. Georgina's father had prize-winning horses, and she once said to a journalist that her "only previous farm experience had been as a girl on her father's farm in Dorsetshire, England where thorough-bred horses were bred and reared."[19] In the 1891 census, "Georgina B. Clark" was a music student, aged nineteen. Other clues of her life before arriving in Saskatchewan are few, but they include a passage in *Wheat and Woman* where she wrote that she had "an intimate knowledge of the life of the educated working woman in Germany, Paris and in England," and that she had "lived with and amongst women-workers."[20] In one of her 1909 articles, Binnie-Clark wrote that before she farmed she "lived for art alone, studied music on the Continent, and latterly became a writer. I visited Canada in 1905 for the purpose of securing 'copy'—and stayed to farm."[21] Georgina may have been the first (and possibly only) member of the family to hyphenate her last name. Her brother Louis, for example, signed his name "Louis B. Clark."[22]

There remain significant gaps in understanding important aspects of Binnie-Clark's life, such as where she was educated, how (or indeed whether) she established a reputation as a journalist, and exactly what she did and where she lived before her arrival in Canada in 1905. It is important to emphasize, as historian Susan Jackel points out in her 1979 introduction to a reprint of *Wheat and Woman*, that it is not clear whether the information provided in Binnie-Clark's own books about herself, her family, and her farming is entirely reliable. But according to her first book, *A Summer on the Canadian Prairie*, she ventured to the Canadian West to visit her brother (Louis, who is "Lal" in the book), who was a homesteader near Fort Qu'Appelle, Saskatchewan. Perhaps she was influenced by Flora Shaw's call for sisters to join homesteading brothers. But as stated above, she wrote that she was a writer in search of "copy." She purchased a farm of 320 acres just a few months later near Fort Qu'Appelle, complete with a house, outbuildings, fencing, and crops. It is not completely clear what she paid for it, but in a 1908 article, "A Woman's Way on the Prairie," Binnie-Clark described how she had to pay for her farm in five instalments each of £200 ($1,500.00). (In *A Summer on the Canadian Prairie* she wrote that the farmer who sold her the farm demanded $5,000, with $1,000 down, another $1,000 when she sold the wheat of the 1905 crop, and the balance at 6 percent.)[23] Also, according to *A Summer on the Canadian Prairie*, she required from her father "sufficient funds to cover the greater part of the first instalment," although she signed the papers without securing her father's permission, claiming she had sufficient income (presumably from her writing) to guarantee the payments. The book also indicates that she purchased the farm initially thinking it would be in partnership with her brother and possibly sister, as she uses the pronoun "we."[24] When there finally was communication from their father, he had included only £100 and stated that "on no condition whatever were we to buy land."[25] Georgina then, according to *A Summer on the Canadian Prairie,* declared she would borrow from her father on the security of the income her work in England would bring her, and run the farm herself. In one of the final passages of the book her homesteading brother tells her, "Ha, ha! A woman work a Canadian farm! Why you would be the laughing-stock of the country, if you could do it, which you can't."[26] She set out to prove them wrong. She also had to prove that she could finance the farm through her writing.

Figure 28. Georgina Binnie-Clark, writer, lecturer, and Saskatchewan farmer. She purchased 320 acres near Fort Qu'Appelle in 1905 and became devoted to the cause of English women farming wheat on the prairies. Courtesy Mr. Dennis Jenks.

As mentioned, Binnie-Clark's own accounts are not entirely reliable if searching for the facts. She changed the names of her family members, her neighbours, and hired men. "Lal," for example, in *A Summer on the Canadian Prairie*, was her brother Louis. His homestead records indicate that he was married and that his wife lived with him on his homestead from March 1906.[27] Yet Lal is presented as a lazy bachelor who wants to abandon his homestead, and Georgina is the one to insist that he stay and prove up. (Louis filed on his homestead of 160 acres in 1904 and proved up in 1907, which meant that he must have been acceptably industrious, as many homesteaders took much longer.) Binnie-Clark's sister, called "Hilaria," must have been Ethel, but if so, it is likely not the case that she hated the rural prairies and farming in the way Binnie-Clark described, as Ethel became a much more permanent resident of the farm than her sister, staying on after Georgina's death in 1947. But for her narrative, it is important to develop Hilaria's distaste for farm life on the prairies, which forms a contrast to Georgina's growing fascination with the West and wheat. And through Hilaria's efforts to find a job as a nurse and domestic servant, readers learn about the limited options for single women in Canada.

THE CANADIAN WEST IN 1905: PROFITS AND PREJUDICE

Arriving in Canada in 1905, Binnie-Clark absorbed the heady atmosphere of optimism about the future that prevailed at that time. The new provinces of Saskatchewan and Alberta were created that year. That season there was a "bumper" crop. An editorial in the *Progress* (Qu'Appelle, Saskatchewan) of 20 July 1905 entitled "A Halo O'er the Grain" began, "Still, the grain keeps growing. Night and day the farmer's profits are swelling, silently, surely. Everywhere is seen the bright and hopeful light of joyous anticipation of the largest crop in the history of the West."[28] Binnie-Clark quite likely read this newspaper and was inspired by this editorial as she visited her brother nearby. It concluded by noting the "stimulus in the air, a spirit of hope in every heart, that causes the prophetic imagination to look into the future when the vast prairie will be teeming with a population of untold millions, when the rich soil shall be made to yield a harvest sufficient to feed the world and when the riches wrested from Mother Nature shall be utilized in revitalizing the afflicted, civilizing the boor, and bettering mankind generally." Binnie-Clark became mesmerized and infatuated with wheat, a "tall mass of living loveliness."[29]

That same year—1905—Frank Oliver was appointed Canada's minister of the interior, in charge of the administration of Dominion (homestead) land. As mentioned in Chapter 3, Oliver was a Liberal member of Parliament from Edmonton, he was devoted to the cause of the development of the West, and he was sceptical that women landowners and farmers had any role to play in that development. He was also made superintendent general of Indian Affairs and doggedly pursued the diminution of First Nations reserves, particularly when they occupied superior agricultural land that was close to a railway. Oliver believed that Indigenous people had no role to play in the development of the West either, and that they retarded and undermined the process and progress of settlement. Intense pressure was placed on the people who occupied reserves in the Fort Qu'Appelle area to surrender their land, particularly where it bordered the main line of the Canadian Pacific Railway (CPR).[30] In many cases this pressure succeeded. In 1907, for example, after relentless pressure from Department of Indian Affairs officials, almost 54,000 acres of reserve land on the Crooked Lake Indian agency was alienated.[31]

In 1905 Binnie-Clark would have quickly learned of another obsession of the time in Western Canada. The "immigration peril" was a concern shared by many of the British and Ontarian settlers, who were the first homesteaders in her district.[32] Icelanders were tolerated, according to a 1905 editorial in the *Vidette* of Indian Head, Saskatchewan, as they were "superior and intelligent, and are closely allied with the Anglo-Saxon element of our own country."[33] But people such as the Doukhobors from Russia and the Galicians (Ukrainians) were another matter. The editorial concluded, "Canada wants no new race and language difficulties; she wants no elements that she cannot assimilate readily." A Presbyterian reverend was quoted in a column in the same paper a few months later, asking, "How are we going to maintain in this new land, which we proudly call 'the Great Britain Beyond the Seas,' those principles and usages and ideals that have made Great Britain so strong and prosperous and influential? We have inherited the genius of the Anglo-Saxon race, a genius that is the product of the thought and toil of a thousand years."[34]

Wanted were Ontarians (of British ancestry) and settlers from Britain, as another Presbyterian reverend, James Farquharson of Winnipeg, wrote in 1910: "The multitudes moving from the Eastern provinces of Canada to the West come to us with ideals much like our own. They are of the same race, they glory in their allegiance to the same government, they acknowledge the same moral standards, they worship God in the same manner. There is rejoicing also in the arrivals from the British Isles, for they, like ourselves, are Celt or Saxon; their literature is ours … they and we are one in claiming as our own the past, the present and the future of the British Empire."[35] By contrast the Ukrainians, according to Farquharson, had many "defects of character," including their "carousals, their drunkenness and brutal fights," as well as "the readiness with which the lie comes to their lips."[36]

The Doukhobors were singled out for particularly harsh condemnation because the women of these communities hitched themselves to ploughs in teams and performed other outdoor labour. Photographs of these women workers were widely published with the clear message that these women were little more than beasts of burden. A description by journalist Jean Blewett was typical, and began with the statement, "The Doukhobor woman is no Venus … hard, incessant work does not tend toward beauty of face or form."[37] Doing men's work out of doors made them masculine. Blewett continued: "Taking her place at the plow while the first furrow is turned in the spring, planting, hoeing, making hay, harvesting the grain, threshing and grinding the same, doing the whole year round a man's work, had given her the figure of a man. She has muscles instead of curves; there is no roundness or softness visible. The sun has burned her face brown and her eyelashes white. Her hands and arms are the hands and arms of a working man."[38] An 1899 article entitled "Women Harnessed to Plows in Manitoba" in the *Woman's Journal* (Boston) admonished the Canadian government for not having taken steps to eradicate this practice, and predicted that "sooner or later some official action will be demanded by the daughters of civilization in neighbouring communities regarding the subjection of their Russian sisters to slavery and drudgery in the harvest field."[39] Binnie-Clark had to confront and contend with these attitudes, as she maintained that British women ought to take up land and perform farm labour. The example of the Doukhobors, however, became useful to supporters of homesteads-for-British-born-women, who argued that the West would then be rid of the "foreigners" who treated women in this manner.

Figure 29. Doukhobor women pulling a plough in Saskatchewan, 1902. There was widespread condemnation of the "slavery and drudgery" Doukhobor women were "subjected" to, although this was not how these women saw their own contribution to the establishment of their farms. Women working in the fields was an aberration to be expunged in the course of establishing the West as a corner of the British Empire. Binnie-Clark had to contend with these views as she called on Englishwomen to farm the prairies. Glenbow Archives, NA-670-45.

CHAMPION OF THE CAUSE IN ENGLAND

Although Binnie-Clark spent stretches of time on her Saskatchewan farm, she also frequently returned to England. According to a 1912 newspaper interview, she spent every winter in England (aside from the winter of 1906–7 that she often lectured about.)[40] Her sister Ethel was the more permanent resident of the farm, and brother Arthur Cameron Binnie Clark also helped out. (He died in Fort Qu'Appelle in 1921.)[41] As Susan Jackel admitted, it is also not clear for how many years, and precisely when she was resident on her Saskatchewan farm.[42]

Binnie-Clark never entirely switched her allegiance or her abode to her Saskatchewan farm and to Canada. She had a flat in London's Chelsea district on Cheyne Walk, on the Embankment with a view of the Thames, from at least the First World War to the late 1930s, although there were times when the flat was rented out.[43] Chelsea, and in particular Cheyne Walk, is a district that has long been associated with writers, artists, and activists, and Binnie-Clark was part of a literary and artistic circle that included a very good friend and neighbour of hers, Dame Ethel Walker, a leading British painter of her day.[44] Walker also lived at the south end of Cheyne Walk on the Thames.[45] Walker, best known for her portraits of women, is today recognized as one of a "large number of significant twentieth-century European artists [who] focused on gay, lesbian and transgender themes."[46] Another close neighbour on Cheyne Walk was prominent feminist Sylvia Pankhurst. Although in a "posh" area today, Binnie-Clark's accommodation was modest; she described hers as the "vagabond end" of Cheyne Walk.[47]

According to her own accounts and from evidence found in family papers, Binnie-Clark's financial situation was always precarious. She had to write, lecture, and take in students to sustain herself and her farm and to purchase the labour she required. She had to learn to milk, make bread, clean out the stables, pickle seed, stook, and to do numerous other chores that she could not afford to have done for her. Binnie-Clark described herself as "desperately short of money" in the winter of 1906–7, and in later correspondence wrote that she was "always more or less hard up."[48] It does not appear that her financial situation ever dramatically improved. (In 1936, for example, she wrote from England to a Fort Qu'Appelle acquaintance asking for the twelve dollars she had loaned her five years earlier.)[49] She did not enjoy the power and privilege bestowed upon men, as she did not qualify for a homestead because of her gender. She was genteel but not well-to-do, and she had to support herself. She would not have been recognized as superior or elite in the Saskatchewan community she adopted; she was keenly aware of her status as an eccentric "green" Englishwoman. She cast herself, however, as well above the people of London's East End, whom she encountered (for the first time, it seems) in an immigrant shed in Quebec in their "grotesque attire" and "squalid degradation."[50] Yet she was critical of what she described as "the creed of every Englishman to dislike or at best tolerate foreigners." She described the Hungarians who settled near her brother, for example, as generous and industrious; they commanded her "unqualified admiration." She cast herself as much more tolerant than her brother, who, she wrote, "imagines he detests them."[51] Her admiration did not extend to "Chinamen," as she called them, providing in *A Summer on the Canadian Prairie* her version of the familiar "no ticky no washy" story.[52]

Binnie-Clark began to attract public attention during a visit to England in 1908 (leaving her farm in the charge of a couple from England), when she started to write articles for the *Canadian Gazette*, published in London, which was a weekly journal aimed at a British readership but consisted of information concerning Canadian commerce, investments, emigration, and Canadians in the metropole. Initially, Binnie-Clark's cause was not the homestead grant for women, but to encourage others among "the class of English gentlewomen from whom she sprang," as well as those of a "lower social grade," to "follow her pathway to the Canadian West," which would be of "infinite benefit to themselves, to the country the relief of their superfluous presence, and to Canada which stands in need of their help in the upbuilding of a vigorous nationality."[53] The message was that an Englishwoman who was "frittering away her life in trivialities may find new life and a career of independence in prairie farming." According to a February 1908 editorial on "The Woman Problem" in the *Canadian Gazette*, Binnie-Clark demonstrated "the satisfaction a cultured Englishwoman may find in the life of a prairie homestead which she herself manages, rearing live stock, growing wheat, and thereby bringing to herself both money and a healthy, satisfying independence."[54] In her columns she mentioned other opportunities for "gentlewomen" in Canada such as nursing, teaching, and housekeeping, but argued that "land-work is far higher than housework, certainly more interesting, and there is no reason at all why women should not adopt it as a healthy, practicable and highly remunerative occupation."[55]

Binnie-Clark's first series of articles in the *Canadian Gazette*, "A Woman, Two Boys and £140," was in the form of letters to a prospective woman homesteader, a widow with two sons. She advised "Mrs. Huntingdon" to head to the prairies, despite the fact she had such limited capital, because she could claim her own homestead, and once her sons reached the age of eighteen they too could claim 160 acres each. Binnie-Clark provided details on a myriad of topics relating to emigrating and establishing a farm on the prairies.[56] A subsequent series, "A Woman's Way on the Prairie," was the story of her own farm, to be told in greater detail in *Wheat and Woman* in 1914. As in her book, she did not try to conceal her mistakes, misfortunes, and calamities. Her point was that "what I struggled through uncomfortably the woman of average intelligence and domestic habit can do at her ease." Nor did she disguise the horrors of the cold and "sea of snow" of her first winter, although she wrote that she "never knew a dull or unhappy moment."[57]

The story Binnie-Clark told in her articles, on the lecture circuit, and finally in *Wheat and Woman* was that her first year's harvest realized £200, but that this was followed by a harvest of wheat that was infested with wild oats and a third harvest damaged by frost. She learned that she had to be very economical with her money, that the farm had to entirely supply the household, that effort had to be put into butter that could be sold, and that there was always a market for pigs. Her message was that it was still possible to make a living out of farming even if grain crops failed.

"A POWERFUL FACTOR IN THE STRENGTHENING OF THE EMPIRE": ORIGIN OF THE HOMESTEADS-FOR-BRITISH-WOMEN CAMPAIGN

Binnie-Clark's 1908 articles in the *Canadian Gazette* led to many inquiries addressed to her concerning women's immigration and settlement in Western Canada. She reported that "women of small capital earnestly seeking a means of self-support" were "constantly applying to me."[58] One letter was from "a little band of six who contemplate coming out with a capital of £500." Another was from "a single woman with a capital of £100 only … [who] wrote to Mr. Obed Smith asking if I could obtain a Government grant of 160 acres, and was most surprised to find that the Canadian Government does not consider the claims of a mere spinster; as for getting land here [in England]—well, the more progressive dailies have fought the battle for years of 'back to the land' in the interests of *the men* only."[59] Binnie-Clark's own rising debts and poor crops had demonstrated that women who had to purchase their land, rather than being able to take advantage of the homestead grant, were at a decided disadvantage from the start.

In a November 1908 article entitled "A Woman's Plea from the West," Binnie-Clark first wrote of the inequities of Canada's Dominion lands legislation, that land was granted to a woman only if the sole head of a family, and not to single women. And it was here she first proposed her "trial scheme" for Englishwomen.[60] She called on the Canadian government to grant "say, twelve quarter-sections annually for three years to women selected and approved by the English agent and at the end of the time allow the result to determine further arrangement." She was brimming with enthusiasm and optimism for the idea, and offered to promote and organize the scheme in England, writing: "The idea is original and full of interest to the world at large; it means advertisement and later it will mean an inestimable investment of English capital in Canadian land. Surely it is worth a little further consideration. As against all the male immigrants you have known to turn out failures, have you ever heard of an Englishwoman immigrant failure?" An editorial in the *Canadian Gazette* supported Binnie-Clark's pleas on behalf of homesteads for women, and called on the Canadian minister of the interior Frank Oliver and the other cabinet ministers to grant land annually for three years to carefully selected and approved Englishwomen.[61] The editors wrote that "the West stands greatly in need of women, and we believe it would be an act of wisdom to give the encouragement of free homesteads to women who have the capital, the independent spirit and proven capacity."

In November 1908 Binnie-Clark wrote from her farm (which she had named "Binning") to the Department of the Interior in Ottawa to ask that officials "give personal consideration to the idea of 'Free Homesteads for Women,'" articulating many of the rationales and arguments she had begun to present in her articles and that she would later develop.[62] She stated her articles had generated a lot of correspondence from Englishwomen eager to follow her lead, and she reported that "as a rule they have agricultural experience. I was a writer." These women had "slender" capital and for them the purchase of land was out of the question, but "given a free homestead, two or three women farming together in a combined capital would be certain to do well." Here she first penned a sentiment she would use in the future, that "if they [Englishwomen] do not get through as much work as a man in a day, they will get through considerably more in a season." Women, she argued, would not have the inclination or opportunity to "roam around during the off season"; they would instead pursue stock raising and dairy produce on their homesteads. "The woman's homestead," she wrote, "will be Home, the centre of life and interest. Schools, Churches, other agents in the process of civilized settlement of the country, can only gain in the woman settler." The "class" of women she had in mind were "chiefly those who, in England, come under the category of working-gentlewomen, women of education" who had capital and had attended an agricultural college or worked on a dairy farm. Binnie-Clark proposed that the government offer a limited number of homesteads to Englishwomen of capability and capital. She was certain that "the experiment would succeed beyond imagination," and that in time it would become law. She was also certain that the offer would be received in the Old Country with the "greatest enthusiasm on the part of all." She saw the only barrier to be "the law" and wrote that "the laws of a Liberal government are always awaiting expansion, and the ear of the true law-giver is always alert for this whispering of Reason."

Superintendent of Immigration W.D. Scott replied swiftly, politely, but firmly and curtly that Binnie-Clark's letter was received and that "I have noted your arguments in favour of giving homesteads to unmarried women, but unfortunately the law does not allow this and the Department does not make a law and has no power to alter it in this particular."[63] Yet this reply did not deter Binnie-Clark, and on her way to England late in 1908 she visited Winnipeg, where she learned that the cause of homestead rights was being pursued by women there. She also stopped in Ottawa, where she had an appointment with Frank Oliver, although he did not keep that appointment.[64] According to her account in *Wheat and* Woman, she met with a deputy minister who simply said: "She can't."

That year a similarly intransigent man was appointed to an influential position in London, and he would become Binnie-Clark's nemesis. In 1908 J. Obed Smith was appointed assistant superintendent of immigration at Canada's London office.[65] He had served as commissioner of immigration in Winnipeg for the previous ten years. Smith was born in England, had homesteaded in Manitoba, and was a lawyer. From the London office, Smith was in charge of emigration to Canada from Europe, and he occupied this position until his retirement in 1924. He was a loyal Liberal. He promoted migration within the Empire, calling on "the great colonizers of the British race to give up the comfort of an English home and put on the glorious armour of courage and of hope, in order to carry forward British civilization and push back the fringe of the wilderness a few feet each year."[66] Yet, as will be discussed later in this chapter, he was utterly opposed to the idea of women farming on their own in Western Canada, whether they were from England or elsewhere. He remained adamant that women migrants could perform only the "humbler duties of domestic work," and worked to ensure that domestic servants were secured for Canada.[67]

It is interesting that like Frank Oliver, J. Obed Smith was implicated in land speculation. In 1907 there was a case heard at Winnipeg in which it was found that Smith was engaged in land deals, admitting that he had used knowledge of land values learned through his position to "make a little money on the side," despite having taken an oath as a civil servant that he would not "disclose without due authority any knowledge which came to him by reason of his office."[68] Smith had been named in a lawsuit by parties to whom he had sold land. In 1907 the opposition in the House of Commons demanded to know "whether an official receiving a salary of $3000.00 a year was to be permitted to engage in land speculation to the detriment of his attention to his public duties, using official information for the purpose." Smith's acts were, it was claimed, "unconstitutional." The Liberal government, however, contended that this was not a violation of his office, that it was an isolated transaction, and that Smith was attentive to his duties. But perhaps this scandal was why Smith was sent overseas.

Binnie-Clark kept up the pressure in her articles, beginning with "Homesteads for Bachelor Women" in February 1909, which started with the argument that the advent of single women homesteaders on the prairies would lead to the quick establishment of schools and churches and other markers of civilization.[69] Through marriage they would bring an end to the preponderance of bachelor men, and rear the next generation: "free homesteads to women will be a powerful factor in the strengthening of the Empire." Binnie-Clark asserted that "there are many ladies in England who, from their knowledge of agriculture, would prove very successful farmers on the prairie, and to others the granting of free homesteads would open the way to relief from a life of genteel drudgery." Answering the question of whether she truly believed women were physically capable of working a homestead, Binnie-Clark wrote that the most progressive farm in her district was, to a large extent, run by a woman whose father was growing wealthy through her efforts. This woman "breaks the land, discs and harrows, and thinks nothing of milking from five to ten cows daily, in addition to her other labours." (This may have been the family she referred to as the "Mazeys" in *Wheat and Woman.*) She drew on this example in subsequent talks and articles, pointing out that this Canadian woman had no claim to the 160 acres "which her Government grants to a male of any nation."[70] Here is the beginning of the argument that was to take centre stage in the homesteads-for-women campaign in the West that Binnie-Clark helped to galvanize: that British and British-Canadian women were more deserving of homesteads than were "foreign" men.

Other of her articles appeared in English journals such as the *Quiver.* In "How Canada Welcomes the Emigrant Girl," Binnie-Clark wrote about staying at the YWCA in Winnipeg and visiting the "Girls' Home of Welcome," and how she met other women immigrants from the "Old Country."[71] She encouraged one young woman from Ireland, who was working at the YWCA but had "done all sorts and conditions of farm work," including ploughing, harrowing, and stoking, to consider farming on a cooperative plan with two or three other women. There were high wages paid for women's labour, and women who pooled their resources could afford to purchase land that was "a safe and sure investment." Once the government realized this would help to benefit the country, "it would extend to women the free grant of 160 acres of land, now limited to men and widows."

Binnie-Clark's articles emphasized that women could perform tasks that were not normally included in the repertoire of feminine behaviour. In "A Fight with Fire," published in the *Pall Mall Magazine* in 1909, Binnie-Clark wrote of how she had fought a prairie fire, beating back flames threatening to destroy her home, barn, granaries, and seed, "until my hands and eyes were as red-hot cinders caught in a whirlwind."[72] The story of the fire was illustrated by a drawing of Binnie-Clark fighting the flames that had almost reached her buildings, and by photographs, including (oddly) one of the "Soo [sic Sioux] village by the western lake of Fort Qu'Appelle," one of a tipi and cart and a man and women with the caption "The way the Indians live," along with one of "homestead quarters" and "the shooting-box of an English settler in the hills by Fort Qu'Appelle." Clearly the message was that perils and dangers such as prairie fires were worth battling in order to bring civilization to this corner of the British Empire.

ARE BOOMING CANADA

ENGLISHWOMEN ARE TRAINING GIRLS TO COME OUT HERE.

Recent Meeting at the Colonial Training School For Girls at Arlesey, Herts, Was Addessed by Practical Observers of Canada's Needs—Miss Binnie-Clark Writes of Her Work in the West.

"Women's Work and Openings in Canada" was the raison d'etre of what was a most interesting meeting held recently at the Country and Colonial Training School for Ladies at Arlesey, Herts. Lady Frances Balfour presided, and the people who contributed speeches and papers on this important and very popular subject were Lady Thomson, who was in Canada with her husband, the president of the British Association, last summer; Mrs. George Cran, author of "A Woman in Canada" (a woman by the way who used her eyes and her trained intelligence); and Mr. G. Bethune Gray, of the Lands Department of the Canadian Pacific Railway. In addition, there was a legacy from Miss Binnie-Clark, the woman farmer in Canada, in the shape of an admirable paper on women farmers. As the girls at Arlesey are being trained in housework, cooking, preserving, pickling and curing bacon, the care of bees, poultry and pigs, gardening, laundry-work and dairy-

MISS BINNIE CLARK

work, they are naturally interested to know what their chances are if they choose to form a little colony, or if they go out simply to plough a lonely furrow in the great Northwest.

Mrs. George Cran, who has been in charge of the C.P.R. stall at the Ideal Home Exhibition, telling women what they can do in Canada, and telling men how to earn homes of their own, is a clever journalist, poetess and art critic. Her new book, "A Woman in Canada," is the result of a careful study of conditions, possibilities, and drawbacks to the life of woman in Western Canada. She is enthusiastic about the Dominion, and especially inasmuch as it offers a solution of the problem of what to do with the superfluous English woman, who is frequently young, capable and attractive, but has the great fault of being superabundant.

Miss Binnie-Clark, who went back to Canada with four girl pupils, a couple of weeks ago, is a living, zealous, charming example of what an Englishwoman can do as a farmer. She has been settled in the Qu'Appelle valley for several years, and has well earned her spurs. She is a well-bred, highly-educated young woman, who treats of her experiences in so matter-of-fact a manner as to inspire the most unenterprising with the conviction that any woman can make good in the West if she gives her mind to it. Her new book, "A Summer on a Canadian Prairie," contains an immense amount of matter valuable to the person looking towards Canada as the Land of Opportunity. The trouble with some of the people intending to settle in Canada is that they are too interested in saying "What has Canada to offer me?" to consider the other equally momentous question "What have I to Offer Canada?"

MAKING GIRL FARMERS

MISS G. BINNIE CLARK RAISING MONEY IN ENGLAND.

She Wants Twenty Thousand Working Women to Put Up $100,000 to Bring Out Englishwomen Who Want to Farm in Canada — Sir Thomas Shaughnessy Approves of Miss Clark's Scheme.

Miss G. Binnie Clark, the Canadian lady farmer, speaking in London at a meeting of the Women's Agricultural and Horticultural International Union, made the interesting announcement that she was raising a sum of $100,000 to place British girls upon the land in the Dominion.

"I am going to get the money from 20,000 working women, from duchesses to factory girls," she said, in the course of her interesting address. "The fund will be used for the purpose of building a 'bridge' from England to Canada for girls who may desire to become farmers. An investment will be made in cottage training farms, each cottage to be built on a section of land capable of keeping twelve tenants, who will work the section. I believe that each well-worked section, with adequate labor and

MISS G. BINNIE CLARK.

horse-power, should turn in an average of $5,000 a year net profit."

Miss Clark stated that she hoped to have a great deal of encouragement from Sir Thomas Shaughnessy, so that the idea may be forwarded in several parts of Canada.

Sir Thomas Shaughnessy has said that he would welcome women settlers in the country on the same terms as men. He also pointed out that the Canadian Pacific Railway and the hotels required 24,000 eggs and 75,000 chickens every week, and these might easily be supplied by women farmers, as the irrigated farms lie close to the railway.

Women must go in for mixed farming, stock-raising, and grain-growing. We must also get the girls a share in Sir Thomas Shaughnessy's scheme of providing ready-made holdings for settlers. Under that plan a girl would reap her first harvest, in all probability, with gratifying success, and in a year's time it is hoped that women of ordinary capacity, with proper application, will be able to take up their own land, and forge ahead towards prosperity.

The idea is that Canada will furnish a fine field for the physically fit and willing woman-worker, and Miss Clark's scheme is receiving the support of the well-wishers of women in every rank of life, both in Britain and in the Dominion.

Sir Thomas Shaughnessy is a very go-ahead Canadian, of Irish parentage, and at present the head of that great railway concern, the Canadian Pacific. He was, before he became president of the company, its chief purchasing agent, and, as such, was actively interested in the development of railway enterprise in the Dominion. He is an enthusiast as regards farming, in all its phases, and has done a great deal in the direction of getting suitable people on the land in Canada. The woman dairy-farmer he encourages to the utmost, believing that there is a prosperous future before all suitable settlers who enter wisely into an industry entirely suited to their case.

Miss Clark's enterprise deserves every commendation, and those who have closely watched her untiring efforts for the provision of a "golden bridge" for the capable gentlewoman with a taste for farming, in any of its phases, between struggle and success, are sanguine as to the practicality of her ideals.

Canada offers, indeed, a promising field for the woman farmer, properly equipped for her task, and doubtless the work of Miss Clark and of the Women's Agricultural and Horticultural Union, with which she is associated, will be crowned with a gratifying resultant ere long.—London Scraps.

Figure 30. Press coverage from 1910 of Georgina Binnie-Clark's activities in England and Canada to promote farming for Englishwomen on the Canadian prairies. Both are from the *Gleichen Call* (Alberta): "Are Booming Canada," 9 June 1910, 7; "Making Girl Farmers," 21 April 1910, 7.

In 1909 Binnie-Clark began to be featured in the Canadian press under headlines such as "Western Suffragette: Miss Binnie-Clark Wants Free Homesteads for Women Who Can Farm," "British Women on Canadian Homesteads," and "Canadian Farms for English Spinsters."[73] It was frequently noted that she always presented a very feminine appearance when she gave her public lectures and talked about an endeavour regarded as distinctly masculine. She was described as "tall, slender and good looking, gracefully dressed in black and white … [she] scarcely looked as if she had combined the duties of farmer and housewife, had plowed her own land and tended without help of any kind 14 horses and cattle and any number of pigs through a whole winter."[74]

At the National Union of Woman Workers in October 1909, Binnie-Clark's talk was on "Conditions of Life for Women in Canada," and her main message was that "the immigration of English women is a matter of vital importance to the Canadian race."[75] She began by speaking about the opportunity for domestic service and argued that women "of refinement" should not fear accepting such positions, but she also spoke of the demand for teachers, stenographers, nurses, landscape gardeners, and vegetable and fruit gardeners. She spoke of the lives of married women and mothers on homesteads and farms and painted a positive picture of the conditions of social and economic life. But she paid the greatest attention to "the finest investment in Canada … my own battleground, the land" and to the cause of homesteads for women. Binnie-Clark read from a letter she had sent to Frank Oliver, in which she had written that "the extension of the free land grant to women should have the same effect on new settlement that deep-ploughing has on the prosperity of the grain-grower: it should work towards Unity, the first condition of prosperity and content." The single women homesteader would be "untrammeled by the special care of husband and children" and would be able to devote energy to the establishment of schools and churches." She concluded her letter:

> English women may not have so direct a claim on Canadian land as the women of Canada, but any country would be the richer for the coming of such Englishwomen as would be prompted to avail themselves of an offer of free land in Canada. Women of trained intelligence, nerve, energy, patience, good-will, foresight, perseverance, courage, power of endurance—limited capital—good comrades, not

> easily driven back from their purpose—Englishwomen, not drawn from any particular class but forming a class of themselves summoned together from all classes by the bugle call of the decree, or desire to labour for a living—or for life.[76]

She ended her talk by mentioning that she had received many letters from women in support of her cause, indicating that women "really want this free land grant," that "it is in the nature of Englishwomen to love outdoor pursuits," and that many needed to support themselves.

Binnie-Clark was developing a position that was radical in several ways. She advocated grain farming on large acreages as the most profitable, rejecting arguments for small holdings and the "lighter branches" of agriculture. She often criticized the home help concept and instead called for the "advent of the hired woman on the land." She wrote that "should I be offered the post of general help on a Canadian farm at a salary of twenty-five dollars a month, or land work at twenty dollars, I should not hesitate to decide on the outdoor occupation, in spite of the lesser remuneration."[77]

Binnie-Clark had many critics in both Canada and England, and one replied to her talk at Portsmouth in 1909. A Miss Beevor, who had visited Canada in the summer of 1909, believed that women should not be involved in the purchase of land, that it was risky and that it amounted to land speculation. She stated that "it is only the exceptional woman who will succeed in this matter of land cultivation."[78] Beevor pointed out that Binnie-Clark had purchased an improved farm and had not done the "pioneer work" herself. She hinted that the government of Canada was wise in not extending the homestead privilege to single women, as they could not obtain agricultural education there except in poultry farming and dairying. She also believed that Binnie-Clark had touched too lightly on the question of solitude, and that she had heard "some sad stories about the break-down of women through excessive work and solitude." She concluded that the "best advertisement for the scheme of getting free land granted to women would be for a few exceptional women to go out, buy land and farm it successfully. Meanwhile, I am afraid that one swallow does not make a summer and one Miss Binnie-Clark won't exactly carry this scheme." Beevor concluded by saying that she loved Canada, however, and that "if I were younger I would be off tomorrow."

But Binnie-Clark's lectures and articles soon garnered considerable attention, interest, and approval. In a series of articles on "How Can I Earn a Living" in the *Woman Worker* (London) in 1909 and 1910, Esther Longhurst wrote about openings for women in the colonies, including farming, and described the experiences and advice of Binnie-Clark under the title "Farming and Freedom."[79] Others could follow her lead if they were "strong and sensible," liked "an outdoor life and did not mind plenty of hard work."

New audiences were reached in 1909 and 1910 when Binnie-Clark published articles in the London *Daily Mail.* Her first, appearing in January 1909, was "A Woman's Farm in Canada," in which she told the story of the purchase of her farm.[80] This first column ended with a plea for homesteads for women that would help her countrywomen to "adopt the same health-giving, somewhat exacting, but in many ways delightful means of self-support" instead of "the ghostly footfall of unemployment, which always lurks alongside the trail from which they view before them the beckoning hand that points with mocking gibe to the hour of superannuation." She expected the right would be granted by the Canadian government "first experimentally, then conditionally, then *gratefully.*" Other columns included "Women Farmers," in which Binnie-Clark wrote that "farm work for a woman is not looked upon as impossible in Canada."[81] She described in greater detail than in previous articles her "Canadian neighbor" who farmed over a thousand acres and never hired labour except at threshing time, and had "for many years entrusted his land work to his eldest daughter. She would plough, drive or harrow day in day out, frequently milking half a dozen cows before and after her field labour." Yet the eldest son had inherited the farm and the daughter, who was "more competent to work a hundred and sixty acres of land than many homesteaders," had no right to the land grant.

With the 1910 publication of *A Summer on the Canadian Prairie,* Binnie-Clark's profile was enhanced. The editors of the *Canadian Gazette* were delighted: "We have read more books on Canadian conditions than we care to recall; in none of them is the touch more sure, more sensitive to realities, and yet more sympathetic."[82] An anonymous reviewer for the *United Empire: The Royal Colonial Institute Journal* was not as glowing, comparing Binnie-Clark's book to Marion Cran's *A Woman in Canada* and Mrs. Humphrey (Mary A.) Ward's *Canadian Born* and finding it to be "inferior to the other two in every respect but that of a convincing realism."[83] Both Cran's and Ward's books, discussed in Chapter 2, conveyed more conservative messages about opportunities for women in Western Canada, with Ward emphasizing marriage as the ultimate destiny. The reviewer was disappointed that *A Summer on the Canadian Prairie* ended abruptly "when the heroine has just gathered in the first sheaves of her first Canadian harvest … and if the tale is as true as it sounds we should like to hear the sequel." Yet there were "scattered among its pages words of wisdom and guidance for the intending settler."

In February 1910 Binnie-Clark was a guest at a London dinner of "lady farmers and gardeners," organized by the Women's Agricultural and Horticultural International Union, and it was noted that she easily held the record for the largest farm.[84] She was asked to reply to the toast of the colonial members of the union, and she spoke in glowing terms of the prospects offered to women by farming in Canada. As usual she appeared in very feminine attire and was described as a "tall, dark-haired, slim young women, with pink malmasons [*sic*] clustering in her black evening gown."[85] In March she spoke at Caxton Hall, Westminster, London, a location that played a central role in the suffrage movement. Her talk "attracted considerable attention."[86] Here she elaborated on why she thought women should farm wheat, saying that "it gives the quickest return." Growing fruit in British Columbia could mean no return for three or four years, while "in the wheat belts, in Saskatchewan and Manitoba your returns are seen in the second year, and you also have immediate profits from poultry and dairy." She reiterated her belief that English women should farm cooperatively, and she stressed that she was "not interested myself in any but educated women at the moment." Although she complimented the "splendid" work of the associations who sent out home helps, she reiterated, "I would like to establish a channel between the educated women of England and Canada."

Speaking to a "select audience at a woman's club in London," also in March 1910, Binnie-Clark "disposed convincingly of the fallacious notion that women, to be successful farmers, must have men to do the rough work."[87] Binding, for example, was "jealously guarded by man," but "this is part of the work excellently suited to women." As reported in the journal *Votes for Women*, there was "something wonderfully alluring in the picture conjured up" by Binnie-Clark's talk of "the large open spaces, the healthy out-of-door life." After quoting Mrs. Pethick Lawrence as stating that "down through the vista of long eras we see the mothers of the human race not only the first builders of the home but … the first tillers of the soil," the author of the article concluded that it was "only natural that women should turn to farming … and that they should be among the most enthusiastic exponents of the modern 'back to the land' movement."

Influential people were present at Binnie-Clark's lectures on many occasions. One of her papers was read at an "at home" at the Colonial Training School for Ladies in May 1910, and chaired by Lady Frances Balfour. Also in attendance were Marion Cran, along with G. Bethune-Gray, manager of the Irrigated Lands Department of the CPR, who "told the audience about the land, and what could be done with it and on it by capable and young women."[88]

In 1910 Binnie-Clark published a series of articles in the *Imperial Colonist* entitled "Are Educated Women Wanted in Canada?," in which she went into detail about opportunities such as nursing, dressmaking, and teaching, with little emphasis on her cause of farming for women and reforming the land laws of Canada.[89] Perhaps she was asked to mute what had become her central message. After that she ceased to be a contributor to the *Imperial Colonist*, and the journal gave no coverage to her lectures or publications. Her cause and her critique were likely becoming too radical for the women behind the British Women's Emigration Association.

In January 1910 Binnie-Clark attended a meeting in London concerning the CPR's "ready-made" farm scheme in Alberta. Held at the large Whitehall Room, the meeting was presided over by CPR president Sir Thomas Shaughnessy, who predicted that the plan would create the most densely populated and most highly productive large body of agricultural land in Canada, which would strengthen and foster imperial sentiment in Canada.[90] Binnie-Clark asked Shaughnessy if the scheme would apply to women, and he replied to the effect that "lady farmers" were welcome, and that there were opportunities for women to raise poultry and eggs for the CPR hotels and dining cars. In subsequent lectures Binnie-Clark complimented the scheme.[91] She hoped that some women would be among the applicants. Perhaps "Jack" May heard this plea. In October 1910 Binnie-Clark visited the colonists at Strathmore, Alberta, writing about her observations in the *Overseas Daily Mail* of London.[92] She found the colonists were "proving themselves Britons of that type which cannot be beaten throughout the length and breadth of the universe," although, alas, drought had ruined the crops and the promised irrigation had arrived too late. She optimistically forecast, however, what would have happened if the land had been irrigated.

Binnie-Clark's popularity reached new heights in 1910, with favourable coverage of her initiatives in Canadian, British, and colonial papers.[93] Reports of her activities were often accompanied by a portrait.[94] She was celebrated as a "living, zealous, charming example of what an Englishwoman can do as a farmer."[95]

TRAINING PUPILS AT BINNING FARM, FORT QU'APPELLE

While on the lecture circuit in England in 1910, Binnie-Clark announced a new initiative to be established on her land in Saskatchewan: a training farm for English girls. The intention was to "build a 'bridge' from England to Canada for girls who may desire to become farmers."[96] She hoped to raise £20,000 collected from "duchesses to factory girls," and the money would be invested in "cottage training farms," with each being built on a section of land that would employ twelve tenants. The plan was that each of these cottage farms would make a net profit annually of £1,000. As a start she was taking four English pupils back with her to Saskatchewan that spring, where she intended to teach them to farm, and each was paying her £52.[97] She hoped that her scheme would have the encouragement of Sir Thomas Shaughnessy, who had said that he would welcome women settlers, and that her pupils could supply the CPR with eggs and poultry.[98] Binnie-Clark also hoped that bringing out pupils from England would be a way of "clearly demonstrating the power of women to work the land, and whether my pupils personally need the Government grant or not, I expect them to fit themselves for the homestead test."

Binnie-Clark's pupils, however, would serve another purpose: providing her with unpaid farm labour. (The Indian residential schools that she admired so much operated on much the same principal.) In her talks, Binnie-Clark advised the woman farmer to take pupils "so as to be provided with free labour and a matron to look after the house—to take, in fact, the part in domestic affairs a man farmer relegates to his wife."[99] Student fees could also help to sustain the farm.

The grand scheme of raising money and establishing cottage training farms never materialized, but Binnie-Clark did train some pupils on her Saskatchewan farm. After her first season she reported success; the students had raised the cleanest crop of Number 1 Northern wheat in the neighbourhood.[100] They had all learned to control a team of four horses pulling several implements, despite the fact that none of them had previous experience with horses. Her pupils had demonstrated "an innate love of animals" that assisted them in all of their farm work. While they were slower at ploughing than male labourers, they were much more thorough at working the land with disc harrows. All of the pupils had hauled water, milked, cleaned stables, shovelled manure, and performed other chores with "good temper and excellent results." This demonstrated, according to Binnie-Clark, that the prejudice against women working out of doors and on the land was "founded on an imperfect knowledge of the facts." She believed that while gardening was a strain on physical endurance, work with implements "not only entails no physical fatigue but is positive physical refreshment." Challenging the division of farm work into men's and women's spheres, she continued: "A conscientious intelligence is necessary in ploughing, but on the disc and harrow cart one sits at ease in the most exhilarating and nourishing air in the world. The work is entirely mechanical, and it is the only one place in the busy world, outside the rest-cure section of a nursing home, where one is free to indulge in day-dreams." The obstacles to women farming were a lack of capital and official encouragement, according to Binnie-Clark, not the physical incapacity of women to perform farm work.

Binnie-Clark's students included some from the prestigious Roedean School near Brighton. One pupil was Kathleen Laughrin, who came out with six others in 1910, having seen an advertisement in the *Times*.[101] An entry in the Fort Qu'Appelle local history written by Derek Harrison, Laughrin's son, provides insight into the sort of adventurous person who was willing to learn about farming in Saskatchewan with Binnie-Clark as instructor.[102] Educated in France and an accomplished musician, Laughrin had travelled extensively. In Paris, she studied with the organist at Notre Dame Cathedral, and in 1903 she was in Russia, where she worked for a year as governess to Count Leo Tolstoy and family. Laughrin had worked as a journalist in London and lived in South America. In 1910, when she arrived in mid-May at Qu'Appelle station there was raging blizzard. This pupil's main memory of her experience with Binnie-Clark was that her bed at Binning was a block of ice; the bed could not be made as the bedding stuck to the frozen wall. In 1914 Laughrin married Roland Harrison, a neighbour of Binnie-Clark's.

Figure 31. In 1910 Georgina Binnie-Clark established a training farm for English girls on her land at Fort Qu'Appelle that she called "Binning." These included pupils from Roedean School, Brighton, as illustrated here. Pupils provided free labour and student fees could help sustain the farm. This student is "stooking," or setting sheaves upright in stooks. Georgina Binnie-Clark, *Wheat and Woman*, 402.

WOMAN'S SUPPLEMENT CANADIAN COURIER

Land and The Woman

By GEORGINA BINNIE-CLARK

At Miss Binnie-Clark's Farm School at Fort Qu' Appelle, the Wealthiest, Like the Poorest, Pupil Must Learn to Perform, Personally, the Duties, Without Exception, Imposed by Simple but Strenuous Farm Life.

IN Britain outdoor occupation for women is the word of the hour, but the obstacle placed in their way by the Canadian Government in refusing women the right to take up homestead land, at present impedes the progress of women towards the place of independence, prosperity or wealth, at which they would undoubtedly arrive in working their own land on the Canadian prairie. It is true that we British women have the alternative of going to our free hundred and sixty acres in Australia or the United States; but Australia is too far off to permit the frequent pleasure of a visit to the old country; and the United States Government very naturally requests one to pass through a form of naturalization; and although in the bitterness of heart towards the narrow and selfish decisions so clearly seen in laws made by men for men, one is sometimes tempted to cut the cord that binds one to one's native land in favour of the country where women have certainly more consideration and a finer opportunity than in those countries where they have neither part nor lot in the franchise, the strength of the imperial and home tie is very strong; and British women, as a rule, refuse to take the severing step which so many of their countrymen have taken without hesitation and without regret.

To the argument that women are not strong enough to fulfil the demand of the homestead law in the matter of field-labour I can only repeat the words I spoke before the National Union of British Women four years ago: "If twenty dollars a month were offered me to do outdoor work on a farm, and twenty-five dollars for the indoor work, I should, without hesitation, accept the easier job at the smaller salary rather than the post sacred to women, entailing the long hours of that daily round which never seems to end." Men place land labour as the bottom degree of toil because it is the hardest they have experienced; had they performed household work for the briefest period they would know how much harder and more trying is the woman's task, which is seldom appreciated, and without standard recognition in the matter of remuneration.

One hour's honest work in a garden makes a greater demand on the body than half a day's work on an implement. Field work by the disc, the harrow, or the rake entails no physical fatigue whatever, and demands but a slender intelligence. Ploughing requires both intelligence and experience, but entails very little physical fatigue except in breaking with the hand plough, and it is more satisfactory in every way to get one's breaking done by outside labour at the local standard of cost per acre. If work on the implements were the sole test of the power of women to produce an income from the land, farming might honestly be recommended as the refuge of the destitute. But it is when one comes down to the chores of stable-cleaning, grooming, milking, wood-bucking, stoning the land, or shocking the sheaves at harvest time—all those tasks where a mind that can soar beyond the menace of monotony must still rely on its patient, splendid, enduring comrade—the body—that the real test is faced. It is to be remembered that to have the power to do all these trying and unfamiliar chores is not necessarily to do them. Given sufficient capital it is always cheaper to pay hire for these meaner tasks and reserve one's own force for development. But the strength of the chain is in its weakest link, and the standard of equipment for the woman farming in Canada must be that the wealthiest comer be able to perform all those duties which her poorest comrade has no choice but to personally perform or leave undone. No pupil is allowed the privilege of living the simple and strenuous life on my cottage home farm and of learning by doing except on this distinct understanding—seven years' farming in good times and bad having taught me that absolute self-reliance at all times and seasons is an indispensable factor to man or woman farming in the North West.

When I came to Canada I understood nothing whatever of farming, but I know as much as one can know of horses until they arrive at the place where the need of the horse is entirely dependent on the woman, from the newly-arrived foal to the ancient and honourable pensioner. Such women farmers as Miss Jack May, Miss May Whittrich and Mrs. Lavington doubtless own a balance sheet on which result has never been forced to the ignominious position of the wrong side. The two first named ladies I know went badly down on grain in their first and frozen season, but I remember marvelling at their good fortune with stock within the first six months of their experiment—their splendid horses, the generous milch-cows, which seemed to produce heifer calves, only, in a country which I had begun to think must be governed by the sign of "Taurus." And pigs! I forget their result, but it was simply great; they had already turned over the original outlay, and still possessed the sows plus the finer members of their families. Also, owing to the skill of Miss Whittrich, their dairy produced an income from the first month of their settlement.

NEW-FOUND "GENTLE ART"

Not a Chariot, Except in the Race of Feminine Independence, is this Four-in-Hand Equipage Used on the Land at "Binning." A Group of Pupils are Shown En Route for Work.

I WORKED, and still work, within the fascination of the wheat clutch, but a visit to Southern Alberta this year has convinced me that at least one-half one's acres should be strongly fenced and dedicated to stock—poultry, pigs, calves and horses. On a 500-acre farm near Calgary was a hog-raiser, with 500 hogs ready for the market, and the Swift packing house ready for every head of his stock, which he placed at a low average, that netted, however, a consoling sum total of $10,000.

In wheat, although tormented by that Judas Iscariot among weeds, wild oats, I have done fairly well. In 1910 I scored the clearest crop in my neighbourhood, which graded 1 Northern, and what I did not sell for seeds sold at a dollar a bushel in May, 1911. But that crop was raised on land I had broken, and the only original and beautiful wheat-field which I found ready-made has cost me hundreds of dollars in wild oats. But horse-breeding I consider to be the safest and most remunerative line for result. For one mare I bought in 1906 I now have four valuable mares and a colt, who is beautiful as a harness and saddle horse, and useful in a team of four on the land. For that mare I gave the very low emergency price of $50, and to-day I place the family at a very low figure in the sum of $1,000.

If wheat is raised, as a rule every side line is neglected; yet on 160 acres from poultry, pigs, and potatoes alone might be drawn an income which would guarantee to the woman independence within a few years, as well as a healthful and happy life. If only Canadian women would unite to insist on the removal of the present disability, which obstructs the woman farmer in the very land which the splendid pluck and endurance and patience of woman held for man in the hard day of the coming of Selkirk and the first agricultural colony in the North West, they would do more for the unity and strength of the Empire than has been done since that splendid and disinterested pioneer laid the great foundation-stone of the prosperity of the prairie—would close for ever the mean and contemptible denunciation of those noble women, who, however mistaken in their occasional method, have fought a painful and disinterested fight for the franchise, merely as a weapon to control with common fairness *the rule of the road of labour*, which, irrespective of sex, is without prejudice, privilege, or the insult of handicap—*God's highway* for humankind, whether they seek life or merely a living.

Miss Binnie-Clark With Her Property "Nanny"—an Animal Bought for Fifty Dollars in 1907 and Now the Mother of Four Farm Horses.

16

Figure 32. "Land and The Woman," by Georgina Binnie-Clark, begins, "In Britain outdoor occupation for women is the word of the hour, but the obstacle placed in the way by the Canadian government in refusing women the right to take up homestead land, at present impedes the progress of women towards the place of independence, prosperity or wealth at which they would undoubtedly arrive in working their own land on the Canadian prairies." Yes, they could go to the U.S. West and obtain 160 acres for free, but "the strength of the imperial and home tie is very strong, and British women, as a rule, refuse to take the severing step." Two of the photographs feature the English students she was training at "Binning." Binnie-Clark appears in the bottom photograph with her horse "Nancy." *Canadian Courier* 12, no. 12, 16 November 1912, 16.

E. Violet Bertram, who in 1913 published a series of articles in the *Canadian Gazette* with the title "Wanderings of a Single Woman," spent some time at an unnamed Fort Qu'Appelle "ranch, demonstrating the feasibility of farming for women in Canada," that was clearly Binnie-Clark's, and had contradictory observations to report.[103] On the one hand, she believed that the experience was of value, as the students had learned about the practical and hard conditions of life on the prairie, and the "ranch owner is always ready to show, explain, expound: ploughing, disking, harrowing ... harnessing, feeding and cleaning the horses." But on the other hand, their teacher was not always adept or competent. Clearly describing Binnie-Clark, Bertram wrote:

> Winter is vacation time here. Miss ___ was therefore immersed in her literary work, and was, in consequence, as absent-minded and unpractical as our old German professor, and this led to hilarious situations. "Thinking of angels," she let the rope of our precious water bucket slip through her fingers to the bottom of the well, but with Bohemian resource and cleverness recovered it with the cunningly bent stove cleaner tied to a slim young tree! Interested in our conversation whilst driving the bobsleigh ... home from Fort Qu'Appelle, the reins would slip through her fingers, and there we would sit helpless, till by fortuitous hills and cajoling cries of "Whoa, Fanny," "Gently, Emma!" the two spirited mares could be persuaded to a standstill. Did we seek the dishcloth, it was found in some position of unmerited honour such as the mantelpiece, the back of the armchair, or handkerchiefwise on her writing bureau!

Bertram left in the spring and concluded that "so large a ranch as this was an impossible undertaking for single women of small means." Yet her training at Binning may have been of some use. In 1915 Miss Violet Bertram, a "co-operative small holder," was present at a conference on Women's Work in Agriculture and Horticulture held at the Royal Horticultural Hall, Westminster (along with Binnie-Clark).[104] Bertram "spoke at length on training applied in Canada, and gave instances of the work women are doing. She laid stress on the urgent necessity for a student to

… study such important subjects as wages, the handling of people, auction rooms and buying and selling generally. She urged co-operation and advised women to work in couples, settle in groups and be ready to take advantage of any change that might come." In 1919 Bertram was running Vanguard Farm in Kent for severely disabled soldiers and sailors.[105] It was a cooperative farm where men and their families settled on small plots. Bertram may have had learned some valuable lessons about farming from Binnie-Clark afterall.

THE FAMOUS FARMER, HER CRITICS, AND SUPPORTERS

Despite her lectures and publications, Binnie-Clark made little headway converting influential men in England to her causes. In January 1912, Binnie-Clark was once again in England, where she attended a talk given by Arthur Hawkes, the special commissioner for immigration for the Dominion of Canada, at the Royal Colonial Institute (RCI), London.[106] She and several other women in the audience, including journalists Currie Love and Mary Agnes Fitzgibbon, were disappointed that nothing was said about opportunities for women in Canada. Binnie-Clark introduced herself as a woman farmer, and she "complained that women could not obtain free land, although any man from any nation could get 160 acres for nothing." She also said that so far only two women had been accepted into the ready-made farm scheme (presumably "Jack" May and Louisa Wittrick, as discussed in the last chapter), even though Sir Thomas Shaughnessy had promised they could enter on the same terms as men. Hawkes addressed much of his reply to Binnie-Clark's critique, providing what he believed would be the "official view" of her request. It was not fair, he said, for a man with a wife and children to be granted a homestead for each. One hundred and sixty acres was adequate for a head of a family. With tongue in cheek, and making a mockery of her cause, Hawkes said: "I will be prepared to make this promise—that I will presently recommend that homesteads shall be granted to single women all through Western Canada on their signing a hard-and-fast undertaking that they will not enter the state of matrimony in the next five years. However, whether the demand for homesteads for—if you will pardon the word—spinsters would be largely increased by facilities being granted I do not know."[107]

This intransigence and mockery did not deter Binnie-Clark. Back in Western Canada that summer, she toured the prairies on a "commission" from the *Canadian Gazette*. Interviewed in Edmonton in August 1912, she was presented as an "ardent suffragette," which was a cause she had not advanced publicly before, although she may well have long been a supporter.[108] It was reported that she was opposed, however, to the militancy and "frantic measures" of the British suffragettes. Binnie-Clark was described as a "charming woman, with very keen perception and the greatest amount of faith in her work as well as in the country she has chosen as her field. A woman of gentle, persuasive personality, convincing in the extreme, who fears not hard work, and who shows great perseverance."

In early 1913, Binnie-Clark gave a series of lectures in England. In March she spoke to the students at the Arlesey Colonial Training School, urging them to start farming in groups in Canada on smaller acreages near cities of the prairies or British Columbia. She assured them that what they were cultivating at Arlesey was exactly what they could grow in Canada. "Beautiful limelight slides" complemented her talk with images of the fruit and flowers of British Columbia as well as of her own farm in Saskatchewan. She also spoke to the Suffrage Club of London in April 1913, which indicates her growing involvement in this cause.[109]

Binnie-Clark's most sustained and fulsome lecture, and given to her most distinguished audience to that date, was her April 1913 paper entitled "Land and the Woman in Canada," presented to the RCI in London. Although other women such as Flora Shaw had spoken before the RCI, they were not permitted to be members. In her paper, which was published in the RCI's journal, *United Empire*, Binnie-Clark's main message was that women, with very little training, were able to plough, cultivate, seed, harrow, harvest, and market crops of wheat. She argued that the woman agriculturalist should aspire to commercial farming and an independent income. Binnie-Clark further asserted that women such as herself, educated and from England, should be eligible for the homestead grant. It was in this lecture that Binnie-Clark clearly articulated the argument that had been hinted at in some of her previous lectures and publications, that it was unjust to reward "foreign" men with land and deny this right to British women who were playing critical roles in the "spade-work of British expansion in this, the supreme place of prosperity among British lands."[110]

These were the themes at the core of her lecture, but Binnie-Clark ranged widely, beginning with the foundations of change in "the once silent plains of the Prairie Provinces," with the settlement at Red River of the Earl of Selkirk and the first harvest of wheat, pointing out that women had played a role in this history and that "history occasionally throws over the past a search-light which discovers the claim of the woman to her share in the land which, over a hundred and thirty years ago, woman helped to win by spirit and to hold by toil." Her message was radical in many ways, as she stressed that the woman contemplating agriculture in Canada should aspire to be a commercial farmer not just for her livelihood, but for her independence. She admitted, however, that smaller acreages could be successful depending on the climate, location, and the market. She described in detail how women could establish various kinds of farm operations in different regions of the West, including British Columbia (starting on five, fifty, or a hundred acres of land on a capital of £100, £500, or £1,000), and how they could emerge after twenty years with £5,000, which was her "symbol of independence." She claimed that near Victoria was "the most exquisite environment [and] … the most perfect conditions for any business that the heart of a woman can desire." Five acres could be acquired for a £100 down payment, and a young woman settler could grow "bulbs by the seashore, fruit of varied and perfect kind, [and] vegetables for which there is always a demand."[111]

Advice for the woman farmer with £1,000 was to farm in the Qu'Appelle Valley like herself, and she made it clear that wheat would always be the main crop of prairie Canada. Binnie-Clark had many economic and demographic statistics and stressed how the dramatic increase in the populations of the prairie cities provided a ready market for the produce of grain, dairy, and market garden farmers. The details might have been somewhat tedious for her audience, as Binnie-Clark itemized how much land to seed to wheat, oats, and barley; how much capital to set aside for land, horses, cows, sows, and poultry; and how much should be spent on the shack, outbuildings, labour, and implements. She concluded that "patience, endurance and energy" was required of the woman farmer, and her audience might have agreed that these were also required to be alert for the entire lecture.

Binnie-Clark complimented the efforts of "Jack" May and her partner, describing them as "the best men of the lot" of the Sedgewick farmers (not realizing that May had already left Alberta) and stating that they were "helping to make Empire through the medium of the Canadian farm."[112] She also declared, when describing how a Canadian government official had warned that the homestead grant would make women "more independent of marriage than ever," that "the woman of today will not have the commercial marriage, or marriage of convenience. She has arrived at the place where, if she cannot have marriage as an inspiration in her life, she refuses it as a mere resource; and to refuse dependence is halfway to independence." Canada, she concluded with indignation, "has not yet outgrown the idea that women are needed for one purpose only."

Lively discussion and debate followed the 1913 lecture at the RCI. Sir Charles P. Lucas was in the chair. He was head of the Dominion Department of the Colonial Office and the author of books on the history of Canada and the British colonies. Other powerful men were in the audience, and they included both critics and admirers of Binnie-Clark. Richard Reid, government agent of Ontario, had no objection to extending homesteading to "the fairer but not inferior sex," and he hoped other Englishwomen would follow Binnie-Clark's lead.[113] Ellis T. Powell (prominent barrister, journalist, imperialist, and spiritualist, and friend of Sir Arthur Conan Doyle) was also in favour, and he too stressed that women who farmed could still be feminine. He was impressed with Binnie-Clark's sound economic knowledge, and he believed that she combined "feminine charm and enterprising resolution which go to make the very best type of the Imperialist woman of the future." He was pleased, however, that ultimately the scheme would lead some of these women to marriage: "If you have women who have pluck and capital to go out to Canada and commence colonising and working there on these lands and building up the Empire, do you not think that these women, either if they remain single and go towards a cheerful independence, or if they become mothers of Imperialists, are doing a work which is of immense moment … towards the ultimate strengthening and consolidation of the Empire which is the centre of all our affections?" These capable women would be "the germ of the very best and grandest Imperialism, which will secure the foundations of the Empire, not only for our generation but for all time to come." Other supporters included Stewart Gray, who was impressed with the farm work done by women in Scotland. Dr. T. Miller Maguire chimed in that in times of war in Germany and Bulgaria, women did a great deal of agricultural work, and he thought it would be much more preferable for the women in England to engage in pastoral pursuits than in factories "working soul-destroying machinery."

J. Obed Smith, however, spoke at the greatest length and was utterly opposed to the idea of women farmers in "this, that, or any other land."[114] He said women were physically incapable of carrying on farming operations, and that he could count on two hands the number of women farming in Canada without the assistance of men. He "dissociated himself entirely from the idea that woman alone could pursue general farming in Canada." Smith was prepared to admit that under special circumstances, women could succeed at poultry and dairy farms, but he insisted that they could not excel at grain farming. That they were not physically capable, he argued, was supported by the curricula of the agricultural colleges of Canada. He asked: "How was it that these excellent institutions did not teach women ploughing, sowing, reaping and various other things that went to make up the life of the farmer? Instead of these they taught [women] sewing cookery, home management, keeping of account, dairying and laundry." He further argued that Canada had deliberately departed from the U.S. legislation that permitted single women to homestead, because it led to the "pernicious practice of procuring two homesteads instead of one" in the case of men and women homesteaders who then married. This legislation, in Smith's view, had led to "disastrous results in the United States," and immigration officials did not desire the same results in Canada.

The next discussant, Jeffrey Bull of Toronto, spoke briefly and agreed with Smith, stating that "it would be most disastrous not only for the woman, but for the reputation of Canada, for any woman to start grain farming in the West."[115] "Disastrous" seems to have been the word of the day.

The sole woman discussant that evening was Miss J.S. Turner of the Arlesey House Colonial Training School, and she directly challenged J. Obed Smith, saying that the Canadian colleges only taught women to cook and sew "because men did not like to do that sort of work themselves."[116] She thought that "any woman who had stamina and common sense had very much better go back to the land than sit about or run after mothers' meetings, or act as sort of junior curate, as so many of our daughters did now." Turner pointed out that Scottish women did half the labour on farms in Scotland, and that "when she was a girl in Lincolnshire women worked on the land and were much better and healthier for it." She had trained many women who had gone to Canada, two to South Africa, and two to Australia, and those who went to Canada had done the best. Many had started out as domestic helps but were now "following Miss Binnie-Clark's example."

One distinguished discussant commented that working in the fields was labour performed by Indigenous women of the colonies, and thus was not considered suitable work for British women. After listening to Binnie-Clark's talk, the former governor of the Bahamas Sir William Grey-Wilson said that in many areas of the world in which he had been posted it was the custom for the women to do all the agricultural work, adding that he was not prepared to admit it was the best of customs.[117] Here was the objection at the heart of the matter: British women farming in the colonies would not be demonstrating a superior domesticity, but sinking to the level of Indigenous people.

Clearly Binnie-Clark still had some distance to go to persuade the influential men of the RCI, the Colonial Office, and Canada's immigration authorities overseas that the homestead grant should be available to unattached English women. The *Canadian Gazette*, however, sprang to Binnie-Clark's defence in an editorial, declaring that her series of lectures was timely and useful and that the theme and text of her address to the RCI "might well have the prophetic words of the great French agricultural statesman, Jules Méline, who says in his book 'The Return to the Land' (1906): 'When shall we make up our mind to provide real agricultural training for women, evoking in them appreciation of the life of the country, and making them realize the dignity and utility of farm work? Of all reforms undertaken in the interests of agriculture, there is none more important or more pressing than this.'"[118] The editors noted that this truth had not yet "come home to any English statesman or agriculturalist."

Critics in Canada were becoming more vocal. The Victoria *Daily Colonist* led the charge in a May 1913 editorial under the headline "Misleading Emigrants."[119] The editorial writer took issue with many of Binnie-Clark's cost estimates for land, livestock, and equipment, and her projections of a comfortable living from five acres if young women of twenty-five followed her advice and settled on Vancouver Island or the mainland close to "industrial populations." Particularly at issue was her estimate of land prices near cities such as Victoria. These were "startling statements," according to the *Colonist*, that were "utterly out of keeping with the facts, and if accepted as true and acted upon by any young woman, would lead to such disastrous results that we can only characterize it as wicked in fact if not in intention." Binnie-Clark was doing "incalculable harm" with her "astonishing statements." The editorial concluded by reminding readers of the acceptable vocations for women, and criticizing schemes to send young Englishwomen to Canada: "There seems to be something very like a conspiracy to get a certain class of young Englishwomen to come to this country. While we are on this subject we may add that the only women of 25 who ought to think of coming here alone to make a living, are those qualified to become schoolteachers, competent stenographers, trained nurses … domestic servants who intend to be servants in fact as well as in name, and women of experience in gardening and farm work generally."

When the text of Binnie-Clark's address to the RCI appeared in the *United Empire*, other objections were raised. Canadian journalist Mrs. Donald Shaw, who was originally from England, wrote to that journal with great disapproval and revilement.[120] Shaw was opposed to women's suffrage, and she wrote articles that lamented the changing world about her. One of her articles began with "What is the world coming to? There seems to be a mad desire just now on the part of a large number of people to tear down and cast aside all the creeds, rules and laws that have in the past built up moral and stable nations."[121] Women farmers, to Shaw, were part of this mad destructive desire. Shaw wrote, "We don't want women farmers in Canada." She believed that "not one woman in a thousand is physically fit" for farm work, and "certainly not one Englishwoman in a thousand." Even if they were capable, Shaw argued, the vocation would not produce a desirable type of woman. Echoing the *Daily Colonist*, she wrote: "Canada does not want women in the fields, but she badly wants women in their own sphere, that is as wives, mothers, cooks, servants, stenographers, teachers and nurses. Surely there is sufficient opening here for women without turning themselves into farm labourers. The idea seems more curious because in Canada women do not work in the fields (that is Canadian women), though they do an enormous amount of work in their houses, and Canadian men have a great aversion to seeing women engaged in outdoor occupations."[122] Shaw recalled that her "own countrywomen" from Britain regarded doing housework as derogatory and asked, "Is it less derogatory or more pleasurable to clear out cowhouses and feed pigs?"

Shaw's letter was quoted at length in the *Daily Colonist,* and the editor of the column "In Women's Realm," Maria Lawson, disagreed with some of her opinions, particularly Shaw's refusal to believe that "the average woman can farm."[123] Lawson wrote that farming on the prairies or in Eastern Canada might be "beyond the strength of most women, but there are many who contend that it is neither impossible nor unsuitable for women to cultivate large gardens or to engage in poultry keeping on small holdings. Englishwomen are engaged in such work in this Province both on the Island and the Mainland, but their success remains to be proven."

In 1913 another critic of Binnie-Clark, Elizabeth Keith Morris, published her book *An Englishwoman in the Canadian West*. Her references were oblique, but there was no doubt whom her remarks were aimed at. At the start of her chapter on "Farming and Fruit Growing," Morris wrote:

> Thrilling and picturesque stories of the lady farmer had assailed our ears, and through these we came to the conclusion that a woman had at last found an Utopian way of earning her own living ... We heard of ... wonderful machinery which turned work into play; and of the golden harvest which awaited those playful efforts at work; and then we came face to face with the facts, which differed in every respect from the fantastic, romantic tales which had been poured into our ears ... for we discovered that only the strong, hardy, eminently practical and really hard-working woman could even hope to reap a good living from that wonderful black loam of the prairies ... after many a heart-breaking experience and the absence of all luxuries and other comforts.[124]

Morris was opposed to Canada's granting the right to homestead to women; the "hard and heavy" work required was unsuitable for them.

WHEAT AND WOMAN

Binnie-Clark's book *Wheat and Woman* (1914) drew together and added much rich detail to the lectures and articles that she had already published. It is a self-deprecating, often humorous account of her first three years of farming, detailing her ignorance of agriculture and the customs of Canada, her mistakes, misfortunes, financial woes, and her adventures—which included being lost on the prairies in a summer deluge and being tossed head first into a snow bank when her beloved horse, Nancy, came to an unexpected and abrupt stop and then bolted, deserting Binnie-Clark. It includes an account of the long and viciously cold winter of 1906–7, perhaps the worst in prairie history.[125] But *Wheat and Woman* is also the story of the courtesy and kindness of Binnie-Clark's neighbours, her love for the prairies and for her animals, her fascination with wheat (a "tall mass of living loveliness"), and her own remarkable persistence and determination.[126] It is a sobering tale of "years of arduous toil and seasons of bitter disappointment," but ultimately the message was that women could succeed if they had capital, fortitude, tenacity, and good humour.[127] It is also a sharp critique of Canadian land laws. The book challenged accepted norms of middle-class femininity; Binnie-Clark never mentioned marriage as the final destination for her or sister, and she did not take kindly to domestic duties such as having to prepare meals for her hired men. "From the beginning," she wrote, "I was perfectly happy working on the land, only I wished it was someone else's turn to get those tiresome three meals a day."[128] And it was radical. The title *Wheat and Woman* was a bold, concise, and deliberate choice; this was not about small holdings and fruit farming or bee keeping.

Wheat and Woman received positive reviews in England and Canada. In the *Times Literary Supplement*, it was praised as a "graphic and clear account of the difficulties encountered … winning her way to practical success through sheer pluck, persistence and … the indispensable equipment of a tough constitution capable of enduring an astonishing amount of hardship and fatigue."[129] The review noted many details, including the "bewildering succession" of inept hired men who were "with few exceptions unsatisfactory and addicted to leaving their employer in the lurch at the most inconvenient moments." Few of the reviewers appeared to agree with or to emphasize Binnie-Clark's central theme that the homestead laws discriminated against women. It was read as the story of one woman's amazing pluck and endurance, and as an eloquent description of life on the prairies. In the *Athenaeum*, *Wheat and Woman* was described as the story of a "singularly brave, cheery and plucky woman of admirable self-control and steadfastness of purpose."[130] The reviewer was pleased that there was only a "hint of something like bitterness in her view of woman's position in the world."

The suffragist journal *Votes for Women* praised the book and Binnie-Clark, and criticized the Canadian government: "Of such stuff are the best pioneers. One would think that Canada or any colony would welcome such a settler with open arms as a valuable asset. Such a settler forms a centre, radiating wholesome energy, intelligence, sympathy, the best the old world has to offer. But the official mind, even in a new country, does not approve of the independent woman, however capable she may be. Man must be the landowner."[131]

Opinions varied. Writing in the *Globe*, Mary MacLeod Moore concluded that *Wheat and Woman* would discourage, rather than encourage, women to take up farming unless they were "as exceptional a woman as Binnie-Clark herself."[132] Moore wrote that "otherwise disaster is fairly sure to overtake her efforts to farm alone, hampered as she is, in the first place, by the Homestead Law, and later by circumstances, climate, loneliness; the difficulties which surround the obtaining of reliable 'hired men' no matter at what price, and many others which develop as time goes on."

Binnie-Clark may have inadvertently placed Canada in the public eye as a less-than-inviting destination for the British gentlewoman.[133] In 1914 in the English newspaper the *Sunday Referee*, a discussion took place about the position of women emigrants to Canada. There were two main objections raised about Canada as a destination. The first was that Canada refused the free grant of land to women available to men, and the second was that there was no dower law. The conclusion was that "Australia, New Zealand and Rhodesia are at present far more suitable for women emigrants than Canada."

In his review in *Westminster Hall and Farthest West Review*, Dan Munday also thought that *Wheat and Woman* might discourage homesteaders from Britain, although he thought it was more honest than the "land-of-promise" literature used to lure them that led to so many abandoned homesteads.[134] He wrote that because of the "close regard for accuracy … the book can be of real value to one contemplating farming on the prairie." Munday noted that while a purpose of the book was to help secure homestead rights for women, this was not mentioned until the last chapter. In his conclusion he wrote that the author "has no intention of settling permanently in Canada." That was, in fact, even more true when the First World War began in August 1914.

Wheat and Woman could not have appeared at a less opportune moment. Almost no one had time or energy for the homesteads-for-women cause in Britain or Canada, and that included Binnie-Clark, but her long-term promotion of women and farming had become timely and vital. Her agricultural skills were now of value at home. She was one of seven agriculturalists appointed by the Ministry of Labour to organize the work of women on the land and assigned the Yorkshire and Lincolnshire districts.[135] One of the last events she attended as "the pioneer woman farmer in Canada" was a 1915 conference in Westminster that she chaired on Women's Work in Agriculture and Horticulture, mentioned above, which was also attended by her former student Violet Bertram.[136] Binnie-Clark declared that "no profession under the sun is so excellent for nervous diseases. In view of the changes which the war is bringing, the cry of 'back to the land' is one which vitally affects women and is of great importance to their economic status."

From the First World War into the 1930s, Binnie-Clark also had a business at 14 Woodstock Street, a small street off Oxford Street, London's main shopping district, called "The Fashion Journals Guild," where she sold patterns for dresses and hats. As a young boy of nine or ten in the 1930s, her great-nephew Dennis Jenks recalls visiting this small, cluttered office that she managed with the assistance of one employee.[137] Just how she juggled her war work on the land, her business, and her farm in Saskatchewan is one of many puzzles about Georgina Binnie-Clark. Her sister Ethel ran the farm while she was gone; in her 1947 will, Georgina left land to Ethel "as a mark of appreciation for the care she bestowed on the whole property during my absence by reason of my illness and the Great War."[138] Georgina returned to her farm in 1926 and 1928, and again in the 1930s, in a final initiative of hers called the Union Jack Farm Settlement, to be dealt with briefly in the conclusion.[139] She continued to promote the British Empire and the settlement of British people in Canada, but her emphasis on women famers was gone. Her writing career slowed and the direction of it changed during the war. She self-published a book for children called *Tippy: The Autobiography of a Pekingese Puppy*, the proceeds of which were to "buy comfort for the wounded soldiers & horses fighting in the Great War for Liberty."[140]

While the number of Binnie-Clark's critics mounted in Canada and overseas by 1914, she had helped to motivate a great number of women and their supporters to organize a homesteads-for-women campaign that followed the same trajectory—gaining strength from 1910 to 1914 but losing momentum in the war years, although it did not disappear altogether. Campaigners in prairie Canada, however, faced formidable and intransigent opponents, and they weakened their own cause considerably by adopting a central strategy of denouncing "foreigners" as unsuitable homesteaders, and requesting the homestead privilege for "British-born" women only, alienating potential supporters.

CHAPTER SIX

"DAUGHTERS OF BRITISH BLOOD" OR "HORDES OF MEN OF ALIEN RACE"?

THE HOMESTEADS-FOR-BRITISH-WOMEN CAMPAIGN

While Georgina Binnie-Clark focused her energies on publishing and lecturing in England about the opportunities for British women farmers in Western Canada and the injustices of Canada's Dominion Lands Act, a similar campaign was gaining steam on the prairies, which the woman wheat farmer of Fort Qu'Appelle helped to motivate and inspire.[1] While supporters of homesteads for women devised many arguments for the entitlement of women to the land grant, they increasingly stressed the rights of British and Canadian-born women, in contrast to the dubious claims of "foreigners," both male and female. The campaigners called for justice and equality, but only for a privileged few. A petition, submitted to the Canadian House of Commons in 1913, asked that the privilege of homesteading be granted to "all women of British birth who have resided in Canada for six months."[2] Faced with a climate that was inhospitable to women farmers, landowners, and voters, and ultimately facing a completely intransigent federal government, supporters articulated an imperialist vision to gain acceptance, to show that they could provide a solution to the problem of the "foreign element" and to demonstrate their fitness for the privileges of citizenship that were denied to them yet available to "foreign" men. Disparaging the suitability of settlers of "foreign" origin justified their own claims for inclusion. Promoters of homesteads for women manipulated ideas about racial and ethnic "others" in an effort to win elite support, while at the same time appealing to an egalitarian code of fundamental justice.

As Pamela Scully has observed about the rhetoric of race in the women's suffrage movement in South Africa, "liberal campaigns for civic rights and equality can in fact depend upon invocations of its supposed antimonies—prejudice and exclusion."[3] Similarly, in the U.S. West, racist and nativist rationales surfaced in the rhetoric of some Anglo-American suffrage activists who were hostile toward the "foreign" men "from the slums of the Old World [who] walk out of the steerage of the ships to become enfranchised citizens and ultimately to vote against giving the suffrage to American-born women."[4] This elitist strategy failed, however, in the case of homesteads for women. The federal government remained intransigent as long as it was in control of Crown or public lands (to 1930), at which point there was little homestead land left. The imperial logic and elitist strategy alienated key constituencies, such as settlers from the United States, who were accustomed to single women having homestead rights and who expected the same privilege in Canada.[5] No matter what the strategy, however, there was little hope for success in confronting deeply embedded views of women as unsuitable and incapable farmers and landowners.

Those who organized for homesteads for women supported other causes that challenged the deliberate crafting of Western Canada as "manly space," where the building block and organizing principle was the authority of the white, property-holding, male head of household.[6] Control of land and therefore wealth was not to be shared with other groups, nor were there to be any hindrances for landowners who wanted to sell or buy. This shaping of "manly space" is illustrated not only in the homestead laws but in the abolition of women's dower rights in 1885 in Manitoba and 1886 in the North-West Territories, which meant that a husband could now sell the family home without his wife's consent or entirely cut her out of his will.[7] Shaping "manly space" also involved a concerted campaign to impose the monogamous model of marriage on the diverse inhabitants of Western Canada.[8] A national identity was to be forged that was distinct from that of the Indigenous people and was distinct, also, from that of the United States. It would be based on an idealized view of a traditional British gender order, of the obedient, submissive wife and the provider, head-of-family husband. All of this was fuelled by an image of the United States as a place of disrupted and dangerous alternatives to the "natural" gender order, and by a determination that pristine and pure Canada would be kept free of the immoral and corrupting influences from the south.[9] Permitting women alternatives to marriage, such as acquiring homestead land for farming, was an indicator of a society run amok.

GALVANIZING THE CAMPAIGN AND A FIRST PETITION

The homesteads-for-women campaign intersected and combined with the call for the reinstatement of dower rights on the prairies and for women's suffrage. Of these campaigns, homesteads for women was the greatest failure. Legislators never wavered on the issue—women never received the right to homestead in Western Canada, except in Alberta after 1930. When the Prairie provinces assumed control of public lands from the federal government in 1930, the right to homestead was abrogated entirely in Manitoba and Saskatchewan, while in Alberta, where there was a little homestead land left, the provincial government drew up regulations that permitted every "person" to apply who was over seventeen, had resided in the province for three years, and was or declared the intention to become a British subject.

Among the early calls for homestead rights for women was one from a 1907 correspondent of the *Farmer's Advocate* writing from Moose Jaw.[10] Like Binnie-Clark, this supporter believed women homesteaders could be a means of strengthening the British fabric of the West. He proposed that all single women over twenty be given the right to enter on a homestead, and he was not at all perturbed that they might marry before they proved up, as "this is exactly what is wanted in giving them homesteads, and I would go further and allow any such homesteader to at once receive patent to her 160 acres as soon as she is married." Echoing Flora Shaw's "sister" scheme, the writer proposed that if young men from Great Britain brought their sisters and each secured 160 acres, "a new immigration movement would take place … We hear much of the 'all-red line of commerce.' This might well be called the 'all-white line of immigration.'" "The benefit," he wrote, "to the whole Northwest, morally, socially, educationally, and spiritually, would be enormous."

When Binnie-Clark visited Winnipeg in late 1908, she met with women who had "already taken up the matter of Homesteads for Women with a deep sense of the injustice of a law which, whilst seeking to secure the prosperity of the country in enriching the stranger, ignores the claim of the sex which bore the brunt of the battle in those early and difficult days."[11] She wrote her own letter to the Department of the Interior at that time (described in the previous chapter), proposing a settlement of English gentlewomen as an initial experiment, and she met with officials in Ottawa.

In 1910 the concept of homesteads for women was still seen as a "novelty" but was gaining traction. The *Toronto Telegram* in January of that year declared support for the idea, noting that the present situation was "both unfair and disadvantageous," and concluding that "if women shrink from the hardships of pioneer life the fact has not been noticed in the history of the west. Then why should they be deprived of participation in its rewards?"[12] Other early voices included that of Louise Langton of Wetaskiwin, who wrote letters to the *Grain Growers' Guide* on a wide range of issues, including suffrage, dower rights, and birth control.[13] She asked, "Must we go on giving birth to daughters whose fate will be the same as ours has been?"[14] Langton proposed that "farm women of the west organize and help in this question of 'homesteads for women'… She made the argument that would eventually become the focus of the campaign, that they had more right to land than "foreign" men, that "women of this great Dominion … [should] join forces, concentrate their powers … so that the same opportunities be given them that are given to the hordes of men with less ability than theirs, and who are pouring into this country every year."[15] Langton's call to action was enthusiastically endorsed in the *Guide* in April 1910. "Onward" wrote, "Here's an emphatic vote in favour of Mrs. Langston's motion … [and] if we cannot organize … we can agitate, discuss, educate, and your page is just the place to begin."[16]

But as Binnie-Clark found, there were formidable opponents. Frank Oliver articulated why he did not support homesteads for women in the House of Commons in April 1910, just a few weeks before Mildred Williams's twelve-day vigil (described in Chapter 3).[17] Oliver was asked by member of Parliament W.J. Roche from Manitoba (later also minister of the interior) if his attention had ever been called to the idea of allowing women to homestead, and the letter of a reverend gentleman in Saskatchewan, published in a Winnipeg newspaper, was read into the record. Reverend W.W. Beveridge recommended allowing women over the age of eighteen to homestead as a means of addressing "a great dearth of marriageable ladies" in the province. He claimed to know of parents of daughters who refused to move west and asked "why that man had not just as much right to homestead and get a quarter section for each of those girls as the man who happened to have four grown-up boys?" Beveridge also knew of men with large families of strong, healthy girls in the Dakotas and Minnesota who would come to Canada if their girls could homestead, but because they could not, they were moving to Montana instead.

Oliver replied that the matter had been brought to his attention frequently, and his answer was that women homesteaders were "not in the interest of the settlement of our country." He was aware of the different land law in the United States but was "not aware that it is an advantageous law." Oliver explained that the purpose of giving free land to homesteaders was to make the land productive, and that "in order that a homestead may be made fully productive, there should be not a single woman upon it, nor even a single man, but there should be both the man and woman in order that the homestead may be fully advantageous to the country. The idea of giving homesteads to single women would tend directly again that idea." He said that it was the job of the single man "to get the woman, and for the woman who wants to settle on land in the Northwest to get the man, rather than that she shall have land of her own ... Our experience is entirely against the idea of women homesteading." It was sufficient to permit land to widows with children old enough to help cultivate the land, according to Oliver.

In the *Manitoba Free Press*, women's page editor Lillian Beynon Thomas (Lillian Laurie) mocked Oliver's reply and pointed out contradictions.[18] Her column began, "Were you ever at a meeting where the men, being in power, were discussing the advisability of giving women something they were asking for? If you have and the men referred to the women as the 'fair sex' then you know that they did not grant the request." Thomas wrote that "nothing was said in the act about having children to cultivate the land and if women are not considered competent to bring the land to a condition of productiveness then the clause permitting women as sole heads of families to homestead is merely a humanitarian provision for the women, and the land has not been considered. To be consistent Mr. Oliver should have the law granting homesteads to women only if there were boys dependent on them for support and old enough to cultivate the land."

Oliver's response in the House of Commons helped galvanize the homesteads-for-women campaign in Western Canada. In late May 1910, a petition to Minister of the Interior Oliver, originating from Edmonton, was published in the *Bulletin*, Oliver's own newspaper, under the headline "Spinsters Want Homesteads."[19] It asked that homestead lands be available to any unmarried woman in Canada over the age of thirty. The central argument advanced in the petition was that unmarried women settlers were as desirable as widows were. It was an injustice to favour widows only, as they often had an inheritance, while a "noble class of women" was just as deserving of land: women who found themselves "at middle age thrown out upon their own resources, the majority of them having had to sacrifice opportunities of marriage and competence for the sake of remaining at home with one or more aged parents to provide and care for them in their old age." The minor children of widows permitted to homestead would become financial assets to their mother, whereas those women who cared for parents had no one to provide for them. Signatures were to be collected from "the undersigned, unmarried women of Canada." A Miss Helen N. Weir of Edmonton was identified as the leader of the "agitation."

The context for the petition was explained in a letter to the *Manitoba Free Press*, where the petition was also published in mid-June 1910. "M.S.T." wrote that a number of women in the Edmonton district had asked her to organize a petition.[20] She was from the United States and had moved to Alberta because of the advertisements she had read about "free land." When she applied for a homestead, however, she was told she was ineligible. "Well, I was surprised, just having refused to join another single woman, who with her father was filing on 160 acres of choice land in Arkansas." She believed there were hundreds of unmarried women who could homestead as successfully as men. She argued that unmarried women who had cared for aged parents "should be rewarded, not looked down upon and called 'old maids' on the bargain counter." She understood that because of the "scarcity of white women … good decent men are degenerating and marrying squaws," and further argued that women were far more capable of homesteading than the many "foreigners who come to this country, men who have never pursued agriculture in their home country and know practically nothing about it." It was later reported in the *Free Press* that the author of this petition had returned to the United States.[21]

MARSHALLING THE ARGUMENTS FOR WOMEN HOMESTEADERS

It is not clear how many signatures this first, Edmonton-based petition received, or whether it was ever submitted to Parliament. There was a fundamental strategic flaw, however, embedded in the petition, as it was organized by an American woman, and the petitioners were women and, of course, non-voters. Canadian legislators could easily dismiss it. Women reformers were divided about the value of petitions but there was agreement that "petitions signed by women are usually treated as a joke by the electors," as prominent activist Nellie McClung told a suffrage rally in 1912.[22] Although petitions were to become the main tactic of the homesteads-for-women campaign, strategies changed considerably after this initial petition that stressed that single women should have the same rights as widows.

The *Grain Growers' Guide* became a focus for the campaign, and women's page editor Isabelle Beaton Graham ("Isobel" in her column "Around the Fireside") was the main voice of the campaign. Born in Ontario, Graham had attended the Alma Ladies College, where, as mentioned in Chapter 2, principal Benjamin F. Austin was an advocate of farming for women.[23] She homesteaded in Manitoba with her husband, Francis Graham, also from Ontario. They had three daughters and one son, and Graham used the example of her own family to point out the inequities of the homestead system, as families with daughters did not have the same option to expand their holdings as families with sons.[24] The Grahams moved to St. Boniface in 1906, where he was a founder of the Grain Growers Grain Company, and she wrote for the *Guide*, founded in 1908. The *Guide* had a cooperative reform agenda, and it supported women's suffrage from its first issue in 1908.[25] Readers of the *Guide* were asked to organize, agitate, and educate on the issues of homesteads for women and dower rights. Isabelle Beaton Graham was involved in the women's suffrage campaign in Manitoba, and was one of the participants in the Mock Parliament in Winnipeg in January 1914. Graham was the speaker of the house, while Nellie McClung was the premier and a delegation of men waited upon the government with a bill for "Votes for Men."[26]

The women's page editors of other major Western publications, including Mary S. Mantle, or Margaret Freeston, of the *Nor'West Farmer*, and Lillian Laurie, or Lillian Beynon Thomas, of the *Manitoba Free Press*, also supported homesteads for women. There were lively debates in many of these publications, including letters to "Prim Rose" of the Western edition of the Montreal-based *Family Herald.*

Binnie-Clark was not particularly active in the campaign in Western Canada (the focus of her lecturing and publishing was England), but she was used as evidence by organizers on the prairies of the interest in and ability of women to farm. Graham had some angles of her story incorrect, believing that Binnie-Clark had arrived in Canada hoping to homestead and had purchased land only after she "was unable to persuade the Dominion government to grant her a free homestead." But Graham applauded her example, writing that she was "a woman of pluck and determination. She came to Canada to farm, to experiment not only for her own benefit but also for the benefit of single women of her own social level left behind in England." Graham wrote that Binnie-Clark would "make a great immigration agent to the old land among women like herself, women of culture and some means, when the Canadian government grants free homesteads to women."[27]

Many arguments were advanced in favour of homesteads for women. A central rationale was evidence that a large number of women wanted to homestead. Supporters pointed to the success of the widows, and to women's interest in obtaining homesteads through purchasing South African scrip (SAS); they had "quietly and promptly availed themselves of the homestead privilege made possible by buying … scrip. This proves conclusively that it is only necessary to give women the opportunity and they are anxiously willing to be self-supporting, and no longer a drag upon the pension list of their masculine relatives."[28] It was pointed out that it was not fair that only women with sufficient money could qualify for homestead land. It also seemed "rather illogical that women can do duty on a scrip, for which they must pay, but cannot on a homestead."[29] Women's ability to purchase and to prove up on homesteads through SAS also made a mockery of the assertion that only men had the strength and stamina to withstand the difficulties of homesteading.

Women wrote to farm journals and to officials of the Department of the Interior stating that they wanted to homestead. In 1910 an Englishwoman, resident in the West for three years who worked as hired help and living with her brother, wrote to the *Nor'West Farmer* that she had read of Binnie-Clark's farming and "would like to see the free land grant for women. I like to see women independent. I don't like the idea of an almshouse at the end of life."[30] An "English Violet" from London wrote to "Prim Rose" of the *Family Herald* in 1913 to say that she would take a homestead if offered to single women.[31] She had worked for two years on a dairy farm on Vancouver Island, and for her farm life was ideal: "The greatest fascination which farm life possesses is that it is so creative, so constructive and so vitally alive." "Farmer's Daughter" wrote that she had spent her life on farms in Ontario and the West and could see no reason why she should not be allowed to homestead, as she was "very ambitious in every line of farm work, thoroughly enjoying it, as I find it ennobling to both mind and soul."[32] "Irish Jill of All Trades" also wrote that she was a farmer's daughter, that she could "drive horses, cut grain, disk, harrow, plough and even drive nails as well as most men. I don't see why women have not as much right to land as men. The average woman works as hard as a man and sometimes harder."[33]

It was not just single and young women who sought homesteads. Married and older women expressed an interest in homesteading due to their family circumstances. A "British born" woman wrote to the *Nor'West Farmer* in 1911 to say that she had lived in Canada for over forty years, that she had married a Canadian and had a family of girls, had worked very hard to raise and educate them, but "now at fifty-eight, I find myself, through no fault of my own, without a home. My husband is old and broken in health, and he has exhausted his homestead rights. I also am not very strong but still could do homestead duties. No doubt there are hundreds in the same position that we are in."[34] Another married woman, who had worked with her husband to prove up on a homestead, wrote to the *Guide* in 1911 that she would soon have no home as her husband had mortgaged their farm and she had no say: "It was my husband who had the rights to the homestead."[35] If she had the right to take a homestead of her own, she would have a home.

The success of the widows who qualified to homestead was also evidence of women's capacity. As "Lochinvar" wrote to the *Guide* in 1911, he "could never see the right or reason of women being unable to make entry for land." His own mother, a widow, "had two homesteads in the West, and I may say this just put her in first class circumstances."[36]

The situation in the Canadian West was often compared to that of the U.S. West, where single women could homestead. A related argument for women's right to homestead was that Canada was losing girls and women to opportunities south of the border. Accounts by U.S. women homesteaders and farmers were published in the *Guide*, such as "Woman on Forty

Acres," written by a woman farmer in Montana who grew wheat, oats, and sugar beets, raised poultry, and had a comfortable home of six rooms.[37]

As a reader wrote to the *Nor'West Farmer*, "If American girls can do this, are we Canadian girls so far behind our American cousins that we can't?"[38] Editor Margaret Freeston replied that she knew two girls who went to the Dakotas because they could not secure homesteads in Canada and were "now the proud possessors of deeds to the land. What a pity that 'good stuff' like these girls were made of should be lost to us!"[39] Will Channon, who wrote to Ottawa from Cordova, Manitoba, in support of homesteads for women in 1910, said this was necessary to "stop many of them going over to the United States where they are privileged of homesteading."[40] A.H. Cunningham from Ravine Bank, Saskatchewan, wrote to the *Guide* that "I have often thought it a shame that in the United States women could take land and here in Canada where there is so much more land they are not allowed the privilege. I have seen women in the States that did their duties far better than the average bachelor."[41] "Canada has never shown any kindness to her women that I ever could see," wrote a woman from Claresholm, Alberta, to the *Guide* in 1912.[42] "Her girls are just as bright and intelligent as those in the United States. The latter were allowed to homestead while Canadian girls were pushed behind the door." She knew of women who had homesteaded in the States, sold out, and bought land in Canada, and she also knew Canadian women going to Montana to homestead and asked, "Why could they not stay at home, as our land is just as good if not better?" "Long Bob," a widower, wrote to the *Family Herald* in 1913 that the women homesteaders of "Uncle Sam's domain … have invariably made a success of it. I cannot see why the women of Canada cannot do as well, or better, as invariably they are of a more rugged character than their southern sisters."[43]

Nellie McClung was acquainted with women homesteaders in the United States, and she used their example to show that they were willing and capable, writing that four girls together were each homesteading a quarter of the same section after having worked in offices and stores, and saving a little money to make a start.[44] They had cleared land of bush with only axes and hoes. McClung knew of one woman who went from Canada to Minnesota to homestead and was the owner of 160 acres. She was careful to stress that this woman had not lost her femininity or "womanly charm," as she was to be married to a neighbouring homesteader.

McClung wrote, "I believe free grants would develop a splendid type of resourceful women for Canada. What a pity the government can't see it."

Many supporters in the initial phase of the campaign were either from the United States or had lived and homesteaded there, or had been neighbours of women homesteaders. "Another Farmer's Wife" from Alberta wrote in 1912 to the *Family Herald* to say that she had had many women homesteaders as neighbours in the United States and that they were "college bred women who made a great difference to their districts to the bachelors especially."[45] She argued that during the "hard times ... between 1893 and 1896," the men abandoned their homesteads but the women "were not so ready to jump from the frying-pan into the fire. They hung on to the homesteads and today they are well-fixed and have their own fine homes. But the men—not so with them; somebody else owns their homes today." She also believed that Alberta "would be far more settled and a better country today, if women had their rights here as they should have." Many women, she believed, including her own daughters who had remained in the United States, would come to Alberta if they had homesteading rights. One woman homesteader in the United States took part in the debate. A "Montana School-Ma'Am" wrote to the *Family Herald* to say that she was living on her 320-acre homestead and was "as happy as a clam in the land of Uncle Sam."[46]

Readers of the women's columns in the farm journals and newspapers of the West were kept up-to-date on the success of women farmers in the United States and elsewhere. In early 1910, Margaret Freeston of the *Nor'West Farmer* wrote about the great scope and variety of agricultural pursuits of women in California, including poultry, fruit, cattle, and horses, and described how they had formed a Women's Agricultural and Horticultural Union. She concluded, "Thus it would seem a 'prosperous farmer' is not necessarily of the masculine gender."[47] The *Nor'-West Farmer* also published articles such as "Women Prize Winners at Scottish Plowing Match."[48] Developments elsewhere reported on in Western Canada included the organization in 1909 of a farm for "spinsters" in Boston, and in 1912 of a colony for women only in Australia, organized by the English Woman's Householders' League.[49] In 1913 the *Family Herald and Weekly Star* ran a story of five sisters who operated a farm of 200 acres in Buckinghamshire, England. There was also coverage of agricultural education elsewhere that was available to women. In a 1910 article, "Girl Graduates in Agriculture," readers of the *Grain Growers' Guide* learned about two sisters who graduated from the agricultural college at Cornell and operated the New York farm they inherited from their father. The author countered the argument that it was a waste to educate women as all would be lost if they married and left the farm, writing that "the work of life goes on just the same after marriage."[50]

Supporters of homesteads for women argued that women had the physical strength and capability to homestead, which they were proving throughout the West by performing homestead duties on the farms of spouses, brothers, and fathers. In a letter to the Department of the Interior, a man from Saskatchewan wrote in 1913 that women worked very hard for years on homesteads, building sod barns and shacks, haying, ploughing, raising poultry and eggs, growing vegetables, planting flowers, "& everything," and that men who had "made good here do it by the help of the wife," as "there is nothing too hard for them to work at it seems."[51] Yet "the wife for all her labour has not an inch of land her own." As "X.Y.Z." wrote to the *Guide* in 1913, "A wife who can rise at four and five o'clock in the morning and wait on a lot of hired men, with the husband in bed, is quite capable of homesteading."[52] In a 1912 letter, "Bronco Buster" wrote that she was alone on a Montana ranch with her father from the age of five, that she went on the round-up every year, that she could "ride any kind of horse, throw a steer and tie him in four minutes, brand a colt and handle the rope in all its forms. I have two belts given me by Teddy Roosevelt and Governor [E.L.] Norris of Montana for expert horsemanship. I can do anything that can be done outside."[53]

Throughout the West on homesteads, farms, and ranches, women and girls worked in the fields and with livestock. This sight could surprise some observers. A government surveyor wrote in 1899 of his first encounter with women at work on a ranch in Alberta:

> This is where I first saw young women on horseback, herding and rounding up cattle. These young women would ride at break neck speed, turning and twisting rapidly in all directions and as fearlessly as experienced cowboys. They mounted and dismounted as gracefully and easily as experienced men. I saw one young woman mount into her side saddle on a fair sized bronco from the level ground. I asked her to dismount and mount again, in order that I

> might see how it was done, and in an instant, she was off and on again from the same level as the horse.[54]

Supporters were also careful to emphasize that women could be feminine and still perform labour out of doors on their homesteads. "Bronco Buster" wrote that she was "just as much of lady as I would have been had it been ten years in a convent" rather than ten years on a ranch, and that "a lady will be a lady no matter where she is or what she has to do."[55] She could do "fancy work," having learned it while taking care of 500 ewes, and she had cooked for a crew of seventeen men.

Homesteading would keep women on the land and away from the evils of the city, offering them a healthy and invigorating environment. Graham argued that it was unfortunate that a daughter raised on a farm had to turn to teaching, dressmaking, or stenography when she had all the necessary skills to work on the land, that "all her soul [would] call aloud for the prairie, for the grating of the plow, for the swish of the binder, and the hum of the threshing machine, never to mention old Brindle or Bess, or the little colt she had raised by hand ... in the name of common sense and common humanity give them a chance to farm and live the life they love and are suited for."[56] Arguments for the strength and stamina women would build on their homesteads dovetailed with beliefs in eugenics. Homesteads for women would develop a "nobler race."[57]

Another widely shared rationale was that homesteads for women would provide a source of wives for bachelors of the West. They would not have to marry women who were "beneath" them in refinement and education. The result would be "contented, prosperous homes, instead of a region of vacant farms, with only the ruins of bachelors' shacks (monuments to a short-sighted policy), to break the monotony of the view."[58]

A central argument advanced by many supporters was that it was an injustice to award free land to families of boys, while those who had girls were penalized. A family with four boys could have five homesteads altogether while a family with all girls could only have one; the family of boys became wealthy while the family of girls became poorer, as pointed out in an editorial in the *Guide* that concluded, "Until the government of our land is entrusted with the power of ordaining the sex of children it does not seem fair that such discrimination should be made as is done in the case of our homestead laws."[59]

The homestead issue was linked to that of dower rights in many ways. As explained in a 1913 *Star Phoenix* article, for a woman to obtain a homestead she had to marry a man and either keep him alive (and they both work to prove it up, although ultimately it would be his property when the patent was granted), or "let him die" (and as a widow, if she had young offspring, she could file on her own land). Valance Patriarche wrote that

> to an independent and wary spinster ... the necessity of a husband brings not only a pause but a full stop. Unlike the Ontario benedict, the married man in the Prairie Provinces may sell, give away, or will away the home without so much as acquainting his wife with his intentions. Just as she has completed three years at hard labor on a farm and is wheezing out hymns of thanksgiving on the melodeon because they own their own land, he may saunter in and tell her he has given it all to the pretty summer visitor on Jones' farm, a proceeding quite within his legal rights. It is not to be wondered at that the hardy perennial spinster desires to bloom alone in prairie soil.[60]

Issues around homestead or farm inheritance were also part of the general critique of the injustices of land ownership and distribution on the prairies. In a 1910 column in the *Grain Growers' Guide*, Graham wrote that "in no country under the sun has woman been more directly responsible for increased land values than in Western Canada" and yet sons, not daughters, inherited farms, based on the rationale that a son "earns or helps to earn the land, therefore the land is sacredly reserved for him."[61] The son might feed the cattle, while a daughter feeds the household; his work was valued, while hers was not. Graham called for daughters to inherit equal shares of farms and estates as a "birthright." In many of Graham's pleas for "equality," however, she also mentioned the entitlement of women, meaning British and/or British-Ontarian women, over the rights of "foreigners." In this column she continued: "Parents who do not dower their daughters equally with their sons are worse than the Dominion government, that will not give homesteads to Canadian women, but prefers rather to dower the unspeakable foreigner."

In letters to the farm journals or to the Department of the Interior, the issues of dower and homestead rights were often intertwined. Mrs.

Thomas McNeil wrote to the minister of the interior in 1913 to say that she had come from Ontario with her husband and eleven children, that they had entered on a homestead in 1909, but that

> after he got his Patent for his Homestead sold it for $2800 and then hit away to Maple Creek with an excuse to buy Horses and to take a purchased Homestead, I have found out that he has drank the most of it by this time and has not took a purchased Homestead yet and about all the satisfaction I can get is that a man in the Saskatchewan can do as he likes with his own property but if he ever does take a purchased Homestead I would never go to live on it. I got hunger enough on this one. I would often have starved only for what my children had sent me.[62]

Mrs. McNeil concluded her letter by saying that "if it is ever in your Power to Help Women to get Homesteads I do hope that God Almighty will reward you for it all."

A fundamental criticism of the homestead legislation was that women were just as deserving of the grant of land as men were. The land grant was cast as a birthright, inheritance, or reward that was owed to women as well as men. As one supporter of the campaign wrote in the *Guide*: "God put both Adam and Eve into the Garden of Eden. Evidently Eve had as much right there and on the land as her husband."[63] As will be discussed later in detail, this rationale was usually bolstered by noting that land that (British or Canadian) women deserved was going to "strangers" or "foreigners."[64]

Women—including married or deserted women—had also earned this birthright, it was contended, as they were directly responsible for increased land values. Mrs. J.R. Long took this position in her letter to the *Nor'West Farmer*:

> There are millions of acres of land lying here waiting to be taken up—any male subject over eighteen years can come and have a half section for the asking and the small entry fee, but a woman who is forced into the world to earn a living for herself and little family cannot have an acre unless her husband is deceased. Is a deserted wife with a family dependent upon her not more worthy of a homestead than perhaps her unworthy husband who may be in

> some other part of the country experiencing no difficulty in securing a homestead? And is a widow who either has no family or a family all married not worthy of some consideration?[65]

Writing the Department of the Interior from Stalwart, Saskatchewan, in 1913, Mrs. Fanny Elizabeth Shepherd asked this very question; she was not eligible for a homestead because her two sons were not minors.[66] She kept house for one of her sons, but when he married she "wanted a roof of my own over my head." She could not afford to purchase land. Shepherd stated she could complete the homestead duties satisfactorily, and she too argued she could "do better than several half-witted fellows about here who have got [homesteads], or ignorant foreigners who cannot speak a word of English."

While "foreign" men were singled out for criticism, some supporters of the campaign extended this to a larger group of males. W.F. Graham wrote from Pettapiece, Manitoba, that there were women in every Canadian city, including teachers, stenographers, and clerks, who were "surely more valuable citizens than the drinking, carousing, cigarette smoking young fellows who loaf about bar rooms, and yet the latter have votes and homesteads and the former have neither."[67]

Although this facet of the argument was muted, perhaps in order to appear non-threatening, supporters of homesteads for women linked homestead and property rights to suffrage, arguing that with homestead rights, women would be landowners and would therefore have to become voters. In a letter to the *Free Press*, "Business Woman" wrote, "Why the Dominion government does not grant a homestead to each and all of our Canadian women who want one bad enough to do all the homestead duties the same as a man, instead of importing foreigners from all over Europe mostly factory and labouring hands, I cannot see, unless they are afraid that with women landowners we would the sooner get the vote."[68] In the *Voice* (Winnipeg), the newspaper of the western trade unions, it was noted that supporters of homesteads for women "probably have in mind the anomalous position the woman will be in who homesteads, if the government will amend the law and grant her that right. She will be a freeholder of the fertile lands of the west ... but will still be in the position of a minor or dependent, denied the right of the franchise. If women should have the right of homestead they should have the right to vote."[69]

The issue of the franchise was also linked to that of the "foreigner" male, as "Business Woman" wrote above. The "foreign" man could not only obtain a homestead but could also vote. As "School Teacher" wrote to the *Manitoba Free Press* in 1910, women's right to homesteads "should go hand in hand with women suffrage. When foreigners receive 160 acres of Dominion land apiece with the franchise thrown in, surely a Canadian woman should receive much more. We have the right of common claim and assuredly deserve this act of common justice from our native land."[70]

The rationale that began as muted but increasingly took centre stage was that homesteads for (some) women would address the "foreign menace." "A Saskatchewan Farmeress" wrote in April 1910 to the *Guide* that "I know of no less than a score of good, honest, respectable girls of proper age, who would be a credit to any neighbourhood or province, and who will do more to improve not only the homesteads but the country, than all the Doukhobors in the province."[71] The corollary of this was that the right sort of woman had to be encouraged to populate the West, and homesteading could entice that kind of woman while domestic service would not. "Jemima" argued in 1912 to the *Nor'West Farmer* that the West needed to attract British and Canadian-born women who might establish dairy and poultry farms, or raise sheep and goats.[72] She ventured to say that if domestic service had been the only thing offered to young men, then few would have settled in Western Canada.

OPPONENTS

Opponents of homesteads for women included powerful men such as Frank Oliver, who drew on a variety of counter-arguments, including that women would not be inclined to marry if they had the right to homestead on their own, and that married couples were required to establish homesteads and family farms on the prairies. Calgary Conservative politician, and later prime minister R.B. Bennett maintained that if separated women were allowed the right to homestead it would encourage couples to part ways. (Opponents did not seem to realize that the homestead laws caused people to postpone or even avoid marriage. As one observer noted, "A certain widow and a certain man are living side by side, and, while they ought to marry, they cannot do so for a period of three years, until the widow has proved up on her homestead."[73])

For opponents, the American West was not a source of inspiration. As discussed in the last chapter, J. Obed Smith told Binnie-Clark following her 1913 presentation to the Royal Colonial Institute that Canada did not want to pursue the same "disastrous" course as the United States had. He elaborated on this some months later in a "despatch," explaining that in the United States, "in nearly every case there was a distinct evasion of the spirit of the law … the American girls took up their homesteads, so did their fiancés. Then they married and had two homesteads, contrary to the spirit of the law."[74] In a 1904 article in the *Globe* (Toronto), a special correspondent commented on differences between the Canadian and U.S. West, noting that the United States "appears to be more liberal in its treatment of the fair sex." He had learned this at his hotel, where he could not get a cooked breakfast and discovered that the dining room waitress was "out on her homestead."[75] He reported that in the United States virtually no improvements were required before patent to a homestead was issued, and included a story of the mayhem that resulted from the lenient divorce laws of the United States and the laws that permitted women to homestead:

> This holding of land by women is responsible for the story about the South Dakota married couple, a farmer and his wife, who held a quarter section, but wanted another one. They determined to take advantage of the lax divorce laws of the State, get divorced, after which, as a single woman, the lady could take up the adjoining quarter section after which they would be remarried. The idea worked out well at first. The divorce and the quarter section were both secured, and the farmer built a house half upon his own and half upon the lady's quarter section. But it was another case of the course of true love. Once divorced the lady fell in love with another man, married him and husband No. 2 secured the coveted quarter section. The story does not tell how the house was divided.

In his 1907 publication, *The Land Laws of Canada and the Land Experience of the United States*, Ditlew M. Frederiksen was critical of the "school marms" who had been permitted to homestead in the U.S. West. Like Smith, Frederiksen found their claims a fraudulent abuse of the homestead laws. He quoted the findings of the 1905 U.S. report of the

Public Lands Commission about entries made by "female school teachers, who spend their vacations on their claims, commute the entries, and leave the country as soon as a better paying position can be found elsewhere."[76] (Frederiksen found, however, that there was even more widespread abuse of the homestead laws by men in both the United States and Canada. Referring to Saskatchewan, he wrote that "what greets the eye frequently is one shack after another without any signs of real fields, stables ... clothes hanging out to dry on the line, or other evidences of progress, family life and civilization.")[77]

"Rural legends" of frozen young women homesteaders of the American West helped to point out their unsuitability and ineptitude. In 1906 it was rumoured that "two girl homesteaders were frozen to death on their claims" in northeast Montana, but it was also reported that "no particulars are obtainable."[78] In 1916 it was widely reported that two teacher homesteaders had been found frozen to death near Havre, in northern Montana close to the Canadian border.[79] The tale had many touching details, including that they were sisters who penned notes saying goodbye to their mother. The story was found to be a hoax.[80]

J. Obed Smith was convinced that women were incapable of the physical labour required on a farm, and other opponents agreed. "Homo" wrote to the *Family Herald and Weekly Star* in 1910, "Show me the woman who will handle horses, plough, pitch hay, stook grain etc. Oh, no. The very first thing she must do after securing her homestead is to hire, marry, or to otherwise obtain a man."[81] He continued: "Every woman in her heart knows full well that she is vastly inferior to man physically. If there are any who do not, they are to say the least, very foolish." (Such letters generally generated many more by women who were performing all of the tasks necessary on a homestead.) Opponents to homesteads for women also claimed that women could not hire and supervise men. The problem would then be idle and vacant land, and "those who live in the west fully realize the great necessity of rapid development of the country."[82]

For context, it is instructive to remember that there was a time in Western Canada when there was debate about whether it was proper for women to learn a host of skills or habits defined as masculine, such as smoking or driving machinery such as an automobile. In 1915 one critic of women's abilities wrote to the *Calgary Daily Herald* that driving a car was "the most severe test one can possibly have on the nerves."[83] He doubted that women would be able to act decisively and without warning to avoid accidents, or that they were strong enough to steer and use the brakes. A Calgary alderman was in favour of a by-law prohibiting women from driving cars, saying, "Women may be and doubtless are perfectly capable of driving an automobile but when they meet a sudden emergency in driving they are apt to lose their heads."[84]

Issues of femininity and propriety were raised by critics of women labouring outdoors. One woman wrote that any farmer husband would be "ashamed to see [his] wife ploughing in the fields."[85] Many commented that woman's place was as wife and mother, and that young women should be striving to marry the bachelors of the prairies who had homes established already. "Homo" wrote, "I am of the opinion that if those few women of today, who are clamouring, shrieking, and wasting their time in a futile attempt to attain that which would be of little, if any, use to them, would devote their time to their children, and other duties for which they were created, they would be rendering a far greater service to their sex."[86] Many insisted (despite the huge volume of letters to the contrary) that "I have yet to meet any single woman who is anxious to go homesteading."[87] "Pencilitus" continued: "What young woman with any intelligence would want to cast her lot on the prairie without any protection and perhaps as far as twenty to forty miles from kith and kin." "Pencilitus" asked what would become of the country if "women were given to grasping after the material things of this universe? What would become of our schools and colleges, our hospitals and kindergartens, and last, but not least, the home?" Young women striving to get ahead of young men in material things would destroy the "law of attraction."

"Silver Knight" agreed that he knew of few Canadian girls who would "forfeit their modesty and 'rough' it for three years at least, even for the sake of getting 160 acres of land for free."[88] He added that Canadian mothers would not want to see their daughters live on a quarter section for three years. "It oftentimes becomes a woman to relinquish her 'rights' and uphold her dignity," he wrote. "Silver Knight" had travelled extensively and knew of no other place where women were "more respected, appreciated and rewarded than in western Canada." The "sons of Canada" treated the women of the region with "chivalry, courtesy, respect." Women had to milk cows morning and night in Ontario, but "it is a very unusual thing for a woman to be seen milking in Western Canada."

Reluctant supporters of land for women advocated that if women were to have homesteads, they should have much smaller acreages. "Eureka" wrote in 1912 from Saskatchewan to propose that 160-acre homesteads be broken up into twenty-acre plots for women to share.[89] They could also share accommodation and save costs, and in this way "make an independent living at poultry raising, dairying, gardening, or raising small fruits."

English travel writer Bessie Pullen-Burry gave some coverage to the homestead campaign in her 1912 book *From Halifax to Vancouver*, but she was decidedly lukewarm toward the idea of encouraging women to emigrate for that purpose. In Winnipeg she met with journalist Ethel Osborne, who was a supporter of the cause, and Pullen-Burry provided a synopsis of the main arguments, but in her opinion, "Canadian women in the West are the worst off of any of their sex among civilised peoples."[90] She learned from a Scottish woman settler that "to say that the conditions of life for educated gentlewomen in Canada were not a daily round of toil and monotony ... would be to obscure and to pervert truth."[91] Dangers lurked everywhere for the women settlers in solitary districts, and the Scottish woman believed it "absolutely indispensable" that women "become practised shots." A young schoolteacher had allegedly recently been "dragged to the woods by a ruffian." Pullen-Burry wrote that "women living on these isolated farms, I assure you, go through periods of mental torture from sheer terror which men never realise until some horrid tragedy within a stone's throw of their own farms makes them uneasy as to the risks run by their womenfolk."[92]

Elizabeth Keith Morris, author of *An Englishwoman in the Canadian West* (1913), opposed homestead rights for women. She was a critic of the "lady farmer," as she referred to Binnie-Clark (as mentioned in the previous chapter), and wrote that the Canadian government wisely limited the homestead right to men, realizing the difficulties and hardships women would confront.[93] She agreed with the "existing opinion amongst farmers in Canada—that the hard and heavy work is unsuitable for women. We heard of odd cases where modern Amazons had many acres under cultivation, but these were exceptional and should not point the way to others." Only a very few would have the physical stamina: "The gently-nurtured, sheltered and irresponsible type of English girl would be mad to dream of following such an occupation, for she is unsuited to any kind of life in the Dominion."[94]

Though their voices were few in the letters columns, "foreigners" objected to what was becoming a central element of the campaign, which was to question the entitlement of "outsiders" to land when British and British-Canadian women were denied homesteads. A "foreigner" wrote to the *Manitoba Free Press* in 1910 to say that the majority of farmers on the prairies were "foreigners of different nationalities," and that they were doing their share to improve the land and that surely they deserved homesteads.[95] (He also believed it was not "a woman's place" to homestead, since women could "get married and let the husband do the work" while having plenty to do with home and offspring.)

It is interesting that in the debates that took place in the farm journals and newspapers of the West, none of the opponents argued that by farming, British or British-Ontarian women would sink to the level of "foreign" women or the Indigenous women of North America or other colonies. Yet this was implied through the widespread coverage of the Doukhobor women who hitched themselves to the plough. A 1911 article that was published in numerous newspapers of the West pronounced that Doukhobor women "have been reclaimed from the plow. No longer do they sweat in the fields of Canada instead of horses … the new world's environments have drawn the women back from the brute level, to which they have been degraded, to the home, with its cooking, its spinning, and its weaving … The melting pot of the western world has recast even the Doukhobors."[96]

HOMESTEADS FOR SOME WOMEN BUT NOT OTHERS

Increasingly, the central rationale in the homesteads-for-women campaign was that land grants should be available to "daughters of British blood" rather than "hordes of men of alien race." Similar arguments were being made by some supporters of women's suffrage. E.A. Partridge, founder of the *Grain Growers' Guide* and a supporter of women's suffrage, argued in a 1909 editorial that it was an "outrage to deny to the highest minded, most cultured native-born lady what is cheerfully granted to the lowest browed, most imbruted foreign hobo that chooses to visit our shores."[97] At the *Guide*, Isabelle Beaton Graham increasingly emphasized this argument for (some) women's homestead rights. In her 1909 column that helped launch the campaign, under the subheading "Consider the Douks," she protested the gift of homestead land to the Doukhobors who "so scandalize civilization."[98] "It is painful to realize that our own Canadian men," Graham wrote, "our fathers and our brothers—deliberately set us aside as undeserving of a share in our country ... to bring in ignorant, uncouth, lawless foreigners to occupy lands that we desire, that we have labored for yet cannot have." In her next, most sustained column on the issue, "Unearned Increments and Woman's Dower," Graham wrote that the federal government preferred to dower the "unspeakable foreigner," while denying to women the proceeds of their own toil.[99]

This argument found many supporters in the pages of the *Guide* and other publications. "Mother Scot," from Alberta, complained that their farm was surrounded by a "colony of aliens whose habits and ways of looking at things make them hopeless as neighbors," and "I often think how unfair it is to give these outlanders the privilege of homesteads and deny that privilege to their own race and blood, when it happens to be of the other sex. Is not the mother—actual or prospective—of sons and daughters of British blood at least as worthy of a share of God's free gift as the hordes of men of alien race who are given free homesteads without a condition?"[100] From Wapella, Saskatchewan, "Lochinvar" mocked the law that permitted any male to homestead while British and Canadian women were denied: "He may be the greatest imbecile in the world, but, if he wears pants and keeps cool he can get the farm. He may come from the ill-fed, ill-bred and illiterate peoples of parts of Europe. He may come from the darkest jungles of darkest Africa. He may be the greatest villain the universe produced, he can get the land, but women, cultured, refined, able to make and keep home happy—not on your life."[101] This writer concluded that it was folly to provide land to "semi-savages," who would take "centuries to mould into a British subject, in preference to a British woman with British pluck, endurance and everything that makes for an enlightened Canadian citizenship."

Graham and other supporters of homesteads for women manipulated fears of the "foreign" or "alien" element that prevailed among the British-Ontarian settlers. Intolerant attitudes toward immigrants seen as undesirable, including Mormons, Ukrainians, Jews, Doukhobors, and Asians, were stridently and widely broadcast in the late nineteenth and early twentieth century in Western Canada.[102] Many of the most prominent newspapermen in the West, such as Frank Oliver and P.G. Laurie, editor of the *Saskatchewan Herald*, Battleford, took the lead in propagating these views.[103] How could "the Greater Britain Beyond the Seas" be forged from the peasantry of Europe?[104] A further "outrage" was that these "aliens" could vote, "men who have just emerged from serfdom … who are ignorant of they very alphabet of the public life of Canada."[105]

Proponents of homesteads for women capitalized on fears of the "foreigner" to connect themselves to issues of national and imperial importance to which they could offer solutions. They were asking for equal treatment, but only for those British and Canadian-born women who qualified for inclusion. Like suffragists in the U.S. West and in other colonial settings, they "manipulated ideas about racial and ethnic 'Others,' usually reinforcing contemporary racialist and racist attitudes, particularly those linking race, sex and 'civilization.'"[106] In Western Canada, however, supporters of homesteads for women could not claim superiority by virtue of their "whiteness," since the "foreign" women they wanted to exclude from the privilege of homesteading were phenotypically similar. It was not particularly clear just who was "white" in Western Canada. As Catherine Hall has observed, the question of "who was white" was seldom straightforward in the colonies of the British Empire.[107] Instead of whiteness, Britishness became the marker of privilege in Western Canada, and a British-Canadian elite dominated business, politics, the law, and education.[108] Leaders of the homesteads-for-women campaign decided to align themselves and identify with this elite, arguing that British-Canadian women settlers would help maintain the hegemony of the group.

The manipulation of fears of racial and ethnic "others" among some supporters of homesteads for women reached a new level in 1911, when the likelihood loomed of a sizeable migration of African Americans from Oklahoma to Alberta and Saskatchewan.[109] They had begun to appear in small numbers in 1905, increasing after 1907 when Oklahoma became a state and the first state legislature passed "Jim Crow" legislation, and again in 1910 when Oklahoma Democrats moved to disenfranchise African Americans. There was a strong reaction against this migration in Western Canada. Graham's columns in the *Guide* were among the most racist, strident, and alarmist, containing utterly fabricated allegations. Her column "The Negro" of 3 May 1911 began,

> Fireside would like well to know what the people, especially the country women of the west think about the negro invasion that is now pouring into the Canadian west and receiving free land grants from the Dominion government, and farming large settlements contiguous to and

> among the whites. There can scarcely be anyone who is not aware of the atrocities committed by members of these terrible communities, the only corresponding punishment for which is the lawless lynching, and even burning at the stake. Already it is reported that three white women in the Edmonton and Peace River districts have been victims of these outrages accomplished in peculiarly fiendish abandon. Where will the end be? ... How many of these industrious, courageous, unprotected, country women must be sacrificed to the horrors of negro attack before the slow and rusty machinery that drives the engine of state can be induced to erect a barricade against so dreadful an evil?[110]

Although it seems like an odd leap after pointing out the vulnerability of women alone on homesteads, the main point of Graham's column on "The Negro" was that women should be given the right to homestead. She concluded that "it should be possible for Canadian women to secure from the government of their fathers, husbands, brothers and sons at least an equal share with the foreign negro, in the rich heritage of the Dominion's homestead lands." This was also Graham's first column to clearly articulate that homesteaders should not be "foreign" women who did not know the "rigors of the country, and who are bound to fail through the discouragements of unexpected hardships. In their interest it is wise to hinder them at the start until fully assured that they understand the undertaking."

In the *Saskatoon Star Phoenix*, Valance Patriarche warned of the "Foreign Menace" that was a "grave concern" and a "hazard that threatens the unity of Canada."[111] She feared that the "native population," by which she meant Canadian and British settlers, would soon be "overwhelmed, lost amid the foreign invasion." Granting single women free homesteads would help to Canadianize this "cosmopolitan element." She explained: "Many wise thinkers are advocating a slower, finer growth for the West, and it is indisputable that the encouragement of Canadian and British women would be a step in the right direction. There is a crying need all through the West for teachers and church workers. On the other hand there is a longing in the heart of many a courageous moral and educated single woman for a home of her own, a chance to labor in the open air, as her own mistress, and to escape that most pitiable end—a worked out woman dependent upon others for her help or support in her old age."

Patriarche concluded that "it is not surprising that the unmarried British woman of sound health considers that, providing she is capable of cultivating the land, she is as valuable an asset to her country as the male unmarried foreigner. Indeed, if she has thought at all she realizes she would be a help to the community where the foreigner is often a detriment."

THE SECOND PETITION: HOMESTEADS FOR "ALL WOMEN OF BRITISH BIRTH"

A second homesteads-for-women petition, prepared by Isabelle Beaton Graham, was announced in the 24 May 1911 issue of the *Guide.*[112] The arguments set forth in the petition were that widows had made successful and desirable settlers; that many others, including unmarried women and widows without young children, desired to homestead; that these women would foster education and health and encourage a "better class of male settlers"; that the homestead laws discriminated against families with daughters; that women contributed their share to the growth and prosperity of the nation and had helped to make Dominion lands valuable; and that the privilege of homesteading would afford women a healthy and economic method of securing an independent livelihood, easing congestion in towns and cities and drawing the population back to the land. The petition then asked that the Parliament of Canada grant the privilege of homesteading to "all women of British birth who have resided in Canada for six months, and if residing with their father or mother or a near relative, are of the age of eighteen years, or if otherwise, are of the age of twenty-one years."

The wording of the petition was deliberately vague on the marital status of the would-be woman homesteader. It could be understood to include both single and married women. In answer to a reader who wrote that she would support the petition if it meant married women as well as single, Graham wrote that "it is certainly intended that any woman, married or single, of British birth shall be eligible to homestead," but that it was "not thought advisable to flaunt the married woman's claim before 'the powers that be.'" She explained that married women were not specifically mentioned in the petition "in the hope that thereby she might pass in unobserved, as it were, but she is certainly there, and who has a better right? It is the married woman, NOT the single man."[113]

There was some debate and uncertainty about whose signatures should be obtained for the petition. In June 1911, Graham thought there should be separate petitions—one for men and one for women—"so that it could easily be ascertained which are the voters and how many, and which are the non-voters."[114] Only women over the age of twenty-one were to sign. But this strategy was shelved when it was later decided that only the signatures of voters (men) should be obtained. Graham explained that "it will be taken for granted that all women desire the homestead privilege for their sisters even though they do not intend to take advantage of it themselves."[115]

Many letters requesting copies of the petition soon appeared in the *Guide.* Supporters sought signatures at summer agricultural fairs and events such as Dominion Day and Orangemen's picnics.[116] Other tactics included postcards and letters sent directly to officials in Ottawa. In 1913 J.H. Perra of Winnipeg wrote to the minister of the interior that "on the strength of the success that the women of the States have made in homesteading and that which the Canadian women are making on scrip which they have bought, can you not see your way to introduce a bill to give the women of Canada the right to homestead. We women of the west feel that our rightful inheritance is wrested away from us and given to strangers and all because we have committed the sin of belonging to the 'female species.'"[117]

The Women's Labour League of Winnipeg endorsed the campaign in August 1911 after a "lengthy discussion upon a point of technicality."[118] They favoured this cause at the time over women's suffrage, as the League had not taken action on a request to circulate petitions for suffrage. The League used Labour Day in September 1911 to get signatures on the homestead petition at an event at River Park, where their display contrasted the ability of "halfbreed" and "foreign" men to get land with the lack of opportunities for British women. Their display created "considerable interest," with cartoons that illustrated the following slogans: "We help men to fight for liberty, need we pray for them to grant it to us?; Is the British woman less capable of ruling a homestead than the halfbreed?; Give the daughters increasing independence that they may be prepared to avoid the tragedy of a misspent life; When God gives me a sister shall I withhold the land from her feet? etc."[119]

Before long, fissures appeared that weakened and undermined the campaign. Readers repeatedly asked Graham why American women were excluded under the wording of the petition. As E.L. Stow, born in the

To His Excellency, The Governor General Of Canada, In Council:

THE PETITION of the undersigned residents of the Dominion of Canada, HUMBLY SHEWETH that:

1. **Whereas** The Dominion Lands Act provides that any person who is the head of a family, or a male who is over the age of eighteen years, may homestead a quarter section of available Dominion lands;

2. **And Whereas** only women who are widows and who have infant children living may secure homesteads;

3. **And Whereas** experience has shown that widows have made successful and desirable settlers;

4. **And Whereas** many women, including widows without infant children and unmarried women, both Canadian born and British, possessing means, are most desirous of, and would take advantage of the right to homestead;

5. **And Whereas** the country would be greatly benefited thereby through the fostering of education of health through the ordinary graces of living; and the greater encouragement of a better class of male settlers;

6. **And Whereas** the Homestead Law discriminates against the man having daughters, providing a birthright dowry only for the homesteader whose children are sons, and none for the homesteader whose children are daughters, and the accident of sex thereby enriches one family and impoverishes the other;

7. **And Whereas** many of the women of Canada, although unable to homestead have entered callings where they do secure their own livelihood, and have thereby contributed their share to the growth and prosperity of the country, it is reasonable to assume that, given the homestead privilege, their consequent action will justify this expansion of favors;

8. **And Whereas** such women have to bear their share of the cost of government, and have largely helped to make Dominion lands valuable, but are nevertheless denied any heritage in them;

9. **And Whereas** the privilege of homesteading would afford them an easy, healthful and economic method of securing an independent livelihood;

10. **And Whereas** the trend of population is flowing, injuriously to Canada, toward congestion in towns and cities; and all over North America the great cry is, "Get back to the land";

11. **And Whereas** homesteads to women would draw the population back to the land,

Now, Therefore, Your Petitioners Humbly Pray:

That as soon as possible a Bill may be introduced by your Government and enacted by the Parliament of Canada, providing that all women of British birth who have resided in Canada for one year and if residing with their father or mother or a near relative and are of the age of eighteen years, or if otherwise, are of the age of twenty-one years, shall be granted the privilege of homesteading.

And your petitioners as in duty bound will ever pray.

Dated this 12th day of June A.D., 1911.

NAME	ADDRESS	OCCUPATION
The Winnipeg Board of Trade		
[illegible] President		
C. N. Bell Secretary		

Figure 33. Homesteads-for-British-Women Petition that was presented to the Parliament of Canada in February 1913 with over 11,000 signatures. It was completely ignored. The petition, which asked that the privilege of homesteading be granted to "all women of British birth," was criticized in the Winnipeg trade union newspaper the *Voice* as a "bald piece of discrimination." Library and Archives Canada, Record Group 15, Department of the Interior, D-II-1, vol. 1105, file 2876596, pt. 2.

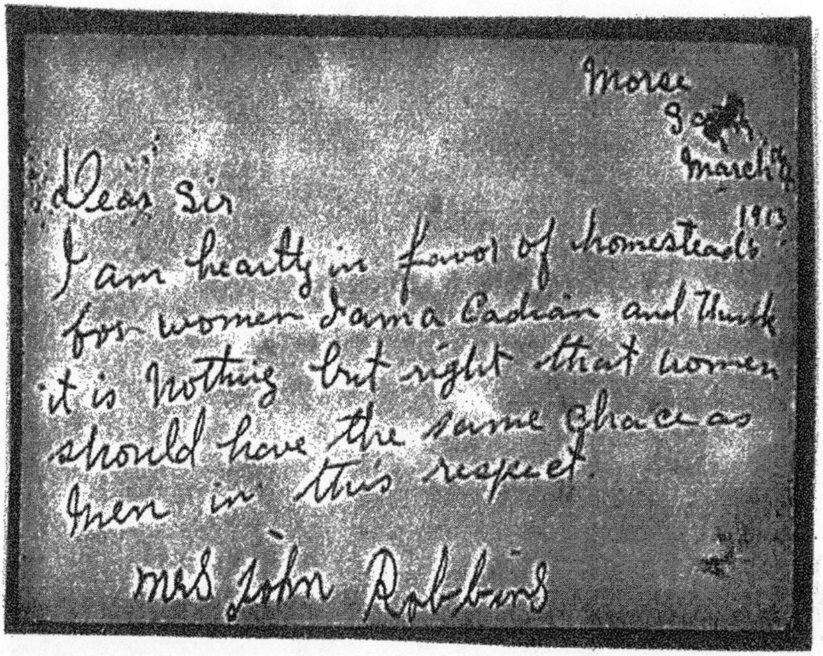

Morse
March 9 1913

Dear Sir
I am hearty in favor of homesteads
for women I am a Cadian and think
it is nothing but right that women
should have the same chace as
men in this respect

Mrs John Robbins

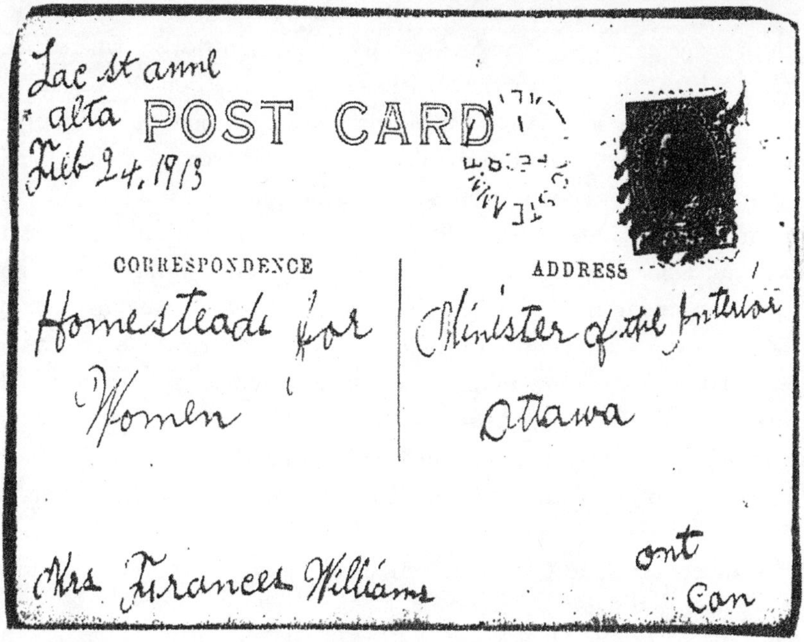

Lac St anne
alta
Feb 24, 1913

POST CARD

CORRESPONDENCE

Homesteads for
Women

ADDRESS

Minister of the Interior
Ottawa

Mrs Frances Williams

ont
Can

Figure 34. Supporters of the homesteads-for-women campaign were asked to send postcards directly to the Department of the Interior in Ottawa. These are two examples from Mrs. John Robbins of Morse, Saskatchewan, and Mrs. Frances Williams, Lac Ste. Anne, Alberta. Library and Archives Canada, Record Group 15, Department of the Interior, D-Ii-1, vol. 1105, file 2876596, pt. 2.

United States but resident in Saskatchewan, wrote, "I do not see why I have not as much right to homestead as a woman of British birth. I am sure I know more about the work of a farm than a Britisher just out a year could do at first." She had "run the binder, stooked, cut, raked, and stacked hay; plowed, disked and harrowed; in fact I think I have done everything necessary on a farm."[120] "Ex-American" wrote, "When I read your petition in Fireside all my fondest hopes were crushed for the petition reads that women of British and Canadian birth be allowed the privilege of homesteading and I first beheld the light of day under the Stars and Stripes."[121] A Mrs. Paterson from Plateau, Saskatchewan, argued that women from the United States should be included, writing that "a great number of the best and pluckiest settlers we have in Western Canada are American women."[122]

On many occasions Graham was obliged to explain her reasoning for excluding all but women of British birth. She wrote on 16 August 1911 that she was "not opposed to the American woman as a homesteader. She is akin to us in every attribute … with the exception of fealty to the British flag. But if we admit any nationality other than British, where shall we, or where can we, draw the line? Instantly the question will be raised, 'Is it in the interest of Canada to admit a heterogeneous mass of foreign femininity to the homestead privilege in Canada? Can we absorb them as fast as they will come? Even as it is the foreign men are a menace and hindrance.'"[123] Graham feared the petition would be unsuccessful if it asked for homestead rights for "women who have no culture whatever, no education, and women who are unlikely to be anything but a drawback to the progress of Canadian institutions for years to come."[124] No one could object, however, to "an influx of law-abiding, industrious, refined and patriotic gentlewomen with some means into the bleak and bare stretches of the West."[125] Graham also insisted that "the American woman has least to complain of inasmuch as she has had the homestead privilege for years and years in her own country."[126]

There was support for Graham's position that American and "foreign" women should be excluded. James Allan, of Cordova, Manitoba, declared he would not have signed the petition if it had not stated "women of British birth."[127] American women, he argued, could not "just step across the line and expect to have the same rights as a Canadian born." Canadian women were entitled because "they should have some birthright in their own country, and British next, because this is part of the British Empire and all the British born subjects should have equal rights." He wrote that he would "oppose to the bitter end any act that would give to the Galician or German girl … the same rights as to our Canadian and British women."

Speaking up for the rights of "foreign" and immigrant women, "Wilhelmina" wrote from Alberta in 1913 to the *Family Herald and Weekly Star* to say that "Canada cannot afford to turn away women of foreign birth."[128] She described her experiences as a homesteader in North Dakota, where she had filed her own claim in a community of other homesteaders. "We built sod houses and sod barns and used flax straw and dry manure for fuel. All this we learned from foreigners, the stout Russians. I have learned many a good lesson from foreigners and hope that they will be carefully protected." She was in favour of homesteads for all males and all females over the age of eighteen, regardless of ethnicity. Some prominent people in the women's movement in Western Canada did not agree with the tactic of excluding "foreign" women. Francis Marion Beynon, who played a critical role in the suffrage campaign in Manitoba along with her sister Lillian Beynon Thomas, was a consistent defender of the rights of the "foreigner," believing that all ethnic groups deserved equal treatment.[129]

Soon there were many voices objecting to the words "of British birth" in the petition. "Is a woman of British birth any more entitled to homestead privileges than one of any other birth who comes here to live, and by so doing, helps build up the country, by helping her husband and neighbors transform a barren prairie to a garden spot of grain?" asked H.G. Ahern, from Claresholm, Alberta. "The women of British birth should not be so selfish and shortsighted as to try to put through a law of this kind … for if they succeed it will be a blot on the degree of their intelligence, and a factor of their lack of Christianity as practiced by them, which our historians will be sorry to relate."[130] M.E. Graham, who acquired signatures at the Kitscoty Dominion Day celebration, reported that a great number of potential supporters of both sexes were not in favour of the clause "of British birth." She added that she personally saw it as a mistake, as there were so many excellent women from the States, and she saw no reason why the homestead law for women should differ from that for men.[131] In a letter sent directly to Ottawa, V.C. Bedier wrote from Chauvin, Alberta, to say that the measures Graham was trying to introduce through the petition ought to fail, "because of it being so narrow let it be for all women … It certainly would be hard to find women less suitable to help build a country than some of these very ones she so very narrowly tries to favour."[132]

The Winnipeg trade union newspaper the *Voice* criticized the petition in an editorial in September 1911.[133] (The *Voice*'s editor was Arthur Puttee, whose wife, Gertrude, hosted meetings of the Women's Labor League that supported the petition.) The *Voice* expressed some sympathy for the cause, as "it strikes anyone as being a grave discrimination against the sex that the government should be offering to all and sundry men throughout the world the right to enter for free lands in Canada … and at the same time refuse that privilege to a Canadian woman who may see this means the road to economic freedom." The editorial disagreed with the petition, however, finding it was

> not conceived on any broadminded lines, and does not provide any incitement for progressive women to enthuse. While the preamble of it may be satisfactory, it will be noticed by those who take the time to read it observingly … that it asks for the right to homestead for "women of British birth" only. How very restrictive this is can only be appreciated here in the west. For a dozen of years people have been pouring in from all the nations of the earth; invited, almost recruited by the government. Although they may have been naturalized in the interim their women folk are still to be debarred from homestead rights if the prayer of the petitioners is granted: indeed, the petition has been specially drawn to debar them. These are the women who would be most likely to want to homestead; and in the large proportion of cases they would be the women most suitable to undertake the hardships attendant theron. It is not often that a public petition includes such a bald piece of discrimination as this and we think the women would be well advised to alter the prayer of the petition or drop it.

The issue of continued support for the campaign was discussed at an October meeting of the Women's Labor League, which decided that while their organization could not discriminate against all nationalities having equal opportunities, the present petition had a chance to pass, being endorsed by prominent men, whereas one with a wider scope might not. The

League was prepared to continue to support the petition, although there was regret that "the measure shuts out several nationalities which might be beneficial to the country." They decided that the words "British birth" were

> inserted mainly to prevent the influx of those European women who are used as beasts of burden by men who cannot afford oxen, and while it has been reported that women may be seen in the prairie provinces hitched to the plow, the league would discountenance any scheme which tended to so degrade women, and it is thought that a bill which granted free homesteads to that class would introduce into this country too many who were willing to continue their old country habits and do the "donkey work" while the men smoked and drank the results of their toil, thus tending to lower the social and moral tone of the country.[134]

Supporters were optimistic in 1911 that a change in the federal government might usher in a new regime more sympathetic to their cause. Frank Oliver and the Liberals were defeated in the September election that year. The Conservative government of Robert Borden appointed Robert Rogers of Winnipeg as minister of the interior in 1911, and when he became minister of public works the next year, Dr. W.J. Roche, member of Parliament for Marquette, Manitoba, was appointed minister of the interior. In 1910 it was Roche who had introduced the issue of homesteads for women in the House of Commons, and he had seemed in favour, arguing that "if this privilege were granted to the fair sex many would go into the west. As there was a surplus of men on the prairies such a movement would assist them in getting helpmates."[135] Once in power, however, Roche's sympathy for the cause disappeared, but that was not immediately apparent. The petition remained the central strategy, and Graham remained steadfast in her insistence on the "British birth" clause as a route to the creation of a "pure" and "moral" colony. She wrote in October 1911: "People are beginning to wake up to the vast conception and imperialistic importance of tendering free homesteads, as an inducement to women of strong moral force and high intellectual ability, to come to our beautiful West and lend their aid in establishing a Canadian colony, a new and clean colony that may, that will in no far-distant future, hold a shining lamp to shed a gleaming light of justice, of honor, of idealistic national purity, of all home comfort, of brotherly love, to all the wide world."[136]

In the fall of 1911 a letter-writing contest on the topic of homesteads for women was featured in the *Guide.*[137] The idea was to explain to the new minister of the interior Robert Rogers the need for and justice of the claim. Five prizes were to be awarded on the topic of "Why women should be granted homestead privileges." The best letters were published in December 1911, and readers were asked to vote on which they felt deserved the prizes.[138] The letters included eloquent pleas that echoed the rationales that have already been outlined here, although either the letter writers themselves or the editor did not include critiques of the "foreigner" being granted access to land. The writers contended that a land of contented, prosperous homes would replace the vacant farms and bachelor shacks; that women could enjoy a healthy open air life rather than factory work and unsanitary surroundings; that women could have property of their own in the event of financial calamity; that families with daughters would not be at a disadvantage; women would be induced to emigrate to the West; and that there would be wives for homesteaders.

Mrs. J.W. Moore in Ernfold, Saskatchewan, put the matter most succinctly in her essay, arguing that women had "as much right to be independent as men," that they had done as much as men to advance the country, that they had endured as many hardships as men and had equally shared the homestead duties only to find that their husbands had mortgaged or sold their land, that girls needed to be encouraged to stay on the farms, and that if allowed to vote, women would use sound judgement.

By late 1911, Graham was replaced as the women's page editor of the *Guide*, apparently in order to pursue the campaign full time, but it may also have been that her views were considered too controversial and extreme, after her racist condemnation of African-American settlers. She was replaced first, and briefly, by Mary Ford, and then by Francis Marion Beynon, who played a critical role in the suffrage campaign in Manitoba along with her sister Lillian Beynon Thomas and Nellie McClung. Beynon had been a consistent defender of the rights of the "foreigner," believing that all ethnic groups deserved equal treatment. She once commented in response to a slur against people of colour, "Because we of the Anglo-Saxon race have been able to bully less militant and aggressive peoples into handing over their territory to us is a poor basis for the assumption that we as a race are the anointed of God and the one and only righteous and virtuous people."[139] Nellie McClung also endorsed ethnic diversity and promoted a vision of Canada as a place where "every race, color or creed will be given exactly the same chance."[140] In 1915 McClung spoke "passionately in defence of the foreign women" on the question of suffrage.[141] At the same time her writing and speeches expressed deep pride in and admiration for the British Empire, and in 1917, she briefly redacted her defence of the rights of "foreign" women when she called for voting rights for Canadian and British-born women only as a war measure. McClung soon withdrew her support for this, however, and acknowledged her error when Beynon criticized her in the *Guide*. There were, however, other suffragists who used the same arguments advanced by Graham, asking how they could be disenfranchised when "untutored" "foreigners" could vote and determine their laws and future. They argued that the female franchise could offset the votes of illiterate immigrants, and that "Canadian women had the well-being of the country more at heart than the average foreign immigrant."[142]

After Graham left the *Guide*, the petition continued to circulate, although under Beynon's editorship there was much less emphasis and far fewer letters published on the issue. The petition was not submitted to Parliament until 1913, when it attracted little attention; the campaign was ultimately an utter failure. The elitist strategy of Graham and other proponents of homesteads for women that excluded rights for "foreign" women weakened rather than consolidated their base of support. Key potential constituencies were alienated, including settlers from the United States. But even without these fissures in the campaign, it seems unlikely that it would have succeeded. The reasons against granting homestead rights to women in Western Canada were clearly articulated in an editorial in the *Nor'West Farmer* of 5 September 1912, explaining why the editors of that journal could not support the cause and wanted nothing to do with the issue of which women should be granted homestead rights. Homesteads for women were opposed "on the simple ground that women are not naturally fitted to become independent, permanent, capable agriculturalists." To bestow 160 acres on every woman who should apply for it was "an unwarranted dissipation of our public domain and a menace to our agriculture." As it was, there were enough "agricultural scaliwags" breaking the spirit of the homestead contract by making the smallest possible amounts of improvements. Capable, lifelong farmers were wanted. Some women might be able to farm on their own, but "the average woman is lacking in the physical strength and natural independence and resource so necessary in a homesteading undertaking."[143]

As historian Bradford Rennie has written, there was considerable support from male farmers in the West for the homesteads-for-women movement, but opinions were divided and there were limitations to this support. Rennie writes that men signed the petition, but "many men opposed the campaign, including delegates to the 1912 Saskatchewan Grain Growers convention, and those in favour in Alberta were not sufficiently concerned to see a resolution on the subject brought before a UFA [United Farmers of Alberta] convention."[144] According to Rennie, it was the homesteads-for-women campaign that helped to build a women's section of the UFA, mobilizing and training women to work for a cause, and encouraging them to join the agrarian movement. But as will be discussed in the next chapter, the demands of organized agrarian women for domestic servants were a priority and this was at odds with, or sat uncomfortably beside, the campaign for homestead rights.

The petition, bearing over 11,000 signatures as well as support from organizations such as the Winnipeg Board of Trade, the three provincial Grain Growers' Associations, the National Council of Women, and Women's Press Clubs across Canada was submitted to Parliament in February 1913.[145] There was no debate on or interest in the issue. Minister of the Interior W.J. Roche simply said "this matter is under consideration" when asked if the petition had been received and what action the government proposed to take. The petition received nothing more than a polite written response from Roche to Isabelle Graham, who was informed that "any matter pertaining to the welfare of the Canadian people will always receive my close and favorable consideration."[146]

LAST GASPS OF THE CAMPAIGN: THE "NATURAL" GENDER ORDER PRESERVED

That was not the end of interest in homesteads for women, but from here on the campaign lost steam. Disappointed in this as well as the dower campaign, organized women focused attention on the vote as a means of achieving their goals. In 1916 voting rights were granted to women, with the exception of Indigenous women, in the three Prairie provinces after years of intense campaigning. The petition remained a main strategy, and the one presented to the premier of Manitoba in 1915 had 39,584 signatures (indicating how comparatively few supporters there had been for homesteads for British women).[147] The First World War also diverted attention away from issues such as homesteads for women. As mentioned in the previous chapter, Binnie-Clark's 1914 book, *Wheat and Woman*, in which she stressed the obstacles faced by the woman farmer in Western Canada, could not have been published at a less ideal time. Even Binnie-Clark herself deserted the cause, returning to England for many years and devoting her attention to other, war-related issues.

Yet supporters had been won through the campaign. A 1915 editorial in the Toronto *Globe* supported the homesteads-for-women cause (minus the preference for "British-born" women only).[148] The homestead laws were a "serious injustice" that "worked injuriously in many ways." The main argument advanced was that as the law stood, the male homesteader "performs settlement duties as if in an obstacle race, without the intention of actual settlement, but with an outlook for speculative development. Were the discrimination against women removed there would be far less of this class of homesteading." The editorial concluded: "The entrance of women into many occupations formerly reserved for men has not caused the social and economic derangements predicted, but has been almost invariably advantageous from the standpoint of progress and development. The change requested in the homesteading law rests on a basis of equity that is unassailable. Neither on grounds of justice nor expediency can it longer be refused."[149]

That women did not have homestead rights in Western Canada to 1930 reflects the goals of the architects of the Canadian West, who imagined and fashioned the region as an extension of the British Empire, distinct from their neighbours to the south. Here the "traditional" and "natural" gender order was to be preserved. White women, preferably of British ancestry, were viewed as the key to order and civilization and to the agrarian ideal, but only if they were firmly tied to the home and domestic sphere. Importing young women as domestic servants rather than holding out the hope of land ownership and possible independence from marriage best served these goals. Promoters of agriculture as a suitable occupation for women in the pages of the *Imperial Colonist* made little impact, nor did the example of the women homesteaders of the American West. Ownership of land (although not working on the land of their spouses, fathers, or brothers) disrupted cherished ideals of British femininity. As Kathryn M. Hunter has written about Australia, "to accept the possibility of women involved in cultivation would have meant a subversion of heterosexuality, particularly when the women involved were single and childless. This would constitute a most inappropriate possession of land."[150] These views were so deeply embedded that even the tactic of allying the cause with that of bolstering the British fabric of the West did not advance the right of women to their own homesteads. But there was more at work than a challenge to cherished ideals of femininity. Architects of the West knew that women were capable of the hard work and deprivation required of homesteaders, but it was useful to insist that they were not, just as the skills of Indigenous farmers were deprecated.[151] Extending homesteading rights to women would mean having to share legal claims to the most valuable resource of the West—land. Improvement of the land and profits from the land were to remain a white male preserve. Nellie McClung wrote in *Maclean's* magazine in 1916, "Women are doing homestead duties wherever homestead duties are being done."[152]

The homesteads-for-women campaign failed for many reasons. It faced formidable opposition from those in authority who wished to keep land, property, and real estate a male preserve. McClung's article in *Maclean's,* for example, was dismissed as "unmitigated piffle" and "gross misrepresentation," and described as full of "wild baseless assertions … and utter disregard for facts." She had gratuitously slandered the homesteaders of Western Canada through her suggestion that women had to perform tasks such as breaking scrub land.[153] Intransigence prevailed at the top level of government. In Canada, women were to marry and to have no options outside of marriage. In 1910 Prime Minister Wilfrid Laurier replied to a single Canadian woman inquiring about a homestead that "I would advise that you take a husband, to whom we will be happy to give the homestead."[154]

The fissures created by the central strategy of the main organizers additionally undermined the cause. Women "of British birth" argued that they were superior to the "heterogeneous mass of foreign femininity" in their midst who should not be entitled to homestead land. They presented themselves as exemplars of a desirable, refined, and respectable British-Canadian femininity, who would introduce all of these qualities to homestead communities. Yet they were asking that they have the land that would permit them to farm and to work outdoors, the very activities for which "foreign" women were condemned. British-Canadian women were threatening to join them, not rise above them, becoming coarse, indecent, and a "remnant of a darker time." The homesteads-for-women campaign gained steam just when it was being proudly proclaimed in the western press that "the melting pot of the western world has recast even the Doukhobors."[155] The melting pot was not, however, supposed to recast British-Canadian women as farmers, sweating in their fields and sinking to the "brute level."

CHAPTER SEVEN

THE PERSISTENCE OF A "CURIOUSLY STRONG PREJUDICE"

FROM THE FIRST WORLD WAR TO THE GREAT DEPRESSION

The First World War brought an end to the organized homesteads-for-(some)-women campaign, although the cause did not die out entirely until 1930. The war also suspended the work of organizations like the Colonial Intelligence League (CIL), dedicated to training and placing British gentlewomen emigrants in Canada in vocations that included farming. Women were needed for farm work at home, and it was dangerous to emigrate by sea. Women in both Britain and Canada devoted themselves to war work, but while a women's land army was created in England and in the United States, and the Ontario government mobilized "farmerettes," there was no such formal organization of women for farm labour on the prairies. Having informed women for years that they were not capable of working the land, it would have been difficult for authorities to suddenly reverse this stand. Yet women on the prairies did perform all varieties of farm work during the war, and it was hoped that the war had proven their capacity to farm. Some women's and men's farm organizations on the prairies continued to request homestead rights for women, adding that this would promote greater production. Even before the war was over there was optimism that British women farmers could find positions and land of their own in Canada, particularly those demobilized from the women's land army or the auxiliary services. This was not to be, however, as authorities remained as intransigent as before, and new rationales emerged to even further limit the homestead right to males, as any available homestead land was to be made available to returned soldiers. Domestic service, along with a few other suitably feminine vocations, remained the only openings for British women in Western Canada. The "curiously strong prejudice" against women farmers and farm labourers persisted and became even more entrenched by the 1930s.[1]

THE FIRST WORLD WAR AND WOMEN'S FARM LABOUR IN BRITAIN AND THE UNITED STATES

The Colonial Training School at Stoke Prior (originally the Leaton Colonial Training Home founded in 1890) closed in 1915.[2] The school had graduated over 700 students, and of these 200 had gone to the colonies, mostly Canada. But after August 1914 there were so few applicants that it was not possible to remain open. The women who had once trained to serve in the colonies were now needed for work on farms at home. But other institutions that trained women for agriculture and horticulture at home, rather than in the colonies, remained open and gained new relevance, vitality, and credibility. The Horticultural College for Women at Swanley introduced short courses in various aspects of agriculture as a war emergency. It was hoped that after the emergency and temporary work required of women on the land that there would be opportunities for a "permanent open-air life" in farms and gardens.[3] Writing in the *Englishwoman*, Alice Martineau stated, "At last the opportunity has come to English women to show the stuff they are made of."[4] And they did.

During the First World War, Britain's food supply was threatened by submarine warfare and factors such as the harsh winter of 1915–16.[5] The Women's Land Army (WLA) in Britain began to take shape in 1915 through the Board of Agriculture, the Board of Trade, and the War Agricultural Committees, although it did not formally begin to recruit until 1917.[6] The purpose of the WLA was for women volunteers to work on the land, taking the place of men serving in the military. Before the formal creation of the WLA there were many smaller, local volunteer groups of women working on the land throughout Britain, such as the mobile hoeing force of girls from the University College of Wales, who attended to the turnip and other root crops.[7] Women who played a prominent role in the creation of the mobile force of women farm workers that became the WLA included Louisa Jebb Wilkins, Meriel Talbot, and Lady Gertrude Denman. Before the war they had been involved in the promotion of agriculture for women, with causes such as small holdings for women and the settlement of British women in the colonies.[8] There were also many women workers on the land during the war who were not members of the WLA.[9] These were rural or village women already in the countryside well before the formation of the WLA; this was work they were accustomed to doing.

Despite the increasing acceptability of agriculture as a suitable vocation for women from about 1900, there remained widespread scepticism and deep-seated prejudice against women engaging in farm labour that was perceived as male. There were many obstacles to overcome, including the attitude of male farmers that women could not take a man's place on the land, and some thought it preferable to recruit old-age pensioners.[10] Demonstrations of women's work on the land, including ploughing, milking, tending cattle, and harnessing draught horses, were staged in 1916, and these were an "outstanding success" in altering the views of farmers and in recruiting women.[11] But there were other challenges. Male farm workers were not happy to have their jobs done by unskilled volunteers, and there was also the fear that if women were employed on farms then the men would become liable for military service. Farm women were not happy to have to feed volunteer women. As the war situation and labour shortage became critical, however, farmers and farm workers reluctantly accustomed themselves to female farm labour.[12] There was an alarming shortage of food by the fall of 1916, and with a crop failure in 1917, famine loomed.

The first appeal for recruits to the WLA was issued in March 1917, and 30,000 women applied.[13] They were to sign up for one of three sections: agriculture, forage, or forestry. A recruit could sign on for six months or a year, had to be prepared to work wherever she was sent, and had to undergo rigorous training. Initially they were offered a small wage and no training, but this did not last long, as higher wages were needed to entice women to take on agricultural work, and training was necessary to convince farmers to hire them. The Selection Committee carefully selected the most suitable women "of good temperament." It is estimated that by the end of 1917 there were 29,000 women employed on farms.

The WLA "land girls" were issued a free uniform. They wore overalls and breeches, but were cautioned to remain feminine. An image was carefully crafted of the land girl as "hard-working, yet feminine, patriotic yet willing to return to the home once the war ended."[14] The WLA *Handbook* given to each recruit stated: "You are doing a man's work and you are dressed rather like a man; but remember that just because you wear a smock and breeches you should take care to behave like an English girl … Noisy or ugly behavior brings discredit, not only upon yourself but upon the uniform, and the whole Women's Land Army."[15]

There was criticism of the uniform, however. A "woman farmer" who wrote to the *Times* of London in 1916 objected that "harm is being done by the ridiculous and vulgar photographs which appear in the Press. I am perfectly ready to employ the right sort of woman. French women and North country girls have found it possible to work in a short petticoat, and they have not required the theatrical attractions of uniform and armlet to induce them to do their duty."[16]

To keep an eye on morals and morale, eighty welfare officers were appointed in 1918 to visit the WLA workers, to make sure they were respecting their curfews and not visiting public houses or communicating with German prisoners of war. To keep their morale up and provide a sense of identity, the journal the *Landswoman*, sponsored by the WLA and the Women's Institutes, started publication in 1918.[17]

In the United States, the American Woman's Land Army (also known as the WLA) was organized in 1918, joining together a number of women's farm and garden committees.[18] These women were also given a wage and basic training, and by the summer of 1918 about 15,000 women in twenty states were working on dairy, livestock, poultry, and grain farms. They too had a journal, the *Farmerette*, that linked them and provided information on jobs, hours, wages, and training camps. Thirty-four women's colleges in the United States offered training for the American WLA recruits. The WLA of the United States also confronted prejudice from men who were unreceptive to female coworkers. The overwhelmingly white, Christian, and middle-class women of the WLA faced criticism that they would develop into a "peasant type of woman."[19] One land worker countered this with her conviction that "women of intelligence will not degenerate mentally or physically through being farm laborers. Rather they will raise labor to their own level, will give it greater dignity."[20]

ONTARIO'S "FARMERETTES"

Although women performed agricultural labour during the First World War all over Canada, there was no comparable concerted program of mobilizing their work, except in Ontario. As part of the campaign for "Greater Production," the Ontario government (Women's Farm Bureau, Trades and Labour Branch of the Department of Public Works) established the Farm Service Corps, calling on women to work on fruit, vegetable, mixed, and dairy farms, to cook for other rural workers, to work in the canneries preserving fruit and vegetables, and to take charge of milk routes.[21] Single women were sought; those with children would be placed only in domestic work on farms. Free transportation was offered for farm workers, who were to make a "solemn declaration" that they would work for not less than three weeks. The Young Women's Christian Association helped with the work by running the camps that housed the workers. Wages varied, depending on the work. For example, on mixed and dairy farms the minimum wage was fifteen dollars per month.

In 1917 the Ontario Government Employment Bureau sent over 800 young women from Toronto to farms, and about 250 were sent from Hamilton and London.[22] They "assisted in all the various operations incidental to truck and fruit farming, some of them driving harrows and rollers, and some even operated 'dust' spraying outfits."

Members of the Farm Service Corps were dubbed the "farmerettes." The term was explained as given "half in playfulness, half in good-natured derision; there have been the suffragettes, and now you see the chauferette … no such word was known among the students of poultry farming, dairying and gardening ten years ago … 'Ette' is in the nature of a diminutive per ex. 'Mignonette,' or 'little darling.' You couldn't call the ladies who go out to help in the farm problem farmers, could you? But farmerette solves the difficulty."[23] Their outfit was "useful and ornamental."[24] They wore "sensible, durable" costumes of khaki smocks and bloomers, cowboy hats, tan shoes, and puttees. Their femininity was still observable, however; they were equipped for hard work but were also "an ornament in the landscape," with their "bewitching curls that insisted on stealing out from under their cowboy hats."

In 1918 a three-week course for farmerettes was offered at the Ontario Agricultural College in Guelph "to assist women to more intelligently cope with the work of a farm and to reduce in this way the amount of time which must necessarily be spent by a farmer in educating his assistant."[25]

Figures 35 and 36. "Farmerettes" of Ontario c. 1917–18. During the First World War Ontario women were mobilized for work on the land to replace male farmers and labourers who were serving in the forces. Members of the Farm Service Corps were dubbed the "farmerettes." There was no similar formal mobilization of women farm workers in Manitoba, Saskatchewan, and Alberta. City of Toronto Archives, William James Family Fonds 1244, items 640 and 640A.

That fall, however, there was another important breakthrough: for the first time "farmer's daughters and farmerettes" who possessed "equal qualifications with the young men" were to be admitted to the college's regular program.[26] There were several young women in the freshman class that fall. The first two Canadian women to graduate with bachelor of science in agriculture degrees were Margaret Newton of Senneville, Quebec, and Pearl Clayton Stanford of Dartmouth, Nova Scotia.[27]

In July 1918 there was great praise for the farmerettes from district agricultural representatives.[28] That June, for example, ninety-five women at Drayton, Ontario, had pulled flax, "applying themselves to the work with wonderful energy and determination."[29] Doubts remained, however, about their capacity to perform certain tasks such as picking apples, as they "can't handle the heavy ladders and baskets," but it was reasoned that as their wage per week was much lower than what was paid to men, less should be expected of them.[30] Ontario Commissioner of Agriculture Dr. G.C. Creelman declared in 1918 that he was now convinced that "women have a place in agriculture," although he admitted that he had been a sceptic when the plan was first proposed by Premier Sir William Hearst in 1917. Creelman had also been opposed to giving women a special course on agriculture at the Guelph Ontario Agricultural College.

Along with the high school boys of the Soldiers of the Soil, the farmerettes paraded in downtown Toronto in April 1918.[31] It was the farmerettes who were seen as a "new species." They were "far more picturesque and useful than the peacetime suffragettes. The farmerettes are a new kind of girl, a pleasing combination of Little Bo-Peep and Little Boy Blue and Jack and Jill all in one." Their clothing, including bloomers, was described in detail, and the article concluded with approval: "If this brand of rural maiden is to come into vogue, there will be no need of a 'back-to-the-land' campaign, the difficulty will be to stop the ebb tide."

Not all was rosy, and there were sceptics and critics. In the *Globe* of 24 March 1916, a letter from a "Patriot Farmer" of Ontario was quoted with approval. The farmer did not believe women of Canada had the capacity for farm work, writing that "women are working on the land in the old country, but people must remember Britain has a class of women who have been trained to work on the land since childhood. We have no such women in Canada, and I would like to see the women here who could do a long, hard day's work pitching hay or sheaves, or pitch manure or such heavy work as that."[32] In his view only "young able-bodied men" were

What a Girl Wears When She Goes A'Farming

Smocks, Breeches, Bloomers and Middies in Styles Approved For Work in the Barn, Field, Orchard and Vegetable Garden.

J. Navy blue jean is the sturdy, good-looking material used for this outfit. The middy blouse is well cut, the cuffs, pockets and front finished with black bone buttons—price, $2.95. The full bloomers button at the knee; and are priced likewise at $2.95.

K. This trim costume is of khaki duck, the belt, cuffs and pockets fastening with black buttons, and the neck with black laces. The middy is $3.50. The breeches, with deep knee cuffs and pockets showing the same black bone buttons, are $3.75.

L. And, of course, the popular white middy is resorted to for variety's sake, this one in the sketch, "The Admiral," being included in many a Farmerette's outfit. Two or three, in fact, are generally put into her trunk, the price being only $1.00 each. The bloomers worn are those in navy blue jean described above. Price, $2.95.

Figure 37. In May 1918 Canada's Eaton's Department Store offered "Costumes for the Farmerette Who's Off to Do her Bit." "Smocks, Breeches, Bloomers, and Middies in Styles Approved for Work in the Barn, field, Orchard and Vegetable Garden" were available. *The Globe* (Toronto), 25 May 1918, 24 (see also 7 May 1918, 16).

needed, who did not have to be assisted and instructed. A year later an Ontario farmer complained about the young women sent to help on his farm, the "sweet things done up in khaki middy blouses and dark bloomers."[33] He found their "tender hands and soft muscles [were] completely unequal to anything like labor with either fork or hoe, and who would think of sending them afield with a spirited team of horses to tread all day the dusty clods or perhaps the miry ground?" A "young lady from the city" sent to help them was scared of their pet cow and shouted at him to "keep the brute away. She verily thought she was in danger of being impaled on the horns of the harmless cow." Farmers, he wrote, could not "afford time to train and superintend the novices, and no half dozen of them could in any way take a skilled man's place."

There was criticism of the housing and treatment of the women land workers from their relatives. One mother of a farmerette complained that their camps were made up of tents discarded by the militia, that there was no protection for them from the "elements or ruffians," and that her daughter's camp was in fact robbed.[34] Following the robbery the girls went to the nearby hotel for breakfast but were turned away, as they "were not gowned in proper style, and their farmerette costume might shock those who staying there." They were forced to go to work without breakfast. The mother further complained that they were treated as "the lowest notch of humanity," and got a pittance in pay that scarcely covered their camp fees.

Women's work on the farms in Ontario was part of a wider campaign to have women free men for the trenches by doing their jobs at home. During the war, for example, about 35,000 women worked in munitions production in Canada.[35] Yet it is striking that photographs of women at work in factories or farms were rarely featured in Canadian First World War propaganda, while these were popular images in British propaganda.[36] When such images were used in Canada, they were accompanied by clear messages that the women had not strayed far from their roles as nurturing mothers; the "unfeminine" behaviour was excused due to the war. Their work was also cast as temporary, as a sacrifice for the emergency and for patriotism. Karen Ann Reyburn found that images of women in agricultural work "contained some elements of domesticity or 'traditional' womanhood."[37] Women were called upon to conserve rather than produce food, and to take charge of vegetable gardens and allotments.

Figure 38. Reminiscent of the postcard of Doukhobor women pulling the plough, this poster conveyed the message that Canadian women were not to be asked to stoop to this behaviour, rather they could purchase and promote the purchase of victory bonds. In Western Canada women were asked to volunteer to help farmers' wives, rather than working in the fields or with livestock. Library of Congress, 2003652830.

WOMEN AND FARM LABOUR IN PRAIRIE CANADA DURING THE FIRST WORLD WAR

In prairie Canada there was no mobilization of women agricultural workers. Paid farm labour remained essentially a male preserve. Labour shortages did become acute, but the farm workers pressed their advantage to demand higher wages.[38] Farmers desired a "cheap and docile" labour force, and preferred to pay "foreign" workers or "aliens" from Europe a lower wage. The government assisted the farmers in finding new sources of labour, including soldiers in training, who were granted leaves to help with the harvest. "City slackers," those who lounged about the billiard halls and theatres, were called upon to enlist so that the trained agriculturalists, the sons of farmers, could remain on the land.[39] As in Ontario, teenage boys were recruited as "Soldiers of the Soil" and awarded a bronze badge. Others who contributed volunteer labour included professional and business men, civil servants, merchants, clerks, and artisans.

There were occasional calls for women to be mobilized for farm work on the prairies. The Saskatchewan Bureau of Labour asked local committees to obtain "kinds of labour not heretofore fully or regularly employed in farming operations such as boys, girls, women, retired farmers, elevator and implement men etc."[40] An editorial in the *Gleichen Call* (Alberta) in January 1916, entitled "Women Should Be Ready to Till the Soil," quoted a patriotic address by the English Earl of Selborne, President of the Board of Agriculture, appealing to "women of every class ... the squire's wife and the farmer's, and the parson's wife and the daughter of the labourer." Selborne had seen for the first time ever "a woman ploughing."[41] The editor of the *Call* noted that the situation was not as grim in Canada, but that women could be seen ploughing in the West and even pulling the ploughs, "although this was done among the foreigners." He called on Canada to "make it fashionable for the ladies to work on the farm," reinforcing the idea that it was decidedly not fashionable, or acceptable, labour.

Women farm labourers were not desired for a variety of reasons, including that they might provide a rationale for conscripting farmers, farmers' sons, and farm workers. These categories were exempted from conscription until the spring of 1918, and in that year in Saskatchewan a report of the Special Committee on Farm Labour recommended that "unlikely or reluctant sources of labour, including women and children," be pressed into service.[42] But this did not happen. Farmers instead reduced labour-intensive farming practices and invested in machinery. In

1918 an "anti-loafing" law threatened every man between sixteen and sixty who was not gainfully employed with a jail sentence.[43]

Throughout the prairies women worked on farms, as they had always done, and they stepped in to do tasks normally done by missing husbands, brothers, fathers, and sons. Women from the cities and towns also pitched in. In 1917 women were reported to be "doing their bit" in the Alberta harvest fields. Alberta's Deputy Minister of Agriculture H.A. Craig reported that he had seen "women wearing overalls, pitching hay, handling rakes and forks with a spirit and efficiency that makes the average harvest hand look like a slacker."[44] The women helping with the 1917 harvest in Minnedosa, Manitoba, were similarly adept: "One was driving a binder. She handled the long-lashed whip and lines of the four-horse team with the dexterity of a man, while the twine-bound sheaves dropped regularly off the carriage as she tripped the lever."[45] When "foreign" farm workers brought in to work on a threshing outfit at Mather, Manitoba, left after one day on the job, women of the district stepped in, and "on most outfits three or four women will be found driving teams."[46]

In Manitoba in August 1917, Brandon's "Telephone Girls" went stooking.[47] The "hello" girls of Manitoba Government Telephones had "caught the fever and had formed a stooking gang," vowing to "not return home until they have stooked one acre each." This was the first time in the Brandon district that "men were supplemented by women workers." There were also thirteen young women among a gang of fifty stookers drawn from a laundry and creamery in Brandon at work that fall.[48]

Calgary organized a small "land army" of its own in 1917, called the Calgary Business Women's National Service Corps.[49] They were "patriotic business girls" who worked in stores, offices, or schools by day, and "instead of going to the golf links and tennis courts during the summer evenings, they were exercising with the hoe, and growing potatoes to increase production." They claimed to "hate Wilhelm, and intend to do everything they can to defeat his object." The city loaned them three acres of raw prairie land and had it ploughed for them. The public was "rather skeptical at first, but eventually they took it seriously, and folk would often drive out in their cars to 'see the girls working.'" For 1918 the plan was to grow a wider range of vegetables on vacant lots in the city. They wore overalls, as skirts impeded their work, and "at first many were reluctant to be seen on the streets in overalls, so they would hurry along on fine evenings wearing rain coats, but towards the end they got over this and

Calgary's Land Army

Which Helps Win the War by Raising Food Ammunition

Miss Veta Lindsay

By Veta Lindsay

Secretary of the Corps

"What's them women doing over there, I want to know."

This enquiry came from a man returning home from his labors, early one summer evening last year.

"Why, they're them there German and Austrian women. You read about them working on the land in their own country, guess they are doing the same here, war economy kind of thing for their own needs, queer creatures aint they? Husky looking, too."

So the conversation continued between the two men on the street car. Presently, when nearing the land under cultivation two more "German and Austrian women" arose from a seat just behind these men. They were dressed in blue overalls and carried themselves in a very workmanlike manner, carrying wicked-looking weapons of torture. Upon closer investigation these proved to be quite harmless garden hoes. The amazement of the men amused the rest of the passengers, as they had no idea they were in such close proximity to alien enemies.

For once, the passersby were wrong. These women working on the land were patriotic business girls, who spent their days working in offices, and stores, and teaching in schools. Instead of going to the golf links, and tennis courts during the summer evenings, they were exercising with the hoe, and growing potatoes to help increase production. For one day last April one of Calgary's business girls became panic stricken with the awful shortage of food, and felt that there were other women who were working on office stools and behind counters who would be willing to go on the land during the evenings and grow something that would help increase production. The matter was then taken up by the press, and quite a number of women came forward and offered to do this work.

An Organization Formed

A meeting was called, and of the number present quite a large precentage indicated their willingness to do what they could. Then an organization was formed, more or less on military lines. It was named the Calgary Business Womens' National Service Corps. Several land owners offered their land for cultivation, and also the city offered its help. It was requested that the city farm grant the use of three acres of land for the purpose of growing potatoes, on the condition that the methods of cultivation meet with the approval of the city. This was sanctioned by the city, and the three acres were loaned to the organization to be cultivated. Several city farm officials gave instruction at the beginning, as most of the members were absolute novices in regard to agricultural work. The City Farm Department also sold the seed potatoes to the organization as at that time it was rather late to start and there was a scarcity of good seed potatoes. There were three kinds used, the Round Red, Lily White and Early Harvest. The, Round Red turned out the best, but the Lily White were the largest potatoes although not so prolific as the others. The price paid was $1.75 per bushel and 15 bushel to the acre was an average.

The land which was cultivated was just raw prairie land, and therefore very heavy to work. The City had it plowed before it was handed over to be worked, but the girls decided to have it disced again. Several times it was gone over. That of course had to be paid for by the organization.

It took some hard work to make the trenches to drop the potatoes into. And during the two weeks that it took the girls to put these potatoes in, there was much back aching, and many grunts and groans heard in various offices. The public was rather skeptical at first, but eventually they took it seriously, and folk would often drive out in their cars to "see the girls working." You may be sure if there were any available helpers they were at once commandeered for work, or else they would move away pretty quickly. However, if they did not help that night, they would come back another evening in working togs, and join in the work. Also there were a few men from the various offices who had been recruited by some of the stenographers to give a hand occasionally.

Potato Production Platoons

The work was divided into sections, a lieutenant being in charge of each section. There were three sections, one Sunday school section, one Community section, where all worked together, and the other Individual section, where each girl had a small piece to work for herself.

After the potatoes were planted and until the time for the potatoes to be hoed arrived, the girls had a little time for other things. The rows were then cultivated by a cultivating machine, and afterwards the girls went over them with the hoes, but this did not take very much time or work.

When these mundane but very necessary tubers were ready to be taken up, a special effort was made through the press to enlist volunteer aid, and quite

AT THE END OF A PERFECT DAY
This photo was taken late one Saturday afternoon during the digging season.

Figure 39. Although never mobilized for work on the land during the First World War as they were in Britain, the United States, and Ontario, women on the prairies contributed to work on the land and to food production. Calgary teachers and office workers formed their own "land army" in 1917, working in the long summer evenings on three acres provided by the City of Calgary. Their official name was the "Calgary Business Women's National Service Corps." *Grain Growers' Guide*, 10 April 1918, 32.

did not mind being seen in man's attire." According to the *Grain Growers' Guide* they all "had lots of fun on the land, and thoroughly enjoyed the experience in spite of the fact that it was hard work."

Women's volunteer "reserve corps" were organized in other urban centres of the prairies during the First World War, but without any attention to farm work. The object was to "be able to defend themselves in case of danger" and to "prepare so that in an emergency the women of the city could undertake the performance of all the duties of an army back of the firing line." There were first aid, telegraph, and telephone sections, and the women were trained in the use of rifles and riding. They also raised funds through events such as dances.[50]

Women from other regions offered to help on prairie farms. In August 1917 there were 2,000 women from British Columbia available and willing to help with the prairie harvest.[51] They had just finished the fruit harvest in that province, and the B.C. Consumers League which had organized them was prepared to take immediate steps to send them once given the green light from the National Service Commission. Perhaps permission was never received, as there is no record of an influx of women harvesters from British Columbia.

There were women from eastern Canada in the wartime harvest excursions who travelled west by train. Most were from Quebec and the Maritimes. This was not an entirely new departure, as women and children had come from the east to help with the harvest prior to the war.[52] During the war, however, eastern women were recruited not to help in the fields but to assist the "farmer's wife who finds herself at harvest time with a bunch of hungry men to cook for and no help available."[53] The Canadian Northern Railway announced in August 1917 that for the first time women would be coming west in numbers that were large enough to warrant special cars, and that policemen would travel on every train to protect them.[54] While the majority of the women were going to do household work in farm homes, particularly cooking, some had declared they were willing to work in the fields if needed.

As in the example of women harvest excursioners, women's war work remained restricted to the domestic realm, limiting their work in the fields, even in the last months of the war. Scepticism remained about the ability of women to farm. A 1916 article, "Women and the Farm: A Mistake to Think That Women Are Capable of Hard Work," that appeared in the western press (reprinted from the Victoria *Daily Colonist*) presented the view that "it is a mistake to think that women can bear as heavy burdens and lift as great weights as men can. The plow and the axe are not implements which women should be asked to use."[55] Yet there was some room for compromise, as the (familiar) argument was made that young women were suited to the "lighter branches" of agriculture. The article concluded, however, that this activity was temporary, that while some women after the war might claim the right to high wages, "the majority of women will be only too glad to return to their household duties."

In 1918 there were calls in Alberta for women volunteers, not to work in the fields but to take the place of men who would. As Edmonton journalist Miriam Green Ellis wrote in February of that year, urban women would be of little use on the farm, except to help the farm wife in the house and to liberate her to do work in the fields.[56] Ellis was acquainted with a few women who farmed on their own, and one woman who knew far more about their prize shorthorn cattle than her husband, but these, in her view, were exceptions. Women could, however, work in offices, garages, freight sheds, hotels, restaurants, libraries, as janitors, chauffeurs, and mail carriers, freeing up ex-farmers who could return to the land. In March of that year a meeting was held in Edmonton of women volunteers who were ready to "help out farm women at the cook stove" and replace men in stores and offices.[57]

Journalists, editors, and women's organizations endorsed the idea that women were wanted on the prairies to help with domestic work. Zoa Haight, vice-president of the Women Grain Growers of Saskatchewan, met with the Saskatchewan minister of agriculture in 1918 to say that the question of domestic help for the farms should be put "on a patriotic basis," meaning volunteer labour, as it was in the direct interest of greater production. The *Saskatoon Star Phoenix* set out the classes of women who could pitch in: single women who could work in stores and offices; married women with older children or without children to work in farm homes; married women with domestics who could give them leave for three weeks or more to help in farm homes. Women were admonished for not seeing this work as an obligation. A Toronto *Globe* editorial criticized Canadian women, commenting that "very few have responded to the need of the country in the way in which thousands in France, Belgium and Great Britain have done. The need has not been so acute in the West until now, but by the time the crop is ready to harvest, there will be a need for women to help the farmer's wife, which, if it is not met, means a serious loss to the Allies."[58]

Prairie women, including First Nations women, were encouraged to undertake Red Cross work, to make bandages, and to knit. For some these tasks were added to work in the fields. At a January 1918 meeting of the Women Grain Growers of Saskatchewan, it was noted that it was difficult to find the time for the Red Cross Work. Zoa Haight, "drove a binder for 10 days last fall, and kept up her Red Cross work at night."[59]

In his 1916 book *Canada and the War: The Promise of the West,* which looked forward into the postwar future of the West, J.H. Menzies saw the soldiers as fighting to preserve a gender order that was central to the British Empire. He noted that there would be many more single women after the war, but their place would be primarily in the home and associated domestic vocations. He wrote that men liked qualities and dispositions in women that were "contrary to their own. They think best of the delicacy of form and amiable softness of the other sex, deeming the milder virtues—gentleness, patience, compassion, tenderness, to sit with peculiar grace upon women, who are expected to excel too in piety, faith, hope and resignation."[60] Delicate womanhood was a central component of the "civilization" that the soldiers were fighting to preserve.[61] There were warnings of the masculinization of females in jobs that were normally male. Readers of the Alberta *Empress Express* in 1918 were told that this was happening to women in munitions factories, that "sociologists speak of this as the virility produced by heavy work—forerunner of the Amazon women who are coming."[62]

There were, however, signs of preparations for women to potentially work more visibly and in larger numbers on prairie farms. Beginning in 1916 some women attended the agricultural course at the Alberta Provincial School of Agriculture at Olds. According to the school, this was simply due to the fact that so many young men had been called to the colours, and "under ordinary circumstances it is not necessary for young ladies to take the heavier class of work."[63] In 1918 it was reported that "one young lady, Miss Erma Poedler took the complete course."[64] At the Manitoba Agricultural College in 1918, many of the students in the home economics class were also taking the regular course on operating gas engines and tractors.[65] Yet the work of young women university students on farms on the prairies was rare enough to attract attention. The *Grain Growers' Guide* noted that in 1917 Miss Annie Norrington, a science student at the

University of Manitoba, had worked for the summer as a "hired man" on a farm in that province, and returned for the 1918 season. She ploughed, seeded, hayed, and mended fences.[66]

At the *Grain Growers' Guide,* women's page editor Mary P. McCallum wanted women to have a place in the production and not just conservation of food, and she urged they be employed to feed stock and care for poultry and vegetable gardens.[67] She hoped the government would enlist the "vast army of women workers in Canada today. We have one half of the population of Canada today absolutely overlooked and unorganized for war service on a national basis. Why can women not be given a definite and positive place in the production campaign?" But there was debate in the *Guide* about how women could contribute to the world's food supply and about the suitability of women for farm labour. Agreeing with Miriam Green Ellis, quoted above, in a February 1918 letter to the *Guide,* Mrs. M.E. Graham of Alberta claimed that much of the work on a farm was "beyond the strength of the average Canadian city girl."[68] Graham contended it would take considerable training to equip the city woman to handle a four-horse team and plough. It required strength to stook and pitch hay or sheaves and load manure.

McCallum did not agree with Graham, and she wrote columns that challenged this view, including a feature article in March 1918 on Ruth Hillman of Keeler (discussed in Chapter 4) under the title "Who Said Women Can't Farm: Miss R.M. Hillman … Disproves Any Such Fallacy."[69] There was a lengthy article on "Feminizing the Farm: How Ontario is Promoting Agriculture among Women" by Laura E. Nixon, in a 1918 issue of the *Guide,* that described the skill, energy, and enthusiasm of the farmerettes, who even included former "society butterflies" and who had learned to milk, feed livestock, care for poultry, run machinery, and take on numerous other tasks at the three-week course offered at the Ontario Agricultural College.[70] An article by McCallum, in the fall of 1918, on "Women and Their Gas Wagons" was about how women on farms in the West were able to assist so much more once they learned to drive, making trips to town for marketing and repairs that would have previously been the job of the male farmer, who could instead stay at work on the land.[71] Western women also had learned to drive tractors and enjoyed it, according to McCallum.

Headlines such as "Woman Farmer, Husband in the Trenches, Meets Awful Accident While Preparing Land for Crop" likely did not help the cause.[72] The article described how in May 1917, Mrs. E.P. Arnott, of Elk Point, Alberta, lost an arm and an eye while running the disc behind a three-horse team. Thrown in a runaway when the team suddenly took fright, she was found by the hired man under the disc. Mrs. Arnott survived with the aid of the Canadian Patriotic Fund that paid for her doctor and nurse, and her neighbours rallied to put in the crop on the Arnott farm.

In the final months of the war there was a desperate call for the labour of "every woman and every teenage girl" to assist with the harvest of 1918. In the article "War's Call to Farms: Men Must Fight and Women Must Reap" that was printed in several western papers, it was noted that in Russia, Italy, France, Belgium, and Britain, women were engaged in all varieties of farm work and that "what the women of Canada have done in this line is negligible yet, although there has been some brave pioneering in Eastern Ontario." Accompanied by photographs of women at work in England and Ontario, the article stated that Canada "needed her daughters to rally now," before the grain rotted:

> The time to act is now! It does not matter a scrap what is or ever will be: what her social status, her occupation, her share of this world's goods. There is a new democracy abroad—a wonderful levelling of grades. Usefulness and service are the things that count. Every woman must search her soul and ask herself how she can best help in taking care of the harvest of 1918 … In short every woman and every teenage girl can do something … It is one of the biggest things ever asked of a woman. It is for the sake of our allies. But most of all for our men—"over there."[73]

But the West survived the war without ever forming a women's land army. Why were women of prairie Canada not mobilized for farm work in the same way as they were in Ontario? In fact there was almost an opposite reaction: women were deliberately steered away from field work and toward domestic work in farm homes. Reasons likely included organizational challenges, many of which were overcome in Ontario, but in the West the scale of the work was much more vast and the harvest season shorter. There were the prevailing attitudes discussed above, that women were physically incapable of farm work, but why were beliefs ignored, at least for the duration of the war, in the case of the farmerettes in Ontario?

Did the absence of organized farm labour for women on the prairies also have something to do with the fact that for years before the war, federal government officials and politicians had declared, particularly in answer to calls for homestead rights, that women were not capable of the work required on farms? They could not suddenly seem to reverse this long-standing position.

NEW RATIONALES AND RENEWED EFFORTS: HOMESTEADS FOR WOMEN AND BRITISH WOMEN SETTLERS

While there was no longer a concerted campaign, pressure to permit women the homestead privilege continued during the war years, with the added rationale that women on their own homesteads would address the need for greater production. Another rationale was that if there was to be free land for returned soldiers, women too should be granted this right. Nellie McClung wrote her most sustained article on the topic in 1915, in "Free Land for the Soldier," which had little to say about land for soldiers except for a brief introduction, and a conclusion that asked if nurses would be given land grants.[74] Most of the article reviewed the rationales for the agitation that began years before the war. The emphasis on granting homesteads to women of "British birth" only had been dropped, although McClung anticipated that the land grant would attract "a great many women from the old countries, fine, cultured, educated women, the type we need so badly to settle up our prairies." She mocked the responses of government officials: "They cannot bear to contemplate [a] lovely woman engaged in the menial task of planting potatoes! They say it is not a woman's place. Of course women may plant potatoes for other people, and have been known to do quite as heavy work as that of proving up a homestead so long as she does not do it for herself, it is all right." McClung addressed the concern that there would not be enough land for everyone if returned soldiers were awarded by claiming that only 2.3 percent of land in Canada was under cultivation. Other wartime conditions provided McClung with additional arguments. She knew an English girl, a "brave daughter of the Empire," who was maintaining her brother's Alberta homestead while he was at the front, minding his stock and travelling seventy-five miles to Edmonton to market pigs and fowl. "Yet if this brave girl, this splendid citizen, wished to own an acre of land she must pay for it," McClung wrote. "She may work like a man. She may endure all the hardships and discomfort and loneliness (against which there is no law). But there is no free land for such as she!"

In 1915 the Toronto *Globe* came out in support of an end to discrimination in the homestead law, arguing that extending the right to women would induce rural girls to stay away from cities.[75] Supporters cited the war work of women on the land in Great Britain, where they were encouraged to cultivate the land, which led "naturally to the wish to own land in their own right."[76] Refusal to grant homestead rights was "caused by the survival of the old spirit which refused to allow women to attend university and still in some places, closes the doors of certain professions against them." At a Liberal convention in Winnipeg in 1917, a resolution was adopted asking that women be allowed to homestead on the same terms as men. The overwhelming majority of the delegates supported the resolution, although opponents "voiced the old arguments that women on account of their physical weakness could not possibly stand the rigorous homesteading life."[77]

In 1918 the Local Councils of Women in Saskatchewan began to seriously agitate for homesteads on the same terms as men.[78] According to the Regina *Leader*, "With the need of greater production being emphasized so strongly, there are many women endlessly thinking of what their duty is; and forever wishing they could become producers, by any other means than just becoming servants of some farmer's wife." That year the Alberta Women's Institutes convention called on Canada "to make homesteads as easily available for women as for men."[79] The rationales articulated in the resolution drew on wartime conditions, referring to a conference of representative women of Canada with the war committee of the Dominion cabinet that recommended "wider participation of women in agricultural pursuits" and short courses for women to fit them for agricultural labour. Nearly two dozen women at the Alberta convention spoke in favour of the resolution, describing the outdoor work they did on farms. Some had homesteads, and several spoke of how they operated farm machinery. Cecilia Dahl of Standard, Alberta, "capped the climax when she stated she had run the mower with a baby in her lap." President Isabel Noble said that it had been demonstrated beyond doubt that "homesteads were no trick for women to manage." It was also pointed out at the convention that in the summer of 1918 women expected to show that they were capable of working on a farm "in a way they have never before attempted."[80]

Letters inquiring about women's homestead rights continued to arrive in Ottawa during the war years, and by 1918 there was a new element in the government's response. Estella B. Carter wrote from Maryland in June 1918 to ask if she and three other young women, three teachers and one with a business education, could obtain homesteads in "a good wheat section of Canada."[81] If they got located and liked it, they would be followed by a party of four others. They had taken a course in school gardening at the Normal School. She received the standard answer, and one new addition: "While the Dominion Government offers to settlers in Western Canada free homesteads of 160 acres, a woman is not privileged to make homestead entry unless she is the sole head of a family having minor children dependent on her. Moreover, all the available free land within approximately fifteen miles of any existing railway line has been reserved for purposes of soldier settlement."[82]

The war helped to further masculinize the prairie West in several ways. Beginning in 1917 it became easier for farm labourers to file on homesteads of their own through a War Measures Act that relaxed the residency requirements, allowing them to count farm employment (on the farms of others) "as a like period of residence in connection with their respective entries."[83] They had to submit sworn evidence of farm employment. The cultivation required to earn patent could be performed in two years instead of three. More than 89,000 homesteads were filed on during the war years.[84] Plans for the settlement of returned soldiers in Western Canada began well before the war ended. A Soldier Settlement Act was first passed in 1917 and was confirmed in 1919. Under a March 1917 order-in-council, returned soldiers who had served overseas and who had been honourably discharged were given the prior right of one day to enter on a homestead in the event of land becoming available for settlement.[85] A year later, to facilitate the acquisition of homestead land for returned soldiers, an order-in-council withdrew the privilege of pre-emption and purchased homesteads.[86]

Beginning in 1918, extensive sections of Dominion lands on the prairies were reserved for soldier settlers. There also began a concerted and successful attempt to acquire Indigenous reserve land from the occupants and make it available for returning non–First Nations soldiers.[87] As explained in the House of Commons by the minister of the interior, the idea was to assist and compensate "those brave lads of ours who have gone from our country and who have been subjected to such terrible hardships. They have acquitted themselves in a manner that has won the admiration of the world. They have gone to the front and done their duty like men, and this offer is meant as some recognition on the part of a grateful country ... If by offering this assistance we can place the soldiers upon the soil and increase our production we shall have accomplished what we have in view."[88] The Empire Settlement Act of 1922 also favoured male agriculturalists; veterans and their families.[89]

The issue of whether nurses who served overseas should be granted the right to homestead land under the Soldier Settlement Act was debated in the House of Commons in 1919. Isaac Pedlow, member of Parliament for South Renfrew said that "settler" in the act was defined as "a person who at any time during the war 'has been therein engaged on active service in a military force.' Does not that definition include nursing sisters?"[90] Minister of the Interior Arthur Meighen replied that the act would not apply to nurses, that "the policy of the board was definitely not to include women," and that "the purpose of the Bill is settlement and the only women who come within its provisions are widows of fallen soldiers. They are included because it was felt, first, that they had a special claim, and secondly, because very frequently widows of soldiers have boys growing up who can render material assistance and make the proposition one of actual settlement. The ordinary nurse, I am afraid, could not come within that promising class, and I do not think that returned nurses should, in their own interests, be encouraged to make settlement on land their occupation in life."[91] Pedlow stated that he had already had an application from a nurse who wanted a homestead and asked if the matter would be considered by the department, but the answer from Meighen was again no, that "I do not propose to include women."

Historian Veronica Strong-Boag describes how the First World War nurse Mary Alice Blackwell Turner enlisted others who had served overseas in fighting to acquire the right to homestead, and Turner claimed a Peace River homestead.[92] To clarify the issue, an amendment was made to the legislation in 1920 that formally excluded nursing sisters from the Soldier Settlement Act.[93] This restriction varied throughout the British colonies. The First World War nurses could apply for land in their own right as veterans in Australia and New Zealand, for example.[94] But in Canada, ex-soldiers received homestead land, loans, and in some cases training in farming, none of which was available to the nurses who had served overseas.

There was to be no postwar relaxation of the homestead laws; in fact, new rationales were added for excluding women. Nothing that women did during the war either overseas or at home persuaded federal government officials that women (other than widows with children) should be permitted to homestead. Nor did the fact that most non–First Nations women in Canada (with the exception of Quebec) could vote. A resolution asking that homestead privileges be extended to women on the same basis as men was passed at the 1919 conventions of the United Farmers and Farm Women of Alberta. It read: "Whereas women are taxed for the support of the Government the same as men, therefore we feel that any natural resources that the Government has to put at the disposal of its citizens should be free to all, irrespective of sex, and we most respectfully ask that Homesteading privileges be extended to women on an equality with men."[95] The resolution was sent to the Department of the Interior, which replied that there was no reason why the policy that had been pursued in the past should be changed "in view of the fact that homestead land is getting scarce, and all Dominion Lands within fifteen miles of a railroad are reserved for Soldier Settlement purposes."[96] A departmental memorandum outlined further rationales for not acting upon any such resolution: "Dealing with the question from the standpoint of the welfare of the women, it would not seem good policy to extend the privilege asked for as it would mean the homesteader would be practically isolated from easy access to the market or medical attention, and the position of the homesteader would be made harder in the Provinces of Manitoba and Saskatchewan where the winter climate is more severe than in the Province of Alberta."[97]

"THEY ARE LONGING TO CROSS THE ATLANTIC": BRITISH WOMEN FARMERS FOR CANADA

Interest in placing British women on homesteads and farms in Western Canada did not entirely abate during the war, and there was optimistic anticipation for a new era after the war. In a series of articles on "The Land of Hope" by American-born English journalist Elizabeth Banks, published in the *Lady's Pictorial* in 1917, the cause of British women farmers for Canada was presented once again.[98] Banks believed that the agricultural training many were receiving during the war helped to suit them for the task. She wrote, "To become a farmer, to stake out a claim, is not certainly a job for every woman. It needs strength, excellent health, great determination. But these are qualities in which many women of the Old Country are not lacking as witness the work they are now doing to release the men at the front." Banks called on Canada to give women the same privileges as men with regard to land.

During the war, the perceived problem of "surplus women" emerged once again as a rationale for sending British women to the colonies. It was predicted that there would be an acute imbalance of men and women in the "motherland," that marriage would be impossible for many women, and that they should, "with the faith to venture and the courage to dare, move to those parts of the Empire where they are wanted."[99] Journalist Amy B. Barnard wrote in 1916 that "the Empire is making at this crisis a clear call to the strong, capable daughters of the Motherland to spread British civilization, language, just rule and righteous living in the overseas dominions."[100] She singled out Saskatchewan and Alberta as most in need because "we are in a minority" there, and "our wonderful Empire should be peopled by the British race." The war, according to Barnard, had strengthened the ties between the motherland and the overseas dominion. Barnard emphasized that teachers, nurses, stenographers, and bookkeepers were needed, but she stressed the need for "home helps." In urging the prospective emigrant to think of the prairies, she comforted them that "it is unnecessary for a woman to learn ploughing and rough farming, as some imagine." Yet farm skills were needed for work in the homes of others. Barnard urged that they take a course at the Hoebridge Overseas Training School at Woking, where a "Canadian lady" was introducing students to fruit and vegetable culture, and dairy and poultry work.[101] With the article's emphasis throughout on women's mission to help build a "sturdy race" in the colonies, it was not surprising that it ended with the prediction that "love and a happy marriage" awaited many of the emigrants.[102]

There is no doubt that wartime activities on the land made some women consider agriculture as a vocation, including the "farmerettes" of Ontario, some of whom wanted to continue to farm after the war and to have land of their own.[103] In "Farmerettes Want Farms" (1918), Violet Dickens asked, "Why should land fit for cultivation lie idle while there are women and girls willing to use it and increase production?" Dickens favoured the idea of the government controlling "idle" land in Ontario (as in the West), and she advocated that the government assist women war workers to acquire small farms after the war.

Nurses who had served in the war declared a desire to go "back to the land." In 1920 "Polly Peele," writing for the Toronto *Globe*, said that women as well as men sought peace and calm in the countryside for their "overworked nerves and weary spirits," for which there was "no balm like that of the blue sky overhead and the brown earth underfoot."[104] She described the Ontario six-acre farm called "Cornerways," occupied by two demobilized nurses who preferred the out-of-doors to their former profession. They had poultry and grew apple and cherry trees. Alice Watkins, a graduate of Royal Victoria Hospital in Montreal, had been stationed in Egypt and France. Her partner, Mary Spence, was from Scotland but had been nursing on the prairies before the war. Peele reported that another nurse from England had a position on a nearby farm, where she was doing "the sort of service that, in ante-bellum days, would have been the work of a 'hired man.'"

There had been optimism that the war would usher in a "new day" of opportunity for non-Indigenous women and the vocation of agriculture on the prairies. At the *Grain Growers' Guide*, women's page editor Mary P. McCallum wrote in 1918 that the "war is having the effect of bringing women in our own country to a realization that there is a place in agricultural operations for women. And women are needed in agriculture."[105]

Reflecting this new optimism, Ellen M. Knox, principal of Havergal College, Toronto, included farming in her book *The Girl of the New Day*, which detailed the opportunities that now beckoned. After the war women as well as men, Knox wrote, "are longing for a road lying out of doors, a road lying in and 'about the feet of God.'"[106] She called on girls to take their place "among the world's adventurers and explorers," becoming hewers and blazers of trails.[107] There was a chapter on "The Joy of Farming" and one on "The Call of the West." The war had demonstrated that women were capable farmers, although Knox emphasized the suitability of "lighter branches." Knox wrote that it was "somewhat late in the day" to ask if small farming was "physically within the reach of women"... when "during war time, countless women have tackled that hardest of all farming—Western farming—and 'kept the pot a-boiling' whilst their husbands were away."[108]

Knox urged young women to go to British Columbia, and she echoed the claims Binnie-Clark made in 1913 that a small farm on Vancouver Island could grow from modest beginnings into a "large and profitable venture."[109] She also endorsed the idea of a "colony of capable women, enamoured of farming who are thrilled at new discoveries and new adventures." The best candidates, in her view, were "out-of-door women" "of good stock, Canadian, Scotch and English ... exactly what will bring fresh vitality into places run down and discouraged by unscientific farming and intermarriage."[110] (Intermarriage with "foreigners" or "aliens" was the implied meaning.) They should be "cultured women" who have been "and always will be the true backbone of country as well as town life."

But even Knox herself did not anticipate an entirely "new day." Despite the emphasis on vocations for women, including farming, throughout the book, and contradicting herself in many ways, Knox emphasized the need for suitable women as wives, particularly in her chapter "The Call of the West." (Her final chapter, "The Queen of Them All," was about the most honourable profession—motherhood.) Women were not required on the prairies as cultivators, Knox argued, but as household helps and domestic servants. The "chief mission of women in the West," Knox wrote, was "the converting of shacks into homes."[111] Women of "gentle birth" were needed to partner with the men who had "'bached' in more or less discomfort or married half-breeds as a simple expedient for obtaining a housekeeper." She called on Canadian and English girls to head to the West as their duty: "Surely women who have helped the men out so nobly in their fight against a foreign foe will play their part in the conquering of their own country. It is in these outposts that women are most needed. It is their privilege to lend a hand in the work at which men have far too long struggled single-handed, and it is their duty as well as privilege to help to lay the foundation of the social life of that glorious West that is the true Canada."[112]

Optimism for a "new day" for women was challenged and disputed, however. In "Must We Rely on Girl Labor?," a *Globe* columnist of May 1919 complimented women for "stepping into the breach" and tilling the fields, harvesting, picking fruit, handling stock, and other tasks. They were as hardworking and efficient as men, and their help was of "vital importance."[113] But "women, to say nothing of growing girls, were not meant for farm labor in normal times any more than they were made for freight-handling or coalmining. It was an abnormality of circumstance that put them in agricultural life in actual outdoor work these past two years, and it is a false economic tenet that promises their continued employment." It was "unworthy" to suppose that required food "is to be forthcoming from girl labor."

Land Army workers in England wondered how they might be able to use their experience to make a living after the war, although there were warnings that openings would be limited, as men were returning to farm and garden work, and the "lighter" tasks would be suitable for the wounded ex-servicemen.[114] Given that prospects for positions as farm or garden labourers were dismal, there was interest in how the former land girl could "make good on [her] own land."[115] Emigration to the colonies was one solution. Knox wrote, "Women must emigrate. They see no prospect of betterment in England, and will not go back to the humdrum of pre-war days. They are longing to cross the Atlantic." While Knox thought that there were openings in domestic service for them, she believed it "cheaper and wiser to provide outlets for them on farms."[116]

Anxious to get back into the business of sending "gentlewomen" as settlers to Western Canada, and convinced that a new era had dawned due to women's work on the land during the war, in 1918 Caroline Grosvenor, founder of the Colonial Intelligence League, wrote a "private and confidential memorandum on emigration after the war."[117] The CIL was in its last months of existence, as a process of amalgamation with the British Women's Emigration Association and the South African Colonisation Society was already begun. But Grosvenor, still wanting to address the need for openings for the "educated" woman, mounted arguments for the continuation of the CIL, working in cooperation with other emigration societies. She proposed that the CIL form a "sort of women's overseas corps" divided into two sections: domestic workers and land workers. She was concerned with the great number of women who were to be "thrown out of work," including land workers, and she thought many would want to go to the overseas dominions. These women had learned to work hard and they would "dislike going back to a rather objectless existence. There are already signs that a considerable number will want to go overseas." Grosvenor was convinced that the war had changed attitudes and opened new doors. Canada and Australia desperately needed workers on the land, and "the number of men engaged in this work is alas! bound to be much smaller," while "the old argument that women have neither the physique nor the experience of land work can be met by showing them what women land workers have done in this country during the last three or four years." She proposed that recruits be taken from upper-crust organizations such as the Women's National Land Service Corps and the Voluntary Aid Detachment Nurses, as these were women of "the educated class."

Grosvenor's private memo appears to have been sent to her colleagues in the other organizations, soon to be amalgamated into the Society for the Oversea Settlement of British Women (SOSBW). The CIL, determined to aid only the "educated gentlewoman," was joining with associations that were concerned with working-class girls and women. Only one response to the private memorandum is included in the CIL papers, that of a polite Miss A.L. Vernon, who thought the corps idea to be excellent, but believed that all social classes had to be included in emigration schemes.[118] Vernon wrote that there were many "rough farms where the girl of the Land Army type would get on better than a WNLSC girl."

When the war ended, there were more strident calls for the single women of England to emigrate as that "cruel old phrase, 'superfluous woman'" came back into use.[119] Canada was seen as the most likely destination, but other colonies and dominions of the Empire were included.[120] But little aside from domestic service awaited single women. Not much had changed as a result of women's participation in occupations previously the preserve of men in factories, farms, and forests. The dominions were clear that women were wanted as domestic servants, and as wives and mothers. In 1919 a Canadian official with External Affairs wrote that "no encouragement should be given to skilled women workers to come to Canada."[121] They were urged to emigrate primarily for the men of the dominions who "want to marry but cannot find wives."[122] The highest officials in immigration, both in Canada and England, continued to have a dim view of women farmers and no interest in encouraging them. Superintendent of Immigration W.D. Scott wrote to J. Obed Smith in February 1919: "Personally I am of the opinion that patriotism had much to do with the energy displayed by women in agriculture and the cessation of the war will find very few who will continue."[123] Scott believed that conditions were too difficult for women farmers in Canada and that few took up the career as a matter of choice.

Demobilized or other British women contemplating Canada were warned: "If you want to go to the colonies because you like the man's work you did during the War, and hope to get something of the same kind in the untrammeled new country more easily than you could in England, you are under an illusion. You are far more likely to be forced back into a traditionally feminine occupation in the colonies."[124] Domestic work, nursing, and teaching were the only posts women could possibly obtain in the colonies. Even those with capital who wanted to eventually establish a business, including a fruit or poultry farm, in Canada were urged to go there first as a home help. Once again, as in the pre-war propaganda of emigration advocates, potential colonists were assured that they would find work among families "of gentle breeding, of English or Scotch origin who would treat the girl from the Home Country as a younger sister."[125]

The idea of emigration did appeal, however, to many women in Britain after the war, because of the contraction of employment opportunities there and the backlash they experienced if they wanted to continue in their new vocations. Approval of their work in wartime had been replaced by "often vicious condemnation." They went from being "saviours of the nation" to "ruthless self seekers, depriving men and their dependents of a livelihood."[126] As historian Lucy Noakes has argued, the "new" women of the war, the ex-servicewomen and members of the Land Army, were "troublesome and potentially disruptive."[127] They had been tolerated as a "rather regrettable necessity" during the war, but were "resented by the men they displaced, and criticized for both their allegedly masculine activities and appearance, and, conversely, for their supposed sexual promiscuity."

Those who had served in the three auxiliary services—the Queen Mary's Army Auxiliary Corps, the Women's Royal Navy Corps, and the Women's Auxiliary Air Force—were seen as particularly problematic, "bold," and masculine as a result of their military work. The land girls were reported to be "inured to labour and have learned to love the soil, but now they want a change of scene, many hoping to find it in Canada."[128] The British government was interested in sending these and other women to the colonies in order to help address the problem of unemployment due to demobilization after the war; they were not to be allowed to threaten the employment of ex-soldiers.

A Free Passage Scheme was made available to ex-servicewomen (who had completed a minimum of six months service) as well as to men, to send "trained defenders of the Empires' borders" to the colonies, help strengthen bonds within the Empire, address the issue of "falling numbers of white settlers," and help to balance the numbers of British men and women in the Empire. There was no mistaking the "science" of eugenics sentiments behind support for the emigration of women. An official involved with emigration to South Africa expressed concern about "the danger to the Race both at home and in the Dominions if an active Post-War migration left large numbers of the best strains of Womanhood here unmated while it condemned the best strains of Manhood in the Dominions to Celibacy or to marriage with lower types."[129]

Single women, orphans, and ex-servicewomen appeared to British government officials to be the likeliest candidates for emigration. An Overseas Settlement Committee (OSC) was formed in 1919, and it worked with the organizations that joined together to become the SOSBW.[130] The British government members on the OSC (Lord Alfred Milner, Leo Amery) saw ex-servicemen as settlers and farmers in the colonies, while ex-servicewomen were understood to be future wives and mothers. Representatives from the pre-war emigration societies continued to contend, however, that more than marriage had to be offered to educated women. (The domestic class of emigrant women would be content with domestic work and marriage.) And they insisted that ex-servicewomen deserved recognition for their wartime service and should have opportunities for incomes of their own.

But little had changed; Canada was interested in women as home helps and in men as farmers. OSC delegates to the colonies found the same situation prevailed in all, that there was an urgent demand for domestic servants. Authorities in the colonies seemed to be unwilling to regard ex-servicewomen any differently from other female migrants. Yet the ex-servicewomen interested in emigrating were not willing to undertake domestic work at home. This was "deeply unattractive" employment for ex-servicewomen and other women, and the Free Passage Scheme failed to attract anything like the numbers initially predicted.[131] In 1920 the home economics department of the Macdonald Institute of the Ontario Agricultural College in Guelph established a twelve-month program to provide British ex-servicewomen and ex–Land Army women with training for Canada.[132] The emphasis was mainly on housework and cooking, in order to "re-domesticate" them. (It is not clear how successful this was, but as few took up the offer for free passage, it seems likely that few enrolled in this program.)

OSC commissioners Gladys S. Pott and F.M. Girdler were assigned to visit Canada in April 1919, meeting in Ottawa with ministers and deputy ministers of immigration, labour, and agriculture.[133] They also visited some of the provinces, including Alberta, and consulted with various associations and institutions concerned with women's work. They found an "urgent demand" for cooks and domestic servants, nurses, teachers, and dressmakers. Federal authorities told them that ex-servicewomen were not able "to avail themselves of the special facilities for Land Settlement allowed to demobilized soldiers." The report of the commissioners discouraged women from considering farming, pointing out the hardships of agriculture in Canada for women settlers, including the isolation "which would not make such a life a pleasant one for women." Potts declared in 1920 that "Canada is calling for strong, capable, well-educated women who are willing to take posts as home helps."[134]

In response to a July 1919 enquiry to the federal Department of Agriculture from a woman in Liverpool as to whether there were "prospects in Canada for young women who wish for open air work, whether on fruit or poultry farms, and who have during the war, been working on a farm," a letter was sent to each of the provincial agriculture departments.[135] The replies from the West were the most discouraging. T.M. Molloy of the Saskatchewan Department of Agriculture seemed irritated; they had had "inquiries of this nature from the Dominion Department of Immigration, the Repatriation Committee, the Dominion Council of the Y.W.C.A., the Y.W.C.A. of Great Britain, the Overseas Settlement Office in London." He added:

> I would state that there is practically no demand for women to do farm work in Saskatchewan, and as a matter of fact, we have discouraged the engagement of women for outside farm work preferring to place men in such situations as are available. There is, on the other hand, a very great demand for women for domestic or housework on our Saskatchewan farms, and if your Department knows of any way in which we can secure these women for farms you may direct at least five hundred to this province and we will guarantee situations for all of them. This is provided of course that they are competent and willing to accept domestic service in our farm homes.[136]

The reply from Alberta was similarly negative: there was no work on the land for young English women, but "there is now and doubtless will continue to be a demand for help for farm housework... If you feel that any of these women could be induced to undertake this line of work, we would be pleased to give every assistance possible."[137]

Compiling the results, federal Deputy Minister of Agriculture J.H. Grisdale concluded that "there is very little demand for female labour on the farms in this country, except, of course, as help in farm homes."[138]

New Brunswick and Nova Scotia were the only provinces where there was a small but very seasonal demand. Grisdale found that "the openings for this class of labour anywhere in this country are so limited that a woman would be ill-advised to emigrate to this country unless she had some other means of earning her livelihood should she fail to find employment at agricultural work."

There was some emigration of British ex-servicewomen after the war; one party of seventy-five arrived in Canada in November 1919, destined for the "farming" areas of Canada.[139] "All profess a willingness for household work," but "the tarnished word 'domestic' is never breathed in the Canadian Emigration Office." All had "worn uniform," and "a hardier, healthier seventy-five lot of girls never left this land before," according to one report.[140] In *The Girl of the New Day*, Ellen Knox was enthusiastic about these "seventy-five farm workers, women fully trained and hardened by war service, forerunners of the many to follow ... at this moment taking flight for their first essay in Western Farming. They cannot ... settle down to the tedium of indoor or society life; they ask adventure, hard work and independence."[141] More were anticipated. In June of 1919 the Salvation Army declared that it intended to bring "many hundreds of farm girls to Canada" who had served in the Land Army.[142] That year headlines such as "What Will Canada Do With These Girls?" appeared, with reports noting the "news from England that thousands of women contemplate emigration to Canada next spring, although they have no assured employment."[143] Yet the seventy-five ex-servicewomen proved to not be "forerunners of the many to follow," although there were a few others. In April 1920, eighty-three "demobilized women" who were "deprived of employment in the old country" arrived in Halifax. They had all agreed to "abandon the work of war for the more peaceful pursuits of domestic service."[144] But they did not arrive in the thousands as threatened.

There was an effort in 1919 to deliberately discourage women of the British Land Army from considering Canada as a postwar destination. J. Obed Smith, still the London-based Dominion immigration commissioner, had long been opposed to women farmers in Canada, but he now claimed that Canada's organized women were also opposed. He stated in October 1919 that while British land girls wanted to become "Canadian farmerettes," "the women of the Dominion will not let them in."[145] Smith sent a cable claiming that "opposition of women's associations in Canada to female farming is so determined that this class of immigration will not be allowed." This statement "aroused considerable questioning" in Canada. Mrs. L.A. Hamilton of the Committee on Agriculture for Women of the Canadian National Council of Women demanded to know the names of these associations.[146] She said that to the contrary, her organization hoped that Land Army women might come to Canada, and would help them in every way if they did. Hamilton stated that "their work in England kept us from many deprivations. Moreover, our Government asks for more production, and these are the women trained to put the request into effect." M. Catherine Straith of Toronto, and formerly principal of the Pennsylvania School of Horticulture for Women, wrote to the *Globe* to say that she was not able to discover which women's associations had made these statements and asked, "What justification can there be for discouraging the immigration of a desirable class of citizens who stand ready to solve one of our greatest problems?"[147] She noted the success of women farmers in the United States and Canada, and pointed out that schools of agriculture in Canada recently had admitted women. Straith concluded that "personal prejudice should have no place in a policy for the general welfare of our country. A general survey of conditions should be taken before any pronouncement is made on a subject so vital to national progress as that of immigration of women farmers."

Yet there is no doubt that some women's organizations in Canada were calling for domestic workers; to provide single women with an opportunity to acquire homestead land would have worked directly against this supply of labourers. A Canadian Council of Immigration of Women for Household Service was formed in 1919 that was comprised of representatives from many organizations, including the Women's Christian Temperance Union, the Girl's Friendly Society, the Council of Women, and International Order Daughters of the Empire.[148] This council worked to assure proper accommodation for British domestics, and members agreed to meet all boats and trains. As Mariana Valverde has written, this network of hostels and matrons was established ostensibly to protect and to assist the new arrivals, but it also functioned to "ensure that once in Canada the prospective domestic servants did not escape their fate and seek other kinds of work or relationships with men."[149]

Farm women's organizations on the prairies also called for domestic help, and not for women farmers or farm labourers.[150] In 1920 the Saskatchewan government inaugurated a plan to acquire domestic help from

England. Miss Frances A. Biden was sent to Great Britain to "select and arrange for the transportation of a number of British women and girls."[151]

The CPR also recruited domestic workers in Western Canada. Organizations such as the Calgary Central Women's Colonization Board worked closely with the CPR to secure household workers. While workers from Britain were preferred, "they would not refuse to handle women of other nationalities, particularly from northern European countries."[152] Difficulties included, however, that British girls demanded more money than "immigrant" girls who could not speak English. They preferred to work in Eastern Canada where they got higher wages.

Women as farmers and farm labourers need not apply—that was the prevailing message. Echoing J. Obed Smith's view, Premier of Quebec Sir Lomer Gouin told the Cross-Atlantic Service in May 1920 that Canada did not want British land girls as immigrants, that "work on Canadian farms is too arduous for women. Moreover Canada is not employing women to usurp men's jobs. We need women in women's jobs, especially domestic servants and wives."[153]

Despite deliberate efforts at discouragement, interest remained in agricultural work in Canada for British women. The cover of Florence B. Low's *Openings for British Women in Canada* (1920) featured a woman holding the reins of two horses harnessed for farm work, which illustrated her optimism for women's work as agriculturalists, and for the "freedom, and independence and vitality" of Canada in general, with its "invigorating and exhilarating climate."[154] The book was based on her trip to Canada in 1919–20. Low, too, emphasized that women were needed as domestic workers, teachers, and nurses, and to help solve "the excess of men over women in Canada," but held out other enticing opportunities, including farming.[155] She claimed that Canada would welcome educated women who would, "as wives and mothers ... play a great *role* in the evolution of Canada's great destiny."[156] Low devoted an entire chapter to "Agriculture: A New Occupation for Women." She believed that the work women did on the land during the war had dispelled prejudice and objections.[157] Low did, however, part ways with Binnie-Clark and the idea that women could farm grain on large acreages on the prairies, and she was silent on the subject of homestead rights for women. She wrote: "Agricultural authorities and practical farmers are of opinion that large farming such as wheat farming and stock-raising as practiced in the Prairie Provinces, and in some parts of British Columbia, is quite unsuited to women.

Farming that may involve the clearing of virgin forests, the ploughing up of virgin lands, the use of heavy machinery, and the handling of heavy loads, demands very great physical strength and endurance such as few women possess or should be called upon to exercise."[158]

Because of the severity of the winters, feeding stock, Low found, was a "man's job," and when hired men were required this posed "obvious difficulties for women farmers."[159] She advocated the less threatening small holdings and lighter forms of agriculture: "'intensive farming' on a few acres—fruit-farming, poultry-farming, bee-keeping, is suited to women, and although so few farmers have become farmers on their own account, experts are of opinion that there is no reason whatsoever why in this branch of agriculture women should not be just as successful as men." Low spoke to many experts who supported "small farms" for "competent women," "for there was nothing in such work that required the peculiarly masculine qualities." She also advocated women working in pairs or groups, arguing that "two competent women together should be able to manage a 5–10 acre farm (and home) satisfactorily and profitably." She hoped that a "wealthy imperialist" would step up and fund a women's settlement in British Columbia. While she found interest in the scheme from government and academic authorities, she was cautioned that soldier settlement was the priority.[160]

There was a mild and fleeting expression of interest in hiring former British Land Army members in British Columbia, although their potential as wives was once again highlighted. In 1920 British Columbia took the lead in advocating their emigration and work as labourers, mainly to harvest fruit.[161] A 1920 headline announced that "Women's Land Army to Invade Canada: English Farmerettes Expected to Solve Farm Labor Problem in British Columbia."[162] The women were to take the place of "Orientals," who "can never be relied upon" and who "do not like to be bossed in the fields." The women would work for "one quarter of what the men are asking in this part of the country for the same kind of work." Minister of Agriculture for British Columbia Edward D. Barrow favoured the scheme and announced that a representative group would visit to assess the conditions. Barrow approved because most were "well-born and educated. During the war, for patriotic motives, they went into the fields. Now a majority of them are homeless. Their male relatives perished for humanity, and the women are left to make a living as best they can… They want to come somewhere where they will have a chance for the future. This country could absorb quite a large number of satisfactory farmerettes."[163] He added, however, that "taken from another standpoint they would make excellent wives for pioneer bachelors."

Headlines such as "English Farm Girls for Canada: Thousands Will Seek Opportunities in the Western Provinces" anticipated an influx of former Land Army soldiers, but this did not occur.[164] Brigadier General R. Manley Sims, agent general of Ontario and a critic, did not mince his words. As quoted in the introduction, Sims stated in 1921 that while there might be a few openings for the "demobbed land girls," "it must be remembered that the Anglo-Saxon never willingly accepts the idea of women for out door labor. It is considered, and I think rightly, too rough and too heavy for them. It was a war emergency measure and we don't want it continued."[165]

At the end of the war a plan to bring Britain's war widows to homesteads in Western Canada was proposed but did not materialize. In his 1920 book *Breaking Prairie Sod*, Reverend (Captain) Wellington Bridgeman of Winnipeg, who lost both his sons in the war, was anxious to rid the West of "aliens" and replace them with British settlers, including "fallen heroes' wives and children from England, Ireland and Scotland, and from the Island of Lewis … In this way we would be encouraging community life with our own flesh and blood, who have suffered far more than we, and at the same time would be building up a pure, clean, white British-Canadian commonwealth."[166] Bridgeman assumed the widows would have sons, and that each of these would eventually have a farm and be "a British-Canadian in a British country." In order to facilitate this, Bridgeman argued that "we must let the enemy aliens go. They are still holding thousands of homesteads in all the provinces which our own should be occupying to-day."[167]

Optimism for a new land of opportunity for British women farmers and landowners on the prairies faded. A 1920 article on "The Lure of the Land" in the popular periodical *The Graphic* (London) noted that "work on the land has proved one of the most permanently popular of the war occupations undertaken by women," and that "the farmer has overcome his prejudices so far as to admit that women had proved the equal, and in some classes of work, the superior of men on the farms."[168] The author lamented, however, that while "at home or in our Empire overseas … innumerable women are longing to make good in some form or another of farming activity … the prospects for the educated land-worker in the

Colonies are not at the moment very roseate." Columns in the *Imperial Colonist* were increasingly pessimistic. It reported in 1921 that the "land girls were beginning to wonder if there really is anywhere for women who want outdoor work." They were warned that in Canada, without capital they would have to "combine housework with farm work and they will have to work for all they are worth."[169] Letters and articles in the postwar *Imperial Colonist* emphasized emigration for domestic service and little more. There was much less emphasis on opportunities for single women in the colonies and more on their roles within emigrating families, as wives of soldiers, for example.

Unlike Caroline Grosvenor's now-defunct CIL, the SOSBW discouraged British women from thinking of agriculture as a vocation in Canada. Their 1923 "Handbook for Women Who Are Thinking of Settling Overseas" stated that "there is no demand for women land workers in Canada. The work of the big wheat-growing farms in the prairie districts is not suitable to women, and the rigorous winter, during which little or no cultivation can be carried on in most parts of Canada, results in the engagement of as few permanent labourers as possible, and in all necessary agricultural processes being performed at a very high pressure during the summer months."[170] Women would need to find alternative employment during the coldest months of the year and that difficulty was "almost insuperable." This approach was echoed in Frances B. Low's *Women Out West: Life and Work in Canada* (1924). Almost all mention of women as farmers was dropped, and there was greater emphasis on how the "British housewife" could succeed in Canada.[171]

The annual reports of the SOSBW throughout the 1920s demonstrate that opportunities involving farm work for women were few. In 1925, five women were "placed in agricultural posts in Canada," but all had to have capital.[172] It was the same dismal story throughout the colonies. In 1926 the report on agriculture was brief: "We do not show an encouraging record in regard to this profession. Only seven girls have been placed on farms during 1926 as compared with 22 the previous year." Of these, two young women had gone to New Zealand to raise poultry and fruit, and there was one placement each in Kenya and South Africa. There were no agricultural postings to Canada that year.[173] Throughout the 1920s there were a few reports from women farmers in the colonies, but none from Canada. In 1928, for example, a British woman in Kenya had acquired 367 acres of forest land and she was trying to learn Swahili.[174] As noted in the report for 1925: "Although there are excellent schemes under which people can be absorbed into the Dominions, these are almost entirely restricted to single men for agriculture and to women with knowledge of domestic work."[175]

The 1920s saw occasional resurrections of the idea that British women might one day farm the prairies. A series of articles by a "Woman Farmer in Canada" was published in the London *Daily Mail* in the early 1920s.[176] Though the farm was in Saskatchewan, the author was not Binnie-Clark (who did not return to her farm after the war until 1924). Articles with titles such as "Saving the Crop" and "Getting in the Wheat" chronicled this woman's efforts to cope with treacherous trails that still had huge snowbanks while preparing to sow her wheat in spring, and to save her crop from infestations of grasshoppers. She persevered through these difficulties, but the descriptions may have inspired few to follow her example.

In 1923 Sir Henry Thornton, president of the Canadian National Railway, offered scholarships to four young Englishwomen from the Federation of Young Farmers' Clubs of Great Britain, who were "experts in farming," to tour Canada for four months and to study Canadian agriculture.[177] Two of them attended courses at the Ontario Agricultural College, and two at the Manitoba Agricultural College. But they were not going to be able to stay, even though it was reported that they liked the West and "very much regretted that they could not remain."[178]

In 1925 Emily Pinder, a graduate of Leeds University experimental farm, studied Canadian agricultural methods in Winnipeg "with a view to creating a movement to Western Canada of English farm girls."[179] Pinder was certain that girls on farms in England were "intensely interested in Canada. They are seeking an outlet for their energies and would migrate to the Dominion in large numbers if properly encouraged." She believed that many had sufficient funds to start farms of their own, and would "prove a valuable asset to the development of the western country." No movement of English farm girls to Western Canada occurred.

Rachel Ard of the Kent Committee of the British Overseas Settlement Committee proposed a scheme in 1925 of "training in agricultural schools for daughters of British settlers," but while the headlines describing her "novel scheme" hinted at more than housework for these girls, Ard emphasized the domestic training they required and argued that with this training they would "make admirable wives for the Western farmer."[180] She had spent that summer in the West and had lived in Saskatchewan from 1902 to 1909. Ard proposed that older daughters spend a winter in Canada studying domestic science to put them in the position to train their own mothers when they arrived the next spring. The older daughters so trained could then work as home helps for neighbours.

The cause of British women farmers was hopeless; domestic service beckoned and little else. In "The Girl Emigrant: Her Chances in the Colonies," published in the *Manchester Guardian*, author Muriel Harris declared that there was "little to no room for the university woman in such countries as Canada and Australia. She has already been trained on lines which make her wholly unsuitable for colonial life. At the best her life would be one long, uncomfortable adaptation."[181] Only young women were wanted, those willing to work as domestics and whose ideas and expectations had yet to be formed.

It was difficult for a woman to come to Canada under any other category than domestic servant, unless she was part of a family unit. A special category of "Unaccompanied Women" required an Emigration Permit. In Mabel Durham's *Canada's Welcome to Women* (1929), women were cautioned that "no woman, unaccompanied by husband, father or mother, may go to Canada with the intention of settling there without the sanction of the Superintendent of Emigration, who acts as the representative of the Canadian government in the British Isles."[182] This policy had been adopted to ensure that "none may go to that country seeking employment under any misconception as to the conditions there and the class of workers that is wanted. It will not allow any woman to go to Canada who might be in danger of becoming stranded there, or suffering disappointment." A woman on her own had to demonstrate that she had secured employment or had sufficient funds to provide for her needs while finding employment. British women receiving passage assistance (for domestic workers) had to submit to a medical examination before leaving home.[183] In 1927 the British Women's Emigration League of Saskatchewan protested these requirements, arguing that they were humiliating.

British Columbia became the focus of any lingering hopes for the "educated" British woman after the war, including agriculturalists and farm labourers. The Vancouver Queen Mary Coronation Hostel established by Mary Agnes Fitzgibbon (discussed in Chapter 2) closed in 1917 but reopened from 1922 to 1933, and it continued to concentrate on a narrowly defined category of "gentlewomen by birth," despite being urged to take women who were not necessarily of this description but were educated.[184]

Most of those who emigrated and found work through this hostel in the decade it was open obtained positions as home helps, or in related work in poultry, dairy, sheep, or seed farms. But if the women worked out of doors they still had to combine that with housework. Lois Evans, who worked at a goat ranch on Vancouver Island, wrote: "I am fond of all animals and have worked in England with cows, goats, pigs and poultry but I am keenest on goats. I have been with Miss Payne for 6 months … I did not realize until I arrived that I had all the indoor work including the cooking to do as well as the goats. I have had 5 years with goats and here I do the work that any lad of 14 could do."[185]

Also in British Columbia, the Princess Patricia Ranch near Vernon, the project initiated by Caroline Grosvenor and the CIL, was rented during the war years and moribund by 1920.[186] The Society for Overseas Settlement for British Women that inherited the experiment decided in 1920 to close the ranch, but the resources were transferred to a new location for training women in poultry and dairy farming at Merritt in the Nicola Valley. There were many, mostly financial reasons, for the demise of the Princess Patricia Ranch, but one was that orchard work was seen as less suitable for women than poultry and dairy work. There was the issue of labouring beside Chinese and Indian workers, and ploughing and spraying orchards was thought to be too demanding for women.[187] Other factors, according to historian Andrew Yarmie, were "problems of scale, poor soil conditions, and location and, at times, a weak market undermined the women's determined efforts to succeed."

Throughout the West, there were some advances in the numbers of women farmers, as indicated in the 1931 census and discussed in Chapter 3 (see Table 2). By 1931 there were 6,786 women farmers on the prairies (as compared to 3,575 in 1921). There were 1,493 in Manitoba, 2,952 in Saskatchewan, and 2,341 in Alberta.

Individual success stories continued to be trumpeted. There was May Hazlett, an "English girl" who farmed in the Touchwood Hills of Saskatchewan.[188] Her brother had been killed at Vimy Ridge and left his homestead to her. She was then working as a stenographer in Regina, and even though neighbours of her deceased brother urged her to sell, she decided to become a "farmerette." It was reported in 1921 that she had over one hundred acres under cultivation and a fine herd of cattle. She was going to England to marry her fiancé and return with him to her farm. Hazlett was an "ardent advocate of homesteads for women."

Two Forward sisters (there were four altogether and it is not clear which were the farmers: Maud, Mable, Beatrice, and Clara) of Oak Lake, Manitoba, continued to be celebrated far into the 1920s.[189] (They had appeared in the CPR pamphlets of the early years of the century.) The sisters were "the most amazing examples of woman's heroic pioneer effort crowned with brilliant success."[190] Their parents were from England and they migrated first to Quebec and then to Manitoba. After their father died in 1904, the daughters continued to operate the farm of 1,120 acres. According to a 1925 article in the *Imperial Colonist*, two of the daughters, "unaided, have wrought miracles in transforming the bald, uncultivated prairie into one of the fairest and most prolific farms of the countryside." They did all the work themselves: "Since the father died a man's hand has never guided a plough or seized a fork on the place. Ploughing, seeding, haying, stooking, harvesting, feeding and the other 'chores' of farm life have been carried out solely by the two girls." In a 1922 article readers were reassured that the Forward sisters had "all the feminine charm of womanhood. Their manlike occupation has not given them a masculine character or appearance as some of the older generations might imagine."[191] In 1929 the "Misses Forward" were reported to be specializing in shorthorn cattle, sheep, swine, and poultry. Each year they had a herd of sixty or seventy cattle.[192]

Mary Anderson, who came to Saskatchewan with her family in 1912, personally managed "one of the most successful dairy herds in the province."[193] She inherited the farm from her father in the early 1920s but had long had an interest in the business. The press coverage of her achievements indicates that successful women farmers were still tagged as rare and unusual. A 1923 article concluded, "Though farming in western Canada must be considered in the main a man-sized job and general conditions are such as to discourage the entry of women into the pursuit on any large scale there are continually to be encountered cases of women making undoubted success against great odds all over the country."[194]

Miss Ellen Foss, of Stonewall, Manitoba, was a wheat farmer, and her 1925 crop of Number One Northern was the first carload sent to the Manitoba Wheat Board.[195] She also had a herd of dairy cows. Foss believed "women can succeed on the land as well as men. I myself do much of the practical farm work. I don overalls, drive a team, plough and help with the harvest. Others can do the same if they will."

Isabelle Rogers Bryce, of Arcola, Saskatchewan, and originally from Scotland, won acclaim for her Clydesdale horses in local, national, and international shows.[196] When her husband died in 1915 she took over the management of their Doune Lodge Farm.[197] Her Clydesdale mare won the Reserve Grand Championship in Chicago in 1924. This was first time in the history of the show that the prize went to a woman.[198] In 1928 she was the only woman exhibitor at the Chicago International Livestock Exposition.

Various English women were reported in the 1920s to be so enamoured following visits to the prairies that they decided to take up farming there. These included writer Patricia Carlisle, who purchased an Alberta ranch in 1925 (as discussed in Chapter 4). In 1921 English writer "Mrs. Harold Bayley" declared that she intended to settle on a farm of her own in Saskatchewan after a visit to a farm at Luseland that was owned and managed by a women.[199] Edith Jones, of Leeds, Yorkshire, owned a farm near Plato, Saskatchewan, and had no previous experience with farming when she acquired it in 1924.[200] After two years on her farm she could ride a horse for twenty miles and milk cows. Her crop of wheat was worth $12,000. She claimed her farm "gave me a new lease of life, provided me with work I love, gave me splendid health and now furnishes me with the wherewithal for a long Christmas and New Year's holiday."

Lady Marjorie (Lowther) Rodney, with her husband Lord George Rodney, came to Alberta in 1919, and together they farmed and ranched 1,000 acres near Fort Saskatchewan.[201] Lady Rodney took an active part in the enterprise, particularly the dairy and swine herds. Her pigs were famous and won many prizes. Before purchasing their own land, they had (allegedly) "hired out" as farm hands on a neighbouring ranch to become acquainted with conditions on the prairies. In the 1920s they trained other young British aristocrats (males) on their farm.

Signs of change included the graduation in 1923 of Sheila Marryat with a bachelor of science in Agriculture from the University of Alberta. Marryat was the first woman with this degree at the University of Alberta.[202] Born in London, Marryat moved with her parents to Alix, Alberta, in 1905, settling near her sister Irene Marryat Parlby (rancher, agrarian reformer, and Alberta legislator). Sheila and her sister were true "daughters of the Empire."[203] Their father, Colonel E.L. Marryat, had built and managed British railways in India; brothers of theirs were in Egypt, India, and Shanghai. In Alberta, Sheila Marryat and her partner, Jean Reed, raised poultry and eggs that were sold to the transcontinental dining cars.

She then took a short course in agriculture at Guelph, followed by two years at the Provincial Agricultural School at Olds, Alberta, before enrolling in agriculture at the University of Alberta. Beneath her photograph in the 1923 yearbook Marryat was called "One of the 'boys.'" She said that she preferred the "natural, simple beauty of the farm to the monotonous, superficial, superfluous, superimposed life of the city."[204]

In Saskatchewan, Miss Ethel May Bradford made headlines in 1923 when she was hired to teach the newly established course in bee husbandry at the University of Saskatchewan. It was a great novelty that the course would be "presided over by a lady."[205] Bradford, who raised bees at Wawota, had attracted considerable attention as a lecturer on bee culture with the Saskatchewan Better Farming Train.

Yet there were also signs that little to nothing had changed over many decades. There was only one woman farmer, Miss Nora Fyffe of Qu'Appelle, Saskatchewan, among a party of sixty-eight Canadian farmers who visited England in 1928 under the auspices of the Canadian National Railways and White Star Line, to inspect facilities for handling and marketing Canadian farm produce.[206] And there remained the ever-present emphasis on the need for women as wives and little else. An article that appeared in a 1928 issue of the *Aberdeen Press and Journal* had the headline "Jills for Jacks: Training Girls as Wives for Settlers."[207] "Jills for Jacks," it claimed, was the "new slogan for Colonial immigration. Canada is crying for out for wifely comforts. From the homesteads and even from the prosperous mushroom cities comes the cry, 'We want wives.' The cry is being answered." A training institute to qualify young women for domestic duties on Canadian homesteads was to be established in Glasgow. The "new slogan" was far from new.

LAST GASPS OF HOMESTEADS FOR WOMEN: NEW AND OLD RATIONALES FOR DENIAL

Hopes that homestead rights might be granted to women on the same basis as men continued until 1930. Journalist E.L. Chicanot thought that the renewed interest in the issue of equality with men in the right to file on homesteads was "acutely stimulated by the movement from England of many girls who, having worked on the land or engaged in some other outdoor occupation during the war, were reluctant to resume their humdrum existences and sought a way to continue an out-of-door existence.

They came to Canada because it offered them the opportunity denied at home. They are essentially Canadian women now."[208] The journalist had to admit, however, that the right to homestead on the same basis as men had never been granted to women, and did not make it clear just what opportunities the English women immigrants had taken advantage of.

In the 1920s resolutions calling for homestead rights for women continued to be passed by various organizations and sent along to federal authorities. In 1921 the convention of the Federated Women's Institute, meeting at Edmonton, passed such a resolution.[209] The following year a similar resolution was passed at the convention of the Saskatchewan Grain Growers.[210] It was noted in the Didsbury, Alberta, newspaper in 1925 that a "noticeable feature" of the mail received at the local Dominion Lands Office was the "number of women directing inquiries as to available homestead land."[211]

In 1925 a Miss Nicholson, national secretary of the Imperial Order Daughters of Empire (IODE), wrote to the prime minister on the subject and the reply was: "The question of granting homesteads to women on the same terms as men is not a new suggestion and the Dominion Lands Act enables the Department to grant a homestead entry to a woman who is the head of a family on the same terms as a homestead entry is granted to a man." (This was not correct; the woman had to have a minor child or children.) Nicholson was told that the "free homestead policy was established to attract to Canada settlers who plan to engage in farming and it has never been the policy to grant homesteads to other than heads or potential heads of families."[212] New reasons were added by government officials as available homestead land dwindled. By the mid-1920s the reply was no longer that any available homestead land was reserved for soldier settlers, but that extending homesteads to women was "highly problematical owing to the majority of available Dominion lands now open for entry being more or less remote from settlement, and requiring, in part at least, to be cleared before the land can be broken."[213] Queries from the United States continued. In 1924, for example, a "girl orphan, Canadian by birth" wrote from Niagara Falls, New York, to ask the Department of the Interior if she could take up a homestead and was told no.[214]

In a 1928 memo contained in the Dominion Land Rulings, a Department of the Interior official summed up the "practice of the Department" on the issue of homesteads for women and added that while he did not know what prompted the government to refuse the right to homestead to single women, he could

> imagine one of the main reasons would be that a single woman is unfitted for a great many reasons for the lonely and isolated life led by the majority of homesteaders on prairie farms. Even if this concession were granted I think that very few women would be willing to face the loneliness and hard work entailed by taking up a free homestead. There is also the financial end of the matter, which I think would prove a considerable handicap as unlike men they would be unable to go out and work in the bush during the winter, or in the lumber mills, or work out during the threshing season, in order to earn additional money to develop their homesteads. The matter appears to be purely one of policy.[215]

The same memo had another addition, possibly by the same author, that outlined why the policy should not be changed and noting (as had decades of previous administrators) that women were free to purchase land, and therefore nothing stood in their way of taking up farming as an occupation: "While the past years have brought a tremendous change in the 'sphere' of women, I do not believe that the Department would be warranted in changing its present policy. Land of good quality can be purchased in the West for a moderate price, and land so obtainable is more advantageously situated, as a rule, with regard to churches, markets, etc. A woman who is fully qualified as a farmer need not be debarred from that occupation because she cannot get a homestead. The capital required for homesteading is not very much less than what would buy a farm."[216]

In 1929 resolutions were passed at the United Farmers of Alberta convention and by the Canadian Council of Agriculture at Winnipeg, asking that homesteads be granted to women on the same terms as men.[217] M.L. Burbank, of Carman, Manitoba, wrote to the *Western Producer* in February 1929 that she held out little hope for the resolution, as she had recently written to the Department of the Interior and had received the standard reply that departure from the present practice was not deemed advisable.[218] She wrote, "As I see it, this reply simply means that, in the opinion of the government, land is much too valuable to be giving it away to women, and that securing homesteads for women in Canada looks rather hopeless as long as there are any homesteads worth having." "It is truly amazing," she commented, "that any one can claim that women are not quite as valuable 'heads of families' as men are, or that a new country does not need women quite as much as it does men." Burbank pointed out the fallacy in the argument that few women would be interested, writing that if that were correct, then little homestead land would be "wasted," and that on the other hand, if "free homesteads attracted any considerable number of women surely the country would not suffer from settlers of this type. In any event it would not seem that the privilege of homesteading, with its hard work and deprivations, is an unreasonable 'favor' to ask."

New rationales for excluding women were mingled with the old, including the persistent refrain that "the Anglo-Saxon never willingly accepts the idea of women for out door labour."[219] "Foreign" women immigrants might do so, but this marked them as boorish, coarse, and vulgar. And as quoted in the introduction, Cora Hind, the commercial, financial, and agricultural editor of the *Manitoba Free Press* and women's rights activist, stated in the late 1920s that she did not recommend farming for women in Canada—meaning white women of British ancestry—explaining that: "You see, a woman can't go on the land as she would in England, for so many of the population of the prairies are low type Central Europeans, who, as a matter of course, make their womenfolk work outside. The result of this is that the Canadian farmer—by that I mean a man of British stock—says, 'I will have no "white" women working on my farm,' for he thinks if he does this he is sinking to the level of the 'bohunk.'"[220] Women's choices according to Hind were two: domestic work, and "more domestic work—marriage to a prairie farmer."[221]

As journalist E.L. Chicanot summarized the situation in the *Imperial Colonist* in 1925: "Broadly speaking, Canada does not encourage women to take up alone the pursuit of agriculture on her domain. There are, in any case, far too many men leading solitary lives and vainly hoping for helpmates. The magnitude on which general Canadian farming operations are carried on, with the arduous toil involved … largely precludes the engagement of women individually in these enterprises, no matter how much they love the work nor how much inclination leads them in that direction."[222] Florence B. Low, too, had long since given up mentioning any opportunities for women to farm on their own. In "The Empire's Call to Women" (1928) Low continued to stress the need for migration and mentioned a few opportunities for wage work, but came right to the point: "Unless British girls become the wives of British settlers in the Dominions, their population will be inspired by foreign ideals and a large part of the British Empire overseas will no longer be dominated by British character and British principles."[223]

A 1928 tour of twenty-five English schoolgirls to Canada was organized by the IODE, the SOSBW, and the Canadian and British governments. The tour was intended to strengthen Empire unity and encourage the migration of women, and the schoolgirls represented "highly desirable 'British stock,' of the respectable classes."[224] And they were to convey back to Britain an image of Canada as a thriving British-based society that was modern and technologically advanced. While Canada's agricultural wealth and other resources were displayed to the girls at many locations, there was no mention that they could take any part in developing these resources. The girls were "displayed and naturalized as the most suitable 'stock' to populate Canada."[225] The dream of sending British women to the prairie Canada as farmers was a London cause.

Figure 40. This poster from 1923 illustrates the suitably domestic roles for women on the farms of prairie Canada. She is modern in many ways, as she is distant from the floor-length gowns, corsets, and long hair that restricted previous generations, but she was still to conform to the same expected gender roles of wife and mother. She was not the owner-operator of a farm. Canadian Pacific Archives, Image no. BR 194.

CONCLUSION

Starting in 1930, drought and dust settled over the Canadian prairies for nearly ten years. Very few "imperial plots" had been successfully carved out of the prairie soil by British women farmers. Overwhelming forces combined to ensure that women migrating to the prairies had to perform domestic work. This imperative seems to have grown even stronger over the decades. Women of British birth in Canada, and proponents of their emigration in the metropole, believed they had a strong claim, stronger than women of other ethnicities or countries of origin, to vocations and opportunities other than domestic work in this corner of what they saw as their Empire, including owning and working on the land.

But throughout the period of this study, Canada maintained its "curiously strong" prejudice against any such initiative. A 1930 Canadian Pacific Railway pamphlet *Household Work in Canada for Girls*, published in London, is a stark indicator of how opportunities for the emigrant British woman had shrunk and shrivelled. It was quite distinct from the CPR pamphlets of the earliest years of the twentieth century that featured British women as farmers and landowners. In 1930 domestic service was the only vocation on offer, and this was made clear from the pamphlet's first sentences. "Capable young women from Great Britain" were wanted but were warned they "must be ready to accept Canadian conditions and do domestic work." They had to "pocket their pride" and go "smilingly into Canadian kitchens to cook and serve, and wash up the dishes, to scour pans and polish metal, to scrub and sweep, make beds, shake rugs, and lend generally with a genuine goodwill."[1] A "scheme" had been started in Britain for training those who did not have household experience, with centres in Glasgow, Newcastle, Cardiff, and London.

It was nearly impossible for a girl or woman to emigrate for any other purpose than domestic work. To pursue the "big future" that awaited her and obtain the reduced rate of passage under the Empire Settlement Act, a girl could be nominated by friends or relatives, if they were prepared to employ her in domestic work. She could be nominated by a fiancé, if she came to Canada to marry him, but only if the man was "actually doing farm work." A widow with her children could get the reduced rate if nominated by a farmer who would employ her, but if the children lived with her she would be paid a lower wage. The woman who paid full fare and emigrated to join friends or relatives in Canada had to be examined by a doctor of the Department of Health, who would sign her Identification Card. She also had to "produce a letter, in the original envelope, from the friends, as proof that there is a home in Canada" that had to be shown at the time of the medical examination.[2]

This narrow range of opportunities was worlds away from the vision Georgina Binnie-Clark had of British women colonists raising grain on their valuable imperial plots that would help to make the prairies British by displacing Indigenous people and eradicating the need to bring in "foreign" settlers. Yet she and the other advocates of this vision had faced insurmountable obstacles. The homestead laws discriminated against single women. Powerful administrators of the laws in Canada over the decades were utterly opposed to the idea of women farmers. They drew on deeply entrenched and tenacious views of women as either physically incapable of the work required, or if they were able to do the work it would make them masculine. They did not want women to be independent of marriage. British migrant women were central to the plot of carving into the very landscape what was seen as the timeless, natural gender order of females for the hearth and men for the field. It was vital to recreate this order as the foundation of society in this outpost of the British Empire to demonstrate that it was modern, appealing to settlers of the right sort, and superior to the Indigenous societies of the previous centuries and the chaotic nation to the south. A key marker of civilization was this gender order, particularly important to uphold and buttress in a colony. A symbol of a darker and more primitive age was women at work in the fields; an activity that was allowable (and even necessary) out of public sight, but would never have official or visible sanction or encouragement. Women from Russia or Indigenous women might be more accustomed to this work, but they too had to conform to the gender order that was at the heart of the colonial order.

British women in the metropole and in Canada who wanted to broaden opportunities in the colonies beyond the roles of wives, mothers, and domestic labourers stressed that they were enthusiastic, devoted imperialists, patriotic building blocks of a British West, superior to both Indigenous men and women and those of "foreign" lands, including Americans. They drew on a "gendered ruralism" to claim the right to participate in the "Great Game." They would help to consolidate the Empire, plant British culture and civilization and crowd out the "foreigner."[3] But they would remain wholesome, nurturing, and feminine. For women to own and work on the land was potentially threatening and dangerous; advocates tried to raise the profile and acceptance of these endeavours by presenting this as an imperialist undertaking that would nurture and nourish a British race in this outpost of Empire. But authorities in Canada worked consistently over decades to ensure that very few women would be able to take up the challenge of owning and farming land.

While this study is largely a history of dashed hopes and plans for imperial plots, it has uncovered a great many women, not just British women, who farmed or ranched on the prairies, some quite successfully. Many more would have liked to do so but were discouraged or prevented, through the land laws and through the intransigence of politicians and officials in various departments, including the Department of the Interior and Department of Immigration. Expressions of the deep and profound opposition at all levels of government in Canada to British women migrants as anything but domestic servants remained pronounced and strident in the 1920s. This was well after women (except those of First Nations) could vote in most of Canada (except in Quebec). The world had not been turned upside down, as some had predicted. Why the continued opposition? The woman farmer was still regarded as a disruptive and troublesome deviation from a "true" and "normal" feminine identity.

Land and farming on the prairies remained overwhelmingly a masculine enterprise, and the war had helped to further this aim.

The same attitudes prevailed with respect to First Nations reserves far into the twentieth century. While women worked on the small farms and gardens of these communities, they were given no official encouragement or sanction or assistance. In the twentieth century the various Department of Indian Affairs initiatives on reserves, such as community farms, band farms, cooperative farms, and corporate farms, involved males only.[4] Indigenous women were encouraged to participate in "Indian Homemakers Clubs" from the late 1930s, and these stressed suitably feminine activities such as sewing, canning, and handicrafts (although the clubs did become settings where women organized to address social, economic, and educational needs of their communities).[5]

Georgina Binnie-Clark's final initiative at her Saskatchewan farm is a bellwether of the changing times. She had totally given up her campaign to attract British women as farmers to the prairies, but she continued to work for the cause of the British Empire with the establishment of the Union Jack Farm Settlement (UJFS) in 1930 for British immigrant families. She persisted with this until at least 1937. Unfortunately the inauguration of the project coincided with the start of the ten-year Depression that hit rural Saskatchewan more severely than all other regions of Canada. Evaporating with the crops and water of the West was any enthusiasm for British or any other settlers. The purpose of the UJFS was to assist British immigrant families to adapt to the conditions of the West by teaching them farming and assisting them to find work. Binnie-Clark believed that "such families are the most eligible type for the 'army of occupation' we need for the guardianship of the King's Dominions Overseas."[6] "In the Union Jack Farm Settlement," Binnie-Clark wrote, "we try to accomplish for human beings what the Experimental Farms, established throughout Canada by the Canadian government, have accomplished for the care and development of all that is most valuable in the life of seeds and plants and birds and stock."

There was little enthusiasm for Empire settlement schemes in Canada through much of the 1920s, and they were a hopeless, lost cause as the Depression deepened.[7] Binnie-Clark's plan was also frustrated because the homestead privilege was no more in Saskatchewan; there were new "purchase provisions" for vacant land, but these were available only to those who had resided in the province for five years.[8] Binnie-Clark also unsuccessfully sought royal sponsorship for the project, which she hoped to attract by setting aside, as a mark of allegiance, an acre in each farm to be known as the "King's Acre," a promise she kept on her own land.[9] A "Birthday Book for the Farm Settlement of the Canadian Prairies," compiled by Binnie-Clark and published in 1935, was also a fund-raising strategy.[10] It seems unlikely to have been successful in raising funds. The UJFS project received no significant financial backing and it limped along, remaining in operation until 1937.

Although fondly remembered in the Fort Qu'Appelle community, Binnie-Clark was also seen as eccentric. And she was considered "no farmer." Her sister Ethel did more to keep the farm going. How otherwise could Georgina have sustained her lecturing and writing career in England? In the local history of Fort Qu'Appelle, there is a special section on Binnie-Clark.[11] She "caused a sensation ... because she was a woman farmer," and she "lives on in local legend." One story told by a hired hand who worked for her in the early 1930s was that she had "ended a discussion over who was going to clean a seeder" by telling him, "Paton, if I'd wanted to be dictated to by a man, I would've married one and let him keep me." She was remembered as kind and generous with children. But the overwhelming lasting impression was of "benign eccentricity: of britches and leggings and a large floppy hat, worn seven days a week on the farm and off ... of the cats that slept on the flour bag in the kitchen and the horses that were kept as pets long after they were of no use on the farm." When I visited Georgina's farm (still owned by great-nephews in England) on a warm August day one hundred years after she bought her land, it was fitting that there were horses grazing there, by the dilapidated shack that her sister Ethel had lived in up until her death in 1955. Georgina died in London in 1947, just short of her seventy-seventh birthday, and Ethel scattered her ashes over her Fort Qu'Appelle fields.

It is ironic that Binnie-Clark's goal of homesteads for women had a measure of success (in Alberta only) just at the time when she had deserted the cause. In 1930 Manitoba, Saskatchewan, and Alberta took control of their natural resources, including land, from the federal government. Alberta was the only province to enact homestead legislation similar to the former federal model, but it granted women the same rights as men. The Alberta Lands Act permitted homestead entry to "persons of the full age of 17 years, British subjects or with the intention of becoming British subjects who had resided in the province for a period of at least three years."[12] The homesteader had to have been resident in the province for at least three years. It was a way of trying to keep the West British through a method that Binnie-Clark would have approved. In Alberta there was immediate interest from women: in August 1931 there were a total of 863 homestead entries, and of these 327 were women.[13] By early 1933, more than 2,000 women had answered the "call of the land."[14] They would have faced many challenges, including that the best land in the province had long been occupied, and that their homestead careers were beginning just as the Great Depression gripped the West. This movement of women onto the land in Alberta also gripped the public imagination, making headlines in newspapers as far away as the *New York Times*.[15]

While Binnie-Clark may have been "no farmer," there were many women on the prairies who were, but they faced obstacles, including "restraining myths" that persist to this day. Females are seen as "not farmers." They are still regarded as not the natural or likely inheritors of a farm. A 2015 article in the *Globe and Mail* about the end of an era in the operation of a prairie family farm since 1925, written by daughter Carrie Tait, began, "One day, when my sister and I were little, our dad walked into the kitchen and said something that has haunted us our whole lives. 'I am glad I had girls,' he said, 'so they don't have to grow up to be farmers.'"[16] Perhaps with the present perilous state of the family farm it is welcome that daughters are understood to have other choices and priorities, and do not have to face the pressure and expectation that they will carry on with the farm. But this also indicates the persistence of the belief that farms are masculine.

In a recent collection of memoirs from rural Canada, farmer Marianne Stamm wrote of how she falters when asked to identify her occupation despite having farmed in Switzerland, British Columbia, and Alberta since she was a "six year old steering a tractor on a pioneer farm."[17] Stamm continued, "Some might say I wasn't really a farmer—I was just a farmer's daughter. They don't understand." She was the mechanic and machinery operator in the family and chief tractor driver as a girl, and later with her husband established a successful grain farm. People then said she was "a farmer's wife," Stamm wrote and continued, "I was that—I was married to a farmer. Being married to a farmer didn't automatically make me a farmer, though, anymore than being married to a teacher or doctor would make me one myself. Not just the farmer's wife. I was a farmer too."[18] Women still battle to be able to identify themselves as farmers, to be seen as legitimate farmers, even if they have farmed all their lives. This battle is no longer required for other vocations that were exclusively masculine in the past such as being a doctor, lawyer, pharmacist, welder, or a host of others. Farming has uniquely retained its masculine association.

A study of female farmers in Canada in the late twentieth century found that they continued to face constraints and issues of legitimacy that made many of them feel that they were not "real" farmers.[19] They confronted "restraining myths" that limited what women could do or know, and these myths "maintained and reinforced the traditional gender relations of farming by controlling the definition of who real farmers are." The three central restraining myths were (1) the "myth of male technological know-how," the idea that men knew more about and were more adept with machinery and technology; (2) the "myth of farming alone," which cast men as capable of farming on their own even if they hired labour, while if women hired labour they were not regarded as capable of farming "alone" and were thus not legitimate farmers; (3) the "myth of physical strength" that does not recognize that some women are as strong as some men, and that women have always done heavy work on farms.

Opposition remained strong in England as well. An "undercover academic" who lived in a picturesque English village and published her findings in 2007 found that various categories of persons, including single women, were stigmatized and excluded.[20] The childless single woman transgressed the norms of the rural idyll. She was seen as a moral threat to the family unit, particularly by other women. If women were not wives and mothers, "thus transgressing traditional rural stereotypes about women's place, their experiences were constructed as inferior or even as threatening, because (married) motherhood was presumed to be the primary identity for adult women."[21] Authors Frances Watkins and Ann Jacoby drew on sociologist Erving Goffman's concept of stigma as an "*undesired* differentness." Those who are stigmatized, according to Goffman, "are seen by others as 'not quite human' and so the legitimate target for discrimination." The end result of stigmatization is social exclusion, with "individuals being denied access to the benefits of belonging to the dominant group."[22] It is interesting that Goffman was born in small-town Alberta (Mannville) and grew up in the town of Dauphin, Manitoba. His understandings of stigmatization must have drawn on his experiences in rural Western Canada.

In 1949 Elsie Hart of the United Farmers of Canada (Saskatchewan Section) and a farmer expressed anger at the absence of any progress.[23] A "brilliant" young woman graduate of the University of Saskatchewan with a degree in agriculture, specializing in horticulture, had applied for a position with the Horticulture Division of the Experimental Farms Service of the Canadian government. She had been told that her application would not be considered because only males would be "acceptable for the present and future vacancies." Hart wrote: "Which means: It was very fine of you young woman to spend four years of your time to scientifically educate yourself in an important branch of agriculture but you must now get yourself some apple seeds and cherry seeds and grow nice apple trees and cherry trees or go to the U.S.A. or some other country where your knowledge and talent will be recognized and appreciated. Equality of opportunity regardless of sex!—Bah."

That obstacles in Canada remained insurmountable is testament to the success of the project of crafting the prairies as a colony of the British Empire where a "natural" or "normal" gender order would be preserved, despite the challenges and criticisms, including by British-born women who wanted a corner of the colony to call their own. The presence of an array of other models of femininity, of Doukhobor women, for example, served to strengthen and justify resolve to eliminate women from work on the land. The profits to be gained from land and crops by men such as Frank Oliver and J. Obed Smith also strengthened resolve. It is interesting, however, to "think back" in time and realize that for farmers like Maxi'diwiac (Buffalo Bird Woman), eliminating women from work on the land would have been a perversion of an acceptable gender order. Asked if young men worked in the fields, Maxi'diwiac laughed heartily and replied, "Certainly not."[24] She owned and cultivated her own land, provided for her family, and she processed, marketed and sold her products. Women of the Plains villages were totally in charge of the agronomy that was the main economic activity of their region. The farming methods and crops that Maxi'diwiac and other Hidatsa and Mandan women developed over centuries endure to this day. Corn is today the number one cereal crop worldwide, and it plays a major role in the economies of Canada and the United States. It is the major agricultural crop of the United States, with over 84 million acres under cultivation on some 400,000 farms, and the third most valuable crop of Canada.[25]

NOTES

INTRODUCTION

1 Provincial Archives of Manitoba (PAM), homestead file 74916 W½ 21-12-15-W1. Thanks to Eric Hallatt, archivist. Elizabeth Cameron, who signed her name with an X, was from Nova Scotia. She became the owner of this land in 1883.

2 Clipping, Isabelle Beaton Graham, "Homesteads for Women: A Western Woman's View of Man's Duty to Women," n.d., n.p. (1910), Library and Archives Canada (LAC), Record Group 15 (RG 15), Records of the Department of the Interior, vol. 1062, file 2029532.

3 Verdon, "Middle-Class Women's Work and the Professionalization of Farming."

4 Saxby, *West-Nor'-West*, 31–32.

5 The literature on settler colonialism is vast and growing. See, for example, Veracini, "'Settler Colonialism': Career of a Concept"; and Jacobs, "Parallel or Intersecting Tracks? The History of the U.S. West and Comparative Settler Colonialism."

6 Wolfe, "Settler Colonialism and the Elimination of the Native," 387.

7 Anon., *The New West*, preface, n.p.

8 Jones, "Gentlemen Farmers in Canada," *Leicester Chronicle and the Leicestershire Mercury*, 25 April 1885, 1.

9 Ibid.

10 Carter, *Lost Harvests*.

11 Anon., *The New West*, preface, n.p.

12 Ibid.

13 Levine, "Introduction: Why Gender and Empire?," 6; Tosh, *Manliness and Masculinities*, 183–85.

14 "A Greeting 1910," *African Standard*, 29 Jan. 1910, 8.

15 Damusey, "The Prairie," *Canadian Magazine* 56, no. 6 (April 1921): 486.

16 Wilson, "Manly Art."

17 Casid, *Sowing Empire*, xxii.

18 Spence, *The Prairie Lands of Canada*, 6.

19 Osborn, "Our Western Chivalry," *Morning Post*, 14 July 1900, 5. See also Henderson, "'No Money, but Muscle and Pluck': Cultivating Trans-Imperial Manliness for the Fields of Empire, 1870–1901."

20 Levine, "Introduction: Why Gender and Empire?," 7.

21 Losurdo, *Liberalism*; McKay, "The Liberal Order Framework."

22 Perry, "Women, Racialized People, and the Making of the Liberal Order," 275.

23 Ibid., 276.

24 "How to Use Our Newest Colony," an interview with Mr. Arnold White, *Pall Mall Gazette*, 4 July 1885, 15.

25 Jacobs, "Parallel or Intersecting Tracks?," 158.

26 Carey, "'Wanted! A Real White Australia,'" 136.

27 Carter, "Britishness, 'Foreignness,' Woman and Land."

28 Carter, *Capturing Women*.

29 "The Doukhobors: Queer Russian Sect Which Has Become Canadianized," *Reflector*, 8 Aug. 1911, 2.

30 Levine, "Introduction: Why Gender and Empire?," 7.

31 Lawrence, *Genteel Women*.

32 McClintock, *Imperial Leather*, 6.

33 Ganley, "What's All This Talk about Whiteness?," 13.

34 Carter, "Britishness, 'Foreignness,' Women and Land."

35 "Woman Changing to Masculinity?," *Saturday News*, 17 Dec. 1910, 11.

36 Ibid.

37 "Tiller," "The Female Farmer," *Sunday Times*, 27 May 1906, 3.

38 Provincial Archives of Alberta (PAA), homestead file 1724101, reel 2843.

39 James, *Hanna North*, 606.

40 Ibid., 607.

41 West, *Homesteading*, 201.

42 Kluth, "Mr. and Mrs. Reinhart Kluth," 75–77.

43 Mrs. Ed Watson, "Pioneering in Saskatchewan," Saskatchewan Archives Board (SAB), R-176, BP W44Z 1924.

44 McClung, "Speaking of Women," *Maclean's*, 10 May 1916.

45 Gleadle, *Borderline Citizens*, 77.

46 Binnie-Clark, "Land and the Woman in Canada," 498.

47 Ibid., 506.

48 Ibid.

49 Anon., *Our Western Lands*.

50 For example, one group of friends of Oliver received an irrigation grant in Alberta of over 380,000 acres in 1906 which they soon sold for an enormous profit. Gilpin, *Prairie Promises*, 5–6; Schmidt, *Growing Up in the Oil Patch*, 65.

51 Young, *On Female Body Experience*, 21.

52 Binnie-Clark, *Wheat and Woman* 1979, 308. Binnie-Clark is quoting the response that Cora Hind received from Frank Oliver when Hind met with Oliver about homesteads for women.

53 Carter, *The Importance of Being Monogamous*.

54 McClung, "Free Land for the Soldiers," *Edmonton Bulletin*, 18 Sept. 1915, 3.

55 Commander, "Opportunities for Educated Englishwomen in Canada Are Not Recognized," *Carbon News*, 13 April 1921, 7.

56 Fripp, *The Outcasts of Canada*, 174.

57 Harrison, *Go West—Go Wise!*, 72.

58 Ibid., 72–73.

59 Weaver, *The Great Land Rush*; Belich, *Replenishing the Earth*.

60 Roe, *"Getting the Know-How."*

61 Lacombe Rural History Club, *Wagon Trails to Hard Top*, 164; PAA, homestead file 524559, reel 2055.

62 *Wagon Trails to Hard Top*, 164.

63 Roe, *"Getting the Know-How,"* 16.

64 Ibid., 16–17.

65 *Vote*, 27 Aug. 1927, 3.

66 McClintock, *Imperial Leather*, 6.

67 Wildenthal, "'She Is the Victor': Bourgeois Women, Nationalist Identities and the Ideal of the Independent Woman Farmer in German Southwest Africa," 80–85.

68 Dinesen, *Out of Africa*, 1.

69 I explore dimensions of this in Carter, *The Importance of Being Monogamous*.

70 Hurt, *The Big Empty*, 5–6. See also Carter, ed., *Montana Women Homesteaders*.

71 Hurt, *The Big Empty*, 8.

72 Binnie-Clark, "Land and the Woman in Canada," 506. The commentary and discussion by J. Obed Smith and others in the audience was published together with Binnie-Clark's address.

73 Ballantyne, "Race and the Webs of Empire"; Ballantyne, "Colonial Knowledge."

74 "Where Women Are Farmers," *Globe*, 19 July 1910, 5.

75 "Women for Canada," *Daily Mail*, 4 April 1921, 6.

CHAPTER ONE

1 Quoted in Hanson, introduction to Wilson, *Buffalo Bird Woman's Garden*, xxii. This book was originally published in 1917 by Wilson as *Agriculture of the Hidatsa Indians*.

2 See, for example, Trigger, *The Huron*.

3 See Kub, "Buffalo Bird Woman's Farming Methods Still in Evidence Today," *Agfax*, 7 Aug. 2013, available at http://agfax.com/2013/08/07/buffalo-bird-womans-farming-methods-still-in-evidence-today/.

4 The best book on Great Plains Indigenous agriculture is Wilson, *Buffalo Bird Woman's Garden.*

5 Bradbury, *Travels in the Interior of America*, 175.

6 Manitoba Culture, Heritage and Recreation, Historic Resources Branch, *The Prehistory of the Lockport Site*, 11.

7 Denig, *Five Indian Tribes of the Upper Missouri*, 109–10.

8 Hanson, introduction to Wilson, *Buffalo Bird Woman's Garden*, xxi.

9 Wilson, *Buffalo Bird Woman's Garden*, 13.

10 Ibid., 114.

11 Ibid., 15.

12 Quoted in Will and Hyde, *Corn among the Indians of the Upper Missouri*, 78.

13 Hurt, *American Agriculture*, 61.

14 Wilson, *Buffalo Bird Woman's Garden*, 27.

15 Quoted in Will and Hyde, *Corn among the Indians of the Upper Missouri*, 54.

16 Quoted in ibid., 136–37.

17 Quoted in ibid., 190.

18 Quoted in ibid., 192–23.

19 Quoted in ibid., 193.

20 Quoted in ibid., 196.

21 Peters, *Women of the Earth Lodges*, 114.

22 Bowers, *Hidatsa Social and Ceremonial Organization*, 203.

23 Peters, *Women of the Earth Lodges*, 120.

24 Catlin, *Letters and Notes on the Manners, Customs and Conditions of the North American Indians*, 189.

25 Matthews, *Ethnography and Philology of the Hidatsa Indians*, 11–12.

26 Wilson, *Buffalo Bird Woman's Garden*, 120.

27 Smithsonian, *Journal of Rudolph Friederich Kurz*, 289.

28 Quoted in Peters, *Women of the Earth Lodges*, 120–21. See also Fritze, "Growing Identity, Growing a Home: Contrasting Functions of Two Nineteenth-Century Gardens."

29 Turner, *Ancient Pathways, Ancestral Knowledge*, 1.

30 Lethbridge and District Horticultural Society et al., *Ethnobotany of the Plants in the Garden of Native Prairie Plants*, 1; http://www.galtmuseum.com/pdf/NativePrairiePlantsGarden-Ethnobotany.pdf.

31 Linklater, *Measuring America*, 223.

32 I have borrowed the term "immaculate grid" from Linklater, *Measuring America*, where it is used as the title of Chapter 12.

33 McKay, "The Liberal Order Framework," 641.

34 Frederick, "John Stoughton Dennis," *Dictionary of Canadian Biography*; http://www.biographi.ca/EN/ShowBio.asp?BioId=39594&query=dennis.

35 Martin, *"Dominion Lands" Policy*, 356.

36 Ibid., 70.

37 Weaver, *The Great Land Rush*, 232.

38 Linklater, *Measuring America*, 84, 166.

39 Conlogue, "Managing the Farm, Educating the Farmer," 4.

40 Quoted in ibid., 3.

41 Boag, "Thinking Like Mount Rushmore," 44.

42 Ibid., 46.

43 Compton, "Proper Woman/Propertied Women," 81.

44 Ibid., 83.

45 Ibid., 86.

46 Ibid., 89.

47 Ibid., 88.

48 Ibid., 3. See also Compton, "Uncle Sam's Farm"; http://digitalcommons.unl.edu/historyrawleyconference/15/. See also LAC, Record Group 17 (RG 17) Records of the Department of Agriculture, vol. 26, f. 2351–2375, and RG 17, vol. 27, file 2382.

49 Compton, "Proper Woman/Propertied Women," 79.

50 Ibid., 80.

51 Ibid., 86.

52 Compton, "Challenging Imperial Expectations: Black and White Female Homesteaders in Kansas."

53 Ibid., 87.

54 Ibid., 94.

55 Chused, "The Oregon Donation Act of 1850 and Nineteenth Century Federal Married Women's Property Law."

56 Gould and Pando, *Claiming Their Land*, iii, 15.

57 Weaver, *The Great Land Rush*, 237.

58 Home, "Scientific Survey and Land Settlement in British Colonialism," 2.

59 Quoted in ibid., 7.

60 Hunter, *Father's Right-Hand Man*, 26–27.

61 Quoted in ibid., 31.

62 Ibid.

63 Spender, ed., *Writing a New World*, 12.

64 Alford, *Production or Reproduction?*, 75.

65 Hunter, *Father's Right-Hand Man*, 24.

66 Ibid., 32.

67 Ibid., 34.

68 Ibid.

69 Ibid., 32.

70 Ibid., 31–32.

71 *Border Watch*, 2 Aug. 1884, 2.

72 Wanhalla, *Matters of the Heart*, 52–53.

73 Paul and Foster, "Married to the Land."

74 Quoted in ibid., 54.

75 Ibid., 68.

76 Wanhalla, *Matters of the Heart*, 52–56.

77 See Harris and Warkentin, *Canada before Confederation*, 123–25.

78 Dennis was a military man who first saw active service during the 1866 Fenian invasion, which did little to enhance his reputation as he was later charged, although acquitted, of endangering his men and deserting them in the face of enemy fire. Dennis escaped the action disguised as a woman, while thirty-four of the men under his command did not. He returned to his surveying career after these embarrassments.

79 Tyman, "Patterns of Western Settlement."

80 Canada, *House of Commons Debates*, 2nd session, 1st Parliament, 32–33 Victoria, v. 2 (Ottawa: Information Canada, 1975), 492.

81 Ibid., 498.

82 Dennis, Jr., "A Short History of the Surveys Made under the Dominion Lands System 1869–1889," Canada, *Sessional Papers* 25, no. 9 (1892): 2.

83 Order-in-council, 1869-0699, "Survey of townships in the [Northwest Territories]-[Minister of Public] works submits system proposed by Lieut. Col. J.S. Dennis," in LAC, Record Group 2 (RG 2), Privy Council Office, Series A-1-a, vol. 270; http://www.collectionscanada.gc.ca/databases/orders/001022-110.01-e.php?PHPSESSIC=vv9ugshn9vqt330oo509ncne978&q1=0699&q2=&13=1869&intererval=20.

84 E.A. Meredith to A. Archibald, 4 Aug. 1870, in LAC, RG 15, vol. 229, file 1 (1871).

85 This section is all from A. Archibald to the Secretary of State for the Provinces, 20 Dec. 1870, in LAC, RG 15, vol. 229, file 1 (1871).

86 Order-in-council, 1871-0708, "Public lands in the Province of Manitoba—Memo, 1871/03/01, from Hon. A. Campbell on subject of [Recommending] rules for survey allotment of woods and [etc]—And that all Crown lands be transferred to the control of the Secretary of State," in LAC, RG 2, Series A-1-a, vol. 285 and 5115; http://www.collectionscanada.gc.ca/databases/order/001022-110.01-e.php?PHPSESSID=hfvknfu2n8abikmq264fioq9i7&q2=public+lands+&q3=1871&interval=20.

87 Canada, *House of Commons Debates*, 6 April 1871, 968.

88 Order-in-council, 1871-0874, "Lands in Manitoba—Hon. A. Campbell submits revised regulations for dealing with—And [recommends] same be approved," 20 April 1871, in LAC, RG 2, Series A-1-a, vol. 286; http://www.collectionscanada.gc.ca/databases/orders/001022-119.01-e.php?&sisn_id_nbr=9032&page_sequence_nbr=1&interval=20&&PHPSESSID=0pv48r468mg1rmuvk2tv812f60.

89 Martin, *"Dominion Lands" Policy*, 140.

90 Richtik, "The Policy Framework for Settling the Canadian West," 617.

91 Morris, *The Treaties of Canada*, 282.

92 Ibid., 315.

93 Carter, "Erasing and Replacing."

94 Morris, *The Treaties of Canada*, 322.

95 Venne, ed., *Indian Acts and Amendments*, 94.

96 Canada, *Sessional Papers*, Annual Report of the Department of Indian Affairs for the year ended 30 June 1895, 117.

97 Canada, *Sessional Papers*, Annual Report of the Department of Indian Affairs for the year ended 30 June 1896, 273.

98 LAC, Record Group 10 (RG 10), Records of the Department of Indian Affairs, vol. 4082, file 486, 315.

99 Canada, *Sessional Papers*, Annual report of the Department of Indian Affairs for the year ended 31 March 1917, 27.

100 Galloway, *I Lived in Paradise*, 48.

101 Goldfrank, *Changing Configuration in Social Organization of a Blackfoot Tribe During the Reserve Period*, 68.

102 Lux, "We Demand 'Unconditional Surrender,'" 667–69.

103 Daschuk, *Clearing the Plains*, 164.

104 Ibid., 185.

105 Turner, *Ancient Pathways, Ancestral Knowledge*, 192.

106 Burnett, *Taking Medicine*.

107 *Cypress Hills Country*, 297.

108 Carter, *Lost Harvests*. See Chapter 6, "Prelude to Surrender: Severalty and 'Peasant' Farming," 193–236.

109 The source of the section by and about Adams Archibald is LAC, RG 15, vol. 227, file, 1, A. Archibald to Secretary of State for the Provinces, 20 Dec. 1870.

110 Ibid.

111 Tough and Dimmer, "'Great Frauds and Abuses.'"

112 Ibid., 206.

113 Quoted in Augustus, "'Half-Breed' Homestead," 57.

114 Dick, *Farmers "Making Good,"* 27.

115 Ibid., 25.

116 Stead, "The Story of Halfbreed Scrip," *Raymond Rustler*, 20 January 1911, 11.

117 Historical Buildings Committee, "67 Main Street: Alloway & Champion Building," 28 Feb. 1986; http://www.winnipeg.ca/ppd/historic/pdf-consv/Main667-long.pdf.

118 Ibid., 2.

119 SAB, homestead file 123419A.

120 LAC, Western Land Grants, search term "Benjamin E. Chaffey"; see, for example, http://www.collectionscanada.gc.ca/databases/western-land-grants/001007-110.01-e.php?q1=&q2=&q3=&q4=&q5=chaffey&q6=&interval=20&sk=21&&PHPSESSID=r21gt83n4nfah59abrj8lhfr10.

121 Eatonia History Book Committee, *A Past to Cherish*, 33.

122 Stead, "Fifty Years in Western Canada: A Sketch of the Career of John Sanderson, the First Homesteader in Western Canada," *Better Farming*, May 1923, 4–5.

123 Carter, "Erasing and Replacing."

124 Venne, *Indian Acts and Amendments*, 43. S.C. 1876 c. 18-70 reads: "No Indian or non-treaty Indian, resident in the province of Manitoba, the North-West Territories or the territory of Keewatin, shall be held capable of having acquired or acquiring a homestead or pre-emption right to a quarter section, or any portion of land in any surveyed or unsurveyed lands in the said province of Manitoba, the North-West Territories, or the territory of Keewatin, or the right to share in the distribution of any lands allotted to the half-breeds."

125 Lambrecht, *The Administration of Dominion Lands*, 106.

126 See the Dominion Lands Act 1872 on the Library Archives Canada website, at https://www.collectionscanada.gc.ca/immigrants/021017-119.01-e.php?&document_code=021017-26&page=1&referer=021017-2210.01-e.html§ion_code=np-land&page_nbr=174&&&&&&&&&&&&PHPSESSID=if7k8pd6tjh43vjqd52vnjnne4.

127 Canada, *Prosperity follows Settlement*, 111.

128 Quoted in Shannon, "Brokers, Land Bankers, and 'Birds of Evil Omen,'" 3.

129 Ibid., 4

130 Ibid., 5.

131 Robertson, *The History of the County of Bruce*, 530.

132 *Journals of the House of Commons of the Dominion of Canada* from 6 Nov. 1867 to 22 May 1869, vol. 1 (Ottawa: Hunter, Rose and Co., 1868): appendix 8, pp. 16–17.

133 Moodie, *Roughing It in the Bush.*

134 "Emigrant Lady," *Letters from Muskoka.*

135 Ibid., 42.

136 Ibid., 137.

137 Ibid., 131.

138 Ibid., 23.

139 Ibid., 64.

140 Ibid., 150.

141 Ibid., 156.

142 Ibid., 181.

143 Ibid., 186.

144 *Regulations under the Free Grants and Homesteads Act* (Canada: s.n., 189?); http://eco.canadiana.ca/view/oocihm.93761/2?r=0&s=1.

145 Ibid., 1.

146 Ibid., 5.

147 "Proclamation by His Excellency James Douglas," no. 15 (151) A.D. 1860, in *Appendix to the Revised Statutes of British Columbia, 1871* (Victoria: Richard Wolfenden, 1871), 61–62. Thanks to Pernille Jakobsen, University of Calgary, for her research on BC legislation.

148 "An Ordinance to amend and consolidate the Laws affecting Crown Lands in British Columbia," no. 144, 1 June 1870, in *Appendix to the Revised Statutes of British Columbia, 1871*, 492–94.

149 "An Act Respecting the Land of the Crown," 1908, c. 30, s. 1. *Revised Statutes of British Columbia* 1911, 1518. Victoria: R. Wolfenden.

150 Ibid., 1518–19.

151 Martin, *"Dominion Lands" Policy*, 393.

152 Allen, "Homesteading and Property Rights," 2.

153 Quoted in Muhn, "Women and the Homestead Act," 287.

154 Ibid., 289.

155 Ibid., 294.

156 LAC, RG 15, Homestead Land Registers from 1872, reel T-2. Thanks to Leslie Hall for her research and analysis of the homestead land registers.

157 Metcalfe, *The Tread of the Pioneers*, entry on Peter Walker, 263–64.

158 PAM, homestead file NE 20-2-3E, reel 2043.

159 Waddell, *Dominion City*, 18.

160 Ibid., 30.

161 LAC, RG 15, Homestead Land Registers from 1872, Reel T-2, 14.

162 LAC, Census of 1881 for Manitoba, district 186 Marquette, Woodlands no. 24, 10.

163 PAM, homestead file SW 24-20-6E, reel 2088.

164 Ibid., homestead file SE 4-16-2-E1, reel 2025.

165 Ibid., homestead file SW 9-14-11-W1, reel 2454.

166 Ibid., homestead file NW 30-9-7 E1, reel 2098.

167 Ibid., homestead file SE 32-12-5-W, reel 2258; Metcalfe, *The Tread of the Pioneers*, 57, 270.

168 PAM, homestead file SW 30-12-8-W, reel 2331.

169 Ibid., homestead file SE 24-12-8-W1, reel 2207.

170 LAC, RG 15, Homestead Land Register, Reel T-2, 80.

171 Ibid., 65.

172 PAM, homestead file NE 15-15-9W, reel 2372.

173 Ibid., Secretary F.R.B. [?] to Secretary, Department of the Interior, 20 March 1897.

174 PAM, homestead file NE 19-12-7-W1, reel 2295.

175 Ibid., homestead file NW 36-12-10-W, reel 2415.

176 Ibid., homestead file NE 33-10-6-E, reel 2088.

177 LAC, RG 15, Homestead Land Register, Reel T-2, 33.

178 Morton, *Manitoba*, 174.

179 Ibid., 177.

180 Friesen, *The Canadian Prairies*, 309.

181 Stead, "Fifty Years in Western Canada," 5.

182 *Manitoba Free Press*, 7 July 1875.

183 Ibid., 26 April 1875, 2.

184 Ibid., 18 June 1875, 2.

185 Ibid., 1 June 1875, 2.

186 Ibid., 9 June 1875, 2.

187 Order-in-council, 1875-0670, "Manitoba Grasshoppers—Acting [Minister of] Interior 17 June—[Recommends] authority to give leave of absence to occupants of Homestead—During prevalence of the plague," in LAC, RG 2, Series A-1-a, vol. 335; http://www.collectionscanada.gc.ca/databases/orders/001022-119.01-e.php?&sisn_id_nbr=6873&page_sequence_nbr=1&interval=20&&PHPSESSID=aqma40uu4ko0tlal1ocoe6v1h4.

188 Order-in-council, 1875-0901, "Relief of settlers in Manitoba rendered destitute by grasshopper ravages—[Minister of Agriculture] 8 September, respecting expenditure of $60,000 authorized by [order in council] 27 August '75 and [employment] of Mr. J.Y. Shantz to purchase supplies," in LAC, RG 2, Series A-1-a, vol. 337; http://www.collectionscanada.gc.ca/databases/orders/001022-119.01-e.php?&sisn_id_nbr=11998&page_sequence_nbr=1&interval=20&&PHPSESSID=aqma40uu4ko0tlal1ocoe6v1h4.

189 Canada, *Sessional Papers*, Annual Report of the Department of the Interior for the year ended 30 June 1875, no. 9, part III; no. 7, vol. 9, 1876.

190 *Manitoba Free Press*, 5 May 1876.

191 Lambrecht, *The Administration of Dominion Lands*, 106.

192 Currie, *The Letters of Rusticus.*

193 Ibid., 38.

194 Ibid.

195 Ibid.

196 Ibid.

197 "How Two Girls Tried Farming" was serialized in the *Manitoba Free Press* in the issues of 22, 23, 24, and 27 March 1875.

198 Ibid., 27 March 1875.

199 Sprague, "Donald Codd," *Dictionary of Canadian Biography*; http://www.biographi.ca/009004-119.01-ephp?BioId=40161.

200 James Cunningham, n.d. (1870s), "Sketch of scheme of construction of portion of Pacific Railway through the fertile regions and settlement of lands along the railway," in LAC, Alexander Mackenzie Papers, MG 26, Reel M-197, 694.

201 See, for example, "Government Aids Homesteaders," *Enterprise*, 23 July 1914, 3.

202 Patriarche, "Husbandless Homesteads Are Wanted in the West," *Saskatoon Star Phoenix*, 17 April 1913; and Thorne, "Woman and the Land," *Globe*, 21 May 1913.

203 Hall, *A Lady's Life on a Farm in Manitoba*, 24.

204 "Shocking Fatality in Manitoba," *New Zealand Herald* 19, issue 6410 (3 June 1882): 7.

205 Anon., "A Study in Homestead Laws: Some Comparison of Canadian and American Practice," *Saturday News*, 31 October 1908, 6.

206 Patriarche, "Husbandless Homesteads Are Wanted in the West," *Saskatoon Star Phoenix*, 17 April 1913.

207 Ibid.

208 "Manitoba," *Toronto Star*, 21 Feb. 1874, 7.

209 Currie, *The Letters of Rusticus*, 18.

210 "Vox," "The Indian Question," *Globe*, 17 Aug. 1881, 7.

211 *Prairie Illustrated* 1, no. 15 (14 March 1891): 11.

212 Levine, "Introduction: Why Gender and Empire?," 7.

213 Ibid.

214 "Where Women Are Farmers," *Globe*, 19 July 1910, 5.

215 Mason, *Woman's Share in Primitive Culture*, 6.

216 "Minutes of Evidence Taken: Immigration to Canada: Mr. Lowe's Evidence," *Journals of the House of Commons of the Dominion of Canada* (from the 7th February to the 10th May, 1878 being the 5th session of the 3rd Parliament of Canada, session 1878), A2-16.

217 Ibid.

218 J. Obed Smith, response to G. Binnie-Clark, in Binnie-Clark, "Land and the Woman in Canada," 509.

219 Lawrence, *Genteel Women*, 180.

220 Canada, *Sessional Papers*, Annual report of the Department of the Interior for the year ended 30 June 1875, xvi.

221 Ibid.

222 Quoted in Emmons, "American Myth, Desert to Eden," 6.

223 *St. Cloud Democrat*, 7 June 1866, 2.

224 Canada, *Sessional Papers*, Annual report of the Department of the Interior for the year ended 39 June 1875, 9.

225 Emmons, "American Myth, Desert to Eden," 6.

226 Ibid., 8.

227 Quoted in ibid., 11.

228 *Manitoba Free Press*, 25 March 1876, 4.

229 Lambrecht, *The Administration of Dominion Lands*, 131.

230 *Manitoba Free Press*, 30 June 1877, 5.

231 Lambrecht, *The Administration of Dominion Lands*, 132.

232 Currie, *The Letters of Rusticus*, 39.

233 Emmons, "American Myth, Desert to Eden," 14.

234 Lambrecht, *The Administration of Dominion Lands*, 34.

235 Richtik, "Manitoba Settlement 1870–86," 182.

236 "Homesteads for Women Asked for," N.d. n.p., in LAC, RG 15, D-II-1, vol. 1105, file 2876596.

237 Patriarche, "Husbandless Homesteads."

238 Lambrecht, *The Administration of Dominion Lands*, 106.

239 Patriarche, "Husbandless Homesteads."

240 *Bow Island Review*, 26 Dec. 1913, 7.

CHAPTER TWO

1 Sykes, "Openings for Educated Women in Canada," 433, 435.

2 Binnie-Clark, "Land and the Woman in Canada," 500, 498, 497.

3 Cran, *A Woman in Canada*, 266.

4 Verdon, *Rural Women Workers in Nineteenth-Century England.* Recent publications are confirming this regional variation; see Richardson, "Women Farmers of Snowdonia"; and Mark Riley, "Bringing the 'Invisible Farmer' into Sharper Focus."

5 Verdon, "Middle-Class Women's Work and the Professionalization of Farming in England."

6 "Ladies as Farmers," *Daily News*, 28 Dec. 1898, 3.

7 Crawford, "Englishwomen and Agriculture," 435.

8 Ibid.

9 Sayer, *Women of the Fields*, 36.

10 Ibid., 52–53.

11 For Western Canada, for example, see Carter, *Capturing Women.*

12 *Mirror* 25, no. 714 (11 April 1835): 233.

13 Sayer, *Women of the Fields*, 41.

14 Ibid., 178.

15 Quoted in Bradley, *Men's Work, Women's Work*, 89.

16 Ibid., 84.

17 Ibid., 82.

18 Ibid., 87.

19 Sayer, *Women of the Fields*, 120.

20 Bradley, *Men's Work, Women's Work*, 87.

21 Davidoff and Hall, *Family Fortunes*, 275.

22 Sayer, *Women of the Fields*, 151.

23 Verdon, "Middle-Class Women's Work and the Professionalization of Farming in England," 402.

24 Bone, "Legislation to Revive Small Farming in England."

25 Smith, *Land for the Small Man*, 2. See also Allen, *Colonies at Home.*

26 "Gardening for Women," *Examiner*, 30 Aug. 1879, 1119.

27 Chesney, "A New Vocation for Women," 341.

28 Ibid.

29 King, *Women Rule the Plot*, 7–10.

30 Warwick, introduction to Bradley and La Mothe, *The Lighter Branches of Agriculture*, xv.

31 Ibid., xx.

32 Wolseley, *In a College Garden*, 112.

33 Cresswell ["The Lady Farmer"], *Eighteen Years on the Sandringham Estate.* Verdon, "The Lady Farmer."

34 Cresswell ["Mrs. Gerard Cresswell"], How the Farming in Great Britain Can Be Made to Pay, 25.

35 Ibid., 24.

36 Ibid.

37 Burton, *My Home Farm.*

38 Ibid., 3.

39 Ibid., 105.

40 King, *Women Rule the Plot*, 108.

41 Levitan, "Redundancy, the 'Surplus Women' Problem, and the British Census." See also Kranidis, *The Victorian Spinster and Colonial Emigration*; Vicinus, *Independent Women.*

42 Vicinus, *Independent Women*, 3.

43 Ibid., 5.

44 "The Field as a Profession for Women: Lady Warwick's Scheme," *Review of Reviews* (June 1898): 578.

45 Ibid.

46 Crawford, "Englishwomen and Agriculture," 428.

47 "Gardening for Women," *Examiner*, 30 Aug. 1879, 1119.

48 Ibid., 1118.

49 Bradley, "The Agricultural Brigade of the Monstrous Regiment of Women," *Fortnightly Review* 63, no. 374 (February 1898): 334. This is in the form of a letter to the editor in response to Janet E. Hogarth, "The Monstrous Regiment of Women," in *Fortnightly Review* 62, no. 372 (December 1897): 926–36.

50 Wolseley, *In a College Garden*, 104.

51 Ibid., 105.

52 Wolseley, *Women and the Land*, 206.

53 Ibid., 208–9.

54 Verdon, "Middle-Class Women's Work and the Professionalization of Farming in England," 398.

55 Bradley, "The Agricultural Brigade of the Monstrous Regiment of Women," 334.

56 Ibid., 337.

57 Worsnop, "A Reevaluation of 'The Problem of Surplus Women' in 19th-Century England," 23.

58 Sayer, *Women of the Fields*, 5, 133–34.

59 Boucherett, *Hints on Self-Help*, vi.

60 Logan, *The Hour and the Woman*, 36–77 (chapter 2).

61 Bodichon, "Reasons for the Enfranchisement of Women" (1866), in Lacey, *Barbara Leigh Smith Bodichon and the Langham Place Group*, 107.

62 *Women's Suffrage Journal*, (1 Sept. 1883): 164.

63 Hansard Parliamentary Debates, House of Commons, 12 June 1884, 96.

64 Darby, "Current Agricultural Topics," *Jackson's Oxford Journal*, 12 Dec., 1891.

65 These statistics were quoted in *Otago Witness*, 8 Feb. 1900, 55.

66 Betham-Edwards, *Reminiscences*, 60.

67 I am using the terms "radical" and "conservative" as described by Worsnop in "A Reevaluation of 'The Problem of Surplus Women' in 19th-Century England," 23.

68 Anonymous, "A Woof for Women," *Agricultural Economist*, 1905, clipping in scrapbook 184, "Common Place Book 1901–6," Papers of Viscountess Frances Wolseley, Hove Central Library.

69 Freer, "Horticulture as a Profession for the Educated," *Nineteenth Century: A Monthly Review* (Nov. 1899): 775.

70 "Gardening for Women," *Examiner*, 30 Aug. 1879, 1118.

71 Anonymous, "Horticulture as a Career for Women," *Times*, 26 Dec., 1907.

72 "Gardening for Women," *Examiner*, 30 Aug. 1879, 1119.

73 Ibid., 1119.

74 Wolseley, *Gardening for Women*, xii.

75 "Ladies Gossip," *Otago Witness* 2397, 8 Feb. 1900, 55; quoted from an article in *Leeds Mercury*.

76 Chesney, "A New Vocation for Women."

77 Opitz, "A Triumph of Brains over Brute."

78 King, *Women Rule the Plot*, 31.

79 Ibid.

80 Ibid.

81 "Lady Farmers: Work at Warwick College," *Tamworth Herald*, 5 Nov. 1904, 8.

82 "Lady Farmers at Studley," *Western Times*, 22 Aug. 1905, 7.

83 Meredith, "Horticultural Education in England, 1900–1940."

84 Ibid., 70.

85 Weston, "Spinster Problem Solved," *Omaha Daily Bee*, 15 March 1908, 5.

86 "Ladies at the Plough," *Essex County Chronicle*, 28 Oct. 1910.

87 "From the Mountain"; "An Industrial Chance for Gentlewomen," *Once a Week* 9, no. 219 (5 Sept. 1863): 291.

88 Postcard, Commonplace Book 185, 1906–8, Papers of Viscountess Frances Wolseley, Hove Central Library.

89 Ibid.

90 Graham, *The Revival of English Agriculture*, 177.

91 Ibid., 177–78.

92 Darby, "Current Agricultural Topics," *Jackson's Oxford Journal*, 12 Dec. 1891.

93 Astor, "Lady Farmers: Women as Agriculturalists," *Harmsworth Magazine* 5 (Aug. 1900–Jan. 1901): 221–27.

94 Ibid., 224.

95 Dale, "Lady-Gardeners," *London Society*, (Aug. 1898): 149–51.

96 Strange, *Toronto's Girl Problem;* Stansell, *City of Women*; Walkowitz, *City of Dreadful Delight.*

97 Strange, *Toronto's Girl Problem*, 5.

98 Jusova, *The New Woman and the Empire.*

99 Young, "Throwing Like a Girl."

100 Bartky, *"Sympathy and Solidarity" and Other Essays*, 17.

101 Green, *The Light of the Home*, 130.

102 Ibid.

103 T.P.W., "The Redundancy of Spinster Gentlewomen," *Scottish Review* (July 1900): 95.

104 Saugeres, "She's Not Really a Woman, She's Half a Man," 642.

105 Ibid., 646.

106 Ibid., 648.

107 Anonymous, "Female Farmers," *Penny Magazine* (16 July 1842): 11.

108 "A Girl Farmer," *Queenslander*, 19 Oct. 1907, 4; "A Professor's Daughter as a Farmer," *Western Gazette*, 15 Nov. 1907, 11.

109 Ibid.

110 Darby, "Current Agricultural Topics," *Jackson's Oxford Journal*, 12 Dec. 1891.

111 "Queen Victoria's Cows," *Qu'Appelle Progress*, 17 Nov. 1892, 3.

112 Verdon, "Middle-Class Women's Work and the Professionalization of Farming in England," 414.

113 "The Successful Woman Farmer," *Daily Mail*, 1 April 1910; "The Woman Poultry Farmer," *Daily Mail*, 15 April, 1910.

114 Verdon, "Middle-Class Women's Work and the Professionalization of Farming in England,"414.

115 "The Empty Lands," *United Empire* 2 (1911): 778.

116 Ibid.

117 Chilton, *Agents of Empire*, 79.

118 Brice, "Emigration for Gentlewomen," *Nineteenth Century: A Monthly Review* (April 1901): 603.

119 Ibid.

120 Chilton, *Agents of Empire*, 90.

121 Barber, "The Servant Problem in Manitoba."

122 Brice, "Emigration for Gentlewomen," *Nineteenth Century: A Monthly Review* (April 1901): 603.

123 Chilton, *Agents of Empire*, 81.

124 Ibid., 95.

125 Levitan, "Redundancy, the 'Surplus Women' Problem, and the British Census" 367.

126 Worsnop, "A Reevaluation of 'The Problem of Surplus Women' in 19th-Century England," 23.

127 Boucherett, "How to Provide for Superfluous Women," 46.

128 Ibid., 45.

129 Ibid., 41–42.

130 This historiography is reviewed in Chilton, *Agents of Empire*, 93–94.

131 Chilton, *Agents of Empire*, 95.

132 Quoted in Gordon, *Politics and Society*, 35.

133 Weston, "Hints for the Single Women of the United Kingdom," *National Review* 17, no. 98 (April 1891): 279.

134 "Tea and Silk Farming in New Zealand," *Chambers Journal of Popular Literature, Science and Arts*, no. 917 (23 July 1881): 469.

135 Weston, "Hints for the Single Women of the United Kingdom," 280.

136 Ibid., 283.

137 Ibid., 284.

138 "Civis Britannicus," "The Need of Women Colonists in South Africa," *Saturday Review of Politics, Literature, Science and Art*, 20 Sept. 1902, 365.

139 M. F-G. (Anonymous), "Should Women Emigrate," *Monthly Review* 27, no. 80 (May 1907): 99–105.

140 "Colonial Training for Gentlemen's Sons," *Chambers Journal of Popular Literature, Science and Arts* 2, no. 95 (Oct. 1995): 684.

141 *Imperial Colonist* 3, no. 25 (Jan. 1904): 11.

142 Vernon, *Leaton Colonial Training Home*, 4–5.

143 Ibid., 12.

144 Ibid., 5.

145 Ibid., 8.

146 *Imperial Colonist* 6, no. 61 (Jan. 1907): 8.

147 "A Farming Hostel for Girls: An Appeal by Lady Warwick," *Review of Reviews* 26, no. 152 (August 1902): 156.

148 Ibid.

149 Ibid.

150 Ibid.

151 Opitz, "A Triumph of Brains over Brute," 51.

152 Ibid., 52.

153 Ibid., 53.

154 *Imperial Colonist* 3, no. 26 (Feb. 1904): 23–24.

155 Ibid., 3, no. 27 (March 1904): 33.

156 "The Woman at Home," *The Review of Reviews* 40, no. 239 (Nov. 1909): 47.

157 Tooley, "Training Girls for Life in the Colonies," *Globe*, 9 July 1910, A4. See Doughty, "Representing the Professional Woman."

158 *Imperial Colonist* 10, no. 121 (Jan. 1912): 17–18.

159 Ibid., 12, no. 148 (May 1914): 79–80.

160 Delahey, "Emma Ducie Active at 100," *Western Producer*, 12 May 1983, n.p., Glenbow Archives Clipping File, "Agriculture-Women."

161 Ibid.

162 Oxendale, "What Should They Know of England Who Only England Know?" See Chapter 4.

163 Gordon, *Politics and Society*, 32.

164 Blakeley, "Women and Imperialism,"136.

165 *Imperial Colonist* 1, no. 1 (Jan. 1902): 4.

166 Ibid., 1, no. 12 (Dec. 1912): 114.

167 Ibid., 2 no. 5 (June 1903): 69.

168 Ibid., 2, no. 5 (May 1903): 59.

169 Ibid., 112.

170 Ibid., 2 no. 2 (Feb. 1903): 21

171 Ibid., 3, no. 25 (Jan. 1904): 3.

172 Ibid., 3, no. 27 (March 1904): 27.

173 Ibid., 28.

174 Ibid., 5, no. 50 (Feb. 1906): 39.

175 Ibid., 5, no. 50 (Feb. 1906): 40.

176 Ibid., 6, no. 65 (May 1907): 6.

177 Ibid., 6, no. 69 (Sept. 1907): 3.

178 Ibid., 6, no. 67 (July 1907): 2.

179 Ibid., 8.

180 Ibid., 10, no. 130 (Oct. 1912): 168.

181 Ibid.

182 Ibid., 10, no. 122 (Feb. 1912): 24.

183 Quoted in Opitz, "A Triumph of Brains over Brute," 52.

184 "Our Special Commissioner," "Empire Migration: What are the Prospects for Educated Women," *Quiver*, Jan. 1919, 611.

185 Taylor, "Conditions of Life for Women in South Africa," 122.

186 Bush, *Edwardian Ladies and Imperial Power*, 151.

187 "South African Women Farmers," *Vote*, 19 July 1927, 237.

188 "The Review of Reviews," *Nineteenth Century* 25, no. 148 (April 1902): 394.

189 *Imperial Colonist* 5, no. 6 (Dec. 1906): 177.

190 Ibid., 6, no. 77 (May 1908): 8.

191 Ibid., 8, no. 104 (Aug. 1910): 127–28.

192 Ibid., 1, no. 12 (Dec. 1902): 112.

193 Ibid., 9, no. 112 (April 1911): 282.

194 Ibid., 9, no. 118 (Oct. 1911): 377.

195 Helly, "Flora Shaw and the Times."

196 Anonymous (Flora Shaw), "Letters from Canada VII, Prairie Settlement—Part 1," Times, 22 Nov. 1898, 6.

197 Helly, "Flora Shaw and the Times," 122.

198 Brice, "Emigration for Gentlewomen," *Nineteenth Century: A Monthly Review* (April 1901): 609.

199 Bernard, "A Training School for Lady Colonists in the Canadian North-West," Times, 5 April 1899, 5.

200 Ibid.

201 Barber, "The Gentlewomen of Queen Mary's Coronation Hostel," 144.

202 Lang, *Women Who Made the News*, 49.

203 Stoddard, "Lally Bernard: An Imperial Daughter," *Canadian Magazine* 46, no. 6 (1916): 513–15.

204 Anonymous (Flora Shaw), "Women and Colonial Settlement," *Times*, 11 April 1899, 8.

205 Quoted in *Leeds Mercury* editorial, 12 April 1899.

206 Ibid.

207 See, for example, *Montreal Gazette*, 22 April 1899, 11; *Leader*, 22 June 1899; *Daily Mail and Empire* (Toronto), 29 April 1899, 15 and 24.

208 Fitzgibbon (Lally Bernard), "Training Schools for Lady Colonists in the Canadian North-West," *Times*, 23 May 1899, 10.

209 *Weekend Herald* (Calgary), 5 Oct. 1899, 4.

210 "M. F-G," "Should Women Emigrate?," *Monthly Review* 27, no. 80 (1907): 99–105.

211 Ibid., 103.

212 *Times*, 26 April 1899, 4.

213 "Women and the West," *Globe*, 16 June 1899, 6.

214 Fitzgibbon, *Times*, 23 May 1889, 10.

215 "Women and the Colonies," *Times*, 1 June 1904, 10.

216 Bernard, "Driftwood," *Globe*, 5 Sept. 1903, 14.

217 Ibid., "Driftwood," *Globe*, 1 June 190, 18.

218 Ibid., "Glimpses of the West," *Globe*, 14 April 1900, 9.

219 London School of Economics (LSE), Women's Library, Records of the Colonial Intelligence League (CIL); King, *Women Rule the Plot*, 51–76; Oxendale, "What Should They Know of England Who Only England Know?," 138–155.

220 Annual Reports CIL, no. 1 (1910), 10, Box 37, CIL Papers.

221 "Unmarried Daughters," *Times*, 7 Dec. 1909, 10.

222 Ibid.

223 Annual Reports CIL, no. 1 (1910), 1, in LSE, Records of the CIL, Box 37.

224 "Women's Emigration," *Times*, 16 April 1910.

225 *Daily Colonist*, 9 April 1911, 8; 14 June 1912, 5; 20 March 1913, 8; 20 June 1914, 2.

226 Grosvenor, "Women Farmers in Canada: British Farm Settlement," *Times*, 27 Feb. 1913, 5.

227 Ibid.

228 Yarmie, "I Had Always Wanted to Farm," 105.

229 Ibid.

230 "Lady Sybil Grey Miner," *Globe*, 18 Sept. 1909, 8.

231 Yarmie, "'I Had Always Wanted to Farm,'" 106.

232 Sykes, *A Home-Help in Canada*, 304.

233 "Ranch for Women," *Ashburton Guardian* vol. 33, no. 8799 (20 Feb. 1914): 6.

234 Ibid.

235 CIL Reference Book: Canada, in LSE, Records of the CIL.

236 Barber, "The Gentlewomen of Queen Mary's Coronation Hostel."

237 Stoddard, "Lally Bernard: An Imperial Daughter," *Canadian Magazine* 46, no. 6 (91916): 514.

238 Barber, "The Gentlewomen of Queen Mary's Coronation Hostel," 150.

239 The *Daily Colonist* editorial is quoted in the *Globe*, 19 July 1913, 6.

240 Yarmie, "'I Had Always Wanted to Farm,'" 113.

241 CIL Minute Book, meeting 16 Oct. 1913, 3, in LSE, Records of the CIL, Box 38.

242 "Mischievous Benevolence," editorial, *Daily Colonist,* 11 July 1913, 4.

243 Seaton, "The Garden Autobiography," 110–11.

244 Cran, *A Woman in Canada*. The book was published in England, Canada and the United States in 1911, and when it first appeared is not clear; it may have been as early as 1909.

245 Cran, *A Woman in Canada*, 14–15.

246 Ibid., 22.

247 Ibid., 39.

248 Ibid., 38.

249 Ibid., 153.

250 Ibid.

251 Ibid., 154.

252 Ibid., 155.

253 "Women Farmers in Canada: A Great Future," *Warwick Examiner and Times* 21 June, 1909, 3.

254 Cran, *A Woman in Canada*, 162.

255 Ibid., 266.

256 Ibid.

257 Smith, "Adventurous Girls of the British Empire."

258 Ibid., 12, 13.

259 Ibid., 4.

260 Ibid., 16.

261 Ibid.

262 Ward, *Canadian Born*. This book was published in the United States with the title *Lady Mereton, Colonist*.

263 Harris, "Hobart and 'Home' in Tasma and Mrs. Humphry Ward."

264 Swan, "Prairie Fires," *Quiver* 48, no. 11 (Sept. 1913): 1044.

265 Ibid., 1053.

266 Ibid., 48, no. 12 (October 1913): 1130.

267 Austin, *Woman*, 35.

268 Ibid.

269 Ibid., 35–36.

270 Hoodless, "Trades and Industries: The Industrial Possibilities of Canada," in *Women of Canada: Their Life and Work*, 92.

271 Ibid., 95.

272 Ibid.

273 Crowley, "Adelaide Sophia Hunger (Hoodless)," *Dictionary of Canadian Biography*, http://www.biographi.ca/en/bio/hunter_adelaide_sophia_13E.html.

274 *Women of Canada: Their Life and Work*, 86.

275 Strong, "Horticulture as a Profession for Women," in *Report on the International Congress of Women*, 319.

276 Yates, "Women in Agriculture," in *Report on the International Congress of Women*, 308.

277 *Women of Canada: Their Life and Work*, 86–87.

278 Ibid.

279 Crerar, "Educated Women for Canada," *Times*, 30 May 1910, 6. On the International Order of the Daughters of the Empire, see Pickles, *Female Imperialism and National Identity*.

280 Rees, *New and Naked Land*, 8.

281 Ibid.

282 Ibid.

283 Ibid., 10.

284 Canadian Pacific Railway Company, *Words from the Women of Western Canada*.

285 Ibid., 4.

286 Ibid., 38.

287 Canadian Pacific Railway Company, *Women's Work in Western Canada: A Sequel to "Words from the Women of Western Canada."*

288 Ibid., 26.

289 Ibid., 38–39.

290 Ibid., 45–46.

291 Ibid., 13–14.

292 Ibid., 13.

293 "Canada for Women," *Daily Mail* 2 March, 1910: n.p.

294 Chapman, "The Argument of the Broken Pane: Suffragette Consumerism and Newspapers," *Media History* 21:3 (2015): 247.

295 Ibid.

296 "Canada for Women," *Woman's Leader and the Common Cause* v. 210 (1913): 28.

297 "A Welcome to Women in British Columbia," *Suffragette*, 7 March 1913, 339.

CHAPTER THREE

1 "Western Farmers Exhibit Brightest Crop Prospects," *Edmonton Bulletin*, 3 Aug. 1909, 1.

2 Brada-Easthill-Roecliffe Historical Society, *Rural Roots*, 82.

3 1906 Census of the Northwest Provinces, Library Archives Canada; http://data2.collectionscanada.ca/e/e049/e001210880.jpg.

4 *Bow Island Review*, 26 Dec. 1913, 7.

5 "Free" is often within quotation marks to indicate that while the Canadian government advertised the grant of 160 acres as free, this was far from the case, as the successful homestead involved considerable cost and labour. See the summary of debates about homestead costs in Russell, *How Agriculture Made Canada*, 238–42.

6 Canada, Dominion Lands Branch, *Homestead Regulations of North-Western Canada with an Abridgement of the Dominion Lands Act* (Ottawa: Department of the Interior, 1903), 3.

7 Grand Trunk Pacific Railway, General Passenger Department, *Land Seekers' Guide*, 22.

8 Dick, *Farmers "Making Good."*

9 This section is taken from Col. G.C. Porter, "Homesteading Widow Raises 10 Children on Crusoe Cuisine," *Winnipeg Evening Tribune*, 13 Feb. 1943, 22; and "Jessie Margaret McGavin, Physician," Memorable Manitobans; http://www.mhs.mb.ca/docs/people/mcgavin_jm.shtml.

10 Richards, "The Story of Beautiful Plains."

11 Schofield, *The Story of Manitoba*, 69–70.

12 1891 Census, Northwest Territories, Library and Archives Canada; http://data2.collectionscanada.gc.ca/1891/jpg/30953_148228-00466.jpg. See also *Moose Jaw Herald*, 11 Sept. 1896, 5; 1 Sept. 1899, 1.

13 Oak Lake Historical Committee, *Ox Trails to Blacktop*, 162–63.

14 Alberta Historical Society, *Cypress Hills Country*, 275–76.

15 Biographical information is taken from the marriage notice of Agnes Katherine Cobb and Francis William Bedingfeld, in *Gentleman's Magazine and Historical Review*, Nov. 1862, 627; information on Agnes Katherine Cobb, later Agnes Katherine Bedingfeld, and her son Francis is also from the U.K. census online from 1861, 1871, and 1881; see, for example, the 1881 census available at http://www.ukcensusonline.com/search/index.php?fn=agnes&sn=Bedingfeld&phonetic_mode=1&event=1881&token=5azQWxpqQ8pu77yZu0Y8-IdxpiGha8ER9SchU-hb_MM. Notice of the death of Lt. Francis W. Bedingfeld is from the *United Service Magazine* 119 (1869): 453.

16 PAA, homestead file 513196, reel 2053.

17 Evans, *Prince Charming Goes West*, 51.

18 PAA homestead file 1208837, reel 2752.

19 Lehr, "The Making of the Prairie Landscape," 11–12; Evans, *The Bar U: Canadian Ranching History*, 76, 78.

20 "The Prince of Wales as Rancher," *Red Deer News*, 19 May, 1920, 9.

21 History Book Society, *Fencelines and Furrows*, 276–78.

22 PAA, homestead file, file 819163, reel 2714.

23 History Book Society, *Fencelines and Furrows*, 277.

24 Pleasantdale and District History Book Committee, *Memories of the Past*, 496–97.

25 Ibid., 497.

26 SAB, homestead file 1591363: SE 28-9-3-W3; and 1774242: NE 21-9-3-W3. See also Mehain and Limerick Historical Society, *Prairie Trails and Pioneer Tales*, 188–92.

27 Coyote Flats Historical Society, *Coyote Flats Historical Review 1905–1965*, 1:63.

28 "Another Oldtimer Passes from the District," *Crossfield Chronicle*, 1 Sept. 1938; Anon., *Prairie Sod and Goldenrod: History of Crossfield and District*, 96.

29 Ghost Pine Community Group, *Memoirs of the Ghost Pine Homesteaders*, 68.

30 Ibid.

31 "Lyster/Sommerville Clan Gather for A Reunion," *Three Hills Capital*, 13 Aug. 2014.

32 Parkbeg History Book Group, *Parkbeg Reflections*, 234–35.

33 Aberdeen Historical Society, *Aberdeen, 1907–1981*, 117.

34 Lacombe Rural History Club, *Wagon Trails to Hard Top*, 568.

35 Webb History Book Committee, *Prairie Memories*, 595.

36 Ibid., 652–53.

37 Yellow Lake History Group, *Treasured Memories*, 531.

38 Parkbeg History Book Group, *Parkbeg Reflections*, 236.

39 Webb History Book Committee, *Prairie Memories*, 1143–44.

40 Notukeu History Book Club, *Next Year Country*, 381.

41 Kenyon, *Lone Rock to Marshall*, 359.

42 Rita Mary Cleveley, "1796 through 1999 … and All the Years Between," unpublished history of the Cleveley family. Thanks to Matthew Ostapchuk, MA, University of Alberta Department of History, for sharing his family history with me.

43 SAB, homestead file 1863456: NE 20-5-1-W3.

44 Ibid., statutory declaration by Mrs. O. Thompson, 14 Sept. 1912.

45 McPherson, "Was the 'Frontier' Good for Women?," 80.

46 This data is from The Last Best West: The Alberta Land Settlement Infrastructure Project at the University of Alberta, with principal investigator Peter Baskerville and co-investigators Sarah Carter and Sean Gouglas. This preliminary data was provided by Peter Baskerville in an email of 14 April 2014.

47 Blaine Lake and District Historical Book Committee, *Bridging the Years*, 476.

48 Ibid.

49 Leonard, *The Last Great West*, 565–66.

50 Thanks to Doris J. MacKinnon, Red Deer, author of *The Identities of Marie Rose Delorme Smith: Portrait of a Métis Woman, 1861–1960*, for providing me with the homestead file of Marie Rose Smith.

51 PAA, homestead file 1390105, reel 2077; LAC, RG 15, Metis Scrip Records, scrip application of Julia Rowland for her deceased son Angus Rowland, form D. no. 2770; Morrow, "The Deville Story," 16.

52 The debates about the cost of homesteading are summarized in Russell, *How Agriculture Made Canada*, 238–42.

53 Church-Staudt, "Agnes (Martin) Balfour: Descendants Uphold Her Heritage," 21. Thanks to Douglas Ramsay for sharing information on Agnes Balfour and family.

54 PAA, homestead file 3268427, reel 2462.

55 Ibid., homestead file 1465905, reel 2789.

56 *Edmonton Bulletin*, 9 Jan. 1906, 3.

57 Advertisement, *Edmonton Capital*, 16 April 1910, 6.

58 "Death of Madame de Tro," *Edmonton Bulletin*, 17 May 1913, 13.

59 Wood Mountain Historical Society, *They Came to Wood Mountain*, 194.

60 LAC, Census of Canada 1911, Saskatchewan, district and subdistrict: Regina, item no. 7690602, 44.

61 Wood Mountain Histortical Society, *They Came to Wood Mountain*, 195.

62 SAB, homestead file 2133402: SW 6-3-5-W3, Marion Pearce to Dominion Lands Office, 11 Dec. 1911.

63 Ibid., F. Nelson to Pearce, 24 Jan. 1912.

64 Ibid., homestead inspector's report, Sept. 1919.

65 Potyondi, *In Palliser's Triangle*, 96–99.

66 SAB, homestead file 2133402, Acting Commissioner of Dominion Lands to Mrs. Frazer, 1928.

67 See Hryrniuk and Korvemaker, *Legacy of Stone*, 11–13.

68 Ibid.

69 John Geddes to the Secretary, Department of the Interior, 23 Oct. 1890, SAB homestead file 425772, SW2-9-5-W2.

70 LAC, Western Land Grants, Mary Ann McNab, SW 2-9-5-W2.

71 Lambrecht, *The Administration of Dominion Lands*, 116.

72 SAB, homestead file 500684: SE 14-14-10-W2.

73 Canada, *Prosperity Follows Settlement*, 111.

74 "Cupid Championed by Miss Rankin in Talk to Congress," *Washington Times*, 8 Dec. 1917, 5.

75 LAC, Census of Canada 1891 for the Province of Manitoba, Selkirk District, Virden Village.

76 *Manitoba Free Press*, 28 Dec. 1882.

77 *Winnipeg Daily Times*, 2 Oct. 1882.

78 Ibid., 30 Sept. 1882, and *Manitoba Free Press*, 28 Dec. 1882.

79 See Kendle, "Thomas Mayne Daly," *Dictionary of Canadian Biography*; http://www.biographi.ca/en/bio/daly_thomas_mayne_1852_1911_14E.html.

80 "Money Flew Fast in the Good Old Tory Days," *Globe*, 5 Jan. 1901, 5.

81 These letters are quoted in "Mr. Daly Had Strong Pull," *Brandon Daily Sun*, 1 Oct. 1908, 1.

82 "Mr. Daly's Homestead," *Brandon Daily Sun*, 16 Oct. 1908, 4.

83 LAC, Census of Canada 1901, Province of Manitoba, District 6 Brandon, Village of Virden, p. 1.

84 *Thomas Mayne Daly*, Manitoba Culture, Heritage and Recreation.

85 Letter, ____ Hall to E.L. Newcombe, 2 April 1896 in Circumstances under which married woman or widow may obtain a homestead entry, LAC, Record Group 13 (RG 13) Records of the Department of Justice, vol. 2247, file int. 25 74/1896.

86 Letter, William Wilson to A.M. Burgess, 28 April 1886, in LAC, RG 13, vol. 2247, file int. 25 74/1896.

87 SAB, homestead file 317719: NW 16-47-26-W2.

88 Ibid., Clerk of the Privy Council to the Minister of the Interior, 18 Feb. 1895.

89 Ellen Margaret Cameron to Department of the Interior, January 1887, in LAC, RG 15, D-II-1, vol. 477, file 130492.

90 Secretary, Department of the Interior to E.M. Cameron, 19 Jan. 1887, in LAC, RG 15, D-II-1, vol. 477, file 130492.

91 Letter, ____ Hall to E.L. Newcombe, 28 Sept. 1893. "Homestead entry of Margaret Spence—half-breed woman with illegitimate children," in LAC, RG 13, vol. 2271, file 150-1893.

92 Letter, Deputy Minister of Justice to Secretary, Department of the Interior, 19 Oct. 1893, in LAC, RG 13, vol. 2271, file 150-1893.

93 Scrip application. Young, Sarah. Address: Stonewall; born 8 Sept. 1885 at Rabbit Point: father: Thomas Young (Whiteman); mother Margaret Spence (Metis); scrip cert.: form E, no. 3492; claim no. 588. vol 1371, in LAC, RG 15, D-II-8-c.

94 Memorandum, Department of Justice, 8 Nov. 1894, in LAC, RG 13, vol. 2247, file int. 25 74/1896.

95 LAC, RG 15, vol. 2108, ruling no. 167, 53–54.

96 LAC, RG 15, Dominion Land Rulings, no. 1504, Memorandum, 27 Aug. 1914.

97 See, for example, SAB, homestead file 2178290: NE 10-3-16 W3 (Mrs. Nettie Blackmer).

98 LAC, RG 15, Dominion Lands Rulings, no. 496-1894, Deputy Minister of Justice to the Secretary, Department of the Interior, 8 Aug. 1894.

99 PAA, homestead file, reel 2434, file 3006361.

100 Canada, *Debates of the House of Commons*, 3rd session, 10th Parliament, vol. 80 (Ottawa: S.E. Dawson, 1906–7), 4813–14.

101 LAC, RG 15, Dominion Lands Rulings, no. 4171, vol. 1971, Department of the Interior circular letter, 21 July 1920.

102 Thwaite, *Alberta: An Account of Its Wealth and Progress*, 306–7.

103 SAB, homestead file 861961: SW 28 25-24-W2.

104 Ibid., James F. MacLean to J.G. Turriff, 30 Jan. 1904.

105 LAC, RG 15, Dominion Land Rulings, no. 4369, Memorandum, 10 Feb. 1921.

106 LAC, RG 15, vol. 2277, file 1895-242, Deputy Minister of Justice to the Secretary, Department of the Interior, 5 March 1895.

107 PAA, homestead file 641486, reel 2074, images 1612–1614: SE 30-4-28-W4.

108 Doughan, "Pioneer Club," *Oxford Dictionary of National Biography*; http://www.oxforddnb.com/templates/theme.jsp?articleid=96079.

109 *Edmonton Bulletin*, 29 May 1912, 3.

110 LAC, RG 15, Dominion Land Rulings, no. 2544, Memorandum, 27 Jan. 1917.

111 LAC, RG 13, vol. 2377, file 105/1895, E. Newcombe to L. Pereira, 31 May 1895.

112 SAB, homestead file 467578: NE 26-26-5-W2.

113 S.C. 1897 60–61 Victoria c. 29 s. 12; Lambrecht, *The Administration of Dominion Lands*, 106.

114 Pollock, *Our Pioneers*, 92.

115 See http://boards.ancestry.com/thread.aspx?mv=flat&m=2835&p=surnames.harvey.

116 LAC, Census of the Western Provinces, 1906; http://data2.collectionscanada.ca/e/e049/e001207780.jpg.

117 Pollock, *Our Pioneers*, 92.

118 Veldhuis, *For Elise: Unveiling the Forgotten Woman on the Criddle Homestead*.

119 PAM, 2255 #375, homestead file NW 28-8-26-W1, Elise Vane to Dominion Lands Agent, Brandon, 19 Aug. 1889.

120 Ibid., Vane to A.H. Smith, Commissioner of Dominion Lands, Winnipeg, 30 Sept. 1889 and Vane to the Minister of the Interior 2 Oct. 1889.

121 Ibid., Anonymous letter to the Commissioner of Dominion Lands, 31 Jan. 1890 from Aweme, Manitoba.

122 Ibid., R.O. Cook to Commissioner of Dominion Lands, Winnipeg, 22 Feb. 1890.

123 Ibid., Percy Criddle to Smith, 26 Feb. 1890.

124 LAC, 1891 Census, district 7 Marquette, subdistrict South Cypress, Manitoba; http://data2.collectionscanada.gc.ca/1891/jpg/30953_148095-00496.jpg.

125 Ibid., for 1901; http://data2.collectionscanada.ca/1901/z/z001/jpg/z000016439.jpg.

126 "Through Silent Night Watches," *Edmonton Bulletin*, 1 Sept. 1908, 1.

127 Watt, *Town and Trail*, 67.

128 "Congratulations," *Edmonton Bulletin*, 3 Sept. 1908, 8.

129 PAA, homestead files, file 1681610, reel 2827; file 1238377, reel 2756.

130 Fullerton, "Our Homesteaders," *Canadian Magazine* 16, no. 3 (January 1916): 253.

131 Anon., "Our Western Lands."

132 LAC, RG 15, Dominion Lands Rulings, vol. 1957, p. 417, Memorandum Oliver to Greenway, 24 Jan. 1910.

133 Ibid., 422, W.W. Cory to T. Greenway, 30 May 1910.

134 Ibid., Memorandum, 23 May 1910.

135 Ibid., Memorandum 16 July 1910, 479.

136 Roy, "A Berkhamstead Boy in the Foothills," 24.

137 Ibid., 17, 29.

138 LAC, RG 15, Dominion Lands Rulings, vol. 1957, 484, Memorandum, A.J. Fraser to F.F. Dixon, 16 June 1910.

139 See, for example, the case of Margrit Hefferman, in PAA, homestead file 119536, reel 2750.

140 LAC, RG2, orders-in-council, no. 2055, "Sale lands Mrs. Marion [*sic*] B. Heath of Leduc..." 1895/07/02.

141 Ibid.

142 LAC, Maria Ann Bell-Heath land patent; http://www.bac-lac.gc.ca/eng/discover/land/land-grants-western-canada-1870-1930/pages/image.aspx?URLjpg=http%3a%2f%2fcentral.bac-lac.gc.ca%2f.item%2f%3fid%3de002979350%26op%3dimg%3dwesternlandgrants&Ecopy=e002979350.

143 PAA, homestead file 1195365, reel 2750.

144 "Took Up Homesteading Illegally," *Minnedosa Tribune*, 8 Sept. 1910, 2.

145 This section is taken from "Got Nine Months: Guilty of Perjury," *Medicine Hat Times*, 25 August 1910, 7.

146 PAM, homestead file SE 12-24-25-W.

147 LAC, 1881 Census, Manitoba, Rockwood Division, Lisgar.

148 LAC, 1891 Census, Manitoba, Marquette, Cypress South.

149 LAC, 1901 Census, Manitoba, Marquette, Dauphin.

150 LAC, 1906 Census, Manitoba, village of Grandview.

151 LAC, RG2, order-in-council, number 1850, "Dominion lands homestead sold Mrs. Delia Bell, homesteader at $3 p. acre," Minister of the Interior, 1910/09/15.

152 PAM, homestead file SE 23-26-27-W of the Principal Meridian, Secretary of the Department of the Interior to Margaret Little, 26 Feb. 1909.

153 Ibid., F. Herchmer to Secretary, Department of the Interior, 24 Feb. 1910.

154 Ibid., Herchmer to F.E. McGregor, 18 April 1910, and McGregor to Herchmer, 7 May 1910.

155 Ibid., Margaret Little to Secretary Department of the Interior, 9 May 1910.

156 Ibid., statutory declaration of Margaret Little, 9 June 1910.

157 Ibid., John A. Watson to Herchmer, August 1910.

158 Ibid., Herchmer to M. Little, 2 Dec. 1910.

159 Ibid., M. Little to Secretary, Department of the Interior, 7 Dec. 1910.

160 Ibid., Herchmer to Secretary, Department of the Interior, 21 Jan. 1911.

161 Ibid., letters patent to Ross Little.

162 "An Enterprising Lady," *Minnedosa Tribune*, 19 Jan. 1911, 2.

163 PAM, homestead file SE 23-26-27-W of the Principal Meridian, William Hughes to Commissioner of Dominion Lands, 12 Jan. 1903.

164 Ibid., homestead file NW 10-26-28-W of the Principal Meridian, Last Will and Testament of William Hughes.

165 Carter, "My Vocabulary Contains No Such Word as Defeat."

166 PAA, homestead file 570088, reel 2062, Clara A. Lynch to W.H. Cottingham, 2 June 1900. All of the rest of the correspondence in this section is from this file. Her land was Section 12, Township 40, Range 1, West of the 5th Meridian. For the history of Bentley, see Bentley and District Historical Society, *Bentley and District Early History.*

167 Turriff to Oliver, 3 April 1901.

168 Lynch to Oliver, 15 May 1901.

169 SAB, homestead file 2487207.

170 SAB, Homestead Index and homestead files.

171 Canada, *House of Commons Debates*, 1907–08, 10 July 1908, 12607.

172 Canada, *House of Commons Debates*, 1907–08, vol. 88, 10 July 1908, 12617.

173 SAB, homestead file 1780808.

174 Canada, *House of Commons Debates*, 1907–08, vol. 83, 25 Feb. 1908, 3782–83; Graham, *A Canadian Girl in South Africa: A Teacher's Experiences in the South African War, 1899–1902.*

175 *Manitoba Free Press*, 17 May 1910; *Daily Phoenix*, 16 May 1910; *Morning Leader*, 17 May 1910.

176 *Toledo Blade*, 23 June 1910.

177 SAB, homestead file 1915194.

178 *Secret Service* 611 (7 Oct. 1910): 29.

179 *Saskatoon Star Phoenix*, 20 Dec. 1917, 3.

180 *Edmonton Bulletin*, 21 May 1910.

181 Ibid.

182 SAB, homestead file 1513986.

183 Eatonia History Book Committee, *A Past to Cherish*, 463.

184 Leonard, *The Last Great West*, 563.

185 SAB, homestead file 2125459.

186 SAB, homestead file 1691732.

187 Stone Diggers History Book Committee, *Prairie Wool*, 181.

188 SAB, homestead file 108200A.

189 Birtles, "A Pioneer Nurse," 2.

190 SAB, homestead file 1773681.

191 SAB, homestead file 1406319.

192 SAB, homestead file 1884227.

193 SAB, homestead file 2138434.

194 SAB, homestead file 2138434.

195 SAB, homestead file 1733160.

196 SAB, homestead file 2092263.

197 Ibid., Jane Gentles to Minister of the Interior, 1 April 1915.

198 Ibid., statement of Jane Gentles, 21 July 1915.

199 *Edmonton Bulletin*, 21 May 1910.

200 See, for, example Bauman, "Single Women Homesteaders in Wyoming"; Garceau, *The Important Things of Life*; Gould and Pando, *Claiming Their Land*; Lindgren, *Land in Her Own Name*; Patterson-Black, "Women Homesteaders on the Great Plains Frontier."

201 Muhn, "Women and the Homestead Act," 286.

202 James Muhn indicates that Mormon women involved in plural marriages were able to file on homesteads until 1878, when the General Land Office ruled that they would no longer be permitted to do so ("Women and the Homestead Act," 290–91). Katherine Benton-Cohen, however, found that Mormon women "finessed homesteading law to accommodate plural marriage or to help children born in Mormon colonies in Mexico to obtain land in the United States." Benton-Cohen, "Common Purposes, Worlds Apart," 431.

203 Memorandum, 8 Nov. 1894, LAC, RG 13, vol. 2247, file int. 25: 74/1896.

204 Anon., *Montana 1909*, 48.

205 Muhn, "Women and the Homestead Act," 283. Many thanks to James Muhn, Land Law Historian for the U.S. Department of the Interior's Bureau of Land Management, for his assistance with my research and for sending me an offprint of this article.

206 Smith, "Single Women Homesteaders," 164.

207 Benton-Cohen, "Common Purposes, Worlds Apart," 435.

208 Lindgren, *Land in Her Own Name*, 20.

209 Ibid., 224.

210 *Hinsdale Tribune*, 21 Dec. 1917.

211 Walker-Kuntz, "Land, Life and *Feme Sole*," 46.

212 Egly Country Club, *Trails, Trials and Tributes*, 40.

213 Geraldine History Committee, *Spokes, Spurs and Cockleburs*, 205.

214 Liberty County Museum, *Our Heritage in Liberty*, 184.

215 U.S. Department of the Interior, Bureau of Land Mangment, General Land Office Records, Sheridan County, Montana; http://www.glorecords.blm.gov/results/default.aspx?searchcriteria=type=patent/st=MT/cty=091/ln=macgregor/sp=true/sw=true/sady=false.

216 Many thanks to Judy Archer, Orillia, Ontario for the photographs and information on her grandmother and aunt.

217 Etta Smalley Bangs, Reminiscence, Small Collections 116, Montana Historical Society Research Center. See also Carter, ed., *Montana Women Homesteaders*.

218 *Edmonton Bulletin*, 27 July 1906, 5; 27 August 1906.

219 Baergen, *Pioneering with a Piece of Chalk*, 88.

220 Cohen, "Women's History Month: Out of Canada: Etta Smalley Homesteaded a New Life," *Missoulian*, 23 July 2007; http://www.missoulian.com/articles/2007/03/16/new/local/news04.txt.

221 MacMahon, "'Fine Hands for Sowing': The Homesteading Experiences of Remittance Woman Jessie de Prado MacMillan," 277–78.

222 SAB, homestead file 3159536: SE 27-4-2-W3.

223 Ibid., T. Rothwell, memorandum to the Minister of the Interior, 21 Feb. 1914.

CHAPTER FOUR

1 Martin-McGuire, "First Nations Land Surrenders."

2 Smith, *Liberalism, Surveillance, and Resistance*, 210–11.

3 Martin-McGuire, "First Nations Land Surrenders," 410.

4 LAC, Census of Canada 1911, item 4991575, subdistrict London, Ontario. Jean C. Laidlaw was forty-five years old, of Scottish ancestry, and born in England.

5 "Woman Rancher Tells of Life: Miss Jean Laidlaw Runs 360 Acres near Pincher Creek, Alberta: Shows Great Pluck," *Globe and Mail*, 6 Feb. 1920, 10.

6 Martin-McGuire, "First Nations Land Surrenders," 329.

7 Ibid., 343.

8 Ibid., 348.

9 Ibid., 354.

10 Ibid., 372.

11 "Famed Prairie Barrister Dies," *Leader-Post*, 2 Aug. 1932.

12 SAB, homestead file 572137: W ½ 4 and all of 6-16-23-W2.

13 SAB, homestead file 861961: SW 28-25-24-W2, letter from Short, Cross, Biggar and Ewing to Frank Oliver, 4 Oct. 1905. Her name is spelled both Buckman and Bucknam in the documents.

14 SAB, homestead file 349942: SW 34-32-13-W2.

15 PAA, homestead file, reel 2033, file 416715.

16 Ibid., ____ to J.G. Turiff, 7 Dec., 1899.

17 Fortier, *Lamoureux*, 27–28.

18 "Un de nos pionnières qui disparaît," *La Survivance*, 4 March 1942, 5.

19 McKenzie, *It's Time to Remember*, 327–28.

20 Ibid., 311–12.

21 Rockwood-Woodlands Historical Society, *Rockwood Echoes*, 78–79.

22 Sonningdale Recreation Board, *Sonningdale Memories*, 406–8.

23 Lindsay v. Morrow, *Reports of Cases Heart in the Supreme Court of Saskatchewan*, vol. 1 (Toronto: Canada Law Co. Ltd., 1909), 516–17.

24 Gleichen United Church Women, *The Gleichen Call: A History*, 207.

25 Glenbow Archives (GA) Canadian Pacific Railway Land Sales. Annie E. Williams purchased four tracts of land in 1908 See http://ww2.glenbow.org/search/archivesCPRResults.aspx.

26 *Gleichen Call*, 28 March 1912, 8.

27 "Mrs. Williams Grew Excellent Flax," *Gleichen Call*, 1 Jan. 1913, 1; "Mrs. A.E. Williams Receives Big Price for Her Seed Flax," *Gleichen Call*, 5 June 1913, 5; "Lady Farmer Raises Record Crop," *Wainwright Star*, 13 Aug. 1913, 2.

28 *Gleichen Call*, 31 Aug. 1916, 1.

29 Gleichen United Church Women, *The Gleichen Call: A History*, 207.

30 See "Alix, Alberta," http://en.wikipedia.org/wiki/Alix,_Alberta.

31 Thanks to Juliet Gayton, Winchester, England, for this genealogical research on Alice Westhead.

32 GA, Canadian Pacific Railway Land Sales, Alice C. Westhead. See http://ww2.glenbow.org/search/archivesCPRResults.aspx.

33 *Calgary Herald*, 7 Sept. 1910.

34 Cavanaugh, "Irene Marryat Parlby."

35 Thompson, "A Woman Rancher in Alberta: A Visit to Quarter-Circle-One Ranch," *Canadian Home Journal*, August 1911; https://archive.org/stream/canadawest0708westuoft/canadawest0708westuoft_djvu.txt.

36 *Edmonton Bulletin*, 29 Sept. 1911, 3.

37 Thwaite, *Alberta: An Account of its Wealth and Progress*, 182.

38 Alix Clive Historical Club, *Gleanings after Pioneers and Progress*, 230–31.

39 See "An English Woman Farmer in Alberta," *Globe*, 7 March 1914, 11; "A Successful Lady Farmer," *Maitland Weekly Mercury*, 20 Dec. 1913, 10.

40 "Law Report High Court of Justice, King's Bench," *Times* 10 Jan. 1903, 12.

41 "Alleged Infringement of Copyright," *Times* 7 Feb. 1910, 3.

42 Hamer Jackson, "How I Made a New Home in Canada," *Daily Mail*, 17 Sept. 1913, 4.

43 GA, Canadian Pacific Railway Land Sales, Mrs. Celesta Hamer Jackson. See http://ww2.glenbow.org/search/archivesCPRResults.aspx

44 "A Successful Lady Farmer," *Maitland Weekly Mercury*, 20 Dec. 1913.

45 "An English Woman Farmer in Alberta," *Globe*, 7 March 1914.

46 On Hamer Jackson lecturing in England, see *Western Gazette*, 16 Jan. 1914, 2; articles on education include C. Hamer Jackson, "Prevention of Pauperism," *Daily Colonist*, 31 May 1914, 4; and "Education in New Country," *Edmonton Bulletin*, 23 August 1923, 6.

47 Ibid. (articles on education).

48 GA, Canadian Pacific Railway Land Sales Database at http://ww2.glenbow.org/search/archivesCPRSearch.aspx.

49 GA, Canadian Pacific Railway Land Sales Database, M 2272, vol. 122, contract number 13081.

50 Ibid., vol. 2272, contract number 25990.

51 Ibid., vol. 99, contract number 29695.

52 Ibid., vol. 78, contract number 1515.

53 Ibid., Canadian Pacific Railway Database.

54 Laut, "Openings for Women in Canada," *Pall Mall Magazine* 40, no. 175 (Nov. 1907), 594–95.

55 "Women as Farmers in Western Canada," *Spokesman-Review*, 14 July 1907, 27.

56 "Monday Interment for Pioneer Resident," *Leader-Post*, 7 March 1949, 16. It is noted that her farm was near the RCMP barracks on Dewdney Avenue in present-day Regina. In the 1901 census Mary V. Gilroy is aged thirty-three, born in May 1867 in Ontario. Her occupation is "Farmer," and she is the head of the household. The only other household member was John Archibald, aged twenty-one. Thanks to Sharon Maier, Regina Public Library Prairie History Room.

57 LAC, 1871 Census; http://data2.collectionscanada.ca/1871/jpg/4396332_00128.jpg.

58 Canadian Pacific Railway Company, *Words from the Women of Western Canada*, 31–33.

59 Ibid., 32.

60 "Canadian Women's Press Club Tour: Girl Farmers and Ranchers in the West Have Made a Success of Their Work …" *Quebec Saturday Budget*, 7 July 1906, 1.

61 "M.H.A.," "How Four Plucky Women Won Out in the Canadian Northwest," *Minneapolis Journal*, 25 July 1906, part 6.

62 Canadian Pacific Railway Company, *Home Life of Women in Western Canada*, 21–22.

63 *Leader-Post*, 7 March 1949, 16.

64 Census research by Sharon Maier, Regina Public Library, Prairie History Room.

65 *Age*, 3 Nov. 1906, 4.

66 *St. John Sun*, 6 Oct. 1906, 10; *Otago Witness*, 30 Oct. 1907.

67 "The Woman Who Would Be a Sailor," *Bay of Plenty Times* 24, no. 3676 (23 March 1898): 2.

68 *Brantford Opinion*, 7 Dec. 1906, 7.

69 "Titled Lady Has Ranch in the West," *St. John Sun*, 6 Oct. 1906, 10; "Canadian Woman Rancher," *Brantford Opinion*, 7 Dec. 1906, 7.

70 "Titled Lady Has Ranch in the West," *St. John Sun*, 6 Oct. 1906, 7.

71 "The Adventures of Lady Ernestine Hunt," *Eastern Daily Mail and Straits Morning Advertiser*, 26 Nov. 1906, 5

72 "Titled Lady Has Ranch in the West," *St. John Sun*, 6 Oct. 1906, 7.

73 Ibid.

74 *L'Abeille de la Nouvelle-Orléans*, 15 May 1910, 6. See also "Handy and Helpful Girls," *Brisbane Courier*, 11 May 1910, 17.

75 "Nurses on Horseback: Picturesque Parade in the West End," *Wairarapa Daily Times*, 17 July 1909, 6.

76 Noakes, *Women in the British Army*, 30–31.

77 "Lady Hunt is a Lieutenant," *Spokane Daily Chronicle*, 28 April 1910.

78 *Star*, 19 June 1909, 3.

79 "A Woman Farmer's Success," *New Zealand Herald* 48, no. 14667 (29 April 1911); *Brisbane Courier*, 19 April 1911, 14.

80 "This Woman Owns Big Farm," *Edmonton Bulletin*, 17 Jan. 1911, 4.

81 LAC, Census of Canada 1911, item number 7745054; http://data2.collectionscanada.gc.ca/1911/jpg/e002098158.jpg.

82 "This Woman Owns Big Farm," *Edmonton Bulletin*, 17 Jan. 1911, 4.

83 "Woman Runs a Big Farm Successfully," *Claresholm Review-Advertiser*, 28 April 1916, 3.

84 McCallum, "Who Said Women Can't Farm? Miss R.M. Hillman of Keeler, Saskatchewan, Disproves Any Such Fallacy," *Grain Growers' Guide*, 27 March 1918, 8.

85 Keeler History Book Committee, *Our Heritage: A History of the Keeler Community*, 345.

86 "A Lady Farmer," *Clarence and Richmond Examiner*, 5 May 1906, 7.

87 "A Lady Farm Laborer," *Wairarapa Daily Times*, 25 May 1906, 6.

88 Admiral William May had one daughter and three sons. The daughter's name was Kinbarra (also his wife's name). In 1881, William and Kinbarra are shown to be in Plymouth, a large naval base. Daughter Kinbarra Swene was born 1882, West Derby District; she died in Edinburgh in 1921 and the death certificate shows that she had suffered from ill health for some time. There are no other births during the period 1878–82 of a girl child called Isobel May born in any of the locations in which the May family was known to have been. Kinbarra Swene Marrow, the daughter born in 1882, is recorded in the England census for 1911 (which took place on 31st March) at the home of her parents in Kensington, London. She is of no occupation and aged 29 years. In none of the post-1911 press reports about "Jack" May is her first name, Isobel mentioned, but this is how her name is recorded in the land ledger of the Canadian Pacific Railway.

Many thanks to Joan Heggie, Research Fellow, School of Social Sciences, Teesside University Middlesbrough, U.K. for her amazingly thorough research on "Jack" May and the Admiral May family.

89 "World's Happiest Girl," *Redcliff Review*, 13 Dec. 1912, 4.

90 "A Woman Farmer," *Border Watch*, 23 May 1906, 4.

91 Ibid.

92 Ibid.

93 "Mrs. 'Jack' May in Alberta," *Saturday News*, 23 Sept. 1911, 8.

94 Ibid.

95 "A Lady Farm Laborer," *Wairarapa Daily Times*, 25 May 1906, 6.

96 "Miss Jack May in Male Attire," *Globe* 15 April 1911, 4.

97 "Provincial Notes: Noted Lady Farmer Settles in Alberta," *Gleichen Call*, 4 May 1911, 5.

98 Thanks again to Joan Heggie, whose research indicates that May arrived on the *Empress of Ireland*. The entry in the passenger list on that ship includes Jack May, destined for Sedgewick, and her age of thirty-five, is first entered in the male column and then is crossed out and written across the female column.

99 *Western Globe*, 19 April 1911, 3.

100 "Girl Posed as a Man to Keep from Starving," *Globe and Mail*, 1 Jan. 1914, 15.

101 "Young Girl Posed as Man," in *Globe and Mail*, 8 June 1918, 13.

102 *Spokane Daily Chronicle*, 1 Dec. 1910, 8.

103 *Gazette Times*, 31 Aug. 1913.

104 "Provincial Notes: Noted Lady Farmer Settles in Alberta," *Gleichen Call*, 4 May 1911, 5.

105 *Daily Colonist*, 14 Aug. 1911, 8.

106 *Kindersley Clarion*, 3 May 1911.

107 "Mrs. 'Jack' May in Alberta," *Saturday News*, 23 Sept. 1911, 8.

108 "Canada's Golden West," *Hawera and Normanby Star* 30 (1912): 2.

109 *Wairarapa Daily Times*, 5 June 1913, 4.

110 GA, Canadian Pacific Railway Land Sales Catalogue; http://ww2.glenbow.org/search/archivesCPRResults.aspx.

111 *Edmonton Bulletin*, 29 April 1911, 5.

112 "Lady Farmers," *Kaipara and Waitemata Echo*, 4 March 1914, 4.

113 "An English Girl's Experience of a Winter in Alberta," *Canadian Gazette*, 25 March 1912, 973.

114 Sedgewick Historical Society, *Sedgewick Sentinel: A History of Sedgewick*, 24.

115 Edwin Snowsell and Frank Snowsell, "Starting Over on a 'Ready-Made' Farm, 1911–16," *Western People*, 4 March 1982, 14–15.

116 Ibid.

117 *Daily Colonist*, 14 April 1912, 8.

118 Rankin, "The Woman Who Never Looks Back," *Canadian Courier* 10, no. 9 (29 July 1911): 16.

119 Love, "Where Opportunity Knocks," 6–12.

120 *Morning Leader*, 1 Oct. 1912, 12.

121 Love, "Where Opportunity Knocks," 7.

122 Ibid., 10.

123 Love, "Farmer-Boy 'Jack,'" *The Lady's Realm*, Nov. 1911, 101–3.

124 "World's Happiest Girl," *Chicago Daily Tribune*, 1 Oct. 1912; "Girl Wears Trousers and Works Big Farm," *Carroll Herald*, 8 Jan. 1913; "World's Happiest Girl," *Redcliff Review*, 12 Dec. 1912.

125 *Tensas Gazette*, 13 Dec. 1912.

126 *Carroll Herald*, 8 Jan. 1913.

127 Love, "Haymaking with Jack May: A Woman's Life on a Canadian Farm," *Quiver* 49, no. 11 (Sept. 1914): 1075–1078.

128 *Sedgewick Sentinel*, 12 Dec. 1912, 4.

129 Ibid., 1 May 1913, 5.

130 Sedgewick Historical Society, *Sedgewick Sentinel: A History of Sedgewick*, 379.

131 "Society Lady Who Prefers the Plow to the Pink Tea," *Edmonton Bulletin*, 21 June 1913, 14.

132 "Women and Land in Canada: Their Disabilities and the Reason," *Globe*, 18 April 1913, 6.

133 Kennedy, "Lady Farmers," *Kaipara and Waitemata Echo*, 4 March 1914, 4.

134 "Jills without Jacks: Bachelor Girls at Spirit River: Pioneer Women of the West," *Nottingham Evening Post*, 24 Jan. 1924, 4.

135 Walker, *Canadian Trails*, 85.

136 Ibid., 84.

137 Sedgewick Historical Society, *Sedgewick Sentinel: A History of Sedgewick*, 15.

138 Ibid., 17.

139 Ibid., 16.

140 Ibid., 197–98.

141 "Another Woman Farmer," *Claresholm Review*, 8 June 1911, 7.

142 *Sedgewick Sentinel*, 7 Nov. 1912, 4.

143 Ibid., 12 Dec. 1912, 4.

144 Kisby, "Vera 'Jack' Holme."

145 Ibid., 122.

146 Boag, *Re-Dressing America's Frontier Past*, 18.

147 Ibid., 19.

148 Ibid., 40.

149 McClintock, *Imperial Leather*, 67.

150 Ibid., 174.

151 Millarville, Kew, Priddis and Bragg Creek Historical Society, *Our Foothills*, 286–87.

152 "She Writes and Ranches," *Oyen News*, 6 May 1925, 5.

153 Ibid.

154 "Woman Author as Rancher: Calgary Experiment," *Devon and Exeter Daily Gazette*, 28 May 1925, 2.

155 Ibid. See also "A Woman Pioneer," *Imperial Colonist* 23, no. 5 (May 1925): 86–87.

156 "She Writes and Ranches," *Oyen News*, 6 May 1925, 5.

157 Millarville, Kew, Priddis and Bragg Creek Historical Society, *Our Foothills*, 287.

158 M.H.A., "How Four Plucky Women Won Out in the Canadian Northwest," *Minneapolis Journal*, 29 July 1906.

159 Delday, *Brooks: Beautiful-Bountiful*, 197.

160 Ibid., 199.

161 Boag, *Re-Dressing America's Frontier Past*, 196.

162 *Saskatoon Star Phoenix*, 8 August 1917, 4.

163 Watanna, *Cattle*, 33.

164 Ibid., 34.

165 Ibid., 144.

166 Yarmie, "'I Had Always Wanted to Farm,'" 112.

167 Saugeres, "She's Not Really a Woman, She's Half a Man," 642.

168 Ibid., 646.

169 Ibid., 648.

170 "A Girl Farmer,"*Queenslander* (Brisbane) 19 Oct. 1907, 4.

171 See, for example, "Women as Farmers," taken from the *New York Tribune*, in the *Herald and News*, 19 July 1907; "Women Farmers of the Great North-West," *Detroit Free Press*, 4 August 1907; "Women as Farmers," *Sun*, 6 July 1907; "Women Homesteading," *Edmonton Bulletin*, 7 August 1907.

172 M.H.A., "How Four Plucky Women Won Out in the Canadian Northwest," *Minneapolis Journal*, 29 July 1906.

173 Alden, "Prosperous Women Farmers," *Farmer's Review*, 19 Nov. 1910, 4.

174 "Lady Settlers in Australia," *Chambers Edinburgh Journal*, 24 Nov. 1849, 334.

175 On this partnership, see also Brown and Martin, "Drysdale, Anne (1792–1853)" in *Australian Dictionary of Biography*, National Centre of Biography, Australian National University (first published in hardcopy by Melbourne University Publishing, 1966); http://adb.anu.edu.au/biography/drysdale-anne-2000. See also Roberts, *Miss D and Miss N An Extraordinary Partnership.*

176 See, for example, Kingston, *Elizabeth Macarthur*; Wymark, "Pioneer Women," *Country Woman* (May 1969): 10–11.

177 See "Penfolds" http://en.wikipedia.org/wiki/Penfolds.

178 Alford, *Production or Reproduction*, 193.

179 "Canadian Women's Press Club Tour: Girl Farmers and Ranchers," *Quebec Saturday Budget*, 7 July 1906.

180 I use this argument in the case of Calgary's Irish settler Caroline "Mother" Fulham, who kept pigs and collected garbage, in Carter, "Britishness, 'Foreignness,' Women and Land," 57.

181 "To the Bachelor Girl," *Redcliff Review*, 19 April 1912, 6.

CHAPTER FIVE

1 Binnie-Clark, *Wheat and Woman*, 303. Unless otherwise specified, all citations to *Wheat and Woman* are to the 2007 edition.

2 *Victoria Daily Colonist*, 22 Oct. 1909, 12.

3 Verdon, "Middle-Class Women's Work and the Professionalization of Farming," 396.

4 Binnie-Clark, *Wheat and Woman* (rpr. 1979), 7.

5 Ibid., 60.

6 Binnie-Clark, *A Summer on the Canadian Prairie*, 27.

7 Ibid., 230, and *Wheat and Woman*, 60.

8 Chilton, *Agents of Empire*, 53.

9 Ibid., 245.

10 The Indigenous people of the reserves surrounding Binnie-Clark's farm had made concerted efforts to farm from the time of the 1874 Treaty Four, and their efforts were met with a measure of success by the early 1880s. Government policies intervened to atrophy this development, however. In particular, the "peasant" farming policy, introduced in the late 1880s, demanded that reserve farmers limit their acreage and grow root, and not grain crops. Indigenous people were prohibited from using labour-saving machinery. A concerted government and settler-supported effort to reduce the size of the reserves gained momentum after the turn of the twentieth century, just at the time of the establishment of Binnie-Clark's farm, and this severely limited the amount of arable land on most Treaty Four reserves. See Carter, *Lost Harvests.*

11 Ibid.

12 Binnie-Clark, *Wheat and Woman*, 58.

13 Ibid., 56.

14 Ibid.

15 Ibid., 57.

16 Ibid., 224–25.

17 Binnie-Clark, *A Summer on the Canadian Prairie*, 218.

18 Thanks to Richard Jenks and Dennis Jenks for sharing "The Family History of Clark." Georgina's father was sometimes listed in the census returns as "Binnie-Clark" and sometimes as plain "Clark." For example, in the 1901 census he was listed as "Arthur W.B. Clark." There were seven children born to Arthur and Maria: Maria Elizabeth (b. 1868), Walter Douglas (b. 1869), Georgina (b. 1872), Louis (b. 1873), Arthur Cameron (b. 1874), Mabel (b. 1874), and Ethel (b. 1880). Georgina's brother Louis signed his name Louis B. Clark. See SAB, homestead file 1328338: SW 6-26-14-W2.

19 "British Women on Canadian Homesteads," *Taber Free Press*, 22 April 1909, 1.

20 Binnie-Clark, *Wheat and Woman*, 304.

21 Binnie-Clark, "Homesteads for Bachelor Women," the *Canadian Gazette*, 4 Feb. 1909, 447–48.

22 SAB, homestead file 1328338: SW 6-26-14-W2.

23 Binnie-Clark, *A Summer on the Canadian Prairie*, 297.

24 Ibid., 299.

25 Ibid., 305.

26 Ibid.

27 SAB, homestead file 1328338: SW 6-26-14-W2.

28 *Progress*, 20 July 1905.

29 Binnie-Clark, *Wheat and Woman*, 236.

30 Carter, *Lost Harvests*, 185–86.

31 Ibid., 186.

32 *Vidette*, 13 Dec. 1905. For the history of the settlement of this district by British-Ontarians, see Dick, *Farmers "Making Good."*

33 *Vidette*, 13 Dec. 1905.

34 Ibid., 14 Feb. 1906.

35 Farquharson, "The Problem of Immigration," 38.

36 Ibid., 43.

37 Jean Blewett, "The Doukhobor Woman," published in *Collier's Weekly* (n.d., n.p.) and in Carrel, *Canada's West and Farther West*, 227.

38 Ibid.

39 "Women Harnessed to Plows in Manitoba," *Women's Journal*, 9 Sept. 1899, 282.

40 "Woman Farmer Visiting the City," *Edmonton Bulletin*, 1 Aug. 1912, 3.

41 Arthur Cameron Binnie Clark (1875–1921) and Ethel Binnie Clark (1886–1955) are both buried in the Lakeview Cemetery, Fort Qu'Appelle.

42 Susan Jackel, introduction, *Wheat and Woman* (rpr. 1979), xiii. In an undated seven-page typed manuscript in the Jenks Papers, Binnie-Clark wrote that she was at her farm in 1926 and 1928, and at that time "I was just pulling out from the embarrassment that awaited me on my return to Canada after my absence during the war and following years." She also noted that "Binning House had been destroyed by fire during the war and never replaced" (2).

43 Binnie-Clark may have had two different homes on Cheyne Walk. On 6 Nov. 1932 she wrote to Dorothy Cooper-Abbs, "Our old house in Cheyne Walk was demolished." She had been renting the flat out for 100 pounds a year and this was an important source of income for her (Derek Harrison Papers). By February 1936, she was living at 125 Cheyne Walk and she lived there until her death in 1947. *Times*, 11 Feb. 1936, 10.

44 Dennis Jenks, conversation, 5 Oct. 2005, London, England. Binnie-Clark was known to family and friends as "Avril."

45 Devas, *Two Flamboyant Fathers*, 213; Holme, *Chelsea*.

46 Youmans, "Walker, Ethel (1861–1951)," *GLBTQ Encyclopedia*; http://eds.a.ebscohost.com/eds/detail/detail?vid=4&sid=5ebbdf3c-7c04-458c-8081-bc12d52e96a7%40sessionmgr4002&hid=4103&bdata=JnNpdGU9ZWRzLWxpdmUmc2NvcGU9c2l0ZQ%3d%3d#AN=40920590&db=qth.

47 Binnie-Clark, *Tippy: The Autobiography of a Pekingese Puppy.* This was a book for children that was "for six pennies or one shilling to buy comfort for the wounded soldiers and horses fighting in the Great War for Liberty." Much of the action takes place on Cheyne Walk.

48 Binnie-Clark, *Wheat and Woman*, 190; Jenks Papers, typed untitled document by Georgina Binnie-Clark, n.d. (c. 1932), beginning on p. 2.

49 Georgina Binnie-Clark to Dorothy Harrison, 21 Feb. 1936, Derek Harrison Papers.

50 Binnie-Clark, *A Summer on the Canadian Prairie*, 30.

51 Ibid., 124.

52 Ibid., 240.

53 "The Woman Problem" (editorial), *Canadian Gazette*, 20 Feb. 1908, 501.

54 Ibid.

55 Binnie-Clark, "Women's Chances in the West," *Canadian Gazette*, 3 Oct. 1908, 28.

56 Binnie-Clark, "A Woman, Two Boys and £140," *Canadian Gazette*, 27 Feb., 28 Feb., and 12 March 1908, 42.

57 Binnie-Clark, "A Woman's Way on the Prairie," *Canadian Gazette*, 7 May 1908, 8.

58 Binnie-Clark, "A Woman's Plea from the West," *Canadian Gazette*, 19 Nov. 1908, 179.

59 Ibid.

60 Ibid.

61 Editorial, *Canadian* Gazette, 19 Nov. 1908, 177.

62 G. Binnie-Clark to the Department of the Interior, 17 Nov. 1908, in LAC, RG 15, D-II-1, vol. 1039, file 1713679.

63 W.D. Scott to Binnie-Clark, 12 Nov. 1908, in in LAC, RG 15, D-II-1, vol. 1039, file 1713679. (Not clear why the response seems to be dated before Binnie-Clark's letter of 17 Nov.)

64 Binnie-Clark, *Wheat and Woman*, 307.

65 John Obed Smith (1864–1937), "Memorable Manitobans," Manitoba Historical Society, http://www.mhs.mb.ca/docs/people/smith_jo.shtml.

66 Smith, "Migration within the Empire," *English Review* (Feb. 1925): 248.

67 Ibid., 247–48.

68 "J. Obed Smith's Land Speculation," *Globe,* 7 March 1907, 1.

69 Binnie-Clark, "Homesteads for Bachelor Women," *Canadian Gazette*, 4 Feb. 1909, 447.

70 Binnie-Clark, "Women Farmers" (from the *Daily Mail*), *Wainwright Star*, 24 March 1910, 2.

71 Binnie-Clark, "How Canada Welcomes the Emigrant Girl," *Quiver* 44, no. 4 (March 1909): 399–403.

72 Binnie-Clark, "A Fight with Fire: A Settler's Experience on the Canadian Prairie," *Pall Mall Magazine* 44, no. 198 (Oct. 1909): 620.

73 *Minnedosa Tribune*, 28 Oct. 1909, 2; *Crossfield Chronicle*, 30 Oct., 1909, 5; *Taber Free Press*, 22 April 1909, 1; *Advertiser and Central Alberta News*, 4 Feb. 1909, 2; *Victoria Daily Colonist*, 22 Oct. 1909, 12.

74 *L'Abeille de la Nouvelle-Orléans*, 14 Dec. 1909, 6.

75 Binnie-Clark, "Conditions of Life for Women in Canada," 110.

76 Ibid., 119.

77 Ibid., 118.

78 Ibid., 120.

79 Longhurst, "How Can I Earn a Living: Canada for the Woman Worker," *Woman Worker*, 23 March 1910, 822.

80 Binnie-Clark, "A Woman's Farm in Canada," *Daily Mail*, 23 Jan. 1909, 4.

81 Binnie-Clark, "Women Farmers," *Daily Mail*, 25 Feb. 1910.

82 Editorial, *Canadian Gazette,* 24 March 1910, 687.

83 "Three Women in Canada," *United Empire* 1 (1910): 413–15.

84 *Western Times*, 11 Feb. 1910, 7.

85 "Girl Farmers," *Colonist* 42, issue 12759 (4 April 1910): 4.

86 "Women Farmers in Canada," *Globe*, 5 March 1910, 6.

87 *Votes for Women*, 18 March 1910, 9.

88 *Canadian Gazette*, 5 May 1910, 132–33.

89 Binnie-Clark, "Are Educated Women Wanted in Canada?," part 1, *Imperial Colonist* 8, no. 98 (Feb. 1910): 22–24; part 2, vol. 8, no. 99 (March 1910): 39–42.

90 *Imperial Colonist*, 13 Jan. 1910, 397–99.

91 "Women Farmers in Canada," *Globe*, 5 March 1910, 6.

92 Binnie-Clark, "Ready-Made Homes: Why the Settlers Are Content" (*Overseas Daily Mail*), *Strathmore Standard*, 22 Oct. 1910, 5.

93 See, for example, Binnie-Clark, "Women Farmers: Experiments in Canada," in *Tamworth Daily Observer*, 9 March 1912, 3; and in *West Gippsland Gazette*, 7 May 1912, 6.

94 "Are Booming Canada—Englishwomen Are Training Girls to Come out Here," *Gleichen Call*, 9 June 1910, 7.

95 Ibid.

96 *Canadian Gazette*, 3 March 1910, 598.

97 "Women Farmers in Canada," *Globe*, 5 March 1910, 6.

98 "Making Girl Farmers," *Gleichen Call*, 21 April 1910, 7.

99 *Glasgow Herald*, 4 March 1910, 5.

100 "Woman Farmers," *Gleichen Call*, 21 March 1912, 6.

101 Thanks to Derek Harrison, Fort Qu'Appelle, for this information about his mother, Kathleen Laughrin Harrison.

102 Fort Qu'Appelle and District History Book Committee, *Fort Qu'Appelle and Area: A History*, 367–68.

103 Bertram, "Wanderings of a Single Woman: Fort Qu'Appelle," 2nd letter, *Canadian Gazette*, 5 March 1913, 795.

104 *Globe*, 14 May 1915, 2.

105 *Gentlewoman and Modern Life*, 19 July 1919, 125.

106 Hawkes, "The Imperial Emigrant," *United Empire* 3 (1912): 207–21.

107 Ibid., 220.

108 "Woman Farmer Visiting the City," *Edmonton Bulletin*, 1 August 1912, 3.

109 "Canada's New Phase," *Canadian Gazette*, 15 April 1913, 39.

110 Binnie-Clark, "Land and the Woman in Canada," 498.

111 Ibid., 501.

112 "Women and Land in Canada: Their Disabilities and the Reason," *Globe*, 18 April 1913, 6.

113 The discussion that followed Binnie-Clark's presentation to the Royal Colonial Institute was published along with her paper "Land and the Woman in Canada," 505–8.

114 Binnie-Clark, "Land and the Woman in Canada," 506.

115 Ibid.

116 Ibid., 507.

117 Ibid., 506–7.

118 *Canadian Gazette*, 12 April 1913, 38.

119 *Daily Colonist*, 8 May 1913, 4.

120 Shaw's letter is quoted in *Daily Colonist*, 19 Oct. 1913, 8.

121 Mrs. Donald Shaw was so "traditional" that I have been unable to find out what her own first name was. See McKay, "Debating Sexuality in Halifax, 1920: Mrs. Donald Shaw and Others," 336. See also Mrs. Donald Shaw, "Where Canada Fails Us," *Canadian Magazine of Politics, Science, Art and Literature* 43 (191): 464–65.

122 Quoted in *Daily Colonist*, 19 Oct. 1913, 8.

123 Ibid.

124 Morris, *An Englishwoman in the Canadian West*, 174.

125 Evans, *The Bar U*, 134–41.

126 Binnie-Clark, *Wheat and Woman*, 236.

127 Ibid., 119.

128 Ibid., 151.

129 "Wheat and Woman," *Times Literary Supplement*, 30 April 1914, 207.

130 "Women and Economics," *Athenaeum*, no. 4527 (August 1914): 148–49.

131 "A Woman Farmer," *Votes for Women*, 14 Aug. 1914, 693.

132 Moore, review of *Wheat and Woman*, *Globe*, 14 Aug. 1914, 3.

133 "No Dower Rights Law and No Free Land Grant for Women," *Edmonton Bulletin*, 5 March 1914, 2.

134 Munday, "A Woman Wheat Grower," *Westminster Hall Magazine and Farthest West Review* 7, no. 4 (May 1915): 15–17.

135 Jenks Papers, handwritten document, "The Union Jack Farm Settlement," p. 113.

136 *Globe*, 30 April 1915, 5; and 14 May 1915, 2.

137 Dennis Jenks to Sarah Carter, email correspondence, 14 Dec. 2005.

138 Last Will and Testament of Georgina Binnie-Clark of 123 Cheyne Walk, Chelsea, London 4 April, 1947, Jenks Papers.

139 In an undated seven-page typed manuscript in the Jenks Papers, Binnie-Clark wrote that she was at her farm in 1926 and 1928, and at that time "I was just pulling out from the embarrassment that awaited me on my return to Canada after my absence during the war and following years." She also noted that "Binning House had been destroyed by fire during the war and never replaced."

140 Binnie-Clark, *Tippy: The Autobiography of a Pekingese Puppy*, dedication page.

CHAPTER SIX

1 Jackel, introduction to *Wheat and Woman* by Georgina Binnie-Clark (rpr. 1979), xx–xxxii.

2 LAC, RG 15, D-II-1, vol. 1105, file 2876595, pt. 1.

3 Scully, "White Maternity and Black Infancy," 70. See also Mehta, "Liberal Strategies of Exclusion."

4 Quoted in Grimshaw, "Suffragists Representing Race and Gender in the American West," 88.

5 On American immigration to Western Canada, see Troper, *Only Farmers Need Apply*.

6 Cavanaugh, "No Place for a Woman."

7 Cavanaugh, "The Limitations of the Pioneering Partnership"; Hawkins, "Lillian Beynon Thomas, Woman's Suffrage and the Return of Dower to Manitoba"; McCallum, "Prairie Women and the Struggle for a Dower Law."

8 Carter, *The Importance of Being Monogamous*.

9 Ibid., 56–57.

10 "Canada's Greatest Need," *Brandon Daily Sun*, 13 Sept. 1907. The column quotes a Moose Jaw correspondent to the *Farmer's Advocate*.

11 Binnie-Clark, *Wheat and Woman*, 307.

12 "What Others Say: Why Not Women Homesteaders?," *Edmonton Capital*, 25 Jan. 1910, 2. This article is reprinted from the *Toronto Telegram*.

13 *Grain Growers' Guide*, 9 March 1910.

14 Ibid., 16 March 1910.

15 Ibid.

16 "Let Us Organize," *Grain Growers' Guide*, 27 April 1910.

17 Canada, *House of Commons Debates*, 30 April 1910, 8488–8490.

18 Laurie, "No Homesteads for Women," *Manitoba Free Pres*, 9 May, 1910, 9.

19 *Edmonton Bulletin*, 21 May 1910.

20 *Manitoba Free Press*, 24 May 1910.

21 Ibid., 18 June 1910.

22 Quoted in Hawkins, "Lillian Beynon Thomas, Woman's Suffrage and the Return of Dower to Manitoba," 76.

23 *Toronto Sunday World*, 22 Feb. 1915, 4.

24 LAC, 1901 Census, item no. 253324, Brandon district, subdistrict Arthur.

25 See "Grain Growers' Guide," *Canadian Encyclopedia*, http://www.thecanadianencyclopedia.com/en/article/grain-growers-guide/.

26 McClung, *The Stream Runs Fast*, 119–21.

27 Ibid.

28 *Grain Growers' Guide*, 23 Feb. 1910, 29.

29 Laurie, "About Women and Men, Especially Women," *Manitoba Free Press*, 9 May 1910.

30 "What about the Future?," *Nor'West Farmer* 29, no. 17 (5 Sept. 1910): 72.

31 "Wishes to Homestead," *Family Herald*, 30 May 1913, 6.

32 "Homesteads for Women," *Family Herald*, 1 Oct. 1913, 6.

33 "Girls Want Homesteads," *Family Herald*, 3 Dec. 1913, 8.

34 "Homesteads," *Nor'West Farmer*, 21 Aug. 1911, 1027.

35 "Speaks from Experience," *Grain Growers' Guide*, 13 Dec. 1911, 9.

36 *Grain Growers' Guide*, 20 Dec. 1911, 24.

37 Ibid., 25 Oct. 1911, 24.

38 *Nor'West Farmer*, 21 Feb. 1910, 230.

39 Ibid.

40 Will Channon to Minister of the Interior, 4 January 1910, in LAC, RG 15, D-II-1, vol. 1062, file 2029532.

41 *Grain Growers' Guide*, 5 July 1911, 17.

42 Ibid., 27 March 1912, 24.

43 "The Homesteading Woman a Success," *Family Herald*, 24 Sept. 1913, 6.

44 McClung, "Free Land for the Soldiers," *Edmonton Bulletin*, 18 Sept. 1915, 3.

45 "The Wife's Share," *Family Herald*, 22 May 1912, 9.

46 "Montana School Ma'Am," *Family Herald*, 7 May 1913, 6.

47 *Nor'West Farmer* 29, no. 2 (20 Jan. 1910): 93.

48 "Women Prize Winners at Scottish Plowing Match," *Nor'West Farmer*, 20 March 1912, 385.

49 "Boston Women Want Farm for Spinsters," *Brandon Daily Sun*, 8 April 1909, 1; "Women Organize Farm Settlement: Great Colony to be Established in West Australia Exclusively for Females," *Family Herald and Weekly Star*, 19 Jan. 1912, 25.

50 "Five Girls Run a 200 Acre Farm," *Family Herald*, 5 March 1913, 6.

51 G. Abrook to Department of the Interior, 24 March 1913, in LAC, RG 15, D-II-1, vol. 1105, file 2876596 pt. 1.

52 *Grain Growers' Guide*, 27 August 1913, 9.

53 "A Daughter of the Plains," *Family Herald*, 14 Feb. 1912, 11.

54 SAB, Department of the Interior, Surveyors Notes, C.F. Aylesworth to C. Douville, 28 June 1899, R-183, no. 9.

55 "A Daughter of the Plains," *Family Herald* , 14 Feb. 1912, 11.

56 *Family Herald and Weekly Star*, 13 Dec. 1911, 10.

57 *Manitoba Free Press*, 1 June 1910.

58 Ibid., 9.

59 *Grain Growers' Guide*, 8 June 1910, 24.

60 Patriarche, "Husbandless Homesteads Are Wanted in the West," *Saskatoon Star Phoenix*, 17 April 1913.

61 Graham, "Unearned Increments and Woman's Dower," *Grain Growers' Guide*, 6 July 1910, 23.

62 Mrs. Thomas McNeil to Dr. Roche, Minister of the Interior, 6 March 1913, in LAC, RG 15, D-II-1, vol. 1105, file 2876596.

63 *Grain Growers' Guide*, 13 Dec. 1911, 9.

64 J. M. Perra to Hon. J.M. Crothers or Dr. Roche, Department of the Interior, 29 April 1913, in LAC, RG 15, D-II-1, vol. 1105, file 2876596.

65 Mrs. J.R. Long, *Nor'West Farmer*, 5 May 1910.

66 Fanny Elizabeth Shepherd to the Department of the Interior, 27 Feb. 1913, in LAC, RG 15, D-II-1, vol. 1105, file 2876596, pt. 2.

67 "Homesteads for Women," *Grain Growers' Guide*, 19 April 1911, 14.

68 *Manitoba Free Press*, 2 June 1910.

69 *Voice*, 15 Sept. 1911, 6.

70 *Manitoba Free Press*, 1 June 1910.

71 "Here Is Progress," *Grain Growers' Guide*, 6 April 1910.

72 "A Plea for the Daughters," *Nor'West Farmer*, 5 Sept. 1912, 1170.

73 Frederiksen, *The Land Laws of Canada and the Land Experience of the United States*, 11.

74 "About Women Homesteading," *Minnedosa Tribune*, 2 April 1914, 4.

75 "Where the Door Stands Open," *Globe*, 22 June 1904, 8.

76 Frederiksen, *The Land Laws of Canada and the Land Experience of the United States*, 6.

77 Ibid., 10.

78 *Bismarck Daily Tribune*, 24 Dec. 1906, 2.

79 *Glasgow Democrat*, 11 Feb., 1916.

80 *Enterprise*, 10 Feb. 1916, 4.

81 "Still Unconvinced," *Family Herald*, 1 June 1910, 11.

82 *Family Herald*, 20 July 1910, 11.

83 *Calgary Daily Herald*, 24 April 1915, 6.

84 Ibid., 21 April 1915, 1.

85 *Family Herald*, 11 May 1910, 11.

86 Ibid., 1 June, 1911, 11.

87 Ibid., 15 Nov. 1911, 11.

88 *Manitoba Free Press*, 16 May 1910.

89 Ibid., 1 Feb. 1912, 9.

90 Pullen-Burry, *From Halifax to Vancouver*, 231.

91 Ibid., 218.

92 Ibid., 219.

93 Morris, *An Englishwoman in the Canadian West*, 175.

94 Ibid.

95 *Manitoba Free Press*, 27 May 1910.

96 The article "The Doukhobors: Queer Russian Sect Which Has Become Canadianized," appeared in July and August 1911 in many western newspapers including the *Reflector* (8 August 1911, 2), *Crossfield Chronicle, Didsbury Pioneer, Claresholm Review, Gleichen Call,* and in November in the *Bow Island Review* (11 Nov. 1911, 6).

97 Quoted in Kulba and Lamont, "The Periodical Press and Western Woman's Suffrage Movements," 274.

98 Graham, "Homesteads for Women: A Western Woman's View of Man's Duty," clipping in LAC, RG 15, D-II-1, vol. 1062, file 2029532, n.d., n.p.

99 *Grain Growers' Guide*, 6 July 1910, 23.

100 Ibid., 15 May 1912, 13.

101 Ibid., 20 Dec. 1911 , 24.

102 Palmer, *Patterns of Prejudice.*

103 Hildebrandt, "The Aspirations of a Western Enthusiast."

104 *Vidette*, 14 Feb. 1906.

105 Ibid.

106 Mead, *How the Vote Was Won*, 7.

107 Hall, "Of Gender and Empire," 49.

108 Carter, "Britishness, 'Foreignness," Women and Land in Western Canada." See also Pickles, *Female Imperialism and National Identity.*

109 Shepard, *Deemed Unsuitable.*

110 *Grain Growers' Guide*, 3 May 1911, 4.

111 Patriarche, "Husbandless Homesteads Are Wanted in the West," *Saskatoon Star Phoenix*, 17 April 1913.

112 *Grain Growers' Guide*, 24 May 1911, 25.

113 Ibid., 14 June, 1911, 21.

114 Ibid.

115 Ibid., 24 May 1911, 25.

116 Ibid., 16 August 1911, 20.

117 Letter, J.H. Perra to J.M. Crother, 29 April 1913, in LAC, RG 15, D-II-1, vol. 1105, file 287659, pt. 2.

118 "Right of Women to Homestead," *Voice*, 4 Aug. 1911, 1.

119 "Woman's Labor League," *Voice*, 8 Sept. 1911, 3.

120 *Grain Growers' Guide*, 11 Oct. 1911, 18.

121 Ibid., 21 June 1911, 21.

122 "Homesteads for American Women," *Grain Growers' Guide*, 19 July 1911, 18.

123 *Grain Growers' Guide*, 16 August 1911, 20.

124 Ibid., 19 July 1911, 18.

125 Ibid., 16 August 1911, 20.

126 Ibid.

127 "Should Be Restrictions," *Grain Growers' Guide*, 20 Sept. 1911, 23.

128 *Family Herald and Weekly Star*, 1 Oct. 1913, 6.

129 Cook, "Francis Marion Beynon and the Crisis of Christian Reformism."

130 *Grain Growers' Guide*, 26 July 1911, 17.

131 Ibid., 6 July 1911.

132 Letter, V.C. Bedier to the Department of the Interior, 25 March 1913, in LAC, RG 15, D-II-1, vol. 1105, file 2876596.

133 "Homestead Rights for Women," *Voice*, 15 Sept. 1911, 6.

134 *Voice*, 20 Oct. 1911, 3.

135 "Roche Wants Free Land for Women," *Minnedosa Tribune*, 5 May 1910, 2.

136 "Homesteads for Women" *Grain Growers' Guide*, 25 Oct. 1911, 18.

137 "Homesteads for Women," *Grain Growers' Guide*, 8 Nov. 1911, 4.

138 Ibid., 13 Dec. 1911, 9–11.

139 Cook, "Francis Marion Beynon and the Crisis of Christian Reformism."

140 Fiamengo, "Rediscovering Our Foremothers Again," 155.

141 Ibid.

142 Quoted in Bacchi, *Liberation Deferred*, 53–54.

143 *Nor'West Farmer*, 5 Sept. 1912, 1142.

144 Rennie, *The Rise of Agrarian Democracy*, 59.

145 Jackel, introduction to *Wheat and Woman* by Georgina Binnie-Clark (rpt. 1979), xxviii.

146 Ibid.

147 Hawkins, "Lillian Beynon Thomas, Woman's Suffrage and the Return of Dower to Manitoba," 97.

148 "Discrimination in Homestead Law," *Globe*, 17 July 1915, 6.

149 Ibid.

150 Hunter, "The Big Picture Problem," 60.

151 Carter, *Lost Harvests*.

152 McClung, "Speaking of Women," *Maclean's*, 10 May 1916.

153 "Speaking of Nellie McClung," editorial clipping, scrapbook 1916–17, Nellie McClung fonds, British Columbia Archives. The clipping is not dated and the newspaper is not identified.

154 The letter from Sir Wilfrid Laurier is quoted in the column "Society in the Capital," by Gertrude Seton Thompson, *Edmonton Bulletin*, 29 April 1910, 3.

155 "The Doukhobors: Queer Russian Sect Which Has Become Canadianized" (see n. 97 above).

CHAPTER SEVEN

1 Grosvenor, "Women Farmers in Canada," *Times*, 27 Feb. 1913, 5.

2 *Imperial Colonist* 13, no. 167 (Dec. 1915): 198–89.

3 "Women on the Land," *Review of Reviews* 52, no. 308 (Aug. 1915): 146.

4 Martineau's article from *Englishwoman* was summarized in "Women on the Land," ibid.

5 White, "Remembrance, Retrospection, and the Women's Land Army in World War I Britain," 165.

6 Twinch, *Women on the Land*, 1–18.

7 Ibid., 20.

8 See King, *Women Rule the Plot*, Chapter 4, "Highly Trained Women of Good Birth."

9 Verdon, "'The work is grand and the life is just what I have always longed for': British Women's Experiences of Working on the Land in the Great War," paper presented at "Women, Land and the Making of the British Landscape," University of Hull, 30 June 2015.

10 Rowbotham, *A Century of Women*, 74.

11 Twinch, *Women on the Land*, 8–9.

12 White, "Remembrance, Retrospection, and the Women's Land Army in World War I Britain," 166.

13 King, *Women Rule the Plot*, 85.

14 White, "Remembrance, Retrospection, and the Women's Land Army in World War I Britain," 165.

15 Quoted in King, *Women Rule the Plot*, 93.

16 "Women on the Land," *Times*, 13 March 1916, 9.

17 Twinch, *Women on the Land*, 33.

18 Riley, *Inventing the American Woman*, 220–21.

19 Gowdy-Wygant, *Cultivating Victory*, 56.

20 Ibid.

21 *Women's Work on the Land: How You May Assist in Food Production This Summer.*

22 "Girls Work on Fruit Farms Last Season," *Globe*, 31 Oct. 1917, 17.

23 *Globe*, 11 July 1918, 2, letter from "M.Y."

24 "Farmerettes Taking Course," *Globe*, 13 May 1918, 8.

25 Ibid.

26 "Guelph Agricultural College to Open 20th," *Globe*, 12 Sept. 1918, 14.

27 "Girls Receive BSA Degree," *Grain Growers' Guide*, 5 June 1918, 1253.

28 *Globe*, 18 July 1918, 8

29 "Girls Start at Flax Pulling," *Globe*, 30 July 1918, 8.

30 *Globe*, 18 July 1918, 8.

31 *Globe*, 25 April 1918, 7.

32 "Organize Ontario's Farm Labour," *Globe*, 24 March 1916, 4.

33 "Farming and Farm Help," *Globe*, 7 March 1917, 15.

34 *Globe*, 30 Nov. 1918, 16.

35 Reyburn, "Blurring the Boundaries," 132.

36 Ibid., 133–34.

37 Ibid., 34.

38 Danysk, *Hired Hands*, 101–3.

39 "Labor Shortage in West," *Claresholm Review*, 13 April 1917, 2.

40 Ibid., 106.

41 "Women Should Be Ready to Till the Soil," editorial, *Gleichen Call*, 13 Jan. 1916, 4.

42 Danysk, *Hired Hands*, 108.

43 "Anti-Loafing Law," *Edmonton Bulletin*, 14 Sept. 1918, 1.

44 "Sufficient Harvest Help in Alberta," *Edmonton Bulletin*, 25 Aug. 1917, 3.

45 "Women in the Fields," *Minnedosa Tribune*, 30 Aug. 1917, 2.

46 "Farm Women to Help with Threshing," *Brandon Daily Sun*, 5 Sept. 1917, 7.

47 "Telephone Girls Will Go Stooking," *Brandon Daily Sun*, 27 Aug. 1917, 2.

48 "General Exodus of Brandonites to Help Garner Grain," *Brandon Daily Sun*, 29 Aug. 1917, 1.

49 Lindsay, "Calgary's Land Army: Which Helps Win the War by Raising Food Ammunition," *Grain Growers' Guide*, 10 April 1918, 32.

50 "Winnipeg Women Still Recruiting Their 'Army,'" *Brandon Daily Sun*, 17 Sept. 1915, 2; "Women Volunteers Are Inspected," *Edmonton Bulletin*, 29 Sept. 1915, 6.

51 "Enlist B.C. Women as Prairie Harvesters," *Daily Colonist*, 22 August 1917, 8.

52 "About Eight Thousand Ontario Harvesters Now on Way to West," *Brandon Daily Sun*, 14 Aug. 1908, 1. It was reported that there were 300 women and children among the 8,000.

53 "Women Harvest Hands," *Brandon Daily Sun*, 22 August 1916, 4.

54 "Women Coming West for Harvest," *Brandon Daily Sun*, 16 April 1917, 8.

55 "Women and the Farm," *Empress Express*, 28 Sept. 1916, 7.

56 Ellis, "Women Volunteers are Needed," *Edmonton Bulletin*, 2 Feb. 1918, 5.

57 "Women Volunteers to Replace Men in Stores and Offices Who Can Help Harvest Work on Farms," *Edmonton Bulletin*, 20 March 1918, 1.

58 "Women for the Farms," editorial, *Globe*, 25 June 1918, 6. This editorial quotes from an editorial in the *Saskatoon Star Phoenix*.

59 "Women G.G. Doing Their Bit," *Grain Growers' Guide*, 9 Jan. 1918, 12.

60 Menzies, *Canada and the War*, 55.

61 Ibid., 40–43.

62 "The Really New Woman," *Empress Express*, 17 Oct. 1918, 7.

63 "Farmerettes Take Ag. Course at Olds," *Coleman Bulletin*, 11 Oct. 1918, 4.

64 Ibid.

65 "Women Learning to Run Tractors," *Empress Express*, 21 March 1918, 3.

66 "College Graduate Farmerette," *Grain Growers' Guide*, 28 Aug. 1918, 1857.

67 "Women for Farm Labor," *Grain Growers' Guide*, 20 Feb. 1918, 386.

68 Ibid.

69 McCallum, "Who Said Women Can't Farm," *Grain Growers' Guide*, 27 March 1918, 618.

70 Nixon, "Feminizing the Farm: How Ontario is Promoting Agriculture among Women," *Grain Growers' Guide*, 4 Sept. 1918, 1876.

71 McCallum, "Women and Their Gas Wagons: Some Experiences of Women Who Drive Their Own Cars," *Grain Growers' Guide*, 25 Sept. 1918, 9.

72 "Woman Farmer, Husband in the Trenches…" *Edmonton Bulletin*, 2 May 1917, 5; "Aid Being Sent by Patriotic Fund to Elk Pt. Woman," *Edmonton Bulletin*, 9 May 1917, 5.

73 "War's Call to Farms: Men Must Fight and Women Must Reap," *Bow Island Review*, 2 August 1918, 3.

74 McClung, "Free Land for the Soldiers," *Edmonton Bulletin*, 18 Sept. 1915, 3.

75 "Discrimination in Homestead Law," *Globe*, 17 July 1915, 6.

76 "The Homestead Law," *Grand Forks Sun*, 29 Oct. 1915, 5.

77 "Homesteads for Women," *Voice*, 10 Aug. 1917, 5.

78 *Morning Leader*, 14 Jan. 1918, 5.

79 "Many Farm Women of Alberta Are Already Engaged in Outside Work Testimony at Convention," *Edmonton Bulletin*, 9 March 1918, 3.

80 "Homesteads for Women in Great Favor," *Edmonton Bulletin*, 11 March 1918, 4.

81 LAC, Record Group 76 (RG 76) Records of the Department of Immigration, vol. 198, file 90212, pt. 5, Estella B. Carter to Deputy Minister, Department of the Interior, 1 June 1918.

82 Ibid., W.D. Scott to Estella B. Carter, 8 June 1918.

83 Danysk, *Hired Hands*, 103.

84 Ibid., 102.

85 LAC, RG 76, vol. 198, file 80212, pt. 5 "Notice to Homesteaders," from J. Bruce Walker, Commissioner of Immigration, 13 March 1917, 5.

86 Ibid., W.D. Scott to M.V. MacInnes, 21 March 1918.

87 Carter, "An Infamous Proposal."

88 Quoted in Lambrecht, *The Administration of Dominion Lands*, 29–30.

89 Pickles, *Female Imperialism and National Identity*, 56.

90 Canada, *Debates of the House of Commons*, Session 1919, vol. 4, 23 June, 3864.

91 Ibid.

92 Strong-Boag, "Making a Difference," 244.

93 Roche, "World War One British Empire Discharged Soldier Settlement in Comparative Focus," 9.

94 Ibid.

95 LAC, RG 15, D-II-1, vol. 1105, file 2876596, pt. 2, Homesteads for Women resolution passed by the Annual Conventions United Farmers of Alberta and United Farm Women of Alberta 1919.

96 Ibid., Memorandum C. Harris to ___ Hume, 25 March 1919.

97 Ibid.

98 An article by Elizabeth Banks is quoted from in *Daily Colonist*, 7 April 1917, 8.

99 Barnard, "Women's Emigration after the War," *Quiver* 51, no. 6 (April 1916): 565.

100 Ibid.

101 Ibid., 566.

102 Ibid., 567.

103 Dickens, "Farmerettes Want Farms," *Globe*, 29 May 1918, 15.

104 Peele, "War Nurses Back to Land: Demobilized Women Prefer Out-of-Doors to Former Profession," *Globe*, 5 June 1920, 10.

105 McCallum, "Girls Receive BSA Degree," *Grain Growers' Guide*, 5 June 1918, 1253.

106 Knox, *The Girl of the New Day*, 200.

107 Ibid., 70.

108 Ibid., 57.

109 Ibid., 52.

110 Ibid., 67.

111 Ibid., 201.

112 Ibid., 211.

113 "Must We Rely on Girl Labor?," *Globe*, 14 May 1919, 13.

114 Our Special Commissioner, "Can an Educated Woman Make Good on the Land?," *Quiver*, May 1919, 534.

115 Ibid.

116 Knox, *The Girl of the New Day*, 66.

117 "Private and Confidential Memorandum on Emigration after the War," 1918, in LSE, Records of the CIL, box 38, minute book, 233.

118 A.L. Vernon to Caroline Grosvenor, 12 Nov., 1918, in LSE, Records of the CIL, box 38.

119 Our Special Commissioner, "Empire Migration," *Quiver*, June 1919, 609.

120 Noakes, "From War Service to Domestic Service," 11.

121 Quoted in ibid., 8.

122 "Empire Migration," *Quiver*, June 1919, 609.

123 Quoted in Yarmie, "I Had Always Wanted to Farm," 113.

124 "Empire Migration," *Quiver*, June 1919, 609–10.

125 Ibid., 611.

126 Quoted in Noakes, "From War Service to Domestic Service," 6.

127 Ibid., 5.

128 "British Women for Dominion," *Globe*, 30 June 1919, 5.

129 Quoted in Noakes, "From War Service to Domestic Service," 10.

130 Ibid., 15.

131 Ibid., 24.

132 *Imperial Colonist* 18, no. 217 (April 1920): 58.

133 "Canadian Openings for Women," *Times*, 12 Nov. 1919, 13.

134 *Gleichen Call*, 27 Oct. 1920, 3.

135 LAC, RG 17, vol. 1351, file 268636, J.H. Grisdale to provincial departments of agriculture, 17 July 1919.

136 Ibid., T.M. Molloy to J.H. Grisdale, 13 Aug. 1919.

137 Ibid., Deputy Minister of Agriculture Alberta to J.H. Grisdale, 2 July 1919.

138 Ibid., J.H. Grisdale to F.C. Blair, 26 Sept. 1919.

139 "British Women Sail for Canada," *Globe*, 17 Oct. 1919, 1.

140 "Is First Party of Women Settlers," *Globe*, 20 Nov. 1919, 1.

141 Knox, *The Girl of the New Day*, 200.

142 "British Women for Dominion," *Globe*, 30 June 1919, 5.

143 "What Will Canada Do with These Girls?," *Wainwright Star*, 27 Aug. 1919, 3.

144 "Demobilized Women to Settle in Canada," *Monitor News*, 16 April 1920, 6.

145 "Women Objectors Not Known Here," *Globe*, 28 Oct. 1919, 10.

146 Ibid.

147 "Farm Women Are Wanted," *Globe*, 3 Nov. 1919, 6.

148 Roberts, "A Work of Empire," 198–99.

149 Valverde, *The Age of Light, Soap and Water*, 127.

150 SAB, Saskatchewan Grain Growers Association Minutes, 31 Jan. 1920, 72. S-B2, F. III-1.

151 *Western Times*, 8 Feb. 1921, 6.

152 Memorandum for Mr. Van Scoy, 15 Nov. 1926, Glenbow Archives, Canadian Pacific Railway Fonds, M 2269, file 732.

153 *Globe*, 10 May 1920, 2.

154 Low, *Openings for British Women in Canada*, 13.

155 Ibid., 10.

156 Ibid., 11.

157 Ibid., 53.

158 Ibid., 54.

159 Ibid.

160 Ibid., 60.

161 Vanderbilt Jr., "Women's Land Army to Invade Canada," *New York Times*, 1 Aug. 1920.

162 Ibid.

163 Ibid.

164 "English Farm Girls for Canada," *Daily Colonist*, 9 Oct. 1920, 1, 6.

165 Kingsmill Commander, "Opportunities for Educated Women in Canada Are Not Recognized," *Carbon News*, 13 April 1921, 7.

166 Bridgeman, *Breaking Prairie Sod*, 244.

167 Ibid., 246.

168 "The Lure of the Land," *Graphic*, 21 Feb. 1920, 275.

169 *Imperial Colonist* 18, no. 227 (July 1921): 94.

170 "Handbook for Women Who Are Thinking of Settling Overseas" (London: Oversea Settlement Department, 1923), 15–16 in LSE, Women's Library, Papers of the Society for the Oversea Settlement of Women, IS0S/12, box FL021.

171 Low, *Women Out West: Life and Work in Canada*, 13.

172 *Annual Reports of the Society for the Oversea Settlement of British Women*, no. 6 (1925): 9.

173 Ibid., no. 7 (1926): 15.

174 Ibid., no. 9 (1928): 57.

175 Ibid., no. 6 (1925): 7.

176 "Saving the Crop," *Daily Mail*, 23 Aug. 1921,4; "A Prairie 'Social,'" 27 Aug. 1921, 4; "The Medicine Man," 22 Feb. 1923, 6; "Getting in the Wheat," 10 May 1923, 8.

177 "English Girls Investigate Canadian Farm Methods," *Blairmore Enterprise*, 7 June 1923, 2.

178 "English Girls Like West," *Irma Times*, 14 Sept. 1923, 2.

179 "British Women Farmers," *Claresholm Review*, 3 July 1925, 3.

180 "Greater Britain: Training Girls for Work in Canada," *Aberdeen Press and Journal*, 3 Nov. 1926, 9; "Canada … Novel Scheme," *Devon and Exeter Daily Gazette*, 1 Nov. 1926, 7.

181 Harris, "The Girl Emigrant: Her Chances in the Colonies," *Manchester Guardian*, 28 Oct. 1926, 6.

182 Durham, *Canada's Welcome to Women*, 5.

183 "Denials Are Issued about Allegations from Saskatchewan," *Globe*, 1 Nov. 1927, 2.

184 Barber, "The Gentlewomen of Queen Mary's Coronation Hostel," 151.

185 Quoted in ibid., 155.

186 Yarmie, "I Had Always Wanted to Farm," 110.

187 Ibid., 109–11.

188 "A Woman Homesteader," *Didsbury Pioneer*, 31 August 1921, 7; "On Easy Street: Women 'Farmerettes' Make Money in Western Canada," *New Oxford Item*, 8 June 1922, 6.

189 Library Archives Canada, Census 1901, Brandon, Manitoba; http://data2.collectionscanada.ca/1901/z/z001/jpg/z000014608.jpg.

190 Chicanot, "Some Canadian Women Pioneers," *Imperial Colonist*, Oct. 1925, 198.

191 "On Easy Street: Women 'Farmerettes' Make Money in Western Canada," *New Oxford Item*, 8 June 1922, 6.

192 "Successful Women Farmers in Canada," *Globe*, 26 March 1929, 11.

193 "Makes Success of Dairying," *Irma Times*, 7 March 1924, 2; "Woman Farmer Makes Success of What Is Now Reckoned Man Size Job," *Edmonton Bulletin*, 23 June 1923, 14.

194 Ibid., *Edmonton Bulletin*, 14.

195 "Women Farmers Raise Wheat in Canada," *Queensland Times*, 13 April 1925, 10.

196 Ibid.

197 Champ, "Heavy Horses at Saskatchewan's Fairs during the 1920s," prepared for the Western Development Museum, Winning the Prairie Gamble, 2005 Exhibit, 10 January 2002, 9.

198 *Imperial Colonist* 23, no. 2 (Feb. 1925): 23.

199 "English Writer Has Yearning for Farm in Western Canada," *Edmonton Bulletin*, 6 Oct. 1921, 7.

200 "Woman Farmer's Success," *Mirror Mail*, 19 Aug. 1926, 3.

201 See PAA, oral interview with Hon. Diana Rodnay, 71.248, 11 July 1971; "Titled Famers Till Canadian Prairies," *Wetaskiwin Times*, 13 Oct. 1927, 2; Lady Rodney, "Where Women Must Be Capable," *Wetaskiwin Times*, 8 March 1928, 3.

202 Chicanot, "Canadian Women's New World," *Woman's Journal*, 18 Oct. 1924, 12.

203 Cavanaugh, "Irene Marryat Parlby," 105.

204 *Evergreen and Gold: The Annual Publication of the Students of the University of Alberta* (1923), 75.

205 "Production of Honey in the Three Prairie Provinces Assuming Large Proportions," *Irma Times*, 2 Feb. 1923.

206 "Canadian Farmers' Tour," *Times*, 9 Jan. 1928, 13.

207 "Jills for Jacks: Training Girls as Wives for Settlers," *Aberdeen Press and Journal*, 12 Nov. 1928, 7.

208 Chicanot, "Canadian Women's New World," *Woman's Journal*, 18 Oct. 1924, 12.

209 "Fair Sex as Farmers," *Carbon News*, 14 July 1921, 6; "Full Discussion of Women's Right to File on Land," *Edmonton Bulletin*, 23 June 1921, 2.

210 "Want Homesteads for Women," *Gleichen Call*, 15 March 1922, 2.

211 "Women Want Homesteads," *Didsbury Pioneer*, 10 Sept. 1925, 7.

212 LAC, RG 15, Dominion Lands Rulings, 6602-6800, vol. 1984, p. 6750, Memorandum, 7 Feb. 1928.

213 Ibid., vol. 1980, p. 5866, Deputy Minister to J. Pope, Under-Secretary of State for External Affairs, 5 Feb. 1925.

214 LAC, RG 76, file 80212 pt. 6, vol. 198, B. Browne to Commissioner of Immigration, 22 March 1924.

215 LAC, RG15, Dominion Lands Rulings, 6602-6800, vol. 1984, p. 6730, Memorandum, 7 Feb., 1928

216 Ibid.

217 LAC, RG 15, Dominion Lands Rulings, 7201-7400, vol. 1987, p. 7261, Memorandum, to Mr. Perrin, 17 April, 1929.

218 *Western Producer*, 14 Feb. 1929, 10.

219 Kingsmill Commander, "Opportunities for Educated Englishwomen in Canada Are Not Recognized," *Carbon News*, 13 April 1921, 7.

220 Quoted in Harrison, *Go West—Go Wise!*, 72.

221 Ibid., 72–73.

222 Chicanot, "Some Canadian Women Pioneers," *Imperial Colonist* 23, no. 9 (Sept. 1925): 177.

223 Low, "The Empire's Call to Women," *Britannia and Eve* 1, no. 2 (5 Oct. 1928): 156.

224 Pickles, *Female Imperialism and National Identity*, 78.

225 Ibid., 88.

CONCLUSION

1 Canadian Pacific Railway, *Household Work in Canada for Girls*, 1.

2 Ibid., 10.

3 Oxendale, "'What Should They Know of England Who Only England Know?,'" 109. Oxendale created the term "gendered ruralism." While she does not provide a concise definition she develops the concept as emerging from the recognition that the time of "muscular" imperialism was over, and there was new concern for racial purity, health and hygiene, and to nurturing these in the colonies. Oxendale writes that "'Ruralism,' with its emphasis on traditional values, allowed for a robustness of character, indeed certain independence in a woman. In all, it provided a metaphor and a reality that allowed an active female role in shaping the meaning and the future of the empire" (109).

4 This is the topic of a forthcoming study by Sarah Carter, with Winona Wheeler, E. Leigh Syms, Robert Coutts, and Bret Nickels, "Growing Pains: The Dynamics of Aboriginal Agriculture in Manitoba."

5 Magee, "'For Home and Country.'"

6 Binnie-Clark, foreword to *A Birthday Book for the Farm Settlement on the Canadian Prairie*, 5. This "birthday book" was compiled by Binnie-Clark as a means of raising funds for the Union Jack Farm Settlement at Fort Qu'Appelle, Saskatchewan. She chose 365 messages from the Bible for each day of the year. Beside each day was a space for the book owner to pledge an amount to the Union Jack Farm Settlement.

7 Schultz, "Leaven for the Lump."

8 Jenks Papers, John Barnett to G. Binnie-Clark, 8 Jan. 1931.

9 Ibid., hand-written document, "The Home Farm Settlement," 1933.

10 Binnie-Clark, *A Birthday Book.*

11 Fort Qu'Appelle and District History Book Committee, *Fort Qu'Appelle and Area: A History*, 18.

12 "Alberta Homestead Regulations Contained in Act," *Wetaskiwin Times*, 2 April 1931, 8.

13 "Alberta Homestead Entries in August," *Wetaskiwin Times*, 17 Sept. 1931, 7.

14 "Women Homesteaders," *New York Times*, 29 Jan. 1933.

15 Ibid.

16 Tait, "Farming: All in the Family," *Globe and Mail*, 4 July, 2015, Section F, 1.

17 Stamm, "I Am … a Farmer," 173.

18 Ibid., 183.

19 Leckie, "Female Farmers in Canada and the Gender Relations of a Restructuring Agricultural System," 227.

20 Watkins and Jacoby, "Is the Rural Idyll Bad for Your Health?"

21 Ibid., 861.

22 Ibid., 853.

23 "Bah! Indeed. Mrs. Elsie Hart in U.F.C. Information, August," *People's Weekly*, 27 Aug., 1949, 4.

24 Wilson, *Agriculture of the Hidatsa Indians*, 115.

25 See Kub, "Buffalo Bird Woman's Farming Methods Still in Evidence Today," *Agfax* 7 August, 2013, available at http://www.epa.gov/agriculture/ag101/cropmajor.html.

BIBLIOGRAPHY

ARCHIVAL SOURCES

Annual Reports of the Society for the Overseas Settlement of British Women

British Columbia Archives
Nellie McClung Fonds

Glenbow Archives (GA), Calgary, Alberta
Canadian Pacific Railway Database
Canadian Pacific Railway Fonds

Harrison, Derek Papers, private collection, Fort Qu'Appelle, Saskatchewan

Hove Central Library, Hove, United Kingdom
Papers of Viscountess Frances Wolseley

Jenks Family Papers, private collection.

Library and Archives Canada (LAC)
Alexander Mackenzie Papers
Census Records
Record Group 2 (RG 2), Privy Council Office Orders-in-Council
Record Group 10 (RG 10), Records of the Department of Indian Affairs
Record Group 13 (RG 13) Records of the Department of Justice
Record Group 15 (RG 15), Records of the Department of the Interior
Dominion Lands Rulings
Homestead Land Registers
Western Land Grants
Record Group 17 (RG 17), Records of the Department of Agriculture
Record Group 18 (RG 18), Records of the NWMP/RCMP
Record Group 76 (RG 76), Records of the Department of Immigration

London School of Economics (LSE), The Women's Library
Records of the Colonial Intelligence League (CIL)

Montana Historical Society Research Center, Helena, Montana
Etta Smalley Bangs, Reminiscence

Provincial Archives of Alberta (PAA), Edmonton, Alberta
Homestead files

Provincial Archives of Manitoba (PAM), Winnipeg, Manitoba
Homestead files

Saskatchewan Archives Board (SAB), Saskatoon, Saskatchewan
Homestead files
Mrs. Ed Watson, "Pioneering in Saskatchewan
Lena Kernen Bacon, "Four Years in Saskatchewan from June 1904 to July 1908"
Saskatchewan Grain Growers Association Minutes

NEWSPAPERS AND PERIODICALS

Aberdeen Press and Journal (Aberdeen, Scotland)

Advertiser (South Australia)

Advertiser and Central Alberta News (Lacombe, Alberta)

African Standard (Nairobi, Kenya)

Age (Melbourne, Australia)

Ashburton Guardian (Ashburton, New Zealand)

Athenaeum (London, United Kingdom)

Bay of Plenty Times (New Zealand)

Better Farming (Chicago, Illinois)

Bismarck Daily Tribune (Bismarck, North Dakota)

Blairmore Enterprise (Blairmore, Alberta)

Border Watch (Mount Gambier, South Australia)

Bow Island Review (Bow Island, Alberta)

Brandon Daily Sun (Brandon, Manitoba)

Brantford Opinion (Brantford, Ontario)

Brisbane Courier (Brisbane, Australia)

Britannia and Eve (London, United Kingdom)

Calgary Daily Herald (Calgary, Alberta)

Calgary Herald (Calgary, Alberta)

Canadian Courier (Toronto, Ontario)

Canadian Gazette (London, United Kingdom)

Canadian Home Journal (Toronto, Ontario)

Canadian Magazine (Toronto, Ontario)

Canadian Magazine of Politics, Science, Art and Literature (Toronto, Ontario)

Carbon News (Edmonton, Alberta)

Carroll Herald (Carroll City, Iowa)

Chambers Edinburgh Journal (Edinburgh, Scotland)

Chambers Journal of Popular Literature, Science and Art (Edinburgh, Scotland)

Chicago Daily Tribune (Chicago, Illinois)

Clarence and Richmond Examiner (Grafton, New South Wales)

Claresholm Adverstiser (1914–16) (Claresholm, Alberta)

Claresholm Review (1904–16)

Claresholm Review-Advertiser (1916–28)

Coleman Bulletin (Coleman, Alberta)

Collier's Weekly (New York, New York)

Colonist (Nelson, New Zealand)

Country Woman (Sidney, Australia)

Crossfield Chronicle (Crossfield, Alberta)

Daily Colonist (Victoria, British Columbia)

Daily Mail (London, United Kingdom)

Daily Mail and Empire (Toronto, Ontario)

Daily News (Perth, Australia)

Daily Phoenix (Saskatoon, Saskatchewan)

Daily Star (Fredericksburg, Virginia)

Daily Telegraph (Tasmania)

Detroit Free Press (Detroit, Michigan)

Devon and Exeter Daily Gazette (Exeter, United Kingdom)

Didsbury Pioneer (Didsbury, Alberta)

Eastern Daily Mail and Straits Morning Advertiser (Singapore)

Edmonton Bulletin (Edmonton, Alberta)

Edmonton Capital (Edmonton, Alberta)

Empire Review (London, United Kingdom)

Empress Express (Empress, Alberta)

English Review (London, United Kingdom)

Enterprise (Harlem, Montana)

Essex County Chronicle (Essex, United Kingdom)

Examiner (London, United Kingdom)

Family Herald (Montreal, Quebec)

Family Herald and Weekly Star (Montreal, Quebec)

Farmer's Review (Chicago, Illinois)

Fortnightly Review (London, United Kingdom)

Gazette Times (Pittsburgh, Pennsylvania)

Gentleman's Magazine and Historical Review (London, United Kingdom)

Gentlewoman and Modern Life (London, United Kingdom)

Glasgow Democrat (Glasgow, Montana)

Gleichen Call (Gleichen, Alberta)

Globe (Toronto, Ontario)

Globe and Mail (Toronto, Ontario)

Grain Growers' Guide (Winnipeg, Manitoba)

Grand Forks Sun (Grand Forks, North Dakota)

Graphic (London, United Kingdom)

Harmsworth Magazine (London, United Kingdom)

Hawera and Normanby Star (Hawera, New Zealand)

Herald (Glasgow, Scotland)

Herald and News (Newberry, South Carolina)

Hinsdale Tribune (Hinsdale, Illinois)

Imperial Colonist (London, United Kingdom)

Irma Times (Irma, Alberta)

Jackson's Oxford Journal (Oxford, United Kingdom)

Kaipara and Waitemata Echo (Helensville, New Zealand)

Kindersley Clarion (Kindersley, Saskatchewan)

L'Abeille de la Nouvelle-Orléans (New Orleans, Louisiana)

La Survivance (Edmonton, Alberta)

Lady's Realm (London, United Kingdom))

Leader (Regina, Saskatchewan)

Leader-Post (Regina, Saskatchewan)

Leeds Mercury (Leeds, United Kingdom)

Leicester Chronicle and the Leicestershire Mercury (Leicester, United Kingdom)

London Society (London, United Kingdom)

Maclean's (Toronto, Ontario)

Macmillan's Magazine (London, United Kingdom)

Maitland Weekly Mercury (Maitland, Australia)

Manchester Guardian (Manchester, United Kingdom)

Manitoba Daily Free Press (Winnipeg, Manitoba)

Manitoba Free Press (Winnipeg, Manitoba)

Medicine Hat Times (Medicine Hat, Alberta)

Minneapolis Journal (Minneapolis, Minnesota)

Minnedosa Tribune (Minnedosa, Manitoba)

Mirror (London, United Kingdom)

Mirror Mail (Mirror, Alberta)

Missoulian (Missoula, Montana)

Monitor News (Monitor, Alberta)

Monthly Review (London, United Kingdom)

Montreal Gazette (Montreal, Quebec)

Moose Jaw Herald (Moose Jaw, Saskatchewan)

Morning Leader (Regina, Saskatchewan)

Morning Post (London, United Kingdom)

National Review (London, United Kingdom)

New Oxford Item (New Oxford, Pennsylvania)

New York Times (New York, New York)

New Zealand Herald (Auckland, New Zealand)

Newcastle Courant (Newcastle-upon-Tyne, United Kingdom)

Nineteenth Century (London, United Kingdom)

Nineteenth Century and After: A Monthly Review (London, United Kingdom)

Nor'West Farmer (Winnipeg, Manitoba)

Nottingham Evening Post (Nottingham, United Kingdom)

Omaha Daily Bee (Omaha, Nebraska)

Once a Week (London, United Kingdom)

Otago Witness (Dunedin, New Zealand)

Overseas Daily Mail (London, United Kingdom)

Oyen News (Oyen, Alberta)

Pall Mall Gazette (London, United Kingdom)

Pall Mall Magazine (London, United Kingdom)

Penny Magazine (Gloucestershire, United Kingdom)

People's Weekly (Edmonton, Alberta)

Prairie Illustrated (Calgary, Alberta)

Qu'Appelle Progress (Qu'Appelle, Saskatchewan)

Quebec Saturday Budget (Quebec City, Quebec)

Queensland Times (Ipswich, Australia)

Queenslander (Brisbane, Australia)

Quiver (London, United Kingdom)

Raymond Rustler (Raymond, Alberta)

Red Deer News (Red Deer, Alberta)

Redcliff Review (Redcliff, Alberta)

Reflector (London, United Kingdom)

Reflector (Mirror, Alberta)

Review of Reviews (London, United Kingdom)

St. Cloud Democrat (Saint Cloud, Minnesota)

St. John Sun (Saint John, New Brunswick)

Saskatoon Star Phoenix (Saskatoon, Saskatchewan)

Saturday News (Edmonton, Alberta)

Saturday Review of Politics, Literature, Science and Art (London, United Kingdom)

Scottish Review (Paisley, Scotland, and London, United Kingdom)

Secret Service (New York, New York)

Sedgewick Sentinel (Sedgewick, Alberta)

Spokane Daily Chronicle (Spokane, Washington)

Spokesman-Review (Spokane, Washington)

Star (Christchurch, New Zealand)

Strathmore Standard (Strathmore, Alberta)

Suffragette (London, United Kingdom)

Sun (New York, New York)

Sunday Times (Sydney, Australia)

Sydney Mail (Sydney, Australia)

Taber Free Press (Taber, Alberta)

Tamworth Daily Observer (Tamworth, Australia)

Tamworth Herald (Tamworth, Australia)

Tensas Gazette (St. Joseph, Louisiana)

Three Hills Capital (Three Hills, Alberta)

Times (London, United Kingdom)

Times Literary Supplement (London, United Kingdom)

Toledo Blade (Toledo, Ohio)

Toronto Sunday World (Toronto, Ontario)

United Empire (London, United Kingdom)

United Service Magazine (London, United Kingdom)

Victoria Daily Colonist (Victoria, British Columbia)

Vidette (Indian Head, Saskatchewan)

Voice (Winnipeg, Manitoba)

Vote (London, United Kingdom)

Votes for Women (London, United Kingdom)

Wainwright Star (Wainwright, Alberta)

Wairarapa Daily Times (Greytown, New Zealand)

Warwick Examiner and Times (Warwick, Australia)

Washington Times (Washington, DC)

Weekend Herald (Calgary, Alberta)

West Gippsland Gazette (Warragul, Australia)

Western Gazette (Yeovil, United Kingdom)

Western Globe (Lacombe, Alberta)

Western People (Ballina, United Kingdom)

Western Producer (Camrose, Alberta)

Western Times (Devon, United Kingdom)

Westminster Hall Magazine and Farthest West Review (Vancouver, British Columbia)

Wetaskiwin Times (Wetaskiwin, Alberta)

Winnipeg Daily Times (Winnipeg, Manitoba)

Winnipeg Evening Tribune (Winnipeg, Manitoba)

Winnipeg Free Press (Winnipeg, Manitoba)

Women's Leader and the Common Cause (London, United Kingdom)

Women's Suffrage Journal (Manchester, United Kingdom)

PUBLISHED PRIMARY SOURCES

Anonymous. *Montana 1909*. Helena, MT: Independent Publishing, 1909.

——. *The New West: Extending from the Great Lakes across Plain and Mountain to the Golden Shores of the Pacific*. Winnipeg: Canadian Historical Publishing, 1888.

——. *Our Western Lands: Some Transactions of the Laurier Administration Exposed in the Sessions of 1906 and 1907*. Ottawa, c. 1908.

Austin, Rev. Principal, ed. *Woman: Her Character, Culture and Calling*. Brantford, ON: The Book and Bible House, 1890.

Bernard, Lally [Mary Agnes Fitzgibbon]. *The Doukhobor Settlements: A Series of Letters*. Toronto: William Briggs, 1899.

Betham-Edwards, Matilda. *Reminiscences*. London: G. Redway, 1898.

Binnie-Clark, Georgina. *A Birthday Book for the Farm Settlement on the Canadian Prairie*. London: The Fashion Journals Guild, c. 1935.

——. "Conditions of Life for Women in Canada." *Women Workers: The Papers Read at the Conference Held in Portsmouth, 1909*, 110–120. London: The Office of the Union, 1909.

——. "Land and the Woman in Canada." Paper read at a meeting of the Royal Colonial Institute on Tuesday, April 8, 1913. *United Empire* 4 (New Series, 1913). London: Sir Isaac Pitman and Sons, 1914, 497–508.

——. *A Summer on the Canadian Prairie.* London: Edward Arnold, 1910.

——. *Tippy: The Autobiography of a Pekingese Puppy.* London: The Fashion Journals Guild, n.d. (ca. 1916).

——. *Wheat and Woman.* Toronto: Bell and Cockburn, 1914. Reprinted with an introduction by Susan Jackel. Toronto: University of Toronto Press, 1979.

——. *Wheat and Woman.* Toronto: Bell and Cockburn, 1914. Reprinted with a new introduction by Sarah Carter. Toronto: University of Toronto Press, 2007.

Boucherett, Jessie. *Hints on Self-Help: A Book for Young Women.* London: S.W. Partridge, 1863.

——. "How to Provide for Superfluous Women." In *Woman's Work and Woman's Culture: A Series of Essays*, ed. Josephine E. Butler, 27–48. London: Macmillan, 1869.

Bradbury, John. *Travels in the Interior of America in the Years 1809, 1810, and 1811.* 1819. Reprint. Lincoln: University of Nebraska Press, 1986.

Bradley, Edith, and Bertha La Mothe. *The Lighter Branches of Agriculture.* Vol. 6, The Woman's Library. London: Chapman and Hall, 1903.

Bridgeman, Rev. (Captain) Wellington. *Breaking Prairie Sod.* Toronto: The Musson Book Co., 1920.

Burton, Mrs. J.H. [Katherine]. *My Home Farm.* London: Longmans, Green and Co., 1883.

Canada. *Prosperity Follows Settlement: Settlers' Experience in Western Canada.* Ottawa: Department of the Interior, 1900.

Canadian Pacific Railway. *Home Life of Women in Western Canada.* Montreal: Canadian Pacific Railway, 1907.

——. *Household Work in Canada for Girls.* London: Canadian Pacific Railway Department of Colonization, Women's Branch, 1930.

——. *What Women Say of the Canadian North-West.* Montreal: Canadian Pacific Railway, 1886.

——. *Women's Work in Western Canada: A Sequel to "Words from the Women of Western Canada."* Montreal: Canadian Pacific Railway, 1906.

——. *Words from the Women of Western Canada.* Montreal: Canadian Pacific Railway, 1903.

Carrel, Frank. *Canada's West and Farther West: Latest Book on the Land of Golden Opportunities.* Toronto: Musson Book Co., 1911.

Catlin, George. *Letters and Notes on the Manners, Customs and Condition of the North American Indians.* New York: Wiley and Putnam, 1844.

Coulton, Sophia. *Our Farm of Four Acres and the Money We Made by It.* With an introduction by Peter B. Mead. 12th London ed. New York: C.M. Saxton, Barker & Co., 1860.

Cran, Mrs. George [Marion]. *A Woman in Canada.* London: W.J. Ham Smith, 1911.

Crawford, Virginia M. "Englishwomen and Agriculture." *Contemporary Review* 74 (September, 1898): 426–35.

Cresswell, Louisa. ["The Lady Farmer."] *Eighteen Years on the Sandringham Estate.* London: The Temple Co., 1887.

——. ["Mrs. Gerard Cresswell."] *How the Farming in Great Britain Can Be Made to Pay.* London: Simpkin, Marshall and Co., 1881.

Currie, David. *The Letters of Rusticus: Investigations in Manitoba and the North-West for the Benefit of Intending Emigrants.* Montreal: John Dougall & Sons, 1880.

Dinesen, Isak (Karen Blixen). *Out of Africa.* London: Putnam, 1937.

Durham, Mabel. *Canada's Welcome to Women.* London: Canadian Northern Railway, 1929.

"Emigrant Lady." *Letters from Muskoka.* London: R. Bentley, 1878.

Farquharson, James. "The Problem of Immigration: European and American." In *Canadian Problems*, edited by W.R. McIntosh, n.p. Toronto: R. Douglas Fraser Presbyterian Publications, 1910.

Fitzgibbon, Mary Agnes. *Trip to Manitoba: Or, Roughing It on the Line.* London: R. Bentley, 1880.

Frederiksen, Ditlew M. *The Land Laws of Canada and the Land Experience of the United States.* Canora, SK, 1907.

Fripp, Edward Fitz-Gerald. *The Outcasts of Canada: Why Settlements Fail. A True Record of "Bull" and Bale-Wire.* Edinburgh and London: William Blackwood and Sons, 1932.

Graham, E. Maud. *A Canadian Girl in South Africa: A Teacher's Experiences in the South African War, 1899–1902.* Toronto: W. Briggs, 1905. Reprinted, edited, and with an introduction by Michael Dawson, Catherine Gidney, and Susanne M. Klausen. Edmonton: University of Alberta Press, 2015.

Graham, P. Anderson. *The Revival of English Agriculture.* London: Jarrold and Sons, 1899.

Grand Trunk Pacific Railway, General Passenger Department. *Land Seekers' Guide.* Winnipeg: General Passenger Department, Grand Trunk Pacific Railway, 1912.

Hall, Mrs. Cecil (Mary). *A Lady's Life on a Farm in Manitoba.* London: W.H. Allen, 1884.

Harrison, Marjorie. *Go West—Go Wise! A Canadian Revelation.* London: Edward Arnold, 1930.

Jack, Annie L. *The Canadian Garden: A Pocket Help for the Amateur.* Toronto: William Briggs, 1903.

Jackson, C. Hamer. *Discoverers and Explorers of North America.* Toronto: Nelson, 1931.

Knox, Ellen M. *The Girl of the New Day.* Toronto: McClelland and Stewart, 1919.

Kurz, Rudolph Friedrich. *An Account of His Experiences Among Fur Traders and American Indians on the Mississippi and the Upper Missouri During the Years 1846 to 1852.* Smithsonian Institution Bureau of America Ethnology Bulletin 115. Washington, DC: Smithsonian Institution, 1937.

Love, Currie. "Where Opportunity Knocks." In *Merchants' and Manufacturers' Record: Calgary, Sunny Alberta and the Industrial Prodigy of the Great West*, 6–14. Calgary: Jennings Publishing Co., 1911.

Low, Florence B. *Openings for British Women in Canada.* London: William Stevens, c. 1920.

——. *Women Out West: Life and Work in Canada.* London: W.T. Cranfield, 1924.

McClung, Nellie. *The Stream Runs Fast: My Own Story.* Toronto: Thomas Allen, 1945.

Marshall, A.C. "Small Holdings for Women." In *Every Woman's Encyclopaedia.* Vol. 2, 1403–1406. London, 1910.

Martin, Chester. *"Dominion Lands" Policy.* Canadian Frontiers of Settlement, edited by W.A. Mackintosh and W.L.G. Joerg, vol. 2. Toronto: The Macmillan Co. of Canada, 1938.

Martineau, Harriet. *My Farm of Two Acres.* New York: Bunce and Huntington, 1865.

Mason, Otis Tufton. *Woman's Share in Primitive Culture.* London: Macmillan and Co., 1895.

Matthews, Washington. *Ethnography and Philology of the Hidatsa Indians.* Washington, DC: Government Printing Office, 1877.

Menzies, J.H. *Canada and the War: The Promise of the West.* Toronto: Copp Clark Co., 1916.

Metcalfe, J.H. *The Tread of the Pioneers.* Toronto: Ryerson Press Printers, 1932.

Moodie, Susanna. *Roughing It in the Bush; Or Life in Canada.* London: Richard Bentley, 1852.

Morris, Alexander. *The Treaties of Canada with the Indians of Manitoba and the North-West Territories.* 1880. Reprint, Toronto: Coles, 1971.

Morris, Elizabeth Keith. *An Englishwoman in the Canadian West.* London: Simpkin, Marshall, 1913.

Osborn, E.B., "Our Western Chivalry," *The Morning Post* (London), 14 July, 1900: 5.

Pullen-Burry, B. *From Halifax to Vancouver.* London: Mills and Boon, 1912.

Report on the International Congress of Women. International Congress of Women. Toronto: Geo. Parker and Sons, 1910.

Robertson, Norman. *The History of the County of Bruce.* Toronto: William Briggs, 1906.

Saxby, Jesse M. *West-Nor'-West.* London: James Nisbet and Co., 1890.

Schofield, F.H. *The Story of Manitoba.* Vol. 3. Winnipeg: S.J. Clarke, 1913.

Seton-Thompson, Grace G. *A Woman Tenderfoot.* Toronto: G.N. Morang, 1900.

Spence, Thomas. *The Prairie Lands of Canada.* Montreal: Gazette Printing House, 1879.

Sykes, Ella C. *A Home-Help in Canada.* London: Smith Elder and Co., 1912.

———. "Openings for Educated Women in Canada." *Journal of the Royal Society of Arts* 61: 3146 (March 7, 1913), 430–438.

Taylor, Frances. "Conditions of Life for Women in South Africa." *Women Workers: The Papers Read at the Conference Held in Portsmouth Arranged by the National Union of Women Workers of Great Britain and Ireland,* 122–128. London: Office of the Union, 1909.

Thwaite, Leo. *Alberta: An Account of Its Wealth and Progress.* Porter's Progress of Nations Series. Chicago: Rand McNally, 1912.

Vernon, A.L. *Leaton Colonial Training Home.* Winchester: Warren and Son, 1905.

Walker, Eldred G.F. *Canadian Trails: Hither and Thither in the Great Dominion.* Toronto: Musson Book Co., 1912.

Ward, Mary Augusta. *Canadian Born.* London: Smith, Elder, 1910.

Watanna, Onoto. *Cattle.* London: Hutchinson and Co., 1923.

Watt, Gertrude Balmer. *Town and Trail.* Edmonton: News Publishing Co., 1908.

West, Edward. *Homesteading: Two Prairie Seasons.* London: T. Fisher Unwin, 1918.

Wilkins, Louisa. *The Work of Educated Women in Horticulture and Agriculture.* London: J. Truscott, 1915.

Will, George F., and George G. Hyde. *Corn among the Indians of the Upper Missouri.* 1917. Reprint, Lincoln: University of Nebraska Press, 1964.

Wilson, Gilbert L. *Agriculture of the Hidatsa Indians: An Indian Interpretation.* Studies in the Social Sciences 9. Minneapolis: University of Minnesota Press, 1917.

———. *Buffalo Bird Woman's Garden: Agriculture of the Hidatsa Indians.* With a new introduction by Jeffery R. Hanson. Saint Paul: Minnesota Historical Society Press, 1987.

Wolseley, Frances. *Gardening for Women.* London: Cassell and Co., 1908.

———. *In a College Garden.* New York: Charles Scribner's Sons, 1917.

———. *Women and the Land.* London: Chatto and Windus, 1916.

Women of Canada: Their Life and Work. National Council of Women of Canada, 1900. Compiled for distribution at the Paris International Exhibition.

Women's Work on the Land: How You May Assist in Food Production This Summer. Government of Ontario Trades and Labour Branch, Department of Public Works, n.d.

SECONDARY SOURCES

Aberdeen Historical Society. *Aberdeen, 1907–1981.* Altona, MB: Friesen Printers, 1982.

Alberta Historical Society. *Cypress Hills Country.* Altona, MB: D.W. Friesen and Sons, 1991.

Alford, Katrina. *Production or Reproduction? An Economic History of Women in Australia, 1788–1850.* Melbourne: Oxford University Press, 1985.

Alix-Clive Historical Club. *Gleanings after Pioneers and Progress.* Alix, AB: Alix-Clive Historical Club, 1981.

Allen, Douglas W. "Homesteading and Property Rights: Or, 'How the West Was Really Won.'" *Journal of Law and Economics* 34, no. 1 (April 1991): 1–23.

Androsoff, Ashleigh. "A Larger Frame: 'Redressing' the Image of Doukhobor-Canadian Women in the Twentieth Century." *Journal of the Canadian Historical Association* 18, no. 1 (2007): 81–105.

Anonymous. *Our Harvest of Memories: Foxdale, Sturgeon Valley, Silver Cliff, Three Creeks, Rayside, Rich Valley.* Altona, MB: Friesen Printers, 1983.

——. *Prairie Sod and Goldenrod: History of Crossfield and District.* Altona, MB: Friesen Printers, 1977.

Armitage, Sue. *Shaping the Public Good: Women Making History in the Pacific Northwest.* Corvallis, OR: Oregon State University Press, 2015.

Augustus, Camilla. "'Half-Breed' Homestead: The North West Metis Scrip Policy, 1885–1887." MA thesis, University of Calgary, 2004.

Bacchi, Carol Lee. *Liberation Deferred: The Ideas of the English Canadian Suffragists, 1877–1918.* Toronto: University of Toronto Press, 1983.

Baergen, William. *Pioneering with a Piece of Chalk: The One-Room Country Schools of Alberta.* Stettler, AB: William Baergen, 2005.

Ballantyne, Tony. "Colonial Knowledge." In *The British Empire: Themes and Perspectives,* edited by Sarah Stockwell, 177–98. Oxford: Blackwell Publishing, 2008.

——. "Race and the Webs of Empire: Aryanism from India to the Pacific." *Journal of Colonialism and Colonial History* 2, no. 3 (2001). doi: 10.1353/cch.2001.0045.

Barber, Marilyn. "The Gentlewomen of Queen Mary's Coronation Hostel." In *Not Just Pin Money: Selected Essays on the History of Women's Work in British Columbia,* edited by Barbara K. Latham and Roberto J. Pazdro, 141–58. Victoria, BC: Camosun College, 1984.

——. "The Servant Problem in Manitoba, 1896–1930." In *First Days, Fighting Days: Women in Manitoba History,* edited by Mary Kinnear, 100–19. Regina: Canadian Plains Research Center, 1987.

Bartky, Sandra Lee. *"Sympathy and Solidarity" and Other Essays.* Oxford: Rowman and Littlefield, 2002.

Bauman, Paula. "Single Women Homesteaders in Wyoming, 1880–1930." *Annals of Wyoming* 58 (Spring 1986): 39–53.

Belich, James. *Replenishing the Earth: The Settler Revolution and the Rise of the Anglo-World, 1783–1939.* Oxford: Oxford University Press, 2009.

Bennett, Jason B. "Apple of the Empire: Landscape and Imperial Identity in Turn-of-the-Century British Columbia." *Journal of the Canadian Historical Association* 9 (January 1998): 63–92.

Bentley and District Historical Society. *Bentley and District Early History.* Bentley and District Historical Society, 1982.

Benton-Cohen, Katherine. "Common Purposes, Worlds Apart: Mexican-American, Mormon, and Midwestern Women Homesteaders in Cochise County, Arizona." *Western Historical Quarterly* 36, no. 4 (2005): 429–42.

Birtles, William. "A Pioneer Nurse." *Alberta History* 43, no. 1 (Winter 1995): 2–6.

Blaine Lake and District Historical Book Committee. *Bridging the Years: Era of Blaine Lake and District, 1790–1980.* Town of Blaine Lake and Rural Municipality of Blaine Lake, 1984.

Blakeley, Brian L. "Women and Imperialism: The Colonial Office and Female Emigration to South Africa, 1901–1910." *Albion: A Quarterly Journal Concerned with British Studies* 13, no. 2 (Summer 1981): 131–49.

Boag, Peter. *Re-Dressing America's Frontier Past.* Berkeley: University of California Press, 2011.

——. "Thinking Like Mount Rushmore: Sexuality and Gender in the Republican Landscape." In *Seeing Nature through Gender*, edited by Virginia J. Scharff, 40–59. Lawrence: University Press of Kansas, 2003.

Bowers, Alfred W. *Hidatsa Social and Ceremonial Organization.* 1963. Reprint, Lincoln: University of Nebraska Press, 1992.

Brada-Easthill-Roecliffe Historical Society. *Rural Roots.* Altona, MB: Friesen Printers, 1987.

Bradley, Harriet. *Men's Work, Women's Work: A Sociological History of the Sexual Division of Labour in Employment.* Minneapolis: University of Minnesota Press, 1989.

Buddle, Melanie. *The Business of Women: Marriage, Family and Entrepeneurship in British Columbia, 1901–51.* Vancouver: University of British Columbia Press, 2010.

Burnett, Kristin. *Taking Medicine: Women's Healing Work and Colonial Contact in Southern Albera 1880–1930.* Vancouver: University of British Columbia Press, 2011.

Bush, Julia. *Edwardian Ladies and Imperial Power.* London: Leicester University Press, 2000.

Carey, Jane L. "'Wanted! A Real White Australia': The Women's Movement, Whiteness and the Settler-Colonial Project." In *Studies in Settler Colonialism: Poltics, Identity, Culture*, edited by F. Bateman and L. Pilkington, 122–39. London: Palgrave Macmillan, 2011.

Carter, Sarah. "Britishness, 'Foreignness,' Women and Land in Western Canada, 1890s–1920s." *Humanities Research* 13, no. 1 (2006): 43–60.

——. *Capturing Women: The Manipulation of Cultural Imagery in Canada's Prairie West.* Montreal: McGill-Queen's University Press, 1997.

——. "Erasing and Replacing: Property and Homestead Rights of First Nations Farmers of Manitoba and the Northwest, 1870s–1910s." In *Place and Replace: Essays on Western Canada*, edited by Adele Perry, Esyllt W. Jones, and Leah Morton, 14–39. Winnipeg: University of Manitoba Press, 2013.

——. *The Importance of Being Monogamous: Marriage and Nation Building in Western Canada.* Edmonton: Athabasca University Press and University of Alberta Press, 2008.

——. "'An Infamous Proposal': Prairie Indian Reserve Land and Soldier Settlement after World War I." *Manitoba History* 37 (Spring/Summer 1999): 9–21. http://www.mhs.mb.ca/docs/mb_history/37/infamousproposal.shtml.

——. *Lost Harvests: Prairie Indian Reserve Farmers and Government Policy.* Montreal: McGill-Queen's University Press, 1990.

——. "'My Vocabulary Contains No Such Word as Defeat': Clara Lynch and Her Battle for Her Alberta Homestead, 1900–1909." *Alberta History* 61, no. 3 (Summer 2013): 2–11.

Carter, Sarah, ed. *Montana Women Homesteaders: A Field of One's Own.* Helena, MT: Farcountry Press, 2009.

Casid, Jill H. *Sowing Empire: Landscape and Colonization.* Minneapolis: University of Minnesota Press, 2005.

Cavanaugh, Catherine A. "Irene Marryat Parlby: An 'Imperial Daughter' in the Canadian West, 1896–1934." In *Telling Tales: Essays in Western Women's History*, edited by Catherine A. Cavanaugh and Randi R. Warne, 100–22. Vancouver: University of British Columbia Press, 2000.

——. "The Limitations of the Pioneering Partnership: The Alberta Campaign for Homestead Dower, 1909–1925." In *Making Western Canada: Essays on European Colonization and Settlement*, edited by Catherine Cavanaugh and Jeremy Mouat, 186–214. Toronto: Garamond Press, 1996.

——. "'No Place for a Woman': Engendering Western Canadian Settlement." *Western Historical Quarterly* 18 (Winter 1997): 493–518.

Chapman, Jane. "The Argument of the Broken Pane: Suffragette Consumerism and Newspapers." *Media History* 21, no. 3 (2015): 238–251.

Chilton, Lisa. *Agents of Empire: British Female Migration to Canada and Australia, 1860s–1930s*. Toronto: University of Toronto Press, 2007.

Church-Staudt, Barb. "Agnes (Martin) Balfour: Descendants Uphold Her Heritage." In *Pioneers! O Pioneers!* No. 4 *Regina Women of the Years*. Regina: Regina and District Old Timers' Association Inc., n.d.

Chused, Richard H. "The Oregon Donation Act of 1850 and Nineteenth Century Federal Married Women's Property Law." *American Journal of Legal History* 29, no. 1 (January 1985): 3–35.

Cohen, Marjorie Griffin. "The Decline of Women in Canadian Dairying." *Histoire sociale-Social History* 17, no. 43 (Nov. 1984): 307–34.

Compton, Tonia M. "Challenging Imperial Expectations: Black and White Female Homesteaders in Kansas." *Great Plains Quarterly* 33, no. 1 (November 2013): 49–61.

——. "Proper Woman/Propertied Women: Federal Land Laws and Gender Order(s) in the Nineteenth-Century Imperial American West." PhD diss., University of Nebraska-Lincoln, 2009. http://digitalcommons.unl.edu/historydiss/19/.

——. "Uncle Sam's Farm: Congress and Free Land Policies in the Nineteenth Century." Paper presented at the 3rd annual James A. Rawley Conference in the Humanities, *Imagining Communities: People, Places, Meanings*, Lincoln, NE, April 12, 2008. http://digitalcommons.unl.edu/historyrawleyconference/15/.

Conlogue, William. "Managing the Farm, Educating the Farmer: *O Pioneers!* and the New Agriculture." *Great Plains Quarterly* 21, no. 1 (Winter 2001): 3–15.

Constantine, Stephen. "Introduction: Empire Migration and Imperial Harmony." In *Emigrants and Empire: British Settlement in the Dominions between the Wars*, edited by Stephen Constantine, 1–21. Manchester and New York: Manchester University Press, 1990.

Cook, Ramsay. "Francis Marion Beynon and the Crisis of Christian Reformism." In *The West and the Nation: Essays in Honour of W.L. Morton*, edited by Carl Berger and Ramsay Cook, 187–208. Toronto: McClelland and Stewart, 1976.

Coyote Flats Historical Society. *Coyote Flats Historical Review 1905–1965*.

Cypress Hills (Alberta) Historical Soceity. *Cypress Hills Country: Our Roots*. Elkwater, AB: n.p., 1991.

Dagg, Anne Innis. *The Feminine Gaze: A Canadian Compendium of Non-Fiction Women Authors and Their Books, 1836–1945*. Waterloo: Wilfrid Laurier University Press, 2001.

Danysk, Cecilia. *Hired Hands: Labour and the Development of Prairie Agriculture, 1880–1930*. Toronto: McClelland and Stewart, 1995.

Daschuk, James. *Clearing the Plains: Disease, Politics of Starvation, and the Loss of Aboriginal Life*. Regina: University of Regina Press, 2013.

Davidoff, Leonore, and Catherine Hall. *Family Fortunes: Men and Women of the English Middle Class, 1780–1850*. London and New York: Routledge, 2002. First published 1987 by Hutchinson Education.

Delday, Eva. *Brooks: Beautiful-Bountiful.* Altona, MB: D.W. Friesen and Sons, 1975.

Denig, Edwin Thompson. *Five Indian Tribes of the Upper Missouri: Sioux, Arickaras, Assiniboines, Crees, Crows.* Norman: University of Oklahoma Press, 1961.

Devas, Nicolette. *Two Flamboyant Fathers.* London: Readers Union-Collins, 1968.

Dick, Lyle. *Farmers "Making Good": The Development of Abernethy District, Saskatchewan, 1880–1920.* Ottawa: National Historic Parks and Sites, 1989.

Dodd, Penny, and Marion Jankunis. "Garden of Native Prairie Plants," Galt Museum, accessed December 8, 2015. http://www.galtmuseum.com/pdf/NativePrairiePlantsGarden-Ethnobotany.pdf.

Doughty, Teri. "Representing the Professional Woman: The Celebrity Interviewing of Sarah Tooley." In *Women in Journalism at the Fin de Siècle: Making a Name for Herself,* edited by F. Elizabeth Gray, 165–81. London: Palgrave Macmillan, 2012.

Eatonia History Book Committee. *A Past to Cherish.* Eatonia, SK: Eatonia History Book Committee, 1980.

Egly Country Club. *Trails, Trials and Tributes.* Fort Benton, MT: 1974.

Emmons, David M. "American Myth, Desert to Eden: Theories of Increased Rainfall and the Timber Culture Act of 1873." *Forest History* 15, no. 3 (Oct. 1971): 6–14.

Evans, Simon. *The Bar U: Canadian Ranching History.* Calgary: University of Calgary Press, 2004.

——. *Prince Charming Goes West: The Story of the E.P. Ranch.* Calgary: University of Calgary Press, 1993.

Farm Women's Union of Alberta. *Pioneers Who Blazed the Trail: A History of High Prairie and District.* High Prairie, AB: South Peace News, 1968.

Farrington, Jessie de Prado. "Rocking Horse to Cow Pony." *New Mexico Historical Review.* Part 1: 30, no. 2 (April 1955): 115–135. Part II: 30, no. 3 (July 1955), 221–251. Part III: 30, no. 4 (October, 1955) 313–339. Part IV: 31, no. 3 (January, 1956), 38–67.

Fenn, Elizabeth. *Encounters at the Heart of the World: A History of the Mandan People.* New York: Hill and Wang, 2014.

Fiamengo, Janice. "Rediscovering Our Foremothers Again: Racial Ideas of Canada's Early Feminists, 1885–1945." In *Rethinking Canada: The Promise of Women's History,* edited by Mona Gleason and Adele Perry, 144–63. 5th edition. Don Mills, ON: Oxford University Press, 2006.

Fort Qu'Appelle and District History Book Committee. *Fort Qu'Appelle and Area: A History.* Fort Qu'Appelle, SK: Fort Qu'Appelle and District History Book Committee, 1996. One copy in the Book and Record Depository of the University of Alberta.

Fortier, Hilaire J. *Lamoureux: Ses Debuts, Ses Pionniers.* Lamoureux, AB: Lamoureux Jubilee Committee, 1955.

Friesen, Gerald. *The Canadian Prairies: A History.* Toronto: University of Toronto Press, 1984.

Fritze, Tamara. "Growing Identity, Growing a Home: Contrasting Functions of Two Nineteenth-Century Gardens." *Studies in the History of Gardens and Designed Landscapes: An International Quarterly* 22:4 (2002): 335–344.

Galloway, Margaret. *I Lived in Paradise.* Winnipeg: Bulman Brothers Ltd., 1942.

Ganley, Toby. "What's All This Talk about Whiteness?" *Dialogue* 1, no. 2 (2003): 12–13.

Garceau, Dee. *The Important Things of Life: Women, Work and Family in Sweetwater County, Wyoming, 1880–1929.* Lincoln: University of Nebraska Press, 1997.

George, Sam. *Botany, Sexuality and Women's Writing 1760–1830: From Modest Shoot to Forward Plant.* Manchester and New York: Manchester University Press, 2007.

Geraldine History Committee. *Spokes, Spurs and Cockleburs.* Fort Benton, MT: River Press, 1976.

Ghost Pine Community Group. *Memoirs of the Ghost Pine Homesteaders.* Three Hills, AB: Ghost Pine Community Group, 1954.

Gilpin, John. *Prairie Promises: History of the Bow River Irrigation District.* Vauxhall, AB: Bow River Irrigation District, 1996.

Gleadle, Kathryn. *Borderline Citizens: Women, Gender and Political Culture in Britain, 1815–1867.* Oxford, UK: Oxford University Press, 2009.

Gleichen United Church Women. *The Gleichen Call: A History of Gleichen and Surrounding Areas, 1877–1968.* Calgary: North West Printing, 1968.

Goldfrank, Esther S. *Changing Configurations in the Social Organization of a Blackfoot Tribe During the Reserve Period (the Blood of Alberta, Canada).* Seattle and London: University of Washington Press, 1966.

Gordon, Peter, ed. *Politics and Society: The Journals of Lady Knightley of Fawsley.* London and New York: Routledge, 2005.

Gould, Florence C., and Patricia N. Pando. *Claiming Their Land: Women Homesteaders in Texas.* El Paso: Texas Western Press, 1991.

Gowdy-Wygant, Cecilia. *Cultivating Victory: The Women's Land Army and the Victory Garden Movement.* Pittsburgh: University of Pittsburgh Press, 2013.

Green, Harvey. *The Light of the Home: An Intimate View of Women in Victorian America.* New York: Pantheon Books, 1983.

Grimshaw, Patricia. "Suffragists Representing Race and Gender in the American West: The Case of Colorado." In *Dealing with Difference: Essays in Gender, Culture and History,* edited by Patricia Grimshaw and Diane Kirkby, 79–81. Melbourne: History Department, University of Melbourne, 1997.

Hall, Catherine. "Of Gender and Empire: Reflections on the Nineteenth Century." In *Gender and Empire,* edited by Philippa Levine, 46–76. Oxford: Oxford University Press, 2004.

Harper, Marjory, and Stephen Constantine. *Migration and Empire.* Oxford: Oxford University Press, 2010.

Harris, Dianne. "Cultivating Power: The Language of Feminism in Women's Garden Literature, 1870–1920." *Landscape Journal* 13, no. 2 (Fall 1994): 113–23.

Harris, Margaret. "Hobart and 'Home' in Tasma and Mrs. Humphry Ward." *Australian Literary Studies in the 21st Century* 28 (2001): 135–44.

Harris, R. Cole, and John Warkentin. *Canada before Confederation: A Study in Historical Geography.* Ottawa: Carleton University Press, 1991.

Hawkins, R.E. "Lillian Beynon Thomas, Woman's Suffrage and the Return of Dower to Manitoba." *Manitoba Law Journal* 27, no. 1 (1999): 45–113.

Helly, Dorothy O. "Flora Shaw and the *Times*: Becoming a Journalist, Advocating Empire." In *Women in Journalism at the Fin de Siècle: Making a Name for Herself,* edited by F. Elizabeth Gray, 110–28. London: Palgrave Macmillan, 2012.

Henderson, Jarett. "'No Money, but Muscle and Pluck': Cultivating Trans-Imperial Manliness for the Fields of Empire, 1870–1901." In *Making it Like a Man: Canadian Masculinities in Practice,* edited by Christine Ramsay, 17–37. Waterloo, ON: Wilfrid Laurier University Press, 2011.

Henderson, Jennifer. *Settler Feminism and Race Making in Canada.* Toronto: University of Toronto Press, 2003.

High River Pioneers and Old Timers Association. *Leaves from the Medicine Tree.* Lethbridge: *Lethbridge Herald,* 1960.

Hildebrandt, Walter. "The Aspirations of a Western Enthusiast: P.G. Laurie and the *Saskatchewan Herald.*" MA thesis, University of Saskatchewan, 1978.

History Book Society. *Fencelines and Furrows.* Calgary: Northwest Printing and Lithographing, 1969.

Holme, Thea. *Chelsea.* London: Hamish Hamilton, 1972.

Home, Robert. "Scientific Survey and Land Settlement in British Colonialism with Particular Reference to Land Tenure in the Middle East 1920–50." *Planning Perspectives* 21 (Jan. 2006): 1–22.

Hryniuk, Margaret, and Frank Korvemaker. *Legacy of Stone: Saskatchewan's Stone Buildings.* Regina: Coteau Books, 2008.

Hunter, Kate (Kathryn M. Hunter). "The Big Picture Problem: Race and Gender in the Histories of Single Farming Women in Victoria, 1880–1930." In *Dealing with Difference: Essays in Gender, Culture and History.* Melbourne: University of Melbourne Press, 1997.

Hunter, Kathryn M. *Father's Right-Hand Man: Women on Australia's Family Farms in the Age of Federation, 1880s–1920s.* Melbourne: Australian Scholarly Publishing, 2004.

Hurt, R. Douglas. *American Agriculture: A Brief History.* Ames: Iowa State University Press, 1995.

——. *The Big Empty: The Great Plains in the Twentieth Century.* Tucson: University of Arizona Press, 2011.

Jacobs, Margaret. "Parallel or Intersecting Tracks? The History of the US West and Comparative Settler Colonialism." *Settler Colonial Studies* 4, no. 2 (2014): 155–161.

James, Jean. *Hanna North: Our Roots.* Hanna, AB: Hanna North Book Club, 1978.

Jusova, Iveta. *The New Woman and the Empire.* Columbus: Ohio State University Press, 2005.

Kalmakoff, Elizabeth Ann. "Woman Suffrage in Saskatchewan." MA thesis, University of Regina, 1993.

Kaye, Frances W. *Goodlands: A Meditation and History on the Great Plains.* Edmonton: Athabasca University Press, 2011.

Keeler History Book Committee. *Our Heritage: A History of the Keeler Community.* Keeler, SK: Keeler History Book Committee, 1990.

Kenyon, Ron. *Lone Rock to Marshall.* Altona, MB: D.W. Friesen and Sons, 1976.

King, Peter. *Women Rule the Plot: The Story of the 100 Year Fight to Establish Women's Place in Farm and Garden.* London: Duckworth, 1999.

Kingston, Beverley. *Elizabeth Macarthur.* Elizabeth Bay, N.S.W.: Historic Houses Trust of New South Wales, 1984.

Kisby, Anna. "Vera 'Jack' Holme: Cross-Dressing Actress, Suffragette and Chauffeur." *Women's History Review* 23, no. 1 (2014): 120–36.

Kluth, Alton E. "Mr. and Mrs. Reinhart Kluth." In *A Historical Tribute to the Pioneers South of the Whitemud,* edited by Harrisland Sewing Club History Committee. Bracken, SK: Harrisland Sewing Club History Committee, 1975.

Kranidis, Rita S. *The Victorian Spinster and Colonial Emigration: Contested Subjects.* London: Macmillan Press, 1999.

Kulba, Tracy, and Victoria Lamont. "The Periodical Press and Western Woman's Suffrage Movements in Canada and the United States: A Comparative Study." *Women's Studies International Forum* 29, no. 3 (May–June 2006): 265–78.

Lacey, Candida Ann, ed. *Barbara Leigh Smith Bodichon and the Langham Place Group.* New York and London: Routledge and Kegan Paul, 1987.

Lacombe Rural History Club. *Wagon Trails to Hard Top: History of Lacombe and Area.* Lacombe, AB: Lacombe Rural History Club, 1973.

Lambrecht, Kurt N. *The Administration of Dominion Lands, 1870–1930.* Regina: Canadian Plains Research Center, 1991.

Lang, Marjorie. *Women Who Made the News: Female Journalists in Canada 1880–1945*. Montreal: McGill-Queen's University Press, 1999.

Langford, Nanci. "First Generation and Lasting Impression: The Gendered Identities of Prairie Homestead Women." PhD diss., University of Alberta, 1994.

Lawrence, Dianne. *Genteel Women: Empire and Domestic Material Culture, 1840–1910*. Manchester: Manchester University Press, 2012.

Leckie, Gloria J. "Female Farmers in Canada and the Gender Relations of a Restructuring Agricultural System." *The Canadian Geographer* 37, no. 3 (1993): 212–29.

Lehr, John C., John Everitt, and Simon Evans. "The Making of the Prairie Landscape." *Prairie Forum* 33, no. 1 (Spring 2008): 1–38.

Leonard, David W. *The Last Great West: The Agricultural Settlement of the Peace River Country to 1914*. Calgary: Detselig Enterprises Ltd., 2005.

Levine, Philippa. "Introduction: Why Gender and Empire?" In *Gender and Empire*, edited by Philippa Levine. Oxford: Oxford University Press, 2004.

Levitan, Kathrin. "Redundancy, the 'Surplus Women' Problem, and the British Census, 1851–1861." *Women's History Review* 17, no. 3 (July 2008): 359–76.

Liberty County Museum. *Our Heritage in Liberty*. Chester, MT: Liberty County Times, 1976.

Lindgren, H. Elaine. *Land in Her Own Name: Women as Homesteaders in North Dakota*. Norman, OK, and London: University of Oklahoma Press, 1991.

Linklater, Andro. *Measuring America: How an Untamed Wilderness Shaped the United States and Fulfilled the Promise of Democracy*. New York: Walker Publishing Company, 2002.

Logan, Deborah Anna. *The Hour and the Woman: Harriet Martineau's "Somewhat Remarkable" Life*. DeKalb: Northern Illinois University Press, 2002.

Losurdo, Domenico. *Liberalism: A Counter-History*. London: Verso, 2011.

Lutz, Otto. *A Mother Braving a Wilderness: Told by Her Son, Otto Lutz*, edited by Thomas Gerwing. Muenster, SK: St. Peter's Colony Jubilee Steering Committee, 1977.

Lux, Maureen K. *Medicine that Walks: Disease, Medicine, and Canadian Plains Native People, 1880–1940*. Toronto: University of Toronto Press, 2011.

——. "We Demand 'Unconditional Surrender': Making and Unmaking the Blackfoot Hospital, 1890s to 1950s." *Social History of Medicine* 25, no. 3 (2012): 665–684.

McCallum, Margaret. "Prairie Women and the Struggle for a Dower Law, 1905–1920." *Prairie Forum* 18, no. 1 (Spring 1993): 19–34.

McClintock, Anne. *Imperial Leather: Race, Gender and Sexuality in the Colonial Context*. New York: Routledge, 1995.

McKay, Ian. "Debating Sexuality in Halifax, 1920: Mrs. Donald Shaw and Others." In *The Challenge of Modernity: A Readers on Post-Confederation Canada*, ed. Ian McKay, 331–345. Toronto: McGraw-Hill Ryerson, 1992.

——. "The Liberal Order Framework: A Prospectus for a Reconnaissance of Canadian History." *Canadian Historical Review* 81, no. 4 (Dec. 2000): 616–45.

McKenna, Katherine M.J. "E. Cora's Hind's Feminist Thought: 'The Woman's Quiet Hour' in the *Western Home Monthly*, 1905–1922." *Journal of the Canadian Historical Association* 22, no. 1 (2011): 69–98.

McKenzie, Tully. *It's Time to Remember: A Hundred Years of Progress Tremaine-Hunterville Area*. Steinbach, MB: Carillon Press, 1975.

MacKinnon, Doris J. *The Identities of Marie Rose Delorme Smith: Portrait of a Métis Woman, 1861–1960*. Regina: Canadian Plains Research Center, 2013.

MacMahon, Sandra Varney. "Fine Hands for Sowing: The Homesteading Experiences of Remittance Woman Jessie de Prado MacMillan." *New Mexico Historical Review* 74, no. 3 (July, 1999): 271–294.

McPherson, Kathryn. "Was the 'Frontier' Good for Women?: Historical Approaches to Women and Agricultural Settlement in the Prairie West, 1870–1925." *Atlantis: A Women's Studies Journal* 25, no. 1, (Fall/Winter 2000): 75–86.

Magee, Kathryn. "'For Home and Country': Education, Activism, and Agency in Alberta Native Homemakers' Clubs, 1942–1970." *Native Studies Review* 18, no. 2 (2009): 27–49.

Manitoba Culture, Heritage and Recreation, Historic Resources Branch. *The Prehistory of the Lockport Site.* Winnipeg: Manitoba Culture, Heritage and Recreation, Historic Resources Branch, 1985.

——. *Thomas Mayne Daly.* Winnipeg: Manitoba Culture, Heritage and Recreation, Historic Resources Branch, 1985.

Marsh, Jan. *Back to the Land: The Pastoral Impulse in England, 1880–1914.* London: Quartet Books: 1982.

Martin-McGuire, Peggy. "First Nations Land Surrenders on the Prairies." Ottawa: Indian Claims Commission, 1998.

Mead, Rebecca J. *How the Vote Was Won: Woman Suffrage in the Western United States, 1868–1914.* New York: New York University Press, 2004.

Mehain, Anne, and Limerick Historical Society. *Prairie Trails and Pioneer Tales.* Altona, MB: Friesen Printers, 1982.

Mehta, Uday S. "Liberal Strategies of Exclusion." In *Tensions of Empire: Colonial Cultures in a Bourgeois World,* edited by Frederick Cooper and Ann Laura Stoler, 59–87. Berkeley, Los Angeles, and London: University of California Press, 1997.

Meredith, Anne. "Horticultural Education in England, 1900–1940: Middle-Class Women and Private Gardening Schools." *Garden History* 31, no. 1 (Spring 2003): 67–79.

Millarville, Kew, Priddis and Bragg Creek Historical Society. *Our Foothills.* Altona, MB: D.W. Friesen and Sons, 1975.

Morgensen, Scott Lauria. "The Biopolitics of Settler Colonialism: Right Here, Right Now." *Settler Colonial Studies* 1, no. 1 (2011): 52–76.

Morrow, John. "The Deville Story." *Alberta History* 12, no. 4 (Autumn 1964): 15–18.

Morton, W.L. *Manitoba: A History.* Toronto: University of Toronto Press, 1967.

Muhn, James. "Women and the Homestead Act: Land Department Administration of a Legal Imbroglio, 1863–1934." *Western Legal History* 7, no. 2 (Summer/Fall 1994): 283–307.

Noakes, Lucy. "From War Service to Domestic Service: Ex-Servicewomen and the Free Passage Scheme 1919–22." *Twentieth Century British History* 22, no. 1 (2010): 1–27.

——. *Women in the British Army: War and the Gentle Sex 1907–48.* London: Routledge, 2006.

Notukeu History Book Club. *Next Year Country.* Notukeu, SK: Notukeu History Book Club, 1980.

Oak Lake Historical Committee. *Ox Trails to Blacktop.* Altona, MB: Friesen Printers, 1982.

Opitz, Donald L. "'Back to the Land': Lady Warwick and the Movement for Women's Collegiate Agricultural Education." *Agricultural History Review* 62, no. 1 (June 2014): 119–45.

——. "'A Triumph of Brains over Brute': Women and Science at the Horticultural College, Swanley, 1890–1910." *Isis* 104, no. 1 (March 2013): 30–62.

Oxendale, Stephanie M. "'What Should They Know Of England Who Only England Know?' Ideas of Englishness, Empire and Organized Women's Emigration, 1902–1927." PhD diss., State University of New York at Binghamton, 2000.

Paice, Edward. *Lost Lion of Empire: The Life of Cape-to-Cairo Grogan*. London: HarperCollins, 2001.

Palmer, Howard. *Patterns of Prejudice: A History of Nativism in Alberta*. Toronto: McClelland and Stewart, 1982.

Parkbeg History Book Group. *Parkbeg Reflections*. Regina: W.A. Print Works Ltd., 1982.

Patterson-Black, Sheryl. "Women Homesteaders on the Great Plains Frontier." *Frontiers* 1 (Spring 1976): 67–88.

Paul, Mandy, and Robert Foster. "Married to the Land: Land Grants to Aboriginal Women in South Australia, 1848–1911." *Australian Historical Studies* 34, no. 121 (April 2003): 48–68.

Perry, Adele. "Women, Racialized People, and the Making of the Liberal Order in Northern North America." In *Liberalism and Hegemony: Debating the Canadian Liberal Revolution*, edited by Jean-François Constant and Michel Ducharme, 274–297. Toronto: University of Toronto Press, 2009.

Peters, Virginia Bergman. *Women of the Earth Lodges: Tribal Life on the Plains*. Norman: University of Oklahoma Press, 1995.

Pickles, Katie. *Female Imperialism and National Identity: Imperial Order Daughter of the Empire*. Vancouver: UBC Press, 2002.

Pleasantdale and District History Book Committee. *Memories of the Past: History of Pleasantdale, Silver Park, Chagoness, and Kinistino Indian Band #91*. Pleasantdale, SK: Pleasantdale and District History Book Committee, 1981.

Pollock, Gwen. *Our Pioneers*. Maple Creek, SK: South Western Saskatchewan Old Timers' Association, 1978.

Potyondi, Barry. *In Palliser's Triangle: Living in the Grasslands 1850–1930*. Saskatoon: Purich Publishing, 1995.

Preston, Rebecca. "'Hope you will be able to recognize us': The Representation of Women and Gardens in Early Twentieth-Century British Domestic 'Real Photo' Postcards." *Women's History Review* 18, no. 5 (November 2009): 781–800.

Ranciére, Jacques. *The Politics of Aesthetics: The Distribution of the Sensible*. London: Continuum, 2006.

Rees, Ronald. *New and Naked Land: Making the Prairies Home*. Saskatoon: Western Producer Prairie Books, 1988.

Rennie, Bradford James. *The Rise of Agrarian Democracy: The United Farmers and Farm Women of Alberta*. Toronto: University of Toronto Press, 2000.

Reyburn, Karen Ann. "Blurring the Boundaries: Images of Women in Canadian Propaganda of World War I." MA thesis, University of Guelph, 1998.

Richards, Irene Lawrence. "The Story of Beautiful Plains," *Manitoba Historical Society Transactions* 3 (1951–52). http://www.mhs.mb.ca/docs/transactions/3/beautifulplains.shtml.

Richardson, Frances. "Women Farmers of Snowdonia, 1750–1900." *Rural History* 25, no. 2 (October 2014): 161–81.

Richtik, James M. "Manitoba Settlement 1870–86." PhD diss., University of Minnesota, 1971.

——. "The Policy Framework for Settling the Canadian West, 1870–1880." *Agricultural History* 49, no. 4 (Oct. 1975): 613–28.

Riley, Glenda. *Inventing the American Woman: An Inclusive History*. Vol. 2, Since 1877. 2nd ed. Wheeling, IL: Harlan Davidson Inc., 1995.

Riley, Mark. "Bringing the 'Invisible Farmer' into Sharper Focus: Gender Relations and Agricultural Practices in the Peak District." *Gender, Place and Culture: A Journal of Feminist Geography* 16, no. 6 (2009): 665–82.

Roberts, Barbara. "'A Work of Empire': Canadian Reformers and British Female Immigration." In *A Not Unreasonable Claim: Women and Reform in Canada, 1880s–1920s*, edited by Linda Kealey, 185–201. Toronto: The Women's Press, 1979.

Roberts, Bev. *Miss D and Miss N: An Extraordinary Partnership: The Diary of Anne Drysdale.* Victoria: Australian Scholarly Publishing, 2009.

Roche, Michael. "World War One British Empire Discharged Soldier Settlement in Comparative Focus." *History Compass* 9, no. 1 (2011): 1–15.

Rockwood-Woodlands Historical Society. *Rockwood Echoes: Ninety Years of Progress 1870–1960.* Steinbach, MB: Derksen Printers, 1960.

Roe, Frank Gilbert. *"Getting the Know-How": Homesteading and Railroading in Early Alberta.* Edmonton: NewWest Press, 1982.

Rowbotham, Sheila. *A Century of Women: The History of Women in Britain and the United States.* London: Viking, 1997.

Roy, R.H. "A Berkhamstead Boy in the Foothills." *Alberta Historical Review* 20, no. 3 (Summer 1972): 17–29.

Russell, Peter A. *How Agriculture Made Canada: Farming in the Nineteenth Century.* Montreal, QC: McGill-Queen's University Press, 2012.

Saugeres, Lisa. "'She's Not Really a Woman, She's Half a Man': Gendered Discourses of Embodiment in a French Farming Community." *Women's Studies International Forum* 25, no. 6 (2002): 641–50.

Sayer, Karen. *Women of the Fields: Representations of Rural Women in the Nineteenth Century.* Manchester and New York: Manchester University Press, 1995.

Sayers, Sean. Review of *The Politics of Aesthetics: The Distribution of the Sensible*, by JacquesRanciére. *Culture Machine* 1 1 0 1, 2005.

Schmidt, John. *Growing Up in the Oil Patch.* Toronto: Dundurn Press, 1985.

Schultz, John A. "'Leaven for the Lump': Canada and Empire Settlement." In *Emigrants and Empire: British Settlement in the Dominions between the Wars*, edited by Stephen Constantine, 121–49. Manchester and New York: Manchester University Press, 1990.

Scully, Pamela. "White Maternity and Black Infancy: The Rhetoric of Race in the South African Women's Suffrage Movement, 1895–1930." In *Women's Suffrage in the British Empire: Citizenship, Nation and Race*, edited by Ian Christopher Fletcher, Laura E. Nym Mayhall, and Philippa Levine, 68–83. London and New York: Routledge, 2000.

Seaton, Beverly. "The Garden Autobiography." *Garden History* 7, no. 1 (Spring 1979): 101–20.

Sedgewick Historical Society. *Sedgewick Sentinel: A History of Sedgewick and Surrounding District.* Sedgewick, AB: Sedgewick Historical Society, 1982.

Shannon, Bill. "Brokers, Land Bankers, and 'Birds of Evil Omen': The Effect of Land Policies on Settlement in Upper Canada Collingwood Township 1834–1860." MA thesis, University of Ottawa, 1989.

Shepard, R. Bruce. *Deemed Unsuitable: Blacks from Oklahoma Move to the Canadian Prairies in Search of Equality in the Early 20th Century Only to Find Racism in Their New Home.* Toronto: Umbrella Press, 1997.

Shteir, Ann B. *Cultivating Women, Cultivating Science: Flora's Daughters and Botany in England, 1760–1860.* Baltimore and London: Johns Hopkins University Press, 1996.

Smith, David. "Instilling British Values in the Prairie Provinces." In *Immigration and Settlement, 1870–1939*, edited by Gregory P. Marchildon, 441–456. Regina: Canadian Plains Research Center, 2009.

Smith, Keith C. *Liberalism, Surveillance, and Resistance: Indigenous Communities in Western Canada, 1877–1927.* Edmonton: Athabasca University Press, 2009.

Smith, Michelle. "Adventurous Girls of the British Empire: The Pre-War Novels of Bessie Marchant." *The Lion and the Unicorn* 33, no. 1 (January 2009): 1–25.

Smith, Minnie. *Is It Just?* 1911. Reprint with a critical introduction by Jenny Roth and Lori Chambers. Toronto: University of Toronto Press, 2011.

Smith, Sherry. "Single Women Homesteaders: The Perplexing Case of Elinore Pruitt Stewart." *Western Historical Quarterly* 22 (May 1991): 163–83.

Sonningdale Recreation Board. *Sonningdale Memories, 1900–1980*. Sonningdale, SK: Sonningdale Recreation Board, 1982.

Spender, Dale. *Writing a New World: Two Centuries of Australian Women Writers*. Sydney: Allen and Unwin Australia, 1998.

Stamm, Marianne. "I Am … a Farmer." In *Country Roads: Memoirs from Rural Canada*, edited by Pam Chamberlain. Halifax: Nimbus Publishing, 2010.

Stansell, Christine. *City of Women: Sex and Class in New York, 1789–1860*. Urbana: University of Illinois Press, 1987.

Stead, Robert J.C. "Fifty Years in Western Canada: A Sketch of the Career of John Sanderson, the First Homesteader in Western Canada." *Better Farming*, May 1923, 4–5.

Stone Diggers Historical Society. *Prairie Wool: A History of Climax and Surrounding School Districts*. Climax, SK: Stone Diggers Historical Society, 1980.

Strange, Carolyn. *Toronto's Girl Problem: The Perils and Pleasures of the City, 1880–1930*. Toronto: University of Toronto Press, 1995.

Strong-Boag, Veronica. "Making a Difference: The History of Canada's Nurses." *Canadian Bulletin of Medical History* 8 (1991): 231–48.

Taylor, Jeffery M. *Fashioning Farmers: Ideology, Agricultural Knowledge, and the Manitoba Farm Movement, 1890–1925*. Regina: Canadian Plains Research Center, 1994.

Thompson, Jane Reid, "'A Stronger and More Independent Self': Single, Middle-Class British Women Emigrants to the Canadian West, 1880–1930." PhD diss., University of Toronto, 2000.

Tosh, John. *Manliness and Masculinities in Nineteenth-Century Britain: Essays on Gender, Family and Empire*. London: Pearson, Longman, 2005.

Tough, Frank, and Kathleen Dimmer. "'Great Frauds and Abuses': Institutional Innovation at the Colonial Frontier of Private Property: Case Studies of the Individualization of Maori, Indian and Metis Lands." In *Settler Economies in World History*, edited by Christopher Lloyd, Jacob Metzer, and Richard Sutch, 205–49. Leiden; Boston: Brill, 2013.

Trigger, Bruce G. *The Huron: Farmers of the North*. 2nd ed. Toronto: Holt, Rinehart and Winston, 1990.

Troper, Harold Martin. *Only Farmers Need Apply: Official Canadian Government Encouragement of Immigration from the United States, 1896–1911*. Toronto: Griffin House, 1972.

Turner, Nancy J. *Ancient Pathways, Ancestral Knowledge: Ethnobotany and Ecological Wisdom of Indigenous Peoples of Northwestern North America*. Vol. 1. Montreal: McGill-Queen's University Press, 2014.

Twinch, Carol. *Women on the Land: Their Story during Two World Wars*. Cambridge: Lutterworth Press, 1990.

Tyman, John L. "Patterns of Western Settlement." *Manitoba Historical Society Transactions* 3, no. 28 (1971–72). http://www.mhs.mb.ca/docs/transactions/3/landsettlement.shtml.

Valverde, Mariana. *The Age of Light, Soap and Water: Moral Reform in English Canada, 1885–1925*. Toronto: University of Toronto Press, 2008.

Veldhuis, Oriole A. Vane. *For Elise: Unveiling the Forgotten Woman on the Criddle Homestead*. Winnipeg: Oriole A. Vane Veldhuis, 2012.

Venne, Sharon. *Indian Acts and Amendments 1868–1975: An Indexed Collection*. Saskatoon: University of Saskatchewan Native Law Centre, 1981.

Veracini, Lorenzo. "'Settler Colonialism': Career of a Concept." *The Journal of Imperial and Commonwealth History* 41, no. 2 (2013): 567–583.

Verdon, Nicola. "Middle-Class Women's Work and the Professionalization of Farming in England, 1890–1939." *Journal of British Studies* 51, no. 2 (April 2012): 393–415.

—— "The 'Lady Farmer': Gender, Widowhood and Farming in Victorian England." In *The Farmer in England 1650–1980*, edited by Richard W. Hoyle, 241–262. London and New York: Routledge, 2013.

——. *Rural Women Workers in Nineteenth-Century England: Gender, Work and Wages.* Woodbridge: Suffolk Press, 2002.

Vicinus, Martha. *Independent Women: Work and Community for Single Women, 1850–1920.* Chicago: Virago Press, 1985.

Waddell, James McKercher. *Dominion City: Facts, Fiction and Hyperbole.* Steinbach, MB: Derksen Printers, 1970.

Walker-Kuntz, Sunday Anne. "Land, Life and *Feme Sole*: Women Homesteaders in the Yellowstone River Valley, 1909–1934." MA thesis, Montana State University, 2006.

Walkowitz, Judith R. *City of Dreadful Delight: Narratives of Sexual Danger in Late Victorian London.* Chicago: University of Chicago Press, 1992.

Wanhalla, Angela. *Matters of the Heart: A History of Interracial Marriage in New Zealand.* Auckland: Auckland University Press, 2013.

Watkins, Francine, and Ann Jacoby. "Is the Rural Idyll Bad for Your Health? Stigma and Exclusion in the English Countryside." *Health and Place* 13 (2007): 851–64.

Weaver, John. *The Great Land Rush and the Making of the Modern World, 1650–1900.* Montreal: McGill-Queen's University Press, 2003.

Webb History Book Committee. *Prairie Memories.* Steinbach, MB: Derksen Printers, 1982.

White, Bonnie J. "Remembrance, Retrospection, and the Women's Land Army in World War I Britain." *Journal of the Canadian Historical Association* 22, no. 2 (2011): 162–94.

——. *The Women's Land Army in First World War Britain.* Houndmills, Basingstoke, Hampshire: Palgrave Macmillan, 2014.

Wilden, Anthony. *Man and Woman, War and Peace: The Strategist's Companion.* London and New York: Routledge and Kegan Paul, 1987.

Wildenthal, Lora. "'She is the Victor': Bourgeois Women, Nationalist Identities and the Ideal of the Independent Woman Farmer in German Southwest Africa." *Social Analysis* 33 (September 1993): 68–88.

Wilson, Catharine Anne. "Manly Art: Plowing, Plowing Matches and Rural Masculinity in Ontario 1800–1930." *The Canadian Historical Review* 95, no. 2 (June 2014): 157–86.

Wolfe, Patrick. "Settler Colonialism and the Elimination of the Native." *Journal of Genocide Research* 8, no. 4 (December 2006): 387–409.

Wood Mountain Historical Society. *They Came to Wood Mountain.* Wood Mountain, SK: Wood Mountain Historical Society, n.d.

Worsnop, Judith. "A Reevaluation of 'The Problem of Surplus Women' in 19th-Century England: The Case of the 1851 Census." *Women's Studies International Forum* 13, no. 1/2 (1990): 21–31.

Yarmie, Andrew. "'I Had Always Wanted to Farm': The Quest for Independence by English Female Emigrants at the Princess Patricia Ranch Vernon, British Columbia, 1912–1920." *British Journal of Canadian Studies* 16, no. 1 (2003): 102–25.

Yellow Lake History Group. *Treasured Memories.* Steinbach, MB: Derksen Printers, 1982.

Youmans, Joyce M. "Walker, Ethel (1861–1951)." *GLBTQ* Encyclopedia. http://www.glbtqarchive.com/arts/walker_e_A.pdf.

Young, Iris. *On Female Body Experience: "Throwing Like A Girl" and Other Essays.* Oxford: Oxford University Press, 2005.

——. "Throwing Like a Girl: A Phenomenology of Feminine Body Comportment, Motility, and Spatiality." In *The Thinking Muse: Feminism and Modern French Philosophy*, edited by Iris Young and Jeffner Allen, 51–70. Bloomington: Indiana University Press, 1989.

Ziff, Bruce, and Sean Ward. "Squatters' Rights and the Origin of Edmonton Settlement." In *Essays in the History of Canadian Law: Volume 10, A Tribute to Peter N. Oliver*, edited by Jim Phillips, R. Roy McMurtry, and John T. Saywell, 446–468. Toronto: Osgoode Society for Legal History, 2008.

INDEX

A

Aboriginal women (Australia), 45–46
adoptions, 175–76, 180
African Americans, 43, 159, 310–11
Agricultural College (Guelph), 127
Ahern, H.G., 317
Alberta Lands Act, 379–80
Alberta Women's Institutes, 346
Alden, Cynthia W., 243
Alix (AB), 144, 212
Allan, James, 316
Allison, Maria, 209
Alloway, Charles, 54, 56
American Woman's Land Army, 330
Amery, Leo, 356
Anderson, Mary, 367
Anishinaabe, 6. *See also* Saulteaux
Archer, Judy, 204
Archer, William, 203
Archibald, Adams, 48, 53
Archibald, John, 405n56
Archie, Agnes, 56
Ard, Rachel, 364–65
Arikara, 31, 35
Arlesey House Colonial Training school, 113, 114, 277
Arnott, Mrs. E.P., 344
Assiniboine, 164, 247, 249
Astor, Phillip, 102
Attridge, Mary, 155
Austin, Benjamin F., 138
Australia, 45–46, 243–44, 297
Awrey, Herbert N., 209

B

Baird, Edward, 195
Balfour, Agnes, 143–44, 159–60
Balfour, Frances, 270
Bangs, Etta Smalley, 204
Bangs, Will, 204
Banks, Elizabeth, 349
Barnard, Amy B., 350
Barrow, Edward D., 361–62
Batchelor, Eliza Ann, 147–48
Batchelor, Thomas, 147
Battersea Polytechnic, 114
Bayley, Mrs. Harold, 368
Bedier, V.C., 317–18
Bedingfeld, Agnes, 151, 152
Bedingfeld, Frank (Francis), 152
bee farming, 369
Beevor, Miss, 267
Bell, Delia, 185–87
Bell, John, 150
Bell, W.G., 186
Belly Fat, Marcia, 50, 52
Bennett, R.B., 303
Bertram, E. Violet, 275–76, 286
Betham-Edwards, Matilda, 96
Beveridge, Isabella, 150, 152
Beveridge, W.W., 290–91
Beynon, Francis Marion, 317, 320–21
Biden, Frances A., 360
Biggar (SK), 197
Binnie-Clark, Georgina: buys farm, 245, 252; and CIL, 131–32; critics of, 133, 281–83; early years, 251–52; as farmer, 245, 246, 254, 258, 260, 269, 379; finances, 258–59; homes of, 409n42, 409n43; as imperialist, 245–47; and Indigenous peoples, 247–51; journalism, 105, 259–60, 263–66, 268–69, 274; later years and legacy, 286, 323; and homesteads-for-women campaign, 14, 235, 259, 260–71, 277–81, 283–85, 289, 294; picture, 253; proponent of British women farming in colonies, 85–86; and *A Summer on the Canadian Prairie,* 254, 268–69; talks and lectures, 276, 277–81; and training farm,

271–76; and UJFS, 378–79, 421n6; *Wheat and Woman,* 283–85

Bird, Maria, 143

Birmingham, Eliza, 196

Birss, James, 153

Birss, Mary Elizabeth, 153

Birtles, Sarah, 195–96

Black, Bessie, 236

Black, David, 236

Blackfoot, 38

Blackmore, Francis, 68

Blackstock, Mary, 175

Blewett, Jean, 256

Borden, Frederick W., 190

Borden, Harold L., 190

Borden, Robert L., 173

Boucherett, Jessie, 95, 107–8

Bradbury, John, 31

Bradford, Andrew, 194

Bradford, Emma, 194

Bradford, Ethel May, 369

Bradley, Edith, 94

Bradshaw, Barbara, 154

Brandon (MB), 126, 150, 168, 169, 338

Brauer, Sophia, 196

Brice, Arthur Montefiore, 106, 122

Bridgeman, Wellington, 362

Briggs, Mary, 205–6

British Columbia, 60–61, 129, 130–31, 132, 340, 361–62, 365–66

British settler women: Canadian interest in attracting, 109–10, 138–41; CPRs promotion for, 141–46, 244; criticism of their plan to farm in Canada, 72, 76, 352, 357–59, 362; discrimination against as homesteaders, 160–69; domestic service of, 375–76; employed as home helps, 116, 117, 375–76; examples of widows homesteading, 148, 149–56; fiction about, 136–37; homesteading in US, 204; and homesteads-for-women campaign, 260–71, 312–22; interest in farming in Canada after First World War, 360–66, 373; need for in Canada after First World War, 349–55; proponents of farming for, 84, 85–87; statistics on as homesteaders, 156–59; and "surplus" problem, 92–97, 350, 354; who purchased land in Canada, 210–16; and First World War, 327–28

British Women's Emigration Association, 107, 116

Brockmann, Clara, 18

Brookes, Isabel H., 155

Bryce, Isabelle Rogers, 368

Bucknam, Matilda, 174, 209

Buffalo Bird Woman (Maxi'diwiac), 29, 31, 33–34, 36, 382

Bull, Jeffrey, 280

Burbank, M.L., 371–72

Burgess, A.M., 170

Burns, Eileen L., 120–21

Burns, Patrick, 121, 153

Burns, Thomas, 150, 152

Burton, Katherine, 92

C

Cairns, Eleanor Bell, 150

Calgary Business Women's National Service Corps, 338–40

Calgary Central Women's Colonization Board, 360

Cameron, Elizabeth, 4, 383n1

Cameron, Ellen Margaret, 170

Cameron, Hugh, 4

Canada, Government of: belief in masculinity of farming, 377–78; and colonial training program for women, 126; and forest tree culture legislation, 81–83; gains control of western lands, 47; and homestead crisis in Manitoba, 70–71; and homesteading eligibility for women, 149, 171–75; and homesteads-for-women campaign, 261, 262, 288, 319, 322, 348, 349, 370–71; and Indigenous peoples, 52–53, 208, 209, 248, 255, 408n10; and M. Cran, 133; scrutiny of widow land owners, 148–49; and Soldier Settlement Act, 347–48, 349; use of US as poor homesteading example, 19, 304. *See also* Dominion Land Act

Canadian Council of Agriculture, 371

Canadian Council of Immigration of Women for Household Service, 359

Canadian Pacific Railway (CPR): and Binnie-Clark training school, 271;

and disease, 52; and eviction of widow homesteader case, 167–69; and hiring home helps, 360; promotion for women settlers, 141–46, 244; publications of, 217, 219, 231–32, 242–43, 375; purchase of its land for homesteading, 216; ready-made farms, 227, 228, 230, 232, 235–36, 270, 276

Canadian Patriotic Fund, 344

Carlisle, Patricia, 238–39, 368

Carlton (SK), 159,

Carlyle (SK), 164

Carruthers, Ellen, 209

Carter, Estella B., 347

Caton, Alice, 216

Cattle (Eaton), 240–41

Chaffey, Benjamin, 56

Chamberlain, Mrs. (Wood Mountain), 239

Channon, Will, 296

cheese making, 101

Chesney, Jane, 98

Chicanot, E.L., 369, 372

Chmelik, Anna, 203

Chmelik, Emily, 203

Chmelik, Mary, 203

Christian of Schleswig-Holstein, Princess, 129

Clark, Arthur Cameron Binnie, 258

Clark, Arthur Walter Binnie, 251

Clark, Ethel B., 254, 260, 286, 379

Clark, Louis B., 251, 252, 254

Clark, William, 35

Cleveley, Sarah, 155–56

Cochrane (AB), 239

Cochrane, Jennie, 197

Codd, Donald, 64, 70, 74, 83

Cohn, Felice, 200

Colonial and Home Domestic Training Branch, 112

Colonial Intelligence League for Educated Women (CIL), 127–33, 242, 327, 353–54

Colonial Training College (at Stoke), 128, 328

colonialism, 6, 8–11, 76–79, 89, 248–51, 281. *See also* imperialism

Colonsay (SK), 195

Colquhoun, Mrs. Archibald, 126

Conklin, Margaret, 179–80

Corbett, Mary Matilda, 65

Corbett, Sarah Jane, 65

corn, 33–34

Courtauld, Katherine, 92

CPR. *See* Canadian Pacific Railway

Craig, H.A., 338

Cran, Marion, 87, 133–36, 268, 270

Crawford, Virginia, 88, 93

Cree, 6, 31, 247, 249

Creelman, G.C., 333

Crerar, Marion, 140

Cresswell, Louisa, 91–92

Criddle, Alice Nicol, 178

Criddle, Percy, 178–79

cross-dressers, 237–38

Crossfield (AB), 154

Cunningham, A.H., 296

Cunningham, James, 74

Currie, David, 72–73, 76–77, 82–83

D

Dahl, Cecilia, 346

Dakota, 6, 49, 247, 249

Daly, Thomas Mayne, 168–69, 170

Damusey, Jack, 7

Day, M.J., 209

De Rothschild, Lionel, 214

De Rothschild, Marie-Louise, 214

de Tro, Margaret, 160, 161, 162

Denman, Gertrude, 329

Dennis, John Stoughton, 39, 46–47, 71, 73–74, 80–81, 386n78

Department of Indian Affairs, 52–53, 208, 209, 248, 255

Department of the Interior, xx, 23, 47, 66, 74, 148–49, 164–65, 170–71, 173, 175–76, 180, 188–89, 197, 197–8, 205, 261, 290, 294, 298, 300, 302, 336–37, 349, 370–71

Department of Justice, 171–72

Devil's Lake (SK), 55

Dickens, Violet, 350

Dinesen, Isak (Karen Blixen), 18

divorced women, 41, 149, 172, 174, 190, 199, 200, 304

Doig, Mrs. (Regina), 172

Dominion City (MB), 63

Dominion Lands Act: 1872 legislation, 57–58, 61, 63; 1876 legislation passed, 3, 30, 61, 62, 71–72, 169; policy on eligibility of women to homestead, 149, 171–72; background to 1876 legislation, 72–79; and case of Mary Briggs, 205–6; conditions which influenced 1876 legislation, 69–71

Douglas, Marguerite, 155

Doukhobors, 10, 255, 256–57, 308–9

Doupe, Catherine, 65

dower rights, 285, 288, 289, 300–301

Doyle, George, 197

Drinkwater, C., 168

Drysdale, Anne, 243–44

Ducie, Emma Roberts, 115

Ducklow, Margaret, 216

Dumont, Peter, 209

Dunn, Maggie, 216

Durham, Mabel, 365

E

Edgar, Valletta Jane Nixon, 65

Edie, George, 68

Edie, Mary Mitchell, 68

Edmundson, Elizabeth, 183, 185

Edmundson, William H., 185

Ellis, Miriam Green, 341

Elm Springs (SK), 156

Empire Settlement Act, 348, 376

eugenics, 299, 355

Evans, Lois, 366

ex-servicewomen (UK), 355–58

F

farm labourers, 328–35, 337–40, 342–45

Farm Service Corps (Ontario), 331–35, 343, 350

farmerettes (Ontario), 331–35, 343, 350

farming: in BC, 361–62, 365–66; belief in masculinity of, 377–78, 380–81; and Binnie-Clark's training school, 271–76; Canadian interest in employing British women in, 109–10, 138–41; and CIL, 127–29, 130–31; in cooperative colonies, 91–92, 351–52, 361; CPR promotion of, 141–46; debate over suitability of women for farm work, 87–88, 100–105; disapproval of women, 14, 15–16, 89–90, 97, 101, 146, 280, 305; European settler view of Indigenous, 31, 34–35, 36–38; examples of successful women in 1920s, 366–69; fiction set on western Canadian farms, 136–37; G. Binnie-Clark as, 245, 246, 258, 260, 269; gender issues concerning, 100–101, 102–3; and health, 138, 139; *Imperial Colonist* view of, 116, 117, 118–21; by Indigenous peoples on reserve, 6, 49–50, 52–53, 247, 378, 408n10; by "Jack" May, 223–35; by land buyers, 211–16; by M. Gilroy, 217–19; by Métis, 56; numbers of women practising in Canada, 139, 366; as occupation for emigrating women, 109–10; as occupation for married women, 96–97; in Ontario, 59–60; and Ontario's Farm Service Corps, 331–35; poor conditions for, 68, 69–71, 83, 146; on prairies during First World War, 328–30, 337–40, 342–45; proponents of women, 85–86, 121–27, 133–36, 138–39, 146; and R.N. Hillman, 221–22; restraining myths of, 15, 380–81; small-holdings movement, 90–92, 109–10, 135, 139, 232, 361; as solution to England's "surplus" women, 92–97; in South Africa, 118–20; training and education in, 98–100, 110–15, 121, 122–23, 124–27, 148, 328, 331, 333, 342–43; of trees, 80–83. *See also* homesteading; Indigenous women

Farquharson, James, 255–56

Favel, Isabella, 56

Fawcett, Millicent, 96

Federated Women's Institute, 370

femininity: and dress, deportment, 103; and G. Binnie-Clark, 246, 266, 269, 279; as imperial ideal, 323–24; role in colonialism, 76–79, 89; and "Jack" May, 207, 223–28, 233; of women farmers, 244, 329–30, 334, 335, 367; of women landowners, 208, 222; of women ranchers, 299; worries farming would destroy, 97, 100–102, 103, 306; as First World War cause, 342

Ferguson, Jane, 177
First Aid Nursing Yeomanry Corps (FANY), 221
First Nations. *See* Indigenous peoples; Indigenous women
Fitzgibbon, Clare Valentine, 123
Fitzgibbon, Mary Agnes, 121, 122–27, 132, 133, 138, 276, 365
Fleming, Jeanette, 240
Ford, Mary, 320
"foreign" migrants: and Doukhobors, 10, 255, 256–57, 308–9; examples of, 159; F.M. Beynon on, 317, 320–21; F. Oliver on, 14, 309; fear of their immigration by Canadians, 255–57; G. Binnie-Clark's view of, 259; and Homestead Act, 43; homestead rights of, 307–8; homesteads-for-women campaign and, 256, 277, 287–88, 300, 302–3, 308–12, 313, 319; and imperialism, 10–11; and manual labour by women, 77, 79, 324–25; statistics on as homesteaders, 157, 159
forest tree culture, 30, 80–83
Forlonge, Eliza, 244
Fort Qu'Appelle (SK), xvii, 24, 80, 209, 249–50, 251–55, 264, 271–76, 287, 379
Forward sisters (Oak Lake, Manitoba), 367
Foss, Ellen, 367
Frazer, James, 163
Frazer, Marion Ferguson, 160, 163–64
Frederiksen, Ditlew M., 304
Free Grants and Homestead Act (Ontario), 58, 60
Freeston, Margaret, 293, 296, 297
Fyffe, Nora, 369

G

Garwood, Eliza Landymore, 154
Geddes, John, 164–65
Gentles, Jane, 198–99, 201
German Southwest Africa, 18
Giller, Amanda, 172–73
Giller, Jean Louis, 173
Gilroy, Mary, 216–19, 405n56
Girdler, F.M., 356
The Girl of the New Day (Knox), 351–52, 353, 358
Gladstone, William, 95
Glynde School for Lady Gardeners, 99, 100
Godkin, Catherine, 176–77
Goodbird, Edward, 33
Goppel, Miss (Priddis), 238, 239
Gordon, Catherine, 155
Gosselin, Emmanuel, 209
Gosselin, Francois, 209
Goueffic, Marie, 159
Gouin, Sir Lomer, 360
Graham, Francis, 293
Graham, Isabelle Beaton: anti-"foreigner" stance, 308–9; as leader of homesteads-for-women campaign, 293, 294, 299, 300; racist views, 310–11; and second petition, 312–13, 316, 319–20, 322; on tree claims, 83
Graham, M.E., 317, 343
Graham, P. Anderson, 101–2
Graham, W.F., 302
Grain Growers' Guide, 293, 308, 320–21, 343
Grandview (MB), 185–86
Grant, Anna, 184
Grant, Oxilla, 183–84
Gray, Stewart, 279
Great Britain: attitudes toward women as farmers, 87–90, 381; emigration after First World War, 355–58; emigration to colonies before First World War, 105–10; problem of "surplus" women, 92–97; small-holdings movement, 90–92; training for colonial farmers, 110–15
Green, Frances Mabel, 216
Green, Sarah, 56–57
Greg, W.R., 93
Grey, Sybil, 130, 133
Grey-Wilson, William, 281
Grisdale, J.H., 357–58
Grosvenor, Caroline, 127–29, 133, 353–54
Guinness, Gwendolen, 115
Guinness, Rupert, 115

H

Haight, Zoa, 341, 342
Hall, Mary, 75
Hallum, Jim, 236
Hamilton, Mrs. L.A., 359
Hanna (AB), 11
Hanson, Grace, 233, 234
Hardisty (AB), 160–62
Hare, Thomas, 175
Harkness, Isadore, 169–70
Harkness, Matthew, 66
Harris, Muriel, 365
Harrison, Roland, 272
Hart, Elsie, 382
Harvey, John, 177
Hawkes, Arthur, 276
Hayden, Ferdinand V., 35, 81
Hazlett, May, 366
health, 138, 139
Hearst, William, 333
Heath, Maria Bell, 184
Heffernan, Margaret, 184–85
Henry, Alexander, 34–35
Hewetson, Mary, 118, 119
Hidatsa, 29, 31–36, 382
Hill, Helena, 236–37
Hill, Louisa, 165–66
Hill, Sarah Jane Castle, 153
Hilliard, Miss (Seattle), 236
Hillis, Lizzie, 11–12, 105
Hillis, Mary, 12
Hillman, Ruth N., 221–22, 343
Hind, Cora, 16, 372
Hodson, F.W., 147
Hoebridge Overseas Training School, 350
Holman, Grandma (Manitoba homesteader), 154
Holme, Vera "Jack," 237
home helps: Binnie-Clark and, 267, 269; as camouflaged domestic service, 86–87; E. Sykes and, 130; as employment of British emigrants, 116, 117, 375–76; in *Imperial Colonist,* 121; need of in Canada after First World War, 350, 354–55, 356–57, 359–60, 365; promotion of jobs as, 106–7
Homestead Act of 1862 (US), 41–43
homesteading: in Alberta after 1930, 379–80; by single women, 57, 169–70, 174–76; pre-emption in BC, 60–61; changing women's eligibility for, 30, 72–79, 83–84, 148, 149, 160–69; claim of women's incompetence at, 73–74, 135; conditions for, 68, 69–71; and dispossession of Indigenous land, 52, 208–9; examples of famous women, 216–37; examples of widows, 148, 149–56, 159–60, 175; exemption of Indigenous peoples from, 57, 61, 62, 75, 388n124; and F. Oliver, 14, 180, 183–84; and fraud, 73, 74, 173–74, 175, 184–89; legislation passed, 48, 57–58; by Métis, 170–71; in Ontario, 58–60; by separated women, 172–74; as social and cultural policy, 61–62; and South African scrip, 190–99; statistics on, 68–69, 156–59; suspicions of fraud in, 177–80, 183–89; through Métis scrip, 209–10; widows roadblocks to, 148–49, 176; women proving up compared to men, 30, 68–69, 200; by women who filed before 1876, 63–68. *See also* farming; homesteads-for-women campaign; United States
homesteads-for-women campaign: during and after First World War, 323, 327–28, 345–49; anti-"foreigner" stance, 256, 277, 287–88, 300, 302–3, 308–12, 313, 319; arguments for, 11, 294–95, 298–303, 320–21; beginnings, 289–94; and CIL, 131; exclusion of Americans from, 313, 316–17; and F. Oliver, 180, 290, 291, 303; first petition, 291–92; and G. Binnie-Clark, 14, 235, 259, 260–71, 277–81, 283–85, 289, 294; and Government of Canada, 261, 262, 288, 319, 322, 348, 349, 370–71; and I.B. Graham, 293, 294, 299, 300; and imperialism, 11, 323–25; last stages of, 369–73; legacy, 286; losing women to US argument, 295–98; and N. McClung, 345–46; opponents of, 281–83, 303–8, 321–22; and racism, 310–11; reasons it failed, 324–25; second petition, 312–24; and suffrage, 302–3, 313
Hoodless, Adelaide, 138–39
horticulture, 22, 79, 90–91, 97, 98, 105, 112, 117, 126–27, 140, 275, 286, 328
House of Commons (Canada), 48, 191, 287, 347–48
Hughes, William, 188–89

Hugonnard, Joseph, 249
Hunt, Ernestine, 219–21
Hunt, Harry Brady, 220
Hunt, Mildred, 203
Hunter, Margaret, 210
Hurcomb, Deborah Jane, 191

I

Iddings, Eva, 201
Imperial Colonist, 116, 118–20, 120–21, 270, 363
Imperial Order Daughters of Empire (IODE), 370, 373
imperialism, British: and fear of immigration, 255–56; and G. Binnie-Clark, 245–47, 274; and gender, 10–11, 376–77; and homesteads-for-women campaign, 11, 323–25; importance of women's femininity to, 76–79, 89, 281; and land survey, 43–44; N. McClung's sense of, 321; and post–First World War emigration from England, 350, 355; prairie Canada as part of, 5–8; and proponents of cooperative farming, 85–86; and relations with locals in South Africa, 119–20; role of widows in, 148; and threat of masculinization of women, 10–11, 324–25, 342; and UJFS, 378–79; and US homesteading, 42–43; use of colonialism in, 8–11; women advocates of, 121, 128, 133, 140, 216; women's place in, 9–11, 105–6, 108–9, 121, 123, 279. *See also* colonialism
Indian Act (1876), 49, 57
Indigenous peoples: and colonialism, 6, 248–51; and disease, 52; dispossession of land, 17, 52, 208–9, 255; excluded from land survey grid, 39, 46; exempted from homesteading, 57, 61, 62, 75, 388n124; farming on reserves, 6, 49–50, 52–53, 247, 378, 408n10; and G. Binnie-Clark, 247–51; and Government of Canada, 52–53, 208, 209, 248, 255, 408n10; homesteaders contact with, 59, 164, 208; homesteading in US, 43; and reserves, 49–53, 51; and Soldier Settlement Act, 347. *See also* reserves, First Nations; treaties
Indigenous women: as farmers, 29, 30–31, 36–38, 50, 382; British view of as exploited by Indigenous men, 76–77; corn cultivation, 33–34; European male view of their farming, 31, 34–35, 36–38; knowledge of farming, 35–36, 38; Maxi'diwiac, 29, 31, 33–34; widows as homesteaders, 49–50
Industrial Farm Colony, 98
Ingleby, Lord and Lady, 154

J

Jackson, Celesta Hamer, 214–16
Jackson, George, 214, 215
Jacobsen, Sebina, 192
Jamieson, Cathy, 154–55
Jefferson, Sophia, 203
Jefferson, Thomas, 39–40
Jenks, Dennis, 286
Jones, Edith, 368
Joyce, Ellen, 116

K

Kainai (Blood), 50
Kealy, O.W., 185
Keay, Grace, 150
Keeler (SK), 221, 343
Kennedy, Lottie, 195
Kennedy, Susannah Jane, 64
Kenya, 18, 363
Keyes, P.G., 175
Kinnaird, Jessie, 155
Kluth, Mary, 13
Knightley, Lady, 108, 116
Knox, Ellen N., 351–52, 353, 358
Kurz, Rudolph F., 36–37

L

Lacombe (AB), 155
Laidlaw, Jean, 208, 403n4
Laird, David, 71, 80
Lambert, Frances, 203

Lambert, Mary, 203
land rushes, 179, 181, 182
land survey grid, 38–40, 46–49, 51
Langham Place Group, 95, 96
Langton, Louise, 290
Laughrin, Kathleen, 272
Laurie, P.G., 309
Laurier, Wilfrid, 324
Laut, Agnes C., 217
Lavelle, Florence, 160
Law, Flora S., 155
Lawson, Maria, 282–83
Leadbeater, Jane, 65
Leaton Colonial Training Home, 111–12, 126
Lepage, Charles, 210
Lepage, Victoria, 210
Letellier de Saint-Just, Luc, 71
Letters from Muskoka (anonymous), 58–60
Lewis, Meriwether, 35
The Lighter Branches of Agriculture (Bradley and La Mothe), 91
Lindsay, Maggie, 211
Lindsay v. Morrow, 211
Lipsett, Ann Jane, 65
Lipsett, Caroline Matilda, 65
Lipsett, Phoebe Louisa, 65
Little, Lemuel, 187, 188, 189
Little, Margaret, 187–89
Little, Roscoe, 188
Livingston, Bertha, 175
Lloydminster (SK), xx, 155
Local Councils of Women, 346
Long, Estelle, 104, 242
Long, J., 104
Long, Mrs. J.R., 301–2
Longhurst, Esther, 268
Love, Currie, 231–32, 233, 276
Low, Florence B., 360–61, 363, 372–73
Lowe, Bob, 222
Lowe, John, 77, 79
Lucas, Charles P., 279
Lucas, Martha, 155
Lumsden (SK), 143–44, 159
Lynch, Clara, 189
Lyndon, Alfred Arthur, 196

M

Macarthur, Elizabeth, 244
Macdonald, Susan Agnes, 123
Macdonald Institute, 356
Macdonald, John A., 123
MacGregor, Carrie Louise, 202–4
MacGregor, Mary Frances, 202–4
MacLean, James, 174
Macleod, Widow, 50
MacMillan, Jessie de Prado, 204
Macoun (SK), 197
Macquarie, Lachlan, 44
Madsen, Hans, 203
Maguire, T. Miller, 279–80
Mandan, 31, 34–36, 382
Maple Creek (SK), 177, 195, 301
Marchant, Bessie, 136–37
marriage, 15, 45–46, 88, 96–97, 134
married women: homesteading in US, 62–63, 96–97, 200; in homesteads-for-women campaign, 312; land owning options for, 149; and South African scrip, 190, 194–95, 196–97, 198–99; who purchased land, 211–16; who wanted to homestead, 295; and First World War work, 341
Marryat, E.L., 368
Marryat, Sheila, 368–69
Marsh, George Perkins, 81
Martin, Kate Smith, 64
Martin, Malcolm, 64
Martin, Thomas, 210
Martineau, Alice, 328
Martineau, Harriet, 95
masculinity, 7–8, 191, 324–25, 347, 377–78, 380–81; and imperialism, 10–11, 324–25, 342
masculinization of women: and farm labour, 233, 237–38, 330, 336, 342, 376; men's fear of, 4, 89, 100, 104, 137, 305, 372; and war work, 342, 355
Mason, Otis T., 77, 78
Matalski, Mary, 191

Matthews, Washington, 36
Maurice, Catherine, 56
Maxi'diwiac (Buffalo Bird Woman), 29, 31, 33–34, 36, 382
May, Isobel "Jack," 105, 207, 222–35, 242, 244, 406n88, 406n98
May, Kinbarra Swene, 406n88
May, William Henry, 223, 406n88
McAskie, James, 66
McAskie, Matilda Graham, 66–68
McBeth, Angus, 50
McCallum, Mary P., 222, 343, 351
McCarthy, D'Alton, 124
McClung, Nellie, 13–14, 15, 293, 296–97, 321, 324, 345–46
McClure, Fanny, 210
McCoy, George, 156
McFadden, Eliza, 175
McGavin, Elizabeth, 149–50
McGavin, James, 149–50
McGavin, Jesse Margaret, 150
McGillis, Norbert, 209
McGregor, Ann, 150
McIntosh, Robert, 56
McKay, Alice, 56
McKee, Rachel, 62–63
McKercher, Isabella, 63–64, 65
McKercher, Janet, 65
McLeod, Mary, 64–65
McMartin, Duncan, 56
McNab, Mary Ann, 164–65
McNab, Samual George, 209
McNeil, Mrs. Thomas, 301
McTavish, J.H., 168
Meighan, Arthur, 348
Medicine Hat (AB), 183, 185
Melfort (SK), 153
Méline, Jules, 281
Menzies, J.H., 342
Métis: opposition to land survey, 47–48; farming by, 56; granted land through scrip, 53–57; women homesteaders, 159, 170–71; farm labourers, 251. *See also* scrip, Métis
Michels, Lena J., 203
midwives, 150, 153–55, 159–60
Milligan, Sarah J., 209
Milner, Alfred, 356
Minto, Mary, 132
Miquelon, Nancy, 209
Molloy, T.M., 357
Moodie, Susanna, 58
Moore, David, 234
Moore, J.W., 320
Moore, Jack, 234
Moore, Mary MacLeod, 285
Moorhouse, Matthew, 46
Moose Jaw (SK), xviii, 150, 155, 181, 289
Mormon women, 402n202
Morris, Elizabeth Keith, 283, 307
Munday, Dan, 285
Munro, Louisa Irvine, 66

N

National Council of Women, 138–39, 359
New Zealand, 44, 46, 120
Newcomb, Caroline, 244
Newton, Margaret, 333
Nicholson, Miss (IODE), 370
Nixon, Laura E., 343
Noble, Isabel, 346
North Battleford (SK), 147
North-West Mounted Police, 53, 125, 155, 193
nurses, 191, 348, 350–51

O

Obie, Ann Yoctorowic, 203
O'Connor, Edith, 119–20
Ojibwa, 6. *See also* Saulteaux
Oliver, Frank: anti-"foreigner" view, 14, 309; appointed minister of the interior, 255; and G. Binnie-Clark, 261, 262; and homesteads-for-women campaign, 180, 290, 291, 303; land speculation of, 384n50; as newspaperman, 194; and women's homesteading applications, 14, 180, 183–84
Ontario, 58–60, 331–35

Openings for British Women in Canada (Low), 360–61
Oregon, 43
Osborn, E.B., 8
Osborne, Ethel, 307
Overseas Settlement Committee (OSC), 356
Overseas Training School for Women, 115

P

Pankhurst, Sylvia, 258
Parkbeg (SK), 154
Parlby, Irene, 212, 368
Parliament of Canada, 322
Partridge, E.A., 308
Paterson, Mrs. (Plateau, Saskatchewan), 316
Patriarche, Valance, 84, 300, 311–12
Pearkes, Louisa, 183–84
Pearkes Jr., George, 183
Pearkes Sr., George, 183
Pedlow, Isaac, 348
Peel, Robert, 96
Peele, Polly, 350–51
Pekisko (AB), 151–52
Penfold, Mary, 244
Perra, J.H., 313
petitions, 292, 293
Pincher Creek (AB), 152, 159, 208
Pinder, Emily, 364
Pipestone (MB), 143
Plowden, Winifred Johnston, 193
Poedler, Erma, 342
Porter, E. Guss, 195
Potts, Caroline Ann, 229
Potts, Gladys S., 356, 357
Powell, Ellis T., 279
Powell, Frances, 153–54
Pratt, Ella F. (Dorothea Alice Shepherd), 73
Prairie Grove (MB), 149
Prince Albert (SK), 169
Princess Patricia Ranch, 130–31, 241–42, 366
Pullen-Burry, Bessie, 307
Puttee, Arthur, 318
Puttee, Gertrude, 318

Q

Queen Mary Hostel, 132, 365–66

R

ranches/ranchers: in BC, 366; E. Hunt, 219–21; examples of, 152, 202, 214, 215; femininity of, 299; home help on, 117; Princess Patricia, 130–31, 241–42, 366; statistics on, 157, 158; successful women in 1920s, 367, 368
Rankin, Jeanette, 166
Rankin, Norman, 231
Red Cross, 342
Reed, Fred, 180
Reed, Jean, 368
Reid, Richard, 279
reserves, First Nations, 6, 11, 17, 20, 49–53, 208–10, 247–48, 378, 408n10
residential schools, 248
Rhodes, B.F., 239
Ritchie, Christina Anne Bethune, 152–53
Ritchie, Dora, 152, 153
Ritchie, Jennie, 152, 153
Ritchie, John T.M., 152
Robbins, Mrs. John, 315
Roblin (MB), 187
Roche, W.J., 195, 290, 319, 322
Rodney, George, 368
Rodney, Marjorie Lowther, 368
Roe, Frank G., 16, 17
Roe, Mary Ann, 16–17
Roedean School, 272
Rogers, Robert, 75–76, 319
Ross, Margaret Campbell, 64
Ross, William, 64
Rothwell, T.G., 205–6
Rowand, Julie McGillis, 159
Royal Colonial Institute (RCI), 276, 277–81

S

Sagen, Mr. (Norway), 195

Salvation Army, 358

Sampson, Katherine, 159

Sanderson, John, 56, 69

Saskatchewan Grain Growers, 370

Saulteaux, 6, 247, 249

Saxby, Jessie M., 5–6

School of Agriculture (Truro), 140

School of Horticulture (Wolfville), 140

Scott, Barbara, 66, 132

Scott, Elizabeth Moffatt, 64

Scott, James, 66

Scott, John, 64

Scott, W.D., 262, 354

scrip, Métis, 20, 23, 53–57, 62, 208–10

scrip, South African (SAS), xvi, 11, 23, 54, 149, 157, 190–99, 201, 294

Sedgewick (AB), 222, 224–25, 228–37, 242, 278, 406n98

Selborne, Earl of, 337

Shadd, Alfred Schmitz, 153

Shaughnessy, Thomas, 270, 271

Shaw, Flora, 121–22, 124, 125

Shaw, Mrs. Donald, 282

Shepherd, Fanny E., 302

Simpson, Julia, 46

Simpson, Madame (Grosse-Isle, Manitoba), 210–11

Sims, R. Manley, 15, 362

single women: allowed to homestead under original act, 57, 61; homesteaders, 57, 169–70, 175–76; emigration from Britain after war, 354, 356; example of homesteaders before 1876 amendment, 169–71; experience farming in Ontario, 58–60; homesteading in US, 18–19, 42, 117, 199–200, 295–98; and homesteads-for-women campaign, 294–95; *Imperial Colonist*'s advocacy of farming for, 116, 117; land owning options for, 149; and land seeking in Australia, 44–46; lose right to homestead, 61, 71–79, 83–84, 117; provisions for homesteading in other jurisdictions, 57–58, 60–61; and South African scrip, 192, 193–94, 195–96; stigma of as farmer, 381–82

Sioux, 247–48, 264. *See also* Dakota

small-holdings movement, 90–92

Smith, Donald (Lord Strathcona), 56, 132

Smith, J. Obed: background, 262–63; on farming women after war, 354, 358–59; opposed to women farming, 14, 280, 305; rejects appeals from women for homesteads, 260; on US homesteading laws, 19, 304

Smith, Marie Rose, 159

Snell, Frederick C., 193

Snowsell, Edwin, 230

Snowsell, Elizabeth, 236

Snowsell, Felicia, 230

Snowsell, Frank, 230

Society for the Oversea Settlement of British Women (SOSBW), 354, 356, 363, 366, 373

Solberg, Johanna, 192

Soldier Settlement Act, 347–49

Soldiers of the Soil, 333, 337

Sommerville, Catherine Corbet, 154

Sorsdahl, Nellie J., 197

South Africa, 112, 116, 118–20, 149, 157, 190–99. *See also* scrip, South African

Spence, Margaret, 170–71

Spence, Mary, 351

Spence, Thomas, 8

Spencer, Mary, 104

Spencer, Sarah, 104

Square Deal (AB), 192

squatters, 156, 157, 159

Stamm, Marianne, 380

Stanford, Pearl Clayton, 333

Stead, Robert J.C., 57

Stimson, Fred, 152

Stott, Hannah, 150

Stow, E.L., 313, 316

Straith, M. Catherine, 359

Strathmore (AB), 120, 270

Street, William, 54

Studley Horticultural and Agricultural College, 98, 112

suffrage: and demolished CPR office windows, 144, 145; fight for in England, 95–96; and "foreign" migrants, 321; and G. Binnie-Clark, 277; and homesteads-for-women campaign,

302–3, 313; in Manitoba, 293; success of campaign for, 322–23; in US, 288

A Summer on the Canadian Prairie (Binnie-Clark), 254, 268–69

Surrey, Hannah, 177

Sveum, Carrie, 195

Swan, Annie S., 137

Swanley Horticultural College, 98, 102, 112, 118, 127, 223, 328

Swift Current (SK), 155, 195–96

Sykes, Ella C., 85, 130

T

Talbot, Meriel, 329

Taylor, Frances, 119

Taylor family (Manitoba), 75

teachers, 191, 193

Templeton, Janet, 244

Texas, 43

Thomas, Lillian Beynon, 84, 148, 291, 293

Thompson, Elizabeth Hopwood, 175

Thompson, Gertrude Seton, 194, 199, 214

Thompson, James, 175, 176

Thompson, Marion T., 175–76

Thompson, Olivia, 156

Thomson, Belle, 209

Thornton, Henry, 364

Tooley, Sarah A., 114

Tosh (Indigenous woman), 251

Training Home for Ladies, 112–13

treaties, 53, 388n124; Treaty One, 6; Treaty Three, 49; Treaty Four, 51, 247, 249, 408n10

tree farms, 80–83

Turner, J.S., 114, 280–81

Turner, Mary Alice Blackwell, 348

Turriff, J.G., 174

Turtle (Maxi'diwiac's mother), 33

Tye, Alice, 209

U

Ukrainians, 255, 256

Union Jack Farm Settlement (UJFS), 286, 378–79, 421n6

United Farmers of Alberta (UFA), 322, 349, 371

United States: Canada's land survey uses model of, 47, 48; Canadian single women moving to, 18–19, 42, 117, 199–200, 295–98; citizens interested in homesteading in Canada, 370; exclusion of Americans from homesteads-for-women campaign, 313, 316–17; experience of homesteading women in, 30, 189, 199–204; farm labouring in, 330; fight of married women to homestead in, 62–63; homestead laws in, 18–19, 41–43, 166, 304–5; and "How Two Girls Tried Farming," 73; land survey grid, 39–40; number of women farmers in, 138; suffrage fight in, 288; and tree farms, 80–81, 83

Utech, Anna, 190

V

Vane, Elise, 177–79

Vanguard Farm, 276

Verndale (SK), 191

Vernon, A.L., 111–12, 354

Victoria, Queen, 105

Virden (MB), 22, 167–69

Volunteer Bounty Act (VBA), 190–91

W

Waddell, Alexander, 64

Waldville (SK), 195

Walker, Eldred G.F., 235

Walker, Ethel, 258

Walker, Mary, 63

Walker, Peter, 63

Walper, Susan, 175

Walsh, Eliza, 44–45

Ward, Mary, 137, 268–69

Warwick, Frances Evelyn 'Daisy,' 91, 93, 98, 100, 112, 117

Watkins, Alice, 351

Watt, Gertrude Balmer, 179

Weir, Helen N., 292

West, Edward, 12, 16

Westhead, Charles G., 212

Westhead, Alice, 144, 212–14

Weston, Jessie, 109–10

Westphal, Marie, 194

Whaley, Hannah J., 68

Wheat and Woman (Binnie-Clark), 283–85, 323

Wheeler, George, 186

Wheeler, T.H., 186

widows: and CPR promotion, 141, 143; Department of Justice's attempt to define, 172; discrimination against as homesteaders, 160–69; emigrating to Canada after First World War, 362; and Empire Settlement Act, 376; examples of homesteading, 148, 149–56, 159–60, 175; as farmers, 121, 147–48, 295, 368; homesteading in US, 41, 200; Indigenous, 49–50; non-farming income of, 159–60; scrutiny of by federal bureaucracy, 148–49, 176; and Soldier Settlement Act, 348; statistics on as homesteaders, 156–59; suspected false claims by, 184–89; suspicions of fraudulent homesteading by, 177–80, 183–84; who homesteaded before 1876, 66–68

Wilhelmina (Alberta), 317

Wilkins, Louisa Jebb, 329

Williams, Annie E., 211–12

Williams, Frances, 315

Williams, Frederick C., 212

Williams, Mildred, 193–94

Willis, Susanna, 167–69

Willis, Thomas, 169

Willoughby, Susan Jones, 209

Willoughby, W.B., 209

Wilson, Gilbert L., 31, 33

Wilson, Isabella, 211

Wilson, William, 169

Wilton, Maria Barron, 65

Wilton, Maxwell, 65

Witter, Daniel, 62–63

Wittrick, Louisa, 225, 229, 234, 235

Wolseley, Frances, 91, 94, 97, 99, 100, 101

A Woman in Canada (Cran), 133–36

Women's Labour League, 313, 318–19

Women's Land Army (WLA), 328–30; after First World War, 352–53, 355; emigration to Canada after First World War, 358, 361–62; during First World War, 327, 328–30

Women's Share in Primitive Culture (Mason), 77, 78

Woodhull, Victoria, 100

Wood Mountain (SK), 157, 159, 163, 205, 239

World War I: and Binnie-Clark, 285, 286; and British farmers in Canada, 86; domestic work during, 340–42; and farm labourers, 328–30, 337–40, 342–45; and Farm Service Corps, 331–35; and homestead application, 198, 201; and homesteads-for-women campaign, 323, 327–28, 345–49; Victory Bonds poster, 336

Y

Yates, Miss (Ontario Agricultural College), 139–40

Young, Sarah, 171

Young, Thomas, 170, 171

Young Women's Christian Association (YWCA), 331

A NOTE ON THE TYPE

The text of this book is set in Adobe Garamond (11/14), designed by Robert Slimbach in 1989 for Adobe Systems. The title text is set in ITC Franklin Gothic Std, designed by Morris Fuller Benton and Victor Caruso for the International Typeface Corporation.